THE AVIFAUNA OF THE ISLAND OF CEYLON

THE
AVIFAUNA OF THE ISLAND
OF
CEYLON

A SYSTEMATIC ACCOUNT,
WITH DESCRIPTIONS OF ALL THE KNOWN
SPECIES OF BIRDS INHABITING THE ISLAND, ALSO
OBSERVATIONS ON THEIR HABITS, NIDIFICATION, & C.,
AND TABLES OF THIER GEOGRAPHICAL
DISTRIBUTION THROUGHOUT INDIA.

James A. Murray

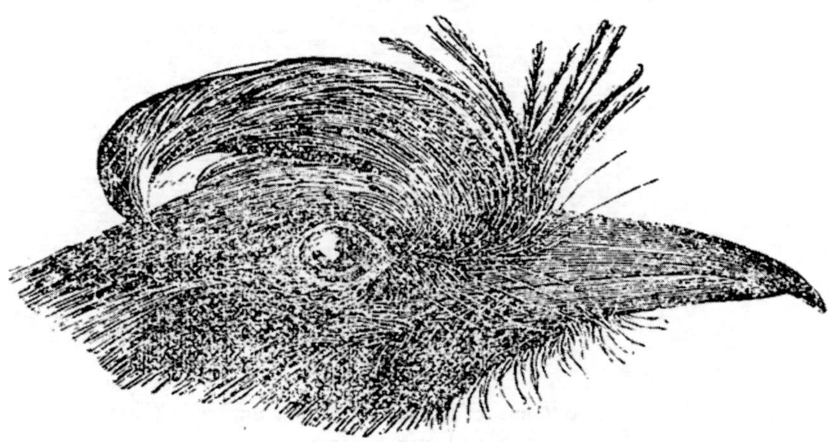

GYAN

Published by

Gyan Publishing House
5, Ansari Road
Daryaganj, New Delhi-110002
Phone: 011-47034999, 9811692060
E-mail: books@gyanbooks.com

Distribution Network
gyanbooks.com
India, USA, Canada, UK, Australia, France

ISBN : 978-81-212-3141-1 (PB)
First Published, London/Bombay, 1890

2nd Impression 2020

Printed at: Gyan Press, Delhi.

The
Avifauna of the Island of Ceylon
Author: James A. Murray

THE AVIFAUNA OF THE ISLAND OF CEYLON.

A SYSTEMATIC ACCOUNT,
WITH DESCRIPTIONS OF ALL THE KNOWN
SPECIES OF BIRDS INHABITING THE ISLAND, ALSO
OBSERVATIONS ON THEIR HABITS, NIDIFICATION, &c.,
AND TABLES OF THEIR GEOGRAPHICAL
DISTRIBUTION THROUGHOUT INDIA.

BY

JAMES A. MURRAY, F.S.A.L.,

MEM. OF THE NATURAL HIST. AND ANTHROP. SOC. OF BOMBAY; MANAGER, VICT. NAT. HIST. INSTITUTE; LATE CURATOR, KURRACHEE MUNICIPAL LIBRARY AND MUSEUM; AUTHOR OF "A HAND-BOOK TO THE GEOLOGY, BOTANY AND ZOOLOGY OF SIND;" "THE PLANTS AND DRUGS OF SIND;" "KURRACHEE TO KANDAHAR;" "THE VERTEBRATE ZOOLOGY OF SIND;" "THE REPTILES OF SIND;" "THE AVIFAUNA OF BRITISH INDIA AND ITS DEPENDENCIES;" AND "THE EDIBLE AND GAME BIRDS OF BRITISH INDIA AND CEYLON."

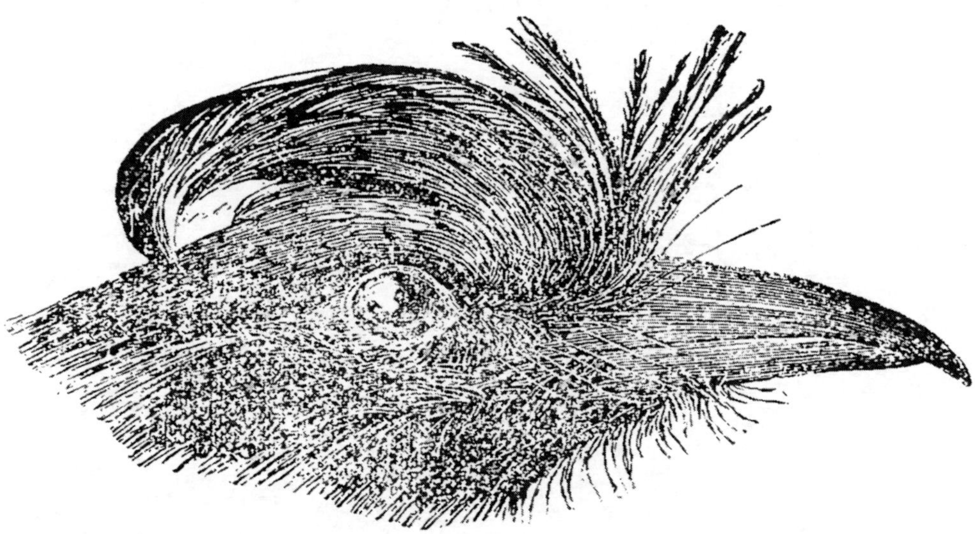

LONDON:—KEGAN, PAUL, TRENCH, TRÜBNER & Co
BOMBAY:—EDUCATION SOCIETY'S PRESS, BYCULLA.

1890.

PREFACE.

SHOULD it be asked whether another work on the Avifauna of the Island of Ceylon was required in addition to such as already exist, the reply shortly is that it was undertaken under the patronage of the Colonial Government of Ceylon, which Government, no doubt, may be presumed to be acquainted with the public wants, in so far that the student, the enquirer, and workers in Ornithology required something systematic to study, with materials collated and brought up to the present time, furnishing also in a brief compass more extended knowledge of the habits, resorts, nidification and geographical distribution of the species of birds inhabiting the Island, as well as all available information in sufficient detail for the discrimination and identification of such species as may be met, without being reduced to the necessity of having to consult periodical literature and works published above a decade ago. It was also undertaken in the hope that, being a subject of special enquiry, and not one included in the "Avifauna of British India and its Dependencies," the severa Governments in India as well as the Home Government, and the several distinguished Independent Princes and Chiefs in India, would extend to it a liberal share of patronage; and this the author very respectfully seeks.

His attention was first particularly directed to the publication of the work by several Ornithologists, with a request to ascertain whether the Colonial Government might not sanction such a work, and so render them less dependent on the older authors, since the publication of whose works,—as valuable as they are,—numerous new species with much additional scattered information have been brought to light and require being blended into a whole. The author has the gratification to find that he has been enabled, with a path strewn with perplexities and heavy clouds over head, to increase very much the knowledge of the geographic distribution of many birds, and to be of some service to Naturalists in general, as well to complete the task he had undertaken, though he regrets very much that owing to insufficient support up to the completion of the work it has not been possible to carry out the plan originally designed in regard to Lithographs and coloured illustrations, &c.

A word in regard to the Introduction. This has been by special request transcribed from my "Avifauna of British India," it being argued as a reason, that, in short, it affords to the student as much as he would wish to know of the external and internal parts of a bird, and gives a sufficiently succinct account of the History of Indian Ornithology.

INTRODUCTION.

BIRDS form one of the most marked and grand divisions of vertebrated animals, as well as the most lovely group in creation. They are oviparous, red and warm-blooded, feathered bipeds, breathing by lungs which are bound by cellular tissue to the inside of the ribs and the sides of the dorsal vertebræ ; there is therefore no distinct thoracic cavity, nor free muscular diaphragm. The cells open directly from the bronchial trunks and, though minute, are large compared with the cells of the lungs of quadrupeds. The interior of the bones, by communicating with the cells of the lungs, are respiratory organs, which communicate circuitously with the trachea. The cells which are continued from the lungs into the cavity of the abdomen, extend to the interior of the trunk, appear in the axillæ, in the neck, and in the region of the pelvis. In fact, every part is impregnated with the air in which they are destined to move. The young of birds, however, have the interior of their bones filled with a thin serous fluid or marrow ; but this is soon displaced by air from the air-cells of the lungs, which gains access at the proximal extremities, to the extent necessary for the various species according to their habits and modes of life. Being intended for flight, their external anatomy or those parts generally visible are specially organized for the purpose. The body is covered with feathers, instead of hair or wool, and the two forefeet of mammals are transformed into wings. As in other classes, the form of structure of the body and all its various members as well as the modifications which these parts assume are discriminating characters which enable the Ornithologist to form conceptions of their respective peculiarities. The primary parts of birds, as of all vertebrates, are the head, body and limbs, under which subordinate members may be classed. The head is composed of the bill and the skull. The latter is joined to the body by a neck. The skull is formed of a thin, nearly diaphanous and continuous plate of bone above, with all the cranial bones anchylosed. The occipital is not separated from the parietal bones by a lambdoidal suture, nor is there a sagittal suture to separate the parietals from the frontal. All these have anchylosed at a very early period. The first cranial vertebræ at the base of the occipital bone is short. The sphenoid bone and the parts in front which form the face are lengthened, while the pterygoid portions of the former are detached. The basilar part of the occipital bone ends in a single condyle, and its position at the lower margin of the foramen as well as its rotundity afford mobility to the connection of the occipital (*A*) bone with the slender circular atlas and the vertebral column generally. The neck being composed of numerous bones (*K*) is rendered flexible, and this enables a bird to preen its feathers both on the upper and lower surface of the body and to sleep with its head turned round and placed under the wing. The face of a bird is movable upon the rest of the skull,—whether articulated as in parrots or not,—the thin nasal (*F*) bones being elastic to a certain extent. The orbits and organs of vision are large, the former being separated only by a thin translucent plate or membrane, while the latter are largely developed in lieu, to a great extent, to the want of the sense of touch. The lower jaw (*P*) moves freely and widens the gape very sensibly. The palatine bones are much developed in length and breadth, and these have between them a large fissure. The nostrils are very various in position, shape, and size, and the upper and lower jaws are also very variable and suited to their habits. In some the mandibles are compressed and lengthened, and terminate in a hook; in others they terminate in a point as in woodpeckers; others again are broad, sharp-pointed, hooked, rounded and hard, or as in ducks long, flat, spoon-shaped and toothed; while birds of prey have a dense horny bill with the edges sharp, strong, and cutting, and the tip hooked. The bill is composed of two pieces corresponding to the jaws of quadrupeds; the upper portion (*a*) is called the upper mandible, which is either continued far back on the forehead and there dilated as to form a casque or helmet, or there is a soft naked skin at the base as in rapacious birds, which is the cere (8); the lower portion (*b*) is the lower mandible. At the base of the upper mandible, concealed or not, and of various shapes, are the nostrils (*c*), while the high medial keel of the bill is the culmen (*d*) and the corresponding keel of the lower mandible is the gonys (*e*). The margins of both mandibles (*f*), commonly called the commissure, is either arched, straight, curved, or festooned, or the upper overlaps the lower; the forehead (*g*) is the region lying close to the nostrils. The body commences with or joins the breast (*o*) and extends the whole length of the sternum or breast-bone. It is succeeded by the abdomen (*q*) and terminated by the vent (*r*) and the under-tail coverts (*s*).

On the upper part of the body are the wings, the interscapularies or back (*t*), lower back (*v*), the rump (*w*), where the upper tail coverts (*w2*) are situated, and last the tail (*x*). The leg, as in quadrupeds, is composed of the thigh (*gg*), tarsus (*hh*), the toes (*ii*), and the claws.

It is scarcely necessary to give a detailed sketch of the internal anatomy of birds, since a knowledge of what is visible to the eye is almost sufficient to determine or classify them generally, or even closely allied groups—though it would no doubt be of much service to the ornithologist to know the various parts or rather the osteology of birds in order that comparisons may be made of the bones of different groups and species. Professor C. J. Sundevall, in an article "On the Wings of Birds," translated for the "Ibis" of 1886, by W. S. Dallas, F.L.S., considers the feather covering of the wings of birds to be of the greatest significance in their systematic arrangement. He says, "It is a truth that every external part of an animal can furnish equally certain indications of affinity or distinction between species as an internal part of the body, and that in this respect no order of precedence can be established *à priori* * * * *." From a physiological point of view, indeed, the internal parts may be regarded as more important than the external, but zoographically we must regard the external parts as possessing an equal, if not greater value, because the characters derived from them can be easily recognized and examined.

Birds have much in common with mammals, and it cannot be denied that there are striking resemblances between individuals of both classes, especially in their habits. The Eagle and the Owl may be said to represent the feline tribe; the Vulture, the Hyæna; the Hawk, the Fox; the Parrots, the Monkeys feeding on fruit; the Ostrich, the Camel; the Cassowary, the Llama; and so on, so far as habits and character are concerned. With a few exceptions, they are essentially creatures of the air, and their organization has been fitted for the purpose; the larger birds, as the Pelican and others, are specially organized for carrying their weight by air sacs under their breasts, besides the bones in their body being filled with air, which make them more buoyant, and facilitate respiration under various pressures of the atmosphere.

Just as is the hair or fur of a mammal or the scales of a snake, the feather is a horny production of the epidermis. According to Professor Huxley, it is devolved within sacs from the surface of a conical papilla of the dermis. The external surface of the dermal papilla, whence a feather is to be developed, is provided upon its dorsal surface with a median groove which becomes shallower towards the apex of the papilla. From this median groove lateral furrows proceed at an open angle, and passing round upon the under surface of the papilla, become shallower until, in the middle line opposite the dorsal median groove, they become obsolete. Mincr grooves run at right angles to the lateral furrows. Hence the surface of the papilla has the character of the kind of mould, and if it were repeatedly dipped in such a substance as a solution of gelatine and withdrawn to cool until its whole surface was covered with an even coat of that substance, it is clear that the gelatine would be thickest at the basal or anterior end of the median groove, at the median ends of the lateral furrows, and those ends of the minor grooves which open into them; whilst it would be very thin at the apices of the median and lateral grooves and between the ends of the minor grooves. If, therefore, the hollow cone of gelatine, removed from its mould, were stretched from within, or if its thinnest part became weak by drying, it would tend to give way along the inferior median line opposite the rod-like casts of the median groove and between the ends of the casts of the lateral furrows as well as between each of the minor grooves, and the hollow cone would expand into a flat feather-like structure with a median shaft as a "vane" formed of barbs and barbules. In point of fact, in the development of a feather, such a cast of the dermal papilla is formed, though not in gelatine, but in the horny epidermic layer developed upon the mould, and as this is thrust outwards it opens out in the manner just described. After a certain period of growth, the papilla of the feather ceases to be grooved and a continuous horny cylinder is formed which constitutes the quill. Shortly, a feather may be said to consist of a tube or quill (calamus), a shaft, and two webs. The tube or quill is horny and transparent, varies in length according to the species, and is fixed in the skin. The shaft or *rhachis* is that part above the quill which is filled with an elastic, corky, white buoyant pith-like substance which bears the vane or web. It is coated on the outer or generally convex side with a horny lamella not unlike the tube, and on the inner or pithy side (also coated, though slightly) is a well-defined groove along its length up to the umbilicus or the small opening into the interior of the tube, which is closed inside by dry membrane. On the side of the shaft, from above the quill or tube, are vane rays or webs. These latter are, in general, fine, filiform, and nearly cylindrical in the smaller feathers, and flattened in the larger ones, as the quills. These, again, are furnished with barbs, barbules and barbicels, which help to give coherency to the entire web.

Then there are the plumules or accessory plumes which, constructed like the larger feathers, issue from the margin of the quill tube below the opening into the interior of the tube, which is regarded as an appendage checked in its growth. This is inconspicuous in gallinaceous birds, as pheasants. The plumules, unlike other feathers, have the vane rays very delicate and fibre-like; two series of barbs issue from them and from the barbs barbicels, extremely fine, entirely disunited, and loose. In the Cassowary and the Emu this *plumula accessoria* is as large as the outer shaft and vane; in others as Grouse and Falcons, about three-fourths the length, downy and incoherent. In the most well-developed feathers, as the quill feathers, the plumule is not present, and in others altogether wanting throughout the whole of their plumage, as in *Strix*, *Columba*, and *Anas*, while in song-birds it is very minute and downy.

Feathers may be divided into those which protect the bird from extreme cold, and those specially intended for flight. Those which are next the body, and commonly known as down, are analogous to the under fur of quadrupeds. These keep the body in an equal temperature, and may be said to resist cold or wet. Birds which lead an aquatic life have these feathers generally more developed than in others, for the manifest intention of affording additional warmth.

The feathers intended for flight are, first, the wing quills, which may be divided into primaries (4), secondaries (5), and tertiaries (6). The primaries may be distinguished from all the others by their greater size and stiffness. These arise from the bones of the hand. In number they are usually 10; the first of which is on the second finger joint, the 2nd, 3rd and 4th upon the first finger joint, and the other 6 upon the metacarpus. In some song birds, however, the number is only 9, and the first feather is either rudimentary or wanting, but never the longest. Secondaries are those which arise from the forearm, and are inserted in the skin on the posterior side of the ulna. They are not so stiff and strong as the primaries, usually shorter than them, more curved and more mobile. The tertiaries are those attached to the proximal end of the forearm, while the scapulars lie over the humerus and scapula.

The feathers on the upper surface of the wing are mostly developed on the cubitus and commonly designated wing coverts. The greater series (3) cover the base or root of the quills, and in general resemble the quill feathers or primaries, and, like them, are destitute of plumules. The second series, or median coverts (2), are also seated in the fold of the skin behind the arm. The smaller feathers behind this series are the lesser coverts (1).

Next is the tail, the feathers of which in the majority of birds are 12 in number, but there are others with as many as 14 to 18;

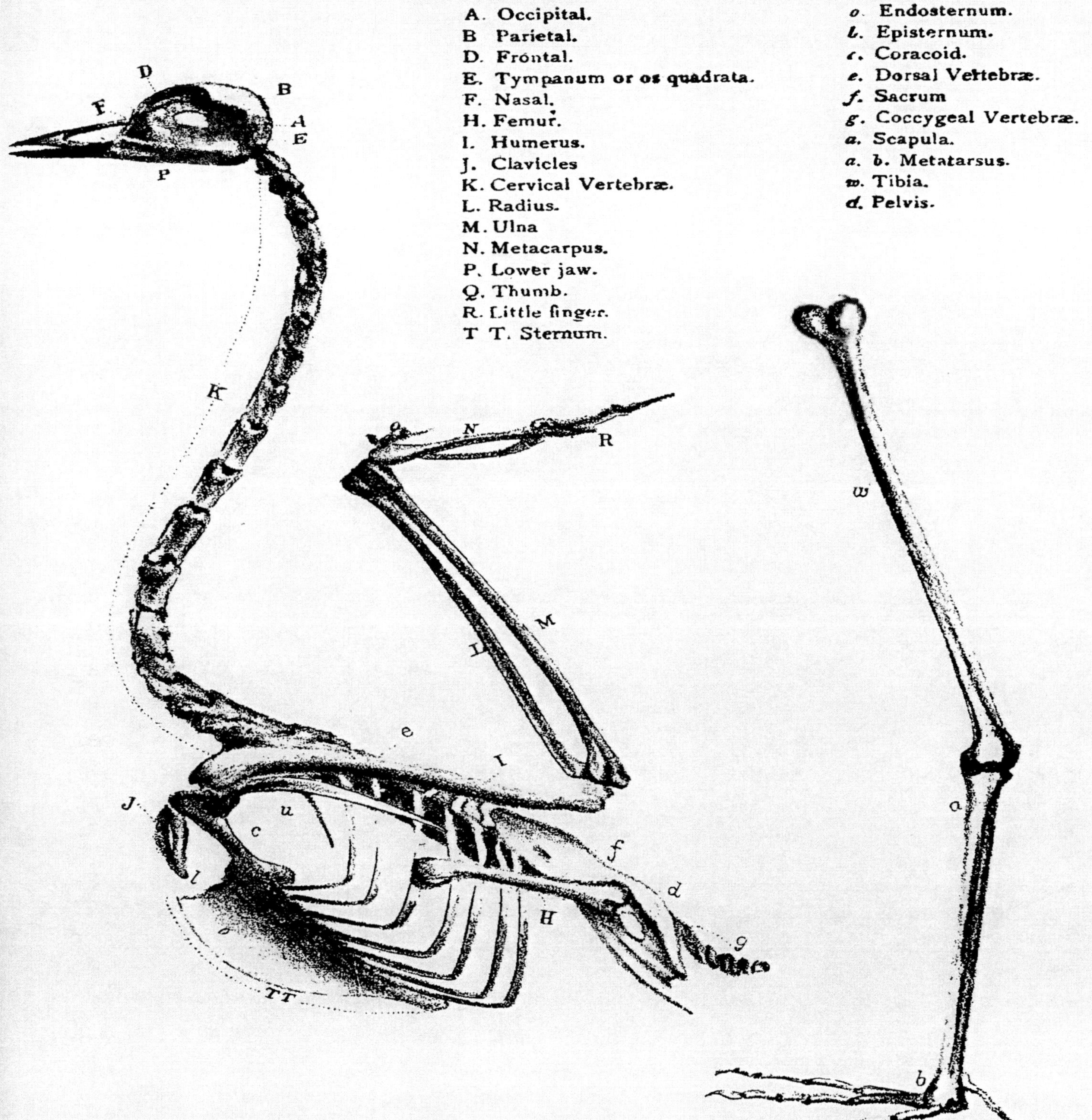

Balearica pavonina (L.).

these act in unison with the wing, during flight, and when expanded act as a rudder. The tail is longest in the Rasorial types and shortest in the natatorial and grallatorials. The tail feathers are covered at the base by the upper and under tail coverts. The tail, as the wing, in its structure shows a peculiar organization specially adapted for various purposes. An even tail is very uncommon; rounded tails are the most prevalent, while the racket tail is exhibited in 2 or 3 groups only as *Edolius*, or *Dissemurus* and *Dissemuroides*, and the lyre-shaped tail exclusively in the Rasorial order.

Of the osteology of birds much will not be said. In the composition of the frame of the body, birds may be said to have false ribs anterior and posterior to the true ribs. These cover nearly the whole short body or trunk, terminate anteriorly in a single articulation with the sternal ribs and pass forwards to be fixed on the sternal appendices on the middle of the trunk. The false ribs do not at all touch the sternum (TT) or breast bone. In the act of respiration the sternum in birds plays a very important part. It is one of the most remarkable and characteristic bones of the skeleton—first, for its great development; next, for the extent to which it covers the trunk, enveloping, as it does, all the internal organs, and by the median carina in front, giving it solidity, as well as strength and power to the pectoral muscles, the limits of attachment of which latter are marked on the external surface. The surface presented by the sternum or breast-bone bears the permanent and powerful muscles of the humerus; the trunk is solid, and the scapula, situated as it is along the side of the vertebral column, gives attachment to the powerful muscles of flight, while the chief support and means of resistance is the coracoid-bone (*c*). The sternum is not of one shape or form throughout the class, but is variable in consonance with the habits of the different orders, and these different shapes, forms and varieties of appearance lend considerable aid to the anatomist and systematist in working out perplexed affinities. In ducks and geese the posterior margin is replaced by membrane. In gallinaceous birds it terminates in narrow, separate bones; this is on account of their habit of running and feeding on the ground; while the high-flying rapacious birds have it solidly anchylosed and ossified. There are no parts of animals which vary so much in form and structure as the atlantal and sacral (*f*) extremities; the parts remotest from the centre of the skeleton are the most mutable in form; and the organs of progressive motion conform most to the medium in which animals reside. These parts vary so much in the same class of animals, that we might almost be induced to imagine that in organs so different as the human hand, and the fin of the porpoise or the wing of the bat, or the forefoot of the mole, all unity of composition was lost; and in passing to different classes we should scarcely expect to find the same element of structure which compose the fin of a fish or the foot of a turtle metamorphosed into the wing of the bird. But these very diversities of form of the same organ, when carefully examined, present the best proofs of the unity and simplicity of the plan upon which all organic forms are constructed.

Anterior to the sternum are the clavicles which unite below and form the furcula or merry-thought bone. These are joined to the sternum by ligament or cartilage—and the width of these serve to keep apart the shoulders, in opposition to the strong exertions of the muscles of the wing in flight.

In most birds—arboreal birds especially—the legs are slender and as light as the wings. These have the long tendons of the flexors and extensors continued to the foot. By the long flexor of the toes passing over the knee and behind the heel, the bending of these joints forces them to grasp mechanically the branches on which they are perched.

The leg bones consist of a short femur, long tibia with an imperfect fibula anchylosed to it; a patella; an anchylosed tarso-metarsal bone (the tarsus) and the toes. The pelvis is much extended longitudinally, and being anchylosed with the vertebral column, affords a large surface for the attachment of the muscles which support the trunk upon the thighs. The long iliac bones are excavated below and receive the kidneys. The ischia and pubic bones are wide and develope in their cavity the eggs, from which they are also expelled.

The muscular system of this class is also adapted for their aërial life and to carry them through the atmosphere. According to Professor Grant, of the Edinburgh College, their irritability or power of contraction is the greatest in the living state, and is the most quickly lost after death, its tenacity after death being generally in the inverse ratio of the degree of activity of that power during life. The muscles are generally more firm and vascular, tougher, stronger, and of a darker colour than in the cold-blooded vertebrates. These properties are most exhibited in the high-flying rapacious birds, and less so in granivorous birds. This muscular force becomes necessary in birds in order that they may fly, either for safety or to pursue their prey through the air, as well as to follow the seasons from latitude to latitude, and to perform their migrations over mountain chains, continents, or the trackless ocean. Though the muscles of the extremities of birds are generally short and thick, the tendons are longer and slender, dense, and often ossified. The form and movements of birds being nearly the same, there is a great uniformity in the disposition of their muscles. Their arms and hands being appropriated for flight, their progressive motion through the air depends chiefly on the action of the *pectoralis major* or the *humerus,* a muscle surpassing in magnitude all the rest in the body and covering nearly the whole of the forepart of the trunk. The muscles of the arm, the forearm, and the hand are inserted high up, and their fleshy portions confined to near their orifice, so that only the long tendons are sent down to the points which are to be moved. There is very little motion in the phalanges of the fingers.

It is not within the scope of this introduction to give an exhaustive or detailed classification of the organs of birds. The osseous system or the organs of support has been touched upon, also the tegumentary organs and those of motion. To detail the organs of connexion, sensibility and sensation, as well as of nutrition and generation, would go far beyond the intended limits of this introduction, while the proper treatment of these would need a more competent writer. *En passant,* however, a few remarks may not be out of place, especially in reference to those organs which the ornithologist and the student must necessarily examine—for instance, the testes. These, it is generally known, lie in front of, and in close proximity to, the kidneys, and although there are certain external characters which would enable the determination of the sex of a bird, yet nothing would be more satisfactory than an examination of this organ of generation—testes or ovaries decide the question beyond doubt. During the breeding or pairing season the testes of all male birds are much developed while the female sex exhibit in the same situation well-developed ovaries which at other times, though present, are small and granular. External sexual differences are more marked in birds than in mammals and other vertebrates; but these are not always reliable, especially in the case of birds, the young and the males of which assume the plumage of the female, or *vice versâ*, at different seasons of the year. The males, with some exceptions, are as a rule larger and more highly coloured.

The voice organs are placed in a glottis, at the bifurcation at the end of the wind-pipe, which is formed of entire rings of cartilage, and the call of each bird is produced by peculiar sets of muscles called the larynx. It is here that that peculiar gift of Nature, the voice of birds, is formed, and this one of all other attributes distinguishes the class from all others in the animal kingdom. The air contained in the cells of the lungs is the force used, while the wind-pipe and the larynx with their contractions, or expansion or movements in the gullet, contribute to the modulations and modifications of the voice. By their song one knows of their happy and cheerful life, and by it the male woos its mate. It is a language which is not even known whether belonging to one family only, or generally intelligible among the class.

The nervous system in birds and the organs of the senses run rapidly to high development.

The sense of sight is also very highly developed in birds, and each class and each family and sub-family will be found to be fitted with organs developed to the extent of their wants and to suit their living condition. The eagle and the raptores generally soar out of human sight, and yet they can see their prey notwithstanding the immense distance. The owl is consigned as a night watchman, and its organs of sight are so adapted that it can only distinguish objects with greater facility in the dusk and when all nature is desirous of repose. It is, however, compensated by a larger or more highly developed sense of hearing. The sense of sight is certainly extremely keen and piercing, and this fact no doubt is an important factor in the solution of the question of the manner in which thousands of miles are traversed by birds in their annual migrations. This must assist them.

It is doubtful whether there is any special development of the sense of taste in birds ; while that of smell, in the absence of any reliable data, may be said to be, if at all, very little developed, except in carrion feeders.

Like quadrupeds, birds may be classified as granivorous, carnivorous, and mixed feeders, or those that partake of both. Granivorous birds are furnished with larger and proportionally longer intestines than carnivorous species. Their food first enters a craw where it reaches entire, but soon undergoes partial dilution by a peculiar liquor secreted from the glands—thence enters another stomach, and eventually the gizzard or true stomach, where, with the aid of powerful muscles, thick and powerful membrane and stones it is triturated and becomes fit for the action of the gastric juices.

In their habits birds are either monogamous or polygamous, the latter exists generally among the Rasores or Gallinacea. Some again live a solitary life till the breeding season, when they begin their courtship and live in pairs, whilst their united efforts are necessary in forming their temporary habitation and in rearing their offsprings. There are also some, as the cuckoo, which leave their eggs to the care of a foster parent. Birds generally evince great affection for their young, and do not leave them till they can feed themselves. A great number or the majority of those known to inhabit India and its dependencies quit the country for the purpose of breeding. Each species associate in flocks and aided by their keen sight, together with the advantage they possess of flying at considerable heights in the air, they are enabled with their instinctive knowledge to discover the route they are to take to migrate—taking, probably, as a guide, the appearance of the atmosphere, direction of winds, &c.; so that without recourse to improbable modes it is not difficult to form an idea of the speed at which they go in transporting themselves to far countries by crossing vast ocean tracts. Without the means of conveying themselves from one place to another they could scarcely subsist for the reason that climatic influences affect their food-supply. This may also be said to be one of the reasons for migrating. Besides the want of food, other causes of migration are the want of a proper temperature of air and a convenient situation for the great work of breeding and rearing their offspring. They either remove from one country or climate to another—or from the inland districts to hills, forest regions, or to sequestered rocks or inlands in the sea, or to vast sandy plains far removed from, or in the vicinity of, the sea or river. And all this is conducted the with greatest punctuality, and the same may be said of their reappearance a few months later. It is also a noteworthy fact, proved by experiments, that birds which affect a certain station or district usually return to it year after year. The question as to how they subsist during their migrations is readily solved, when we consider the velocity of their flight together with the considerable length of time the majority continue on the wing. If we estimate the speed of a bird's flight at a mile in two minutes, it would need but 24 hours to carry it as many as seven hundred miles without taking into consideration favourable wind currents which would probably nearly double the distance. Red-starts and other short-winged birds pass by gradual and slow movement—as is evidenced by their appearance in different countries at different times of the year—but these seldom go further than the inaccessible heights of mountain ranges. Many journey during the night to avoid the dangers of daylight or for the purpose of taking advantage of favourable air currents. What the true reason for migrating is has yet to be learnt. We see their punctuality of departure and return, we note the dates very carefully, the time of their nidification, the composition of the various structures they build for the rearing of their young, also the number of eggs they lay, their colour, size and shape, as well as the changes of their plumage during the breeding season, but beyond this, and conjecture, we have not gone. The nidification of birds is indeed very various, but in consonance with their habits. The high-flying rapacious birds have their eyries on the ledges of high mountains in the most inaccessible parts or on the tops of high trees; the larger ones, including the Vulturinæ, lay but one, and seldom two eggs. The lesser ones, as the Accipitrinæ, build generally on trees or on steeple tops, and lay 2—4 eggs and seldom do more than repair their nests annually. All true vultures lay but a single egg, and their nests, as those of eagles, are built entirely of stout sticks and twigs with a hollow receptacle lined with coarse grass or fine twigs and any soft material. Bones also form a part of the structure. Many birds build in society—occupying trees, mountain ledges, plains, and the eaves of roofs—as sparrows, crows, herons, gulls, terns; and some when robbed of their eggs lay others very shortly after. The situation of the nests, too, are quite in consonance with their habits of life. Owls build in holes in wells, caverns, and in old decayed trees; Woodpeckers in holes in trees; Kingfishers in the banks of streams; the Swallow tribe build nests composed of mud plaster and feathers against the face of a wall, or under a roof or bridge, while others again, as the Byah or Weaver-bird, Honeysuckers, &c., build pensile nests, and all songsters nearly, of the Timeliinæ group, make small nests in bushes or shrubs; and with an instinctive knowledge endeavour to hide their nests by various artifices, as covering them with cobwebs, lichen, or plaster to give them the appearance of the surroundings of the nest.

Of the Avian inhabitants of India nearly one-half are known to breed in the country. A great number go no further than the Himalayan range, while the rest may be said to be resident members, and to breed on the plains.

It is not necessary to refer to the geographical distribution of species, nor to divide the country into geographical regions, as the table at the end of the volume will sufficiently show the first, and the text the latter, while it is patent to all that humid countries comprise birds of bright plumage and those of the plains of duller plumage, and in consonance with the nature of the surroundings. The geographical distribution of species has been worked out from all the materials available.

[As a short *resumé* of the history of Indian Ornithology would perhaps be not uninteresting, what has been written in my Avifauna of British India is transcribed here, prefatory to that of the Island.]

It is above half a century since Major Franklin, who was the first writer on Indian Ornithology, published a paper on the Ornithology of India. This paper appeared in the Proceedings of the Zoological Society of London. Colonel Tickell soon followed by publishing in the Asiatic Society's Journal a list of the Birds of Bhorabum and Dholbum. Another equally energetic naturalist was Col. Sykes, who in 1832 began his Catalogue of the Birds of the Deccan, and continued his studies and publications for some years, not only of birds but of the mammals and fish of the Mahratta Country so designated, while Mr. Brian Hodgson, who was attached as Resident at the Court of Nepaul, added largely to the store of knowledge of the avian inhabitants of the Himalayas. His contributions are spread both in the Indian and Home scientific periodicals, and his valuable MSS. and drawings, so largely referred to in every Ornithological work, are zealously watched over and consulted at the British Museum. Assam was next worked out by MacClelland, and his papers—also published in the Zoological Society's Proceedings in 1839—are full of interest, and particularly as showing the geographical distribution of the Himalayan birds.

Dr. Adam collected in Cashmere, as well as in the North-West Provinces of India; Colonel Tytler in Barrackpore and Dacca; while the names of Hutton and numerous other observers and collectors are prominent in the earlier journals as contributors of interesting notes on habits, nidification, &c., of species in various parts of India.

Mr. Blyth, who is rightly called the Father of Indian Ornithology, " was by far the most important contributor to our knowledge of the Birds of India." Seated, as the head of the Asiatic Society's

Museum, he, by intercourse and through correspondents, not only formed a large collection for the Society, but also enriched the pages of the Society's Journal with the results of his study, and thus did more for the extension of the study of the Avifauna of India than all previous writers. There can be no work on Indian Ornithology without reference to his voluminous contributions. The most recent authority, however, is Mr. Allen O Hume, C.B., who, like Blyth and Jerdon, got around him numerous workers, and did so much for Ornithology, that without his Journal—"Stray Feathers"—no accurate knowledge could be gained of the distribution of Indian birds. His large museum, so liberally made over to the nation, is ample evidence of his zeal and the purpose to which he worked. Ever saddled with his official work, he yet found time for carrying out a most noble object. His "Nests and Eggs," "Scrap Book," and numerous articles on birds of various parts of India, the Andamans and the Malay Peninsula, are standing monuments of his fame throughout the length and breadth of the civilized world. His writings and the field notes of his curator, contributors and collectors are the pith of every book on Indian Birds, and his vast collection is the ground upon which all Indian Naturalists must work. Though differing from him on some points, yet the palm is his as an authority above the rest in regard to the Ornis of India. Amongst the hundred and one contributors to the Science in the pages of "Stray Feathers," there are some who may be ranked as specialists in this department, and their labors need a record. These are Mr. W. T. Blanford, late of the Geological Survey, an ever watchful and zealous Naturalist of some eminence. Mr. Theobald, also of the Geological Survey, Mr. Ball of the same Department, and Mr. W. E. Brooks. All these worked in Northern India, while for work in the Western portion must stand the names of Major Butler, of the 66th Regiment, Mr. W. F. Sinclair, Collector of Colaba; Mr. G. Vidal, the Collector of Bombay, Mr. J. Davidson, Collector of Khandeish, and Mr. Fairbank, each one having respectively worked the Avifauna of Sind, the Concan, the Deccan and Khandeish.

The country referred to in the Avifauna of British India embraces the whole of India, including those recently acquired possessions in (now British) Burmah. Of this latter and most interesting portion of the Indian Empire, Mr. Eugene Oates, of the Public Works Department, has written a connected and detailed account, and it is from the pages of his valuable work I have been able to add much to the knowledge of the Avifauna of the Indian Empire as it now stands. In his Introduction he gives a *resumé* of the Ornithological explorations in that country. Colonel Tickell, whose contributions in the early numbers (1833) of the Asiatic Society's Journal are of much interest, is said to be the first Ornithologist who attempted to work Burmah. His field of work was in Tenasserim, chiefly among the higher hills and mountains to the east of Moulmein, culminating in the peak of Mooleyit, which rises about 6,000 feet above sea level. The late Mr. Blyth, after assuming charge of the Asiatic Society's Museum, found willing contributors in Captain (now Sir Arthur) Phayre, also the late Major Berdmore, Dr. Mason, and others. Mr. Blyth's contributions of the birds of this country also swell the pages of the "Asiatic Society's Journal," as well as those of the "Ibis." His valuable Catalogue of Burmese Birds was his last contribution, and this was published in 1875 by the late Lord Tweeddale as a posthumous work. The latter, recently known as Lord Walden, also interested himself in the Ornithology of Burmah, and his valuable papers have also been published as a posthumous work, edited by Captain R. G. Wardlaw-Ramsay, who explored a considerable portion of Pegu.

The following are other particulars given by Mr. Oates of the work done in Pegu. He says: "Turning now (1883) to those who are engaged in active work in connection with Burmese Ornithology, I come to a small band of hardworking field naturalists. Mr. A. O. Hume in his study and Mr. W. Davison in the field have, for many years past, actively worked Tennascrim." The notes of these Naturalists enrich the pages of Oates' work, as well as of this, culled from both sources.

Other workers in the field of Burmese Ornithology are Mr. W. T. Blanford, Captain Fielden, Dr. Armstrong, Captain Bingham, the late Colonel Lloyd, the late Captain Beavan, Mr. Oliver and Mr. DeWet; also Mr. Hough and Mr. Shopland. The contributions of all these gentlemen are to be found in the pages of "Stray Feathers."

British Burmah, according to Oates, is an irregular, narrow, maritime country, hardly any portion being more than 200 miles from the sea. It lies entirely within the tropics, the most Northern portion of Arrakan being at a short distance from the Northern tropic, and the most Southern point of Tennasserim lying on the 10th degree of North Latitude. The general character of the country may be said to be mountainous, the only flat portions being strips of land along the banks of the larger rivers, and considerable areas at the mouths of these rivers.

The whole of British Burmah where not cultivated is covered with dense growth of vegetation. On the elevated portions, the vegetation is composed of large forest trees and bamboos, and on the low alluvial plains, elephant grass of great height. The climate owing to a heavy rain-fall, is said to be humid, and its effects, to cause the plumage of birds to be of great brilliancy. The same may be said of that portion of the Zoological region which comprises the Himalayas, also Eastern Bengal, and Malabar.

Ceylon is an island which, though from almost time immemorial has always attracted the attention of those interested either in antiquities, archæology, ethnology, geology, and other kindred subjects, its zoology, until very recently, was not investigated, and hence very little has been known. Bibliography, in regard to its scenery and climate, as well as of sporting tours, was not wanting, but of its zoology there were no connected accounts, beyond some important communications published in the Bengal Asiatic Society's Journal by Drs. Davy, Kinnis and Templeton, which were edited by the late Mr. Edward Blyth, whose name in connection with Indian Ornithology still stands as a monument in the annals of Natural

History. These papers excited so much interest that they were immediately followed by others from the pen of Mr. E. Layard, and in 1852 sufficient materials were collected by Dr. Kelaart to enable him to write his "Prodomus Faunæ Zeylanica." While continuing their interest in the zoology of the Island, Drs. Davy and Templeton, also Professor Harvey, worked up the mammals, reptiles, fish, molluscs, &c.

With the united results of the officers abovenamed, and the "Prodomus" of Dr. Kelaart, Major Legge began his researches, and as much as a decade ago wrote his "Birds of Ceylon," an excellently illustrated work. Though it was all that could then be desired, and useful in being descriptive of the Avian inhabitants of the Island, the classification adopted by him was generally inappreciable, while the nomenclature was more or less obsolete, and the synonyms incompletely worked up.

Since Major Legge's publication, the interest in the Ornithology of the country has increased ten-fold, and numerous field-workers, as Messrs. E. E. Green, H. Parker, F. Armstrong and others, have added much valuable information in regard to nidification, as well as made many valuable and important discoveries. These are scattered in various periodicals, and one of the objects of this work is to bring them together, and to present a systematic account of the Avian inhabitants of the Island according to the most modern and generally accepted classification, as adopted in my "Avifauna of British India and its Dependencies." It comprises, like that work, ordinal, generic and specific Descriptions of all the birds, as well as notices of their habits, &c., with also a table showing their geographical distribution. This last is considered the most important portion of the work, as showing what species belonging to the Indian Fauna occur there, and as permitting inferences as to the potential factor in determining their distribution from the Himalayas so far south, and what the conditions are (configural, climatic or nutritive) which preclude other species from having a place in the Fauna.

With the *Table of Contents* of this work before one, the whole topography of the country is easily read. The absence of Vultures in the Island points to an animal of another class having been given a place to in some numbers, as a compensation, and it may be rightly inferred that the Jackal (*Canis aureus*) which hunt in large packs, especially in the low country, do the work which the Vultures in other parts of the world have been assigned. Then come the Buzzards or Harriers, the number of species of which in comparison to the number of other Falconidæ, shows that the country is generally a heavy grass land, over which these species soar for rats, snakes, &c., which infest it, while from the Pandiones which occur, also the Brahminy or Fish-kite, as well as the number of species of Terns and the species which occur of the Accipitrinæ, it cannot but be inferred that the Island is in great part a large undulating plain, diversified by a mountain system of no great extent; and that from this configuration large marshes exist, and that the country is seasonally inundated, and so form extensive tanks in the northern and central regions. The number of species of the Palæorninæ and Gecininæ, also the paucity of songsters among the Passerine birds, point to the hills and valleys formed by the mountain system being clothed with large trees and dense vegetation; and the species of the Fringillidæ which occur lead one to the belief that rice is the chief or only cereal cultivation.

European forms occur, as the storks, curlews, and waders generally, but these are chiefly seasonal visitants. The large tanks, marshes, lakes and marshy plains, also the shallow lagoons on either side of the Island, especially in the Eastern Provinces along the coast between the mainland and the sand formations of the shore, teem with aquatic birds and waders; in fact, in such situations they are simply in myriads. Though in number of species the Grallatores do not number high, but the individual members of each species may be said to be innumerable. The Gallinæ and Anseres, as will be seen, are not many, and it is scarcely explainable why only so few of the latter, as well as the Laridæ, occur, considering the vast extent of sea coast and suitable marshy ground, unless climatal conditions are averse to the Anseres affecting the Island. The Passeres certainly outnumber both the Grallæ and the Anseres, and form nearly two-thirds of the whole Avifauna of the Island.

Of the 375 species known to occur, as many as 232 are found in the moist regions of Bengal; 226 in British Burmah; 197—199 in the moist and hilly regions of the Concan and Deccan, where the average rainfall is about the same as in Ceylon. In the drier regions of India as Sind, Kutch, Guzerat and the Punjab, the distribution of the birds of Ceylon is very small, the latter country containing only 197 species belonging to the Ceylon Avifauna, while in Guzerat and Kutch can only be counted 160—164, respectively. In Southern India and along the Malabar Coast as many as 301 of the Ceylon forms are found, while the Island has no less than 41 species peculiar to itself.

Southern India has been practically worked out by the late Dr. Jerdon. His admirable manual shows the energy he spent in bringing to perfection a system of classification to this day admitted as practically good though not very natural, but yet the foundation for the past quarter of a century of every work on the Avifauna of India; and if there are any who differ from him in certain views, it is because they live in later times, and follow, though not quite, those who base their classifications on internal as well as external structure.

Classification—according to Jerdon—may be said to be the grouping of objects according to their affinities, and their arrangement into divisions of various degrees of magnitude. Its object is to bring together those beings that most resemble each other, and to separate those that differ. By some it has been regarded simply as a convenient method of arrangement for shortening the labour of the naturalist, who, by its means, instead of studying all the characters which each specimen presents, is enabled, by knowing its general position, to confine his attention to a few of the minor details of structure. His labour is thus simplified by the union into one group of all the animals which agree in the most important and essential characters. The Philosophic naturalist has, however, a higher aim, and his object is to discover the natural system, or, in other words, to endeavour to develope the general plan on which the Creator has formed and arranged the numberless species of natural objects.

On comparing certain species with others, we find various degrees of resemblance of structure and general appearance. Those, which are nearest and most close, are called affinities, and more distant resemblances, analogies ; and these are of every degree of nearness or remoteness. The affinities of species may be said to point out their order of succession in nature, and are easily understood and appreciable. Not so, however, the analogies exhibited by many species and groups to others, perhaps very distantly related. These may be resemblances of structure, or of colour, or of habits. Some naturalists explain them by expressing their belief that in every group, great or small, there are certain types of structure, offering fixed characteristic marks, and that analogies are, simply, the representation in one group of a certain type in another, or, to put it in other words, that analogous groups or species simply occupy a corresponding place in their respective classes, orders, or families. This theory of representation has, perhaps, been carried out to too great an extent by certain writers, but, nevertheless, it appears to be founded on nature ; and the existence of these, often unexpected analogies between distant groups and species, clearly manifests the unity of the plan of the animal creation. According to Mr. Darwin's views, such analogies might be explained on the supposition that the resemblances were due to some remote ancestral origin. The colours and markings of some birds appear to be repeated in other groups ; and, in most natural divisions, great variety of form of bills, and also of other parts is exhibited, representing several distinct types ; and, in some more distantly related groups, analogy is shown by habits, by the colour of the eggs, by seasonal change of plumage, &c., &c. Many examples of analogy will be pointed out in the present work.

On beginning at any point in any series of beings, and tracing, step by step, the scale of affinities, we soon find that the supposed chain is interrupted, and that branches strike off in various directions.

That a linear arrangement is quite impossible has long been conceded universally; but what directions the divergencies take, is not agreed on; nor, indeed, have Zoologists of the present day decided that there is a fixed plan for any one class, still less that the same system extends through all. Strickland and, quite recently, Wallace have attempted to show the affinites of some families and orders of birds by means of diagrams.

Certain English Naturalists, and simultaneously, one or more German Botanists, have maintained that, in arranging any series of animated beings, according to their affinities, the tendency is to revert to the point whence they set out, not indeed in an unbroken line, but in a series of circles. Thus the circular system, as it has been termed, has been strained, perhaps, too far by its exponents, but there is no doubt that in many instances this tendency to a quasi-circular arrangement appears to exist in nature, and even Wallace's diagrams show this. It appears, however, according to some, that the affinities of the species of any group are various, and cannot be expressed by figures, every natural group and species being connected not with two only, but with several; and it is possible that any natural group, if we possessed all the forms which it comprised, would present links of transition towards all the other groups of the same family or order. Many examples might be given to show the tendency to a circular arrangement, but I shall content myself by pointing out to the student this supposed feature, to verify, or otherwise, in any group he may be studying. Many gaps of course occur in following the chain of affinities, some very great, others easily bridged over. These of course are stumbling blocks in the way of such as believe in a complete chain or circle; and the fossil remains of birds, hitherto discovered, have not been sufficiently numerous to make these intervals much less.

That a special design is exhibited in Creation there can, I think, be but little doubt. It is admitted by almost all, and most fully and unequivocally, in the best known and most highly organized group the Vertebrata; in all the classes of which a certain archetype of form is preserved, marked and recognizable, however disguised for special ends. It is surely more consonant to our ideas of a Creator to believe that He formed His numberless creatures with certain relations to each other, than to conceive that each was brought to life independently. Indeed, a follower of Darwin might fairly argue that the evidence of design is as clearly shown by the theory of the transmutation of species, as by that of separate individual creation; but Darwin himself, perhaps, lays too much stress on external and fortuitous circumstances as producing varieties, and not enough on the inherent power of change, which, as he clearly shows, is now and then exhibited by various organic bodies.

That species were created at hap-hazard, without any reference to others, either of the same group or more distant ones, is a doctrine so opposed to all the affinities and analogies observed throughout the animated world, that the mind refuses to accept it, and intuitively acknowledges the evidence of design.

That a certain system has been followed, if we allow design at all, must be admitted, but the exponent of the *natural* system—Sharpe, Gadow, Seebohm and others too numerous to mention notwithstanding—has yet to appear. "The tendency of the present age is to accumulate facts and not to generalize, but we have now a sufficiency of facts, and want our Lyell to explain them."

By the consent of most naturalists, all object of nature are divided into kingdoms, sub-kingdoms, classes, orders, families, and genera, and, in some cases, where the families are numerous, tribes, sub-families, and sub-genera are added. Birds are a class of the sub-kingdom Vertebrata, of the Animal kingdom. The Orders of birds are founded chiefly on the form of the bill, and more especially of the feet. Families are characterized by more minute distinctions of the bill and feet, together with characters drawn from the wings, tail, and certain habits, more or less common to all. A genus comprises one or many species closely resembling one another in the structure of bill, feet, wings and tail, and in habits, yet differing, it may be, in colour, size or some minute differences of structure. To give a familiar example, the European Kite and the Common Kite of India are species of the same genus, *Milvus;* and the English Kingfisher and the little Indian Kingfisher are separate species of the same genus Alcedo, each of these genera containing several species. Of late years genera have been greatly divided and multiplied, some of them being classed as sub-genera; but in practice, and till the whole realm of Ornithology is presided over by a master-hand, no distinction can be satisfactorily pointed out, or acted on. When the families of any order are very numerous, they are classed in tribes; and when the genera of any family are numerous, or comprise several distinct forms, they are grouped into sub-families.

In every natural assemblage of forms, whether it be genus, family or order, there is some one form which presents the characters that are common to all, in a more remarkable and complete manner than the rest; and this is called the type of the group. Thus each genus has its typical specie; each family its typical genus, and so on; the type being, in each instance, that form to which our minds naturally revert as best exhibiting the characters that belong to the entire group. Some are very close to the type, others differ from it to such a degree that we might have failed to recognise the connection, were it not for the presence of intermediate links. These are called aberrant forms.

It may be asked, are the divisions, which are here indicated, natural, *i.e.*, marked out by nature, or, in other words, designed? That some of them are so, we may, I think, safely infer from the example already quoted of the Vertebrata. Here we have at least four, some say five, great divisions marked out by nature so broadly that the distinctions are in most cases recognizable and patent to all; and, in each of these classes so clearly marked, that there are certain divisions apparent even to the uninstructed; such, for example, among birds, are the Birds of Prey, Owls, Finches, Game birds, Ducks, &c., &c. Many genera, too, are undoubtedly exceedingly natural and clearly defined, and on the whole, I think, we may conclude that Nature herself (could we but correctly read her lessons) has pointed out most of the divisions ; or, in other words, has varied each group, small as well as great, in a certain and definite method. Many natural divisions, however, appear to grade into each other, and have no definite limits ; yet, for purpose of study, we must assign limits and characters ; and the affinities, by which they are grouped, must be judged of by as many and as constant characters as possible derived from all parts ; but certain typical characters must be assigned.

There are at present above 8,000 species of birds known and described, though much of the civilized world has yet to be explored. When this has been done, what the number may be it is difficult to conjecture, but this large number has been arranged by Naturalists into six large orders, founded entirely on the organs of manducation and prehension. These are :—

I.—Raptores, or birds of prey.
II.—Insessores, or perching birds.
III.—Gemitores, or pigeons.
IV.—Rassores, or game birds
V.—Grallatores, or waders.
VI.—Natatores, or swimming birds.

Though this is the basis of classification, there is a tendency in the present day to split and divide these, and to upset the order of arrangement, owing to structural and external characters combined being made the basis, hence we see in a very recent classification, viz., "Oates' Catalogue of Indian Birds in the British Museum," crows taking the lead in the Natural System ! ! ! In another the Raptores are placed after the Parrots, and the Passeres hold the first place, as in the following rather mixed arrangement:—

I. Passeres ; II. Macrochires ; III. Pici ; IV. Coccyges ; V. Psittaci ; VI. Striges ; VII. Accipitres ; VIII. Steganopodes ; IX. Herodiones ; X. Anseres; XI. Columbæ ; XII. Gallinæ ; XIII. Geranomorphæ ; XIV. Limicolæ ; XV. Gaviæ ; XVI. Tubinares ; XVII. Pygopodes. It is needless to defend these systems ; it cannot be done ; the oldest system must survive..

Raptores, or birds of prey, are distinguished by their crooked bill and claws, by means of which they are enabled to overcome, and in the order of nature to prey upon, other birds and small quadrupeds, to keep that necessary balance so needful. They hold the same rank among birds as the *Carnivora* among the quadrupeds. They are divided into two families, the diurnal and nocturnal, the latter being the owls, which issue at dusk. The diurnal species are the eagles, vultures, kites, falcons, hawks, &c. They are readily distinguished by having their nostrils placed in a naked skin or cere, and their feet bearing three toes before and one behind and their eyes placed laterally; while the *Striges*, or nocturnal species, have their nostrils covered with stiff hairs, the outer toe reversible; eyes large and directed forwards. The Passerine birds form the largest class. They are all very nearly alike in structure, and are divided according to the position of their exterior toe, those having the midtoe united to the middle by one or two joints only; and those with the exterior toe united to the middle one as far as the last joint but one. The next order is that of the Climbers or Scansores, vith both the outer and great toe directed backwards. Following this are the Gallinaceous birds, or Rasores of some: birds of heavy gait, short, rounded wings, heavy flight, such as peafowls, game jungle cock, &c. The Waders or Grallatores, comprising the 5th order, are distinguished by the naked tarsus and a portion of their thighs also, their long legs, which they lay back under the tail feathers in flight. The last are the web-footed birds, as the ducks, characterized by their webbed feet, and generally broad, spathulate bills. A more detailed account of the orders, sub-orders, families and sub-families into which these have been divided will be found under the respective headings in the body of the work; which cannot from its nature have much pretensions to originality.

It is only as a descriptive handbook of the birds of the Island of Ceylon that this work should be regarded. The idea of writing it did not originate wholly with myself, but besides the trouble and inconvenience experienced by me in looking up literature for determining species received from the Island, there was a general conviction among all my correspondents and numerous working cabinet and field naturalists that a work of this kind in a moderate compass would be welcomed as supplying a desideratum, especially if all the knowledge extant of the birds of Ceylon were put together under one consecutive serial number. Numerous valuable works have been laid under contribution in preparing the work, especially Sharpe, Seebohm and Gadow's Catalogues; Jerdon's valuable Manual; Oates' Birds of British Burmah; Stray Feathers; Ibis; Hume's Nests and Eggs, &c., &c., all of which have been referred to under the synonyms of species, and thus avoiding the use of inverted commas wherever they may have been required. In doing this latter I would crave the indulgence of all authors for the privilege I have taken, in this way, of so largely adding from their valuable works, to the existing knowledge of the distribution of the Avifauna of Ceylon. I only trust that this small effort will find public favour. It has been made as complete as possible, so that naturalists will find it to be an unpretending manual to guide them in adding to the present accumulation of facts much of what is at present hidden and unknown to science.

In concluding this Introduction, it only remains for me to acknowledge the valuable assistance received in this attempt to collate the scattered information regarding the Avifauna of the Island of Ceylon into a systematic account, and, as stated in the Prospectus, arranged according to the most modern and generally accepted classification. Among those to whom I am under special obligation I would mention Mr. W. H. Parker who very kindly sent me valuable notes of the nidification and distribution of the Birds in the Island; also Mr. F. Armstrong who, besides his notes, furnished me with numerous skins for examination. To Mr. W. F. Sinclair, the Collector of Kolaba, I am especially indebted for specimens from the Kolaba district, of the order *Steganopodes* which added to the existing knowledge of the distribution of the species of this order which are not only rare but of a roving disposition. Besides this I have received other very material assistance from him, which has in a great measure enabled me to complete the Avifauna of British India as well as this work. To Lieutenant Henry E. Barnes, D.A.C., I am also indebted for many valuable notes in regard to nidification, &c., while the kindness of Mr. Mahon Daly in sending me birds from South India and also eggs has helped me considerably with the distribution table.

I have also to tender my acknowledgments to Mr. H. M. Phipson for assistance given in precisely the most important direction, *viz.*, in furnishing me with the opportunity of consulting several important works which would have been otherwise inaccessible to me. Mr. Edgar Thurston of the Central Museum, Madras, has also very kindly assisted me in sending such references as I required from books in the Public Library under his charge.

VICTORIA NATURAL HISTORY INSTITUTE,
RIPON ROAD
BYCULLA, BOMBAY.

J. A. M.

SYSTEMATIC TABLE OF CONTENTS.

96/173 Collocalia Linchi, p. 173 ;
211/156 Amadina striata, p. 121 ;
127/74 Stoparola sordida, p. 81 ;
188/132 Zosterops Ceylonensis, p. 138 ;
178/122 Parus atriceps, p. 126 ;
182/130 Cinnyris zeylanica, p. 134 ;
150/105 Pycnonotus hæmorrhous, p. 109 ;
134/110 Thamnobia fulicata, p. 114 ;
240/250 Excalfactoria chinensis, p. 235 ;
208/158 Amadina Kelaarti, p. 163 ;
159/121 Alcippe nigrifrons, p. 125 ;
192/139 Hirundo javanica, p. 144 ;
168/83 Prinia inornata. p 90 ;
200/148 Anthus rufulus. p. 154 ;
169/91 Cisticola cisticola, p. 96 ;
147/106 Pycnonotus lutæolus, p. 110 ;
137/96 Merula Kinnisi, p. 100 ;
86/225 Halcyon smyrnensis, p. 208 ;
132/111 Copsychus saularis. p. 115.
103 Corone splendens, p. 53.

LIST OF ILLUSTRATIONS.

THE

AVIFAUNA OF THE ISLAND

OF

CEYLON.

ORDER—ACCIPITRES.

Bill short, strong, stout, covered at the base with a cere or naked skin and strongly curved; the tip perpendicular; nostrils open. Legs and feet muscular and strong, the latter armed with powerful curved, sharp, elongated talons capable of being bent under the feet. Toes four, three in front and one behind.

The Accipitres or Raptores vary greatly in size. The Vultures and Eagles comprise some of the largest of the feathered tribes, while the Falcons are small. The order comprising these is analogous to the feline quadrupeds, and forms a distinct and primary one in the class of birds. They are readily recognized by their strong hooked bill, the upper mandible of which is longer than the lower. The edges in some are festooned or toothed to assist in the operation of tearing their prey. They are notoriously the most muscular and powerful. The muscles of their legs and feet are of great strength to enable them to strike down or hold their prey. The greater number are suited for rapid flight and live on prey got by their own courage and exertions. The Vultures, however, are slothful, large bodied, and, not unlike the Hyæna, feed upon carrion and act the part of scavengers.

The males are always smaller than the females, and owing to this difference in size of the sexes, and the almost totally different plumage of the various stages of growth of the members, from the young to the adult, they are difficult to determine, even with large series of specimens. In number and species they are not many—taking them world-wide—compared with the Insessores or perching birds. For special reasons in the economy of nature they are not prolific, but propagate slowly. Many lay but one egg, others two, and none of the order are known to lay more than four, nor to breed more than once a year.

The order is divided by Sharpe (*Cat. Acc. Br. Mus.*) into three sub-orders, *viz.*, Falcones, Pandiones, and Striges; four families, *viz.*:—Vulturidæ, Falconidæ, Bubonidæ and Strigidæ, and these again into nine sub-families

The members of 7 (seven) only occur in Ceylon, the exceptions being the Polyborinæ and Sarcoramphinæ.

The following is the division of the Accipitres :—

SUB-ORDER—Falcones.
Family—Vulturidæ.
Sub-Family—Vulturinæ.
Family—Falconidæ.
Sub-Family—Accipitrinæ.
,, Buteoninæ.
,, Aquilinæ.
,, Falconinæ.
SUB-ORDER—Pandiones.
SUB-ORDER—Striges.
Family—Bubonidæ.
Sub-Family—Buboninæ.
,, Syrniinæ.
Family—Strigidæ.

These comprise the Vultures, the Falcons, and the Owls, the two former are diurnal, and the latter nocturnal birds of prey.

SUB-ORDER—FALCONES.

Toes without feathers; outer toe not reversible ; eyes lateral ; cere soft and fleshy, generally not hidden by bristles. Facial disc none. Plumage compact.

Family—VULTURIDÆ—VULTURES.

Upper mandible not toothed, sometimes sinuate. Head and neck more or less bare or clothed only with short down. No true feathers on crown of head.

Members of the Sub-Family—Vulturinæ—or Vultures Proper, the scavengers of all tropical countries, are not represented in Ceylon.

Sub-Family—NEOPHRONINÆ—SCAVENGERS.

Bill lengthened, slender ; nostrils longitudinal, nearly in the middle of the bill, perforated, and without bony septum.

Gen. Neophron.—*Savigny*.

Characters, same as those of the family.

1. Neophron ginginianus, *Lath.*, *Ind. Orn.* i. p. 7; *Blyth*, *Ibis*, 1866; *Jerd.*, *B. of Ind.* i. p. 12, No. 6; *Sharpe*, *Cat. Acc. Br. Mus.* p. 18; *Hume*, *Str. F.* vol. i. p. 150; *Rough Notes* i. p. 39; *Murray*, *Hdbk. Zool.*, *&c. Sind*, p. 105; *id.*, *Vert. Zool.*, *Sind*, p. 64; *Legge*, *B. Ceylon*, p. 64; *Murray*, *Avif. Br. Ind.* i. p. 9, No. 8.—The WHITE SCAVENGER VULTURE, or PHARAOH'S HEN OF BRUCE.

Adult.—Yellowish or creamy white. Quills black, neck hackles long, lanceolate, tinged somewhat rusty; secondaries dark brown, and like the quills, internally ashy white at base. Head bare, throat with a little scanty down; a few white feathers in front of the eye. Irides reddish brown; cere and face turmeric yellow; bill pale horny brown; feet and legs yellowish white.

Length.—21 to 22 inches; wing 15·5 (not reaching the tip of the tail); tail 9·5; tarsus 3·4; culmen 2·9.

Hab.—In Ceylon this species is very rare, but throughout India it is a permanent resident and breeds from February to April on cliffs, old mosques, &c., seldom on trees, making a rude nest of twigs, lined with rags, &c. Eggs variously coloured, the ground colour usually a dirty white, blotched and smeared with reddish brown, or marked all over with deep red, with blotches at the larger end.

Family—FALCONIDÆ—Falcons.

Bill usually short and compressed; tip elongated, curved and sharp. Commissure of upper mandible distinctly toothed or festooned. Head always covered with true feathers.

Sub-Family—BUTEONINÆ.

Bill small and moderate, with the tip hooked. Wings moderate; tail generally short; tarsus with scutæ in front and behind; tibia longer than tarsus. Outer toe connected to middle toe by interdigital membrane.

Gen. Circus.—*Lacep.*

Upper mandible slightly festooned; lower emarginate. Nostrils round, with no bony excrescence. Tarsi long and slender, naked; wings long; the first quill not so long as the fifth, the third and fourth longest; cere large, surrounded with a ruff of setaceous curved plumes.

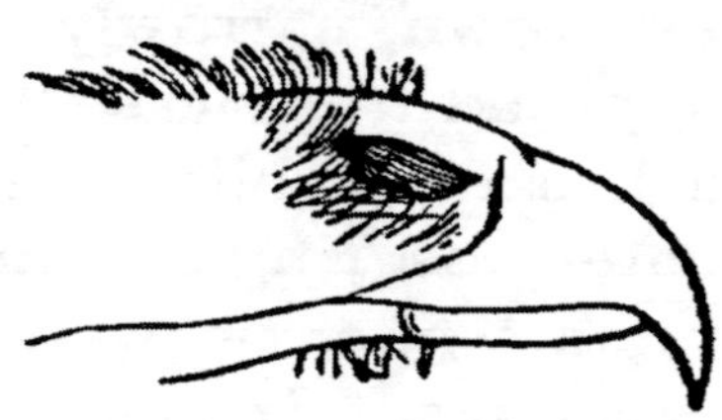

2. Circus cyaneus, *Linn., Sys. Nat.* i. p. 126; *Yarrell, Br. B.* i. p. 94; *Sharpe, Cat. Acc.* p. 52; *Boie, Isis,* 1822; *Gould, B. Eur.* i. pl. 33; *Jerd., B. Ind.* i. p. 95; *Gould, B. Gt. Bt.* 1867; *Hume, Rough Notes* ii. p. 93, No. 50; *Str. F.* i. pp. 160, 418; *Reid, Cat. B. Prov. Mus. N.-W. P. and Oudh*; *Murray, Avif. Br. Ind.* i. p. 10, No. 9.—The Hen Harrier.

Adult Male.—Upper parts, chin, throat, cheeks, ear coverts, and sides of the neck, and breast bluish ashy, paler on the wing coverts and tail, the former also slightly margined with whitish and the scapulars slightly tinged with fuscous. Frontal plumes and lores whitish; feathers of the nape pure white. Forehead and supercilium whitish. 1st 6 primaries blackish both above and below, the outer webs, towards the tips, more or less suffused with silvery grey; the inner webs white at the bases. Secondaries silvery grey on the outer webs and tips, with black shafts and an indistinct subterminal band. Tail ashy grey, tipped with white, the middle tail feathers entirely uniform pale ashy grey, white-shafted, the lateral ones becoming less grey and white on the inner webs, with from 6 to 8 imperfect, and sometimes almost obsolete transverse ashy bars. *Upper tail coverts white. Under surface from below the breast, including the thighs, the axillary plumes, and under wing coverts white* (in the adolescent stage slightly suffused with very pale bluish grey). Cere yellow; bill bluish black; irides yellow; legs and feet bright yellow; claws black.

Length.—17 to 19 inches; wing 12·2 to 13·8; tail 8·1 to 9·0; tarsus 2·5 to 2·9; bill from gape 1·16.

Young Male.—Above brown; bright rufous on the head and neck. Upper tail coverts white with rufous brown mesial lanceolate streaks. Tail tawny, fulvous at tip, with four broad black cross bands. Young females with rufous cross bars on the tail.

Adult Female.—Crown of the head, hind neck, and nape reddish fawn or pale tawny fulvous, the feathers broadly streaked mesially with dark brown. Forehead, a narrow supercilium, lores, and cheeks, and a streak over the ear coverts fulvous white; basal two-thirds of feathers of the nape white; ear coverts and cheeks rufous, streaked with brown. Quills brown, tipped with whitish, and with 3 to 5 dark brown transverse bars on the inner webs *2nd, 3rd, 4th, and 5th primaries emarginated on the outer web.* Scapulars, interscapulary region, lower back and rump, also wing coverts brown, spotted with large oval tawny buff marks. Upper tail coverts pure white with sometimes lanceolate rufous brown spots on the shafts. Tail white at the extreme base, the central feathers grey brown, narrowly tipped with white or rufescent white, and crossed with 4 to 5 broad transverse bars of darker brown; lateral tail feathers similar but with broader white tips, and the interspaces on the outer webs creamy buff, the outermost tinged with rufous; sides of neck and under surface of body yellowish white, brown-shafted, and with more or less conspicuous ovate rufous-brown spots. Irides reddish brown.

Length.—19·5 to 21·6 inches; wing 14·5 to 15·6; tail 10 to 10·9; tarsus 3·1 to 3·17.

Hab.—Ceylon, where it is uncommon, and throughout Europe. Occurs also in all countries bordering the Mediterranean and extending in winter to N. India. (*Sharpe.*) In India the Hen Harrier is common about the outer ranges of the Himalayas; from Abbottabad to Kumaon in the Punjab; Sind, N.-W. Provinces, and Oudh, also the Central Provinces. It has been obtained in Meerut, Bareilly, Etawah, Saugor, Nagpore, Chanda, and Goona (*Hume*); also in Beloochistan, S. Afghanistan, Nepaul, Eastern Turkestan, and Gilgit.

This species is not known to breed in India. Dr. Scully, in his contribution to the Ornithology of Eastern Turkestan, says it is a permanent resident in the plains of Kashgaria and breeds there. The nest, he says, is placed in long grass jungle; and adds that he often observed the bird sailing low over rush-grown marshes and bare fields with a wonderfully long sustained flight. It never seems to tire and always appears keenly intent on looking for its prey, every now and then suddenly dropping down among the reeds as if shot, but soon rising again to resume its hunting. He does not, however, give any particulars of its nidification, except as to the position of the nest. In Europe it is said to be placed on the ground and the materials used are small sticks and coarse grass. Eggs 4—5; in colour pale white or skimmed milk-blue; 1·67 × 1·33 inches.

3. Circus melanoleucos, *Forst.*, *Ind. Zool.* p. 12, pl. 11; *Vieill.*, *N. Dict. d' Hist. Nat.* vi. p. 465; *Jerd.*, *B. Ind.* i. p. 99, No. 53; *Sharpe*, *Cat. Acc. B. M.* p. 61; *Stray F.* i. p. 98; *id.*, iii. p. 33; vi. p. 11; *id.*, vii. p. 250; *Hume*, *Rough Notes* ii. p. 307; *Holdsw.*, *P. Z. S.* 1872, p. 414; *Legge*, *B. Ceylon*, p. 9; *Oates*, *B. Br. Burm.* ii. p. 172; *Murray*, *Avif. Br. Ind.* i. p. 12, No. 10.—The PIED HARRIER.

Adult Male.—The whole head, chin, *throat*, neck all round, *upper breast*, nearly two-thirds of the back, scapulars (except the undermost one or two), primaries, and a broad band across the wing black. Wing coverts silvery grey, often broadly tipped with brown. Primary coverts and secondaries silvery grey, except the innermost, which are black. Lower portion of back, rump, and upper tail coverts wnite, the latter with two or three broad cross bars of black or ashy grey. Tail pale silvery dove colour or silvery grey, narrowly tipped with white; below and the inner webs also broadly margined with white. Under surface from lower breast, including wing lining and axillaries, pure white. Bill and cere black. Irides and feet yellow.

Length.—16 to 17·15 inches; wing 13·70 to 14·4; tail 8·5 to 10; tarsus 2·98 to 3·13; culmen 1.

The young male as described by Mr. Hume has the whole head, neck, and back of neck clove brown, each feather broadly margined with pale rufous. Upper back and scapulars uniform clove brown; lower back and wings of a slightly lighter shade. Some of the longest feathers of the back with two obscure, terminal, rufous spots, one on each web; edge of the wings rufous white and many of the lesser coverts faintly or boldly margined with fulvous or rufescent. Upper tail coverts pure white, dark shafted, and with a conspicuous oval, rufous brown subterminal spot. Tail feathers a somewhat greyish pale-brown, narrowly tipped with fulvous white and with broad, rather dark brown transverse bars. Lower parts buffy or rufous white, with central rufous brown stripes, broad on the lower breast and abdomen, almost obsolete on the chin and the thigh coverts. Inner webs of primaries pale rufous white, barred with darker brown, the bars wider and more conspicuous on the under surface. Wing lining rufous buff; axillaries the same, with darker shafts and two or more broad, irregular transverse red brown bars. Winglet, greater primary coverts, and bases of the outer webs of the later primaries grey, with broad transverse brown bars.

The adult female is larger than the male, and has a slaty grey wash on the back. Wing 15·4; tail 10; tarsus 3·13 inches.

Hab.—Ceylon, and Mr. Sharpe gives Eastern Asia, eastern side of the Indian Peninsula and Burma, northwards to Mongolia, Amoor land and Northern China. It occurs in Nepal, Burma, Assam, and Eastern Bengal generally, (extending westward to Mirzapoor), also almost throughout the Himalayas; from the valley of the Burhampooter to Afghanistan. It has been noted from Bengal, Rajputana, Central India, the Central Provinces, the Concan, Deccan South India, British Burma, and Nepaúl.

Nothing is known of the nidification of this species. Dr. Jerdon, however, remarks in his Appendix, that he has every reason to believe it breeds in Northern India.

4. **Circus pygargus** (*Linn.*), *Sharpe, Cat. Acc. B. M.* p. 64. Circus cineraceus, *Cuv., Regne. An.* i. p. 338; *Jerdon, B. of India* i. p. 97, No. 52;

Hume, Rough Notes ii. p. 303; *Shelley, B. Egypt* p. 184; *Murray, Hdbk. Zool., &c., Sind*; *id., Vert. Zool. Sind p.* 88; *Legge, B. Ceylon* p. 12; *Oates, B. Br. Burm.* ii. p. 173; *Murray, Avif. Br. Ind.* i. p. 13, No. 11. Falco pygargus, *S. N.* i. p. 48.—MONTAGUE'S HARRIER.

Adult Male.—Above blue grey; throat, breast, and wing coverts darker, the latter slightly mottled, and with a terminal spot of a dark ash colour. Primary coverts and secondaries silvery grey, tipped with white, and with two bands of black, one of which is hidden by the greater wing coverts. Primaries black, the inner ones greyish at the tips and on the inner web. Secondaries grey with a black band. Tail grey or greyish white, the two outer feathers banded on their inner webs with rufous, the others dusky, with fine ashy black bands. Upper tail coverts white, shading into ashy grey. Lores whitish. *Abdomen, flanks, thighs, and under wing coverts white, streaked with fawn*; the axillaries with spots of the same colour. Cere greenish yellow. Feet and irides yellow.

Length.—18 inches; wing 14 to 15; tail 9·5; tarsus 2·3.

The adult female differs from the male in being nearly uniform brown with scarcely any fulvous margins to the feathers. The hind head and neck are streaked with fulvous, as also the sides of the neck and facial ruff. Feathers under the eye whitish. *Outer margin of 5th primary entire; notch in second primary an inch or more distant from tip of coverts.* Upper tail coverts white; tail brown, tipped with paler brown and banded with five bars of darker brown. Under surface of body buffy white, the feathers with rufous centres; legs yellow; irides hazel.

Length.—19 to 19·5 inches; wing 15·3; tail 8·7; tarsus 1·4; culmen 1·1 to 1·2.

Hab.—Ceylon; in India it has been found in Sind, Punjab, N.-W. Provinces, Oudh, Bengal, Rajputana, Central India, the Central Provinces, Kutch, Behar, Guzerat, the Concans, Deccan, South India, and British Burmah. Occurs also in Beloochistan, Afghanistan, and Nepaul. Sharpe gives its distribution as Europe generally, ranging in winter through Palestine and along the Nile to Abyssinia South Africa, and India.

It is, like the last, a winter visitant to India generally. Like the last, it flies low, skimming along the surface of the ground in search of prey. It frequents open jungle and cultivated fields, preying on birds, reptiles, insects, &c. It has not been known to breed in India. In England it is said to make its nest on the ground, generally among furze. The eggs are white, or greenish white, sometimes faintly spotted with reddish-brown. Size 1·58 × 1·33 inches, and seldom above four in number.

5. Circus macrurus (*S. G. Gmel.*), *Sharpe, Cat. Acc. B. M.* p. 67; *Murray, Hdbk. Zool., &c., Sind*, p. 115; *Legge, B. Ceylon* p. 17; *Oates, B. Br. Burm.* ii. p. 175; *Murray, Avif. Br. Ind.* i. p. 14, No. 12. Circus swainsonii, *Smith, S. Afr. Q. Journ.* i. p. 384; *Gray, Gen. B.* i. p. 32; *Jerd., Birds of Ind.* p. 96, No. 51; *Hume, Rough Notes* ii. p. 298. Circus pallidus, *Sykes, P. Z. S.* 1832, p. 80; *Shelley, B. Egypt* p. 183; *Hume, Str. F.* i. p. 160; *Murray, Vert. Zool. Sind* p. 88; *Reid, Cat. B. Mus. N.-W. P. and Oudh.* Accipitur macrourus, *S. G. Gmel., N. Comm. Petrop.* xv. p. 439.—The PALE HARRIER.

Adult Male.—Above pale bluish grey, scapulars slightly darker; eyebrow and sides of face white; under surface of body greyish white. Quills blackish brown; the secondaries ashy grey, tipped with white, and the primaries washed with ashy grey, white at base of inner web; other quills white underneath. *Upper tail coverts white, banded with ashy grey.* Tail feathers—except the two middle ones, which are uniform ashy grey—banded grey and white; the tips and under surface of all the feathers white. Bill black; feet and irides yellow.

Length.—17·5 to 18·5 inches; culmen 1·15; wing 13·5 to 14; tail 8·8 to 9 5; tarsus 2·75.

Adult Female.—Above brown, the feathers of the head and hind neck streaked, and of the upper surface and lesser wing coverts margined and tipped with rufous. Forehead, supercilium, and a spot below the eye white. Cheeks and ear coverts dark brown, slightly streaked with tawny. Quills dusky brown, the primaries externally shaded with ashy grey, and like the secondaries obsoletely barred darker and tipped with buffy white. *Outer margin of 5th primary entire*; *notch in second primary nearly or quite hidden by coverts*; upper tail coverts white, banded or spotted with dark brown. Tail with the two centre feathers ashy brown and with six blackish brown bands, the rest with four bands, those on the outer feathers being pale rufous. Under tail coverts rufescent. Under wing coverts buffy white, spotted and streaked with brown. Cere greenish yellow; feet yellow; irides brownish.

The young, in the livery of which Mr. Hume says he has numerous specimens, is shortly described by Mr. Sharpe as being brown, like the old female, but not so much variegated above, with tawny margins to the feathers; under surface entirely pale fawn colour (rufous buff—*Hume*), the facial ruff of this same colour, and therefore contrasting in marked prominence with the dark brown cheeks and ear coverts, the flank feathers and axillaries with indistinct brown central streaks; frontal feathers, superciliary streak and spot under the eye whitish; upper tail coverts white, spotted with pale rufous; tail much as in the female, but the dark bars only five in number.

Length.—18 to 20·5 inches; wing 14 to 14·5; tail 10 to 10·5; tarsus 2·8 to 3.

Hab.—Ceylon, Europe, Africa, and throughout India, China, and Burmah. Has been noted from the N.-W. and Central Provinces, Punjab, Sind,

Beloochistan, Afghanistan, Persia, Mesopotamia, S. India, Kutch, the Concans and Deccan, Kattiawar, Behar, Nepaul. In India and the Indo-Burmese Countries it is a winter visitant, arriving about the middle of September and leaving again in March. Generally found along rivers.

Nothing is known of its nidification anywhere in India, no birds having ever been seen in India after March or the middle of April.

6. **Circus æruginosus** (*Linn.*), *Savigny, Syst. Ois. Egypt* p. 90; *Hume, Rough Notes* p. 314; *id., Nests and Eggs* p. 51; *Shelley, Birds Egypt* p. 181; *Jerd., Birds of Ind.* p. 99, No. 54; *Sharpe, Cat. Acc. B. M.* p. 69; *Murray, Hdbk. Zool., &c., Sind,* p. 116; *Hume, Str. F.* i. p. 100; *Murray, Vert. Zool., Sind,* p. 89; *Dresser, B. Eur.* v. p. 415; *Legge, B. Ceylon* p. 5; *Oates, B. Br. Burm.* ii. p. 176; *Murray, Avif. Brit. Ind.* i. p. 16, No. 13; *Reid, Cat. B. Mus. N.-W. P. and Oudh.* Falco æruginosus, *Linn., S. N.* i. p. 130.—The MARSH HARRIER.

Adult Male.—Above dark brown, the feathers of the upper surface edged with rufous; the smaller wing coverts buffy and centred brown; primary coverts and secondaries bluish ashy, tipped very slightly with pale white. Primaries blackish brown, paler at the tips, whitish at base of inner web. Upper tail coverts greyish white and tinged with rufous. Tail bluish ash or uniform grey, slightlv fulvescent beneath. Head, neck, and breast pale rufous or creamy buff, with dark brown streaks; under parts reddish brown or pale rufous, as also are the thigh coverts, the latter in some spotted or margined with white; under wing coverts buffy white, the axillaries with brown shaft stripes. Cere greenish yellow; legs and irides yellow; claws black.

Length.—19 to 22·5 inches; wing 16; tail 9 to 10; tarsus 3·25; culmen 1·55.

Adult Female.—Larger; length 23 inches; wing 17; tail 10 to 11; tarsus 3·8.

The young bird is uniform reddish brown, the head, neck, and cheeks in some stages being yellowish, rufous white, or white with brown stripes on the crown; upper tail coverts rufous btown.

Hab.—Ceylon, Europe generally, China, Japan, N.-E. and S. Africa, and throughout India, and Burmah. In Sind and the Punjab it occurs in great numbers, frequenting the maritime districts, rivers, marshes, lakes, and inundated fields, feeding on rats, mice, frogs, fish, &c. It occurs also in the N.-W. Provinces, Oudh, Bengal, Rajpootana, Kutch, Kattiawar, Jodhpore, North Guzerat, Central and Southern India, the Deccan and Concans, and in fact throughout India; also in Beloochistan, Persia, Mesopotamia, Afghanistan, Eastern Turkestan, Gilgit, Nepaul, Malacca, and Upper Pegu. Said sometimes to remain and breed in India. Eggs, 3—6, pale bluish green.

Gen. **Astur**.—*Gm.*

Bill broad at base, compressed to tip, festooned in the middle. Nostrils oval, situated anteriorly in the cere. Wings long.; 3rd, 4th, and 5th quills longest. Tarsi long, scutate.

7. Astur trivirgatus, *Tem., Pl. Col.* i. pl. 303; *Cuv., Regne An.* p. 332; *Jerd., B. Ind.* i. p. 47, No. 22; *Wallace, Ibis,* 1868, p. 6; *Sharpe, Cat. Acc. B. M.* p. 105; *Legge, B. Ceylon* p. 20; *Oates, B. Br. Burm.* ii. p. 177; *Murray, Avif. Brit. Ind.* i. p. 17, No. 15. Astur palumbarius, *Jerd., Madras Journal,* p. 85. Lophospizia trivirgatus, *Kaup., Contr. Orn.* 1850, p. 65; *Hume, Rough Notes* p. 116; *Stray F.* v. pp. 8, 502.—The CRESTED GOSHAWK.

Adult Male.—Above slaty grey, the upper tail coverts blackish and tipped with white. Head and neck clearer slaty grey, including a conspicuous occipital crest, the sides of the neck somewhat tinged with rufous; quills browner than the back; primaries with rufescent shafts, barred above with dark brown, much plainer underneath where the quills are white at the base of the inner web. Tail ashy brown, paler at tip, crossed with four bands of dark brown; throat white with a distinct black moustachial streak on each side and a broad medial line; chest clear tawny rufous; rest of under surface white, broadly banded with pale rufous, each bar of this colour having a conterminous brown bar; the thighs thickly barred with ashy brown without any rufous tinge. Under tail coverts white; under wing coverts white, spotted with brown or rufous brown; axillaries similarly barred. Bill black, plumbeous at base. Cere orange yellow. Cheeks and orbits orange; feet yellow; irides orange yellow.

Length.—14 to 16 inches; wing 7·8 to 8·5; tail 6·3 to 7; tarsus 2·1 to 2·2.

Adult Female.—Much larger. Length 17·5 to 18 inches; wing 9·5 to 9·7; tail 8·0; tarsus 2·5 to 2·7.

Young.—Brown above, with a fully developed occipital crest. Upper tail coverts banded with darker brown and tipped with white. Tail with five cross bands of darker brown. Under surface of body white; throat as in the adult; breast broadly streaked with pale rufous or dark brown; lower breast, thighs, and abdomen barred with pale rufous, darker on the thighs; under tail coverts white, with a few narrow rather indistinct cross bars; under wing coverts buff, spotted and barred with dark brown.

Hab.—Ceylon and Southern India, also Assam, Burmah, Java, Borneo, Sumatra, and the Phillipine Islands. Nothing is known of its nidification in India. In Ceylon Mr. F. B. Armstrong took a nest in the middle of May in the Bogawantalawa district at 4000 feet elevation. The nest, he says, was placed in a tree in heavy jungle about 30 feet from the ground and made of small stricks lined with dead leaves. He got one egg with a pale bluish white ground, with spots and blotches of rich brown; the other egg was devoid of any markings. The larger Nepaulese race is provisionally separated by Mr. Sharpe as *A. indicus.*

8. Astur badius, *Kaup., Ibis*, 1847; *Sharpe, Cat. Acc. Br. Mus.* p. 109 (Sub-sp. A.); *Legge, B. Ceylon* p. 23; *Murray, Avif. Br. Ind.* i. p. 18, No. 16. Micronisus badius, *Bp. Consp.* i. p. 33; *Jerd., B. Ind.* i. p. 48, No. 23; *Blyth, Ibis*, 1863; *Hume, Rough Notes* p. 117; *Murray, Hdbk. Zool., &c., Sind; id., Vert. Zool. Sind*, p. 108. Accipiter badius, *Strickl., Ann. Mag. N. H.* xiii. p. 33.—The SHIKRA OR BROWN HAWK.

Young.—Head, nape, neck behind, back, scapulars, wing and upper tail coverts ashy, dusky, or pale earthy brown, the feathers on the head slightly darker, and all edged with pale rufous, the feathers of the neck with their white bases showing through. Lores and eyebrow white; sides of the face and ear coverts pale brown, tinged with rufescent and mesially streaked with darker; chin and throat white, with a mesial dark brown throat stripe; breast and abdomen whitish with large longitudinal drops—oval on the upper breast—of a pale rufous colour. Vent and under tail coverts white; under wing coverts buff, streaked and barred with dark brown; thigh coverts also barred. Primaries brown, their inner webs buffy, and barred with dark brown; secondaries brown, barred darker on both webs and margined and tipped with buffy; tail ashy brown, with 5—6 broad dark brown bands, narrower and about nine on the outermost feathers, the interspaces and tips of all buffy white. Cere yellow; bill dusky with a bluish tinge. Iris pale yellow; feet yellow.

In the adult plumage the upper parts are bluish grey; the nape is mottled with white, and the white bases of the scapular feathers show through in some specimens; the primaries are dusky black, with their inner webs of a buff colour and barred darker brown, nearly black; the secondaries are bluish grey and also barred. The tail is ashy grey, and tipped with white, the bars on the lateral tail feathers 9 to 11 in number, and of a dark brown colour. The throat stripe is less distinct than in the young, and the entire lower surface is barred with white and rufescent brown. The abdomen, thighs, and under tail coverts unspotted white; rest as in the young. The adult female is like the male but larger.

Length.—Adult male, 13·5 inches; wing 7·9; tail 6·3; tarsus 2.

Length.—Adult female, 14·5; wing 8·3; tail 6·4; tarsus 2·15.

Hab.—Ceylon, and the Indian Peninsula generally, extending to Assam and Burmah, and also to Beloochistan, Persia, and Afghanistan. Occurs in Oudh, Bengal, Central Provinces, Rajputana, Central India, Kutch, Kattiawar, Guzerat, Concan, Deccan, and Southern India. Breeds in April and May in Sind, Punjab, and the N.-W. Provinces on large lofty trees on the edges of streams or lakes, laying usually three or four eggs, oval or pyriform in shape, smooth, fine, glossless shells of a pure, delicate bluish white, as a rule without markings, or at most thinly sprinkled all over with very faint greyish specks and spots. In size the eggs vary from 1·5 to 1·63 inches in length and from 1·2 to 1·26 in breadth. It is commonly trained by natives, being easily reclaimed and expert in striking a quarry.

Gen. **Accipiter.**—*Briss.*

Bill short, much compressed, festooned. Nostrils oval, rather oblique, situated on the forepart of the cere, and partly hidden by setæ. Wings moderate, rounded, and with the 4th and 5th quills longest. Tarsi long.

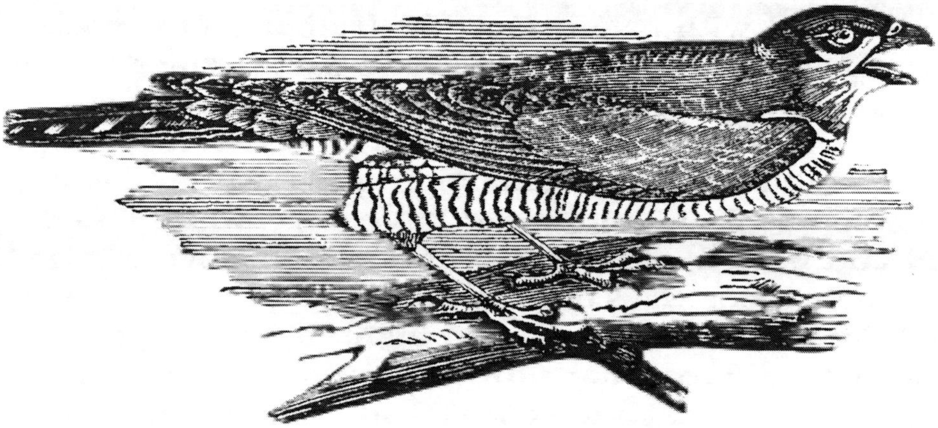

9. Accipiter nisus, *Linn., Syst. Nat.* i. p. 130; *Pall., Zoogr. Rosso. As.* i. p. 370; *Gray, Gen. B.* i. p. 29; *Jerd., B. Ind.* i. p. 51, No. 24; *Hume, Rough Notes* i. p. 124; *id., Nests and Eggs Ind. B.* p 25; *Sharpe, Cat. Acc. Br. Mus.* p. 132; *Murray, Hdbk. Zool., &c., Sind,* p. 110; *id., Vert. Zool. Sind; Legge, B. Ceylon* p. 27; *Oates, B. Br. Burm.* ii. p. 181; *Murray, Avif. Brit. Ind.* i. p. 21, No. 19. (*Basha*, the female; *Bashin*, the male, Hind.)—The EUROPEAN SPARROW-HAWK.

Young.—Head, nape, neck behind, back, scapulars, and wing coverts dusky brown, darker on the upper back, the feathers margined with rufous, the occiput and nape with white mottlings, caused by the broad white bases of the feathers showing through. Lores and eyebrow white; chin and throat and sides of the neck white, the feathers with mesial dark streaks. Ear coverts the same. Rump and upper tail coverts like the back, the feathers with dark shafts and tipped rufous. Primaries and secondaries dusky brown, basally rufescent white on their inner webs and barred with dark brown. The tips of the secondaries rufous or rufescent white; inner web of the tertiaries subterminally white, and margined at the tips with pale rufous. Tail ashy brown above, greyish white on the under surface, tipped whitish and with five dark brown bands; breast, abdomen, flanks, and thigh coverts barred with rufous brown and white. Under tail coverts white. Under wing lining buff, with spots and transverse dark brown bars.

Adult Male.—Head, nape, hind neck, wing coverts, back, and scapulars slaty, with a bluish tinge, the nape mottled white, and some of the tertials basally white. Upper tail coverts and scapulars with indistinct dark shafts. Tail, like the back, tipped white, and with four dark brown bands. Primaries dark brown, their inner webs rufescent white, and crossed with darker brown, nearly black bars; secondaries slaty, also rufescent white on their inner webs and barred across with dark brown. Chin and throat white, with a rufous tinge; breast, flanks, and abdomen barred with bright rufous and white. Thigh coverts the same. Under tail coverts white. Under wing coverts barred with rufous and dark brown. Bill horny or dark horn blue; cere, base of lower mandible, and legs yellow; iris orange.

Length.—13 inches; wing 8·15; tail 6·3; tarsus 2·3. Females larger and of a duller tint. Length 15·5; wing 9·3 to 9·5; tail 7; tarsus 2·5.

Hab.—Ceylon, the whole of Europe and Northern Asia, extending in winter into Algeria, N.-E. Africa, the Indian Peninsula, and China. (*Sharpe.*) Occurs throughout Sind, Punjab, N.-W. Provinces, Oudh, and Bengal; also throughout the Western Presidency, in Rajputana, Central India, Kutch, Guzerat, Concan, Deccan, Southern India, and in Beluchistan, Persia, Mesopotamia and Afghanistan; also British Burmah, Upper Pegu, Tennaserim, and Nepaul. Affects gardens and cultivation. It is much used for hawking, and is said to be easily tamed, and owing to its courage a better bird than the Shikra for the quarry. Breeds during May and June in the Himalayas in wooded valleys, laying four bluish white eggs, blotched with red.

Mr. Hume in his "Rough Notes," p. 128, describes in detail the Dove-Hawk (*Accipiter melaschistos*) from Simla as a new species, which Mr. Sharpe thinks is only a dark race of this species.

10. Accipiter virgatus, *Reinw.*, *Temm. Pl. Col.* i. pl. 109; *Vig.*, *Zool. Journ.* i. p. 338; *Gray*, *Gen. B.* i. p. 29; *Jerd.*, *B. Ind.* i. p. 52, No. 25; *Hume*, *Rough Notes* i. p. 132; *Jerd.*, *Ibis*, 1871, p. 243; *Sharpe*, *Cat. Acc. Br. Mus.* vol. i. p. 150; *Legge*, *B. Ceylon* p. 26; *Oates*, *B. Br. Burm.* ii. p. 182; *id.*, *Str. F.* x. p. 182; *Murray*, *Avif. Brit. Ind.* i. p. 22, No. 20; *Stray F.* vol. ii. p. 141.—The BESRA SPARROW-HAWK.

Adult Male.—Head and neck dusky black, sides of the neck washed with rufous, nape mottled with white; ear coverts and face light dusky; throat buffy white; wing coverts blackish slate colour. Quills dark brown, unbarred above; under surface ashy, pale rufous near the base of the inner web and barred with blackish. Tail ashy grey above, much paler below, with three transverse bands of slaty black. Abdomen and under tail coverts white, rest of under surface bright ferruginous or vinous chestnut, paler on the thighs; under wing coverts yellowish ochry; axillaries barred with brownish. Cere pale lemon yellow; bill black, plumbeous at base. Legs and feet pale orange yellow. Irides yellow.

Length.—11 to 11·25 inches; wing 6·5 to 6·6; tail 5·75 to 6·6; tarsus 1·9 to 2·2.

Adult Female.—A little larger than the male.

Length.—13 inches; wing 7·4 to 8; tarsus 1·9 to 2·2.

The plumage of the various stages of the young of this species is so very variable, that it is not possible to give a description which would suit, but the following from *Rough Notes* is the usual type of coloration of specimens from the Punjab, in the Kurrachee Museum. Head, nape, back, mantle, and upper tail coverts dusky cyaneous, darkest on the head. Nape mottled with white. Tail slaty grey, brownish on lateral feathers, and with seven narrow transverse bars on the inner webs and four broad blackish bars on both webs of the other ten feathers. Sides of neck and coverts dusky, the latter with traces of rufous striæ. Chin and throat white with one central blackish stripe; a streak of white over the eye. Breast deep ferruginous at the sides, the central portion having the feathers a mixture of blackish, deep ferruginous and white. Sides, flanks, and upper abdomen ferruginous, imperfectly barred with white; lower abdomen white, barred with pale ferruginous. Tibial plumes white, closely barred with rusty grey; under tail coverts white.

Hab.—Ceylon and throughout the Indian Peninsula nearly. Occurs in the Concan and Deccan, Rajputana, in South and Central India; also in the Punjab, N.-W. and Central Provinces, the Himalayas, and S. Andamans. Mr. Wallace gives it from Malacca, Timor, and Java, and Dr. Jerdon says extends to Assam, Burmah, and Malayana. Mr. Thompson (*Rough Notes*) is confident that it breeds in the forests of Gurhwal from March to May, but nothing certain is known. In Ceylon, however, according to Mr. H. Parker, F.Z.S., the usual breeding season is from May to July. The nests, he says, are generally built in large trees, and are shapeless structures of small sticks, about 30 feet off the ground. Eggs bluish white, blotched with reddish brown. In parts of India it is caught where fairly numerous and much used by falconers for the quarry. It is said, however, to be a difficult bird to train, but when trained fetches a considerable price, being speedy and active, especially at partridges, quails, doves and snipe.

Sub-Family—BUTEONINÆ.

Bill small and moderate, with the tip hooked. Wings moderate; tail generally short; tarsi with scutæ in front and behind; tibia longer than tarsus. Outer toe connected to middle toe by interdigital membrane.

Gen. Buteo.—*Cuv.*

Bill short with hooked tip; margin of upper mandible slightly festooned; nostrils oval. Lores clothed with bristle-like feathers. Wings long; 3rd, 4th, and 5th quills sub-equal and longest; inner webs of 1st four quills strongly notched. Tarsus bare or feathered on the upper third only.

11. Buteo plumipes, *Hodgs. in Gray's Zool. Misc.* p. 81; *id., P. Z. S.* 1845, p. 37; *Jerd., B. Ind.* p. 91, No.; *Hume, Rough Notes* p. 285; *Jerd., Ibis,* 1871, p. 340; *Str. F.* iv. pp. 358-371; *Sharpe, Cat. Acc. B. M.* i. p. 180, *pl.* vii.; *Legge, B. Ceylon* p. 31; *Oates, B. Br. Burm.* ii. p. 184; *Murray, Avif. Brit. Ind.* i. p. 25, No. 23. Buteo japonicus, *Bp. Consp.* i. p. 18; *Jerd., Ibis,* 1871, p. 337. Buteo vulgaris, *Blyth, Ibis,* 1863, p. 20.—The HARRIER BUZZARD.

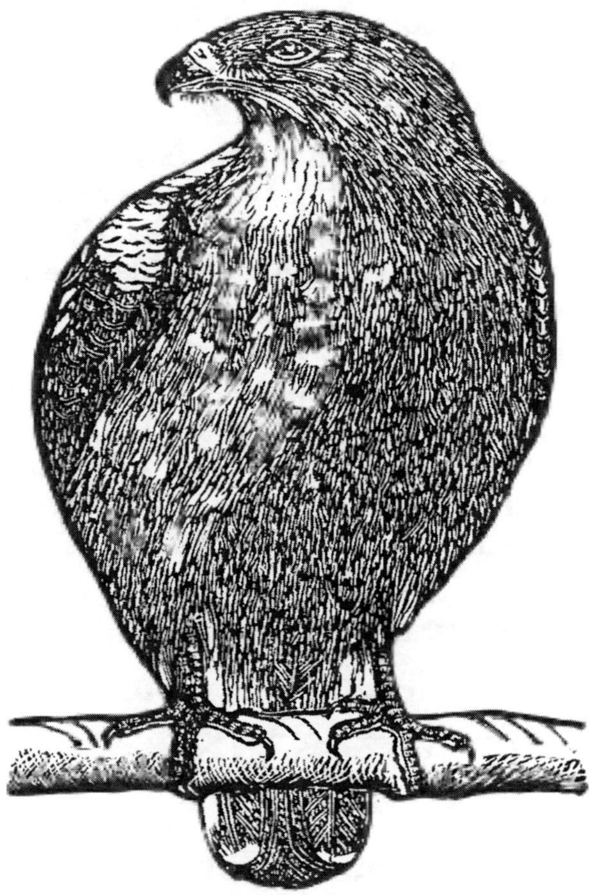

Adult—Above dark purplish brown, the feathers rufescent on their margins; sides of face and neck rufous, the feathers mesially streaked with brown; lores whitish. Upper margin of ear coverts dark brown; cheeks blackish, forming a strongly pronounced moustache. Under surface of body rufous, streaked with blackish on the chin and less distinctly on the throat; chest almost uniform rufous with a black shaft stripe; lower breast fulvous white, irregularly barred with rufous brown; thighs rufous with fulvous margins to the feathers; lower abdomen, vent, and under tail coverts creamy buff. Primaries blackish; secondaries paler with whitish tips and irregularly mottled or barred with brown; tail brown with an indistinct purplish subterminal band, a white tip, and 3 to 4 other distinguishable bars of darker brown.

Length.—21·5 inches; wing 15·7; tail 9; tarsus 3; culmen 1·35.

Aged specimens are everywhere dull smoky brown, the wing coverts and scapulars lighter; primaries dark brown, inclining to purplish brown near the tips; the inner web buffy white, barred with brown; shafts whitish; secondaries like the back; tail uniform smoky brown with whitish shafts and pale whity brown tips with obsolete remains of cross bars. Sides of face and neck and entire under parts uniform smoky brown.

Length.—20 inches; wing 15·4; tail 9; tarsus 3.

Hab.—Ceylon; the Travancore Hills of Southern India, the Himalayas, the Northern portions of the Tenasserim province of British Burmah, Nepaul and Sikkim and eastwards to China and Japan.

Mr. Bourdillon in *Str. F.* states that this is a winter visitor in Travancore during December, January, and February, preferring high open country, where two or three may be seen steadily quartering the ground and occasionally pouncing on some mouse or lizard. As to the iden'ity of this species with *plumipes* there is still a set controversy owing to the very variable plumage of the Buzzard in all their different stages. Messrs. Hume, Blyth, Sharpe, Dresser, and Gurney have worked hard to find out the points of distinction between the Indian species of Buzzards, but no satisfactory conclusion has yet been come to. Mr. Sharpe has, however, in his Catalogue, fairly well given a key to seventeen species of *Buteo* from all parts of the world. I doubt whether anything could be made of the Indian or Ceylonese species.

Sub-Family—AQUILINÆ—EAGLES.

Bill strong, more or less lengthened, festooned but not toothed; tarsus reticulate behind, more than half the length of the tibia. Outer toe only connected to middle toe by membrane. Wings moderate. 4th quill usually longest.

Gen. **Nisætus**.—*Hodgs.*

Bill much hooked at tip; cere large; nostrils large, elliptic; upper mandible festooned; tarsus feathered to the toes. No elongated occipital crest.

12. Nisætus fasciatus, *Vieill., Mem. Lin. Soc. Paris*, p. 152; *Sharpe, Cat. Acc.* p. 250; *Strickl., Orn. Syn.* p. 61; *Murray, Vert. Zool. Sind* p. 77; *Legge, B. Ceylon* p. 36; *Murray, Avif. Brit. Ind.* i. p. 36, No. 32. Falco bonelli, *Tem.*, *Pl. Col.* i. pl. 288. Aquilla bonelli, *Less.*, *Man. Orn.* i. p. 83; *Gould*, *B. Eur.* i. p. 7; *Shelley*, *Birds of Egypt* p. 206. Eutolmætus bonelli, *Blyth*, *J. A. S. B.* xix. p. 174; *Hume*, *Rough Notes* i. p. 189. Pseudætus bonelli, *Bp.*, *Cat. Ois. Eur. Parzud.* p. 1; *Hume*, *Stray Feathers* i. p. 158. Nisætus bonelli, *Jerd.*, *B. of Ind.* i p. 67, No. 33; *Murray*, *Hdbk. Zool.*, *&c.*, *Sind*, p. 100.—The CRESTLESS HAWK EAGLE.

Adult Female.—Above deep brown, the feathers white at base, some of them paler margined; eyebrow and sides of neck streaked with white. Sides of the face white; cheeks streaked with brown; ear coverts inclining to rufous. Under surface white with dark shaft stripes; flanks irregularly barred and marked with dark brown arrow-head markings. Feathers of the tarsus more or less pale brown, varied with dark brown and irregularly spotted with white; under wing coverts white, streaked with black; the lower ones entirely black with white tips; axillaries white, barred and streaked with blackish. Quills deep brown, mottled on the inner web with white. Tail ashy brown, inclining to grey, with 5 to 6 indistinct bars of brown near the base, and a broad sub-terminal band of dark brown; the tips of the feathers fulvous; cere and gape dingy yellow, bluish about the nostrils, Bill horn black. Feet whitish brown, tinged with yellow. Iris yellow.

Length.—26 inches; culmen 2·5; wing 21; tail 11·5; tarsus 4.

Adult Male.—Length 27—29 inches; wing 18—19·6; tail 11; tarsus 3·5. (Sharpe, *Cat. Acc.*)

Hab.—Found in Ceylon, Southern Europe and the Mediterranean. Breeds nearly throughout India. In Sind and the Punjab during December and January, and in the Himalayas according to Hume in April and May. It occurs in the N.-W. Provinces, also in Persia, Beloochistan, and Southern Afghanistan, Kutch, Guzerat, the Deccan, Concan, and Southern India; also Kattiawar, the Carnatic, Nepaul, Assam, and in fact the entire Indian Peninsula.

This Eagle breeds on trees, or on ledges of precipitous rocky cliffs. The nest is from 4 to 6 feet in diameter, made of sticks, with scarcely any depression, except in the middle for the reception of the eggs. The lining of the nest is usually of green twigs and leaves. The number of eggs is usually two, but three have occasionally been found. They vary in shape and size, also in colouring; generally they are oval, unspotted pale greyish or faintly streaked and blotched with pale yellowish or reddish brown. In size they vary from 2·56 to 3 inches in length and from 1·95 to 2·22 in breadth.

13. Nisætus pennatus, *Gm.*, *Sys. Nat.* i. p. 272; *Tem.*, *Pl. Col.* i. pl. 33; *Sharpe*, *Cat. Acc.* i. p. 253; *Legge*, *B. Ceylon* p. 40; *Oates*, *B. Br. Burm.* ii. p. 189; *Murray*, *Avif. Br. Ind.* i. p. 37, No. 33; *id.*, *Vert.*

Zool., Sind, p. 78. Aquila pennata, *Vig., Zool. Journ.; Gray, Gen. B.* 14; *Jerdon, B. of Ind.* p. 63, No. 31; *Loyard, B. S. Afr.* p. 10; *Murray, Hdbk. Zool., &c., Sind.* Hieratus pennatus, *Kaup., Mus. Senck.* iii. p. 260; *Blyth, J. A. S. B.* xv. p. 7; *Hume, Rough Notes* i. p. 182; *Str. F.* vol. vii. pp. 74, 198; viii. p. 162.—The DWARF OR BOOTED EAGLE.

Head and neck behind, and on the sides, rufous or pale orange brown, the feathers lanceolate and streaked mesially with dark brown; some of the lengthened feathers entirely dark brown and forming a not very apparent crest. A narrow superciliary stripe; a band from the angle of the mouth below the ear coverts, and a central chin stripe dark brown. Ear coverts rufescent brown; back, scapulars, and wing coverts sepia brown; the median wing coverts and some of the scapulars broadly edged with fulvous white, forming a conspicuous wing band; rump and upper tail coverts like the back, the latter shading from dull fawn brown to buffy white on their margins and tips. Tail dull sepia brown, shaded with ashy, tipped with fulvous white, and with 4—5 indistinct bars of darker brown more distinct on the under surface. Primaries dark brown, inclining to ashy white basally on their inner webs; secondaries indistinctly barred with dull brownish white. Under surface of body rufous, buffy, or fulvous white, deeper on the breast, and streaked with dark brown, the streaks disappearing on the abdomen, thighs, and under tail coverts, which are white. Under wing coverts white, with a few narrow shaft streaks. Cere and gape bright wax yellow; bill bluish black, pale blue at the base; feet pale wax yellow; iris pale brown.

Length.—Female 19 to 24 inches; wing 15·5 to 16; tail 9 to 9·25; tarsus 2·8. The young bird is paler beneath, the breast rufous or fulvous with a white shoulder spot, and white lores and forehead. The upper tail coverts are whitish, and the tail distinctly barred on both webs.

Adult Male.—Smaller than the female. Length 19 inches; wings 13·7; tarsus 2·4.

Hab.—Sind, the Punjab, N.-W. Provinces, Oudh, Beloochistan (Quetta), Persia, and Afghanistan; also the Concan, Deccan, and throughout the Indian Peninsula and Ceylon. Hume says it breeds in Spain in April and May, and that Mr. Theobald found a nest in the Salem district at Huroor. The eggs were two in number; one which reached him, he says, was a very broad oval, ground colour dead white, devoid of gloss, and thickly blotched and streaked throughout with reddish brown. Size 2·13 × 1·78 inches.

Gen. Lophotriorchis.

Nostrils visible; no chin tuft; crest long and wedge-shaped; bill short, high at the base, with a prominent festoon; tarsi feathered to the base.

Head of Lophotriorchis kieneri.

14. Lophotriorchis kieneri, *Geoff. St. Hil., Rev. Zool.* 1845, pl. 35; *Sharpe, Cat. Acc. Br. Mus.* i. p. 255; *Legge, B. Ceylon*, p. 43; *Murray, Avif. Brit. Ind.* i. p. 38, No. 34. Spizaetus kieneri, *Gray, Gen. B.* i. p. 14; *Hume, Rough Notes* i. p. 216; *id., Str. F.* i. p. 311. Limnaetus kieneri, *Strickl., Ann. Nat. Hist.* xiii. p. 33; *Jerd., B. Ind.* i. p. 74, No. 37.—The RUFOUS-BELLIED HAWK EAGLE.

Above black, slightly shaded with brown. Occipital crest 2·4 to 2·5 inches long; feathers of the nape white at the base. Ear coverts mixed white, black and rufous; cheeks, throat and breast pure white with a few narrow black shaft lines; rest of under surface including under wing and tail coverts tawny rufous, streaked with black shaft stripes, broader on the flanks; wings black, some of the feathers externally brownish, the inner lining of quills whitish ashy with a few blackish bars on the inner webs of the primaries; secondaries narrowly tipped with white; tail black, very narrowly tipped with whity brown and with 6—7 indistinct bars of dark brown; lower surface of tail ashy white with a subterminal brown bar. Cere and feet yellow; bill plumbeous; irides brown.

Length.—21 to 25 inches; wing 14 to 16; tail 8·5 to 9·5; tarsus 2·9 to 3; culmen 1·5.

Hab.—Ceylon, the Indian Peninsula, Travancore and Burma, extending to Borneo and Sumatra. Not uncommon in Lower Bengal, extending to the Himalayas. Mr. Inglis gives it from N.-E. Cachar, and Wallace from the Phillippines. Nothing is known of its nidification. It is said to have a rapid and elegant flight and to mount and soar well.

Gen. Neopus.—*Hodgs.*

Bill moderate, bending from the base, much hooked at the tip, with a slight festoon in the upper mandible; cere large; nostrils ovoid oblique; wings exceeding the tail, which is long and slightly rounded; primaries emarginate; claws nearly straight

15. Neopus malayensis, *Tem., Pl. Col.* i. pl. 117; *Horsf. and Moore, Cat. B. M. E. I. Co.* i. p. 381; *Jerd., B. Ind.* i. p. 65, No. 32; *Hume, Rough Notes* i. p. 187; *Sharpe, Cat. Acc. B. M.* p. 257; *Legge, B. Ceylon* p. 470, *App.* 1289; *Hume and Dav., Str. F.* vi. p. ii.; viii. p. 82; *Oates, B. Bm.*

Burm. ii. p. 190; *Murray, Avif. Brit. Ind.* i. p. 38, No. 35. **Heteropus** malayensis, *Hume, Nest and Eggs Ind. B.* p. 33.—The Black Eagle.

Uniform brown black, somewhat darker beneath. Upper tail coverts barred with white, feathers of the tail more or less distinctly barred with ashy; quills mottled with white or greyish white near the base and faintly barred on their inner webs. Cere, gape, and feet deep yellow; bill greenish horny, black at the tip; iris dark brown.

Length.—Male.—27·5 to 29·5 inches; wing 22 to 22·7; tail 12·8 to 14; culmen 2·05; tarsus 3·4.

Female.—30·5 to 31·5; wing 23 to 25·5; tail 14 to 14·75; tarsus 3·62 to 3·75.

Hab.—Ceylon, the Indian Peninsula generally, Burmah, the Malayan Peninsula to Java and Sumatra. It occurs in Malabar, in the Wynaad, Coorg, the Western Ghats, Travancore, Central India, the Punjab, N.-W Provinces, throughout the Himalayas, and Nepal.

Jerdon says it is a bird of easy, graceful, and elegant flight, always soaring and circling about at no great height, with hardly any flapping of its wings. It lives chiefly on eggs of birds and nestlings. It nests on the ledges or on the face of cliffs and lays from 2 to 3 eggs, a pale yellowish white, with a few brown specks and spots. One egg in Mr. Hume's possession is said to be richly blotched and mottled all over (most densely towards the small end) with somewhat brownish red. In length the eggs vary from 2·5 to 2·68 inches, and in breadth from 1·88 to 2·02 inches. Hume's collection of these eggs were from Bussahir and Koolo, and were obtained in January.

Gen. **Spizaetus**.—*Vieill.*

Form aquiline; bill short, high at the base, curved, hooked at the tip; upper mandible with a festoon; wing short; tail long and square; tarsi moderate, feathered to the base; inner toe without the claw shorter than the outer.

16. Spizaetus nipalensis, *Hodgs., J. A. S. B.* v. p. 229, pl. 7; *Gray, Cat. Acc.* p. 8; *Blyth, J. A. S. B.* xix. p. 333; *Hume, Rough Notes* i. p. 210; *Sharpe, Cat. Acc. B. M.* p. 267; *Murray, Avif. Br. Ind.* i. p. 39, No. 36. Limnaetus nipalensis, *Jerd., B. Ind.* i. p. 73, No. 36; *Holdsw., P. Z. S.* 1872, p. 411.—The Spotted or Hodgson's Hawk Eagle.

Adult Male.—Crown of the head, occipital crest, ear coverts, cheeks, sides of the neck and nape blackish brown; the occipital crest, which is usually from 2·5 to 4 inches in length, is tipped with white, and the feathers on the nape, cheeks, and sides of neck edged with tawny; chin and throat white or fulvous white with a broad streak of black down the centre; back, scapulars, wing coverts and secondaries deep brown, the feathers with darker transverse bars; upper tail coverts a lighter brown than the back, narrowly tipped with white, and with broad transverse white bars; tail pale brown, narrowly tipped with white, and with 4—5 broad transverse, deep brown bands which are broader than the interspaces; neck in front and upper breast a mixture of brownish and fulvous white, the feathers broadly centred with blackish brown; rest of under surface, including tarsal feathers which reach to between the inner and middle toes, brown, barred transversely with white or fulvous white; under wing coverts white or fulvous white, also barred or spotted with brown; cere and bill black; feet dirty yellowish white; iris yellow.

Length.—28 to 29 inches; wing 18·5 to 19; tail 13 to 13·2; tarsus 3·9 to 4; culmen 1·9.

The adult female is larger than the male. Length 29·25 to 32 inches; wing 18·5 to 18·7; tail 12·6 to 13; tarsus 4·2 to 4·4.

Mr. Hume in *Rough Notes* describes a young male as having the whole of the head, back, and sides of the neck and ear coverts rufous buff, each feather with a narrow dark brown central stripe, a long conspicuous occipital crest black and narrowly tipped with white; scapulars and interscapulary region hair brown, the feathers paling at the margins and towards their bases to a pale wood brown; rump and upper tail coverts dingy, somewhat rufous wood brown; central tail feathers a sort of olive brown, very narrowly tipped with white with a one inch subterminal and four other half inch broad transverse dark brown bands; wing coverts, except the greater primary coverts, a rather pale wood brown with dark brown centres, paling into the margins; secondary greater coverts almost wholly white on their inner webs; quills and primary coverts umber brown; 2nd to 5th primaries emarginate on their outer webs and obscurely barred with dingy buff; chin and throat pure white, also the base of neck in front, breast and abdomen—the feathers tipped with rufous buff and black shafted near the tip; lower tail coverts, flanks, and tibial plumes pale rufous brown, barred obscurely with white; axillaries the same, with spots forming imperfect bars; under wing coverts barred with dingy rufous or hair brown.

Hab.—Ceylon, Southern India generally, and Travancore; also the Punjab, N.-W. Provinces, the Himalayas, and Khasia.

This species as far as is at present known breeds in the Himalayas during March, April, and May. Its nest, not unlike other eagles, is made of sticks, and is said to be either hidden in a dense forest or projecting from the face of some inaccessible cliff. The normal number of eggs is two, in shape a broad regular oval, almost symmetrical at both ends. Shell coarse, dull, and glossless; the ground colour a slightly greenish white spotted thinly with reddish brown and with numerous large blotches and streaks of very pale inky purple. Size 3·78 by 2·23 inches. (*Hume*.) Hodgson's Hawk Eagle is a shy forest bird and confines itself to deep wooded hills ascending far into the interior of the Himalayas, where it feeds on pheasants, hares, and partridges.

17. Spizaetus cirrhatus, *Gmel., S. N.* i. p. 274; *Bp., Consp.* i. p. 29; *Hume, Rough Notes* i. p. 206; *Sharpe, Cat. Acc. B. M.* p. 269; *Murray, Avif. Br. Ind.* i. p. 40, No. 37. Falco Ceylonensis, *Gmel., S. N.* i. p. 275. Limnaetus cristatellus (*Temm.*), *Jerd., B. Ind.* i. p. 71, No. 35; *Holdsworth, P. Z. S.* 1872, p. 411; *Stray F.*, vol. iv. p 356; *id.*, vol. vii. p. 33. Spizaetus Ceylonensis, *Legge, B. Ceylon*, pp. 55, 1209.—The CRESTED HAWK EAGLE.

Adult Male.—Head, nape, and upper back brown, the feathers with a mesial dark brown shaft streak; occipital crest 3·9 to 4·9 inches, black, with or without white tips, and with white bases. Cheeks and ear coverts pale brown, the feathers with a very narrow mesial dark brown stripe; throat white, with a broad white central streak and with a distinct moustachial stripe on each side; breast and upper abdomen pure white inclining to rufous, the feathers with a broad dark brown central stripe on the terminal half; lower abdomen, vent, under tail coverts, and tibial plumes uniform brown, also the lower back, rump, and upper tail coverts. Under wing coverts rufous brown, with dark shaft stripes; the lower series white, centred or barred with blackish brown. Axillaries a paler brown. Quills brown, barred with darker brown. Secondaries tipped with buff or buffy white, the innermost paler than the back, and the barrings very conspicuous. Wing coverts dark brown, the greater series margined paler. Tail pale brown with three and a broad sub-terminal dark brown band, broader than the interspace between it and the next. Cere pale yellow; feet and iris yellow.

Length.—Male—25 to 26 inches; wing 16; tail 11; tarsus 3·9 to 4.

Length.—Female—29 to 32 inches; wing 17·5 to 17·8; tail 12·51 to 12·57; tarsus 4·1.

Hab.—Ceylon, Central and Southern India, the Central Provinces, Guzerat, and Nepal. It has been found in Travancore, the Western Ghauts, Madras, the Neilgherries, Seoni, Raepoor, Etawah, Mundla and other localities in the Central Provinces; also at Mount Aboo, in Guzerat and South Concan.

Mr. Bourdillon in *Stray Feathers,* iv. 356, says of it, that it is very daring, frequently making a dash amongst chickens, when, if it misses, it retires to some neighbouring tree to concert a fresh plan of attack. It usually keeps to well-wooded tracts and feeds generally upon small birds as quail and pigeons, and at times on snakes and lizards; and Mr. Vidal in *Stray Feathers,* vol. vii., p. 31, adds that he had heard of one having been seen attacking a mongoose. Mr. Vidal has taken the eggs of this Hawk Eagle in the South Concan. He says it breeds during December and January and as late as April. The nests he says are large and comparatively deep stick structures loosely put together with the twigs hanging down untidily, built very high up, as a rule, in forks of rees. They are always profusely lined with green mango leaves. The old birds make no attempt to defend their nests. Out of 32 nests examined by Mr. Vidal, none contained more than one egg or one young bird. The largest egg measured 3 inches × 2·1 and the smallest 22·5 × 1 85. In shape they vary greatly, but the usual type is a moderate oval pointed at the smaller end. Colour a dull greenish white, sometimes unspotted and sometimes faintly streaked at the larger end with reddish brown. It is unglossed and has a pale green lining.

Gen. **Spilornis**.—*Gray*. Hæmatornis.—*Vigors*.

Bill straightened at the base; wings short; head crested; crest feathers rounded; tarsi plumed; toes scutellate at base of claw.

18. Spilornis melanotis, *Jerd., Madras Journ.* xiii. p. 165; *Sharpe, Cat. Acc. B. M.* p. 289, Sub-sp. a; *Davison and Wenden, Stray F.* vol. vii. sp. 74; *Ball, id.* p. 299; *Vidal, Stray F.* ix. p. 33; *Butler, id.* ix. p. 373; *Murray, Avif. Br. India* i. p. 46, No. 42. Hæmatornis spilogaster, *Bly., J. A. S. B.* xvi. p. 351. Spilornis spilogaster, *Blanf., J. A. S. B.* 1871, p. 270. Spilornis davisoni, *Hume, Stray F.* i. pp. 305, 422; *id.*, iv. pp. 281 358. Spilornis rutherfordi, *Swinh., Ibis,* 1870, p. 85; *id., P. Z. S.* 1871; *Wald., Ibis,* 1870, p. 298. Spilornis bacha, *Holds.* (*non Le Veill.*), *P. Z. S.* 1872, p. 412. Spilornis spilogaster, *Legge, B. Ceylon,* p. 61.—The SOUTHERN OR LESSER HARRIER EAGLE.

Young.—Above brown, with large spots of dark brown near the end of each feather, which is slightly tipped with fulvous, the bases of the feathers white, the upper tail coverts tipped and barred on the outer web with the same; wing coverts blackish brown, the least ones apically margined with white; the greater series whity brown, more or less entirely white on inner web, mesially streaked with dark brown, widening into a spatulate apical spot. Quills dark brown, tipped with white; the secondaries more broadly barred across with blackish brown, very distinct underneath, where the inner webs are for the most part white. Tail ashy brown, tipped with white, and crossed with three broad bands of darker brown. Head and neck all round white, with a narrow shaft stripe and a diamond-shaped apical spot of dark brown. Ear coverts and cheeks nearly uniform brown. Under surface of body white, with broad streaks of brown on the breast, becoming very narrow and linear on the flanks; thighs narrowly barred with brown. Under wing coverts white, with large oval spots of rufous brown on the innermost, and having bars of brown on the lower series.

Adult Female.—Head much crested, jet black, with conspicuous white bases to the feathers, those of the nape tipped with dull ochraceous; rest of upper surface of body purplish brown, paler on the interscapulary region; the wing coverts blacker, with remains of white tips, which are less distinct on the scapulars, but very broad on the upper tail coverts. Quills brown, tipped with white and mottled slightly on the outer web, but more on the inner with the same; all the quills dark brown at base and having a broad subterminal band of blackish brown, the primaries showing a second dark brown band near the base; the inner web of the quills below whitish, showing the bands very distinctly. Tail black, narrowly tipped with whitish and crossed with a very broad median band of pale whity brown; sides of face and chin blackish with a distinct greyish band, the latter showing slight tips of fulvous to the feathers; rest of under surface pale ochraceous brown, with distinct but irregular transverse lines of dark brown; the rest of the under surface with large white spots, rather oblong in shape, mostly margined above and below with black, changing to bars on the thighs and under tail coverts. Under wing coverts and axillaries light rufous with very distinct oval spots of white.

Adult Male.—Smaller. Length 26 inches; wing 16·5; tail 12; tarsus 3·5. Chest perfectly uniform brown with no traces of cross barrings on the under surface; breast and lower parts very largely and distinctly spotted with white; cere, loral skin, and gape bright yellow; bill slaty plumbeous at base, bluish black at tip and on culmen; feet pale dingy yellow; iris intense yellow. (*Sharpe.*)

Cere, orbital skin, and legs yellow; irides orange; bill bluish, black at the tip. The following are comparative measurements of this species and *S. cheela* in inches:—

	S. cheela. *Adult.*	*S. melanotis.* *Adult.*
Length	28 to 30	24 to 26.
Wing	18·5 „ 20·5	15 „ 16·8
Tail	12 „ 13	10·8 „ 12·5
Tarsus	4·15 „ 4·5	3·65 „ 3·75

Hab.—Central and Southern India, the Andamans to Ceylon and China. Occurs in both the Northern and Southern Concans, the Deccan, Travancore, Raipur, and other localities in the Central Provinces from the Ganges to the Godavery, Orissa, and also in Lower Bengal.

The Lesser Harrier Eagle affects marshy and hilly forest tracts, especially where there are rice and other cereal cultivations. It feeds chiefly on frogs, mice, and small birds. The only record of its nidification is in a paper in *Str. F.* by Mr. Vidal on the Birds of the South Concan. In Ceylon the nest building, according to Mr. H. Parker, is in progress in March, and the egg is laid at the end of that month or early in April. In May the young are generally hatched out. Two nests were taken by Mr. Vidal during March, and the eggs in his possession measured respectively 2·75 × 2·25 inches and

2·65 × 2·12 inches. They are said to be broad ovals, slightly pointed at the smaller end, white, streaked all over with reddish brown, and with a confluent cap of the same shade at the large end.

Gen. **Haliætus**,—*Savigny*.

Bill stright at the base, longish, compressed, curved towards the tip, which is much hooked; margin of upper mandible sinuate; wings long; 4th and 5th quills sub-equal, longest; tarsus plumed for nearly half its length; lower hal of tarsus scutellate.

Head of Haliætus albicillus.

19. Haliætus leucogaster, *Gm., S. N.* i. p. 257; *Vig., Zool. Journ.* i. p. 336; *Jerd., B. Ind.* i. p. 85; *Sharpe, Cat. Acc. B. M.* p. 307; *Str. F.* ii. 149; iii. 324-335; iv. 422-461; vi. 17; vii. 199; ix, 32; *Legge, B. Ceylon*, p. 67; *Hume, Str. F.* viii. p. 82; *Oates, B. Br. Burm.* ii. p. 199; *Murray, Avif. Br. Ind.* i. p. 53, No. 48. Cuncuma leuçogaster, *Hume, Rough Notes* i. p. 259; *id., Nests and Egg Ind. B.* p. 48; *Wall, Ibis*, 1868, p. 15; *Armstrong, Str. F.* iv. pp. 422-461.—The WHITE-BELLIED SEA EAGLE.

Adult.—Head, neck all round, breast, abdomen, under tail and wing coverts white, the outermost of the latter shaded with grey; the greater series ashy grey with white bases; body above ashy grey shaded with brown. Primaries cinereous black; also the secondaries, but tipped narrowly with white; tail black, broadly tipped with white. Cere and orbital ridge bluish lead tinged with green; legs and feet yellowish. Irides olive brown.

Length.—28 to 30 inches; wing 22 to 24; tail 9 to 9·5; tarsus 3·1 to 4; bill from gape 2·25.

The adult female is larger. The young is described by Mr. Sharpe (*Cat. Acc.*) Head and neck dark brown, streaked with buffy white; throat sandy buff, the feathers paler centred; rest of under surface rufescent brown with distinct buffy shaft streaks widening towards the apex; under tail coverts for the most part white, irregularly mottled with reddish brown. Above brown, the feathers margined paler, and with dull whitish shaft stripes; lower back and rump rather darker than the rest of the back, and with distinct white streaks; quills deep brown; secondaries paler and tipped with buffy white; the quills with more or less distinct darker brown bars; tip of inner web whitish below for the greater part of its length; tail dark brown, tipped with whitish and crossed with three ill-defined bars of paler brown, much mottled with darker brown and shaded with whitish.

Hab.—Ceylon, and the whole of India, including British Burmah and the Tennaserim province, also Assam and the Malay Archipelago, the Andamans and Nicobars. Occurs in the Concan, Deccan, Central, Northern and Southern India, Punjab, N. W. P. and Bengal. A permanent resident in most parts, breeding on lofty trees.

Mr. Vidal has taken the eggs in October, November, and December in the Southern Concan. The nests are gigantic platforms, built of strong, thick sticks, and are fully 5 feet in diameter. The normal number of eggs is one, and sometimes two have been found; they are greenish white, unspotted and glossless, from 2·7 × 2·04 to 3· × 2·06 inches. Mr. Vidal's experience is that the same nests are used year after year after being repaired, and that they they build on large trees in cocoanut and other gardens. As its English name implies, it feeds chiefly upon fish.

Gen. **Haliastur**.—*Selby*.

Bill stout, curved and hooked. Nostrils circular with bony margin all round. Wings very long, the 4th quill longest; tail slightly rounded; tarsi plumed at the knee, and covered with scutæ.

20. Haliastur Indus, *Bodd., Tabl. Pl. Enl.* 25; *Gray, Gen. Birds* i. p. 18; *Jerdon, B. of Ind.* i. p. 101, No. 55; *Hume, Rough Notes* ii. p. 316; *S. F.* vii. 251; i. p. 160; *Murray, Hdbk. Zool., &c., Sind,* p. 116; *Gray, Cat. Acc. B. M.* i. p. 313; *Hume, Str. F.* iii. p. 35; *Blyth, B. Burm.* p. 64; *Oates, Str. F.* v. p. 142; *Legge, B. Ceylon,* p. 76; *Hume & Dav., Str. F.* vi. p. 22; *Cripps, Str. F.* vii. p. 251; *Hume, Str. F.* viii. p. 82; *Scully. Str. F.* viii. p. 227; *Oates, Str. F.* x. p. 181; *id., B. Br. Burm.* ii. p. 201; *Murray, Avif. Brit. Ind.* i. p. 56. No. 50. Haliætus indus, *Sch. Mus. P. B.* p. 19.—The MAROON-BACKED OF BRAHMINY KITE.

Adult.—Head, neck, throat, entire breast, and as far as the middle of the abdomen white, with dark brown shaft stripes; rest of the plumage maroon, or rufous chestnut, paler on the secondaries, the tail paling into a fulvous white at the tip. Quills black, rufescent at the base of inner web; under wing coverts deep maroon, with dark shaft stripes; cere brownish; feet greenish yellow; irides brown.

Length.—20 to 21 inches; wing 14·75 to 16; tail 7 to 8.

The young bird is a rather deep brown above, the feathers tipped with rufous. Head, neck, and lower parts pale rufous, streaked paler.

Hab.—Ceylon and India generally. Recorded from Sind, the Punjab, N.-W. Provinces, Kutch, Kattiawar, Ajmere, Concan, Deccan, Tranvancore, Upper Pegu, Nepal. Generally affects trees near water in parties of from six to a dozen. Breeds wherever it occurs from the middle of February to the beginning of April. The nest is always on a tree near by water, and is not unlike that of *Milvus govinda*. The normal number of eggs is two, but it is not uncommon to find three. In shape they vary much; but typically they are very perfect, moderately broad ovals, slightly compressed towards one end; in colour greyish white, speckled or spotted with pale dingy brown or reddish brown. Size 1·89 to 2·28 × 1·5 to 1·79.

Gen. **Milvus.**—*Cuv.*

Bill short, straight at the base, well curved and hooked at tip. Upper mandible with a rounded festoon. Nostrils oval, oblique. Wings long. Tail forked or emarginate. Tarsi short, plumed at the knees, and with scutæ in front below.

21. Milvus govinda, *Sykes, P. Z. S.* 1832, p. 81; *Jerd., B. of Ind.* p. 104, No. 56; *Hume, Rough Notes* ii. p. 320; *Sharpe, Cat. Acc. B. M.* p. 325; *Stray Feathers*, i. p. 160; *Murray, Hdbk. Zool.,&c., Sind,* p. 116; *id., Vert. Zool. Sind,* p. 90; *Legge, B. Ceylon,* p. 80; *Murray, Avif. Brit. Ind.* i. p. 57, No. 51.—The Common Pariah Kite.

Adult Male.—Above brown or rufous brown, the head and neck rufescent with dark central stripes. Scapulars and wing coverts edged with buff, the wing coverts with dark central stripes. Quills and greater coverts dark brown, the quills albescent near the base and mottled with brown. Tail ashy brown, tipped with buffy white and barred with brown; the under surface pale brown, or whitish, and also mottled and barred. Throat albescent with brown shaft-stripes. Under parts dull rufous brown, buffy on the vent and under tail coverts, and with brown shaft stripes; the feathers of the breast somewhat fulvescent. Under wing coverts rufous brown, with dark brown centres to the feathers. Cere and gape yellow. Bill horny black. Feet yellowish. Irides yellowish.

Length.—20 to 23 inches; wing 18·5 to 19; tail 13; tarsus 2·25.

Hab.—Throughout India. In Ceylon it is not numerous, and according to Mr. Parker rare in the Hambantotta districts, visiting occasionally the inland tanks in the north. A resident scavenger. Breeds on house tops, old mosques, and flat-roofed buildings,—seldom on trees,—during January, February, and March. It occurs also in Beloochistan, Afghanistan, and Nepal.

Gen. **Elanus**.—*Savigny*.

Bill small, ridge (without cere) greater than half of middle toe without claw; tip much hooked and lengthened; edge of upper mandible slightly sinuate. Cere small; nostrils oval. Loreal space feathered. Wings reaching to end of tail, pointed; 2nd quill longest; the 1st emarginate near the tip. Tail short. Tarsi short, plumed above, covered with small round scales. Middle claw keeled.

22. Elanus cæruleus, *Desf. Mem. Acad. R. des Science,* p. 503, pl. 15; *Sharpe, Cat. Acc. B. Mus.* i. p. 336; *Legge, B. Ceylon,* p. 85; *Hume, Str. F.* viii. p. 83; *Oates Str. F.* x. p. 181; *id., B. Br. Burm.* ii. p. 205; *Murray, Avif. Brit. Ind.* i. p. 59, No. 55. Falco melanopterus, *Daud. Traite,* ii. i. p. 152; *Bree, Birds Eur.* i. p. 108. Elanus melanopterus, *Leach, Zool. Misc.* p. 5; *Jerd., Birds of Ind.* i. p. 112, No. 59; *Sharpe, P. Z. S.,* 1869, p. 570; *Hume, Rough Notes* ii. p. 21. *id., Nests and Eggs Ind. B.* p. 56; *Str. F.* i. pp. 21, 163; *Murray, Zool., &c., Sind,* p. 117; *id., Vert. Zool. Sind,* p. 92.—The Black-winged Kite.

Adult.—Entire upper parts ashy grey, lighter on the head; forehead, eye-brow, lores and sides of face white; ear coverts ashy grey; supercillium dark brown or black; lesser and median wing coverts and winglet glossy black; greater coverts concolourous with the back. Axillaries and under wing coverts white; inner lining of wing dark grey; primary coverts and quills ashy grey, the latter white at the base and black-shafted. Tail ashy, the two centre feathers greyish; entire under parts white. Cere, orbits, and feet yellow; bill black; irides crimson.

Length.—13 inches; wing 10·6 to 11; tail 5·6; tarsus 1·4.

Hab.—Ceylon and South India generally; also South-Eastern Europe and Africa. Very widely distributed. Recorded from Egypt, Gambia, Transvaal, South Africa, and the Mediterranean; also from Kutch, Kattiawar, Jodhpore, Sambhur, North Guzerat, the Concan and Deccan, Pegu, Burmah and Nepal. Breeds almost throughout Upper India. Nest circular, composed of small twigs and sticks, and lined with fine grass roots and fibres. Eggs bluish white or creamy, streaked and blotched with pale yellowish brown or brownish red.

As to the habits of this species there is not much recorded; it usually flies low, skimming above the surface of the ground, or hovers in the air much like a kestrel, but dropping suddenly to the ground. It is not uncommon to see it perch on telegraph wires, on the bare end of a bough, or on some dry tree in the vicinity of water. It feeds chiefly on rats, mice, beetles, grasshoppers, and other insects.

It is a resident in Ceylon and affects forests. Breeds in the Kurnegalla districts from May to August. In India it breeds from November to January.

Gen. **Pernis**.—*Cuv.*

Bill curved from the base; the margin straight; lores clothed with scale-like feathers; tarsi short, reticulate, half plumed in front; scales on toes transverse; wings and tail long.

23. Pernis ptilonorhynchus, *Steph., Gen. Zool.* xiii. pl. 35; *Holdsw., P. Z. S.* 1872, p. 414; *Sharpe, Cat. Acc. B. M.* p. 347; *Legge, B. Ceylon*, p. 89; *Murray, Avif. Br. Ind.* i. p. 61, No. 57. Pernis cristata, *Cuv., Regne An.* i. p. 335; *Jerd., B. Ind.* i. p. 108, No. 57; *Hume, Rough Notes* ii. p. 330; *Stray F.*, vol. iii. p. 448; vol. ix. p. 375. Pernis ptilorhynchus, *Salvad., Ucc. Born.* p. 9; *Hume, Nest and Eggs Ind. B.* p. 55; *Oates, B. Br. Burm.* i. p. 207.—The HONEY BUZZARD.

Adult.—General colour above and below rich chocolate brown, with indistinct black shaft stripes; the crown and sides of head, as well as the throat, ashy grey; the lower throat blackish; quills and tail brownish ashy, the latter with 3 dark bands, the uppermost hidden by the upper tail coverts, the terminal one tipped with greyish white; crest variably developed; cere black, greenish towards commissure and nostrils; gape and lower mandible pale blue; feet bees'-wax-yellow; irides yellow.

Length.—24 to 25·5 inches; wing 15·5 to 16·5; tail 11·5 to 12·75; tarsus 2·1 to 2·2. The female is larger. The intermediate and young stages of the Honey Buzzard are so very variable, that it is scarcely necessary to describe them. Mr. Sharpe says: "Great variations exist in the tone of the intervening stages, the colour varying from tawny to fulvous brown, while the extent of black stripes on the throat is also a very variable character." Again, he adds, under "Obs." "that the young of *P. ptilonorhynchus*, if they happen to be crestless, are undistinguishable in plumage from the immature of *P. apivorus*; and I have seen young birds from India which I could not separate from European examples. A natural inference is that these may not be *P. ptilonorhynchus*, but *P. apivorus*, the young of which may migrate to India in the winter." Mr. A. O. Hume's remarks are also to nearly the same effect.

Hab—Ceylon, the whole of India except Sind; the Himalayas, Burmah, the Malayan Peninsula, Sumatra and Java, also Nepaul.

Breeds in May and June, on trees, making a moderate-sized nest of sticks and twigs lined with leaves or grass; eggs normally 2 in number, spherical nearly, or a very broad oval, white or buffy with red, reddish brown, or blood red markings and varying in size from 1·82 to 2·2 in length and from 1 5 to 1·9 in breadth. The food of the Honey Buzzard is young birds, frogs, mice, bees, and reptiles generally. It has a rapid flight, soars very high and gracefully, and glides through the air without apparent effort. It is easily tamed, bears confinement well and does not show the fierceness of other birds of prey. Another species, *Pernis brachypterus*, Blyth, has been mentioned in *Stray Feathers*, vol. iii., p. 36, as having been found in Upper Pegu. The description is certainly very curt, and I have seen birds answering it from the Punjab and the Deccan The extremely variable character of the plumage of the intermediate and crested stages of the species leaves room to doubt its validity.

Sub-Family—FALCONINÆ—Falcons.

Bill short, suddenly curved from the base; upper mandible distinctly toothed; nostrils either round, oblique, or linear oval; cere short; tarsi slender, naked; hinder aspect reticulate. Outer toe only connected to mid-toe by interdigital membrane; tibia longer than tarsus.

Gen. Baza.—*Hodgs.*

Bill small, much hooked, grooved on its side; upper mandible with two sharp teeth on each side, lower with 3-4; lores covered with feathers; nostrils transverse, narrow; head crested; wings moderate; the 3rd quill longest, the 1st three slightly emarginate towards the tip; tarsi covered with small smooth hexagonal scales; claws small, subequal.

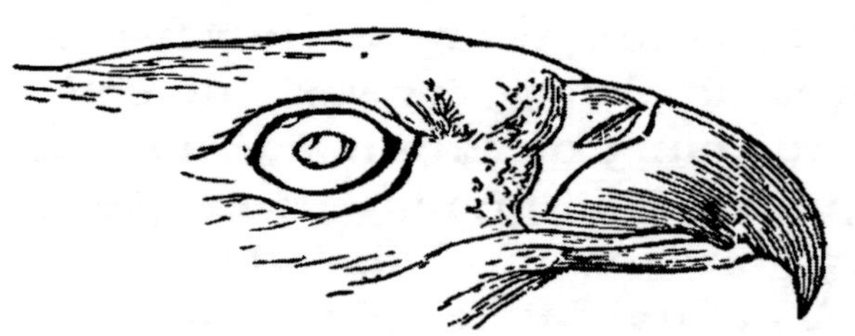

24. Baza lophotes, *Tem. Pl. Col.* i. pl. 10; *Gray, List, Gen. B.* p. 4; *Blyth, Cat. B. Mus. Soc. Beng.* p. 17; *Jerd., B. Ind.* i. p. 111, No. 58; *Blyth, Ibis,* 1863, p. 11; *Wall., Ibis,* 1868, p. 19; *Hume, Rough Notes* p. 337; *Holdsw , P. Z. S.* 1872; *Sharpe, Cat. Acc. B. M.* p. 352; *Hume, Str. F.* vi. p. 24; viii. p. 191. *Legge, B. Ceylon*; p. 98; *Oates, B. Br. Burm.* ii. p. 208; *Murray, Avif. Br. Ind.* i. p. 62, No. 58.—The Black Crested Kite.

Above glossy greenish black with a very long occipital crest; thigh coverts under tail and under wing coverts also glossy greenish black; quills black, greyish underneath; outer webs of the secondaries deep chestnut at base and towards the tip which is greenish black; rest of the feathers white; scapulars and some of the coverts next them white internally and tipped chestnut, forming a conspicuous interrupted white wing band; tail greenish black above, ashy grey beneath; entire sides of the face and neck as well as the throat black, tinged with brown; foreneck and chest white, forming a very broad band followed by an indistinct line of blackish feathers, and another broad band of chestnut covering the upper breast; lower breast creamy white and banded with chestnut, narrow on the lower part and flanks; thighs, lower abdomen, under tail coverts and underwing coverts greenish black, the lower ones of the latter ashy grey; bill and legs plumbeous; irides dark brown.

Length.—13 to 14 inches; wing 9 to 9·85; tail 5· to 5·7; tarsus 1·3 to 1·5

Hab.—Southern India, Ceylon, the Malayan Peninsula, Lower Bengal, Assam, Tipperah and the Tennaserim provinces of British Burma.

Of the nidification of this species nothing is known. It is said to frequent thick forests and to be more or less gregarious.

25. Baza ceylonensis, *Legge, Birds of Ceylon*; *Stray F.* iv. p. 247; viii. p. 444.—The CEYLON CRESTED KITE.

Lores blackish; head brownish tawny; centre of forehead and crown black, edged with rufous; occipital crest 1¾ inches in length, black, conspicuously tipped with white; the feathers of the hind neck deeply edged with rufous tawny, the centre parts being black; back, scapulars, rump, upper tail coverts, primary and lesser wing coverts blackish brown, the latter the deepest and with a cinerous tinge; upper tail coverts paler than the back; median and greater wing coverts pale or fulvous brown; quills black, the outer webs with smoky grey bars, the corresponding band on the inner web being brown; tertials and secondaries tipped with white; tail dark smoky grey, tipped greyish white and with four blackish bars, the terminal one about 1½ inches in depth; cheeks and ear coverts slaty grey with dark shafts, the dark feathers of the occiput passing round to meet the latter region; chin and throut buff with a broad mesial black streak; sides and lower part of foreneck with the upper edge of the pectoral region tawny cinerous, the feathers with brownish shafts; below this, the under surface, under tail and under wing coverts are white, with broad rufescent brown edges; iris yellow, also the tarsi and feet; bill blackish leaden; lower mandible pale at base; cere dusky plumbeous.

Length.—To front of cere 16·5; culmen 0·10; total length 17·5; wing 11·7; tail 7·5; tarsus 1·5; bill to gape 1·2.

Hab.—Southern India (The Wynaad), and Ceylon (Kandy district). Nothing is known of its habits, &c.

Gen. **Falco**.—*Linn.*

Nostrils round with a central tubercle. First one or two quills notched internally, second quill longest; tarsus feathered at the knee; toes long, scutellated.

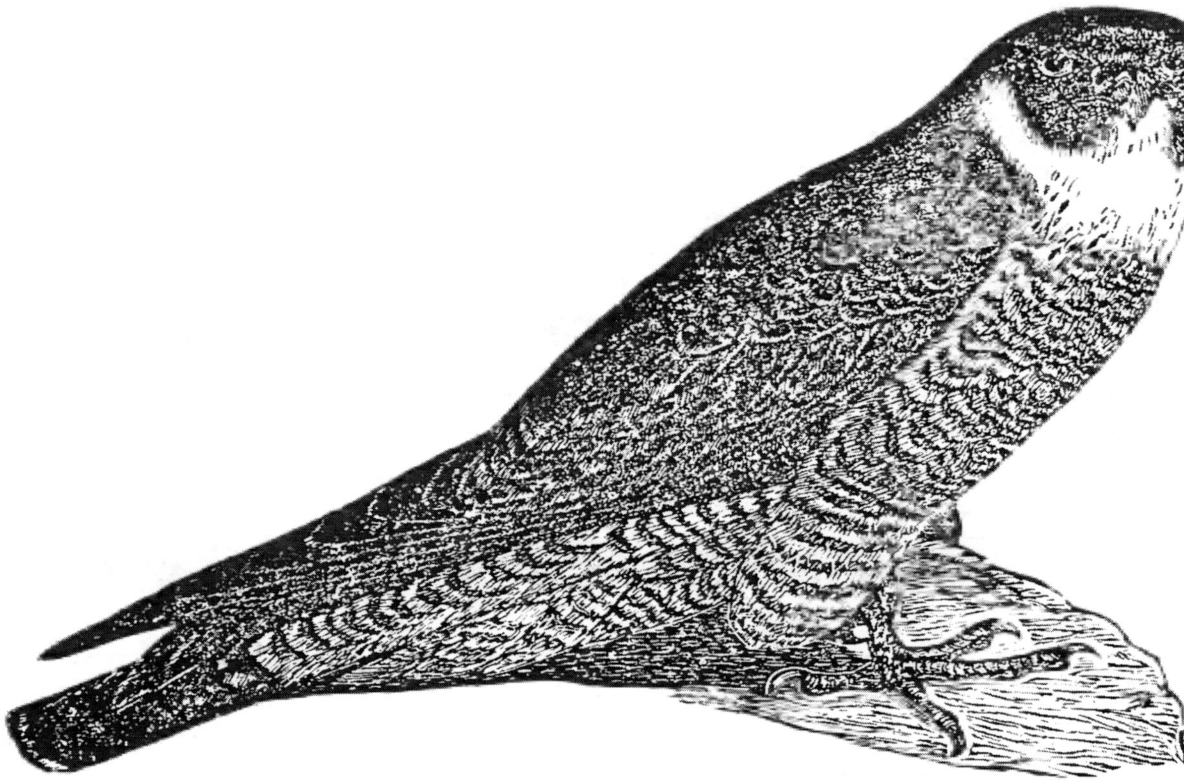

26. Falco communis, *Gm., S. N.* p. 270; *Less., Traite*, p. 88, pl. 16; *Sharpe, Ann. N. H.* xi. p. 222; *id., Cat. Acc. B. M.* p. 376; *Murray, Avif. Br. Ind.* i. p. 68. Falco peregrinus, *Gmel., S. N.* vol. i. p. 272; *Jerdon, Birds of India* vol. i. p 21; *Ibis*, 1871; *Grey, Cat. Br. Mus.* p. 11; *Hume, Rough Notes* vol. i. p. 49; *Sharpe, Cat. Acc. Br. M.* p. 376; *Murray, Hdbk., Zool., &c., Sind*, p. 106; *Legge, B. Ceylon* p. 101; *Oates, B. Br. Burm.* ii. p. 214. *Bhyri* (the female), *Bhyri Bacha* (the male). Hind. Falco atriceps, *Hume, Ibis*, 1869, p. 356; *id., Rough Notes* i. p. 58; *id., Ibis*, 1871, p. 24; *Jerd., Ibis*, 1872, p. 2. Falco Brookii, *Sharpe, Ann. N. H.* (4) ii. pp. 20, 222 1873.—The Peregrine Falcon.

Adult Male.—Above bluish grey, paler on the rump and upper tail coverts, and barred with blackish. Head, neck, upper part of mantle and wing coverts blackish, with grey barring, more or less indistinct on the latter. Cheeks, ear-coverts and a short moustachial band blackish. Forehead, sides of neck, chin, throat, under surface of body and breast white, the latter with a tinge of pale fawn, as also the lower abdomen; the chest with a few narrow black shaft stripes almost disappearing in old individuals; abdomen with some small heart-shaped spots, some similar marks on the under tail coverts also. Thighs transversely barred with narrow black lines. Quills brownish black, primaries slightly shaded with greyish, the secondaries clearer grey, crossed by dull blackish bars, the smaller median quills tipped white. Tail feathers greyish, broadly barred with black and tipped with white. Bill bluish, black at the tip; cere, legs and feet yellow; claws black; iris hazel-brown.

Length.—15 to 16 inches; culmen 1·2; wing 12·2 to 12·7; tail 6·5. (*Adult female* similar to the adult male, but larger. *Length*, 17 to 19 inches; culmen 1·35; wing 14·5; tail 7·5; tarsus 2·3.)

The young bird is brown, all the feathers edged with pale buff shading into whitish; under surface of the body whitish, the throat unspotted, all the rest of the feathers dark brown in the centre, lower flanks barred; head more edged with whitish; cheek stripe brown. Wing darker than the back; the inner webs spotted or barred with rufous. Tail feathers brown, broadly tipped with white; the outer web spotted and the inner one barred with pale rufous more or less distinct

Hab.—Ceylon. A very widely distributed species. A winter visitant to India. Occurs in Sind, Punjab, N.-W. Provinces, Oudh, Bengal, Rajpootana, Kutch, Central and South India, Guzerat, Concans and Deccan; also Beloochistan, Persia and S. Afghanistan. Rare in Pegu and Tennaserim. Has also been found in Nepaul.

The Peregrine is believed to breed below Ferozepoor along the banks of the Indus, but nothing certain is known. Mr. Hume, in his "Rough Notes," mentions having had a nestling shot by a shikaree in the interior of the Himalayas not far from Kotegarh. In Europe it builds on rocks and cliffs. Eggs 2, 3 or 4, of a light russet-red colour, marbled over with darker shades, patches, and streaks of the same. Nest composed of sticks, seaweed, hair, and other such materials. The flight of the peregrine is extremely rapid, and by repeated beatings of its wings. 150 miles an hour has been calculated as its rate of flight. It is much prized in falconry on account of its courageous spirit and fearlessness. The food of the species consists principally of birds, such as seagulls, partridges, plovers, grouse and ducks; but it also feeds on hares, rats, &c. It has frequently been known to stoop upon and carry off game from before the sportsman.

27. Falco peregrinator, *Sundev., Phys., Tidskr. Lund.* 1837, p. 177, pl. 4; *Gray, Gen. B.* i. p. 19; *id., Cat. Mam. and B. Nepal Hodgs.* p. 44; *Blyth, J. A. S. B.* xix, p. 321; *Jerd., B. Ind.* i. p. 25; *Hume, Rough Notes* i. p. 557; *id., Nests and Eggs* p. 14; *Jerd., Ibis*, 1878, p. 237; *Sharpe, Ann. and Mag. Nat. Hist.* xi. p. 223, 1873; *id., Cat. Acc. B. M.* i. p. 382; *Str. F.* v. p. 500; *id.*, vii. p. 428; *Legge, B. Ceylon* p. 106; *Oates, Str. F.* x. p. 178; *Gurney, Ibis*, 1882, p. 291; *Murray, Avif. Br. Ind.* i. p. 69, No. 65. Falco shaheen, *Jerd., Madr. Journ.* x. p. 81; *id., Ill. Ind. Orn.* pls. xii. and xxvii.—The Shaheen Falcon, or Indian Peregrine.

Adult.—Head, nape, neck, interscapulary region, cheek-stripe and wing coverts deep black, the latter shaded with bluish grey; lower back, rump and upper tail coverts slaty or bright bluish grey, the latter with remains of or without obsolete blackish cross markings; quills black, externally washed with greyish, the inner web with a few nearly obsolete rufous bars; secondaries tipped with fulvous; tail bluish grey, the tips tawny, the blackish bars nowhere distinct; chin, throat and upper breast white; rest of under surface rufous, or tawny ferruginous; flanks, thighs and under tail coverts with a few spots or bars; under wing coverts rufous with black bars. Cere yellow; bill slaty, blue black at tip; feet yellow; iris deep brown.

Length.—16 to 16·5 inches; wing 12·25 to 12·77; tail 6·5 to 6·8; tarsus 2·2 to 2·25.

Hab.—Ceylon and the whole of India to Nepaul; also British Burmah and Afghanistan, extending into Western Asia.

The Shaheen Falcon, like the Peregrine, is much prized in falconry. All the peculiarities which are sought for in the Peregrine are also exhibited in this species, which is considered a better bird. Its native habits have not been studied much. It however affects both rocky hills and forest land, and destroys much game. It has been found breeding in Central and Southern India during March and April, building on inaccessible cliffs. In Ceylon Mr. Parker says it frequents a precipice at Periya Puliyankulam, 9 miles N.-E. of Vilankalam.

28. Falco severus, *Horsf., Tr. Lin. Socy.* xiii. p. 135; *Blyth, Ibis,* 1863, p. 8; *Sharpe, Cat. Acc. B. M.* p. 397; *Legge, B. Ceylon* p. 110; *Oates, B. Br. Burm.* ii. p. 216; *Murray, Avif. Br. Ind.* i. p. 74, No. 70. Hypotriorchis severus, *Gray, G. B.* i. p. 20; *Jerd., B. Ind.* i. p. 34, No. 14; *Hume, Rough Notes* i. p. 87; *Stray F.* iv. p. 354; and pp. 533-5.—The INDIAN HOBBY.

Adult.—Dark slaty blue above, black on the cheeks and ears; beneath deep unspotted rusty red. Cere, orbital skin, and legs reddish yellow; bill plumbeous.

Length.—Male, 10·5 inches; wing 9; tail 4·5.

Mr. Sharpe (*Cat. Acc.*) describes an adult female as being black above, with a slight slaty grey shade, more distinct on the lower back, rump and tail, with the bars on the latter obsolete; head, cheeks and ear coverts black; under surface of body bright chestnut; throat and sides of neck creamy white, the latter with a slight wash of chestnut; under wing coverts bright chestnut, some of the lower ones barred with black. Primaries black with a few rufous bars near the base. Cere, orbits and feet yellow; bill bluish black, yellow at base; iris dark brown.

Length.—13·5 inches; wing 8·5 to 8·75; tail 4·5 to 4·62; tarsus 1·15.

Hab.—Ceylon, Northern and Southern India (Nilghiris, Travancore Hills,) Barrackpore; also the lower ranges of Kumaon and Gurhwal and the Himalayas generally. Out of India proper, Mr. Sharpe gives the Indo-Malayan sub-region and Nepaul. It is supposed to breed in the dense forests of Gurhwal.

29. Falco chiquera, *Daud, Traite* ii. p. 121; *Blyth, Cat. Mus. As Socy. Beng.* p. 14; *Sharpe, Cat. Acc. Br. Mus.* p. 403; *Legge, B. Ceylon* p. 110.; *Murray, Avif. Br. Ind.* i. p. 74, No. 71. Hypotriorchis chiquera, *Gray, Gen. B.* i. p. 20; *Jerdon, B. Ind.* i. p. 36, No. 16; *Murray, Hdbk. Zool., &c., Sind*, p. 108. Chiquera typus, *Bp., Rev. Mag. de Zool.* p. 536, 1854; *Hume, Str. F.* i. p. 157. Lithofalco chiquera, *Hume, Rough Notes* i. p. 91; *Anderson, P. Z. S.* 1871, p. 681. The *Turrumti*, Hind.—The RED-HEADED MERLIN.

Adult Male.—Crown, nape, back, and sides of the neck chestnut; forehead white; sides of the face, chin, throat and neck white, except a faint, short, moustachial stripe; eyebrow and a narrow streak below the eye black; back, scapulars, tertiaries, wing and primary coverts and secondaries slaty blue, the feathers with dark shafts and barred with dark brown. Primaries dark or blackish brown, their inner webs barred with white; under wing coverts white, barred with blackish brown; breast white, some of the feathers with dark shaft-streaks; rest of under surface white, barred transversely with black. Tail like the back, the feathers barred with black, tipped white and with a broad subterminal black band. Cere, orbits and feet yellow; claws black; bill greenish, yellow at base, black at the tip; irides light brown.

Length.—11·5 to 12 inches; wing 8·25; tail 4·75 to 6; tarsus 1·5; culmen 0·85.

The adult female is similar to the male, but larger. *Length.*—13 inches; wing 9; tail 6·5; tarsus 1·5 to 1·55.

Hab.—Ceylon and throughout the Indian Peninsula. Recorded from Sind, Punjab, N.-W. Provinces, Bengal, Nepaul, Kutch, Kattiawar, Jodhpore, and N. Guzerat; also Beloochistan, Persia and Afghanistan.

Affects open country in the vicinity of cultivation. It is said to be easily reclaimed and flown at partridges and quails, which it pursues very perseveringly. Like the European Sparrow-hawk, it is a very courageous bird, and the propensity for attacking larger birds of prey than itself seems to be more developed. Jerdon says it even drives away the *Wokhab* (*Aquila fulvescens*) from the vicinity of its nest or perch. In India it breeds in February, March, April and May, nearly everywhere on trees; nest fixed in a fork near the top. Eggs 3—4 in number, variable in shape; in colour, they are pale yellowish brown, with from a few reddish brown specks to a nearly uniform dark brownish red, obscurely mottled and blotched with a somewhat purer and darker. Size 1·6 to 1·75 in length, and 1·25 to 1·32 in breadth.

30. Cerchneis tinnuncula (*Linn.*), *Boie, Isis,* 1828, p. 314; *Sharpe, Cat. Acc. B. M.* p. 425; *Legge, B. Ceylon* p. 114; *Hume, Str. F.* viii. p. 81; *Scully, Str. F.* viii. p. 223; *Murray, Avif. Br. Ind.* i. p. 77, No. 74. Falco tinaunculus, *Linn., Syst. Nat.* i. p. 127. Tinnunculus alaudarius, *Gray, Gen. Bird* i. p. 21; *Jerd., B. Ind.* i. p. 38, No. 17; *Blyth, Ibis,* 1863; *Hume, Rough Notes* p. 96; *Murray, Hdbk. Zool., &c., Sind,* p. 108; *Oates, B. Br. Burm.* ii. p. 217. Cerchneis saturata, *Hume and Dav., Str. F.* vi. p. 3. (*Narzi,* the female; *Narzanak,* the male, Hind.)—The KESTREL.

Adult Male.—Forehead buffy white; crown of the head, nape, neck behind and on the sides, blue grey, the feathers with narrow dark shaft-stripes. Eyebrow buffy white; sides of the face, except a dark moustachial stripe, silvery white; chin and throat, also the under tail coverts, unspotted buff. Upper back, scapulars, tertiaries and wing coverts brick-red or vinaceous, the feathers with a subterminal heart-shaped black spot, larger on the tertiaries. Primaries and their coverts, and secondaries dark brown, the primary coverts margined with rufous; outer secondaries narrowly edged and tipped with fulvous or buffy white, and the primaries barred on their inner webs with white; the inner primaries with bars of a rufescent hue. Lower back, rump, upper tail coverts and tail blue grey, the tail with a broad subterminal black band and tipped with white; breast, abdomen and flanks rufous fawn, the feathers on the breast and flanks with mesial dark streaks, which take an oval shape lower down. Thigh coverts unspotted rufous fawn. Under wing coverts white, with a buffy tinge, and spotted black. Bill bluish-horn, black at the tip and yellowish at the base. Cere, orbits and legs yellow. Irides brown.

Length.—12·5 to 13 inches; wing 9·5 to 10; tail 6·5 to 6·7; culmen 1·75; tarsus 1·6.

The adult female is less rufous in colour above, and with the subterminal spots wider and forming bands. The head is rufous with longitudinal streaks; tail rufous, banded with dark brown, tipped with white and with a subterminal black band as in the male.

Hab.—Ceylon and throughout India to Nepaul. A winter visitant, arriving in India in August and leaving in April. Breeds in the Himalayas, from Afghanistan to Sikkim, also in the Suliman range and the hills that divide Sind from Khelat, and in the Nilghiris. Hume says, that in the Himalayas it lays in April, May and June, and in the Nilghiris as early as the last week in February, and in March and April. It nests either in rocky ledges or on trees, or in holes of cliffs. Hume adds that he has authentic accounts of the Kestrel's nest being taken in ruined buildings both in Cashmere and Kumaon. Eggs 3 to 6 in number, broad ovals, more or less pointed or compressed towards one end, ground colour brick or blood red, speckled and blotched with darker red; size 1·16 to 1·65 × 1·13 to 1·30.

31. Cerchneis amurensis (*Radde*), *Homey, J. F. O.* 1868, p. 251; *Sharpe, Cat. Acc. B. M.* p. 445; *id., Str. F.* iii. p. 303; *Legge, Str. F.* iii. p. 362; *id., B. Ceylon* p. 119; *Hume, Str. F.* viii. p. 81; *Oates, Str. F.* x. p. 178; *id., B. Br. Burm.* ii. p. 219; *Murray, Avif. Br. Ind.* i. p. 79, No. 77. Erythropus amurensis, *Gurney, Ibis,* 1868, p. 251. Erythropus vespertinus, *Swinh., Ibis,* 1861, pp. 253, 327; *Jerd., B. Ind.* i. p. 40, No. 19; *Hume, Rough Notes* i. p. 160; *Jerd., Ibis,* 1871, p. 243. Hypotriorchis concólor, *Gurney, Ibis,* 1866, p. 127. Falco vespertinus, var. amurensis, *Radde, Reis Amurl Vog.* p. 230, pl. i., *fig.* 2, *a, b, c.*—The RED LEGGED HOBBY.

Adult Male.—Above leaden black, paler on the lower back and secondaries; greater wing coverts and primaries washed externally with silvery grey; tail greyish black above, paler below; under surface of body pale grey; lower abdomen, thighs, vent and under tail coverts bright chestnut; under wing coverts and axillaries pure white. Cere, orbits and feet dark orange; claws whitish; bill yellowish horn colour, blackish at tip; iris hazel.

Length.—9·5 inches; culmen 0·75; wing 9; tail 5·3; tarsus 1·15.

The adult female is dull leaden grey above, darker on the interscapulary region, clearer on the scapulars, lower back and rump, all the feathers crossed by indistinct bars of black; tail bluish grey crossed by a broad subterminal and other narrow bars of black; quills brownish black, externally washed with grey and barred with white about half way up the inner web; crown of the head, lores, feathers round the eye, and a slight moustachial streak dull blackish; sides of the face, neck and throat unspotted creamy white, also the breast; the latter with mesial streaks of black on each feather; flanks barred; thighs, vent and under tail coverts pale rufous; under wing coverts white with black spots.

Length.—10·5 inches; culmen 0·75; wing 9·5; tail 5·3; tarsus 1·1.

Hab.—Mr. Sharpe gives Amoor Land, N. China, Nepaul, E. Coast of Africa and Natal. It migrates during winter to India and Ceylon. It has been found in the Punjab, N.-W. Provinces, Central India, the Concan, Deccan, and also in N.-E. Cachar and British Burmah.

Its habits are quite like those of the Lesser Kestrel, building in communities and hunting in company for grasshoppers and other insects.

SUB-ORDER—PANDIONES.

Outer toe reversible; toes devoid of feathers; eyes lateral; no facial disc; plumage close and compact. Nostrils not concealed by bristles.

Gen. Pandion,—*Savigny.*

Bill short, rounded above and curved from the cere. Upper mandible with a slight festoon. Nostrils small, obliquely transverse; wing lengthened; second quill longest; distance between tips of primaries and secondaries greater than length of tarsus; legs naked; tarsi with reticulate scales.

32. Pandion haliætus, *Lin., Syst. Nat.* i. p. 129; *Sharpe, Cat. Acc. B. M.* i. p. 450; *Less., Man. d'Ornithology* i. p. 86; *Sw. and Rich., Faun. Bor. Am. Birds* p. 20; *Gould, Birds of Eur.* pl. 12; *Bp., Consp.* i. 16; *Jerd., B. Ind.* i. p. 80, No. 40; *Hume, Rough Notes* i. p. 234; *id., Stray Feathers,* i. p. 159; *Blanford, Eastn. Persia,* p. 114; *Murray, Hdbk. Zool., &c., Sind,* p. 110; *id., Vert. Zool. Sind,* p. 81; *Shelley, B. Egypt* p. 203; *Legge, B. Ceylon* p. 122; *Oates, Str. F.* x. p. 179; *id., B. Br. Burm.* ii. p. 220; *Gurney, Ibis,* 1882, p. 594; *Murray, Avif Br. Ind.* i. p. 80, No. 78. Pandion indicus, *Hodgs. in Gray's Zool. Misc.* p. 81. *Muchee-Mar,* Sind; *Much Murrung,* Hind.—The OSPREY.

Head and nape white, the feathers of the forehead and crown with dark brown stripes; a dark brown streak from the eyes over the ears; upper plumage rich hair brown; quills blackish; tail pale brown with dark bars, whitish on the inner web; beneath pure white with some brown spots on the breast, longitudinal in youth, broader in advancing age, and tending to coalesce in the fully adult; irides bright yellow; legs and feet plumbeous yellow; bill black.

Length.—Female—26 inches; wing 20; tail 9; tarsus 2·4.

Hab.—Ceylon and nearly throughout the Indian Peninsula in suitable localities. Recorded from Sind, Beloochistan, and Persia; also the Punjab, N.-W. Provinces, Bengal, British Burmah, Nepaul, Kutch, Kattiawar, Concan and Deccan, and occurs also all over Europe and Africa, N. and S. America, China and Japan. Very widely distributed. Most abundant along the coasts, large rivers and lakes. In Ceylon Mr. H. Parker says it visits the larger tanks in the interior of Northern and North-West Provinces, where its favourite perch is the stump of some dead tree standing in the water.

Mr. Sharpe (*Cat. Acc.* p. 450) remarks that "Ospreys seem to get whiter on the head with age; the mottling on the breast is strongly marked in all old birds, and that the tail becomes more uniform brown with age, so that a strongly barred tail is a sure sign of immaturity."

It is believed the Osprey breeds in the Valley of Kumaon, where Mr. Hume says he saw the nest of one. Mr. Thompson believes it breeds on the Ganges above Hurdwar. Nothing certain is however known. In the British Isles it is said to make a large nest either on trees, on rocks, or about old ruins near large pieces of water, and to lay 2 or 3 eggs, oval in form, and typically have a white ground, here and there clouded with pale purple and very richly blotched and streaked, most densely towards the large end with deep red, becoming in its intensity almost black.—Size 2·52 × 1·89 to 1·93.

Gen. **Polioaetus**—*Kaup.*

Tarsus feathered in front for one-third its length, scutellate in front. Distance between tips of primaries and secondaries less than length of tarsus.

33. Polioaetus ichthyaetus, *Horsf., Tr. Linn. Socy.* xiii. p. 136; *Sharpe, Cat. Acc. B. M.* i. p. 453; *Kaup., Contr. Orn.* 1850, p. 73; *Jerd., B. Ind.* i. p. 81; *Hume, Rough Notes* ii. p. 239; *id., Nests and Eggs* p. 43; *Legge, Str. F.* iii. p. 363; *id., B. Ceylon* p. 72; *Oates, B. Br. Burm.* ii. p. 221; *Murray, Avif. Brit. Ind.* i. p. 81, No. 79. Haliaetus plumbeus, *Hodgs, J. A. S. B.* vi. p. 367.—The EASTERN WHITE OR BAR-TAILED FISHING EAGLE.

Adult Male—Head and neck all round ashy grey; breast a little lighter brown than the back; wings darker; primaries blackish; under surface of wing leaden brown with a whitish spot at the base of the primaries; tail white with a terminal bar of brown; abdomen, vent, thighs, lower flanks and under tail coverts white; under wing coverts ashy brown. Cere and bill blackish; feet dirty yellowish white; iris brown.

Length.—26 inches; wing 18; tail 10; tarsus 3·75; culmen 2·3.

Adult female.—Similar but larger. *Length.*—29 inches, with a wing of 20·4 and tarsus 3·9.

The young bird is lighter brown above, all the feathers edged and tipped with whitish; feathers beneath pale reddish brown, with mesial pale streaks; thighs white, mottled with reddish brown; quills as in the male with a larger white basal patch below; tail fulvous brown, mottled with dark brown: tip uniform dark brown, forming a distinct band.

Hab.—Ceylon, and India generally; Punjab, N.-W. Provinces, Oudh, Bengal, Rajputana, Central India, the Southern Mahratta Country (Dharwar), Central Provinces, Kutch, the Concan and British Burmah, extending to Nepaul and Assam. Breeds in Ceylon in December and January, and from January to as late as April chiefly in the N.-W. Provinces of India and Bengal (although it may be found breeding in other parts or India), building a nest of stout sticks on high trees on the bank of some river or in the proximity of some considerable piece of water. The nest is usually lined with some soft material as grass, weeds and green leaves; this latter is generally the uppermost layer on which the eggs are laid. Eggs normally three in number, a broad and perfect oval in shape; texture rough and pitted, and with a slight gloss, and unspotted white—2·72 to 2·8 inches in length, and from 2·1 to 2·15 in breadth.

SUB-ORDER—STRIGES

or

NOCTURNAL BIRDS OF PREY.

Head large, eyes surrounded with a circle of radiating feathers forming a facial disc and directed forwards; ears large. Nostrils generally hidden by stiff bristles; feet generally feathered to the toes; outer toe reversible; tibia more than double the length of tarsus; plumage soft and fluffy.

Family—BUBONIDÆ.

Hinder margin of sternum with two or more distinct fissures or clefts; furcula free, not attached to keel of sternum; inner margin of claw of middle toe not serrated; mid toe longer than the inner one.

Sub-Fam.—BUBONINÆ,—Eagle and Scops Owl

Ear conch not larger than the eye, and without an operculum.

Gen. Ketupa.—*Lesson*.

Bill long, strong, straight at base, moderately compressed and hooked. Wings do not reach the end of the tail; tarsi naked, reticulate; soles of feet with tiny prickles; ear tufts large.

34. Ketupa ceylonensis, *Gmel., Syst. Nat.* i. p. 287; *Gray, Gen. Birds* i. p. 38; *Jerd., Birds of Ind.* i. p. 133, No. 72; *Hume, Rough Notes* ii. p. 379; *id., Nests and Eggs Ind. B.* p. 64; *Str. F.* i. p. 341; ii. p. 469; *Sharpe, Cat. Striges*, p. 4; *Murray, Hdbk., Zool., &c., Sind*, p. 119; *id., Vert. Zool. Sind*, p. 92; *Legge, B. Ceylon* p. 127; *Hume, Str. F.* viii. p. 83; *Oates, B. Br. Burm.* ii. p. 149; *Murray, Avif. Brit. Ind.* i. p. 83, No. 81.—The Brown Fish-Owl.

Adult.—Above fawn-brown, the feathers broadly centred black and mottled brown and fulvous on both webs; feathers of the hind neck thinly barred with brown; the ear tufts with dark central longitudinal streaks; quills dark brown, the primaries tipped and spotted on their outer web with creamy, the same spots on the inner webs, dull fawn-brown; secondaries dark brown, with less distinct spots and bars, and more mottled with brown; tail brown with a fulvous tip, and 3 or 4 pale fulvous bands; chin and throat white streaked with dark brown; loreal plumes whitish; under surface of body fulvous-fawn or vinaceous-rusty, all the feathers mesially streaked with broad black centres and with wavy bars; disc rusty with dark brown stripes; cere greenish grey; bill pale horny yellow; legs and feet dusky yellow; irides bright yellow.

Length.—21 to 24 inches; wing 16·25; tail 8; tarsus 2·65.

Hab.—Ceylon, India, Assam and Tenasserim. I have had it at Khandalla and Poona in the Deccan. At Madras it is not uncommon, as also in Nepaul and Behar, Sind, Beloochistan, Afghanistan, N.-W. Provinces, Oudh, Bengal, Punjab; also Rajpootana (scarce), Central India, the Central Provinces, Concan, Deccan, South India, British Burma and Nepaul. There is no record of its occurrence in Kutch and Guzerat.

Breeds throughout Ceylon and India from December to March or April, making its nest on a shelf of rock, clay cliffs, or high banks near water; seldom or never on trees. In the Manaar district in Ceylon, Mr. Parker found a young bird on a tamarind tree. Normally this species lays two eggs, very perfect broad ovals, white, with in most specimens the faintest possible creamy tinge. The shell is close-grained and compact, freely pitted over its surface, but more or less glossy. In size they vary from 2·29 to 2·44 in length, and from 1·84 to 1·94 in breadth. In Sind it affects the forests and apparently also breeds in holes of decayed trees. Of its food it is not particular. Fish, young birds, quails and partridges, it is quite partial to.

Gen. **Bubo**.—*Auct.*

Nostrils oval, situated in the anterior margin of the cere; cere not inflated. Ear tufts distinct; tarsi never naked.

35. Bubo nipalensis, *Hodgs, As. Res.* xix. p. 172; *Sharpe, Cat. Striges,* p. 37, *Legge, B. Ceylon* p. 131; *Hume and Dav., Str. F* vi. p. 30; *Hume, Str. F.* viii. p. 83; *Oates, B. Br. Burm.* ii p. 152; *Murray, Avif., Brit. Ind.* p. i. 86, No. 85. Huhua nipalensis, *Hodgs., J. A. S. B.* vi. p. 362; *Jerd., B. Ind.* i. p. 131, No. 71; *Blyth, Ibis,* 1866, p. 254; *Hume, Rough Notes,* p. 378; *id., Str. F.* i p. 431. Bubo orientalis, *Blyth, Cat. B. Mus. As. S. B.* p. 34. Huhua pectoralis, *Holds., P. Z. S.* 1872, p. 416.—The FOREST EAGLE OWL.

Adult.—Above brown, narrowly tipped and banded across with tawny buff over the whole of the upper surface, these bars less distinct on the crown, but broader and deeper coloured on the hind neck; outermost scapulars tipped and spotted with yellowish buff on the outer web, forming a distinct shoulder patch; primary coverts nearly uniform dark brown, with faint indications of lighter brown bars; quills dark brown, barred darker; tail dark brown, broadly tipped with whitish and crossed with six other bands of fulvous; face dusky brown with whitish shaft streaks; feathers above the eye blackish; ear tufts 3·1 inches long, dark brown, notched and barred with fulvous or white on the inner web; cheeks with white stiff feathers mesially streaked with brown; chin whitish; rest of under surface of body white, washed here and there with fulvous and barred across with dark brown; under tail coverts the same, also the under wing coverts.

Length.—23 to 25 inches; wing 16·5 to 18·1; tail 11; tarsus 3·2; bill at gape 2·5, horny yellow; irides brown.

Hab.—Ceylon, also Southern India and the Himalayas, ranging eastward into Tennaserim; found also in Malabar.

I have nothing to record in regard to its nidification. It preys on rats, snakes, hares and pheasants. Mr. Gurney in *P. Z. S.* 1884, p. 558, plate 52, gives an excellent figure of this large owl, from a living specimen in the Zoological Society's Garden, captured as a nestling on a precipitous ledge of a lofty mountain in the Karenne Country to the N.-E. of Pegu. It has lived in the Gardens since 1878, at which time a note was made of the circumstances of its capture, (*P. Z. S.* 1878, p. 790), under the name of ***Bubo*** (*Huhua*) *orientalis.* Mr. Gurney now has no doubt that it is really an example (now fully adult) of *H. nipalensis*. Mr. Gurney says "the present is probably the most eastern example of *Huhua nipalensis*, of which the locality has as yet been ascertained, as there appears to be considerable doubt whether a young owl obtained by Col. Tickell on the Mooleyit Mountain in Tennaserim belonged to this species or to its congener, *H. orientalis*. Mr. Blyth held the former opinion (*Ibis*, 1872, p. 89), and Mr. Hume advocated the latter in *Stray F.* vol. vi. p. 31. Capt. R. G. Wardlaw-Ramsay possesses a specimen of *H. nipalensis* in immature dress, which was shot at Tonghoo, a locality nearly as far eastward as that from which the bird now in Regent's Park was obtained. Col. Godwin-Austen has recorded a much more northern specimen of this species obtained in the Darrang District of Assam (*J. A. S. B.*, vol. xiv., pt. 2, p. 68); while Mr. W. T. Blanford records its occurrence (*J. A. S. B.* vol. xli., pt. 2, p. 154) in the Tista Valley in Sikkim, and Hodgson in *Asiatic Researches*, vol. xix., p. 173, says it is found in all parts of the kingdom of Nepaul. Major Fitzgerald obtained the young of this species in the Darjeeling District, and says (*Ibis*, 1878, p. 19), that though not a common bird, it is met with in most parts of the Himalayas in the more temperate valleys. The presumption in favour of the Malabar bird being identical with *H. nipalensis* is strengthened by the fact of this species being an inhabitant of Ceylon."

Gen. **Scops**.—*Sav.*

Ear tufts large, ear orifice moderate. Lateral margin of bill somewhat curved; cere not inflated; nostrils oval, situated in the anterior margin of the cere. Wings long, reaching nearly or quite to the tip of the tail; 3rd and 4th quills longest; tail short; toes generally feathered; tarsi never naked.

I quite agree with Messrs. Sharpe and Hume, that it is most difficult to understand the owls, especially the species of the *Genus Scops*, which are in every way the most difficult to identify.

Mr. Sharpe has, however, done something towards characterizing the various species, and had necessarily from want of a large series of skins to make "races" or "sub-species." He says, "these races *do* exist in nature, and they may be called by whatever name Naturalists please. 'Varieties,' 'races, 'sub-species,' 'climatic forms,' &c., but it has seemed to me better to keep these forms distinct from one another, than to merge them all in one species and thus to obliterate all records of natural facts which are plain enough to the practised eye of the Ornithologist though difficult to describe in words."

36. Scops sunia, *Hodgs., As. Res.* xix. p. 175; *id. in Gray's Zool. Journ.* p. 82; *Blyth, J. A. S. B.* xiv. p. 182; *Jerd., Ill. Ind. Zool.* pl. xli.; *Sharpe, Cat. Striges* vol. ii. p. 67; *Legge, B. Ceylon* p. 139; *Murray, Avif. Br. Ind.* i. p. 93, *No.* 91. Ephialtes sunia, *Gray, Cat. Mamm., &c., Nepaul, Coll. Hodgs.*, p. 51; *Holdsw., P. Z. S.* 1872, p. 418. Ephialtes Bakkamæna, *Blyth, Ibis*, 1866, p. 255. Scops pennatus, *Hume, Nest and Eggs Ind. B.* i. p. 65. Ephialtes pennatus, *Hume, Rough Notes* ii. p. 386.—Hodgson's Scops Owl.

Adult.—Above clear cinnamon rufous, nearly uniform, most of the feathers with a narrow central shaft line of black, a little broader than on the crown; scapulars externally yellowish buff or pure white, with a black subterminal bar; wing coverts rufous like the back with the same dusky black shaft lines, broader on the greater series, which are white at the tips of their external webs; the spurious quills externally whitish, broadly barred with dark brown; primary coverts cinnamon, with a spot of yellowish white near the tip of the outer web, the inner web blackish brown; quills dull cinnamon rufous with faint cross-bars of brown, almost obsolete on the innermost secondaries, less distinct on the outer ones, but plainer on the primaries, many of the light interspaces on the outer webs of the latter inclining to whitish; tail cinnamon, the centre feathers nearly uniform, with only faint indications of narrow blackish cross-bars, these are broader and more distinct on the outer feathers, the exterior ones having slight indications of whitish spots on the light interspaces; lores white, the elongated bristly shafts blackish at tip; over the eye a patch of white feathers narrowly margined with black at their tips; sides of face cinnamon with silvery white shaft lines to the feathers; behind the ear coverts a distinct ruff of deep cinnamon feathers broadly terminated with black; plumes on the chin whitish; chest cinnamon, some of the feathers buffy white at the tips, with broad mesial streaks of black; rest of under surface of body for the most part white, broadly streaked down the centre with black, barred with cinnamon and freckled and grizzled with zigzag lines of blackish; under tail coverts white, slightly washed with cinnamon at the tips, and with few indications of a central dark brown streak; under wing coverts yellowish, those near the edge of the wing rufous mottled with brown; edge of wing white; bill dusky horn; feet fleshy brown; iris bright yellow.

Length.—5·7 to 7·5 inches; wing 5·3 to 5·7; tail 2·5; tarsus 0·9 to 1·0 (*Sharpe*).

The above description is by Mr. Sharpe, taken from a Nepaul skin collected by Mr. Hodgson.

Mr. Sharpe observes that some specimens show considerable differences, principally on the breast and abdomen, both the Penang and Madras specimens having the central black streaks very indistinct on the under parts, while they vary *inter se* in the mottling of the abdomen. Mr. Sharpe's description answers exactly to a specimen of Scops very near *pennatus*, now in the Kurrachee Museum, collected at Kurrachee, except that the tibial and tarsal plumes are unspotted white, also the under tail coverts; another specimen has the tibial and tarsal plumes rufous fawn, with faint indications of small brown spots; the primaries too have the outer webs broadly barred with yellowish white and dark brown.

Hab.—India generally, ranging down to Ceylon and the Malayan Peninsula, as far as Penang. Recorded from Madras, Penang, and Nepaul; also Sind, the

Punjab, and the lower ranges of the Himalayas to Darjeeling, and everywhere where *pennatus* occurs. I cannot from the series I possess of these Scops sufficiently separate them.

In my opinion it bears the same relation to *pennatus* as *plumipes* of the Himalayas does to *S. lettia.*

37. **Scops malabaricus**, *Jerd., Madr. Journ.* x. p. 89; *Sharpe, Cat. Striges*, p. 94, Sub-Sp. B.; *Str. F.* vol. v. p. 135; *Bourdillon, B. S. Travancore, Str. F.* vol. vii. p. 34; *Hume, Str. F.* vol. vii. p. 361. Descr; *Legge, B. Ceylon* p. 139; *Murray, Avif. Brit. Ind.* i. p. 98, *No.* 95. Scops griseus, *Jerd., Madr. Journ.* xiii. pt. 2, p. 119. Scops lettoides, *Blyth, J. A. S. B.* xiv. pl. i. p. 182 (*ex. Jerd. Ms.*). Ephialtes malabaricus, *Hume, Rough Notes* ii. p. 402; *Jerd., Ibis,* 1871, p. 348. Scops indicus, *Gmel., Stray Feathers* v. p. 135; vii. pp. 359,5 06. Scops bakkamæna, *Forst., Hume, Nest and Eggs Ind. B.* p. 69; *Legge, B. Ceylon,* pp. 135-1210. Ephialtes griseus, *Hume, Rough Notes*, p. 398; *Murray, Hdbk. Zool., &c., Sind,* p. 221.—The MALABAR SCOPS OWL.

A prominent tuft of disunited-webbed, bristly white feathers (with dark naked tips to the shafts, and traces on those nearest the eye of dark cross bars) on each side of the upper mandible at its base; a faint tinge of buffy at the anterior angle of the eye; rest of the lores, feathers below and behind the eyes, including ear coverts, loose-webbed, silky and greyish white with traces of faint minute transverse brown bars; chin white; the feathers of the extreme tip somewhat bristly and curving upwards round the lower mandible; across the throat and upwards, immediately behind the ear orifice, as far as the base of the aigrettes, a band of creamy or pale buff feathers, with numerous minute, transverse, wavy brown pencillings and bars; those from the aigrettes to the sides of the throat with conspicuous dark brown tippings, which form the defining line of the disc, and a few of those in the centre of the throat with similarly coloured spots at the tips; forehead and a broad supercilium running up the inside webs of the aigrette feathers, and a curved band at the back of the head, extending from the point of one aigrette to the point of the other, a silvery grey or greyish white, the feathers with dark brown shafts and numerous minute transverse pencillings of that colour, and some of them with terminal spots; centre of forehead, top of head, a triangular space surrounded by this grey band, a rich dark brown, purest on the centre of the forehead with small twin spots or imperfect transverse bars and mottlings, to a greater or less extent, of pale buff; the outside webs of the aigrettes are similar, as are the feathers of the band outside and contiguous to the curved grey band, which latter seems continuous with the dark line of the outer webs of the aigrette, while the former seems to start immediately above the centre of the eye; below the dark band at the base of the neck is another band of very similarly marked feathers, but whereas the dark brown predominates in the former, the buff much predominates in the latter. The back, rump, upper tail coverts, scapulars, wing coverts, except the greater ones of the primaries, a mixture of pale brownish grey and pale buffy, with dark brown central streaks, and numerous transverse wavy brown pencillings and mottlings. In the outside line of the scapulars the buff is very pure, and in some positions conspicuous, and while the rump, upper tail and lesser wing coverts are dingier and greyer, the centre of the upper back and the median and secondary wing coverts show more of a pale buff; the primary greater coverts are very dark brown with broad transverse buffy mottled bars; the quills are darkish brown, with numerous broad transverse greyish more or less dingy white bars, much more conspicuous on the outer webs; with the exception of a few bars on the upper portion of the outer web of the earlier primaries, which are unmottled and slightly tinged with creamy, all the rest of these bars are closely mottled and pencilled with brown; the second, third and fourth primaries are just perceptibly emarginate on the outer webs, and the first to the fourth are conspicuously notched on the inner webs; the sides of the neck behind the dark line, the breast, sides, abdomen and thigh coverts, a sort of creamy grey, very soft and silky, the feathers with narrow rich brown central streaks and numerous minute irregular, wavy, transverse pencillings; greater portion of wing lining, vent feathers and lower tail coverts silky greyish white, the latter, some of them, with dark central streaks towards the tips; tarsal feathers silky greyish white, with a faint buffy tinge towards the joint, and with several narrow, somewhat irregular transverse brown bars; tail feathers greyish brown, with imperfect transverse mottled bars of very pale dingy buff, and with the interspaces, too, more or less mottled with the same colour. Toes and claws pale greyish brown. Soles creamy white; pads and papillæ much developed and soft; irides brownish yellow or dark brown; bill dark brown; cere dusky grey.

Length.—7·88 to 9 inches; wing 5·6 to 6·75; tail 2·5 to 3·37; tarsus 1·06 to 1·19.

The above is Mr. Hume's description of *Scops indicus, Gm.*, which, he says (on page 506, vol. vii. *Str. F.*) is identical with *Scops griseus* (*malabaricus* of *Sharpe, Cat. Striges, B. M.*) and *Scops bakkamœna* of *Forster*. Sharpe, however, does not in his references to the literature of this species allude to the names given by Gmelin and Forster.

Hab.—Ceylon, and Southern India. Recorded from the Punjab, N.-W. Provinces, Oudh, Bengal, Central India, Madras, Malabar Coast, Travancore, Eastern and Western Ghauts, North Guzerat, and Ratnagiri (S. Concan). Like the preceding species, it occurs in Sind, but is uncommon, and affects wooded districts only.

Breeds in holes of trees; nest commonly lined with leaves; eggs white, glossy and spherical. Nests have been taken during March and April in Sind, Central Provinces (Etawah), and near Hansi.

38. Scops minutus, *Legge, Ann. and Mag Nat. Hist.* 1878, i. p. 175; *id., B. Ceylon* p. 142; *Hume, Str. F.* vii. p. 145.—The CEYLON SCOPS OWL.

General hue above dark brown; head, back, rump, scapulars, tertials and wing coverts crossed with transverse spots of ochraceous, spotted finely, and closely vermiculated on the rest of their surfaces with grey and ochraceous grey, surrounding transverse irregular markings of blackish; hind neck barred with white and margined with buffish; outer scapulars white on the outer web, with terminal spots and bars of black, edged with rufous; primaries and secondaries brownish rufous, mottled with blackish brown, their inner webs banded broadly with the same; outer web of first five primaries banded with 5 white dark margined bars; tail brownish, crossed with 5—6 bars of buffy white. Loreal plumes black, their bases white; facial disc grey; ruff pale rufous, feathers edged and centred with brown; foreneck and under surface of the body white, stippled with iron grey; chin whitish; irides yellow; bill olivaceous brown; feet fleshy brown; cere greenish.

Length.—6 inches; culmen 0·55; wing 4·85; tail 2·1; tarsus 0·8.

Hab.—Ceylon.

Gen. **Ninox**.—*Hodgs.*

Head small; disc obsolete; bill short, cere large; wings long and pointed, the distance between it and the tip of the tail equal to, or less than the tarsus; distance between tip of first primary and that of the third equal to, or greater than, the length of tarsus. Tarsus not twice the length of the middle toe, feathered toes clad with bristles.

39. Ninox scutulata, *Raffl., Tr. Linn. Soc.* xiii. p. 280; *Jerd., B. Ind.* i. p. 147; *Armstrong, Str. F.* iv. p. 373; *Hume, Rough Notes* p. 420; *Sharpe, Cat. B. Br. Mus.* ii. p. 156; *Bl. and Walden, B. Burmah*, p. 67; *Hume, Str. F.* viii. p. 84; *Kelham, Ibis*, 1881, p. 37; *Legge, B. Ceylon*, p. 145; *Murray, Avif. Br. Ind.* ii. p. 108, *No.* 104. Athene scutulata, *Gray, Gen. B.* i. p 35; *Wald., Ibis*, 1868, p. 22. Ninox hirsutus, (*Tem.*), *Hume Str. F.* iii. p. 40; *id.*, 1874, pp. 141. 469, *et* 1875, p. 441. Ninox Burmanica, *Hume, Str. F.* iv. p. 285; *Hume* and *Davison, S. F.* vi. p. 40; viii. p. 84; ix. p. 245. Ninox innominata, *Hume, Str. F.* iv. p. 286; v. p. 16.—The BROWN HAWK-OWL.

Head, sides of the face and also of the neck chocolate brown; forehead, lores and chin whitish with mesial dark streaks; whole upper surface, including wing coverts and tertiaries dark chocolate brown, the scapulars with large concealed white spots; primaries and secondaries dark brown, barred with white on the inner webs; a few of the primaries edged with rufous; throat rufous streaked with brown; breast rufous chocolate, each feather edged with white; rest of under surface rufous chocolate, barred with white; tail ashy brown, paler at tip and with 5—6 dark bars, the basal one concealed; under tail coverts pure white; under wing coverts and axillaries rufous, barred with white; edge of the wing whitish.

Irides bright yellow; cere dull green; bill bluish black; culmen and tip of lower mandible yellowish green; feet pale yellow.

Length.—11 to 12·5 inches; wing 8 to 8·75; tail 4 to 5·5; tarsus 1·1 to 1·15.

Hab.—Ceylon. Rare in the Punjab, and N.-W. Provinces, also in Rajputana and the Deccan. All the more wooded countries, as the Carnatic, the Malabar and Rutnagherry coasts and also in Central India. Lower Bengal and the Himalayas, extending through Assam, Burmah, Malaya to Nepaul, and to China and Japan. The Brown Hawk-Owl frequents the skirts of dense forests. It is nocturnal in its habits, issuing forth at dusk. It seats itself generally on stumps of dead trees, whence it swoops, or rather skims along the surface of the ground or water in search of insects, which are its chief food, and Jerdon says, occasionally mice or reptiles. It has a peculiar call which it frequently utters at night, resembling, as Tickel says, the cries of a strangling cat; Buchanan likens it to the cry of a hare when caught by hounds, and Elliot, "the cries of a child." Oates says its note resembles the word *Whoo-wuk*, repeated several times.

Nothing is known of its nidification.

Gen. **Glaucidium**.—*Boie.*

Nostrils tubular in the middle of a swollen cere; wing short and rounded, the distance between it and the tip of tail much greater than the length of the tarsus, which is feathered and is as long as the mid toe; 1st quill shorter than the next four, emarginated; 4th and 5th about equal. Tail rounded.

40. Glaucidium radiatum, *Tick.*, *J. A. S. B.* ii. p. 572; *Sharpe*, *Ibis*, 1876, p. 259; *Walden*, *Ibis*, vol. vi. 1876, p. 343; *Sharpe*, *Cat. Striges B. M.* p. 217; *Legge*, *B. Ceylon* p. 152. Athene radiata, *Bly.*, *J. A. S. B.* xv. p. 281; *Jerd.*, *B. Ind.* i. p. 143, No. 77; *Ball*, *Str. F.* ii. p. 383; *Str. F.* iv. p. 373; vi. p. 36; *Hume*, *Rough Notes* ii. p. 409; *id.*, *Nests and Eggs*, *Ind. B.* i. p. 70; *Vidal*, *B. South Concan*, *Str. F.* p. 39.—The JUNGLE OWLET.

Above dusky brown, barred with rufous buff or rufescent whitish, rather broader on the hind neck; outer web of scapulars whitish with a few dusky spots or bars; wing coverts rufescent, the bars broader than on the back; edge of the wing white; some of the outer webs of the greater coverts with large white spots; primaries and their coverts and secondaries dark brown, banded with rufous, the bands on the secondaries narrower than those on the primaries; tail dark brown, *narrowly tipped with whitish and with eight narrow white bands;* chin, throat, and cheeks whitish; rest of under surface barred, except the centre of the body, which is barred transversely with dusky and whitish, the bars on the sides of the breast rather fulvous; under tail coverts white, with brown spots. Bill and feet greenish horny; iris golden yellow; claws dusky.

Length.—8 to 8·5 inches; wing 4·9 to 5; tail 2·85 to 3; tarsus 1·0.

Hab.—Ceylon and India generally, from the Himalayas southwards through the Peninsula, but not extending far below the Nilghiris. Recorded from the N.-W. Provinces, Bengal, the Central Provinces, the Concan, Malabar and Travancore, also Rutnagherry, South India on the Nilghiris, British Burmah (?) and Nepaul. Whether this species is distinct from *malabaricum* or not, has not been quite settled. Much has been written on the various phases of plumage of both these species, and it is argued that this is due to climatic influence. Sharpe, however, keeps the northern and southern forms distinct, calling *malabaricum* a sub-species of *radiata*. I have not had a sufficient number of specimens of the two forms, and hence cannot give an opinion. I follow Sharpe in keeping both separate till some one with enough materials will decide the points raised.

The Jungle Owlet breeds in the early part of the summer in holes of trees during April, May and June.

The eggs are pure white, round and measure 1·2 by 1·0. The young are generally fully fledged by the end of June. It is easily tamed, and in confinement will eat readily of raw or cooked meat, insects, frogs, &c. Both adults and young are excessively noisy, and when teased make a peculiar hissing chattering tremulous noise. The cry, according to Mr. R. Thompson, is a too-roo-roo-roo, &c., drawn out to a considerable length, and resembles that of the Common Guana or Monitor Lizard.

41. Glaucidium castanonotum, *Blyth, Cat. B Mus. A. S. B.* p. 39; *Kelaart, Prodr. Faun. Zeyl.* p. 27; *Sharpe, Cat. B. Br. Mus.* ii. p. 215; *Legge, B. Ceylon,* p. 149. Tænioglaux castanonotus, *Bp., Rev. et Mag. de Zool.* 1854, p. 544. Noctua castanonota, *Schl., Mus. P. B. Striges,* p. 34. Athene castaneonota, *Gray, Handl. B.* i. p. 39; *Hume, Rough Notes* ii. p. 412; *Holdsw., P. Z. S.* 1872, p. 418.—The RUFOUS-BACKED JUNGLE OWLET

Head and neck dark brown, narrowly banded with ochraceous; hind neck banded and spotted with white; ear coverts rather darker than the head and barred similarly; lores brown, barred with ochraceous, the bases of the feathers white; cheeks white, forming a triangular patch; chin whitish; throat crossed with a band of dark brown feathers and barred with ochraceous, like the sides of the neck, with which it is continuous; upper surface of the body deep rufous chestnut, with remains of blackish cross bars more or less visible on the back and greater wing coverts; some of the outer median coverts slightly notched with fulvous, the rest uniform chestnut like the back; primary coverts dull brown, with a few rufous bands externally; primaries dull brown, barred with rufous brown on the inner web, the outer web having a corresponding spot of rufous on the outermost primaries; secondaries also dark brown, banded with rufous on the outer and with fulvous on the inner web, these bands much less distinct on the inner secondaries; upper tail coverts blackish brown, narrowly banded with fulvous, exactly resembling the tail, which has eight narrow fulvous bands, including the terminal ones; sides of the breast blackish brown, narrowly barred with ochraceous; rest of the under surface of the body white, streaked down the centre with brown, with which colour the flanks are also barred; under tail coverts whitish; leg feathers fulvous, barred with brown; under wing coverts whitish, with a few brown spots near the outer edge of the wing, the greater series whitish at base, brown at tip; inner lining of the wing dull and slightly rufous brown, spotted on the outer and barred on the inner web with pale rufous inclining to fulvous on the latter; bill yellow; feet greenish brown.

Length.—8·7 inches; wing 5·5; tail 2·7; tarsus 0·9.

Hab.—Ceylon, to which island the species is peculiar.

Sub-Family II.—SYRNIINÆ.—Hooting Owls

Wings moderate, somewhat rounded; tarsus feathered. Head larger than in the last; ear conch larger than the eye, with large operculum shutting in the ear; facial disc distinct; wings long; 2nd and 3rd quills longest.

Gen. Syrnium.—*Savigny.*

Head not so large as in the *Striges.* No ear-tufts; toes thickly feathered with hair-like bristles or entirely bare; feet stout. Ears moderately large and operculate.

42. Syrnium indranee, *Sykes, P. Z. S.* 1832, p. 82; *Horsf. and Moore, Cat. B. M. E. I. Co.* i., p. 83; *Jerd., B. Ind.* i. p. 121, No. 63; *Holdsw., P. Z. S.* 1872, p. 415; *Hume, Str. F.* 1873, p. 429; *Legge, Str. F.* 1874, p. 349; *id., B. Ceylon,* p. 155; *Murray, Avif. Br. Ind.* i. p. 121, No. 117; *Sharpe, Cat. B. Br. Mus.* p. 282. Bullaca indranee (*Kaup*), *Hume, Rough Notes* ii. p. 347.—The Southern Wood-Owl.

Above hair brown, darkest on the head and neck; the greater coverts, scapulars, and tertiaries banded with white, the outer scapulars being almost white with brown bars; rump and upper tail coverts also faintly barred with fulvous; quills brown, barred with pale fulvous on both webs, and with narrow whitish bars and a white tip; disc black round the eye, with a pale whitish upper edge or supercilium, rufous externally; ruff brown with some white markings; beneath pale fulvous white, narrowly and closely barred with brown; quills and tail beneath dusky brown, with white bars; bill pale greenish; irides deep brown; claws horny reddish.

Length.—19 to 21 inches; wing 13 to 14; tail 8 to 9; tarsus 2·5; mid toe and claw 2·5; toes feathered three-quarters of their length, with strong scuta; wings reach nearly to the end of tail. The above is Dr. Jerdon's description. He gives the habitat as throughout Southern India, in Ceylon and the Malayan Peninsula, not yet in Burmah.

Family—STRIGIDÆ.

Hinder margin of sternum entire, with no distinct cleft; inner margin of middle claw serrated. Head large, densely feathered. Eyes surrounded with a circle of radiating feathers; between the anterior portion of the facial area a frontal patch of small stiff feathers always present. Bill short, covered by stiff bristles. Feet feathered to the toes.

Gen. **Strix**.—*Linn.* (*in pt.*)

Nasal fossæ large; nostrils lunate. Wings reaching far beyond the tail; tail short, slightly rounded; 2nd quill longest; tarsi scantily feathered.

43. Strix flammea, *Lin.*, *S. N.* i. p. 133; *Tem.*, *Man. d'Orn.* i. 91; *Gould*, *B. Eur.* i. pl. 36; *Murray*, *Vert. Zool.*, *Sind*, p. 101. Strix Javanica, *Gm.*, *S. N.* i. p. 295; *Jerd.*, *Mad. Journ.* x. p. 85; *id.*, *Birds of Ind.* i. p. 117, No. 60; *Hume*, *Nests and Eggs Indian Birds*; *Murray*, *Hdbk. Zool.*, *&c.*, *Sind*, p. 119; *Legge*, *B. Ceylon*, p. 164; *Murray*, *Avif. Br. Ind.* i. p. 122, No. 118. Strix indica, *Blyth*, *Ibis*, 1860, p. 25; *Hume*, *Rough Notes* ii. p. 342; *id.*, *Str. F.* 1873, p. 163, *et* 1875, p. 37.—The INDIAN SCREECH OWL.

Head pale buff, mottled with light grey, each feather tipped with a white spot and edged darker; neck silky white, sometimes tinged yellowish and with small brown spots; the ruff the same, with darker tips; chin, throat, and breast, and the under parts white, the feathers of the breast and abdomen with small black specks; scapulars and back pale buff, mottled with grey, each feather with a terminal dark-edged white spot; primaries buff on the outer web and paler on the inner, edged with white and barred with brown, the outer web finely speckled; tail pale buff, with 4—5 dark bars, the tip whitish, and the inner web of the lateral feathers pure white; under tail coverts and tarsal plumes white; under wing and thigh coverts white with small dark spots; facial disc pure white with a rufous spot in the corner of each eye. Bill yellowish white; irides black; cere flesh coloured.

Length.—13 to 14 inches; wing 11; tail 2·5; tarsus 2·5 to 2·75.

Hab.—Ceylon, and throughout Europe, India, Beluchistan, Afghanistan and extending through Burmah. Oates says it is abundant in Pegu and Arrakan, and Capt. Bingham records it from near Moulmein. In Burmah it is found chiefly in woods. It breeds in holes of trees or in the ground. Eggs 5 in number.

Gen. **Phodilus**—*Isid. Geof. St. Hilaire.*

Facial disc irregular, the area above the eye being not equal to that below it. Wings rounded, reaching to nearly the tip of the tail; 1st quill equal to the 10th; tarsus feathered, inner toe longer than midtoe; outer toe reversible.

44. Phodilus badius, *Horsf., Tr. Lin. Soc.* xiii. p. 139; *id., Zool. Research. Java,* pl. 37; *Isid. G. St. Hilaire, An. Sc.* xxi. p. 201; *Jerd., B. Ind.* i. p. 119, No. 62; *Wall., Ibis,* 1868, p. 26; *Gray, Handl. B.* i. p. 52; *Gould, B. Asia,* pl. xxii.; *Walden, Ibis,* 1872, p. 365; *Hume, Rough Notes* ii. p. 346; *id., Str. F.* 1873, p. 429; *Hume and Dav., S. F.* vi. p. 27; *Hume, Str. F.* viii. p. 83; *Oates, S. F.* x. p. 181; *id., B. Burm.* ii. p. 166; *Sharpe, Cat. B. Br. M.* ii. p. 309. Phodilus assimilis *Hume, Str. F.* p. 429; *id. Str. F.* v. pp. 137, 353; *Legge, B. Ceylon,* p. 161. Strix badia, *Horsf., Zool. Research. Java,* pl. 37; *Tem. Pl. Col.* i. p. 318.—The Bay Screech Owl.

Forehead and anterior half of the crown delicate pinkish white; remainder of the crown and nape very deep chestnut; the whole upper plumage, wings, and tail lighter chestnut; quills banded black on the inner web; the first two or three on the outer web also; the first primary and first primary-covert as well as the winglet with their outer webs white and with broad transverse dark bars as on the quills; tail with more or less perfect bars on both webs; the feathers of the other parts each with a small black mark, and those of the greater wing coverts, scapulars and tertiaries with some white shaft spots; feathers round the eye deep chestnut; disc whitish, marked with chestnut; under surface fulvous pink, sparingly spotted with brown, except on the tarsi and under tail coverts; bill fleshy white; toes pale livid; irides brown.

Length.—11 to 12 inches; wing 7·3 to 7·5; tail 3·3 to 3·5; tarsus 1·7 to 1·9. Females slightly larger.

Hab.—Ceylon and nearly all India to the North, ranging through Burmah, Pegu, Java, Borneo, and the Eastern Himalayas. Mr. Thompson records it from Dehra Dhoon, and Jerdon obtained specimens at Darjeeling and on the Khasia Hills. In Burmah Captain Feilden obtained it at Thayetmyo, and Captain

Wardlaw-Ramsay at Toonghoo and on the Kharen Hills, east of Toonghoo. The Ceylonese race is somewhat smaller in measurements, but taking a series of both, this is not very apparent. The back too is slightly darker in tint. These, however, are not sufficient to constitute a new species, notwithstanding the dark brown, instead of chestnut brown, patch at the base of the first two or three primaries on the under wing lining.

Nothing is known of the habits of the Bay Screeh-Owl, nor anything of its nidification. The natives assert that it approaches the tiger with the same familiarity as *Pastor Jalla*, Horsf., does the buffalo, and does not fear to alight on the tiger's back.

In beginning the second Order, *viz.*, the *Passeriformes*, or Perching Birds, I follow Mr. Bowdler Sharpe in the arrangement of the orders and sub-orders, as well as the various divisions and sections which this most extensive group cannot but contain. Mr. Sharpe explains that the system of classification for the higher groups of Passerine birds followed in his work is that of Professor A. H. Garrod, who, after an exhaustive consideration of many points in their anatomy, has established his classification on several characters after devoting his attention to the characters given by Professor Sundevall and Dr. Elliott Coues. For the lower groups he follows as far as possible the divisions of Professor Sundevall's "Tentamen" without adopting their exact order. All the great ornithologists have been consulted, and such authorities as Professor Garrod, Mr. Wallace, Professors Baird and Ridgeway have helped him in his great work, which cannot but be of the greatest assistance to students and working ornithologists.

ORDER II.—PASSERIFORMES.

Perching birds, with a nude oil gland and colic cæca. *Cf. Garrod, P. Z. S.*, 1874, p. 119. (*Sharpe, Cat. Pass. B. B. Mus.*)

SUB-ORDER I.—PASSERES.

Anomalogonatous birds with the second, third, and fourth toes directed forwards and the hallux backwards; the *flexor longus hallucis* muscle independent of the *flexor perforans digitorum*, the cæca coli short but at the same time of characteristic shape; oil gland nude; palate ægithognathous; *tensor patagii brevis*, specialized and quite peculiar. (*Garr.*)

DIVISION I.—ACROMYODI.

Sub-Division I. Passeres Normales.

Section A.—*Turdiformes.* Typical or Thrush-like Passeres, with 10 primaries, the first more or less markedly reduced in size. (*Cf. Wallace.*)

GROUP I.—COLIOMORPHÆ.

Bill stout, generally of large size, not deflected at all or very little so. Chin angle produced before the line of the nostrils; cutting edge of lower mandible simple; tongue thick and fleshy, the tip horny, slight, divided or split in various ways; feet in most strong and large with the claw of the midtoe oblique. (*Cf. Sund. Av. Tent.*); *Sharpe, Cat. Pass. B. B. Mus.*

Family.—CORVIDÆ.

Bill without a distinct sub-terminal notch in the upper mandible; hallux strong; its claw not as long as the midtoe and claw. Toes normal.

Many of the birds which constitute this family are nearly alike in their plumage and habits. It includes the Rook, the Raven, the Magpie, the Crows, the Jackdaw, the Chough, and others. Members of this family are found in almost every part of the known world. While some feed on earthworms, insects as well as reptiles, others act the part of scavengers by feeding on putrid flesh and removing noxious matter. Though restless and noisy—the crows especially—they are active and sagacious, and have strong propensities for thieving. In general the family constitutes many which are readily tamed and taught to talk or articulate words. As for the Corvus genus, every one could testify to their voracious habits. They have been known to commit much havoc in some countries, that it became necessary to set a price on their heads. They are monogamous, and live in a kind of society. They moult only once a year.

Gen. Corone.—*Kaup*

First primary longer than the foremost secondaries, but not longer than the inner. Nasal bristles directed horizontally over the nostrils; tarsi stout, scutate.

45. Corone splendens, *Vieill., N. Dict. d' Hist. Nat.* viii. p. 44; *Tem., Pl. Col.* ii. pl. 425; *Gray, Gen. B.* ii. p. 315; *Jerd., B. Ind.* ii. p. 298; *Hume, Str. F.* vol. viii.; *Murray, Hdbk. Zool., &c., Sind*, p. 173; *Legge, B. Ceylon*, p. 349; *Murray, Avif. Br. Ind.* p. 130, No. 127. Corvus impudicus, *Gray, Handlist B.* ii. p. 14; *Hume, Str. F.* i. p. 206; *Str. F.* ii. pp. 418, 493; *Murray, Vert. Zool. Sind*, p. 176; *Oates, B. Burma* p. 398. Corone insolens, *Hume, Str. F.* 1875, p. 144; *Sharpe, Cat. B. Br. Mus.* vol. iii. p. 34; *Oates, B. Burma* vol. i. p. 399.—The COMMON INDIAN CROW.

Nasal bristles, crown of head, lores, sides of face, chin, throat, back, wings and tail glossy black with purplish, or steel-blue reflections; lower abdomen, flanks, vent, under tail and thigh coverts dull black; nape, hind neck, sides of the neck, and part of the upper back a greyish drab; breast and upper part of the abdomen dark ashy; under wing coverts and axillaries dull black; bill and legs black; irides deep brown.

Length.—16 to 17 inches; wing 11 to 11·25; tail 7; bill at front 1·12.

Hab.—Ceylon, and throughout India to the foot of the Himalayas, Assam, B. Burmah, Tennaserim and Malacca.

The Indian House Crow like its congeners, is extremely social, and lives about towns feeding on almost anything and everything; dead mice, rats, putrid flesh, fruit, &c., in fact, is a general scavenger. Breeds from the middle of March to the beginning of June, laying generally four eggs of a greenish colour, marked with various shades of brown. The nest is made of twigs, lined with grass, hair, rags, or any other soft material.

I do not separate *splendens* and *insolens*. From an examination of a large series of *insolens* sent to me by Mr. Calthrop from Tonghoo, Karenne, and other parts of Burmah and Tennaserim, I have come to the conclusion that it cannot be specifically separated from *splendens*. If shades of colour, especially of grey and brown, are to constitute species, Ornithology will soon reach a state of confusion, from which it will never be extricated. Races and sub-species sound well, but both help to make what never should be.

46. Corone macrorhynchus, *Wagl., Syst. Av. Corvus, sp.* 3; *Hume, S. F.* v. p. 461; *Legge, Birds Ceylon* p. 346; *Hume, S. F.* viii. p. 105; *Murray, Avif. Br. Ind.* i. p. 131, No. 129. Corvus Levaillantii, *Les traite,* p. 328; *Hume, Nests and Eggs* p 411; *id., Str. F.* ii. p. 295; *Anderson, Yunnan Exped.* p. 589. Corvus culminatus (*Sykes*), *Jerd., B. Ind.* ii. p. 295. Corvus Vaillantii (*Less.*), *Bl. B. Burm.* p. 86; *Oates, S. F.* v. p. 159. Corone macrorhynchus, *Sharpe, Cat. B. Br. Mus.* iii. p. 38; *id., Cat. B. Br. Mus.* iii. p. 39; *Oates, B. Br. Burmah* i. p. 397.—The INDIAN JUNGLE CROW.

Whole upper plumage deep black glossed with purple, blue and green; bill, legs, and feet black; irides dark brown.

Length.—19 to 21 inches; tail 7·6 to 9·2; wing 12·2 to 14; tarsus 2·3; bill from gape 2·3.

Hab.—Ceylon, and the whole Continent of India, also the Andaman Islands, the Indo-Burmese countries and China, extending to Eastern Siberia. Southerly it extends down the Malayan Peninsula to Sumatra, Java, Borneo and Timor. In India it is found in Sind, Punjab, N.-W. Provinces, Oudh, Rajputana, Central India, the Central Provinces, Concan, Deccan and South India, also in British Burmah and Nepaul.

It will be seen that *Levaillanti* has been made a synonym of *macrorhynchus*. Sharpe, makes the former a sub-species, but it must not stand thus. Hume has worked out the Crows to some purpose, and, like him, I am of opinion, that these two cannot be specifically separated. Except from Kutch and Guzerat, I have had specimens of this species from all parts of India for examination, and not less than 13 from various parts of Burmah and Tennaserim, and though in a few the pale bases to the feathers are apparent, in others it is either absent (though from one locality) or distributed here and there over different parts of the body. This may be a sign of nonage.

The Jungle Crow does not affect forests only, but it also frequents towns and villages, associated with the House Crow; also shallow pools of water after inundations, and generally in rice fields. Mr. H. Parker of Kurnegalla, Ceylon, also notices this fact, and says that he saw them at this in the Southern Province, where they were catching the fry and devouring them. To do this they fly over the water and fish like a tern. Nesting and breeding season the same; also the eggs, though slightly larger.

Gen. **Cissa**.—*Boie.*

Bill strong, robust, moderately long, slightly curved and hooked. Eye surrounded by a fleshy ring. Head crested; nostrils basal; wings rounded; tail long; hind toe and claw large.

47. Cissa ornata (*Wagl.*), *Blyth, Ibis*, 1867, p. 299; *Schl., Coraces*, p. 69; *Gray, Handl. B.* ii. p. 7; *Holdsw., P. Z. S.* 1872, p. 461; *Sharpe, Cat. B. Br. Mus.* iii. p. 87. Pica ornata, *Wagl., Isis*, 1829, p. 749. Cissa puella, *Blyth, Cat. B. Mus. As. Soc. B.* p. 93; *Layard, Ann. and Mag. Nat. Hist* (2) xiii. p. 213. Cissa pyrocyanea, *Gould, B. Asia part.* 1. (*Ex. Licht. MSS.*). Kitta ornata, *Bp., Consp.* i. p. 166. Kitta speciosa, *Bp.* t. c. p. 370 (*lapsu*). Citta ornata, *Licht., Nomencl. Av.* p. 9.—The Ceylon Magpie.

General colour deep blue, shading off into bright cobalt on the rump and upper tail coverts; head and neck all round as well as the chest chestnut; the rest of the under surface deep blue, shading off into brilliant cobalt on the abdomen and flanks; thighs ultramarine; wing coverts rich ultramarine, rest of the wing chestnut on the outer web, blackish on the inner one, the innermost secondaries shaded with blue on the inner web, the first primary black, washed with blue externally; tail deep blue, more or less shaded with cobalt, and broadly tipped with white, before which is a tolerably broad bar of black; under wing coverts blue, shading off into grey on the innermost, the inner lining of the quills blackish, externally edged with chestnut and inclining to rufous near the base of the inner web; bill red; bare skin round the eye crimson; feet coral red; iris light brown.

Length.—17 inches; wing 6·5; tail 10·5; tarsus 1·8; culmen 1·6. (*Sharpe.*)

Hab.—Ceylon, where it breeds from December to February. Eggs bluish green, spotted and streaked with umber brown and blue grey. Size 1·3 × 1·1.

Fam.—ORIOLIDÆ.

Bill long, strong, moderately broad at the base, hooked, and distinctly notched at the tip; nostrils in front of the base of the bill and quite bare; tail rather short; tarsi short; feet small; claws curved.

Gen. **Oriolus**.—*Lin.*

Characters those of the family; the culmen keeled; wings with the 1st quill very short, second shorter than the third, which is the longest; upper tail coverts long. Lores feathered, but generally with a small bare space behind the eye. Outer toe syndactyle. Nostrils lateral.

48. Oriolus diffusus, *Sharpe, Cat. B. Br. Mus.* iii. p. 197; *Legge, B. Ceylon,* p. 355; *Murray, Avif. Brit. Ind.,* p. 147, No. 151. Oriolus indicus, *Jerd., Ill. Ind. Orn.* pl. 15; *id., B. Ind.* ii. p. 109, No. 471; *Salvad, Ucc. Born* p. 275; *Hume, Str. F.* vii. p. 132; *Bl. and Walden, B. Burm.* p. 139; *Hume and Dav., Str. F.* vi. p. 329; *Hume, Str. F.* viii. p. 99; *Oates, B. Br. Burm.* i. p. 211. Oriolus cochinchinensis, *apud David et Oust. Ois. Chine,* p. 132. —The BLACK-NAPED ORIOLE.

Above and below bright yellow; lores, and a band through and above the eye continued to the nape, on each side black; primaries and secondaries black, tipped and edged narrowly with yellowish white, the latter more broadly, outer webs of tertiaries and a portion of the inner webs next the shaft yellow; primary coverts black, tipped broadly with yellow; inner webs of greater coverts black, also the winglet; tail black, tipped with yellow; the central pair narrowly and the others progressively broader towards the outer feathers.

The young have the feathers of a greenish tinge, and dark shafted on the breast and abdomen, the band on the nape indistinct; tail greenish with yellowish tips; irides and eyelids pinkish; legs and feet plumbeous; bill pinkish red.

Length.—9·6 to 10 inches; wing 5·85 to 6; tail 3·85 to 4; tarsus 1 to 1·05; culmen 1·25 to 1·4.

Hab.—Ceylon and the Indian Peninsula to Tennaserim, China, and Mongolia. Oates says it appears to be a winter visitant to British Burmah. Blyth records it from Arrakan. It is said to be common about Pegu, Rangoon, and in the Irrawady delta. Davison met with it in Tennaserim from Thatone to Malewoon during winter. Jerdon procured it in the Malabar jungles, and mentions it as having been procured at Dharwar, and to be found also near Calcutta.

The Black-naped Oriole affects forests, large groves and gardens. It feeds on fruit and insects, and is strictly arboreal in its habits.

49. Oriolus melanocephalus, *Linn., S. N.* i. p. 160; *Jerd., B. Ind.* ii. p. 110, No. 472; *Hume, Nests and Eggs Ind. B.* p. 301; *Blyth, B. Burm.* p. 139; *Sharpe, Cat. B. Br. Mus.* iii. p. 215; *Oates, S. F.* vii. p. 48; *Cripps, Str. F.* vii. p. 99; *Anderson, Yunnan Exped.* p. 660; *Hume, Str. F.* vii. p. 99; *Legge, B. Ceylon,* p. 358; *Oates, B. Br. Burm.* i. p. 214; *Murray, Avif. Br. Ind.* i. p. 149, No. 155. Oriolus Ceylonensis, *Bonap., Consp.* i. p. 347; *Jerd., B. Ind.* ii. p. 311; *Hume, Str. F.* i. p. 439. Oriolus Himalayanus, *Legge, B. Ceylon,* p. 358.—The BLACK-HEADED ORIOLE.

Above and below bright golden yellow; head, chin, throat and upper breast black; scapulars and wing coverts bright yellow; winglet and primary coverts black, the latter yellow for their terminal half, forming a large alar speculum; upper wing coverts yellow; first primary black; the others black, tipped with yellow, which increases in extent towards the secondaries, the innermost of which have the entire outer web yellow; base of primaries yellow; tail yellow, the two central feathers with a broad subterminal bar of black; the next on either side with a patch of black.

The female is not unlike the male, but the yellow is less bright and has an olivaceous or a greenish tinge. The young is duller in colour everywhere, the forehead is streaked with black, the feathers of the crown and nape edged with yellowish; throat white, streaked with black. Bill lake red; irides rich red; legs plumbeous.

Length of adult male and female—9·5 to 10 inches; wing 5·4 to 5·55; tail 3·4 to 4; tarsus 1· to 1·05; culmen 1·15 to 1·3.

Hab.—Ceylon, and throughout the Peninsula of India, extending down the Malay Peninsula. Occurs throughout Burmah; also in Cochin-China and Siam. It is found in the Punjab, N.-W. Provinces, Bengal, Rajputana, Central India, the Concan, Deccan, South India, the Malabar Coast, the Carnatic, Pegu, Tennaserim, the Andamans and Nepaul. I do not follow Sharpe in separating *O. ceylonensis*, either as a distinct species or sub-species, nor Captain Legge in calling the larger form *O. himalayanus*. Mr. Sharpe (*Cat. B. Br. Mus.*) observes, that *O. ceylonensis* "although rather smaller than Himalayan examples, has the alar speculum larger than in the Cingalese form, and he looks upon it as intermediate between the continental and insular birds. *O. ceylonensis* is not at all a good species, and perhaps in a large series would be found to be inseparable,—*which it certainly is* from *O melanocephalus*."

The Black-headed Oriole affects both the densest forests and open jungles, also orchards and gardens. Oates says, its exquisite call of five whistling notes is one of the most charming sounds heard in the jungle, and it seems to be uttered at all hours of the day and almost all the year round. It feeds chiefly on fruit. Jerdon says the figs of the Banian, peepul and other *Fici*, also mulberry, blossoms, and buds. It nests from March to June, generally at a considerable height from the ground. The nest is suspended between two twigs, and in shape is like a cup. The materials used are leaves, fine twigs and vegetable fibres. Eggs 2 to 3, pinkish white, spotted with black; they are often white and unspotted; the average of 10 might be said to be 1·14 × 77 inch.

Family—DICRURIDÆ—Drongo Shrikes.

Bill rather large, wide at base, thick, culmen curved and keeled, tip notched; rictal bristles moderately developed; nostrils basal, concealed by short plumes; tail usually long and furcate; outer feathers generally much lengthened. Plumage generally black or steel blue.

Gen. **Buchanga**.—*Hodgs.*

Bill moderate, despressed at base and slightly hooked; culmen keeled and notched at tip; rictal bristles strong; frontal plumes dense, but not elongated to form a crest. Plumage black; tail forked.

50. Buchanga atra, *Herm., Obs. Zool.* p. 208; *Murray, Vert. Zool. Sind*, p. 126; *Sharpe, Cat Passerif. B Br. Mus.* p. 246; *Legge, B. Ceylon* p. 386; *Murray, Avif. Br. Ind.* i. p. 386, No. 161. Dicrurus macrocercus, *Viell., N. Dict.* ix. p. 588; *Jerd., Mad. Journ.* xiii. pt. ii. p. 121; *id., B. of Ind.* i. p. 427, No. 278; *Gray, Gen. B.* i. p. 286; *Str. F.* iv. p. 278; vi. p. 213; vii. p. 272; *Murray, Hdbk., Zool., &c., Sind*, p 137. Buchanga albirictus, *Hodgs., Ind. Rev.* p. 326; *Hume, Str. F.*, 1873, p. 178; *Ball, Str. F.*, 1874, p. 402. Dicrurus balicassius, *Sykes, P. Z. S.* 1832, p. 86 (*nec. L.*).—The COMMON DRONGO SHRIKE OR KING CROW.

Head, hind neck, back, upper tail coverts, lesser and median wing coverts glossy blue-black; a white spot at the gape; chin, throat, lores, sides of the face, and under surface of the body black, less glossy than the upper surface, and with a greenish cast; greater and primary coverts black, glossed greenish, also the secondaries and tertiaries; primaries and tail duller black; the inner webs of the primaries and under surface of the tail dusky. Young with whitish lunules on the under surface of the body. Bill and legs black; irides red.

Length.—12 inches; wing 5·75; tail 6·25 to tip of outer feather; tarsus 0·9.

Hab.—The whole of India and Ceylon, extending to Assam, the Indo-Chinese region, China, Formosa and Burmah. Occurs also in Java, Siam, Cochin-China, the N.-W. Himalayas, Nepal, Beluchistan and Afghanistan. It is found throughout the Punjab, N.-W. Provinces, Oudh, Bengal, Rajputana, Central India, Kutch, Guzerat, Konkan, Deccan, Travancore and South India generally. According to Oates, it is a common bird in Burmah and Pegu. In the latter it is common from October to January. Dr. Armstrong found it common in the Irrawaddy delta; Davison found it common in Tennaserim from Moulmein to Malewoon, and Captain Bingham met with it at Tounghoo.

The King Crow is chiefly found in open jungle, and seldom or never in forests. It is a conspicuous bird everywhere about a station. Its presence is readily known simply by its cheerful and pretty notes. Perched on a telegraph wire, wall, or on a bare branch, its sweet notes are uttered, not forgetting now and again its rather harsh cry. A couple of pairs within one's grounds often make their chattering, as if one to another, for half an hour at a time, sound disagreeable. Its loquacity is unsurpassed, especially in the early morn. It is often seen on the backs of cattle, sheep and goats when out grazing in company with *Acridothera tristis* or *ginginianus*, the common crow, and not unfrequently *Neophrons*.

The food of the King Crow is chiefly insects of sorts, as grasshoppers, mantises, bees, wasps, ants, dragon flies, moths and butterflies. I don't know that it has a predilection for any thing higher than members of the Invertebrates. During the breeding season, which lasts from May to July, March to April, and August and September, according to locality, the King Crow is very pugnacious. It pursues and drives away every bird it suspects, even hawks, kites, and crows, especially when the female is sitting for incubation. It places its nest generally in the fork of the outer branches of a tree, selecting generally an *Acacia*. The nest is cup-shaped and shallow, and made of fine twigs and grass; in some instances lined outside with cobwebs and inside with a little hair or feathers. Eggs generally 4 in number, reddish or pinkish white, prettily streaked, spotted and blotched with brick red or brown.

51. Buchanga longicaudata (*A. Hay*), *Jerd.*, *Mad. Journ.* xiii. p. 121; *Jerd.*, *B. Ind.* i. p. 430, No. 280; *Wald.*, *P. Z. S.* 1866, p. 549; *Hume*, *Nests and Eggs* p. 189; *Hume*, *Str. F.* iii. p. 97; *Wald.*, *in Bl. B. Burm.* p. 130; *Sharpe*, *Cat. B. Br. Mus.* iii. p 249; *Hume and Davison*, *Str. F.* vi. p. 213; *Legge*, *B. Ceylon* p. 390; *Tweedd.*, *Ibis*, 1878, p. 74; *Hume*, *Str. F.* viii. p. 91; *Scully*, *Str. F.* viii. p. 270; *Oates*, *Str. F.* x. p. 202; *Murray*, *Avif. Br. Ind.* i. p. 155, No. 162. Dicrurus himalayanus, *Tytler*, *Ibis*, 1868, p. 200. Buchanga Waldeni, *Beavan*, *Ibis*, 1868, p. 497; *Oates*, *B. Burm.* i. p. 220.—The DARK-ASHY OR LONG-TAILED DRONGO.

Whole upper plumage including the wings and tail blackish ashy, with a greenish gloss; sides of the face, frontal plumes, and under surface of the body dark ashy, paler towards the vent; under tail coverts dull greyish white, paler and nearly white at the tips; under wing coverts similarly tipped; in old or fully adult birds, these whitish tippings are absent. Bill and legs black; iris red.

Length.—11 to 11·5 inches; wing 5·5 to 5·6; tail, including outer feathers, 6·5 to 6·7; tarsus 0·8; culmen 1.

Hab.—India generally, the Indo-Burmese countries, Ceylon, N.-W. Himalayas to Nepaul and Ladakh. Found in Travancore and Southern India generally; also on the Malabar coast, Wynaad, Coorg, the Nilghiris, Bengal, Punjab, N.-W. and Central Provinces. In Southern and parts of Western India, it is a permanent resident, also in S. Pegu. Davison found it in Tennaserim, from Moulmein to Mergui. In Upper Pegu it is said to be replaced by *B. leucophæa*.

Its habits are quite those of *B. atra*, but unlike it, it inhabits or rather affects forests, and has a pleasant song. Breeds during April and May. Nest similar to that of *B. atra*. Eggs, 3—4 in number, typically white with brick red spots.

52. Buchanga cærulescens, *Linn.*, *Syst. Nat.* i. p. 134; *Sharpe*, *Cat. B. Br. Mus.* iii. p. 252. Dicrurus cærulescens, *Vieill.*, *N. Dict. d' Hist. Nat.* ix. p. 587; *Jerd.*, *Madras Journ.* x. p. 239; *Bly.*, *Ann. and Mag. Nat. Hist.* xiv. p. 47; *Jerd.*, *B. Ind.* i. p. 432, No. 281; *Murray*, *Avif. Br.*

Ind. i. p. 157, No. 165. Buchanga insularis (*Sharpe, Sub.-sp. a.*) Buchanga cærulescens, *Holdsw.*, *P. Z. S.* 1872, p. 439 (*nec. L.*) *Eastern Districts of Ceylon.* Buchanga leucopygialis, *Blyth, J. A. S. B.* xv. p. 298; *Holdsw.*, *P. Z. S.* 1872, p. 439.—The White-bellied Drongo.

Whole upper plumage, including wings and tail, slaty grey, with a metallic steel blue gloss; chin, throat and breast ashy brown, glossed with steel blue on the sides of the neck and sides of the upper breast; abdomen and lower tail coverts white; under wing coverts ashy brown and slightly glossed; thighs glossy black; bill and feet black; iris lake-red.

Length.—9·5 to 9·6 inches; wing 4·75 to 5·05; tail 3·65, to tip of outer feathers 5; tarsus 0 8; culmen 0·95.

Hab.—Ceylon, and India generally. Recorded from Malabar, the slopes of the Nilghiris, Madras, Nellore, Central India, Calcutta, Central Provinces, Behar, Kattyawar, N.-W. Himalayas to Nepaul.

The White-bellied Drongo affects well-wooded districts generally. It is seldom seen in clearings, groves, or near habitations. Like other species of *Buchanga*, it seizes its prey on the wing, and has the usual sweet song and harsh cry of the family. I do not specifically separate the Ceylonese races. Among my series of skins from Southern India, the Himalayas, Central India, and the N.-W. Provinces, numbering 62, are a number which answer the descriptions of the sub-species made by Mr. Sharpe, and which gradually merge into typical *cærulescens*. *B. insularis* and *cærulescens* have the abdomen and under tail coverts white, and the form characterized as *leucopygialis* have the vent and under tail coverts white, shading into brownish on the abdomen.

Gen. **Dissemuroides**.—*Hume.*

Outer tail feathers produced and recurved at tip; forehead with a few bristles.

53. Dissemuroides edoliformis (*Blyth*), *Sharpe, Cat. B. Br. Mus.* iii. p. 256.. Dicrurus edoliformis, *Blyth, J. A. S. B.* xv. p. 297. Dicrurus lophorinus, *Gray, Hand-l. B.* i. p. 285. Dissemurus lophorinus, *Holdsw., P. Z. S.* 1872, p. 439; *Legge, B. Ceylon*, p. 396.—The Ceylon Racket-tailed Drongo.

Female.—General colour above black with a metallic green shade, rather more purplish on the head and on the neck hackles; wings metallic steel green; inner secondaries the same; rest of the quills black, glossed externally with steel green; tail feathers black, glossed with steel green on the outer webs; forehead crested; plumes deep black, as also those of the lores and sides of the face; under surface of the body black, glossed with steel green, more metallic on the tips of the feathers of the breast and producing a slightly spangled appearance; under wing coverts black, glossed with metallic green; bill and legs black; iris dull brownish red. (*Legge.*)

Length.—12·3 inches; wing 5·6; tail 5·2; to tip of outer feather 7·2; tarsus 0·95; culmen 1·25.

The adult male is similar but larger, the wing measuring 6 inches.

Hab.—Ceylon in the Southern Province.

Gen. **Dissemurus.**—*Gloger.*

Crest more full and developed, and falling back on the forehead; tail forked, the outermost pair with the outer web gradually thinning off; shaft bare for some distance, and terminating in a racket.

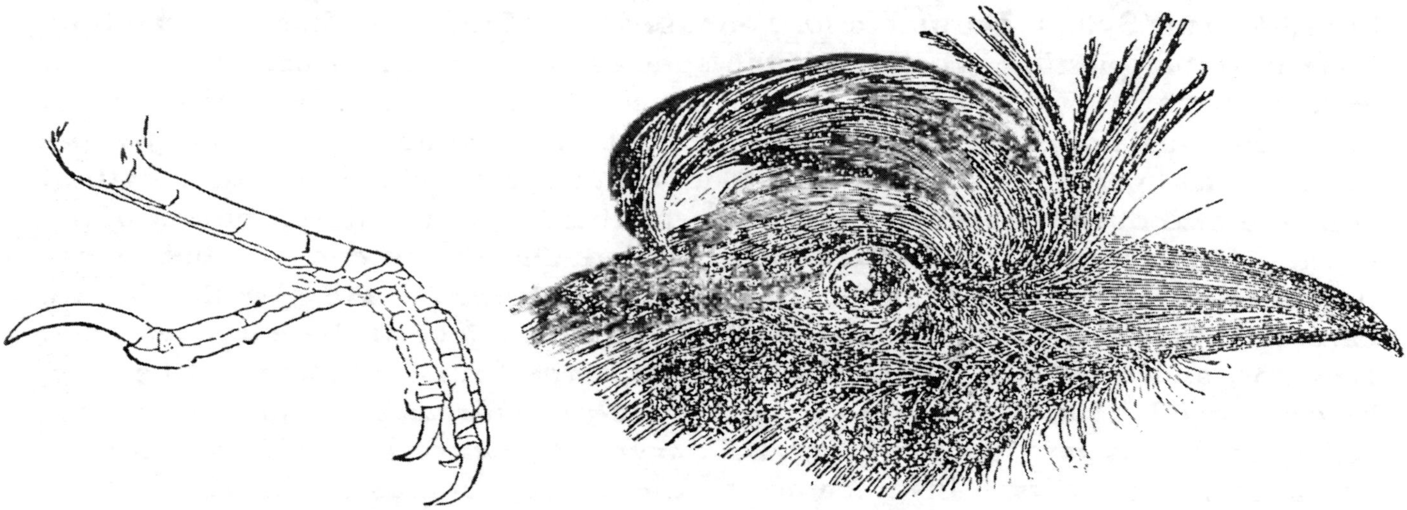

Claw and head of Dissemurus paradiseus.

54. Dissemurus paradiseus, *Linn.*, *Syst. Nat.* i. p. 172; *Bl. in Wald. B. Burm.* p. 128; *Armstrong, Str. F.* iv. p. 321; *Sharpe, Cat. B. Br. Mus.* iii. p. 258; *Tweedd., Ibis,* 1878, p. 80; *Hume and Davison, Str. F.* vi. p. 219; *Legge, B. Ceylon,* p. 399; *Hume, Str. F.* viii. p. 192; *Bingham, Str. F.* ix. p. 174; *Oates, Str. F.* x. p. 203; *id., B. Br. Burm.* i. p. 225; *Murray, Avif. Brit. Ind.* i. p. 160, No. 168. Dicrurus platurus, *Vieill., N. Dict. d' Hist. Nat.* i. p. 588. Edolius Rangoonensis, *Gould, P. Z. S.,* 1836, p. 50. Edolius grandis, Gould, *P. Z. S.*, 1836, Chibia malabaroides, *Hodgs., Ind. Rev.* i. p. 325. Dicrurus retifer, *Jerd., Mad. Journ.* x. p. 241. Edolius cristatellus, *Blyth, J. A. S. B.* xi. p. 171. Edolius brachyphorus (*Temm.*), *Bonap., Consp. Av.* i. p. 351. Edolius paradiseus (*Linn.*), *Jerd., B. Ind.* i. p. 435. Edolius malabaricus (*Scop.*), *Jerd., B. Ind.* i. p. 437. Dissemurus malabaroides (*Hodgs.*), *Hume, Nests and Eggs Ind. B.* p. 123; *id., Str. F.* iii. p. 101. Dissemurus grandis (*Gould*), *Hume, Str. F.* viii. p. 92; *Oates, Str. F.* viii. p. 166; *id., B. Br. Burm.* i. p. 225.—The GREAT RACKET-TAILED DRONGO.

Whole plumage black, glossed with steel blue, except on the inner webs of the quills, the throat, lower abdomen and vent. The outer pair of feathers in both sexes lengthened and furnished with a racket; in the young the gloss is less developed, and the under wing coverts are tipped with white; bill, legs and feet black; irides red (brown in the young).

Length.—14 inches; wing 6·6; tail 7; outer feathers 13 to 15; tarsus 1·15; culmen 1·3.

Hab.—Ceylon and the Indian Peninsula, Andaman Islands, Indo-Chinese and Indo-Burmese Countries, the Malayan Peninsula, Java andBorneo; also Sumatra, Cochin-China and Nepaul. It is recorded as occurring from the Himalayas to the Eastern Ghats as far South as N. L. 15°; also at Nellore, Goomsoor, Central and S. India, N.-W Provinces, Lower Bengal, the Sunderbuns, Assam, Sylhet, Burmah and Tennaserim. Mr. Sharpe has very carefully gone into the question, whether all the species hitherto described as distinct, were so or not. *Brachyphorus* from Borneo, appeared to be a distinct form, but there was not sufficient ground upon which it could be specifically separated. The specific characters held to constitute a species were the length of tail, the size of the rackets on the outer feathers, and the development of the crest. These Mr. Sharpe has carefully studied, and the outcome is that he has united all under one species (*Dissemurus paradiseus*). He says that after a careful study of what has been written on the subject of these racket-tailed Drongos, and after comparison of the series in the British Museum collection, he has arrived at the conclusion that between *D. malabaroides* (a very full-crested form) of the Eastern Himalayas and *D. brachyphorus* of Borneo, an unbroken chain of races exists. Blyth came to the same conclusion in 1849. Mr. Sharpe adds that he does not see that the labours of ornithologists have tended to upset this conclusion. His review of these species ends with the following remarks:—"Finding it however, quite impossible to define exact specific characters for these supposed species, I have united them under one name, and merely keep the specimens arranged under different headings; for I fully believe that a larger series will only show more connecting links, and that it will be found more and more impossible to give spectific characters for those differentiated under the various titles mentioned."

The Large Racket-tailed Drongo affects forests, and well-wooded districts. Like the Drongos in general it selects the extreme end of a bough or branch for its perch, which it now and again leaves for the purpose of capturing a passing insect. It always returns to the same perch. Its song is said to be rich and mellow, especially during the breeding season. The nest is built in a fork on the very tip of a bough on the highest tree in the place, and almost inaccessible. In structure it does not differ from that of its congeners. The eggs, usually three in number, are white or pinkish, marked with reddish brown.

Gen. **Irena**.—*Horsf.*

Bill stout, of moderate length; culmen rather elevated and slightly arching from the base, tip notched; nostrils covered with short plumes. Wings with the 4th quill longest; tarsus short.

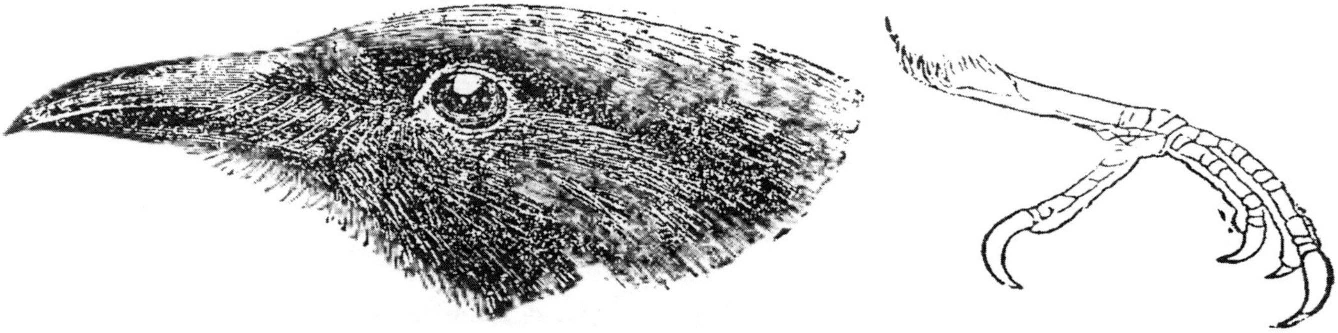

Head and claw of Irene puella.

55. Irena puella, *Lath., Ind. Orn.* i. p. 171; *Jerd., B. Ind.* ii. p. 105; *Stol., J. A. S. B.* xxxix. p. ii. p. 318; *Wald., Ibis*, 1871, p. 170; *Hume, Nests and Eggs* p. 298; *Hume, Str. F.* ii. p. 226; iii. p. 130; *Bl. and Wald., B. Burm.* p. 138; *Armstrong, Str. F.* iv. p. 326; *Bourdillon, Str. F.* iv. p. 400; *Wardlaw-Ramsay, Ibis*, 1877, p. 467; *Hume and Dav., Str. F.* vi. p. 328; *Hume, Str. F.* viii. p. 99; *Legge, Birds Ceylon* p. 466; *Sharpe, Cat. Birds B. Mus.* vi. p. 177; *Bingham, Str. F.* ix. p. 184; *Oates, Str. F.* x. p. 211; *Oates, B. Br. Burm.* p. 209; *Murray, Avif. Br. Ind.* i. p. 161, No. 169—The Fairy Blue Bird.

Whole upper plumage, including the lesser wing coverts, brilliant glistening cobalt blue. Sides of the head, quills and tail deep black; the secondaries and central tail feathers with a shade of blue; lores, feathers over the eye, sides of neck and entire under surface, also the thighs and under wing coverts, black; under tail coverts purplish black.

The female has the whole of the upper plumage dull prussian blue, brighter on the rump and upper and under tail coverts; primaries and secondaries dark brown, also the greater wing coverts, primary coverts, and tertiaries, but these with a bluish tinge on their outer webs.

Bill and legs black; iris crimson.

Length.—10 to 10·3 inches; wing 5; tail 4·2 to 4·4; tarsus 0·85; culmen 0·95 to 1.

Hab.—Ceylon, the Malabar Coast, Southern India generally, and Travancore; also Assam, Arrakan, and British Burmah. It also occurs in Siam and Cochin-China, in the Khasia Hills, Cachar, and the Andamans.

The Fairy Blue Bird affects evergreen, dense, woody forests, and is more abundant in the hilly tracts than in the plains. It is found in the Pegu Hills down to Rangoon; in the Irrawaddy delta, and according to Davison, in all the evergreen forests of Tennaserim. It is generally found in pairs, but parties of 6 or 7 are not uncommon. Capt. Bingham found the nest in Tenasserim. It was cup-shaped in form, and in structure like that of a Drongo. Eggs, two, greenish white, marked with brown.

Family.—PRIONOPIDÆ.

Bill with a notch in the upper mandible. Nostrils more or less covered with plumes. Tail moderate, rounded or square, and of 12 feathers.

Sub-Family.—PRIONOPINÆ.

Bill higher than broad, wings short, not reaching the tip of the tail.

Gen. **Tephrodornis.**—*Swainson.*

Bill moderately hooked and notched at tip; a few rictal bristles; nostrils covered with procumbent plumes; wings moderate; tarsus and toes short. Outer toe longest and slightly syndactyle.

56. Tephrodornis pondicerianus. *Gmel., S. N.* i. p. 939; *Bly., J. A. S. B.,* 1846, p. 305; *Jerd., B. Ind.* i. p. 410, No. 265; *Murray, Vert. Zool., Sind,* p. 123; *Hume, Str. F.* i. p. 435; *Murray, Hdbk., Zool., &c., Sind,* p. 134; *Legge, B. Ceylon,* pp. 372, 1214; *Murray, Avif. Brit. Ind.* i. p. 162, No 170. Tephrodornis indica, *G. R. Gray, Cat. Hodgs. Coll. B. Br. M.* p. 90. Tentheca leucura, *Hodgs., Ind. Rev.* i. p. 447.—The COMMON WOOD-SHRIKE.

Head, hind neck, scapulars, back and rump ashy brown; the feathers of the rump edged white; superciliary streak fulvous white; a dark brown streak from the nostrils to the ear coverts; upper tail coverts dark brown; wings dusky brown; tail dark brown, the two outer feathers white, and margined dusky on the outer web at the tip; basally they are dark brown; chin and throat white; breast and upper abdomen greyish brown; lower abdomen, vent and under tail coverts white; bill dusky horn; legs plumbeous; irides greenish yellow.

Length.—6·5 to 7 inches; wing 3·5; tail 2·75; bill at front 0·62.

Hab.—Ceylon and India generally, also Burmah, extending to the foot of the Himalayas. Occurs in the Deccan, North Guzerat, Kutch, Kattiawar and the Carnatic; also Assam and Bengal, in small flocks. In Sind it is a seasonal visitant, arriving in April, breeding and leaving the Province early in September. I obtained nestlings in May and June, and during July and August. Of the eight specimens collected, five were young birds. None were seen in September. Its presence is easily known by a very pretty, unmistakable little song, quite unlike that of any of the *Laniinæ.* It is generally lined with fine fibre and hair. According to Mr. H. Parker, the nest is glued on to a lateral branch of some small tree or low bush, and usually in a fork. They breed from March to July. The eggs are 2–3 in number, greenish white, with large brown blotches, or pale rust colour confined to the larger end. In length they vary from 0·69 to 0·8 inch; and in breadth from 0·57 to 0·65 inch.

57. Tephrodornis affinis. *Blyth, J. A. S. B.* xvi. p. 473; *id., Cat. B. Mus. A. S. B.* p. 153; *Bp., Consp.* i. p. 358; *Hume, Str. F.* 1873, p. 434; *Sharpe, Cat. B. Br. Mus.* iii. p. 276. Tephrodornis pondiceriana, *apud. Holdsw., P. Z. S.* 1872, p. 437.—The ALLIED WOOD-SHRIKE.

Adult (*Male*).—Above slaty grey, with only a slight trace of a paler eyebrow; wing coverts grey like the back; the greater series ashy brown like the quills, which are externally washed with grey; lower rump white; upper tail coverts black; tail feathers blackish; the two outermost white with blackish bases and a black spot at the tip of the feather; nasal bristles and lores greyish brown; the feathers above and below the eye and the ear coverts deeper black; cheeks and chin white; rest of the under surface ashy with a pinkish shade, gradually becoming white on the abdomen and under tail coverts; under wing coverts cinerous; the edge of the wing white; bill dusky; feet dusky lead colour; iris dull yellow. (*Holdsworth.*)

Length.—6·4 inches; culmen 0·8; wing 3·35; tail 2·45; tarsus 0·65.

Adult Female (Colombo; *Legge*).—Similar to the supposed male above described, but duller in colour, browner above and below washed with ashy brown, extending well into the throat, the eyebrow rather whiter or more distinct.

Length—6 inches; culmen 0·75; wing 3·3; tail 2·5; tarsus 0·65. (*Sharpe.*)

Hab.—Ceylon, near Newara Eliya and Colombo. Habits and nidification similar to those of *T. pondiceriana.*

Gen. **Hemipus.**—*Hodgs.*

Characters as in *Tephrodornis;* bill more depressed, and wider at base; 3rd quill nearly equal to 4th.

58. Hemipus picatus. *Sykes, P. Z. S.* 1832, p. 25; *Sharpe, Cat. B. Br. Mus.* iii. p. 307; *Jerd., B. Ind.* i. p. 412; *Hume, Nests and Eggs,* p. 178; *id., Str. F.* i. p. 435; iii. p. 93; *Hume and Davison,* vi. p. 207; *Hume, Str. F.* viii. p. 91; *Legge, B. Ceylon,* p. 375; *Murray, Avif. Brit. Ind.* i. p. 164, No. 174.—SYKES'S PIED SHRIKE.

Whole upper plumage, with the lores and ear coverts glossy black; rump feathers broadly tipped with white; chin, vent, and upper tail coverts pure white; the remainder of the lower plumage pale vinaceous; the cheeks and the sides of the neck white, produced so as to form an indistinct white collar round the neck; lesser wing coverts black; median coverts black, broadly tipped with white, the outer greater coverts black; primary coverts and quills black, the later secondaries broadly edged with white; tail black, all but the central feathers tipped with white, which extends over the whole outer web of the outermost feathers; bill black; iris hazel; eyelids plumbeous; legs plumbeous brown.

Length.—5·4 inches; wing 2·5; tail 2·4; tarsus 4·5; culmen 7.

Hab.—Ceylon, South India, Travancore, N.-W. Provinces, Oudh, Central India, Concan, Deccan, British Burmah and Tennaserim.

The Little Pied Shrike is generally seen in small parties of five or six, wandering about from tree to tree, every now and then darting on insects in the air. It has a pleasant song, which, however, is not often heard. It frequents thick forests, and like the Drongo, perches on the outer branches of a tree. According to Davison it also searches the leaves like a Wood Shrike. A nest taken by Mr. Davison at Ootacamund, was a small shallow cup made of grass and roots, covered with cobwebs and lichens and sparingly lined. It was placed on a branch of a tall tree and contained three eggs, which were pale greenish marked with umber-brown. Jerdon says the markings of the eggs he obtained at Darjeeling were a few rusty red spots.

GROUP.—CICHLOMORPHÆ—Thrush-like Passeres.

Wings with 10 primaries, the first markedly smaller; angle of chin shortened; rictal bristles generally present. Bill notched, curved at the tip, acuminate; nostrils nearer the cutting edge of mandible than the culmen.

Family ARTAMIDÆ.—Swallow Shrikes.

Bill moderate wide at the base, deep and slightly curved; commissure slightly curved; nostrils basal, with a minute tuft of bristles at their base; tarsus short and strong; claws well curved, acute; wings long; 1st quill minute, 2nd longest; tail short. (*Jerd.*) Plumage grey. They are called Swallow Shrikes, owing to their feeding like the swallows in the air.

Gen. Artamus—*Vieill.*

Characters those of the Family.

59. Artamus fuscus, *Vieill., Nouv. Dict. d'Hist. Nat.* xvii. p. 297; *Jerd., B. Ind.* i. 441, No. 287; *Hume, Nests and Eggs Ind. B.* p. 194; *Blyth, B. Burm.* p. 127; *Hume, Str. F.* iii. p. 102; *Armstrong, Str. F.* iv. p. 321; *Dav. et Oust. Ois. Chine*, p. 101; *Cripps, Str. F.* vii. p. 273; *Sharpe in Rowley's Orn. Misc.* iii. p. 191; *Legge, B. Ceylon*, p. 666; *Hume, Str. F.* viii. p. 92; *Oates, Str. F.* x. p. 203; *id., B. Br. Burm.* i. p. 396.—The Ashy Swallow Shrike.

Lores black; head and neck ashy grey, also the back, scapulars, rump and shorter upper tail coverts, but these with a rufescent or vinous tinge; longer upper tail coverts white; tail dark grey, tipped with whitish; wings and their coverts deep grey; quills narrowly margined wtth white near the tips and on portions of the inner webs; breast, abdomen, under wing and under tail coverts pale purplish brown, the latter finely barred with ashy. Bill pale blue, darker at the tip; legs slaty; irides dark brown.

Length.—7 to 7·3 inches; wing 5·2; tail 2·5; tarsus 0·65; bill from gape 0·95.

The young are barred above, the quills are broadly margined with whitish, and the under wing coverts tipped with rufous.

Hab.—Throughout nearly the whole of the moist regions in India and Ceylon. Jerdon says it is more abundant in the wooded districts, especially where palm trees abound, more particularly the Palmyra palm. He found them most abundant in the Carnatic, the Madras Coast, the Northern Circars, and Bengal; rare in the Deccan and Central India. Occurs also at Darjeeling, and spread throughout Assam and British Burmah. It has been found at Arracan, Tenasserim and Pegu in large flocks. The nests are built on palm trees, and are made of grass, twigs and fibres. Eggs, 4 in number, whitish, marked at the larger end with yellowish brown and lilac.

Artamus leucorhynchus, a species with the rump and lower surface of the body white and the back and wings chocolate brown, is found in the Andamans.

Family.—CAMPOPHAGIDÆ.

Bill moderate, vertically deep, broad at base; culmen arched; rictal bristles feeble; tail long, rounded; feathers of lower back and rump rigid in most genera; tarsus short.

Gen. Graucalus.—*Cuv.*

Bill of moderate length, strong and wide at base, the culmen curved, hooked and slightly notched; rictal bristles not much developed; wings long and pointed; tail moderate, slightly rounded.

60. Graucalus Macii, *Less.*, *Traite* p. 349; *Jerd.*, *B. Ind.* i. p. 417, No. 270; *Wald.*, *Ibis*, 1872, p. 311; *Blanf.*, *J. A. S. B.* xli. pt. ii. p. 156; *Hume, Nests and Eggs* p. 181; *id.*, *Str. F.* ii. p. 204; *Ball*, *Str. F.* ii. p. 400; *Bl.*, *B. Burm.* p. 123; *Anderson*, *Yunnan Exped.* p. 647; *Legge*, *B. Ceylon* pp. 360, 214; *Sharpe*, *Cat. B. Br. Mus.* iv. p. 34; *Hume*, *Str. F.* viii. p. 91; *Scully*, *Str. F.* viii. p. 267; *Murray*, *Avif. Br. Ind.* i. p. 170, No. 182. Graucalus layardi, *Bl.*, *Ibis*, 1866, p. 35; *Jerd.*, *Ibis*, 1872, p. 117; *Legge*, *Ibis*, 1875, p. 287; *Murray*, *Vert. Zool.*, *Sind*, p. 124.—The Indian Cuckoo-Shrike.

Head, neck, back, rump, upper tail coverts and scapulars french-grey; primaries and their coverts black, externally edged with whitish; secondaries french-grey on the outer webs, and margined and tipped whitish; the inner webs dusky; tail with the two centre feathers grey, tipped with white; the rest black, broadly tipped with white. A narrow frontal line, lores, below the eye, and at the gape black. Sides of face and ear coverts darkish grey beneath; the neck and breast french-grey; upper abdomen lighter, with numerous dull white transverse lines; lower abdomen, vent and under tail coverts white; under wing coverts and axillaries white, with a few cross lines of grey at the edge of the wings; bill blackish; irides rich lake; legs plumbeous.

The female is paler in colour throughout and has not the black on the face; generally there are present nearly obsolete barrings on the under surface. The young have the upper plumage tipped and margined with pale ferruginous, and the under surface nearly pure white.

Length.—11·8 to 12 inches; wings 6·5 to 7; tail 5 to 6; tarsus 1 to 1·05; bill at front 1.

Hab.—The Indian Cuckoo-Shrike is found over all India, from the Himalayas to the extreme South. It is abundant in Southern India and S.-E. Ceylon (*Parker*), spread over the whole of British Burmah, recorded from Nepaul, Pegu, Assam, and Port Blair; also the N.-W. Provinces, Punjab, Oudh, Bengal, Rajputana, Kutch, Kathiawar, Jodhpoor, North Guzerat and Travancore. Blyth records it from Arrakan, Mr. Davison from Tennaserim, and according to Dr. Tiraud it is found in Cochin-China. It affects thin forest, jungles, gardens, orchards, avenues and thick growths of high bushes. Feeds chiefly on insects as caterpillars, mantides, locusts, and grasshoppers, and probably also small fruit. Jerdon says it is rather a shy bird, flying before you from tree to tree uttering as it alights two or three rather sweet and mellow notes, but it has also a very harsh rattling scream. It flies in an easy undulating manner, with but few flappings of its wing. Its flesh is said to be eaten by the natives. Breeds almost everywhere about the beginning of the rains. Nest usually placed in the fork of a lofty branch of a tree, constructed of fine twigs and grass, cup-shaped in form. Eggs three, of a greenish colour, marked with spots and blotches of brown and pale purple.

Gen. **Pericrocotus.**—*Boie.*

Bill short, rather broad at base, and high; culmen slightly curved; wing long, 4th and 5th quills longest; tail long, lateral feathers graduated; tarsi and feet short and feeble.

Mr. Sharpe has properly, like most authors, placed this group of brightly coloured birds next to the *Campophaginæ*. The Minivets form a group of species very similar to each other; the males being for the most part clothed in black and red (vermilion red), and the females in dusky and yellow. They associate in small flocks and are always found on trees, actively hopping from branch to branch in search of insects, upon which they feed.

61. Pericrocotus flammeus (*Forst.*), *Sws., Zool. Ill.* p. 52; *Tem , Pl. Col.* 263; *Boie, Isis* 1828, p. 321; *Jerd., Ill. Ind. Orn.* pl ii. *m.* and *f.*; *id., B. Ind.* i. p. 420, No. 272; *Holdsw., P. Z. S.* 1872, p. 438; *Sharpe, Str. F.* iii. p. 95; iv. pp. 207, 394; v. pp. 175, 197; *Sharpe, Cat. B. Br. Mus.* iv. p. 75; *Hume, Nests and Eggs Ind. B.* p. 182; *Legge, B. Ceylon* p. 363; *Murray, Avif Br. Ind.* i. p. 775, No. 191.—The ORANGE MINIVET.

Whole head, nape, neck, upper back, wings, and central tail feathers shining blue black; lower back, rump, upper tail coverts, wing spot to the fifth primary, tips of some of the coverts, and entire under surface deep crimson; lateral tail feathers the same, but with black bases.

The female has the forehead tinged with yellow, the head and back grey; the rump, wing spots, lateral tail feathers and entire under surface yellow; wings and tail dusky, the pair next the middle feathers edged narrowly with yellow. Bill and legs black; irides dark brown.

Length.—7·5 to 8 inches; 3·5 to 3·7; tail 3·9 to 4; culmen 0·37; tarsus 0·6.

Hab.—Ceylon, Southern India, in the Circars, along the Coromandel and Malabar Coasts to Travancore; also in the Concan.

The Orange Minivet is abundant in all the more wooded parts of its habitat, and generally keeps to the topmost branches of high trees. It keeps continually flying from branch to branch, and is incessantly on the move, catching insects. It breeds on the Nilghiris during June and July. The nest is a comparatively massive little cup composed of fine twigs and plastered over with lichen-like cobwebs. It is usually placed in the fork of a slender bough. Eggs a palish green, thickly streaked and spotted chiefly at the large end with pale yellowish brown and dingy purple.

62. Pericrocotus peregrinus, *Lin., Syst. Nat.* i. p. 342; *Jerd., B. Ind.* i. p. 432; *Hume, Nests and Eggs* p. 184; *Bl. and Wald., B. Burmah* p. 124; *Hume, Str. F.* i. 177; iii. p. 96; *Sharpe, Str F.* iv. p. 209; *Hume, Str. F.* v. p. 179; viii. p. 91; *Oates, Str. F.* viii. p. 166; *Legge, Birds Ceylon* p. 366; *Sharpe, Cat. B. Br. Mus.* iv. p. 76; *Murray, Vert. Zool., Sind,* p. 125; *Murray, Avif Br. Ind.* i. p. 176, No. 194. Pericrocotus malabaricus, (*Gm.*), *Hume, Str. F.* v. p. 182; *Oates, B. Br. Burmah* i. p. 245.—The SMALL MINIVET.

Upper surface of body ashy grey; a narrow frontal band, lores, chin, throat and ear coverts blackish; wing coverts black, the lesser series edged with dull grey, and the greater with a narrow orange tip; quills dusky black, duller toward the tips; the bases of the primaries, except the first three, orange red, forming a conspicuous wing patch; rump and upper tail coverts bright vermilion; tail black, the four outer feathers on each side widely tipped with orange; the breast vermilion, also the upper abdomen and flanks, fading on the lower abdomen, vent and under tail coverts to yellowish; under wing coverts and edge of the wing yellow; thigh coverts dusky black. Bill and legs black; irides brown.

Length.—6 inches; wing 2·55; tail 3; bill at front 0·45.

The female is light grey above, the throat white, also the eye streak; sides of forehead and lower parts whitish, tinged with yellow on the breast, abdomen, and under tail coverts; the flanks and under wing coverts brighter yellow; quills light brown; the primaries with narrow white edgings; the wing spot yellow; rump vermilion; colour of bill and legs as in the male.

Length.—6·25 inches; wing 2·75; bill 0·45; tail 3·1.

Hab.—Ceylon, India, Burmese countries, Andamans and Java. Occurs in the N.-W. Himalayas, South and Central India, Nepaul, the Punjab, N.-W. Provinces, Oudh, Bengal, Rajputana, Deccan, Kutch, Kattiawar, Jodhpore, and N. Guzerat. In Sind it is a winter visitant, arriving in August and remaining till about the end of December.

The Small Minivet is most abundant wherever it is found, and like the other species of the genus is a restless bird. It is usually found in small parties. Breeds from about the end of April to the end of June. The nest is a very neat cup, made of very fine twigs, and coated thickly with cobwebs, to which are attached dead leaves, &c. The cobwebs are the nests of a species of spider which build on trees an almost circular papery covering; with these this Minivet lines the outside, making the nest appear as if there were knotty excrescences growing on it. The nest is usually placed high up and in a fork at the end of a bough. Eggs three in number, pale green, marked with reddish brown.

Gen. **Lalage**.—*Boie.*

Shrike-like birds of soft plumage; feathers of the lower back and rump rather stiff; bill stout and moderately hooked; rictal bristles almost wanting; wings longer than the tail; under tail coverts long.

63. Lalage sykesi, *Strickl., Ann. Nat. Hist. Ser.* i., xiii. p. 36; *Sharpe, Cat. B. Br. Mus.* iv. p. 89; *Legge, Birds of Ceylon* pp. 369, 1214; *Murray, Avif. Br. Ind.* i. p. 181, No. 202. Volvocivora sykesi, *Jerd., B. Ind.* i. p. 414, No. 268; *Hume, Nests and Eggs* p. 179; *Bl., B. Burm.* p. 123; *Hume, Str. F.* viii. p. 91. Campophaga sykesi, *Oates, B. Br. Burm.* i. p. 234.—The Black-headed Cuckoo-Shrike.

Head, neck, upper back, chin, throat and upper breast black; lower breast and abdomen pale grey, gradually passing to white on the vent and lower tail coverts; lower back, scapulars, lesser wing coverts, rump and upper tail coverts grey, the latter margined paler; median wing coverts black, tipped and broadly margined for their terminal half on the outer webs with grey; greater wing coverts black, narrowly margined greyish; primaries and secondaries black, the primaries with a narrow white margin on their outer webs and a large white patch on their inner webs, the secondaries rather broadly margined and tipped with white ; tail with the central feathers grey, the rest black, broadly tipped with white.

The female has the head and the upper plumage grey, paler on the rump and upper tail coverts, the latter barred with dusky ; cheeks, sides of the neck and the whole of the lower plumage whitish or albescent, closely and narrowly barred transversely with black, the bars becoming obsolete on the abdomen ; vent and under tail coverts white ; quills and wing coverts dark brown, each feather margined with greyish white ; ear coverts greyish, mottled with brown ; the feathers white shafted ; tail with the central pair of feathers grey, narrowly tipped with white, the rest blackish or dark brown, broadly tipped with white, the outermost with the white tippings, mottled with brown.

The young are similar to the adult female ; adults have the bill black, also the legs and feet ; iris brownish red.

Length.—7·5 inches ; wing 4 ; tail 3 ; tarsus 0·8 ; bill from gape 0·85.

Hab.—Ceylon, and the whole Peninsula of India, Central and Southern India, Bengal, the Concan and Deccan, and, according to Blyth, Upper Pegu. It hunts usually in small parties, and occasionally, according to Jerdon, singly or in pairs, flying from tree to tree, and slowly and carefully examining the foliage, prying searchingly all around and under the leaves to discover a suitable morsel. It continues its search, hopping and flying, from branch to branch till the tree has been well inspected, when the flock flies off together to another tree. Caterpillars and other soft insects are its favourite food. Dr. Jerdon adds that it is usually a silent bird but has a harsh call, and mentions having in June heard a male giving out a clear whistling call as it was flying from tree to tree. It affects wooded tracts, but not deep forests. Mr. Blewitt found the nest of this species in Bundelcund in July. It was placed at the end of two small out-shooting branches of a Mowa tree, and was slightly made of thin twigs and roots, and partially covered with spider's web. The eggs, two in number, were green, mottled with dark brown.

Family.—MUSCICAPIDÆ.

Passerine birds of very varied form, embracing a large number of Genera, connecting the woodshrikes with the thrushes, with ample rictal bristles, wide, depressed or shallow bills. They are all chiefly insectivorous. Their wings are moderate and not adapted for long and speedy flight, but are capable of rapid and powerful sallies.

Gen. Hemichelidon—*Hodgs.*

Bill much depressed and shallow, wide at base, slender and narrowed at tip, which is faintly hooked ; gape wide ; rictal bristles moderate ; wings long

3rd and 4th quills sub-equal and longest; 1st quill minute; tarsus feeble; lateral toes unequal.

Head of Hemichelidon ferruginea.

64. Hemichelidon ferruginea, *Hodgs., P. Z. S.* 1845, p. 32; *Hume, Nests and Eggs* p. 207; *Sharpe, Cat. B. Br. Mus.* iv. p. 122; *Murray, Avif. Brit. Indi.* i. p. 184, No. 206. Butalis ferruginea, *Bl., B. Burm.* p. 104; *David et Oust. Ois. Chine* p. 121. Alseonax ferruginea, *Jerd., B. Ind.* 1. p. 460, No. 299; *Hume and Dav., Str. F.* vi. p. 277; *Bingham, Str. F.* ix. p. 175; *Oates, Str. F.* x. p. 204; *Oates, B. Br. Burm.* 1 p. 276.—The FERRUGINOUS FLYCATCHER.

Forehead and crown of head dark brown; orbital feathers pale buff; lores and ear coverts rufescent brown; back, scapulars, lesser wing coverts, rump and upper tail coverts, rusty or reddish brown, becoming deeper (chestnut) on the latter and on the rump; median and greater coverts brown, edged and tipped with chestnut; quills dark brown, the later secondaries and tertiaries edged with rusty brown; under surface of quills buffy; tail reddish brown; lower throat with a patch of white, the rest of the under surface chestnut; the throat rufescent brown; bill dusky, yellowish at base of lower mandible; legs pale fleshy; irides dark brown.

Length.—5 inches; wing 2·75; tail 2·0; tarsus 0·5; bill from gape 0·65.

Hab.—Ceylon, the Carnatic, N.-W. Provinces, British Burmah, Nepaul, and Sikkim. The Ferruginous Flycatcher is a rare visitant to the plains of India. Jerdon says he did not hear of its occurrence away from the Himalayas. He records it from Ceylon, and I have had three specimens sent to me for identification by Mr. William Mayberry of Kuduganava, obtained by him in January 1888. It is common in the neighbourhood of Darjeeling, from 4,000 to 8,000 feet. In Burmah it is a winter visitor. It is recorded from Bankasoon in Tenasserim; Oates procured specimens near Pegu, and Captain Bingham secured a specimen in the Thoungyeen Valley. It extends southwards through the Malay Peninsula, and is found in Cochin-China. It frequents, according to Jerdon, dark, open forests without underwood, and pursues insects from a low branch, or the stump of a fallen tree.

It breeds in the Himalayas. The structure of the nest, as well as the number, size, and shape of the eggs, is the same as in the preceding species—colour a sort of buff, minutely and feebly freckled with brownish red; size 0·64 × 0·5.

Gen. **Alseonax**.—*Cabanis*.

Bill more lengthened than in *Hemichelidon*, less swallow like, being narrower in front and deeper vertically; 3rd and 4th quills subequal.

65. Alseonax latirostris, *Raffles*, *Trans. Lin. Soc.* xiii. p. 312; *Jerd.*, *B. Ind.* i. p. 459, No. 297; *Hume and Henders.*, *Lahore to Yark.* p. 185, pl. v.; *Hume*, *Str. F.* ii. p. 219; *Brooks*, *Str. F.* iii. p. 276; iv. p. 273; v. p. 470; *Sharpe*, *Cat. B. Br. Mus.* iv. p. 127; *Scully*, *Str. F.* viii p. 276; *Legge*, *B. Ceylon*, p. 415; *Hume*, *Str. F.* viii. p. 92; *Brooks*, *Str. F.* ix. p. 225; *Murray*, *Avif. Brit. Ind.* p. 185, No. 207. Butalis terricolor, *Bl.*, *J. A. S. B.* xvi. p. 120. Muscicapa cinereoalba, *Tem. and Schleg.*, *Faun. Jap. Aves*, p. 42, pl. 15. Alseonax terricolor, *Jerd.*, *B. Ind.* i. p. 460, No. 298; *Brooks*, *Str. F.* iii. p. 234. Butalis latirostris, *Bl.*, *B. Burm.* p. 104; *Oates*, *B. Br. Burm.* i. p. 277.—The Brown Fly-Catcher.

Above greyish brown or dark brown, the feathers of the crown centred darker; lores and orbital ring white; scapulars, tertiaries, and secondaries dark brown; wing coverts the same, all but the primaries edged with rusty; tail dark brown, the outermost feathers narrowly tipped with whitish; under surface of body white, tinged with pale ashy on the breast, flanks, and sides of the throat.

Immature birds have broad fulvous margins to all the feathers of the upper plumage. Bill, legs and claws black; base of lower mandible yellow; in the immature, except the tip, which is dusky, the whole lower mandible is yellow.

Length.—5 to 5·2 inches; wing 2·75 to 2·85; tail 2·5 to 2·85; tarsus 0·5; bill from gape 0·7.

Hab.—Ceylon, Malabar Coast, South India, N.-W. Provinces, Oudh, Central India, the Concan, Deccan. British Burmah, and Nepaul. Extends to Cochin-China.

The Brown Fly-Catcher is a winter visitor to Burmah. It is said to be a resident of Southern India and Ceylon, but nothing appears to be known of its nidification. Oates says that in Pegu some birds would appear to stay all the year round, or to nest close by, having shot both adult and young in July. It is abundant, according to him, in the southern half of Pegu. Captain Wardlaw-Ramsay got it at Tounghoo. Mr. Blyth received it from Arrakan, and Davison says he observed it in the southern half of Tenasserim. It extends down the Malay Peninsula to the Archipelago, and is found spread over China in winter. Its habits are quite those of the other species. Jerdon says it is very sedentary, sitting motionless on a branch and darting out occasionally to capture an insect on the wing.

66. Alseonax muttui (*Layard*), *Sharpe*, *Cat. B. Br. Mus.* iv. p. 132, Butalis muttui, *Layard*, *Ann. and Mag. N. H.* 1854. xiii. p. 127; *Legge*, *B.*

Ceylon, p. 417. Alseonax terricolor (*nec. Hodgs.*), *Holdsw., P. Z. S.* 1872, p. 441; *Legge, Str. F.* 1875, p. 366. Alseonax flavipes, *Legge, Str. F.* 1875, p. 367.—The EARTHY BROWN FLY-CATCHER.

Above ochraceous brown, shaded with olive on the head and neck; upper tail coverts rufous; tail brown, narrowly edged with rufescent on the outer web and with fulvous on the inner one; wing coverts dark brown, edged externally with ochreous brown; greater coverts and quills dark sepia brown, edged externally with rufous; primary coverts sepia brown; lores, feathers in front of and round the eye dull white; ear coverts and sides of the head olive brown; cheeks light ochreous brown, the fore part mottled with white; throat, centre of breast and abdomen white; foreneck and sides of the breast light ochreous brown; flanks and thighs pale fawn buff; under tail coverts whitish, rather fulvescent at their tips; under wing coverts and axillaries orange buff. (*Sharpe.*) Bill blackish brown, the lower mandible fleshy yellow; legs and feet pale yellow; iris reddish brown.

Length.—5·2 inches; wing 2·85; tail 2·25; tarsus 0·55, culmen 0·6. (*Legge.*)

Hab.—Ceylon.

Gen. **Muscicapa**, *Linn.;* Butalis, *Boie.;* Erythrosterna, *Bp.*

Wings pointed and long; bill rather long, depressed, wide throughout, except at tip; second primary longer than the secondaries and nearly the length of the third; nasal bristles scanty.

67. Muscicapa albicilla, *Pall., Zoogr. Rosso.-Asiat.* i. p. 462; *Aves, tab.* i.; *Sharpe, Cat. B. Br. Mus.* iv. p. 162; *Oates, B. Burm.* i. p. 278; *Murray, Avif. Bri. Ind.* i. p. 188, No. 211. Erythrosterna leucura. (*Gm.*), *Jerd., B. Ind.* i. p. 481, No. 323; *Bl., B. Burm.*, p. 103. Erythrosterna albicilla (*Pall.*), *Anders., Yunnan Exped.* p. 621; *Hume and Dav., Str. F.* vi. p. 233; *David et Oust. Ois Chine*, p. 120; *Scully, Str. F.* viii. p. 280; *Hume, Str. F.* viii. p. 93.—The WHITE-TAILED ROBIN FLY-CATCHER.

Male in Summer plumage.—Upper plumage and wings olive brown, the latter margined paler; upper tail coverts black; tail black, the four outer pairs of feathers white for about two-thirds of their length from the base; lores mixed ashy and white; chin and throat orange; ear coverts, cheeks and a band passing round the orange of the throat pure ashy, extending on to the upper breast in some; rest of lower plumage ashy white.

In winter the male loses the orange on the chin and throat and the plumage on the under surface of the body is tinged with buff; orbital ring white.

The female is like the male in summer; bill dark brown, yellowish at the gape; iris hazel brown; legs black.

Length.—5 to 5·1 inches; wing 2·75; tail 2·0 to 2·1; tarsus 0·65; bill from gape 0·6.

Hab.—Ceylon; also the N.-W. Provinces, Oudh, Bengal, Concan, and, perhaps, the Deccan, as well as British Burmah and Nepaul. Jerdon says it is found "throughout the whole of India." This statement is certainly incorrect. It is not known from South India, though it occurs in Ceylon. In Northern and Central India it is not uncommon, but everywhere, even in British Burmah, as a winter visitant. According to Oates it is common in Pegu, and spread over the whole division from November to March. It is recorded from Arrakan, and Mr. Shopland got specimens at Akyab. At Tounghoo Captain Wardlaw-Ramsay obtained specimens. It is spread over the whole of Tenasserim. It is said to summer in Eastern Siberia and North China.

The White-tailed Robin Fly-Catcher affects gardens, orchards, groves and low jungle chiefly. It appears to be strictly arboreal, playing about on the branches of trees searching for insects, and never descending to the ground.

68. Muscicapa hyperythra (*Cab.*), *Sharpe, Cat. B. Br. Mus.* iv. p. 163; *Legge, B. Ceylon*, p. 427; *Murray, Avif. Brit. Ind.* i. p. 188, No. 212. Erythrosterna hyperythra, *Holdsw., P. Z. S.* 1872, p. 442, pl. 17; *Hume, Nests and Eggs Ind. B.* p. 217. Siphia hyperythra, *Cab., Journ. F. Ornith.* 1866, p. 391; *Hume, Str. F.* vii. p. 376.—The WHITE-TAILED ROBIN OR RUFOUS-BREASTED FLY-CATCHER.

Upper surface brownish grey, turning to a purer grey on the rump and upper tail coverts; tail black, with the basal halves of the lateral rectrices white, the upper tail coverts, especially the longest, are blackish in parts, especially on the outer webs; lower surface a bright red-brown or rusty-red, except on the middle of the abdomen, which is pure white; the red-brown colour is most intense on the throat and breast, lighter and mingled with albescent on the sides of the abdomen and lower tail coverts; tibial plumes grey; loreal region somewhat dotted with white; sides of the head and neck pure grey, separated from the red-brown of the throat and breast by an irregular blackish line; under wing coverts tinged with rusty yellow; feet and upper mandible brown, the lower yellow; 4th quill longest, fifth longer than the third, 2nd about equal to the 8th.

Length.—5·33 inches; wing 2·88; tail 3·3; tarsus 0·8. (*Cabanis.*) The distinguishing characters of this species are the rich orange-brown of the throat and breast, and the black stripe running from the bill down the sides of the neck to the breast and terminating below the bend of the closed wing; bill dusky above, yellow beneath; irides dark brown. (*Holdsworth.*)

Hab.—Ceylon, Central India and the N.-W. Provinces; also Cashmere.

The Rufous-breasted Fly-Catcher appears to have the usual habits of the other species. According to Brooks it breeds in Cashmere at from 6,000 to 7,000 feet elevation. There is no record of its nest having been found in India.

Gen. **Pratincola**, *Koch. Syst. d. Baier. Zool.* p. 190.

Bill short, straight, wider at the nostrils than high; nostrils hidden; second primary longer than the secondaries, the first not half the length of the second.

69. Pratincola caprata (*Linn.*), *Blyth, J. A. S. B.* xvi. p. 129; *Bp., Consp.* i. p. 305; *Jerd., B. Ind.* ii. p. 123, No. 481; *Hume, Str. F.* 1873, pp. 182, 379; 1874, pp. 413, 477; 1875, p. 134; 1877, p. 229; 1876, p. 259; *Str. F.* 1875, p. 238; *Murray, Vert. Zool., Sind,* p. 141; *Oates, B. Br. Burm.* i. p. 281; *Legge, B. Ceylon,* p. 430; *Blanfd., Eastern Persia* p. 144; *Murray, Hdbk. Zool., &c., Sind,* p. 145; *id., Avif. Brit. Ind.,* p 194, No 217. Motacilla caprata, *Linn., S. Nat.* i. p. 325. Œnanthe caprata, *Vieill., N. Dict.* xxi. p. 433. Saxicola bicolor, *Sykes, P. Z. S.* 1832, p. 92. Pratincola atrata, *Blyth, J A. S. B.* xx. p. 177; *Jerd., L. Ind.* ii. p. 124, No 482. Pratincola bicolor, *Hume, Nests and Eggs Ind. B.* p. 314.—The White-winged Black Robin.

Adult Male.—Head, neck all round, throat, breast, sides of the face, back, wings, tail and entire under surface black; under wing coverts black; vent, under tail coverts, rump, upper tail coverts and wing patch white; some of the feathers of the lower abdomen very slightly edged with white. The young male is dark brown, the feathers of the upper and lower surface with brownish edgings; the quills dark brown with whitish tips, and the lower abdomen, vent and upper tail coverts, as well as the wing patch, white. The female is dusky brown, the feathers edged pale, and with dark centres to the feathers of the head, scapulars and back; rump and upper tail coverts rufescent; tail dark brown, as also are the wing coverts and quills, but margined with lighter brown; beneath pale reddish or ochraceous brown, whitish on the throat; vent and under tail coverts white, with a slight rufous tinge; bill and legs black; irides dark brown.

Length.—5 to 5·4 inches; wing 2·75; tail 2·1; tarsus 0·8; bill at front 0·45.

Hab.—Ceylon, India generally (Southern India), Burmah, Java, and Philippines. In the Indian region it extends to the Himalayas, and is extremely common throughout Sind, the Punjab, Beloochistan, S.-E. Persia and S. Afghanistan, at Chaman, Gulistan, Dubrai and Kandahar; also occurs all along the Western Coast, Kutch, Kattiawar Jodhpore, North Guzerat, the Deccan and Concan. Breeds in Sind and the plains generally during March and April. Eggs usually three, pale greenish white, speckled finely with brown.

Gen. **Hypothymis**.—*Boie.*

Bill of moderate length, broad, triangular, suddenly narrowed, straight, tip hooked, and with a distinct notch; rictal bristles numerous; nostrils with a few hairs above it; 4th and 5th quills of wing subequal and longest; tarsus short; head with scale-like velvety plumes.

70. Hypothymis ceylonensis. *Sharpe, Cat. B. Br. Mus.* iv. p. 277; *Legge, B. Ceylon* p. 408. Myiagra azurea, *Holdsw., P. Z. S.,* 1872, p.

440 (*nec. Bodd.*). Hypothymis azurea, *Murray, Avif. Brit. Ind.* i. p. 201, No. 228, *pt.*—The CEYLONESE BLUE FLY-CATCHER.

Adult Male.—An indistinct patch on the nape, and a narrow frontal line black; sides of the face, throat and foreneck light azure blue; rest of under surface white, washed with bluish; the whole remaining plumage with the lesser wing coverts blue; greater wing coverts black, externally edged with blue; wings brown, narrowly edged with blue; tail brown, suffused with blue on the central pair of feathers and on the outer webs of the others; and with either a very narrow nearly obsolete white tip, or this is wanting; bill pale blue or plumbeous; inside of mouth yellow; legs blue; iris dark brown; edges of eyelids blue.

Length.—5·8 to 6·4 inches; wing 2·8; tail 2·5; tarsus 0·7; culmen 0·55 to 0·75.

The female has the head above azure blue, the sides of the head, chin and throat duller; breast greyish brown; abdomen flanks and under tail coverts white, tinged with grey; wings black; rump and upper tail coverts brown; tail darker brown, the outer edges washed with blue and all but the central feathers tipped with white.

Length.—6·5 inches; wing 2·95; tail 3; tarsus 0·7.

Hab.—Ceylon. This species is barely separable from *H. azurea*, a race found in India generally, and ranging through the Burmese countries to Pegu, Tenasserim, and the Malay Peninsula; also China, Cochin-China, and the Indo-Burmese countries; also occurs in the Punjab, N.-W. Provinces, Oudh, Bengal, Central India, the Concan, Deccan, South India, Pegu, British Burmah generally, and Nepaul. It affects every description of jungle, also gardens, orchards, and bamboo groves. It is an active bird and ever on the move, darting on insects and capturing them on the wing. It breeds in the low, warm, well-wooded valleys of the sub-Himalayan ranges up to 3,000 feet, from May to August, and in Ceylon during June and July. The nest is a delicate cup, made of green grass and coated with cobwebs, and is generally placed in the fork of a tree, or a bamboo, not far from the ground. The eggs, 3 to 4 in number, are white, or white with a salmon tinge, speckled and spotted with pale red and purple, or reddish pink; size 0·69×0·53. The bird, according to Mr. Parker, sits very close.

Gen. **Rhipidura**.—*Vig. and Horsf.*

Plumage of the head full, no elongated crest; bill rather long, depressed, wide, except at tip, which is slightly hooked and notched; nostrils overhung by long nareal bristles; rictal bristles long and slender; wings with the first 4 quills unequally graduated; tail lengthened, rounded or graduated; tarsus moderate; lateral toes unequal.

71. Rhipidura albifrontata, *Sharpe, Cat. B. Br. Mus.* iv. p. 338; *Oates, B. Br. Burm.* i. p. 268; *Murray, Vert. Zool. Sind.* p. 129; *Legge, B.*

Ceylon p. 412; *Murray, Avif Brit. Ind.* i. p. 210, No. 237. Rhipidura albofrontata, *Frankl., P. Z. S.*, 1831, p. 116; *Blyth, J. A. S. B.* xii. p. 935. Leucocerca albofrontata, *Jerd., Madras Journ.* xi p. 12; *id., B. Ind.* i. p. 452; *Hume, Nests and Eggs* p. 201; *Blyth and Wald., B. Burm.* Leucocerca aureola, *Hume, Str. F.* i. p. 436; iii. p. 104; viii. p. 92. Leucocerca burmannica, *Hume, Str. F.* ix. p. 175 (footnote).—The WHITE BROWED FANTAIL.

Head, neck, lores, and sides of the face slaty black; a broad frontal band, extending over the eyes to the nape, white; throat white, the feathers black at their bases; lower throat black, slightly edged with white; back and wing coverts ashy brown, the latter, including the primary coverts, tipped with triangular spots of white; axillaries dark brown, edged with whitish; breast, abdomen, under tail and thigh coverts white, the feathers of the latter with black bases; tail dark brown, all except the centre ones broadly tipped white; bill and legs black; irides deep brown.

Length.—6 to 6·7 inches; bill at front 0·5; wing 3·3 to 3·15; tail 3·6; tarsus 0·75.

Hab.—Ceylon and India generally, to Burmah, Pegu and N.-W. Himalayas. Common in the Punjab, N.-W. Provinces, Oudh, Central India, Rajputana, Kutch, Kattiawar and Jodhpore; also in Southern India, the Concan and Deccan, especially in gardens. Breeds from March to August. The nest is a very neat cup, made of fine fibres, &c., covered on the outside and inside with cobwebs, and usually attached towards the end of a low branch. Eggs 2 to 3 in number, not unlike those of the preceding.

Gen. **Terpsiphone.**—*Gloger.*

Bill long, wide, depressed at base, narrowing at tip, hooked and notched, the culmen keeled; rictal bristles numerous, long and stout, not reaching beyond half the length of the bill; wings rather long and somewhat pointed; tail long, cuneate, with the central feathers greatly elongated in the males. Head crested.

72. Terpsiphone paradisi, *Linn., Syst. Nat.* i. p. 224; *Sharpe, Cab. Passerif.* p. 347; *Cat. Mus. Heine. Th.* i. p. 58. Muscicapa paradisi, *Cuv. Regne. Anim.* 1817, i. p. 344; *Sykes, P. Z. S.* 1832, p. 84; *Jerd., Ill. Ind. Orn.* pl. 7. Tchitrea paradisi, *Less., Traité*, p. 386; *Gray, Gen. B.* i. p. 259; *Hume, Ibis*, 1869, p. 9; *Jerd., B. Ind.* p. 444, No. 288; *Str. F.* 1873, pp. 403, 474; 1875, p. 102; *Murray, Hdbk. Zool. &c., Sind*, p. 138.—The PARADISE FLY-CATCHER.

Adult Male.—Head with a long occipital crest; sides of face, neck, and entire throat glossy steel green; above and below pure white, some of the feathers more or less black shafted; quills black, externally white; the edges of the innermost quills white, with a longitudinal dark mark down the centre; tail feathers elongated, 12—13 inches in length.

Adult Female.—Crown of head and crest glossy greenish black; lores, sides of face, sides of neck, and throat greyish · rest of under surface of body white;

the flanks greyish and tinged with rufous ; back, wing coverts and inner secondaries bay ; tail light chestnut ; bill bluish ; legs and feet pale blue ; irides dark brown.

Length of Male.—Including elongated tail feathers, 17 inches ; bill 0·85 ; wing 3·65 ; tail 5·5 ; middle feathers 13. *Female, length,* 7·5 ; wing 3·45 ; tail 4.

Hab.—Ceylon and India to Nepaul and Cashmere. Abundant on the Malabar Coast and in Southern India. Occurs in the Punjab, N.-W. Provinces, Oudh, Bengal, Rajputana, Central India, Kutch, Kattiawar, Jodhpore, and N. Guzerat. In Sind it is a winter visitant, arriving in September.

The Paradise Fly-Catcher is more or less a permanent resident of forest and wooded districts of India, and although it occurs in open districts as Sind and Rajputana, it is only a winter visitant in those parts. The highest elevation it has been found at is about 5,500 feet. Jerdon says it is very partial to bamboo jungle. In its habits it is restless and wandering, flitting continually from branch to branch and tree to tree, and feeds on flies and other insects, always capturing them on the wing, sometimes picking them off a leaf or bough. It breeds throughout the outer ranges of the Himalayas, in the warmer valleys, up to 5,500 feet, also in the Dhoon Terai, Oudh, and the Central Provinces. The season lasts from May to July. The nest is cup-shaped, and composed of moss, fibres, and grass, ornamented on the outside with white silky cocoons. Eggs 3 to 4 in number, longish oval in shape ; in colour pinkish white, speckled with brownish red ; size 0·81 × 0·6.

In regard to the change of plumage of the Paradise Fly-Catcher, I entirely agree with Mr. Sharpe's views, *viz.*, that the changes are not seasonal but due to age.

The nestlings in their first dress has a dull chestnut plumage, with the under surface of the body (abdomen) white, and this is the plumage of the females of the first year, except that the sides of the breast are greyish. In the second year the chestnut becomes duller, and this is the first stage of the males, which also have the steel green crown, crest and throat. In the following stage the long red tail is acquired, the quills and primary coverts are edged with white, and the inner secondaries only retain some of the rufous of the back. This is certainly the breeding plumage of the male in the second year. It is during the third year that the male changes to the full white plumage during autumn. Once the white plumage is assumed there is no further change, either by moult or other means, and the birds are said to breed and live throughout the rest of their lives in their white plumage.

Gen. **Culicicapa**.—*Swinhoe.*

Head subcrested ; bill moderately broad, flattened, outline bowed in towards the tip ; nareal bristles long and strong ; rictal bristles slightly shorter ; wing rather pointed ; 1st quill shorter than the second ; 4th and 5th very little longer than the third ; tarsus short, feeble ; tail nearly even.

73. Culicicapa ceylonensis, *Swainson, Zool. Ill Ser.* i. pl. xiii.; *Sharpe, Cat. B. Br. Mus.* iv. p. 369; *Oates, B. Br. Burm.* i. p. 274; *Hume, Str. F.* viii. p. 92; *Scully, Str. F.* viii. p. 275; *Legge, B. Ceylon,* p. 410; *Murray, Avif. Br. Ind.* i. p. 214, No. 242. Cryptolopha cinereocapilla, *Hutton, J. A. S. B.* xvii. p. 689; *Jerd., B. Ind.* i. p. 455, No. 295. Myiolestes cinereocapilla (*Vieill.*), *Hume, Nests and Eggs Ind. B.* p. 205; *Ball, Str. F.* 1874, pp. 404, 406; *Wald., B. Burm.* p. 132. Culicicapa cinereocapilla, *Hume, Str. F.* iii. p. 104.—The GREY-HEADED FLY-CATCHER.

Head, neck and breast ashy, darker on the crown, where the feathers are dark centred; under surface bright yellow; the under wing coverts slightly paler; lores and edges of the eyelids whitish; back, rump, scapulars and upper tail coverts greenish yellow; wings and their coverts dark brown; the outer webs of all the feathers, except the first two primaries, edged with bright greenish yellow; the lesser wing coverts more broadly edged with the same on both webs; tail dark brown, the outer webs of all except the outer pair edged with greenish yellow; bill brown, paler at gape; mouth yellow; iris dark hazel; legs yellowish brown.

Hab.—Ceylon, and the greater portion of India, extending through the Burmese countries down the Malay Peninsula to the islands of Java, the Philippines, and Celebes. (*Sharpe.*) According to Jerdon the Grey-headed Fly-Catcher is dispersed from the Himalayas to the Nilghiris, and spreads on the other side of the Bay through Assam, into Arrakan, Burmah, and Tenasserim. In South India, on the summit of the Nilghiris, it is very common. Towards the north and in Central India it is occasionally met with, and is not rare in Lower Bengal. Oates found it spread over the whole of Pegu as a winter visitor, both in the hills and plains. Davison states it is generally distributed throughout the whole of Tenasserim. Captain Bingham found it in the Thoungyeen Valley, and Captain Wardlaw-Ramsay in the hills in Karin. It prefers rather dense jungle in general, or shady groves and tangled thickets, is tolerably active and lively, making frequent sallies after small insects. It is often seen in small parties, occasionally singly or in pairs, and has a pleasant, but feeble, chirping song. It breeds in the Himalayas and in the Nilghiris at considerable elevations. Hutton obtained a nest at Mussoorie. It was placed against the trunk of a tree. It is sometimes placed against a rock. In shape the nest is like a watch-pocket, made of moss, and fixed to the moss of the tree by spider's web and lined with fine fibres. It breeds during April and May. The eggs, 4 in number, are dingy yellowish white, minutely spotted with pale greenish brown, or purplish grey, with a broad ring of the same near the large end; size 0·62 × 0·48.

Gen. Stoparola.—*Blyth.*

Bill short, depressed; the culmen not equal to twice its breadth at the gape; tip hooked; rictal bristles numerous; wing rather long; 3rd, 4th and 5th quills subequal; tail moderate; tarsus short.

74. Stoparola sordida (*Walden*), *Sharpe, Cat. B. Br. Mus.* iv. p 449. Glaucomyia sordida, *Wald., Ann. and Mag. Nat. Hist., Ser.* 4, v. p. 218; *Hume, Str. F.* 1875, p. 401. Stoparola melanops, *Layard, Ann. and Mag. Nat. Hist.* xiii. p. 127 (*nec V.*) Eumyias sordida, *Holdsw., P. Z. S.* 1872, p. 441; *Legge, Ibis,* 1874, p. 18; *Sharpe, Trans. Linn. Soc.* New Series, i. p. 326.—The CEYLON VERDITER FLY-CATCHER.

Above dusky grey, washed with greenish; forehead and feathers over the eye cobalt; wing coverts like the back, the lesser series tinged on the outer ones with brighter cobalt; quills, and greater coverts dusky brown, externally edged with greyish blue; tail brown, the feathers edged with a wash of greyish blue; sides of the face and throat dusky grey, washed with cobalt; breast and sides of the body dusky grey; abdomen and under tail coverts whitish; thighs dusky grey, the feathers tipped with white; frontal line, feathers in front of and below the eye, also at angle of mouth and base of chin, black; under wing coverts white; edge of wing light bluish; bill black; legs and feet blackish lead colour; iris dull reddish brown.

Length.—5·8 inches; wing 3·09; tail 2·6; tarsus 0·75; culmen 0·5.

Hab.—Ceylon, on the Kandy hills.

Gen. **Siphia**.—*Hodgs.*

Bill moderately wide; length of culmen equal to twice the breadth of the base at gape, slightly hooked at tip and notched; nostrils covered by bristles and frontal plumes; wings pointed and long, but not reaching to the tip of the tail; 4th quill longest; hind claw moderate and curved, not as long as the hind toe; toes scutate at base of claws; tarsus as long as hind toe and claw.

75. Siphia rubeculoides (*Vigors*), *Sharpe, Cat. B. Br. Mus.* iv. p. 445; *Oates, B. Br. Burm.* i. p. 287; *Legge, B. Ceylon* i. p. 424; *Murray, Avif. Brit. Ind.* i. p. 225, No. 258. Phœnicura rubeculoides, *Vig., P. Z. S.* 1831, p. 35; *Gould, Cent. Him. B.* pl. 25, fig. 1. Cyornis rubeculoides, *Blyth, J. A S. B.* xii. p. 941; *Jerd., B. Ind.* i. p. 466, No. 304; *Blyth and Wald., B. Burm* p. 103; *Hume, Nests and Eggs Ind. B.* p. 211; *id., Str. F.* iii. p. 204; *Hume and Dav., Str. F.* vi. p. 227; *Anders., Yunnan Exp.* p. 619; *Hume, Str. F.* vii. p. 92.—The BLUE-THROATED REDBREAST.

Male.—Forehead and streak over the eye glistening blue; lores and feathers at the base of the bill black; ear coverts dusky blue; cheeks, sides of the neck, *throat and chin dusky blue-black*; whole upper plumage dark blue; tail black-shafted, the feathers brown on their inner webs; wings dark brown, the feathers narrowly edged with dark blue; lesser wing coverts bright blue; the larger coverts brown, edged with dark blue; breast and abdomen bright ferruginous, running up to a point on the throat; lower abdomen and under tail coverts white; under wing coverts pale ferruginous; bill black; iris brown.

The female has the upper plumage olive brown, tinged with ferruginous, strongly so on the forehead, feathers round the eye and upper tail coverts; lores albescent; *chin, throat and breast ruddy ferruginous*; abdomen and under tail coverts white.

Length.—5·7 inches; tail 2·4; wing 2·75; tarsus 0·75; bill from gape 0·7.

Hab.—Ceylon and India generally, extending to the N.-W. Himalayas, Nepal, Sikkim, and the Burmese countries.

The blue-throated Redbreast visits the plains of India during the winter months. It is rare in the south of India, and occurs both on the Eastern and Western Coasts. In the Punjab, N.-W. Provinces, Oudh and Bengal it is tolerably common. At Darjeeling it is found at from 4,000 to 6,000 feet elevation. In British Burmah it is also a winter visitor. It is recorded from Arrakan, and is found both in the hills and plains of the Pegu District from October to April. Mr. Davison says it is common throughout Tenasserim and is a permanent resident. It breeds in holes in banks. Captain Hutton found two nests at Mussoorie; they were made of moss and hair-like fibres. The eggs, four in number, were dull pale olive, or olive green faintly clouded with clay colour and marked with dull rufous. Size 0·72 × 0·52.

76. Siphia tickelliæ (*Blyth*), *Sharpe, Cat. B. Br. Mus.* iv. p. 448; *Oates, B. Burm.* i. p. 289; *Legge, B. Ceylon* p. 421; *Murray, Avif. Brit. Ind.* i. p. 225, No. 259. Cyornis tickelliæ, *Blyth, J. A. S. B.* xii. p. 491; *Jerd., B. Ind.* i. p. 367, No. 306; *Hume, Nests and Eggs* p. 212; *id., Str. F.* i. p. 436; *Ball, Str. F.* ii. p. 405; *Hume, Str. F.* iii. p. 468; *Wald. in Bl. B. Burm.* p. 103. Cyornis banyumas (*nec. Horsf.*), *Jerd., B. Ind.* i. p. 466, No. 305.—TICKELL'S BLUE REDBREAST.

Above light blue; forehead cobalt; a narrow frontal line and space in front of the eye blue black; cheeks, ear coverts and a narrow line across the chin at the base of the bill dark blue; the ear coverts washed with lighter blue; wing coverts cobalt blue; quills and tail light blue externally and dusky brown on the inner webs; two centre feathers and inner secondaries nearly entirely blue; entire throat and breast orange rufous; under wing coverts and axillaries, also the lower abdomen and under tail coverts, white; sides of the breast and edge of the wing and thighs blue.

Length.—5·3 to 5·8 inches; wing 2·8 to 2·9; tail 2·3 to 2·5; tarsus 0·7; bill from gape 0·75.

The female is similar to the male, but paler, and has no black on the chin and face; the frontal line and lores are dull white; the ear coverts greyish blue, with whitish shaft streaks.

Hab.—Ceylon and India generally, ranging to British Burmah.

Tickell's Redbreast is recorded from the N.-W. Provinces and Oudh, also Bengal, Kattiawar, Rajputana, Central India, the Central Provinces, the Carnatic,

Malabar Coast, Guzerat, Concan, Deccan, South India and British Burmah. It breeds during May and June throughout Central India, the Nilghiris, and the Western Ghauts, nesting in the hole of a tree or wall. The nest is made of moss and dry leaves, rather a clumsy structure; according to Mr. Parker, outwardly a mere heap of soft dead leaves and fine fibres, with almost always moss in or out. The eggs are greyish white (dull brownish pink? *Hume*), speckled with dull reddish brown; size 0·61 × 0·48. It affects open forests, groves, and gardens.

77. Siphia nigrorufa (*Jerd.*), *Sharpe, Cat. B. Br. Mus.* iv. p. 455; *Legge, B. Ceylon.* p. 425; *Murray, Avif. Brit. Ind.* i. p. 227, No. 261. Saxicola nigrorufa, *Jerd., Madras Journ.* x. p. 266. Ochromela nigrorufa, *Blyth, J. A. S. B.* xvi. p. 129; *Jerd., B. Ind.* i. p. 492, No. 300; *Hume, Nests and Eggs Ind. B.* p. 207; *id., Str. F.* 1876, p. 396; *Fairbank, Str. F.* 1877, p. 401.—The Black and Orange Fly-Catcher.

Head, nape and back of neck dusky black; cheeks and upper surface of body orange-rufous; wings black, the quills browner, white edged along the inner web; tail orange; thighs dusky, under wing coverts pale orange; rest of under surface of body orange-rufous, rather buffy on the middle of the abdomen; bill black; legs dirty reddish; irides hazel brown.

Length.—4·7 to 4·9 inches; wing 2·4; tail 1·9; tarsus 0·8.

The female is dusky on the head, also on the wings; wing coverts washed with orange.

Hab.—Ceylon and Southern India.

Jerdon says it has only been found on the summit of the Nilghiris and in Ceylon. It frequents the dense forests, preferring shady, damp and swampy places. Breeds on the Nilghiris. Eggs, 2 to 3, pale salmon in colour, 0·7 × 0·53; nest a large ball of dry sedges placed in a bush.

Family.—TURDIDÆ.

Bill slender but rather wide and depressed; *wings long and flat, with a very small bastard primary not more than half the length of the second*, the latter generally longer than the secondaries. Composed of birds generally migratory.

Sub-Family.—SYLVIINÆ—Grey Warblers.

The young in first plumage differ very slightly in colour from the adult, both being unspotted above and below. In rare instances in which the upper parts are spotted in the adult the spots are less conspicuous in the young. (*Seebohm.*)

Gen. Sylvia.—*Scop.*

Bill Sylviinæ, generally with more or less dark underneath; nostrils in a groove. Tail nearly even, generally with white on the outermost tail feathers;

bastard primary not extending beyond the primary coverts, or not more than 0·3; 2nd primary generally shorter than the 3rd and 4th; feet and tarsus stout, latter scutellated in front. The males of many have dark heads.

78. Sylvia affinis, *Blyth, Cat. B. Mus. As. Soc.* p. 187; *Hume, Str. F.* vii. p. 60; i. p. 197; ii. p. 332; iii. p 272; *Jerd., B. Ind.* ii. p. 209, No. 582; *Murray, Hdbk. Zool., &c., Sind*, p. 163; *Seebohm, Cat. B. Br. Mus.* v. p. 19; *Legge, B. Ceylon* p. 538; *Murray, Avif. Br. Ind.* i. p. 236, No. 277. Sylvia curruca, *apud Jerd., B. Ind.* ii. p. 209; *apud. Blf., East. Persia* ii. p. 175; *Murray, Vert. Zool., Sind*, p. 161.—The ALLIED GREY WARBLER.

General colour pale slaty or brownish grey; supercilium indistinct; wings and tail brownish; outermost tail feather on each side white on their outer webs; chin, throat, belly, and under tail coverts, also axillaries and under wing coverts, white, tinged greyish brown on the breast and flanks; bill and legs brown; irides light brown.

Length.—6 inches; wing 2·5; tail 2·25; bill at front 0·51.

Hab.—Ceylon and nearly all India; Sind, Punjab, N.-W. Provinces, Behar, Deccan, Kutch, Guzerat, Kattiawar, Jodhpore and Sambhur; also Beloochistan, Persia, S. Afghanistan and Turkestan. Seebohm says it breeds throughout Siberia, extending northwards almost to the limit of forest growth.

Gen. **Phylloscopus**.—*Boie.*—WILLOW-WARBLERS.

Bill Acrocephaline, pale underneath, slender, small, straight, with a few short rictal bristles; wings long, flat, and pointed, or short and rounded as in those which inhabit the plains and breed in the mountains near by; bastard primary small; greater wing coverts with pale tips in the spring plumage; *axillaries and under wing coverts yellow.*

This genus comprises a group of birds, mostly of small size, familiarly known as Willow or Tree Warblers, tolerably abundant throughout India during winter—a very few only of which are known to breed in the Himalayas. They are exclusively fly-catchers or insectivorous, feeding on minute insects and flies, which they pick off leaves and branches or capture in the air, and may be said to be strictly arboreal. The majority have their summer residence in Europe or Western Asia, and migrate thousands of miles in winter. Seebohm says: "In their breeding range these birds are palæarctic, ranging from the Atlantic to the Pacific, one species being known even to cross Behring's Straits into Alaska." Those which breed in the Himalayas ascend till they reach a palæarctic climate.

No mesial line on the crown:

79. Phylloscopus nitidus, *Blyth, J. A. S. B.* xii. p. 965; xiv. p 591; *Jerd., B. Ind.* ii. p. 193, No. 559; *Hume, Str. F.* 1873, p. 197; *Legge, Ibis*, 1874, p. 22; *Seebohm, Ibis*, 1877, p. 72; *id., Cat. B. Br. Mus.* v. p. 43; *Murray, Hdbk. Zool., &c., Sind*, p. 162; *id., Vert. Zool.*,

Sind, p. 159.; *id.*, *Avif. Brit. Ind.* i. p. 240, No. 283. Phyllopneuste nitida (*Blyth*), *Adam*, *Str. F.* 1873, p. 382.—The GREEN WILLOW-WARBLER.

Head, nape, back, scapulars, rump and upper tail coverts yellowish green; supercilium extending to the nape yellow; lesser wing coverts and tips and edges of the median ones like the back; greater wing coverts brown, edged with yellowish green and tipped yellow, forming a conspicuous wing band; primaries, their coverts and secondaries brown, edged on their outer webs with yellowish green: 2nd primary intermediate in length between 6th and 7th; exposed 1st primary 0·55 to 0·6; edge of the wing, under wing coverts and *entire under surface yellow or yellowish green*; in some specimens albescent on the chin; bill dusky brown; the lower mandible pale; legs light brown; irides dark brown.

Length.—4·5 to 4·75 inches; wing 2·5; bill at front 0·5.

Hab.—Ceylon; also Southern India, Sind, Punjab, N.-W. Provinces, Oudh, Bengal, Concan, Deccan and Nepaul, breeding in the Himalayas and wintering in the plains.

80. Phylloscopus viridanus, *Blyth, J. A. S. B.* xii. p. 967; *Jerd.*, *B. Ind.* ii. p. 193, No. 560; *Brooks*, *Ibis*, 1872, p. 31; *Scully*, *Str. F.* iv. p. 148; *Seebohm*, *Ibis*, 1877, p. 73; *Hume*, *Str. F.* vi. p. 356; *Legge*, *B. Ceylon* p. 555; *Murray*, *Avif. Brit. Ind.* p. 241, No. 284. Phyllopneuste viridanus, *Blyth and Wald.*, *B. Burm.* p. 105. Phylloscopus seebohmi, *Hume*, *Str. F.* v. p. 355.—The INDIAN WILLOW-WARBLER.

Similar to *Phylloscopus nitidus*, except that the upper plumage is tinged with dull olive green, and the quills narrowly tipped with pale white also, that the *greater coverts only are tipped with pale yellowish white*, and so forming only one wing bar; 3rd, 4th and 5th primaries longest; 2nd intermediate in length between 7th and 8th, sometimes between 6th and 7th; 2nd primary 0·5 to 0·65.

Length.—4 inches; wing 2·3 to 2·5; tarsus 0·75; culmen 0·45 to 0·5.

Hab.—Ceylon and the Himalayas up to Cashmere, where it breeds. In winter it is found all over India nearly. It has been recorded from Arrakan, in Tenasserim at Thatone, Moulmein, and Tavoy, and extends through the Indo-Burmese countries (?) to Cochin-China. In India proper it is recorded as having occurred in the N.-W. Provinces, Oudh and Bengal, also Rajputana and Southern India; also from Nepaul. Mr. Brooks found its nest in Cashmere at an elevation of 11,000 feet. It was a domed structure, placed on the steep bank side of a ravine full of birch trees, but it did not contain eggs.

81. Phylloscopus magnirostris, *Blyth, J. A. S. B.* xii. p. 966; *Jerd.*, *B. Ind.* ii. p. 191, No. 556; *Brooks*, *Str. F.* iii. p. 243; *Seebohm*, *Ibis*, 1877, p. 77; *Hume and Dav.*, *Str. F.* vi. p. 355; *Hume*, *Str. F.* viii. p. 102; *Seebohm*, *Cat. B. Br. Mus.* v. p. 47; *Oates*, *B. Br. Burm.* i. p. 82;

Legge, B. Ceylon p. 553; *Murray, Avif. Brit. Ind.* i. p. 242, No. 287. Phyllopneuste magnirostris, *Bl., B. Burm.* p. 105.—The LARGE-BILLED WILLOW-WARBLER.

Above dark olive green, slightly darker on the head and somewhat greener on the rump; eye stripe pale yellowish white; lores and feathers behind the eye brown; ear coverts yellowish white, suffused with brown; wing coverts and wings brown, edged with olive, the median coverts with small and the greater coverts with large yellowish white tips, forming two distinct wing bars; tail brown, edged with olive green on the outer webs and tipped paler beneath; the inner webs, except those of the central tail feathers, with a narrow greyish white margin. Under surface of body pale greyish yellow, greyest on the breast and flanks; axillaries, under wing coverts and thighs greyish yellow. Bill much decurved at tip, the rictal bristles well developed; upper mandible dark brown; under mandible pale, darker towards the tip; legs, feet and claws bluish brown; 4th and 5th primaries longest; 2nd intermediate between 7th and 8th; 1st primary 0·6 to 0·75. Irides earthy brown; legs carneous, bill horny.

Length.—5·4 inches; wing 2·7; tail 2·2; bill from gape 0·65.

Hab.—Ceylon; also South India, the Punjab, N.-W. Provinces, Oudh, Bengal, Central India, the Central Provinces, Deccan, British Burmah, Cashmere and Nepal. It has been recorded from Arrakan by Blyth. Davison is said to have procured it in Tenasserim, and Mr. Hume records it from the Malay Peninsula. It is generally spread over Ceylon, the whole Peninsula of India, and the Andamans. It summers in the Himalayas up to Cashmere, where it breeds, and extends to Sikkim.

Mr. Brooks, who met with this species in the Himalayas, says: "The conditions this bird require are wooded cliffs or very steep rocky banks impracticable for man, and plenty of flowing water below. Above a roaring torrent it is in its element and sings most vigorously.

Gen. Acrocephalus.—*Naum.*

Bill large, depressed and broad at the base, with moderately developed rictal bristles in two species only; the bill is as slender as in *Locustella;* wings moderately long; 3rd and 4th quills generally longest; bastard primary minute in one or two species only, extending in length beyond the primary coverts; tail more rounded than in *Hypolais*.

82. Acrocephalus stentoreus, *Hemp. et. Ehr. Symb. Phys. Aves* fol. b.b; *Heugl., Orn. N. Afr.* i. p. 287; *Shelley, B. Egypt* p. 95; *Blf., East Persia* ii. p. 194; *Legge, B. Ceylon* p. 541; *Murray, Avif. Brit. Ind.* i. p. 257, No. 309. Agrobates brunnescens, *Jerd., Madr. Journ.* x. p. 269. Acrocephalus brunnescens (*Jerd.*), *Blyth, Cat. B. Mus. As. Soc.* p. 181; *Jerd., B. Ind.* ii. p. 154, No. 515; *Hume and Henderson, Lahore to*

Yarkand, p. 214, pl. xvi.; *Murray, Hdbk. Zool., &c., Sind,* p. 152; *Str. F.* vol. ii. p. 330; iii. p. 369.—The INDIAN GREAT REED-WARBLER.

Above light olive brown, with a very slight ferruginous tinge, paler on the rump; wings and tail dark brown; the quills and lateral tail feathers pale edged; supercilium buffy white, chin white; throat greyish white, as also is the breast, but with a fulvous tinge; rest of under surface yellowish or fulvous white; bill dark brown, fleshy at base of lower mandible; irides yellowish; legs slaty brown.

Length.—7·5 to 8·5 inches; wing 3 to 3·35; tail 3; tarsus 1 to 1·1.

Hab.—Ceylon and India generally, extending to Nepal. In Ceylon, Mr. Parker says he met with this species at one tank in the Manaar district. He adds that it is a permanent resident at Tissa, southern provinces, and breeds there in July, in which month he found a nest containing two eggs. It is a cool season visitor in the northern provinces. As the village tanks dry up in March and April, all the birds that are dependent on them leave the district, and this Reed Warbler among them. His observations are to the effect that its distribution depends probably upon local circumstances in this manner. It vacates its quarters when the reeds are bent or lie down, and returns to the same spots when the food supply and the shelter that it requires are renewed; but that it is certainly not a regular migrant in the N.-W. Province of the island, since it has been procured there by him in January, March, May, July and August. The eggs are 5—6 in number, and bear a close resemblance to those of *Locustella certhiola*—rosy white, speckled with reddish brown. The nest is a deep cup attached to the reed stems near the water level, and consists entirely of rough grass stems exteriorly interspersed with feathers. Inside it is lined with finer grass stems. The bird is a great skulk, and to observe it in a clump of reeds one must step well into them, crouch down, and remain perfectly quiet for a few minutes. It soon overcomes its feeling of prudence, and will then be seen noiselessly working its way up to another among the rushes. Occasionally it may be seen perched with head high and tail depressed on nearly vertical dead branches of low trees, uttering its strange harsh note in reply to some comrade in the reeds below. Appears to be a resident in Egypt; breeds in Turkestan and the highlands of Persia; also in Cashmere and Nepal. (*Seebohm.*) In Sind it breeds in August. It is probably also a resident of Beloochistan and Afghanistan, where it occurs in some numbers. Recorded from Rajputana, North Guzerat and Kutch.

83. Acrocephalus dumetorum, *Blyth, J. A. S. B.* xviii. p. 815; *Jerd., B. Ind.* ii. p. 155, No. 516; *Dresser, B. Eur.* pt. liii.; *Seebohm, Cat. B. Br. Mus.* v. p. 96; *Legge, B. Ceylon* p. 545; *Murray, Avif. Brit. Ind.* p. 258, No. 310. Calamodyta dumetorum (*Blyth*), *Gray, Handlist B.* p. 207. Salicaria eurhyncha, *Severtz., Turkest. Jevotn.* pp. 66, 128; *id., Str. F.* 1875, p. 425.—BLYTH'S REED-WARBLER.

Upper parts olive brown; supercilium very pale, nearly obsolete; wings and tail slightly darker brown, narrowly edged paler on the outer webs; beneath brownish buff, paler on the chin and throat; under wing coverts buffy white; bill dusky, fleshy at base of lower mandible; legs pale horn brown; irides yellowish.

Length.—6 inches; wing 2·5; tail 2·3; bill 0·7.

Hab.—Ceylon; also South India, in Travancore and the Nilghiris. Occurs in Europe; breeds in the Himalayas, and winters in Sind, Punjab, N.-W. Provinces, Deccan, the Carnatic, Central India, Bengal to Assam, and Nepal. Breeds in the Himalayas at altitudes up to 7,000 feet. Nest a globular structure, similar to that of the last. Eggs, 4 in number, white, speckled with rufous. Size about 0·62 × 9·5.

Gen. **Locustella**.—*Kaup*.

Bill slender, about half as long as the head; rictal bristles weak; forehead without hairs; 1st primaries very small; 2nd reaches nearly to the tip of the wing; tail rounded.

84. Locustella certhiola (*Pall.*), *Seebohm., Cat. B. Br. Mus.* A. p. 114; *Hume, Str F.* viii. p. 100; *Oates, B. Br. Burm.* i. p. 102; *Legge, B. Ceylon* p. 548; *Murray, Avif. Brit. Ind.* i. p. 259, No. 312. Motacilla certhiola, *Pall., Zoogr. Rosso-Asiat.* i. p. 509. Locustella rubescens, *Blyth, J. A. S. B.* xiv. p. 582; *Jerd., B. Ind.* iii. p. 160. Locustella temporalis, *Jerd., B. Ind.* ii. p. 160. Calamodyta doriæ, *Salv., Atti. R. Ac. Sc. Tor.* iii. p. 531; *Sharpe, Ibis*, 1876, p. 41, pl. ii., fig 2.—The LESSER OR RUDDY REED-WARBLER.

Upper parts russet brown, greyer on the head, more tawny on the rump and upper tail coverts, and paler on the edges of the wing coverts; tail feathers blackish brown, irregularly margined with rufous brown, and broadly terminated with whitish; stripe over the eye and a streak from the bill under the cheeks and ear coverts yellowish buff; ear coverts hair brown; under wing coverts whitish; primaries and secondaries dark brown, narrowly edged with rufous brown; under surface buff, paler on the throat and upper breast, which and the whole breast are spotted with black brown. In the next stage the throat and breast are unspotted, and the whole under surface, including these, are brighter yellow; the rump is also unstreaked or almost so; the rectrices are not so broadly tipped white, and the eye streak, chin, throat, and the whole lower plumage are yellowish buff. In spring the adult birds have the head blackish brown, each feather narrowly edged with pale reddish brown. An unmarked reddish brown collar is present in some; the back, scapulars, and wing coverts dark blackish brown, rather broadly edged with reddish brown; the rump is also reddish brown; the upper tail coverts reddish brown with a central spot of black; outer tail feathers nearly all black, with scarcely any rufous margins; towards the middle the feathers become less black and more margined with rufous, the central pair being rufous with only a black shaft; all the feathers are tipped with white; chin, throat and centre of abdomen whitish; rest of the under parts delicate buff; bill dark brown; legs whitish; irides sepia brown.

Length.—5·5 inches; wing 2·3; tail 2·2; tarsus 0·85; bill from gape 0·7.

Hab.—Central and Eastern Siberia, where it breeds. It passes through China on migration, and winters in Ceylon, India, the Burmah Peninsula, and the Islands of the Malay Archipelago. In India it is found in the N.-W. Provinces, Oudh, Bengal, and Central India, also Assam. It also recorded from the Khasia Hills. In Burmah Oates says it occurs in Pegu, and probably also in Arrakan and Tenasserim. It summers in Siberia and occasionally straggles into Europe, when it is shy, and is seldom seen except by accident. Oates says that in Burmah it swarms in inundated paddy fields to an incredible extent. After the 16th December the bird disappears entirely. Quoting Dybowsky, Oates has it that it makes its nest in a tuft of grass close to the ground, and lays five or six eggs, which are rosy white, speckled with reddish brown.

GROUP—BRADYPTERI.

Aberrant Reed Warblers with 10—12 tail feathers, and allied to the Grass-Warblers.

Gen. **Schœnicola**.—*Blyth.*

Bill moderate, rather deep, much compressed; culmen slightly curved; rictal bristles moderate, few; wings moderate, slightly rounded; 4th quill longest, 3rd equal to the 5th; tail moderate, the feathers broad; under tail coverts long, reaching to more than half the length of the tail; tarsus long; plumage lax.

85. Schœnicola platyura (*Jerd.*), *Blyth, J. A. S. B.* xiii. p. 374; *Jerd., B. Ind.* ii. p. 73, No. 442; *Hume, Str. F.* 1878, p. 37; *id., Str. F.* 1879, p. 97; *Brooks, Str. F.* 1881, p. 209; *Hume,* t. c. p. 211; *Legge, Birds Ceylon* p. 532; *Murray, Avif. Brit. Ind.* i. p. 270, No. 330; *Hume, Str. F.* 1880, pp. 234-260; *Butler, Cat. B. Bom. Pres.* p. 43; *Sharpe, P. Z. S.* 1881, p. 920; *id., Cat. B. Br. Mus.* vii. p. 110. Timalia platyura, *Jerd., Madr. Journ.* xiii. p. 170.—The Broad-tailed Reed-Bird.

Upper surface russet or rufous brown, including the ear and wing coverts; quills dusky, externally margined with russet-brown, the innermost secondaries the same on both webs; tail russet-brown, obscurely banded with dusky brown under certain lights; the outer feathers darker and tipped with ashy; lores whitish; supercilium fulvous, also the cheeks and sides of the neck; throat, centre of breast, and abdomen whitish, the former washed with fulvous on the lower parts, also the sides of the body, flanks, thighs, and under tail coverts—the latter washed with ashy at the tips; under wing coverts and axillaries buffish white. Bill horny yellow, 0·4; legs fleshy yellow; irides yellowish brown.

Length.—5·8 to 6·3 inches; wing 2·5 to 2·65; tail 2·6 to 2·8; tarsus 0·8 to 0·85.

Hab.—Ceylon and Southern India (Belgaum, Travancore, Wynaad, at the foot of the Nilghiris). According to Jerdon the Broad-tailed Reed-Bird affects reeds in swampy places. In their actions and habits, Captain Butler says: "These birds resemble *Chætornis striata*, and in the breeding season rise constantly into the air, chirruping like that species, and descending afterwards in the same way on to some low bush or tussock of grass, sometimes even on to the telegraph wires. They are fearful little skulks. If you attempt to pursue them, at once they disappear into the grass, from whence it is almost impossible to flush them again unless you all but tread on them. They breed in September. The food of the Broad-tailed Reed-Bird consists chiefly of insects." Captain Butler's notes, in *Str. F.* ix., p. 262, quoted by Mr. Hume, in regard to the nidification of this species are to the effect that the nest is composed of coarse grass, with an entrance on one side, built in long grass, and about a foot from the ground; the eggs, he says, have a purplish white ground, sprinkled all over with numerous small specks and spots of purplish brown and purple (brownish red, almost black in some), with a cap of the same at the large end. They are moderately broad ovals, with but little gloss. Size 0·73 × 0·6.

Gen. **Prinia**.—*Horsf.*

Bill of moderate length, stoutish, slightly deeper than broad at nostrils; culmen moderately curving, and not exceeding the length of hind toe and claw; rictal bristles well developed, 2 to 3 on each side; wings short and rounded, the first three primaries nearly equal; 4th and 5th generally longest; tail graduated, long, and of 10 feathers; tarsus long; claws moderately curved.

86. Prinia inornata, *Sykes, P. Z. S.* 1837, p. 89; *Jerd., Mad. Journ.* xi. p. 4; *Blyth, J. A. S. B.* xiii. p. 376; *Sharpe, Cat. B. Br. Mus.* vii. p. 195; *Oates, B. Brit. Burm.* i. p. 114; *Murray, Avif. Br. Ind.* i. p. 279, No. 340. Sylvia longicaudata, *Tick., J. A. S. B.* ii. p. 576. Prinia fusca, *Hodgs., Gray's Zool., Misc.* p. 82; *id., P. Z. S.* 1845, p. 29. Prinia adamsi, *Jerd., B. Ind.* ii. p. 170, No. 533; *Hume, Nests and Eggs* p. 335; *id., Str. F.* viii. p. 101. Drymoipus inornatus, *Jerd., B. Ind.* ii. p. 178, No. 543; *Hume, Nests and Eggs* p. 346; *Hume and Henderson, Lahore to Yarkand*, pl. xvii. fig. 1; *Brooks, Str F.* iii. p. 495; vii. p. 468. Drymoipus longicaudatus, *Jerd., B. Ind.* ii. p. 180, No. 544; *Butler, Str. F.* iii. p. 483; *Brooks, Str. F.* iv. p. 229; *Hume, Str. F.* iv. p. 407. Drymoipus fuscus, *Hume, Nests* *and Eggs* p. 348. Drymoipus terricolor, *Hume, Nests and Eggs* p. 349; *Brooks, Str. F.* iv. p. 229; *Hume, Str. F.* iv. p. 407. Drymoipus longicaudus, *Hume, Nests and Eggs* p. 350. Drymœca longicaudata, *Bl., B. Burm.* p. 118; *Hume, Str. F.* viii. p. 101. Drymoica fusca, *Hume, Str. F.* viii. p. 101. Drymœca insularis, *Legge, Birds of Ceylon*, pp. 529, 1216, pl. xxv. fig. 2. Prinia blanfordi, *Wald. in Bl., B. Burm.* p. 118; *Oates, B. Br. Burm.* i. p. 112. Drymoipus extensicauda (*Swinh.*), *apud Oates, Str. F.* iii. p. 340. Drymoica blanfordi, *Hume and Dav., Str. F.* vi. p. 349.—The Indian Wren-Warbler.

Winter.—Upper plumage and tail rufous brown, the feathers on the crown dark centred, the tail feathers tipped pale ashy, with a black subterminal spot more distinct when seen from below; wings brown, edged with bright rufous; under surface of body fulvous, rather darker on the breast, flanks, and under tail coverts; thighs dark rufous. The young in first plumage are very rufous.

In breeding plumage the upper surface is ashy or greyish brown, with indications of dark centres to the feathers, especially of the head; wings dark brown, edged with ashy white or brownish ashy; the primary coverts and quills with narrow rufous brown edges, and the inner secondaries with fulvous brown; tail pale brown with dusky cross bars under certain lights; all, except the centre feathers, white at the tip, and a tolerably well defined subterminal bar of blackish; lores, supercilium, cheeks and ear coverts white, the latter tinged with fulvous; under surface of the body pale yellowish buff, whiter on the throat; thighs tawny rufous; sides of upper breast ashy; axillaries and under wing coverts yellowish white; bill black; legs and feet pale yellowish fleshy; iris hazel brown (*Brooks*), orange yellow (*Oates*).

Length.—In summer 5·25; in winter 6 inches; wing 1·9 to 2; tail in summer 2·25; winter 3 inches; culmen 0·4; tarsus 0·8.

Hab.—Ceylon; South India from Mysore to Cape Comorin, and the whole of India, ranging westward into Sind, eastward through Assam, the Burmese countries, Southern China, Formosa, and Hainan. Occurs throughout Sind, parts of Beloochistan and Southern Afghanistan, Punjab, N.-W Provinces, Oudh, Bengal, the Concan, Deccan, South India, Behar, Khandesh, Cachar, all Burmah and Nepaul. Oates says it is an amusing little bird. Perched on the summit of a stalk of elephant grass, it gives out its monotonous song, consisting of one note repeated some twenty times; then, with its ample tail held at right angles to the back, it skips away to the bottom of the next tuft only to reappear on the summit with its persistent little song. These birds seem hardly able to regulate their flight. They seldom fly more than twenty yards, and in this short space they appear in imminent peril of turning sundry somersaults, for the bill on these occasions points to the ground, while the tail bent well over the back is nearly horizontal. The Indian Wren-Warbler breeds wherever it is found. The nest is cylindrical or oval in shape, made entirely of fine grasses most strongly woven together; although the walls can be seen through, yet they resist any ordinary efforts to tear them asunder. Altogether the nest is a beautiful specimen of bird architecture. The eggs, usually 4 in number, are pale blue, marked with spots and scrawls of purplish brown.

87. **Prinia sylvatica,** *Jerd., Madr. Journ.* xi. p. 4; *Blyth, J. A. S. B.* xiii. p. 376; *Murray, Avif. Brit. Ind.* p. 280, No. 341. Prinia neglecta, *Jerd., Madr. Journ.* xiii. p. 130. Drymoica sylvatica, *Blyth, J. A. S. Beng.* xvi. p. 458; *id., Cat. B. Mus. As. Soc.*, p. 142. Drymoica jerdoni, *Blyth, J. A. S. B.* xvi. p. 459. Drymoica neglecta, *Gray, Gen. B.* i. p. 164; *Ball, Str. F.* ii. p. 218. Drymoipus validus, *Jerd., B. Ind.* ii. p. 182. Drymoipus sylvaticus, *Jerd.* t. c. p. 181, No. 545; *Hume, Nests and Eggs Ind. B.* p. 351. Drymoipus jerdoni, t. c. p. 180; *Hume, Str. F.* 1873, p. 437; 1874, p. 453. Drymœca valida, *Blyth, Ibis*, 1867, p. 302; *Hume, Str. F.* 1879, p. 101; *Legge, B. Ceylon* p. 525. Suya gangetica, *Blyth, Ibis*, 1867, p. 23; *Hume, Str. F.* 1877, p. 138; 1878, p. 6; 1879, p. 101. Drymoipus rufescens, *Hume, Nests and Eggs Ind. B.* p 351; *Butler, Str. F.* 1875, p. 484; *Hume*, t. c. p. 484; *Brooks, Str. F.* 1876, p. 229. Drymoipus insignis, *Hume, Nests and Eggs Ind. B.* p. 351. Drymœca rufescens, *Hume, Str. F.* 1879, p. 101. Drymœca neglecta, *Hume*, t. c. p. 101, *Dav. and Wenden*, t. c. p. 407; *Vidal, Str. F.* 1880, p. 480.—The JUNGLE WREN-WARBLER.

Breeding Plumage.—Above dark brown, slightly paler on the lower back and rump; head and hindneck dusky ash brown; lores dull white; no supercilium present; ear coverts dusky brown, with obscure yellowish shaft lines; cheeks and under surface of body yellowish white; the abdomen pure white; sides of breast ashy; flanks fulvescent; thighs tawny brown; under tail coverts pale yellowish white; upper tail coverts and centre tail feathers pale reddish brown, crossed with obscure dusky bars under certain lights, the near feathers brown along the outer web and white on the inner, shaded more or less with pale sooty brown; external tail feathers almost entirely white; lesser and median wing coverts, also scapulars, dark brown with ashy margins; greater coverts margined with reddish brown, also the quills. *In the winter plumage* the tail feathers have no white on the inner web, but the external feathers are tipped with white, and have a tolerably distinct subterminal black bar; bill brown black; irides hazel; legs and feet yellowish.

Length.—6·3 to 6·5 inches; wing 2·55 to 2·6; tail 2·85 to 3·3 in winter plumage; tarsus 0·9; culmen 0·55.

Hab.—Ceylon, and the whole of India south of the Himalayas. Recorded from the N.-W. Provinces, Bengal, Assam, Concan, Deccan, Central and Southern India, Malabar Coast, Travancore, Nepaul and Cashmere.

Habits same as the last. Mr. Hume in his *Nests and Eggs, Indian Birds,* refers to the nidification of this species under all the synonyms quoted above. Generally it may be said that the nest is a deep cup, made of grass, well woven and neat, usually fixed in a thorny shrub, and lined with a little soft down. Eggs, 2 to 4, pale blue, with larger purplish brown blotches, or unmarked.

Gen. **Burnesia**.—*Jerd.*

Bill longer and more slender than in Prinia. Culmen exceeding the length of hind toe and claw; rictal setæ fine and minute, not reaching beyond nostrils; plumage streaked; tail of ten feathers, strongly graduated.

88. Burnesia socialis (*Sykes*), *Sharpe, Cat. B. Br. Mus.* vii. p. 208; *Murray, Avif. Brit. Ind.* i. p. 282. Prinia socialis, *Sykes, P. Z. S.* 1832, p. 89; *Jerd., Madr. Journ* xi. p. 3; *id., Birds Ind.* ii. p. 170, No. 534; *Blanf., Ibis,* 1867, p. 464; *Butler, Str. F.* 1875, p. 479; *Fairbank, Str. F.* 1876, p. 259; *id.,* 1877, p. 406; *Vidal, Str. F.* 1880, p. 67. Prinia stewarti, *Blyth, J. A. S. B.* xvi. p. 455; *Jerd., B. Ind.* ii. p. 171, No. 535; *Hume, Str. F.* 1875, p. 480; *id., Str. F.* 1876, p. 497; 1878, p. 319; 1879, p. 101. Prinia brevicauda, *Legge, B. Ceylon,* p. 521. Cisticola poliocephala (*Anders.*), *Sharpe, Cat. B. Br. Mus.* vii. p. 257.—The DARK-ASHY WREN-WARBLER.

Crown of the head and back, also upper tail coverts, dark slaty grey; lores and a streak above the eye buffy white, a dark spot in front of the eye; ear coverts and cheeks light tawny buff, slaty grey along the upper margin of the former; rump with a few tawny buff feathers on each side; lesser and median coverts like the back; greater coverts dusky brown, externally edged with light brown; tail feathers light brown, with a subterminal broad bar of black and tipped white; throat whitish, slightly washed with fulvous; lower throat, foreneck, chest, breast, sides of the body, flanks, thighs and under tail coverts tawny buff, paler on the latter; abdomen white; under wing coverts and axillaries light tawny buff; upper mandible black; lower pale horny; legs dull yellowish brown; iris brown.

Length.—4·6 to 5 inches; wing 1·8; tail 1·8; tarsus 0·8.

The young bird is rufous brown above, a little more dusky on the head; rump and upper tail coverts brighter rufous; tail rufous brown, tipped with fulvous white, and with a subterminal black bar; an ochraceous superciliary streak present.

Hab.—Ceylon to Nepaul, Assam, (Northern, Southern, Central and Western India generally). Recorded from north of the Godavery, the N.-W. Provinces, at Agra, Cashmere, Punjab, the Deccan, Concan, Kattiawar, Saugor, the Nilghiris, Khandeish, and Dehra Doon.

Its habits are those of *Burnesia flaviventris*, except that, unlike *flaviventris*, it also frequents gardens, hedges, and vegetable crops. Eggs usually reddish white or brick red, with numerous darker red spots at the large end. Nest similar to that of *flaviventris*.

Gen. **Sutoria**.—*Nicholson*.

Bill long and slender, rather wide at base; rictal bristles few; culmen exceeding the hind toe and claw in length; 5th and 6th quills longest and equal; tail of 12 feathers, strongly graduated or rounded, with the middle tail feathers elongated beyond the rest and pointed. The birds of this genus, also of *Orthotomus*, are remarkable for the beautiful nests they make.

89. Sutoria sutoria (*Forst.*), *Sharpe, Cat. B. Br. Mus.* vii. p. 215; *Oates, B. Br. Burm.* i. p. 107; *Murray, Avif. Brit. Ind.* i. p. 285, No. 346. Motacilla sutoria, *Forst., Ind. Zool.* p. 17. Motacilla longicauda, *Gm., Syst. Nat.* i. p. 954. Orthotomus longicauda, *Moore, P. Z. S.* 1854, p. 81; *Jerd. B. Ind.* ii. p. 165, No. 530; *Hume, Nests and Eggs* p. 331; *Hume, Str. F.* iii. p. 135; *Bl. and Wald., B. Burm.* p. 120; *Murray, Vert. Zool., Sind,* p. 151. Orthotomus edele (*Tem.*) *apud. Bl. and Wald., B. Burm.* p. 120. Orthotomus sutorius, *Sharpe, Ibis,* 1877, p. 109; *Oates, Str. F.* v. p. 158; *Hume and Dav., Str. F.* vi. p. 345; *Hume, Str. F.* viii. p. 101; *Scully, Str. F.* viii. p. 305; *Legge, B. Ceylon* p. 517.—The INDIAN TAILOR BIRD.

Forehead and crown rufous; back of head and neck ashy, with a very faint rufous tinge; sides of nape with dark brown setæ on each side; back, scapulars, rump and upper tail coverts yellowish green; edge of wing white; primaries and secondaries brown, edged with olive green, more distinct on the secondaries; all, for two-thirds their length, narrowly margined basally on the inner webs with whitish; under wing coverts buffy white; tail light brown, the central feathers greenish, and the lateral ones edged on the outer web with the same and tipped with white; chin, throat, breast, belly and under tail coverts white; the flanks cinereous; a dark spot on each side of the throat; bill horny brown, paler on the under mandible; legs brown; irides reddish yellow.

Length.—6 to 6·5 inches; wing 1·9 to 2; tail 3·5; bill at front 0·5.

Hab.—Ceylon, and throughout India to Nepaul and Cashmere, also British Burmah. Common in the Deccan, Concan, Kutch, Kattiawar and North Guzerat, also the Punjab, N.-W. Provinces, Oudh, Bengal, and Central India. In Sind it is common in all the open country studded with trees, and affects the acacias chiefly. Breeds in July and August. Eggs, 2 to 4, white, spotted with reddish brown, thicker and closer at the larger end. Nest made of leaves, stitched with cotton or fibre, and lined with wool and cotton.

Gen. **Cisticola**.—*Kaup*.

Bill shorter and slightly more slender than that of *Phyllergates* and *Prinia;* rictal bristles two on each side and well developed; wings short; 1st quill short, 2nd generally equal to 7th and shorter than the 6th; tail of 12 feathers, shorter than in *Prinia,* broader than in both *Prinia* and *Phyllergates* and somewhat rounded; tarsus long; feet proportionally large, with the lateral toes nearly equal and the claws not so much curved as in *Prinia*.

The genus *Cisticola* forms a small group of small birds averaging in total length 3 to 4·5 inches, nearly all possessing a streaked plumage, and frequenting chiefly grass and reeds. In respect to the changes of plumage of this group, after examining all the available material in different Museums and in the collections of Naturalists, Mr. Sharpe gives his conclusions in Vol. vii. of the *Cat. B. Br. Mus.* p. 235. He says:—"(1) The male and female are more or less different in the breeding plumage, the tendency being in the male to have a uniform coloured head, while the female's is striped. (2) The female's winter plumage resembles her summer dress, but is rather more mealy and the tail is longer. (3) In the autumn moult the male passes into a winter plumage, when he resembles the female. (4) The first winter plumage of the young bird resembles that of the old female, and that they have longer tails. (5) The male is always larger than the female." "There are," he adds, "probably some exceptions among the plain backed species." The range is given as the whole of Africa and Madagascar, South Europe and countries bordering the Mediterranean, eastwards to India, Ceylon, the Burmese countries and China, as well as Japan, the Malayan Peninsula, and throughout the whole of the Indo-Malayan sub-region.

Nest a roundish ball of dry grass, with a circular entrance on one side near the top. Eggs, 3 to 4, white, speckled all over with reddish brown and pale lavender, rather densely at the larger end. It is like the *Malacocerci*, nearly always seen in flocks of half-a-dozen or more flying from bush to bush, scarcely ever leaving a bush without having examined it from the top to the root stalks.

90. Cisticola gracilis (*Franklin*), *Sharpe, Cat. B. Br. Mus.* vii. p. 253; *Oates, B. Br. Burm.* i. p. 119. Prinia gracilis, *Frankl., P. Z. S.* 1831, p. 119; *Jerd., Madr. Journ.* xi. p. 3; *id., Birds Ind.* ii. p. 172. No. 536; *Hume, Nests and Eggs Ind. B.* p. 341; *Wald. in Blyth, B. Burm.* p. 119; *Hume, Str. F.* iii. p. 136; viii. p 101; *Brooks,* t. c p. 476. Prinia hodgsoni, *Blyth, J. A. S. B.* xiii. p. 376; *Jerd., B. Ind.* ii. p. 173, No. 538; *Hume, Nests and Eggs* p. 342; *Wald. in Blyth B. Burm.* p. 119; *Hume, Str. F.* iii. p. 136; *Legge, Str. F.* iii. p 203; *id., B. Ceylon.* p. 523; *Oates, Str. F.* vii. p. 480. Prinia albogularis, *Wald., Ann. Nat. Hist.*, Series 4, vol. v. p. 219. Drymœca gracilis, *Dresser, B. Eur.* iii p. 13. Prinia rufula, *Godw.-Austen, P. Z. S.* 1874, p. 47; *id., J. A. S. B.* xliii. pt. ii. p. 165; *Hume, Str. F.* iii. p. 397; *id.* t. c. viii. p. 101.—FRANKLIN'S GRASS-WARBLER.

Above, including the wings and tail, ashy grey, the wings edged with pale rufous; tail with a subterminal patch of brown on each feather *tipped with whitish*, and obsoletely across with dusky under certain lights; ear coverts whitish in front, greyish behind; lores and feathers above the eye dusky; cheeks chin, throat, abdomen, vent and under tail coverts white or yellowish white; *breast ashy, forming a band across;* under wing coverts and axillaries white or yellowish white; sides of the body and flanks slightly tinged with ashy; bill black; legs and and feet yellowish fleshy; irides reddish yellow.

In winter plumage the upper parts, including the tail, are rufous brown; the wings brown, broadly edged with rufous; the tail with subterminal dark patches and white tips; lower plumage white, tinged with fulvous; supercilium whitish.

Length.—3·7 to 4·2 inches; wing 1·75; tail 1·55 to 2·15; tarsus 0·7; culmen 0·5; from gape 0·55.

Hab.—Nepaul to Bhootan and throughout the more moist regions of India and Ceylon, ranging eastwards into the Burmese countries as far south as Pegu. It is also recorded from Malayana. It occurs also in the Concan, Deccan, and Bengal. In Central and Northern India, and on the Vindhian hills near Mhow and at Saugor, it is said to be not uncommon, also in the Nepaul Terai and lower bills. In Southern India it is recorded from the Malabar Coast, the Wynaad, the slopes of the Nilghiris and on the Eastern Ghauts, while in British Burmah it occurs throughout Pegu and Arrakan. It has been met with in Tenasserim also, and has been got in Karin by Captain Wardlaw-Ramsay.

Franklin's Wren-Warbler affects brushwood and the outskirts of tree forest, where there is a plentiful undergrowth of grass. In such localities it is abundant. It breeds throughout the rains, making a nest very like that of the Tailor Bird but smaller, sewing the leaves together with cotton, and with the same material, as wool and soft vegetable fibres lining the nest. The eggs, 3 to 4 in number, are pale blue with some brown or reddish spots.

91. Cisticola cisticola (*Tem.*), *Sharpe, Cat. B.* vii. p. 259; *Oates, B. Br. Burm.* i. p. 115; *Murray, Avif. Brit. Ind.* i. p. 292, No. 356. Sylvia cisticola, *Tem., Man. d' Orn.* i. p. 228; *id.*, pl. col. 6, fig. 3. Prinia cursitans, *Frankl., P. Z. S.* 1831, p. 118. Cisticola schœnicola, *Bonap., Comp. List. B. Eur. and N. Am.* p. 12; *Jerd., B. Ind.* ii. p. 174, No. 539; *Hume, Nests and Eggs* p. 343; *id., Str. F.* i. p. 439; iii. p. 137; *Blyth, B. Burm.* p. 119; *Oates, Str. F.* v. p. 158. Salicaria brunniceps, *Tem. et Schleg. Faun. Jap. Aves.* p. 134, pl. 20. Cisticola munipurensis, *Godw.-Austen, P. Z. S.* 1874, p. 47; *id., J. A. S. B.* xiii. pt. ii. p. 165, pl. ix., fig. 2; *Hume, Str. F.* iii. p. 397; viii. p. 101. Cisticola cursitans, *Dresser, B. Eur.* iii. p. 3; *Hume, Str. F.* v. p. 90; *Hume and Dav., Str. F.* vi. p. 349; *Hume, Str. F.* viii. p. 101; *Legge, B. Ceylon* p. 531. Cisticola homalura, *Hume, Str. F.* v. pp. 93, 350; viii. p. 101.—The Rufous Grass-Warbler.

Forehead rufescent; crown, hindneck and back dark brown, all the feathers margined and edged with rufous; rump and upper tail coverts rufous; primaries and secondaries dusky brown, edged on their outer webs with pale rufous; tertiaries dark brown, edged and tipped with pale rufous; edging near the tips and the tips whitish; tail dusky brown above, pale brown below, the feathers with a broad subterminal band of black tipped with white; the dark spots and white tips more distinct on the under surface; chin and throat whitish or rufescent white; breast and belly rufescent; vent and under tail coverts paler; bill dusky brown; the under mandible paler; irides brownish.

Length.—4·5 to 4·75 inches; wings 2 to 2·25; tail 1·75 to 2; bill at front 0·25.

Hab.—Ceylon and India generally to Nepaul; British Burmah, S.-W. Europe, Africa, Egypt, Arabia, Deccan, Concan, Kutch, Kattiawar, Jodhpore, and N. Guzerat; also Bengal and Central India.

Affects the tamarisk jungles along the banks of rivers and thin jungle generally, and breeds in July and August. Nest a deep purse, beautifully made of vegetable down, and placed in a tuft of soft grass. Eggs, usually five, white, speckled with reddish.

Sub-Family—TURDINÆ.

Gen. **Geocichla**.—*Kuhl.*

This genus, as now revised, includes a number of well-known and very familiar genera, such as *Zoothera, Oreocincla, Turdulus, Cichlopasser, Chamœtylus* and *Psophocichla,* and forms a well-defined group of a number of birds commonly known as Ground-Thrushes. The characters of this group as given by Seebohm in the Vth Vol. of the British Museum Catalogue are briefly these: "Basal portion of the outside web of all the secondaries and of many of the primaries white, occasionally tinted with buff, but abruptly defined from the brown of the rest of the quills. Axillaries parti-coloured, the basal half white, the terminal half black, slaty grey or brown; under wing coverts the same, the basal portion, however, *being black and the terminal* half white. Young generally spotted on the back and breast. Bill moderately stout, somewhat wide at base, gently arched throughout, and moderately hooked at the tip; rictal bristles more or less developed; wing more or less rounded; tail of 12 to 14 feathers (14 in three species only); toes long; plumage generally soft and silky, usually mottled above and spotted beneath, and dull blue and ferruginous in colour. Peculiar to the Indian region."

Tail twelve feathers.

92. Geocichla citrina (*Lath.*), *Seebohm, Cat. B. Br. Mus.* v. p. 172. Turdus citrinus, *Lath., Ind. Orn.* i. p. 350. Geocichla citrina (*Lath.*), *Jerd., B. Ind.* i. p. 517, No. 355; *Hume, Nests and Eggs, Ind. B.* p. 229; *Blyth, B. Burm.* p. 99; *Oates, Str. F.* v. p. 151; *Hume and Dav., Str. F.* vi. p. 250. *Hume, Str. F.* viii. p. 94; *Legge, B. Ceylon* p. 457; *Scully, Str. F.* viii. p. 283; *Hume, Str. F.* ix. p. 101; *Oates, B. Br. Burm.* i. p. 3; *Murray, Avif. Brit. Ind* i. p. 298, No. 365. Geocichla andamanensis, *Wald., Ann. and Mag. Nat. Hist.,* 1874, p. 56. Geocichla albogularis, *Blyth, J. A. S. B.* xvi. p. 146. Geocichla innotata, *Blyth, J. A. S. B.* xv. p. 370.—The ORANGE HEADED GROUND-THRUSH.

Whole head, neck, breast, belly and flanks orange buff, darkest on the head and albescent on the chin and throat; vent, thighs and under tail coverts pure white; back, rump, upper tail coverts, scapulars and smaller wing coverts dark bluish grey; some of the wing coverts near the edge of the wing tipped white, the larger wing coverts, primaries and primary coverts dark brown, exteriorly edged with ashy; inner webs of primaries white at their bases; under wing coverts dark slaty grey basally and white terminally; the bases of the secondaries and some of the primaries white on their inner webs; two centre tail feathers and most of the outside web of the remainder dark slate grey, the rest dark brown; outermost feathers generally paler at tip and frequently tipped with white; bill dark brown or horny black; iris dark hazel; legs and feet fleshy.

Length.—8·5 to 8·8 inches; wing 4·6; tail 3; tarsus 1·3; bill from gape 1·1.

Young birds differ in having the feathers of the upper parts edged with pale yellowish instead of ashy.

Hab.—Throughout the whole range of the Himalayas from Nepaul to Assam up to about 5,000 feet elevation, descending to the plains during winter, being then found in Northern, Central and Southern India, and Burmah, straying also as far south as Ceylon. Jerdon says it is found in most of the forests and well-wooded districts of Northern and Central India, extending rarely as low as N. lat. 16°. In the neighbourhood of Calcutta it is not uncommon, also at Darjeeling and in the warmer valleys in Sikkim. In British Burmah, according to Oates, it is a constant resident.

It keeps to woods and shady gardens, and, like the last, prefers bamboo jungle. Like others of its kind, it feeds on the ground. It is not a shy bird, and does not retreat far from villages. It is said to have a pretty song during the breeding season, but otherwise is silent. The nest is usually built in the forks of high trees, made of grasses, moss, stalks, and roots. Eggs, 3 to 4, pale greenish, freckled with rufous, forming a patch at the large end. Size 0·3 to 1·1 inch in length by 0·7 to 0·82 in breadth.

93. Geocichla wardi (*Jerd.*), *Seebohm, Cat. B. Br. Mus.* v. p. 178. Turdus wardi, *Jerd., J. A. S. B.* xi. p. 882; *Legge, B. Ceylon* p. 453. Merula wardi (*Jerd.*), *Blyth, J. A. S. B.* xvi. p. 146. Cichloselys wardi (*Jerd.*), *Bp., Compt. Rend.* xxviii. p. 5; *Hume, Nests and Eggs*, p. 231. Turdulus wardi (*Jerd.*), *Jerd. B. Ind.* i. p. 520, No. 357. Turdus (Cichloselys) wardi, *Brooks, Str. F.* 1875, p. 237. Oreocincla pectoralis, *Legge, Str. F.* 1876, p. 244; *Hume, Str. F.* 1877, p. 202.—WARD'S PIED GROUND-THRUSH.

Upper parts black; whole head, neck, lores, chin, throat, breast and ear coverts black; wing coverts, innermost secondaries, upper tail coverts and most of the tail feathers more or less conspicuously tipped with white; quills dark brown, their outer webs black and edged with white for some distance, where they cease to be emarginated; under surface white, the flanks with broad, subterminal, irregular crescentic black bands; base of axillaries white, terminally black; bill and legs yellow; irides brown; supercilium white.

Length —8 to 9·6 inches; wing 4·6; tail 3·6; bill at front 0·75; culmen 1·1.

The female is olive brown above; the supercilium and spots on the wing coverts are fulvous white; throat brownish white.

Hab.—The Himalayas, wintering in the plains of India; southwards as far as Ceylon. Occurs in Southern India on the Nilghiris, also in the Carnatic and Nepaul, the Punjab, and N.-W. Provinces (Mussoorie, Nynee Tal). At Mussoorie Captain Hutton found the nest early in April. It breeds in June and July, making a pretty nest of green mosses and fibres in the fork of trees. The eggs are usually 4 in number, pale verditer, spotted with sanguine brown. Size 1·06 inches in length by 0·76 in breadth. It is very regular, somewhat elongated, oval, only slightly compressed at one end.

94. Geocichla spiloptera (*Blyth*), *Seebhom, Cat. B. Br. Mus.* v. p. 167. Oreocincla spiloptera, *Blyth, J. A. S. B.* xvi. p. 142; *Blyth, Cat. Soc.* p. 160; *Kelaart, Prodr. Cat.* p. 122; *Layard, Ann. Nat. Hist.* 1853, p. 270; *Blyth, Ibis,* 1867, p. 303; *Holdsw., P. Z. S* 1872, p. 446; *Legge, Ibis,* 1874, p. 18; *id., Str. F.* 1875, p. 367. Turdus spilopterus (*Blyth*), *Gray, Handl. B.* i. p. 254 No. 3693; *Legge, Birds Ceylon* p. 451, pl. xix.—The Spotted Ground Thrush.

Above russet brown, paling into olive brown on the head; lores pale grey, no eye stripe; median and most of the greater wing coverts dark brown, tipped with white; quills brown, margined externally with russet brown; tail russet brown, the two lateral feathers obscurely tipped pale, and all obscurely barred with transverse bands; under surface of the body white; flanks and sides of the breast tinged with brownish; ear coverts, cheeks and breast with blackish fan-shaped terminal spots; basal half of axillaries white, terminal half brown; bill dark brown, paler at base of lower mandible; 4th and 5th primaries sub-equal and longest; 2nd about equal to the 8th; legs greyish brown.

Length.—Wing 3·6 to 4·0 inches; tail 3· to 3·4; tarsus 1·3 to 1·4; culmen 0·8 to 0·95. (*Seebohm.*)

Hab.—Ceylon, where it is said to be confined to the central hill country about Newara Eliya.

95. Geocichla imbricata (*Layard*), *Seebohm, Cat. B. Br. Mus.* v. p. 159. Zoothera imbricata, *Layard, Ann. and Mag. Nat. Hist.* xiii. p. 212; *Jerd., B. Ind.* i. p. 509 (*note*). Oreocincla nilgherriensis, *Blyth apud Jerdon, Ibis,* 1872, p. 139; *apud Holdsw., P. Z. S.* 1872, p. 446. Oreocincla imbricata (*Layard*), *Hume, Str. F.* 1873, p. 437; *Legge, B. Ceylon,* p. 455, *pl.* xix., *fig.* 2. Oreocincla gregoriana, *Nevil, Str. F.* i. p. 437.—The Ceylonese Ground Thrush.

Above dark olive brown, the feathers with a terminal crescent-shaped dark band; those of the head with also a faint indication of an ochreous subterminal one; wing coverts and secondaries dark olive brown on their inner webs and ochraceous on the outer; lores pale grey; no eye stripe; quills brown, edged externally with ochraceous; four central and two outside feathers of the tail olive brown, remaining three of the lateral feathers on each side darker olive brown; lateral feathers tipped with white, and all more or less obscurely barred; under parts ochraceous buff, each feather with narrow transverse, terminal crescent-shaped black band, nearly obsolete on the chin, centre of belly and under tail coverts; axillaries white on the basal half, and black terminally; under wing coverts black on the basal half and white terminally; bill dark brown, paler at base of under mandible; 3rd, 4th and 5th primaries nearly equal and longest, 2nd between the 5th and 6th or 6th and 7th; legs greyish brown.

Length.—Wing 4·5 to 4·9 inches; tail 2·75 to 3·3; tarsus 1·1 to 1·15; culmen 1·15 to 1·28.

Hab.—Ceylon, to which island it is confined, breeding in the mountain forests and descending into the jungle during the cold season. (*Sharpe.*)

Gen. **Merula**.—*Leach.*

Bill slightly more lengthened generally than in *Turdus*, compressed at tip and notched. Nostrils plumed at base; rictal bristles short and strong; feet strong. Distributed in greater number in the neotropical than in the Australian, oriental, or palæarctic regions.

96. Merula Kinnisi, *Blyth, J. A. S. B.* xx. p. 177; *Kelaart, Prodr. Cat.* p. 122; *Blyth, Ibis,* 1867, p. 304; *Holdsw., P. Z. S.* 1872, p. 446; *Seebohm, Cat. B. Br. Mus.* v. p. 252. Turdus kinnisi (*Blyth*), *Legge, B. Ceylon,* p. 449.—The Ceylonese Ouzel.

Above sooty black, obscurely edged with dark slaty grey; no eye stripe; wings and tail blackish brown, margined externally with dark slaty grey; under surface of the body, axillaries and under wing coverts dull black or dusky blackish, the feathers obscurely margined with dark slaty grey; bill orange yellow; 4th and 5th primaries subequal and longest; 2nd intermediate between 8th and 9th; bastard primary 0·85 to 1·15; legs and feet, also claws, yellow.

Length.—Wing 4·0 to 4·5 inches; tail 3·25 to 3·7; tarsus 1·2 to 1·39; culmen 0·89 to 1·0.

Hab.—Ceylon. Breeds on the hills and descends into the villages during the cold season. Has been found at 7,000 feet at Newara Eliya.

Gen. **Monticola**.—*Boie.*

This genus is placed by Seebohm in his *Cat. B. Br. Mus.* after *Erithacus*. There are certainly links which Mr. Seebohm may have considered sufficient to establish its position, but, taking both the external and internal structure of the group, there can be little doubt that its systematic position is between the Ouzels and the Chats, instead of after the latter. The genus *Monticola* is shortly characterized as having, like the Ouzels (males), an unspotted under surface; the bill, too, is long, and the tail comparatively short; and, as Mr. Seebohm puts it, "never as many as four times the length of the culmen." The bill is long, slender, straight, and moderately hooked at the tip, and either entire or faintly notched; nostrils apert, plumed at the base; rictal bristles small and numerous; wings long, the third quill generally the longest; tail short and even; tarsus moderate, 1 to 1·2 inches in length. All the Indian species have blue chins and throats and chestnut breasts and abdomen. The females have a barred under surface,

97. Monticola cyanus, *Linn.*, *Syst. Nat.* i. p. 296; *Gmel.*, *Syst. Nat.* i. p. 834; *Lath.*, *Ind. Orn.* i. p. 345; *Murray*, *Avif. Brit. Ind.* i. p. 312, No. 385. Monticola cyana (*Linn.*), *Boie*, *Ibis*, 1822, p. 552; *Shelley*, *Birds of Egypt*, p. 70; *Blf.*, *Eastern Persia* ii. p. 155. Petrocossyphus cyaneus (*Linn.*), *Boie*, *Isis*, 1828; *Jerd.*, *B. Ind.* i. p. 511, No. 351; *id.*, *Ill. Ind. Orn.* p. 20; *Hume and Henders.*, *Lahore to Yarkand*, p. 190; *Heugl.*, *Syst. Uebers.* p. 29; *Sharpe and Dresser*, *B. Eur.*; *Murray*, *Hdbk.*, *Zool.*, *&c.*, *Sind.* Cyanocincla cyanus (*Linn.*), *Str. F.* 1874, p. 407; vol. vi. p. 247; *id.* iii. p. 112.—The Blue Rock Thrush.

Male—Head, neck, and back indigo blue, with a faint metallic lustre on the head; lores dusky greyish; wings, their coverts and tail dark brown; the outer webs of the feathers indigo blue; under surface of body cobalt blue; the abdomen and the under tail coverts with faint streaks and spots of whitish.

Female.—Of a dingy brown, scarcely tinged above with indigo or cobalt blue; some of the feathers edged whitish; under parts fulvous with dusky transverse bars, including the under tail coverts; bill black; legs black; irides brown,

Length.—8·5 to 9 inches; wing 4·5 to 5; tail 3·75 to 4; bill at front nearly one inch.

Hab.—Southern Europe, North Africa, Beloochistan, Persia, Afghanistan, wintering throughout the peninsula of India and Ceylon. Recorded from all India, Tenasserim, Cashmere, Nepaul, and North-West Himalayas. Extremely common in the Concan and Deccan, Kutch, Kattiawar, Jodhpore, Sambhur, and North Guzerat; also in South India. Frequents gardens, pagodas, &c. Breeds in the Himalayas, laying 4 eggs, pale blue, spotted with brown; has a fine gloss; size 1·0 × 0·73 inches.

Gen. **Erithacus**.—*Cuv.*

In this genus, as revised, there are only sixteen known species, six only being found in India. The bill is small or of mean length, generally black above and paler on the under mandible; rictal bristles small or nearly obsolete; wings moderate; tail short, more or less rounded, and of 12 feathers; tarsus long, slender, and not scutellated, except occasionally in young birds.

Three species of the six which occur in British India are known to breed in the Himalayas. In habits they closely resemble the Redstarts. They feed mostly on the ground, insects generally being their chief food.

99. Erithacus brunneus (*Hodgs.*), *Seebohm, Cat. B. Br. Mus.* v. p. 302, Larvivora brunnea, *Hodgs., J. A. S. B.* vi. p. 102, 1837 (female); *Legge, B. Ceylon*, p. 446. Larvivora cyana (*Pall.*), *apud. Hodgs., J. A. S. B.* vi. p. 102, 1837 (male); *apud. Jerd., B. Ind.* ii. p. 145, No. 507; *apud Hume, Nests and Eggs Ind. B.* p. 324. Larvivora superciliaris (*Jerd.*), *Blyth, Ibis*, 1867, p. 16; *Brooks, Str F.* 1875, p. 240; *Fairbank, Str. F.* 1876, p. 259.—The Indian Blue Robin or Wood-Chat.

Upper surface dull dark blue; lores, forehead at base of bill, cheeks, and ear coverts black, shading into dull dark blue on the sides of the neck; supercilium white; wings and their coverts brown, their outer webs more or less suffused with dull dark blue; tail brown; the two centre feathers and the outer webs of the others more or less suffused with dull dark blue; under surface of body orange chestnut, shading into white on the centre of the abdomen and under tail coverts; axillaries and under wing coverts grey, more or less suffused with pale blue; bill dark brown, paler at base of under mandible; rictal bristles nearly obsolete.

The female has the upper surface olive brown, slightly suffused with chestnut on the upper tail coverts; the under surface is chestnut brown, paler on the chin and throat and white on the centre of the abdomen and under tail coverts. Birds of the year resemble the female.

Length.—6 to 6·2 inches; wing 2·8 to 3; tail 1·7 to 1·95; culmen 0·5 to 0·6; tarsus 1· to 1·1.

Hab.—Ceylon, the Himalayas from Cashmere to Sikkim, the Nilghiris, and Travancore. Jerdon records it from near Calcutta. At Darjeeling it is said to be common; also about Madras. It frequents open forests in the hills, perching low and descending to the ground to pick up insects. Breeds on the Himalayas and the Nilghiris. Mr. Davison in *Nests and Eggs* says the nest was in a hole in the trunk of a small tree about 5 feet from the ground, and was composed chiefly of moss, but mixed with dry leaves and twigs. The egg taken by Mr. Davison was an elongated, slightly pyriform oval, the ground colour a pale slightly greyish green, thickly mottled and streaked with pale brownish red; size 0·9 × 0·67.

99. Erithacus cæruleculus (*Pall.*), *Seebohm, Cat. B. Br. Mus.* v. p. 308; *Murray, Avif. Brit.* p. 317, No. 393. Motacilla cærulecula, *Pall., Zoogr. Rosso Asiat.* i. p. 480. Cyanecula suecica, *Linn., Sys. Nat.* i. p. 336; (*Partim*), *Brehm., Vogt. Deutschl.* p. 350; *Gray, Gen. B.* i. p. 182; *Heugl, Orn. N. O. Afr.* i. 336; *Shelly, B. Egypt*; *Blf., East. Persia* ii. p. 169; *Hume and Dav., Str. F.* vi. p. 337; *Legge, Birds of Ceylon*, p. 433; *Murray, Str. F.* vii. p. 112; *id., Hdbk., Zool., &c., Sind*, p. 152; *Shelley, Ibis*, 1881; *Str. F.* ix. p. 330; viii. p. 304. Cyanecula cæruleculus (*Pall.*), *Bp. Consp.* i.

p. 206; *Gray, Handlist B.* i. p. 223; *Jerd., Birds Ind.* ii. p. 152, No. 514.—The INDIAN BLUE-THROAT.

Head, neck, back, wings and wing coverts pale brown; the feathers of the head slightly centred, darker, and the wing coverts and quills edged paler; lores dark brown; supercilium buffy white; chin, cheek, throat, and breast cobalt blue, with a large ferruginous or chestnut spot in the centre of the throat and breast; below the blue of the breast a black band, followed by a chestnut one; rest of under surface buffy white; tail rufous or pale ferruginous, the two centre feathers and the terminal third of the others dark brown, lighter on the outermost; ear coverts silky rufescent brown; bill dusky; gape yellow; legs dusky brown; irides dark brown.

Length.—5·5 to 6·5 inches; wing 3; tail 2 to 2·25. The female is like the male, but without the pectoral gorget; the throat, chin, and neck buffy white, with a line of dusky brown from the base of the side of the lower mandible continued to, and across the breast; rest of under surface buffy white.

Hab.—Ceylon, also Europe, Asia, and North Africa generally. Winters in the plains of India. Common in Sind, Punjab, N.-W. Provinces, Bengal, and the whole of India to Nepaul and Cashmere; also in Beloochistan, S.-E. Persia, Afghanistan, and E. Turkistan. It has been recorded from Arrakan, and is found nearly throughout British Burmah. Its habits are quite those of its congeners, frequenting thick brushwood and long grass jungle in the vicinity of water.

Family.—TIMELIIDÆ.

Sub-Family.—BRACHYPODINÆ.

Rictal bristles scanty or numerous, generally strong; tarsi short, not longer than the length of the bill measured from the gape; legs and feet strong and short; wings moderate; bill variable, more or less wide and depressed at base.

Gen. **Ægithina.**—*Vieill.*

Bill moderate; culmen shorter than the tarsus, somewhat compressed, slightly curved and hooked at the tip; rictal bristles scanty, not extending beyond the hind edge of the nostrils, which are apert; wing short and rounded; 4th, 5th, and 6th quills generally sub-equal and longest; tail even and short; tarsi short, scutellate.

This genus contains three good species, *i.e.*, *Æ. viridissima*, *tiphia* and *nigrolutea*, and twice as many races. Mr. Hume, in *Stray Feathers*, 1877, p. 423, and Mr Sharpe, in *B. M. Cat.*, have both exhaustively treated the subject; and so far Mr. Sharpe, the latest writer, says that Mr. Hume's conclusions with regard to *Æ. tiphia* and it's races are thoroughly borne out by the series of specimens he has examined. It is scarcely necessary to say that the changes of plumage in "*tiphia*" and its races are still not quite understood. Mr. Sharpe's account of the results obtained by him are given as follows. He says :—

"1. *Æ. viridissima* and *Æ. nigrolutea* are both distinct species. *Æ. tiphia* is the most widely spread form, and embraces five races, or sub-species, which cannot be infallibly recognized.

2. The females of all the races of *Æ. tiphia* cannot be recognized one from the other.

3. In Southern India and Ceylon the full-plumaged birds are black on the head and back. Birds with more or less black are found in other parts of the Indian Peninsula and the Burmese countries; but black-backed birds are rather the exception than the rule. In the Malayan Peninsula, however, black-backed birds again occur, not to be distinguished from South Indian specimens.

4. In East Central India there is a black-backed form like *Æ. zeylonica*, but easily distinguished by its paler colouration. This race is noticed by Mr. Hume in *Str. F.*, 1877, p. 439.

5. *Æ. scapularis* from Java never has any black on the males, which appear to resemble the females, excepting in being a little darker on the wings.

6. *Æ. viridis* from Sumatra and Borneo is the *Æ. scapularis* of authors from the abovementioned Islands. From an examination of numerous individuals, I am certain that it never has a black-backed plumage; and it might be considered a distinct species were it not that the adult males can be matched by others from Ceylon in the stage of p. .mage which they assume before getting the black head and back, but when they are brilliant yellow below with black wings and tail the lores and forehead of *Æ. viridis* is also brilliant yellow. This is peculiar to the adult Bornean birds."

100. Ægithina tiphia (*Linn.*), *Hume, Nests and Eggs Ind. B.* p. 295; *Oates, Str. F.* v. p. 157; *Sharpe, Cat. B. Br. Mus.* vi. p. 7; *Oates, B. Br. Burm.* i. p. 202; *Murray, Avif. Brit. Ind.* ii. p. 9, No 416. Motacilla tiphia, *Linn., Syst. Nat.* i. p. 331. Motacilla zeylonica, *Gm., Syst. Nat.* i. p. 964. Iora zeylonica, *Jerd., B. Ind.* ii. p. 101, No. 467. Iora typhia, *Jerd., B. Ind.* ii. p. 103, No. 468; *Blyth and Wald., B. Burm.* p. 137; *Hume, Str. F.* v. p. 428; *Anders., Yunnan Exped.* p. 660; *Legge, B. Ceyl.* p. 490; *Hume, Str. F.* viii. p. 99.—The Common Dwarf Bulbul.

Adult Male in Summer plumage.—Lores, forehead, crown and back black, the feathers of the mantle yellowish white at base and showing through; rump greenish yellow; upper tail coverts and tail black, also the lesser wing coverts; the greater coverts black, tipped with white; the median coverts white, the white tippings forming a double bar across the wing; quills black; the primaries narrowly edged with yellow, and the secondaries fringed with whitish at the tips; sides of the head and neck, lores and eyelids glossy black; lower edge of eyelids, cheeks, ear coverts, chin, throat, breast and under surface of body deep intense, or bright yellow, fading off into paler or greenish yellow on the lower abdomen, vent, under tail coverts and sides; a large tuft of silky white plumes on either flank; thighs yellowish green, with dark brown bases; under wing coverts white, washed with yellowish; axillaries white.

The *female* is yellowish green above, with rather more yellow on the head; mantle long and silky; tail green, with a narrow yellowish edge; wings with two bars across; median coverts dusky green, with broad white tips; greater coverts blackish, tipped with white; quills dusky blackish, narrowly edged with pale yellowish; lores, sides of the head and face, also round the eye and under surface of the body bright yellow, the sides washed with greenish; axillaries and under wing coverts as in the male. In winter the male loses all the black of the upper parts except on the tail and wings, while the immature have not the black even on the wings and tail. Feet and claws plumbeous; iris yellowish, olive grey, or hazel; bill bluish, darker on the culmen.

Length.—5·1 to 5·4 inches; wing 2·4 to 2·6; tail 1·85 to 2·0; tarsus 0·7; bill from gape 0·7; culmen 0·6.

Hab.—Ceylon, South India, the Punjab (?), N.-W. Provinces, Oudh, Bengal, Rajputana, Central India, the Central Provinces, Kutch, Concan, Guzerat, Deccan, British Burmah, Nepaul, and Sikkim.

The Dwarf or White-winged Green Bulbul is common in all the places mentioned above. Jerdon mentions Nagpore, Saugor, and Jaulnah as some localities. It is a very widely spread species, and, owing to the changes of its plumage, is difficult to identify with any degree of certainty. In Assam, Arrakan, Pegu, and Tenasserim, it is abundant. Captain Wardlaw-Ramsay met with it in Karenne. In the Indo-Burmese countries, Siam, Cochin-China, and the Malay Peninsula to Singapore, it is abundantly met with. It frequents orchards, low trees and brushwood, actively and restlessly searching the twigs, leaves, and smaller branches for insects, which are its chief food. It does not, according to Jerdon, confine itself to cultivated ground, but is also a denizen of the open spaces of jungles. Its flight is performed by a succession of quick vibrations of the wing, and causes a loud whirring sound, When searching for food it keeps up a continuous loud warble or a peculiar querulous note.

The breeding season of this Bulbul is from May to September, building usually on the upper surface of a horizontal bough at a height of from 10 to 25 feet from the ground. The nest is not unlike that of a *Leucocirca.* It is cup-shaped, but not very compact, with an egg cavity of 2 inches diameter on an average, and lined with fine grass stems. The general structure is of fine fibres and grass, coated on the outside with cobwebs. The eggs, usually three in number, are greyish white, or with a creamy or salmon tinge, streaked with long pale brown, brown or reddish brown markings, confined chiefly to the large end. In shape they are moderately broad ovals and slightly pointed at one end. In size the average may be said to be 0·6 to 0·76 × 0·51 to 0·57.

Gen. **Chloropsis**.—*Jard. and Selby.*

Bill moderate, *longer than the tarsus*, and variable; the culmen keeled and more or less curved; tip bent down and notched; nostrils basal, long; rictal bristles scanty; wing rounded, moderately long; the 4th and 5th quills subequal; tail moderate, even.

This genus comprises birds of bright grass green plumage. All are marked or varied with blue and yellow markings about the head, neck, or wings.

101. Chloropsis malabarica (*Gmel*), *Sharpe, Cat. B. Br. Mus.* vi. p. 22; *Murray, Avif. Brit. Ind.* ii. p. 14, No. 421. Turdus malabaricus, *Gmel., Syst. Nat.* i. p. 837. Phyllornis malabaricus, *Blyth, J. A. S. B.* xiv. p. 566; *Gould, B. Asia*, pt. xiii.; *Jerd., B. Ind.* ii. p. 99, No. 464; *Fairbank, Str. F.* 1876, p. 258; *Bourdillon*, t. c. p. 400; *Hume, Str. F.* 1879, p. 99; *Legge, B. Ceylon*, p. 488.—The MALABAR GREEN BULBUL.

Adult Male.—Bright grass green; wing coverts like the back, the lesser series bright greenish cobalt, forming a shoulder patch; quills blackish, externally green, and edged with brighter green; tail dull green, the inner webs blackish; forehead bright orange; no orange across the foreneck, which, like the breast, is green; lores, a circle of feathers round the eye and below it, under part of the cheeks as well as the entire thorax black; ear coverts and sides of neck green; moustachial streak cobalt; under surface of body light green; edge of the wing blue; bill blackish; legs and feet plumbeous; irides light yellow brown.

Length.—7·3 to 7·5 inches; wing 3·5 to 3·75; tail 2·7 to 3; tarsus 0·8; culmen 0·9.

The female is smaller and has the forehead green, and the throat patch and moustachial stripe smaller.

Hab.—Ceylon, the forests of Malabar and Southern India, occurring also in Travancore, on the Eastern Ghauts, forests of Central India, and throughout the northern half of Ceylon. Jerdon mentions it from Wynaad, Coorg, and on the sides of the Nilghiris up to about 4,000 feet elevation. It has also been reported from the Deccan. In its habits the Malabar Green Bulbul does not differ from those of *C. aurifrons*. Their food consists of insects. The male bird, he says, frequently sits on the summit of a tree, and gives utterance to a series of notes, which at times becomes a rather sweet song. They feed a good deal on fruit too and the nectar of flowers. They are not at all shy, and may be met with in gardens and compounds just as frequently as in deep forests.

102. Chloropsis jerdoni (*Blyth*), *Sharpe, Cat. B. Br. Mus.* vi. p. 26; *Jerd., Madr. Journ.* xiii. pt. 2, p. 124. Phyllornis jerdoni, *Blyth, J*

A S. B. xiii. p. 392; *Jerd., B. Ind.* ii. p. 97, No. 463; *Holdsw., P. Z. S.* 1872, p. 451; *Ball., Str. F.* 1874, p. 410; *Hume, Nests and Eggs Ind. B.* p. 294, *Fairbank, Str. F.* 1876, p 259; *id.*, 1877, p. 406; *Ball.*, t. c. p. 215; *Hume, Str. F.* 1879, p. 99; *Legge, B. Ceylon*, p. 485; *Murray, Avif. Brit. Ind.* ii. p. 15, No. 423.—JERDON'S or the COMMON GREEN BULBUL.

Above light grass green; the head dull yellow, shading into the emerald green of the occiput and nape; anterior edge of eyelid and lores black, also the feathers below the eye, the cheeks and throat; ear coverts dull yellow, separated from the black throat by a similar band which extends from behind the eye down the sides of the neck on to the lower throat, where it forms a gorget; moustachial streak violet cobalt; shoulder patch turquoise blue; quills blackish brown, edged externally with green, the primaries yellow towards the tips of the outer webs; inner secondaries green; tail green; under plumage emerald green, deeper on the sides; under wing coverts and axillaries green, with greyish bases; edge of wing emerald green; bill blackish; legs and feet plumbeous or pale lavender; iris brown or pale brown. (*Legge.*)

Length.—7·8 inches; wing 3·45; tail 3; tarsus 0·75; culmen 0·8.

The *female* has not the black throat, which is pale turquoise blue, and is much smaller.

Hab.—The greater part of the Continent of India, but does not extend to Lower Bengal or the sub-Himalayan districts. It is common in Ceylon; also, according to Jerdon, in the Western Provinces of India and in the jungles of the Eastern Ghauts. In the open country of the Carnatic, Travancore. Mysore, and Hydrabad it is said to be rare, but not so in Central India, at Mhow, Saugor, &c., and through the jungles of Chota Nagpore up to Midnapore.

Its habits are quite those of the other species.

Tickell says it is an excellent mocker, and imitates the notes of almost every small bird of the country.

The Common Green Bulbul breeds in July and August, but eggs have been taken in different parts during April, May, and June also. The nest is a shallow cup composed entirely of vegetable fibres worked over fine roots or stems. The eggs are rather elongated ovals, white or creamy white in colour, and sparingly marked, chiefly at the large end, with specks, spots and minute blotches, lines, &c., of blackish and reddish or purplish brown; in size they vary from 0·8 to 0·92 × 0·56 to 0·63.

Sub-Family.—PYCNONOTINÆ.

Head generally crested or sub-crested. Plumage usually full, and with hairs or bristles arising in many instances from either the head or nape. Sexes usually alike and plain in colour. Inhabitants of forests, jungles, orchards and groves. Food—fruit and insects.

Gen. **Hypsipetes.**—*Vigors.*

Bill moderately long, nearly straight; culmen very slightly arched; nostrils long, with a few scanty hairs at base; wings longer than in *Chloropsis*; 4th and 5th quills generally the longest, 3rd sub-equal; tail long, square, emarginate; legs and feet short; tarsi not scutellate in front.

103. Hypsipetes ganeesa, *Sykes, P. Z. S.* 1832, p. 86; *Jard. and Selb., Ill. Orn., 2nd Ser.* iv. pl. 2; *Blyth, J. A. S. B.* xiv. p. 574; *Jerd., B. Ind.* ii. p. 78; *Fairbank, Str. F.* 1876, p. 258; *Hume*, t. c. p. 400; *id., Str. F.* 1879, p. 598; *Legge, B. Ceylon*, p. 469; *Murray, Avif. Br. Ind.* ii. p. 19, No. 428. Hypsipetes nilgherriensis, *Jerd., Madr. Journ.* 1839, p. 245; *Jerd., B. Ind.* ii. p. 78, No. 446; *Hume, Nests and Eggs Ind. B.* p. 280; *id., Str. F.* 1873, p. 438; *Fairbank, Str. F.* 1877, p. 405.—SYKES' BLACK BULBUL.

Above dark slaty grey or grey brown, paler beneath; wings and tail brown; head sub-crested, metallic black; sides of face slate grey, no black stripe on cheek; bill coral red or orange vermilion in skin; feet orange yellow.

Length.—8·5 to 9 inches; wing 4·5; tail 4 to 4·15; tarsus 0·7 to 0·75; culmen 1 to 1·1.

Hab.—Hill ranges of Southern India, extending on the western side along the Western Ghauts to the Mahableshwar Hills and to Matheran and Ceylon. Sykes' Bulbul breeds from March and April to June. The nest is placed in some dense clump of leaves or parasitic plant (in Southern India), which covers nearly every acacia and other tree. It builds a cup-shaped nest, neatly and firmly made of green moss, grass, stalks and fibres. Eggs similar to those of *psaroides;* 1·0 to 1·7 × 0·7 to 0·8.

Gen. **Xenocichla.**—*Hartl.*

General characters like those of *Criniger*, but with conspicuous hairs springing from the nape. Nostrils oval, bare, and with a posterior membrane.

104. Xenocichla icterica (*Strickl.*), *Sharpe, Cat. B. Br. Mus.* vi. p. 96; *Murray, Avif. Brit. Ind.* ii. p. 33, No. 448. Criniger ictericus, *Strickl., Ann. Nat. Hist.* 1844, xiii. p. 411; *Jerd., B. Ind.* ii. p. 82; *Hume, Nests and Eggs Ind. B.* p. 282; *Bourd., Str. F.*, 1876, p. 800; *Fairbank, Str. F.* 1877, p. 405; *Hume, Str. F.* 1879, p. 61. Pycnonotus ictericus, *Blyth, J. A. S. B.* 1844, xiv. p. 570.—The YELLOW-BROWED BULBUL.

Above bright olive yellow or olive green; wing coverts the same; quills dark brown, their outer webs edged with olive yellow; tail dull olive yellow, dusky along the inner webs and towards the tips; lores, a narrow eyebrow and feathers round the eye bright yellow; ear coverts yellow, shaded with olive; cheeks and under surface of body bright yellow; the sides and breast washed with olive; under wing coverts and axillaries bright yellow; bill black; legs and feet dusky slatish; iris red or blood red.

Length.—7·4 to 8 inches ; wing 3·4 to 3·7 ; tail 3 ; tarsus 0·8 ; culmen 0·75.

Hab.—Ceylon and Southern India, not ranging higher than Bombay. (*Sh.*) Recorded also from Malabar, Coorg, and Travancore. Jerdon says it prefers mountainous regions, and that it is abundant on the slopes of the Nilghiris, living in small flocks and keeping up a continual mellow warble when flying from tree to tree. Breeds from March to May. Nest a small shallow cup hung between two twigs, and composed of excessively fine twigs. It is lined with hair-like grasses, and attached by cobwebs. Eggs two to three in number, of a pinkish salmon colour, with a dark ring at the thick end, and speckled more or less thickly over the whole surface of the egg with pale brownish red or pink. Size 0·9 to 1·03 × 0·64 to 0·7.

Gen. **Pycnonotus**.—*Boie.*

Bill rather long, thin and slightly curved ; rictal bristles strong ; legs and feet stoutish ; tarsi with a single scute at insertion of feet ; toes scutellate ; head more or less crested, but not conspicuously so.

105. Pycnonotus hæmorrhous, *Blyth, J. A. S. B.* xiv. p. 566; *id.*, xv. p. 50; *Gray, Gen. B.* i. p. 237 ; *Jerd., B. Ind.* ii. p. 94, No. 462 ; *Str. F.* 1875, p. 292 ; *Sharpe, Cat. B. Br. Mus.* vol. vi. ; *Murray, Handbk., Zool., &c., Sind* ; *Legge, B. Ceylon*, p. 482 ; *Murray, Avif. Br. Ind.* ii. p. 34, No. 449. Hæmatornis hæmorrhous, *Swains., Faun. Bor. Amer. B.* p. 485. Pycnonotus pusillus, *Gray, Gen. B.* i. p. 237 ; *Str. F.* 1878, p. 258 ; *Hume, t. c.* p. 456 ; *Str. F.*, 1877, p. 246. Molpastes hæmorrhous, *Hume, Str. F.* 1879, p. 98.—The COMMON MADRAS BULBUL.

Head crested, black ; chin and throat black ; neck, back and wing coverts brown, more or less pale edged ; upper tail-coverts white ; tail brownish black, tipped with white ; breast brown, all the feathers edged with white or ashy ; lower abdomen and vent white ; flanks and thigh coverts light brown ; under tail coverts crimson ; under wing coverts whitish. Bill black ; legs greenish or slaty green ; irides deep brown.

Length.—7·75 to 8 inches; wing 3·4; tail 3·4; tarsus 0·8; bill at front 0·9.

Hab.—Ceylon, Southern and Central India (Mhow), Travancore, Deccan, Concan, Malabar, Kutch, Kattiawar, Jodhpore and North Guzerat; also the Punjab, N.-W. Provinces, Bengal and Oudh. In Sind it appears to be a permanent resident, breeding from June to August. Eggs 2—4, white, speckled with lake red or deep claret.

This is the common Bulbul of all India. It is found in gardens, orchards, Babool groves, and wherever there are any clumps of trees, but never in forests, either associating in small families or in pairs restlessly flying about from tree to tree in search of fruit and insects. It does much damage in gardens, where it picks off blossoms of cherries and flower buds. It is commonly caged throughout India, or kept tied by a cord round the waist. Being pugnacious they are made to fight for small prizes, and when being trained for this purpose are fed on minced meat and a compound made of wheat, flour, sugar and milk boiled together, otherwise dates and other seasonal fruit. Breeds chiefly in June and July—many often as early as April and as late as the middle of August. Nest generally a compact structure composed of delicate stems, dry leaves and grass, with a little lining of any soft material. Eggs 3—4 in number. In shape the eggs are rather long ovals, slightly compressed or pointed towards the small end. The markings are very various, and as Mr. Hume says, take almost every conceivable form defined and undefined specks, spots, blotches, streaks, smudges and clouds; their combinations are as varied as their colours, which embrace every shade of red, brownish and purplish red. In length the eggs vary from 0·7 to 0·89 and in breadth from 0·6 to 0·72.

106. Pycnonotus luteolus (*Less.*), *Gray, Gen. B.* i. p. 237; *Murray, Avif. Brit. Ind.* ii. p. 39, No. 457. Hæmatornis luteolus, *Less., Rev. Zool.* p. 354. Pycnonotus flavirictes, *Strickl., Ann. Nat. Hist.* xiii. p. 413. Ixos luteolus, *Jerd., B. Ind.* ii. p. 84, No. 452; *Hume, Nests and Eggs Ind. B.* p. 283; *Ball, Str. F.* 1874, p. 410; 1876, p. 235; *Fairbank*, t. c. p. 258; *Hume*, t. c. p. 415; *Fairbank, Str. F.*, 1877, p. 405; *Ball*, t. c. p. 417; *Hume, Str. F.* 1879, p. 98; *Legge, B. Ceylon*, p. 475.—The White Eye-browed Bush Bulbul.

Above olive brown, more olivaceous on the lower back and rump, where there is a perceptible tinge of greenish yellow; lores, eyelids, supercilium, also a streak under the eye dull white; ear coverts light brown, washed with olive and with narrow whitish shaft streaks; forepart of cheeks yellow, forming a short moustachial streak; foreneck, forepart of cheeks, breast, and flanks pale ashy brown, washed with olive; chin yellow; throat dingy white; wing coverts and quills brown, externally olive yellow; tail light brown, the feathers margined with olive; under tail coverts yellow; under surface of body pale yellowish white, rather deeper yellow on the axillaries and under wing coverts; bill blackish; legs dark plumbeous; iris blood red.

Length.—6·5 to 7 inches; wing 3·35; tail 3; tarsus 0·85; culmen 0·7.

Hab.—Ceylon, also Central and South India. It is recorded from Madras, Malabar and Trevandrum. Jerdon says it is a tolerably common bird in many parts of the south of India; rare in others. Common in the low jungles of Malabar and in the bushy jungle and gardens in the Carnatic, also throughout the Northern Circars to Goomsoor. Common in Midnapore. (*Hume.*) It is usually seen alone and avoids observation. It flies from bush to bush with a fine, loud, clear, thrush-like warble, and feeds entirely on fruit. It breeds about Bombay. According to Mr. Hume it builds in a bush a rather loose structure of twigs lined with fine grass roots, &c., cobwebs and wool being used to tie it firmly to its support. Eggs 2—4 in number, reddish white, with darker lake red spots. They are elongated ovals and measure 0·92 × 0·62.

Gen. **Kelaartia** (*Blyth*), *Jerd.*, *B. Ind.* ii. 86

Bill short, somewhat stout and wide, strongly notched; the culmen curved and not so long as the mid toe; gonys nearly straight; head fully crested, the feathers rounded; rictal bristles feeble; tarsus longer than in the genus *Pycnonotus*.

107. Kelaartia penicillata (*Blyth*), *Jerd*, *B. Ind* ii. p. 86; *Sharpe, Cat. B. Br. Mus.* vi. p. 162; *Holdsw., P. Z. S.* 1872, p. 450; *Legge, Ibis*, 1874, p. 20; *id., Str. F.* 1876, p. 245; *id., Birds Ceylon*, p. 480, pl. 23, *fig.* 1. Pycnonotus penicillatus, *Blyth, J. A. S. B.* xx. 1851, p. 178; *Kelaart, Prodr. Cat.* p. 123; *Layard, Ann. and Mag. Nat. Hist.* 1854. xiii. p. 125. —The Yellow-eared Bulbul.

Upper surface of the body olive greenish; quills dusky brown, edged externally with olive green; innermost secondaries dark olive green; tail dark olive brown, margined with yellowish externally, the tips of the outer feathers narrowly edged yellow; head sub-crested; forehead and crown brown, the feathers of the nape dusky brown, washed with olive and faintly edged with olive yellow; a streak of white from the nostrils and forming behind a tolerably distinct supercilium; lores and sides of the face dusky brown, a line of bright yellow over the ear coverts and a spot of the same colour in the middle of the ear coverts; cheeks, chin and throat white; lower throat bright yellow; foreneck, breast, and sides of the body olive yellow tinged with greenish on the sides of the breast; abdomen and under tail coverts bright yellow; under wing coverts, axillaries and edge of wing yellow; bill black (*Sharpe*); tarsi and feet dark leaden blue; iris red.

Length.—7·5 to 8 inches; wing 3·1 to 3·4; tail 3·1 to 3·2; tarsus 0·9; culmen 0·65. The female is slightly smaller.

Hab.—Ceylon, from 3,500 to 4,000 feet elevation.

Gen. **Rubigula**, *Blyth.*

Bill as in *Otocompsa*, but broader than it is high; rictal bristles moderate; tail slightly rounded or nearly even. Head more or less crested; feathers of the back lax and decomposed.

108. Rubigula melanictera (*Gmel.*), *Walden, Ibis*, 1866, p. 321; *Blyth Ibis*, 1867, p. 304; *Holdsw., P. Z. S.* 1872, p. 451; *Legge, Str. F.* 1875, p. 368; *id., Birds of Ceylon* p. 477; *Sharpe, Cat. B. Br. Mus.* vi. p. 168. Muscicapa melanictera, *Gmel., List. Nat.* I. p. 941. Ægithina atricapilla, *Vieill., Nouv. Dict. d'Hist. Nat.* I. p. 176. Rubigula aberrans, *Blyth, J. A. S. B.* xv. p. 288. Pycnonotus atricapillus, *Blyth, Cat. B. Mus. A. Soc.* p. 211; *Layard, Ann. and Mag. N. H.* xiii. p. 125. Pycnonotus nigricapillus, *Kelaart, Prodr. Cat.* p. 123. Rubigula gularis, t. c. p. 123. Brachypus gularis, *Bp. Consp.* I. p. 264 (*nec Gould*).—The YELLOW BREASTED or BLACK-HEADED BULBUL.

Upper surface of the body dull olive yellow, paler on the rump; quills brown, externally edged with olive yellow; tail dusky brown, edged with olive near the base, all except the two central feathers with a white spot at tip; crown of head and nape, also the sides of the face, glossy black; throat and entire under surface of the body bright golden yellow; sides of breast and flanks washed with olive; under wing coverts and axillaries yellow. (*Sharpe.*) Bill black; legs and feet blackish; iris dull red;

Length.—6·3 to 6·5 inches; wing 2·7; tail 2·6; tarsus 0·6; culmen 0·8.

Peculiar to Ceylon, inhabiting forest tracts to 5,000 feet.

Gen. **Myiophoneus.**—*Temm.*

Bill large, strong, compressed, of moderate length, hooked at tip, and much higher than broad at nostrils; rictal bristles few or almost wanting; nares round with some frontal plumes and hairs at their base; wings long, rather pointed; 4th and 5th quills nearly equal, the 5th generally the longest, tail moderate; tarsus large, stout, entire, or with a subterminal scute.

These birds are generally known as Whistling Thrushes. They are birds of fairly large size, black plumage, glossed or enamelled with blue, and their bills are either yellow or black. They have a range from Turkestan to Afghanistan and the whole of India and Ceylon, throughout the Burmese countries and China. According to Sharpe apparently absent in the Malayan Peninsula, but re-occurs in Java and Sumatra.

109. Myiophoneus Blighi (*Holdsworth*), *Sharpe, Cat. B. Br. Mus.* vii. p. 13. Arrenga Blighi, *Holdsworth, P. Z. S.* 1872, p. 444, pl. 19; *Gould, B. Asia pt.* xxviii., 1876. Myiophoneus blighi, *Legge, B. Ceylon*, p. 463, pl. 20, figs. 1, 2.—BLIGH'S WHISTLING THRUSH.

Head, throat and hind neck coal black; interscapulars black; scapulars, wing coverts and breast cerulean blue, the bases of the feathers of these parts black; lesser wing coverts bright smalt blue; wings and tail brownish black, the quills obscurely edged with blue; upper tail coverts and bases of the rectrices edged with chocolate brownish; under surface of the body, including the under tail coverts, the same, the bases of the feathers brown; bill, legs and feet black; irides brown.

Length.—8 to 8·5 inches; wing 4·2 to 4·4; tail 3·1 to 3·5; tarsus 1·4 to 1·5; bill from gape 1·25.

The female is of a brighter tint than the male, but the wing spot is lighter in colour. The young is dark brown above and rufous below, the feathers of the forehead, throat, foreneck and breast are centred with yellow brown.

Hab.—The hills of Ceylon, affecting dense jungles.

Mr. F. B. Armstrong very kindly sends me the following extract:—

"Mr. E. E. Green discovered a nest in March of 1888, and wrote to the *Taprobanian* to the following effect:—

"On the 1st instant (March), I found what I believe to be the nest of *Myiophoneus Blighi*—Bligh's Whistling Thrush. The nest was placed on a sheltered ledge of rock by the side of a waterfall, and hidden by surrounding ferns. It was a very compact, solid structure of moss and fern roots, the top forming a level platform, in which a small and rather deep cavity was sunk for the eggs. The platform exceeded in area the hollow space, and when first found the fresh body of a small fish was lying upon it, its head having apparently been just devoured. The fish was a stone loach (about three inches long), many of which were swimming in the pool immediately below. In the hollow of the nest was a single egg, bluntly oval, with a smaller and larger extremity; colour dull greenish white, stained with pale-reddish at the larger end.

"I was unable to get a sight of the birds, though I heard them in the bushes close by uttering the complaining note common to many of the thrushes. I have on many former occasions seen specimens of what I believe to be *M. blighi* frequenting this stream.

"On the 8th instant I revisited the nest, thinking that the full complement of eggs would have been deposited, and hoping to shoot one of the birds for identification; but the nest was deserted and the single egg had disappeared. Is it possible that the egg can have been transported by the parent birds to a place of safety? The nest was situated in such a position that rats or other small animals could not have reached it; and, being in an unfrequented corner and entirely concealed, it is improbable that any of the estate coolies could have robbed it.

"Upon taking down the abandoned nest, its construction showed that it must have been rebuilt upon the same spot for many seasons."

Gen. **Thamnobia**.—*Swains.*

Bill slender, as wide as high at the nostrils, slightly arched throughout; wings shortand rounded, the 4th and 5th quills longest, the primaries hardly exceeding in length the secondaries and tertiaries; tail moderate, broad and rounded, the outer feather on each side shorter than the longest by the length of the tarsus.

110. Thamnobia fulicata (*Lin.*), *Jerd., Mad. Journ.* x. p. 264; *Blyth, J. A. S. B.* xvi. p. 139; *Layard, Ann. and Mag. Nat. Hist.* xii. p. 226; *Jerd., B. Ind.* ii. p. 121, No. 419; *Hume, Nests and Eggs Ind. B.* p. 307; *Fairbank, Str. F.* 1876, p. 459; *Hume, Str. F.* 1877, p. 406; *id., Str. F.* 1878, ii. p. 55; *Ball l. c.* p. 216; *Legge, B. Ceylon*, p. 440; *Murray, Avif. Br. Ind.* ii. p. 64, No. 493.—The BROWN-BACKED INDIAN ROBIN.

Above glossy blue-black; wings *with a large white spot formed by the lesser wing coverts;* median and greater coverts white, tipped with glossy blue-black; primary coverts and quills brown, margined externally with blue-black; lores, sides of the face and *under surface of body glossy blue-black*; lower abdomen and under tail coverts bright chestnut; bill, legs and feet black; irides brown.

Length.—6 to 6·8 inches; wings 2·5 to 2·7; tail 2·75; tarsus 1·0; culmen 0·55.

The female is larger and dusky brown, more sooty on the back and rump, the white shoulder patch is wanting, and the upper tail coverts are blue-black; under tail coverts chestnut; feathers round the eye fulvous; cheeks and under surface of the body ashy brown, darker on the abdomen, sides of the body and flanks.

The young are entirely sooty brown with paler margins to the feathers; under tail coverts ferruginous.

Hab.—Ceylon, also Central, Southern and Western India.

The Indian Robin affects villages, and their neighbourhood, chiefly ruins of old houses and mud-walls; also rocky and stony situations. It is usually seen in pairs, briskly hopping about on the ground or flitting from a branch to the ground, or *vice versâ*, or from one large boulder to another, continually jerking its tail upwards on to the back of its head. In India it breeds from February to May, building its nest among rocks, in mud walls, in roofs of houses, or under tussocks of grass, but in Ceylon Mr. Parker says May to August in the S. Provinces, and April to September in the Northern.

The nest is a neat structure of grass, roots and hair. The eggs are round ovals, moderately glossed, and of a greyish white or pale bluish white ground, thinly sprinkled here and there, and in some all over with spots and specks of pale yellowish brown. Size 0·68 to 0·76 inch × 0·55 to 0·56.

Gen. **Copsychus**.— *Wagl.*

Bill moderately long and strong; culmen slightly curving and bent at the tip; nostrils basal, large; rictal bristles very scanty; wings with the 4th and 5th quills longest, the 3rd sub-equal; tail graduated; tarsus scutellated, moderately long and short; mid toe long; claws curved.

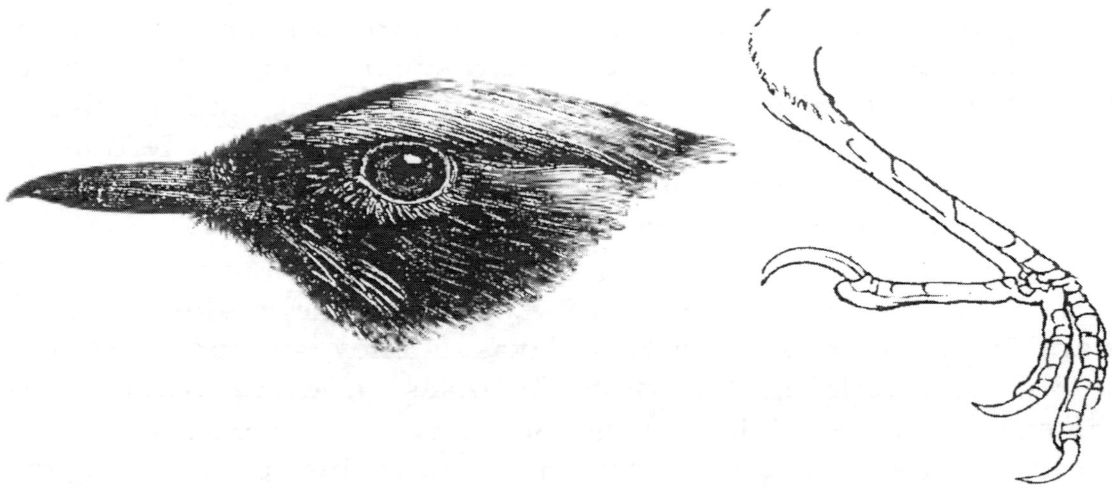

Head and leg of Copsychus saularis.

111. Copsychus saularis (*Lin.*), *Wagler, Syst. Av.* 1827; *Blyth, J. A. S. B.* xi. p. 889; *Jerd., B. Ind.* ii. p. 114, No. 475; *Hume, Nests and Eggs Ind. B.* p. 303; *Hume and Henderson, Lahore to Yarkand,* p. 202; *Hume, Str. F.* ii. p. 230; iii. p. 133; *Bl., B. Burm.* p. 100; *Oates, Str. F.* v. p. 157; *Hume and Dav., Str. F.* vi. p. 332; *Legge, B. Ceylon,* p. 433; *Hume, Str. F.* viii. p. 99; *Sharpe, Cat. B. Br. Mus.* vii. p. 62; *Oates, B. Br. Burm.* i. p. 21; *Murray, Avif. Brit. Ind.* ii. p. 65, No. 495. Gracula saularis, *Linn., Syst. Nat.* i. p. 165. Copsychus mindanensis (*non. Gm.*), *Blyth, J. A. S. B.* xvi. p. 139; *Hume, Str. F.* 1873, p. 459; *Salvad., Ucc. Borneo,* p. 254. Copsychus ceylonensis, *Sclater, P. Z. S.* 1861, p. 186. Copsychus musicus, *Wald., Ibis,* 1872, p. 203; *Tweed., Ibis,* 1877, p. 302; *Hume and Dav., Str. F.* 1878, i. p. 33; *Hume, Str. F.* 1879, p. 99. Copsychus andamanensis, *Hume, Str. F.* 1873, p. 231. Kittacincla melanoleuca, *Less., Rev. Zool.* 1840, p. 354.—The INDIAN MAGPIE ROBIN or the INDIAN DHAYAL BIRD.

Head, neck all round, back, wings, chin, throat, breast, central tail feathers, upper abdomen, and edge of the wing black; lower abdomen, vent and under tail coverts, also the shoulder of the wing, some of the outer webs of the secondaries and also the outer tail feathers white; under wing coverts white.

The female is dark grey where the male is black, with a slight gloss on the upper surface; under surface white; wings as in the male; central tail feathers dark brown; outer feathers white; throat grey; under wing coverts and axillaries white; bill and legs black; irides brown.

Length.—8 to 8·5 inches; wing 3·8 to 4·2; tail 3·6; tarsus 1·05; culmen 0·8.

Hab.—Ceylon and all over India, eastward to Assam and as far south as Pegu. It is recorded from Central and South India, also from Nepal,

Darjeeling, Kumaon, Pegu and the Andamans, and as a race (*musicus*), Malacca, Penang, Siam and Java.

The geographical distribution of the Dhayal bird, Sharpe says, is of great interest; so gradual is the transition of one supposed species to the other, and so uncertain are the characters for their specific separation, that he has deemed it best to recognize but a single actual species, and in this I agree, especially when hybrids have to be given consideration to. Jerdon says it is generally seen alone or in pairs, usually seeks its prey from a low perch or hops a few steps to pick up insects, which are its chief food.

It breeds, according to Hume, but sparingly throughout the plains of Upper India; also in the N.-W. Provinces of Ceylon. The majority resort to the Dhoons and Terais that skirt the Himalayas. They lay from the end of March to the end of July, building their nests in holes in trees, banks or walls, or under the eaves of huts. The nest is composed of coarse grass of flower-stalks intermixed with fine roots and dry tendrils of climbing plants. Eggs 5—6 in number, of a pale bluish green, thickly spotted and blotched with purplish brown, and showing an imperfect ring of nearly confluent blotches at the larger end.

Gen. **Cittocincla**.—*Sclater*.

Bill more slender than in *Copsychus;* tail very long, graduated; wings rounded; tarsus slender.

112. Cittocincla tricolor (*Vieill.*), *Sharpe, Ann. and Mag. Nat. Hist.* (5) x. p. 49; *id., Cat. B. Br. Mus.* vii. p. 85; *Murray, Avif. Brit. Ind.* ii. p. 68, No. 498. Turdus tricolor, *Vieill., N. Dict. d'Hist. Nat.* pt. xx. p. 291. Copsychus macrurus, *Wagl., Syst. Av. Art.* Copsychus, *Sp.* Cercotrichas macrurus, *Boie, Isis,* 1831, p. 542; *Hume, Nests and Eggs, Ind. B.* p. 306; *Ball, Str. F.* 1874, p. 412; *Hume t. c.* p. 477; *Hume and Oates, Str. F.* 1875, p. 13; *Ball, t. c.* p. 293; *Fairbk., Str. F.* 1876, p. 259; *Inglis, Str. F.* 1877, p. 36; *Oates, t. c.* p. 157; *Hume and Davison, Str. F.* 1878, i. p. 333; *Ball, Str. F.* 1878, p. 216; *Hume, Str. F.* 1879, pp. 64, 99; *Butler, Cat. B. Bom. Pres.* p. 47; *Vidal, Str. F.* 1880, p. 66. Kittacincla macrura, *Gould, P. Z. S.*, 1836, p. 7; *Blyth, J. A. S. B.* xvi. p. 139; *Jerd., B. Ind.* ii. p. 116, No. 476; *Walden, P. Z. S.*, 1866, p. 550; *Godwin-Aust., J. A. S. B.* xii. p. 142. Cittocincla macrura, *Sclater, Ibis,* 1886, p. 109; *Beavan, Ibis,* 1867, p. 445; *Legge, Ibis,* 1875, p. 396; *id., B. Ceylon,* p. 437; *Oates, B. Br. Burm.* i. p. 22.—The SHAMA.

Head, neck, upper breast, back, scapulars, wing coverts and tertiaries glossy black; rump and upper tail coverts white; lower breast, abdomen, sides, flanks, and under tail coverts, also the under wing coverts, chestnut; thighs white; edge of the wing black; also the primaries, their coverts, and secondaries; central pair of tail feathers black, the others black with broad white tips.

The female is olive brown, where the male is black; the wing coverts and quills are edged with ferruginous, and the lower surface is dull chestnut, whitish on the abdomen; tail much shorter. Bill black; legs and feet fleshy white; irides dark brown.

Length.—*Male*—11 to 11·8 inches; wing 3·45 to 3·65; tail 7 to 7·4; tarsus 1·05; culmen 0·7. *Length.*—*Female*—7 to 7·2 inches; tail 4·4 to 4·6.

Hab.—Ceylon, Southern and Central India; sub-Himalayan region, westward from the Ganges to Assam, through the Burmese countries to Siam, Cochin-China, and Hainan, down the Malayan Peninsula to Java. According to Jerdon, it is common in the dense and lofty jungles of Malabar, especially in the upland districts, also in the Wynaad; more rare in the Eastern Ghauts. It extends to the hill tracts of Assam, Sylhet, Burmah and Malacca, and also to Ceylon, where, according to Mr. Parker, it is found all through the North Western, North Central and Northern Provinces, and breeds from April to July, laying 3—4 eggs. The nest Mr. Parker found in a hole in a dead stump of a tree. It was a thin structure, formed, he says, of fine fibre and a little fine grass. In British Burmah it is spread abundantly wherever there is thick jungle. It is said to be almost always solitary, to perch low on branches, and to secure prey from off the ground. It is a charming songster, and its song, according to Jerdon, is chiefly heard in the evening, just before and after sunset. He says it is a most gushing melody of great power, surpassed by no Indian bird. It is caught and caged, and in confinement imitates the song of other birds. The Shama breeds in April and May. Mr. Hume gives an account of Mr. Davison's finds of two nests in April and May at Shymootee, and on the road to Meeta Myo in Tenasserim. The nests were found in holes of old stumps of trees. The eggs, four in number, are said to be moderately broad ovals, a good deal compressed towards the small end, and exhibiting a slight pyriform tendency; the shell is fine and compact, and has a slight gloss. The ground colour is a dull greenish stone colour, everywhere densely freckled with a rich raw sienna brown and dull purplish markings. Size 0·87 to 0·89 × 0·6 to 0·62.

Group.—CRATEROPODES.

The Crateropodes are characterized by their strong and stout legs and feet, and a short and rounded wing as well as a compressed bill, which is various in form and length. Including non-Indian species, and all those at present known from various parts, it presents a large assemblage of birds of diverse and varied aspect of plain, sombre and in some varied and generally lax plumage. In it are comprised the laughing thrushes, shrike thrushes, the thick-billed finch thrushes, the jay thrush, the tit thrushes, as well as the scimitar, spiny and other true babbling thrushes. They are social and gregarious in their habits, feed on the ground either on insects, grain, seeds, fruit, &c. Some affect open spots or groves, others delight in climbing through interlaced hedges and thickets, in which also they build. The majority lay eggs of a blue colour. Two-thirds of the recognized genera are Indian, and the rest are either African or peculiar to Australia, New Guinea, China, and the Malayan Peninsula. The majority of the Indian representatives belong to the great Himalayan mountains ranging east, west and north-west, a few only are residents of the plains, and a smaller number are found in the hill ranges of Bengal extending to Tenasserim, from north to south, alike in the hills and plains.

Gen. Argya.—*Lesson.*

Bill shorter than the tarsus, much compressed, slightly curving from the base, and barely hooked at the tip; commissure slightly curved; nostrils apert; its operculum stout and swollen; a few pale short rictal setæ; wings short, not so much rounded as in *Gampsorhynchus*; 4th, 5th and 6th quills nearly equal and longest; tail moderately long and broad; tarsus stout and scutellate; claws curved.

113. Argya rufescens (*Blyth*), *Sharpe, Cat. B. Br. Mus.* vii. p. 389. Malacocercus rufescens, *Blyth, J. A. S. B.* xvi. p. 453; *id., Cat. B. Mus. As. Soc.* p. 141; *Bp. Consp.* i. p. 373; *Kelaart, Prodr. Cat.* p. 122; *Layard, Ann. and Mag. Nat. Hist.* xii. p. 271; *Legge, B. Ceylon,* p. 497, pl. xxi. fig. 2. Layardia rufescens, *Jerd., B. Ind.* ii. p. 67; *Holdsw., P. Z. S.* 1872, p. 449; *Blyth, Ibis,* 1867, p. 300; *Legge, op. cit.* 1874, p. 18; *id., Str. F.* 1875, p. 368; *Hume, Str. F.* 1879, p. 97.—The Ceylon Pufescent Babbler.

Above, including the wing coverts and inner secondaries, warm earthy brown; quills reddish brown, margined on their outer webs with olive brown; tail the same, but more rufous, and with indistinct transverse bars, only seen in certain lights; head and nape light ashy; lores, cheeks and ear coverts rufous, the latter rather darker and paler-shafted; throat and breast rufous; sides and under surface of the body, also the thighs and under tail coverts, rufous brown; under wing coverts and axillaries light tawny; bill orange yellow; legs and feet dull chrome yellow; orbital skin pale greenish yellow; irides greenish white.

Length.—9·3 to 10·8 inches; wing 4·0 to 4·2; tail 4·85; tarsus 1·4; bill from gape 1·0 to 1·1.

Hab.—Ceylon, to which island it is confined. Extends over the western and damp portions of the island and through the western highlands to the main range. (*Sharpe.*) Breeds during May and June.

Pomatorhinus —*Horsf.*

Bill long, the culmen longer than the tarsus, compressed, pointed, and much curved throughout; nostrils barely apert; rictal bristles minute and a few only; wing equal to or longer than the tail, rounded; 5th and 6th quills longest; tail long or moderate; tarsi stout, shorter than the culmen.

114. Pomatorhinus melanurus, *Blyth, J. A. S. B.* xvi. p. 457; *Bp. Consp.* i. p. 220; *Kelaart, Prodr. Cat.* p. 122; *Layard, Ann. and Mag.*

Nat. Hist. xii. p. 271; *Blyth, Ibis,* 1867, p. 301; *Legge, J. A. S. B. Ceylon Branch,* 1870-71, p. 41; *Holdsw., P. Z. S.* 1872, p. 447; *Legge, Str. F.* 1873, p. 437; *id., Str. F.* 1876, p. 245; *Whyte, Str. F.* 1877, p. 202; *Hume, Str. F.* 1878, p. 383; *Legge, B. Ceylon,* p. 501.—The CEYLON BLACK-TAILED SCIMITAR BABBLER.

Above dark olive brown; wing coverts the same, but washed with ashy on the edge of the wing and the primary coverts; quills dusky brown, washed with dark olive brown; tail blackish brown, washed with olive brown on the margins and barred indistinctly with dusky under certain lights; crown of head darker olive brown than the back; base of forehead, a line along the sides of the crown, eyelids, lores and ear coverts black; supercilium, upper edge of the eyelid, cheeks, throat and under surface of the body white; sides of neck washed with rufous; flanks, thighs and under tail coverts dark olive brown, the sides of the breast faintly streaked with white; irides brownish red, dull or reddish brown; orbital skin and eyelids dull blue. (*Sharpe.*) Bill gamboge yellow, more or less blackish at the base; legs and feet plumbeous. (*Legge.*)

Young birds are ferruginous above and on the sides of the body.

Hab.—Ceylon, where it is distributed throughout the central and southern hills. It is recorded from Newara Eliya and Suffragam; also Buddyarna. Breeds from December to February.

Gen. **Garrulax**.—*Less.*

Bill nearly straight, rather long, moderately stout, the culmen shorter than the tarsus, gently curved towards the tip, which is slightly hooked and notched; nostrils rounded, pierced in the anterior part of the nasal depression, more or less impended by nareal tufts; rictal bristles long and strong, not reaching much beyond the nostrils; the feet outstretched does not reach the end of the tail; wings moderate, 5th and 6th quills generally the longest; tail long, much rounded; legs and feet strong; claws long.

Birds of moderately large size, the largest averaging 12 inches; plumage lax and disunited; coloration plain; head crested or not.

115. Garrulax cinereifrons, *Blyth, J. A. S. B.* xx. p. 176 (1851); *Kelaart, Prod. Cat.* p. 122; *Layard, Ann. and Mag. Nat. Hist.* xii. p. 270; *Blyth, Ibis,* 1867, p. 300; *Holdsw., P. Z. S.* 1872, p. 448; *Legge, Ibis,* 1874, p. xx.; *id., B. Ceylon,* p. 1199, pls. 21-22, fig. 2; *Sharpe, Cat. B. Br. Mus.* vii. p. 447.—The GREY-FRONTED GARRULAX.

Adult.—General colour above rufous brown, the wing coverts like the back, the one near the carpel bend of the wing edged with ashy grey; quills dark brown, externally rufous brown, the primaries paler, the innermost secondaries almost externally rufous brown; tail feathers dark brown, washed with rufous brown near the base; head and nape grey, as also the lores, sides of the face, and ear coverts; cheeks, throat and under surface of body light rufous buff, paler on the abdomen, the cheeks and chin slightly washed with grey; sides of body darker rufous brown, also the thighs; under tail coverts light rufous brown, with fulvous bases to the feathers; under wing coverts and axillaries light rufous buff; quills dusky brown below, fulvescent along the edge of the inner web; bill black, the inside of the mouth greenish yellow; legs and feet plumbeous brown; the claws dusky horny; posterior part of tarsus bluish; eyelid plumbeous; iris white. (*W. V. Legge.*)

Length.—10 inches; culmen 1·05; wing 4·2; tail 4; tarsus 1·5.

Young.—Iris dull grey, with a dark outer circle; bill black, the gape and base of lower mandible yellowish; eyelids greenish yellow; legs and feet olivaceous brown, soles yellowish fleshy, claws yellowish brown; forehead and head as in the adult, the nasal plumes and the grey of the crown not continued so far back; the back is deeper rufous than in the adult, and the wing coverts likewise are more intense; chin not so white, and the throat and under surface more fulvescent. In the first plumage the feathers of the chest and breast are fluffy. This dress appears to be quickly put off; and in the next or yearling plumage the iris is pearly grey, or in some white, with a tinge of reddish; gape and eyelid yellow; legs and feet bluish brown. There is scarcely any perceptible difference in the grey of the occiput, but the foreneck is paler and more fulvescent. (*W. V. Legge.*)

Hab.—Peculiar to the island of Ceylon, where it occurs up to an elevation of 3,600 feet in humid and inaccessible jungles. It seems only to be found in the central provinces; as, according to Legge, it is not known from the jungles of the south-eastern, eastern, or northern division of the island.

Gen. **Crateropus.**—*Swainson.*

Bill short or moderate, much compressed, rather deep, and curving from the base; nostrils apert; a few short rictal bristles; wings short, rounded, 4th, 5th and 6th quills nearly equal and longest; tail moderately long and broad; tarsus stout; frontal plumes rigid; general colour sombre grey, mixed more or less with rufescent, and the feathers mesially striated with dusky.

116. Crateropus striatus (*Swains.*), *Sharpe, Cat. B. Br. Mus.* vii. p. 481. Malacocercus striatus, *Swains., Zool. Illustr. N. S.*, pl. 127; *Jerd., B. Ind.* i. p. 59; *Blyth, Ibis*, 1867, p. 300; *Holdsw., P. Z. S.* 1872, p. 449; *Hume, Str. F.* 1878, p. 385; *id., Str. F.* 1879, p. 97; *Legge, B. Ceylon* p. 494. Malacocercus bengalensis (*non Blyth*), *Kelaart, Prod. Cat.* p. 122; *Layard, Ann. and Mag. Nat. Hist.* (2) xii. p. 271.—The Striated Babbler.

Above earthy brown, tinged with greyish brown on the head, mantle and back, the latter with central obscure streaks; lower back, rump and upper tail coverts uniform light earthy brown, the latter slightly fulvous; wing coverts ashy brown with pale shaft lines, the greater series narrowly edged with pale ashy; quills brown, the outer webs of the secondaries and primaries edged with ashy, the secondaries obscurely barred with dusky; tail dark brown, the base of the middle feathers for some way ashy, all barred with dusky under certain nights; lores and feathers round the eye dull white; cheeks and ear coverts light ashy, with narrow pale shaft lines to the latter; throat and chest ashy, washed with fulvous brown on the chest, breast and flanks; centre of abdomen, under tail coverts and thighs fawn buff, the latter slightly washed with brown; under wing coverts and axillaries fawn colour; bill yellowish white; eyelid yellowish; irides white.

Length.—9·8 to 10 inches; wing 3·95; tail 4·25; tarsus 1·25; culmen 0·95.

Hab.—Ceylon and Ramesvarum Island. In Ceylon in low country only. Breeds in the southern provinces in July; in the northern from January to July. Eggs, 4 in number only.

GROUP.—TIMELIÆ.

This group contains chiefly the Wren, Grass, Tree, Ground and Thrush Babblers, which are considered to be the most typical of the *Timeliinæ*, and closely affined by their general appearance to the *Muscicapinæ*. They vary much in the form of their bill, some having it long, slender, and much bent downward at the tip, others more arched and notched; others again broader and with the tip but slightly bent downwards. The plumage of the group is generally of a sombre tint; the head is either crested, or sub-crested, and in some not crested. The wing is either equal to, or longer than the tail, and very seldom shorter than it, which again is in most of the families graduated. Their habits, too are various.

Gen. **Pyctorhis**.—*Hodgs.*

Bill rather short, strong and deep; rictus bristled; orbits nude; 4th and 5th quills longest.

117. Pyctorhis nasalis, *Legge, Ann. and Mag. Nat. Hist.* iii. p. 169; *id., Birds Ceylon* p. 512; *Hume, Str. F.* 1879, p. 95; *Sharpe, Cat. B. Br. Mus.* vii. p. 512. Chrysomma sinensis (*non Gm.*), *Kelaart and Layard, Prodr. App.* p. 58; *Layard, Ann. and Mag. Nat. Hist.* xii. p. 272. Pyctorhis sinensis (*non Gm.*), *Holdsw., P. Z. S.* 1872, p. 448; *Legge, Ibis*, 1875, p. 290.—The Black-billed Grass Babbler.

Above reddish brown, darker on the head, and rufous on the wings; inner webs of primaries and secondaries dusky; tail dull brown, with very indistinct or nearly obsolete dusky cross bands; a stripe from the nostrils through the eye; chin, throat, and entire under surface white; bill black, also the nasal operculum; legs and feet dull yellow, extremites of toes dusky; eyelids chrome yellow; irides golden yellow.

Length.—6·25 to 6·5 inches; wing 2·75; tail 3·5; bill at front 0·5.

Hab.—Ceylon, where it is generally distributed in the southern parts. The nesting of this species is exactly similar to that of *P. sinensis*. Mr. Sharpe from a series of specimens in Capt. Wardlaw-Ramsay's collection holds this species as distinct from the Indian race. The nest is typically cone-shaped (apex downwards), from 5 to 6 inches in depth and 3 or 4 in diameter at the base, with the cone sometimes or rather often truncated according to the situation of the nest. The base of the cone is uppermost, and in it is the egg cavity. The whole structure is compactly woven with blades of grass and strips of fibrous bark, and more or less coated exteriorly with cobwebs. The number of eggs is from 2 to 3. They vary a good deal in shape and size, as well as in colouring. Eggs usually two, and sometimes three in number, prettily marked on a dusky or pinkish ground with streaks, spots and blotches of a brick red and brown colour. Affects chiefly the low tamarisk jungle, in which it also builds its nest. Oates says that in Burmah it affects grass jungle of all descriptions, and is much more common in such situations. Though creeps through grass without very perceptibly moving it, its pleasant and oft-repeated notes are sufficient to show its whereabouts.

Gen. **Dumetia**.—*Blyth*.

Bill moderate, rather compressed, pointed, and *with a subterminal notch;* culmen slightly curving from the base; rictal bristles small and few; wing short and rounded; 4th, 5th and 6th quills nearly equal; tail moderate; tarsus stout. *Frontal feathers stiff with rigid shafts.*

118. Dumetia albigularis, *Blyth, J. A. S. B.* xvi. p. 453; *id., Cat. B. Mus. As. Soc.* p. 140; *Layard, Ann. and Mag. Nat. Hist.* xii. p. 272; *Gould, B. Asia*, part 12; *Jerd., B. Ind.* ii. p. 26, No. 398; *Hume, Nests and Eggs Ind. B.* ii. p. 247; *Butler, Str. F.* 1875, p. 471; *Fairb., Str. F.* 1876, pp. 258, 265; *Bourdillon, t. c.* p. 399; *Butler, Str. F.* 1878, p. 94; *Legge, B. Ceylon* p. 505; *Hume, Str. F.* 1879, p. 96; *Vidal, Str. F.* 1880, p. 63; *Sharpe, Cat. B. Br. Mus.* vii. p. 514; *Murray, Avif. Brit. Ind.* ii. p. 132, No. 601.—The WHITE-THROATED WREN-BABBLER.

Above ashy olive brown, slightly more fulvescent on the rump, the feathers of the back, also of the lesser and median wing coverts, with pale shaft lines; greater coverts and quills light brown, edged with ashy olive brown, a little darker on the outer webs of the primaries; tail light brown, the feathers indistinctly cross-rayed under certain lights, shaded with ashy, and tipped with a narrow edging of whity brown; feathers of the crown stiffened; forehead rufescent, with blackish shafts; lores and eyelids whitish; ear coverts olivaceous ashy; cheeks and under surface of body bright sienna buff; throat, centre of breast and abdomen white; thighs more fulvous; axillaries sienna buff with white bases; under wing coverts bright sienna buff; irides greenish-white or white; upper mandible dusky or pinkish brown with fleshy margins; lower mandible fleshy, the tip dusky; legs and feet reddish dusky.

Length.—5·7 to 5·9 inches; wing 2·15; tail 2·45; tarsus 0·8; culmen 0·6.

Hab.—The peninsula of India, ranging from Travancore along the West Coast as high as Khandeish, and occurring again on Mount Abu.

In Ceylon it is said to be found all over the low country in all parts of the island. It affects bushy jungle, ravines, thick hedge-rows, &c., and is usually found in small parties skulking along one after the other, under and through from bush to bush, not unlike species of *Malacocercus*. It feeds on small insects. Breeds from February to September. Hume in his *Nests and Eggs* has an account of its nesting from Miss Cockburn of Kotagherry. The nest was constructed on a coffee-tree and contained three eggs, which were white and profusely covered with reddish spots of all sizes. The nest was small and nearly globular, and constructed of broad flaggy grass, without any lining or admixture of other material. In shape, Mr. Hume says, the eggs are moderately elongated ovals. The shell is very fine and smooth, and has, in some, a rather bright gloss. In length the eggs vary from 0·7 to 0·75 inches and in breadth from 0·5 to 0·53.

Gen. **Elaphrornis**, *Legge, B. Ceylon*, p. 514.

Bill moderate, about the length of the middle toe and claw, straight, curving gently to the tip and with a sub-terminal notch; nostrils with a tuft of nareal bristles at the base; gape smooth; wings short and rounded, the 4th, 5th and 6th quills the longest; tail short and graduated, with soft and flexible feathers; tarsus long and strong; mid toe nearly as long as the bill. Nuchal plumelets trifid and distinct.

119. Elaphrornis palliseri (*Blyth*), *Legge, B. Ceylon*, p. 514, pl. xxiv. fig. 2; *Sharpe, Cat. B. Br. Mus.* vii. p. 517. Brachypteryx palliseri, *Blyth, J. A. S. B.* xx. p. 178; *Kelaart, Prodr. Cat.* p. 102; *Layard, Ann. and Mag. Nat. Hist.* xii. p. 269; *Holdsw., P. Z. S.* 1872, p. 443, pl. xviii.—PALLISER'S WREN BABBLER.

Above dark brown, olivaceous on the head and neck; wing coverts brown, washed externally with olivaceous brown; quills dark sepia brown, their outer webs edged with olive brown; upper tail coverts ruddy brown; tail brown, the feathers with double dusky transverse bars, only visible under certain lights; lores and a faint supercilium ashy white; sides of face and ear coverts ashy brown, with ashy shaft lines; cheeks and throat pale fawn-colour; rest of under surface ashy olive with a tinge of green, centre of abdomen pale yellowish; under wing coverts and axillaries dark olive brown; (*Sharpe*) bill black, slaty at the base beneath; legs and feet brown or purplish brown.

Length.—6·2 inches; wing 2·45; tail 2·7; tarsus 1·05; culmen 0·65.

Hab.—Ceylon, in the higher mountain ranges of the Island to above 5,000 feet.

Gen. **Scotocichla**.—*Sharpe, Cat. B. Br. Mus.* vii. p. 522.

Bill moderate, straight, compressed, gently curved, notched and hooked at the tip; rictal bristles feeble; wings much rounded, 5th 6th, and 7th quills longest, and sub-equal; tail less graduated than in *Dumetia*, moderate, the distance between the tip of the outer and the tip of the central feathers, less than the length of the hind toe without claw; tarsus uniform; hind claw not more than half the length of the hind toe; nostrils shut in with a membrane, in the anterior portion of which the rounded nasal aperture is pierced.

120. Scotocichla fuscicapillum (*Blyth*), *Sharpe, Cat. B. Br. Mus.* vii p. 523. Drymocataphus fuscicapillus, *Blyth, J. A. S. B.* xviii. p. 815; *Kelaart, Prodr. Cat.* p. 122; *Layard, Ann. and Mag. Nat. Hist.* xii. p. 269. Pellorneum fuscicapillum, *Blyth, Ibis,* 1867, p. 301; *Hume, Str. F.* 1879, p. 96. Drymocataphus fuscicapillus, *Holdsw., P. Z. S.* 1873, p. 447; *Hume, Str. F.* 1873, p. 299 (note); *Legge, Ibis,* 1874, p. 19; 1875, pp. 393, 410. Pellorneum fuscicapillum, *Legge, B. Ceylon,* p. 509, pl. xxiii. fig. i.—The Ceylon or Brown-capped Babbler.

Above brown, the feathers of the mantle, wing coverts and back, with mesial fulvous streaks; lower back and rump uniform brown; quills pale brown, margined on their outer webs with reddish brown, more fulvous on the primaries; upper tail coverts and tail olive brown, the latter tipped with rufous; head blackish brown, the feathers with rufous shaft streaks; lores, supercilium, sides of face and neck vinous brown; entire under surface of body sienna brown, the flanks, abdomen and under tail coverts rather paler and more fulvescent; under wing coverts and axillaries like the breast; irides from light to dark red; eyelids olivaceous; upper mandible deep brown, lower flesh-color.

Length.—6·4 to 6·8 inches; wing 2·5 to 2·8; tail 2·4 to 2·6; tarsus 1· to 1·1; mid toe 0·75.

Hab.—Ceylon. Widely distributed in the north, central and south-west. In S.-E. Ceylon it is one of the commonest birds; also all Ceylon north of the Kandian Hills to 6,000 feet.

Mr. Parker says a party of five or six may often be seen walking about on the ground under the bushes, and turning over the leaves in search of insects. He adds that during the breeding season this Babbler is very pugnacious, and is ready to accept any challenge. Its common and loudly reiterated note, "to-*meet*-you," appears to be merely a call—such as the caw of a crow, for instance; but even a poor attempt at imitating its more prolonged series of notes never fails, according to his experience, to cause the bird to make its way straight up to one, provided that one remains perfectly still. The bird approaches silently but unhesitatingly, sometimes flitting from twig to twig, but quite as commonly walking along the ground. He noticed that it was silent in May and June in parts of the Northern Province. A nest is said to have been found in Ceylon belonging to this species.

Gen. Alcippe.—*Blyth.*

Bill short, moderately stout and compressed; culmen curved, hooked and notched; a few rictal setæ; wings moderate, rounded, 4th and 5th quills generally equal; tail moderate or rather short, very slightly rounded; tarsus stout; head sub-crested. Birds of small size and plain sombre plumage ranging through the hills of Southern and Western India and Ceylon, also the Himalayas and the hills of N.-E. Bengal.

121. Alcippe nigrifrons, *Blyth, J. A. S. Beng.* xviii. p. 815; *Kelaart, Prodr. Cat.* p 122; *Layard, Ann. and Mag. Nat. Hist.* xii. p. 269; *Blyth, Ibis*, 1867, p. 302; *Holdsw., P. Z. S.* 1872, p. 446; *Legge, Ibis*, 1874, p. 18; *id., Str. F.* 1875, pp. 157, 367; *Hume, Str. F.* 1878, ii. p. 383; *id., Str. F.* 1879, p. 95.; *Legge, B. Ceylon*, p. 507, pl. xxvii. figs. 2—3; *Sharpe, Cat. B. Br. Mus.* vii. p. 625. Malacopteron nigrifrons, *Gray, Hand-l. B.* i. p. 317.—The BLACK-FRONTED QUAKER THRUSH.

Above fulvous brown, also the flanks, thighs and under tail coverts; wing coverts the same; quills dusky, edged on their outer webs with fulvous brown; tail brown, margined with fulvous brown, and crossed transversely with dusky visible only under certain lights; crown of the head fulvous brown; forehead black with stiff glossy feathers; lores, orbital ring and ear coverts black; cheeks and under surface of the body white; axillaries light tawny buff, whitish at base; bill dark brown; margins of the upper and lower mandibles fleshy; irides yellowish white.

Length.—4·7 inches; wing 2·05; tail 1·95; tarsus 0·85; culmen 0·6.

Hab.—Ceylon. According to Legge, the tint of the upper surface of this species varies accordingly to locality, southern and western examples being rusty brown, and those inhabiting the hills olivaceous; northern examples are said to be intermediate between the two. Breeds from March to October in the N. W. and N. Central Provinces. Mr. Armstrong notes its nesting in Bogawantalawa and Pundaloya districts, 4,500 feet, from April to June. The nest is said to be a shapeless ball of leaves, and is generally placed in a shrub about 3 to 4 ft. from the ground. The eggs, 3 in number, are white, spotted with brownish red and bluish grey, and measure 0·74 × 0·56. Mr. Parker says some eggs are almost unspotted. The shape varies from an elongated and compressed to a very stumpy blunt oval, some being almost elliptical in outline. The average size of 20 eggs is given by Mr. Parker as 0·73 × 0·54. The length, he adds, varies from 0·70 to 0·77, and the breadth from 0·52 to 0·60.

Family.—PARIDÆ.

Tarsus generally short or moderate; feet fitted for perching; wings and tail moderate; bill various, strong, somewhat conic; plumage variegated. All are arboreal in their habits.

Sub-Family.—PARINÆ.

Bill typically rather short, less than the head in length, somewhat conic, stout, and without a notch; nostrils lateral or basal, the nares tufted; wings moderate, rounded, 3rd to 5th primaries longest, the first very short; tail varying in length and shape, long in a few only; tarsi and feet short and stout; hind toe long; claws curved; plumage soft, woolly and lax. In colour they are mostly sober compared with the *Liotrichinæ*; the principal colours however are white, black, yellow and blue; crown of the head generally crested. All the species are non-migratory, and are chiefly confined to the Himalayas; a few only extend to the hill regions of Central and Southern India. In their habits they are strictly arboreal, actively climbing about and clinging to the twigs and flowering branches of trees and continually flitting from spray to spray, and suspending themselves in all kinds of attitudes. They are noted for the peculiarly elegant construction of their nests, which are composed of the softest materials; and many of them are fastened to the extreme end of a small branch that projects over water; they also nidificate in holes of trees or even in walls, and occasionally on the ground. A few build pendulous nests. Their principal food consists of insects, which they find in the opening buds or in flower cups, but they also feed on seeds and fruits. They are indefatigably industrious.

Gen. **Parus**.—*Lin.*

Bill short, subulate, more or less conical, blunt at tip and without a notch; nostrils round, hidden by recumbent frontal feathers; tail rounded or square; tarsus scutate; head often crested. The well-known genera, *Lophophanes*, *Cyanistes*, *Melanochlora*, and *Machlolophus*, have all, at the hands of Dr. Gadow, become synonyms of *Parus*.

122. Parus cinereus, *Bonn. et Vieill.*, *Tabl. Cont. Meth.* p. 506, (1823), *ex Levaill; Blyth, J. A. S. B.* xvi. p. 460; *Bp.*, *Consp. Av.* p. 229; *Kelaart, Prodr. Cat.* p. 121; *Gould, B. Asia*, pt. x. pl.; *Jerd.*, *B. Ind.* ii. p. 278; *Walden, Ibis*, 1869, p. 315; *Holdsw.*, *P. Z. S.* 1872, p. 460; *Hume and Henders.*, *Lahore to Yarkand*, p. 167; *Cock. and Marsh.*, *Str. F.* 1873, p. 384; *Ball, Str. F.* 1874, p. 417; *Wardlaw-Ramsay, Ibis*, 1880, p. 62; *Gadow, Cat. B. Br. Mus.* viii. p. 16; *Murray, Avif. Brit. Ind.* ii. p. 182, No. 668. Parus atriceps, *Horsf.*, *Trans. Lin. Soc.* xiii. p. 160; *Sykes, P. Z. S.* 1832, p. 92; *McLell.*, *P. Z. S.* 1839; *Temm.*, *Pl. Col.* 207, fig. 2; *Sykes, P. Z. S.* 1832, p. 92; *Jerd.*, *Madr. Journ.* 1840, p. 7; *Legge, B. Ceylon*, p. 557; *Oates, B. Br. Burm.* p. 125. Parus nipalensis, *Hodgs.*, *Ind. Rev.* p. 31; *Blyth, J. A. S. B.* xi. p. 459; *Blyth and Wald.*, *B. Burm.* p. 112; *Scully, Str. F.* 1879, pp. 329-367; *Blanf.*, *J. A. S. B.* 1869, ii. p. 181. Parus cæsius, *Tick.*, *J. A. S. B.* (*fide auctt.*); *Swinhoe, P. Z. S.* 1871, p. 361; *Hume, Nests and Eggs Ind. B.* ii. p. 405; *Brooks, Str. F.* 1875, p. 253; *Butler, ibid*, 1875, p. 491; *Hume, ibid*, 1876, p. 402; *Hume and Dav.*, *ibid*, 1878, p. 376; *Dav. and Wenden, ibid*, 1879, p. 95. Parus commixtus, *Swinh.*, *Ibis*, 1868, p. 63; *Blyth and Wald.*, *B. Burm.* p. 111; *Hume, Str. F.* 1878, i. p. 376.—The Grey Indian Titmouse.

Forehead and crown to the nape, also the chin, throat, and a large patch on the breast, continued as a mesial abdominal line to the vent, black; sides of the neck black, connecting the black of the nape and breast; under surface of the body pale rufescent ashy; upper tail coverts, and lesser and median wing coverts ashy blue; greater coverts black, tipped with whitish; primary coverts and quills blackish, edged externally with ashy blue; outer tail feathers white, brown at the base; the next pair bluish on the outer web and white terminally, the inner webs blackish with a white stripe, the third outer pair with a small white tip; the remainder blackish on the inner and bluish on the outer webs. Bill black; iris brown; legs and feet plumbeous.

Length.—5·5 inches; wing 2·6; tail 2·6 to 2·8; tarsus 0·65; culmen 0·46.

Hab.—Nearly all over India from the Himalayas to Ceylon, also in Afghanistan. Extends to the southern half of China as well as to Java and Lombock. It is found in Nepal, Bhootan, Assam and through Central India to the Nilghiris. It extends all along the range of the western ghauts north to Khandeish. Occurs also in the hilly regions of Nagpore and at Saugor. Gilgit, Cashmere, Peshawur, Mussoorie, Simla, Kumaon, Nepaul, Behar, Khandeish, Madras, Travancore, Bhootan, Upper Assam and Bhamo, are also given as localities. Oates says it is irregularly distributed over Pegu. He found it at Thayetmyo, and again met with it west of the Irrawaddy, towards the foot of the Arrakan hills. In Tenasserim it is rare. It is a familiar bird wherever found. It is known to breed in the Himalayas, also on the Nilghiri hills and the Northern and Southern Provinces of Ceylon, where Mr. Parker took nests in April. Hume says it breeds throughout the more wooded mountains of the Empire, wherever these attain an altitude of 5,000 feet to even 9,000 feet. In the Nilghiris the breeding season is from February to May, and in the Himalayas from March to June. The nests are placed in holes in banks, in walls of buildings or of terraced fields, in outhouses of dwellings or deserted huts and houses, and in holes in trees, and, very frequently, in deserted nests of Woodpeckers and Barbets. The eggs are a broad oval, but somewhat elongated and pointed towards the smaller end. Colour pinkish white, sprinkled with pale purplish, thickly so towards the large end, where they form a heavy zone of red blotches, spots and streaks Size 0·65 to 0·7 in length, and in breadth from 0·5 to 0·58.

The North-Western race (Affghanistan and Turkestan) is named *P. bocchariensis.* It is said to be a larger and paler race, being pale or french grey above.

Family.—LANIIDÆ.

Bill strong, short, or of moderate length, notched or toothed at the tip; gape wide, with rather rigid rictal bristles; tarsus short and strong, and covered with large scutes on both sides; nostrils basal and of various forms; wings with ten primaries, the first small; tail of twelve feathers; toes four; midtoe largest.

This large family, including the genera found outside of India Proper, has been divided by Dr. Gadow into 5 sub-families, viz., *Gymnorhinæ,* comprising genera in the Australian region and Borneo; *Malaconotinæ*, comprising genera found in Africa, Madras and India, one genera only (*Pterer ythrius*) being found in the hilly and mountainous districts of the Indian region. The next is *Laniinæ*, in which are comprised four genera, the genus *Lanius* only being Colonial, but the species, however, extend their range into the Palæarctic and African regions in the old world; and following this are *Pachycephalinæ* and *Vireoninæ*, both unrepresented in India and Ceylon. Dr. Gadow, however, places, *Tephrodornis grisola* in the *Pachycephalinæ* sub-family, but this cannot stand there, nor can *P. cyanea*, both of which are true Niltavas without tarsal scutes.

Sub-Family.—LANIINÆ—TRUE SHRIKES.

Bill stout, strong, deep, laterally slightly compressed; culmen bent, and ending in a hook with a well-developed notch; nostrils partially covered with feathers and bristles and non-operculated; tail graduated or square; wings moderate, the first primary variable in length; the third, fourth (fifth) primaries the longest; tarsus short and stout. Birds of sombre and lax plumage, which is either black, grey, rufous or white, never red, green or blue; found throughout the Palæarctic, Indian, Colonial and African regions. They feed on insects and small birds, pouncing on their prey from their perch, invariably returning with their victim to the same spot to feed. The young are barred across.

123. Lanius erythronotus (*Vigors*), *Gray, Gen. B.* i. p. 290; *Blyth, J. A. S. Beng.* xv. p. 302; *Jerd., B. Ind.* i. p. 402, No. 257; *Murray, Hdbk. Zool., &c., Sind*, p. 134; *id., Vert. Zool. Sind*, p. 121; *id., Zool. Beloochistan and Southern Afghanistan*, p. 52; *Swinhoe, Birds of South Afgh., Ibis*, 1884, p. 104; *Gadow, Cat. B. Br. Mus.* viii. p. 263. Collurio erythronotus, *Vigors, P. Z. S.* 1831, p. 42; *Gould, Cent. Him. B.* pl. xii. fig. 2; *Hume, Str. F.* 1873, p. 174; *id., Nests and Eggs, Ind. B.* p. 167. Lanius caniceps, *Blyth, J. A. S. Beng.* xv. p. 302; *Gadow, Cat. B. Br. Mus. Sub-sp. a.* viii. p. 265; *Legge, B. Ceylon*, p. 383; *Murray, Avif. Br. Ind.* ii. p. 205, No. 702.—The RUFOUS-BACKED SHRIKE.

A black frontal band continued through the eyes to the back of the ear coverts; head, neck and upper back pale ashy grey; lower back, rump, upper tail coverts, lower scapulars, flanks, lower abdomen and vent rufous, a little lighter on the vent; chin, throat and upper breast white, in some a buffy tinge; primaries dusky with a small white spot at the base, and the edge of the wing white; secondaries dusky, faintly margined whitish on the external webs in some specimens, in others absent; tertiaries and wing coverts dark brown or blackish, edged and margined on the external web with whitish; tail, with the central feathers, black or dark brown, lateral feathers greyish brown, edged and tipped whitish. Bill and legs dark brown; irides dark brown.

Length.—9·75 to 10 inches; wing 3·5 to 3·75; tail 4·5 to 5.

The young has the head, neck and mantle ashy brown; the back, rump and upper tail coverts pale orange rufous; all the feathers of the upper surface paler at tip, and barred with dusky brown; the wing feathers edged with dull rufous; tail ashy brown, marked with indistinct wavy lines across.

Hab.—Ceylon, and India generally. It is found also in Afghanistan, Punjab, N.-W. Provinces, Cashmere and the N.-W. Himalayas, extending throughout India nearly to Ceylon. Common in Sind and the Malabar Coast, also the Nilghiris, and the better portion of the Carnatic and Central India, as well as Lower Bengal. It is recorded from all parts of Sind, from Murree, Kotegurh, Cashmere, Rajkote, Kamptee, and the Concan and Deccan. It breeds, at least the majority of the birds, in N -W. Himalayas, the Nilghiris, Pulneys, Arrakan hills. the Rajmahal hills and in Ceylon, where Mr. Parker got two broods in a year from a nest in his compound. They breed early in February, also in March and April. March to July, and often very late in August, is the period. 4 to 6 eggs is the usual number, and the colouring is not unlike that of *Lanius tephronotus*. In length the eggs vary from 0·93 to 1·0 inch, and in breadth 0 7 to 0·72.

It will be seen that I do not admit *L. caniceps* to specific rank. It is only a paler species, and the amount of rufous varies so much in birds from the Malabar Coast, the Deccan and the Nilghiris, that placed alongside in a line of 40 or more specimens from different parts of India, no very distinct character can be obtained. *Caniceps* is in my estimation only a climatic race.

124. Lanius cristatus, *Linn., Syst. Nat.* i. p. 134; *Jerd., B. Ind.* i. p. 406, No. 261; *Wald., Ibis,* 1867, p. 212; *Beavan, Ibis,* 1870, p. 312; *Holdsworth, P. Z. S.* 1872, p. 436; *Ball, Str. F.* 1873, p. 65; *Hume, t. c,* p. 65; *Hume, Nests and Eggs Ind. B.* p. 175; *Blyth and Wald., B. Burm.* p. 121; *Fairbank, Str. F.* 1876, p. 256; *Armstrong, t. c.* p. 316; *Hume, Str. F.* 1877, p. 29; *Butler, Str. F.* 1877, p. 228; *Legge, B. Ceylon,* p. 377; *Hume, Str. F.* viii. p. 91; *Bingham, Str. F.* ix. p. 172; *Gadow, Cat. B. Br. Mus.* viii. p. 271; *Oates, B. Br. Burm.* i. p. 252; *Murray, Hdbk. Zool., &c., Sind,* p. 134; *id., Vert. Zool. Sind,* p. 122; *Murray, Avif Br. Ind.* ii. p. 207, No. 704. Lanius phœnicurus, *Pall, Zoogr. Rosso-As.* i. p. 405; *Wald., Ibis,* 1867, pl. 5, fig. 2, p. 215; 1871, p. 173.—The BROWN SHRIKE.

A broad band from the lores through the eyes to the ear coverts dusky brown; head, tail and upper tail coverts rufous; back rufous brown; streak over the eye white; throat white; rest of under surface fulvous; wings dusky; the tertiaries margined rufous brown; tail rufous brown. The young birds and females have the feathers of the head, wing and lower parts edged with brown and whitish. Bill horny above, below pinkish white; irides brown.

Length.—8·9 inches; wing 3·50; tail 3·92; bill at front 0·50.

Hab.—Colombo, Kandy, Southern India generally, the Deccan, Bengal, N.-W. Provinces, Sind, Punjab, Nepaul, Mussoorie, Bhootan, Assam, Pegu and Tenasserim; also from Lake Baikal to the Malay peninsula, and from Yarkand to the east coast of China. Occurs during the winter months only, throughout India, the Andamans and British Burmah.

125. Lanius lucionensis, *Linn., Syst. Nat.* i. p. 135; *Wald., Ibis,* 1867, p. 125; *Hume, Str. F.* ii. p. 199; *Wald., Trans. Zool. Soc.* ix. p. 171, pl. xxix., fig. 1; *David et Oust. Ois. Chine*, p. 99; *Legge, B. Ceylon*, p. 378; *Hume, Str. F.* viii. p. 91; *Gadow, Cat. B. Br. Burm.* i. p. 251; *Murray, Avif. Br. Ind.* ii. p. 207, No. 705. Lanius Schwaneri, *Wald., Ibis,* 1867, p. 223.—The PHILLIPINE SHRIKE.

Forehead and a distinct supercilium greyish white; the feathers immediately at the base of the upper mandible, the lores, and a broad streak passing through the eye and covering the ear coverts, black; the whole upper plumage and scapulars liver brown, tinged with rufous on the rump and upper tail coverts; tail brown, tinged with rufous and tipped paler; chin, throat and sides of neck white; remainder of lower plumage pale buff; lesser coverts white, the remaining coverts and all the wing dark brown, edged with rufescent, more broadly so on the tertiaries than elsewhere. The young have the upper plumage brown, closely barred with black, and the lower plumage yellowish or buffy white; all the feathers, except those on the chin, throat, centre of breast and abdomen barred with dark brown; legs and feet dull leaden blue; the upper mandible horny brown, edged whitish near the gape, the terminal third of the lower mandible horny brown, the basal two-thirds bluish or fleshy white; irides brown. (*Davison.*)

Length.—8 inches; tail 3·8; wing 3·5; tarsus 1; bill from gape 0·9. (*Oates.*)

Hab.—Tenasserim, in the extreme south, where Oates says it is only a rare straggler. In winter it is said to be found in the Malay peninsula, the Andaman Islands, and the Phillipine Islands. It passes through China on migration, and is said to have occurred in Ceylon. A specimen in my possession from that Island however exactly fits the description, and there is no doubt more would be found.

The *adult female* differs from the male in having the ear coverts and lores more brownish, and the under parts paler. The young are brownish rufous above, brighter on the upper tail coverts; no grey on the head; loral region and a supercilium dingy white or cream colour; head, hind neck, mantle and upper tail coverts showing faint dark vermiculations; wing coverts and secondaries brown, broadly edged with rufous, each feather with a dark brown submarginal line; ear coverts and a small spot in front of the eye dark brown; chin, throat, middle of abdomen and under wing coverts creamy white; rest of under surface strongly washed with creamy or even with rufous, and marked with numerous dark brown cross vermiculations.

Group.—CERTHIOMORPHÆ.

Bill entire, and not notched.

Family.—CERTHIIDÆ.

Bill either straight and subulate, or slender, long, acute, entire and much curved; culmen keeled; tarsi comparatively short, covered anteriorly with transverse scutæ, except in *Tichodroma*, in which genus they are nearly fused together; sides of the tarsus with one long scutum; feet large; toes more often syndactyle; hind toe and claw large; wing and tail variable in size and structure, the wing with ten primaries.

This family of Tenuirostral or slender-billed Passerine birds are commonly known as *Creepers*. They are for the most part adapted to live upon the trunks and branches of trees, and to feed upon insects which infest the bark. The form of the bill is either long or short, slender or stout, and capable of penetrating very hard substances. They cling with their feet to the perpendicular surface of trees, resting upon the stiff quills of their tail, and creep from the base to the summit of the stem, with short jerking movements, searching every crevice as they ascend. They are divided into *Certhiinæ*, or true Creepers, and *Sittinæ*, or Nuthatches, the latter having affinities for the Woodpeckers.

Sub-Family.—SITTINÆ.

Bill slightly longer than the head, nearly straight, subulate and compressed at the tip; nostrils in a coriaceous groove, exposed or hidden by the frontal plumes; wings long and pointed; first primary short; tail short, rounded or square; tarsi short, anteriorly covered with transverse scutæ.

Nuthatches, like woodpeckers, climb with great facility up, down and around the trunks and branches of trees, but unlike them do not use their tail to assist them; usually they alight on trees with their head downwards, and it is said they sleep in that position. They feed on insects and nuts of kinds, some build in holes of trees, and others on the face of perpendicular cliffs. In the case of *S. syriaca*, which is common both in Afghanistan and Beloochistan in the Bolan Pass, the nests are made of mud plasters and cowdung in the form of a projecting cone with the entrance inclined downwards. All about the walls, within a radius of 2 or 3 feet, pieces of rag, feathers, &c., are placed in small chinks, or plastered on to the wall. When breeding in holes of trees, the holes are cemented till a small entrance is formed.

126. Sitta frontalis (*Swains.*), *Horsf.*, *Tr. Lin. Soc.* xii. p. 162; *Vig.*, *Mem. Raffl.*, p. 670; *Tick.*, *J. A. S. Beng.* ii. p. 579; *McLell.*, *P. Z. S.* 1839, p. 165; *Oates*, *B. Br. Burm.* i. p. 134; *Gadow*, *Cat. B. Br. Mus.* viii. p 358; *Murray*, *Avif. Br. Ind.* ii. p. 218, No. 723. Orthorhynchus frontalis, *Swains.*, *Zool. Ill. 1st Ser.*, pl. 2. Dendrophila frontalis, *Swains.*, *Classif. B.* ii. p. 318; *Jerd.*, *Mad. Journ.* xi. p. 218; *Blyth*, *J. A. S. Beng.* xvi.

p. 580; *Mason, Burmah*, p. 280; *Jerd., B. Ind.* i. p. 388, No. 253; *id., Ibis*, 1872, p. 21; *Holdsworth, P. Z. S.* 1872, p. 435; *Hume, Nests and Eggs Ind. B.* i. p. 161; *Legge, Ibis*, 1874, p. 16; *Ball, Str. F.* 1874, p. 397; *Bourdillon, Str. F.* 1876, p. 393; *Fairbank, Str. F.* 1877, p. 399; *Hume and Dav., Str. F.* 1878, p. 201; *Legge, B. Ceylon*, p. 560; *Hume, Str. F.* 1879, p. 459. Dendrophila corallina (*Rich.*), *Hume, Str. F.* 1874, p. 473; 1875, p. 89; *Sharpe, Str. F.* 1876, p. 436; *Anders., Zool. Exped. Yunnan*, p. 633.—The VELVET-FRONTED BLUE-NUTHATCH.

A broad band on the forehead and a long supercilium black; ear coverts lilac; chin and throat whitish; rest of the upper plumage, including the wing coverts, fine cœrulean blue, with a slight purplish shade; quills and primary coverts deep black, edged with blue; central pair of tail feathers blue, the rest black, largely tipped and margined with blue; under wing coverts deep black; under surface of the body pale vinous brown. Bill bright cobalt blue; legs sienna yellow; orbital skin lemon yellow; iris light straw yellow

Length.—4·5 to 5 inches; wing 2·9; tail 1·7; tarsus 0·7; culmen 0·65.

Hab.—From the Himalayas to Ceylon, throughout the Burmese countries, Java, Borneo and the Phillipines. According to Jerdon, it is found over the greater part of India in suitable localities. He found it on the Malabar Coast, on the summit of the Neilgherries, in Central India, in Goomsoor, and also on the Himalayas. In Ceylon as well as in Assam, Burmah and Malayana, it is not uncommon. Oates says it occurs over every portion of Pegu where there is thick forest, but is commoner on the hills than elsewhere. Davison found it throughout Tenasserim, and Captain Bingham in the Thoungyeen valley. The species is generally found in small companies of 5 or 6, affecting trees and brushwood. They nest during February and March, and lay 3—4 eggs of a whitish colour, spotted with red and purple.

Group—CINNYRIMORPHÆ.

Bill long, always pointed and curved; tongue extensile. No rictal bristles. Colours metallic.

Family—NECTARINIIDÆ.

Bill of various lengths, generally long, always much pointed, and more or less curved. Nostrils basal, rounded, covered by membrane. Rictal and nasal bristles wanting, wings moderate, first primary small; third to fifth primaries form the tip of the wing; tongue long, protractile, and ending in a tube, which is divided anteriorly; tarsus anteriorly covered with transverse scales; hallux and claws stout.

The Honeysuckers, or Sunbirds as they are called, are noted for the brilliant and metallic splendour of their plumage, and may be said to take the place in India of the humming birds of America. The principal ground colours are yellow and green, with the addition of other ornamental and metallic colours, which are generally, with the pectoral tufts, characteristic of the male bird. The central tail feathers of many are elongated. The sexes differ much in colour, the females being dressed in plain yellow, greenish yellow, or pale fawn yellow. They live chiefly on minute insects, and on the nectar of flowers. Nests pensile ; eggs generally two, white.

Gen. **Cinnyris**.—*Cuv.*

Bill longer than the head, strongly curved, and much pointed; culmen keeled ; no rictal bristles; first primary short ; third, fourth and fifth longest ; tail shorter than the wing ; tarsus covered with transverse scales.

127. Cinnyris asiatica (*Lath.*), *Less.*, *Man. d'Orn.* ii. p. 36 ; *Vieill, N. Dict. d'Hist. Nat.* xxxi. p. 493 ; *Shelley, Monogr. Nect.* p. 181, pl. 57 ; *Legge, B. Ceylon*, p. 566 ; *Gadow, Cat. B. Br. Mus.* ix. p. 57 ; *Murray, Avif. Br. Ind.* ii. p. 228, No. 733. Cinnyris orientalis, *Frankl.*, *P. Z. S.* 1831, p. 122. Cinnyris currucaria, *Sykes*, *P. Z. S* 1832, p. 98. Nectarinia mahrattensis, *Jard.*, *Monogr. Sun-Birds*, pp. 222, 264, pl. 24 (1843). Nectarinia asiatica, *Blyth*, *Cat. B. Mus. As. Soc. B.* p. 224 ; *Gould*, *B. Asia*, pt. 8, pl. 2. Arachnethra asiatica, *Reichb.*, *Handb. Scansoriœ*, p. 295, No. 691, pl. 579 ; *Jerd.*, *B. Ind.* i. p. 370, No. 234 ; *Beavan*, *Ibis*, 1865, p 414 ; *Walden*, *Ibis*, 1870, p. 20; *Hume*, *Nests and Eggs Ind. B* p. 151 ; *Ball*, *Str. F.* 1874, p. 396 ; *Hume*, *Str. F.* 1875, p. 87 ; *Armstrong*, *tom. cit.* p. 313 ; *Blyth and Wald.*, *Cat. B. Br. Burmah* ; *Butler*, *Str. F.* iii. p. 492 ; *Hume and Dav.*, *Str. F.* ii. p. 190 ; *Murray*, *Hdbk. Zool., &c., Sind*, p. 132 ; *id.*, *Vert. Zool.*, *Sind*, p. 119. Arachnethra intermedia, *Hume*, *Ibis*, 1870, p. 436 ; *Jerd.*, *Ibis*, 1872, p. 18; *Hume*, *Nests and Eggs*, *Ind. B.* p. 154.—The PURPLE HONEYSUCKER.

Summer plumage.—Head, neck, throat, breast, and back glossy greenish purple; abdomen purplish black ; tail dull black, faintly white-tipped ; wings dull black ; a tuft of crimson and yellow feathers on the flanks behind the axil. In the winter garb, or non-breeding plumage, the upper parts are dull olive green, beneath yellow ; shoulder and stripe from chin to vent brilliant glossy violet ; wings and tail dusky. The female is olive grey above and olive yellow beneath ; the breast and throat deep yellow ; wings dusky ; tail black. Bill and legs black ; irides reddish brown.

Length.—4·5 inches ; wings 2·25 ; tail 1·5 ; bill at front 0·75.

Hab.—Ceylon ; throughout India to Burmah ; also Nepal and Upper Pegu. Occurs in Beloochistan, S. Persia, S. Afghanistan, South India, Travancore, the Deccan, Kutch, Kattiawar, Jodhpore, and N. Guzerat. It is everywhere extremely common, and breeds during June and July, laying two eggs, which are greenish white, speckled and marked with deep grey. The nest is pendulous usually suspended from the end of the branch of a tree and composed of wool, fibres, leaves, grasses, &c., with a hole at nearly the bottom for an entrance.

128. Cinnyris lotenia (*Linn.*), *Cuv. Regn. Anim.* i. p. 412; *Bp. C. A.* i. p. 408; *Shelley, Monogr. Nect.* p. 177, pl. 56; *Gadow, Cat. B. Br. Mus.* ix. p. 60; *Murray, Avif. Br. Ind.* ii. p. 229, No 735. Cinnyris politus, *Vieill., N. Dict. d' Hist. Nat.* xxxi. p. 500; *Jerd., Madr. Journ.* xi. p. 225. Nectarinia lotenia, *Jard., Monogr. Sun-birds*, pp. 220-263, pl. 23; *Blyth, J. A. S. B.* xii. p. 978; *Gould, B. As.* pt. viii. pl. 111. Arachnethra lotenia, *Cab. Mus. Hein.* i. p. 105; *Reichenb., Handb. Scansoriæ*, p. 294, pl. 579; *Jerd., B. Ind.* i. p. 372; *Walden, Ibis*, 1870, p. 23; *Holdsworth, P. Z. S.* 1872, p. 434; *Legge, B. Ceylon*, p. 563.—The LARGE PURPLE HONEYSUCKER.

Above brilliantly glossed with metallic green and purple; throat and breast rich purple; a narrow bright maroon collar or band below this and the sooty brown abdomen; flanks and under wing coverts sooty brown; pectoral tufts pure yellow. Bill and legs black; irides dark brown.

Length.—5·5 inches; wing 2·15 to 2·3; tail 1·5; tarsus 0·65; culmen 1·1 to 1·3. The female like that of *C. asiatica* is silky or greyish white on the under surface.

Hab.—Southern India and Ceylon. According to Jerdon common along the Malabar Coast, and the more wooded parts of the Carnatic as about Madras and other large towns.

129. Cinnyris minima, *Sykes, P. Z. S.* 1832, p. 99; *Sykes, J. A. S. B.* iii. p. 543; *Jerd., Madr. Journ.* xi. p. 226; *Legge, B. Ceylon*, p. 572; *Shelley, Monogr. Nect.* p. 143, pl. 46; *Gadow, Cat. B. Br. Mus.* ix. p. 62; *Murray, Avif. Br. Ind.* ii. p. 230, No. 736. Nectarinia minima, *Tick., J. A. S. B.* ii. p. 277. Nectarinia minuta, *Jard., Monogr. Sun-birds*, pp. 224-265. Leptocoma minima, *Horsf. and Moore, Cat. B. Mus. E. I. Co.* ii. p. 742; *Jerd., B. Ind.* i. p. 369; *Hume, Str. F.* 1877, p. 42; *id., Nests and Eggs, Ind. B.* i. p. 150; *Fairbk., Str. F.* iv. p. 392.—The TINY HONEYSUCKER.

PLATE.

Entire crown metallic green; throat metallic violet; ear coverts and loral region black; hind neck and sides of neck and a broad collar across the foreneck and chest, also the back and wing coverts, rich bright sanguine or blood-red; rump and upper tail coverts metallic amethystine purple; *no distinct pectoral tufts*; under surface of the body pale lemon yellow. In winter plumage the male resembles the female, but retains invariably the amethystine rump, and usually a little red about the shoulder of the wing. (*Hume.*) The female is olive brown above, has a red rump, and the under parts are pale yellowish buff.

Length.—3·5 inches; wing 1·9; tail 1·2; tarsus 0·52; culmen 0·58.

Hab.—South-Western India and Ceylon. Found on the west coast of India, also on the Nilghiris to about 3,000 feet elevation, the Malabar Coast and Travancore.

130. Cinnyris zeylonica (*Linn.*), *Vieill, N. Dict. d' Hist. Nat.* xxxi. p. 507; *Hahne, Vogt.* pt. 7, pl. 4; *Vieill, Enc. Meth.* ii. p. 594; *Hume,*

Cinnyris Minimus

B.E

Str. F. v. p. 270; *Cripps, tom. cit.* p. 267; *Legge, B. Ceylon*, p. 569; *Shelley, Monogr. Nect.* p. 137, pl. 45; *Murray, Avif. Br. Ind.* i. p. 230, No. 737. Certhia zeylonica, *Linn., Syst. Nat.* i. p. 188, No. 23. Nectarinia zeylonica, *Jard., Monog. Sun-birds*, pp. 213, 261, pl. 20; *Blyth, J. A. S. B.* xii. p. 976; *Gould, B. Asia*, pt. 19, pl. 40. Leptocoma zeylonica, *Cab. Mus. Hein.* i. p. 104; *Jerd., B. Ind.* i. p. 368, No. 232; *Beavan, Ibis*, 1865, p. 232; *Ball, Str. F.* vii. p. 232; *id., Str. F.* vii. p. 208; *Godw.-Austen, J. A. S. B.* 1870, p. 267; *Hume, Nests and Eggs Ind. B.* p. 147. Nectarophila zeylonica, *Reichb., Handl. Scans.* p. 282, pl. 570, figs. 3885-87.—The AMETHYST-RUMPED HONEYSUCKER.

Head above and lesser wing coverts bright metallic glossy purplish green; upper back, scapulars and median wing coverts maroon brown; lower back and upper tail coverts metallic lilac, shaded with blue; tail brownish black, the outer feathers paler at the tips, the rest very slightly edged with metallic violet; remainder of the wing dark brown; the greater coverts and quills edged with rufous brown; cheeks and ear coverts deep coppery brown, shading into dull brown behind the ear coverts; under surface of the body sulphur yellow; chin and throat metallic lilac; sides of the neck and a pectoral collar maroon brown like the back; sides of the body and under wing coverts white. Bill and legs black; irides reddish brown.

Length.—4·1 to 4·5 inches; wing 2·25; tail 1·45; tarsus 0·75; culmen 0·65.

The adult female is ashy olive brown above; tail black, broadly tipped with white; crown ashy grey; foreneck silky white; a white eyebrow and a dark streak through the eye; chest and centre of abdomen sulphur yellow; under tail coverts paler yellow.

Length.—3·6 to 3·9; wing 2·1.

Hab.—Ceylon, the Indian Peninsula and Assam; not found in Sind and the N.-W. Provinces of India, otherwise it is generally spread throughout India, from the extreme south to Bengal, extends through Dacca into Assam. Abundant in Madras, Malabar, Mysore, Coorg, Pondicherry, the Carnatic, Deccan, Singbhoom, Maunbhoon, Kamptee, Sumbulpoor and Khasia hills. Seen in every garden flying from flower to flower. The species has not much of a note. Blyth describes it as having a week shrill chant followed by frequent low chirps analogous to that of *Certhia familiaris*. In Calcutta, as well as in Madras, many are taken daily with birdlime for sale. It is said to lay at least twice a year, in February and August, and sometimes in December. The breeding season, Hume says, is variable. The nests are generally attached to the terminal twigs of branches, from 10 to 30 feet from the ground. In shape they are purse-like, with the aperture near the top. According to Mr. Morgan, the bird often selects a cobweb in which to build its nest, and this is so ingeniously built, that it is impossible to detect the existence of the nest unless the cobweb is examined. An average-sized nest is about 5·6 inches in length and about 3 in diameter. It is composed of very fine grass or vegetable fibre, and the inner or egg chamber is lined with feathers or vegetable down, while the exterior is ornamented with flower buds, lichen, &c. Eggs, two in number; in shape and size quite like those of *C. asiatica*. Hume describes them as moderately broad ovals, a good deal elongated and usually pointed towards one end; the shell is delicate and close-grained and almost devoid of gloss; the ground colour varies considerably; in some it is nearly pure white, but generally it is a dingy greenish or brownish white, much freckled, clouded and streaked with minute greyish brown or brown markings, which commonly form an irregular zone round the larger end, and sometimes a confluent cap. In others the whole surface is finely and closely speckled so as to entirely conceal the ground colour.

Family—MELIPHAGIDÆ.

Bill variable in length, but always with a prominent culmen, broadened out at the base, curved, and almost always with a slight notch; maxilla serrated. Nostrils basal, situated in a large unossified groove which is quite soft and membranous, either longitudinal and with a well-developed coriaceous operculum, or oval, and situated in front of a coriaceous groove; never entirely covered with feathers. Tongue protractile, bifid, each half broken up into numerous stiff horny fibres, so as to form a brush; wings, tail and tarsus variable in shape and length, plumage greenish or greenish yellow; in the *Myzomelinæ* red, generally nude wattles on the ears or cheeks or round the eye. (*Gadow.*)

This family is divided by Dr. Gadow into three sub-families, viz., 1, *Myzomelinæ*; 2, *Zosteropinæ*; and 3, *Meliphagine*; three species of the second of which only are known in India.

Sub-Family—ZOSTEROPINÆ.

Bill shorter or equal to the length of the head; a ring of whitish feathers round the eye; 1st primary absent or very short.

Gen **Zosterops**.—*Vig.*

Bill of about the same length as the head, wide at base, somewhat conic, acute at the tip and slightly but distinctly notched; culmen slightly curved; rictus smooth; eyes surrounded by close-set minute white feathers; nostrils longitudinal, exposed; wings moderate; 1st primary extremely short; sometimes absent; 3rd and 4th primaries longest and forming the tip of the wing; tail short, even; tarsus moderate, covered in front with a few scales; toes strong; outer syndactyle.

131. Zosterops palpebrosa (*Temm.*), *Blyth, J. A. S. B.* xiv. p. 563; *Bp., Consp. Av.* i. p. 398; *Kelaart, Prod. Cat.* p. 121; *Jerd., B. Ind.* ii. p. 265, No. 631; *Stol., J. A. S. B.* xxxvii. p. 51; *Beavan, Ibis*, 1868, p. 82; *Brooks, Ibis*, 1869, p. 57; *Holdsw., P. Z. S.* 1872, p. 458; *Hume, Nests and Eggs Ind. B.* p. 397; *Cock. and Marsh., Str. F.* 1873, p. 356; *Adams, l. c.* p. 384; *Hayes Lloyd, Ibis.* 1873, p. 412; *Legge, Ibis,*

1874, p. 22; *Ball*, *Str. F.* 1874, p. 417; *Hume*, *Str. F.* 1875, p 143; *Brooks*, *l. c.* p. 252; *Butler*, *l. c.* p. 491; *Blyth and Wald.*, *B. Burm.* p. 110; *Fairbk.*, *Str. F.* 1876, p. 260; *id.*, 1877, p. 407; *David and Walden*, *Str. F.* 1878, p. 84; *Butler*, *Cat. B. Sind*, p. 42; *Legge*, *B. Ceylon*, p. 582; *Hume*, *Str. F.* 1879, p. 104; *Vidal*, *Str. F.* 1880, p. 69; *Butler*, *l. c.* p. 413; *Hume*, *l. c.* p. 413; *Gadow*, *Cat. B. Br. Mus.* ix. p. 165; *Murray*, *Vert. Zool. Sind* p. 174; *Murray Avif. Brit. Ind.* ii. p. 242, No. 748. Sylvia palpebrosa *Temm.*, *Pl. Col.* 293, fig. 3 (1824). Zosterops Madraspatensis, *Jerd.*, *Madr. Journ.* xi. p. 7. Zosterops nicobarica, *Blyth*, *J. A. S. B.* xiv. p. 563. Zosterops simplex, *Swinh.*, *Ibis*, 1861, p. 331; *Gould*, *B. Asia*, part xxiii., *Hume*, *Str. F.* 1878, vol. ii. p. 403; *id.*, *Str. F.* 1879, p. 104. Zosterops nicobariensis, *Hume*, *Str. F.* 1874, p. 242; 1879, p. 104. Zosterops palpebrosa-nicobariensis, *Hume*, *Str. F.* 1876, p. 291.—The WHITE-EYED TIT.

Head, nape, back, scapulars, rump and upper tail coverts siskin green, yellowish on the upper tail coverts; chin, throat and upper breast canary yellow; eyes with a circle of white feathers; lower breast, abdomen and flanks white with a bluish tinge; vent, under tail and thigh coverts yellow; primaries, secondaries and tertiaries brown, edged externally with the colour of the back, all margined white on their inner webs, except the innermost tertiaries; edge of wing and under wing coverts yellowish; tail brown, the feathers margined on their outer webs with greenish, and on their inner webs with whitish. Bill blackish brown; legs horny brown.

Length.—4·5 inches; wing 2·3; tail 1·7; bill at front 0·33 to 0·4; tarsus 0·75.

Hab.—Ceylon; India generally to Assam, Arracan, and Nepaul, and also Sind (probably Kutch), Rajputana, Deccan, Concan, Central and Southern India, also the Burmese countries eastwards into South China, Andaman Islands, and Nicobars. Found wherever it occurs in small flocks moving from tree to tree with a low twitter, searching for insects among the leaves. It breeds throughout India, sparingly in the hotter parts, and abundantly in the Nilgiris and other ranges of the Peninsula to their very summit, and in the Himalayas to an elevation of 5,000 or 6,000 feet. The breeding season lasts from January to September; sometimes they have two broods. The nest is a soft delicate little cup, sometimes very shallow and at other times deep, and, as a rule, suspended between two twigs. The materials of which it is made are various, as fine grasses, grass roots, fibres, thread, floss-silk and cobwebs. The eggs are usually two in number, and pale blue in colour, and vary in length from 0·53 to 0·7 and in breadth from 0·42 to 0·58.

Mr. A. G. Cardew's experience in the Nilgiris is that out of a dozen nests or more at least five-sixths were built in the common *Berberis aristata.* The eggs, always two, are a delicate blue with a greenish tinge. Breeds February—April. It is known as Pa-Chit-Tam or Flower-Small-Bird.

132. Zosterops ceylonensis, *Holdsworth, P. Z. S.* 1872, p. 459, pl. 20, fig. 2; *Swinhoe, Ibis,* 1873, p. 228; *Layard, P. Z. S.* 1873, p. 205; *Legge, Ibis,* 1874, p. 22; *Holdsw., t. c.* p. 123; *Legge, Ibis,* 1875, p. 410; *Hume, Str. F.* 1879, p. 104; *Legge, B. Ceylon,* p. 585; *Sharpe, Cat. B. Br Museum,* ix. p. 173. Zosterops annulosus (*nec Sws.*), *Kelaart, Prodr. Cat.* p. 121; *Layard, Ann. and Mag. Nat. Hist.* xii. p. 267.—The Ceylon White-Eyed Tit.

Above, including the wing and primary coverts, rump and upper tail coverts, dull olive green; median and greater coverts the same, but edged slightly with yellowish; quills and tail dusky; edged on the inner web with white and on the outer with olive green; the edges of the primaries tinged with yellowish; crown of the head a shade more dusky than the back; orbital ring white; ante-ocular spot dusky; ear coverts and cheeks, olive green; throat, fore-neck and chest bright olive yellow, greener on the sides of the breast, which is light ashy grey; under tail coverts bright yellow; axillaries and under wing coverts white tinged with yellow; bill blackish, slaty at the base beneath: legs pale leaden; irides variable, from yellowish brown to reddish brown.

Length.—4·5 inches; wing 2·25; tail 1·8; tarsus 0·65; culmen 0·55.

Hab.—Ceylon. Habits same as the last.

Section.—FRINGILLIFORMES.

Wings with generally *nine* primaries; the first well developed and long, except in *Prionochilus* and *Pardalotus*.

Family.—DICÆIDÆ.

Bill moderate, broad at the base, the culmen curved; tip entire; wings with nine primaries; habits nearly similar to those of the Sun-birds.

Gen. Dicæum.—*Cuv.*

Bill creeper-like, broad at the base, tip entire, culmen curved; wings with the first three primaries sub-equal, the second slightly the longest; tail short, exceeding the wing in length. Birds of small size.

133. Dicæum erythrorhynchum (*Lath.*), *Blyth and Wald., B. Burm.* p. 143; *Fairbk., Str. F.* 1877, p. 399; *Hume and Dav., Str. F.* 1878, p. 196; *Hume, Str. F.* 1879, p. 90; *Vidal, Str. F.* 1880, p. 57; *Butler, t. c.* p. 390; *Oates, B. Br. Burm.* i. p. 334; *Murray, Avif Brit Ind.* ii. p. 249, No. 757. Certhia erythrorhynchos, *Lath., Ind. Orn.* i. p. 299. Dicæum minimum, *Blyth, Ann. and Mag. Nat. Hist.* xx. p. 316; *Tytler, op. cit.* xiii. p. 373; *Bp., Consp. Av.* i. p. 374; *Jerd., B. Ind.* i. p. 374, No. 238; *Beavan, Ibis,* 1865, p. 416; *Hume, Nests and Eggs Ind. B.* p. 155; *Ball, Str. F.* 1878, p. 208; *Legge, B. Ceylon,* p. 574; *Butler, Cat B. B. Pres.* p. 30.—The Small Flower-Pecker.

The whole upper plumage ashy olive, the feathers of the crown darker centred; tail dark brown; wing and coverts brown, edged with ashy olive;

lores, sides of the head and face pale ashy brown ; the ear coverts streaked with narrow whitish shaft lines ; under surface of the body pale ashy with a buffish tinge; under tail coverts buffy white ; under wing coverts and axillaries white. Bill pale fleshy with a dusky tip ; legs plumbeous ; iris brown.

Length.—3·2 inches ; wing 1·8 ; tail 1 ; tarsus 0·5 ; culmen 0·4.

Hab.—Ceylon, Lower Bengal and Central and Southern India as far as the Eastern Himalayas and Assam, extending through Arracan to Moulmein in Tenasserim. Recorded from Nepal, Madras, Belgaum, Dacca, Khandalla in the Deccan, Poona and Bombay. Breeds in the Deccan and the Nilgiris ; nesting habits same as those of the other species of the genus. Eggs, 2—3, pure white.

Gen. **Prionochilus**, *Strickl.*

Bill stout and finch-like, occasionally with tomical serrations, broader than high at nostrils, gape without wattles; tail short, not exceeding the tip of the wing by as much as the length of the tarsus ; wing with a distinct bastard primary; nostrils only a narrow slit; tarsus large ; inner toe shorter than the outer.

134. Prionochilus squalidus (*Burton*), *Sharpe, Cat. C. Br. Mus.* x. p. 73; *Murray, Avif. Brit. Ind.* ii. p. 251, No. 761. Pipra squalidus *Burton, P. Z. S.* 1836, p. 113. Fringilla agilis, *Tick., J. A. S. B.* ii. p. 578. Piprisoma agile, *Blyth, J. A. S. B.* xiii. p. 395; *Jerd., B. Ind.* i. p. 376, No. 240; *Hume, Nests and Eggs Ind. B.* p. 158; *Beavan, Ibis,* 1867, p. 430, pl. x.; *Hume, Str. F.* i. p. 434; *id.*, viii. p. 90; *Legge, B. Ceylon,* p. 579; *Scully, Str. F.* viii. p. 260; *Oates, Str. F.* x. p. 198; *id., B. Br. Burm.* i. p. 338.—The Thick-billed Flower-Pecker.

Whole upper plumage and lesser wing coverts ashy brown with a slight olive tinge on the rump and upper tail coverts; quills brown, externally edged with olive; median and greater series of coverts the same ; tail blackish, edged with green on the outer webs of the feathers and a bar of white on the two outermost ; sides of face and ear coverts ashy brown ; cheeks and under surface of the body greyish white with a faint tinge of yellowish; foreneck and breast with indistinct dusky stripes ; chin and throat yellowish white ; an indistinct or obscure line runs down either side of the throat from the base of the lower mandible to the breast ; sides of the body, flanks and thighs washed with ashy brown ; under tail coverts white ; under wing coverts and axillaries white. Bill plumbeous, blackish at tip; iris orange yellow; legs dark plumbeous.

Length.—3·6 to 4 inches ; wing 2·3 to 2·4 ; tail 1·25 to 1·3 ; tarsus 0·6 ; culmen 0·35.

Hab.—Ceylon, and the whole of India, except the drier parts up to the Himalayas, occurring in the N.-W. portion of the range, and in Nepal, extending to Tenasserim. Jerdon found it on the Malabar Coast and Ceylon, most commonly in jungly districts. He procured it at Goomsoor, on the Eastern Ghauts and in the Deccan. Blyth got it in the Midnapoor jungles, while in Pegu and Tenasserim and the hill tracts of Bengal it is said to be common. It has been recorded from Darjeeling, the N.-W. Himalayas, Manbhoom, Madras, Jhansi (Bundelkund), Bangalore, Mirzapore and Ramnuggur.

It breeds from the middle of February to the end of May, according to locality, making a nest of various materials, but small in shape and size; a full-bottomed purse-like bag, which is hung from a small twig, and has the aperture near to the top. The number of eggs is 2—3, varying in size and shape, elongated ovals, white in colour, and marked with reddish brown.

135. Prionochilus vincens, *Sclater, P. Z. S.* 1872, p. 729; *Holdsw., t. c.* p. 483; *Legge, J. A. S. (Ceyl. Branch)*, 1873, p. 13; *Sclater, Ibis*, 1874, p. 2, pl. 1, figs. 1, 2, ; *Legge, t. c.* p. 23; *Holdsw., t. c.* p. 126; *Hume, Str. F.* 1876, p. 493; *id., Str. F.* 1879, p. 90; *Gould, B. Asia*, pt. 31, 1879. Pachyglossa vincens, *Legge, B. Ceylon*, p. 577, pl. 26, figs. 1, 2 —The CEYLONESE FLOWER-PECKER.

Above glossy leaden blue-black, also the rump, which is slightly greyer, the wing coverts, lores, sides of the face, ear coverts, cheeks, throat, chest and sides of the chest; quills black, edged with leaden blue; upper tail coverts black, edged with plumbeous grey; tail black, all but the four central feathers, with a white terminal white spot; breast and under surface of the body yellow, the flanks behind washed with ashy olive; thighs and under tail coverts white, slightly washed with yellow; under wing coverts and axillaries white, mottled with black on the edge of the wing; bill black, lower mandible paler at base; legs and feet blackish brown; irides reddish.

Length.—3·8 inches; wing 2·35; tail 1·15; tarsus 0·55, culmen 0·45.

The adult female has the head and hind neck bluish ashy, changing into the olivaceous brown of the back, which is overcome with dark olivaceous green on the lower back and rump; tail brownish black, the terminal spots only on *three* outer pairs of feathers; length 3·9 to 4 inches; wing 2·15 to 2·3.

Hab.—Ceylon.

Family.—HIRUNDINIDÆ.

Broad-billed Passeres, with nine primaries. Bill short, depressed, compressed at the tip, more or less curved; gape very wide; wings long and pointed; tarsi short; feet feeble.

Sub-Family.—HIRUNDININÆ or SWALLOWS.

Bill short, flat, nearly triangular, compressed at the tips with a slight emargination; gape large; rictal bristles wanting: two first quills generally equal;

tail various, even, slightly emarginate or deeply forked; tarsus and toes feathered in some; plumage dense and soft, and always glossy. Nests usually made of mud or intermixed with hair, feathers, grass, &c., and plastered against rocks, walls, or under roof of buildings, culverts, bridges, &c.

Gen. Cotile.—*Boie*.

Bill smaller than in *Hirundo*, weak, depressed, broad at the base, and barely hooked at the tip; nostrils with an overhanging superior membrane, the nasal aperture being longitudinal; wings long, 1st primary generally the longest and longer than the tail, which is even and without any indentation or fork on the inner web of the outer tail feathers; tarsus slightly longer than in *Chelidon*; toes smaller and weaker; some species with a small tuft of feathers above the hind toe.

136. Cotile obsoleta, *Cab., Mus. Hein. Th.* i. p. 50; *Heugl., B. N. O. Afr.* i. p. 163; *Sharpe, P. Z. S.* 1870, p. 301; *Blanf., Ibis,* 1875, p. 214; *Murray, Vert. Zool. Sind*, p. 104; *Sharpe, Cat. B. Br. Mus.* x. p. 111. Ptyonoprogne pallida, *Hume, Str. F.* 1873, pp. 1, 417; *Blanf., Ibis,* 1873, p. 214. Cotyle obsoleta, *Blanf., East Pers.* ii. p. 217; *Legge, B. Ceylon*, pp. 598, 1217; *Murray, Avif. Brit. Ind.* ii. p. 258, No. 771. Ptyonoprogne obsoleta, *Hume, Str. F.* 1879, p. 84; *Butler, Cat. B. Sind.* p. 13.—The Pale Crag Martin.

The whole upper surface a very pale greyish earthy brown, very much paler than the same parts in either *P. rupestris* or *Cotyle sinensis*, the quills only slightly darker, yet sufficiently so to contrast pretty markedly with the scapulars, back, rump and upper tail coverts; the lateral tail feathers and all but the external feather on each side with a large oval white spot on the inner web as in *rupestris*, and with dark shafts, and a darker tint on the web, near the shaft, as in that latter species. Lower surface as in *rupestris*, but much paler, the whole of the chin, throat, breast and abdomen being white, with only a faint fulvous or rufous tinge; wing lining and lower tail coverts the same pale earthy grey brown as the upper surface. Bill black; legs and feet horny brown; irides dark brown. (*Hume, Str. F.* vol. 1, p. 417.)

Male, Length.—5·35 to 6 inches; expanse 12·25 to 13; wing 4·4 to 4·7.

Female, Length—5·25 to 5·5; expanse 12·3; wing 4·5 to 4·75; tail from event 1·8 to 2; tarsus 0·4.

Hab.—N.-E. Africa; Ceylon, found also in Beloochistan, Kutch and N. Guzerat. In Sind it arrives during winter, but is less common than the preceding species, and generally affects hilly situations.

Gen. Hirundo, *Linn.*—True Swallows.

Bill broad at the base, triangular and compressed at the tip; wings long; tail long, furcate or subfurcate, the outer feathers on each side emarginate on the inner web, and generally elongated to a great extent; nostrils lateral, with a distinct superior membrane; tarsus moderate, nude; feet moderate.

137. Hirundo rustica. *Linn., Syst. Nat.* i. p. 343; *Gould, B. Eur.* ii. pl. 54; *Yarrell, Br. B.* ii. p. 213; *Hodgs., Icon. ined Br. Mus. Passeres.* pl. 8; *Bp., Consp. Av.* i. p. 338; *Jerd., B. Ind.* i. p. 157, No. 82; *Godwin-Austen, J. A. S. B.* xxxix. p. 94; *Hume, Nests and Eggs*, p. 72; *id., Str. F.* 1874, p. 155; *Dresser, B. Eur.* iii. p. 477, *Hume, Str. F.* 1875, p. 451 (pt.); *Blanf., East. Pers.* ii. p. 215; *Legge, B. Ceylon*, p. 587; *Hume, Str. F.* 1879, p. 84; *Vidal, Str. F.* 1880, p. 43; *Reid, Str. F.* 1881, p. 16; *Davidson, Str. F.* 1882, p. 292; *id., Str. F.* 1883, p. 346; *Seebohm, Hist. Br. B.* ii. p. 171; *Murray, Vert. Zool. Sind*, p. 102; *id., Avif. Brit. Ind.* ii. p. 259, No. 772.—The COMMON SWALLOW.

Before giving a description of this species it is due to Ornithologists, who have not access to the works issued by the British Museum, to transcribe here Mr. Sharpe's observations in regard to "*Hirundo rustica and its allies*," and every working Ornithologist will agree with him, that "the races of Chimney Swallows are by no means easy to decipher, notwithstanding that they have been the subject of much discussion." He recognizes only five species. "Mr. Dresser," he says in his *Birds of Europe*, "does not distinguish the Eastern Chimney Swallow (*H. gutturalis*) from *H. rustica*, and says that the latter merges gradually into *H. erythrogastra*, as it proceeds eastwards." This certainly was my belief, but Mr. Sharpe thinks otherwise, and has given the latter sub-specific rank. He goes on, "I say nothing about the *probability of hybridization** taking place between the various forms of *H. rustica*, for at present we have no positive evidence of such being the case; but I would draw attention to the fact that although, in my opinion, *H. Savignii* does not occur in Palestine, the examples of *H. rustica* from that country are permanently more rufous than those from any part of Europe." How is this to be accounted for? According to Mr. Sharpe—and it is possible too—"it may be due to a strain of *H. Savignii* from adjoining localities. They are, however, always to be distinguished even from young *H. Savignii*, and are to be matched by specimens from different parts of Europe." The same difficulties attend the determination of the swallows which winter in Burmah, where many specimens occur which are puzzling to the Naturalist. They may be hybrids between the various races of *H. rustica*; and nothing but continued study by field naturalists can solve these points in question. It seems to me that a case of hybridization between *H. rustica* and *H. tytleri* would result in offspring very difficult to distinguish from *H. erythrogastra.* More recently Mr. Seebohm has reviewed the question. He recognizes five races. *H. rustica*, according to this author, has a wide summer range in Europe, extending to the valley of the Yen-e-say, but it is said to winter in "Sind and West India." Mr. Sharpe continues and adds his experience

* The italics are mine.

"that it shares to a great extent the winter quarters of the Eastern Chimney Swallow, called by Mr. Seebohm *H. rustica* var. *gutturalis*, and that it is quite possible it accompanies the latter occasionally back to its summer home. There are many places where both races occur together in winter; and the Burmese countries appear to be the winter residence of at least four of the Chimney Swallows—*H. rustica*, *H. gutturalis*, *H. erythrogastra* and *H. tytleri*. Speaking of *H. rustica* var. *horreorum*, Mr. Seebohm says that it winters in Burmah, "where it has been re-named *H. tytleri*." This is not strictly correct, for although specimens from Lake Baical are identical with the North-American bird, and undoubted examples are in the British Museum from Burmah; yet they cannot be said to be identical with *H. tytleri*, which is a distinct race leading on to *H. Savignii*, which it resembles in its deep chestnut under surface, while it retains the broken breast band of the *H. gutturalis* and *H. horreorum* type."

Male.—Forehead light chestnut; body and wings glossy steel-blue; primaries and secondaries black; tail feathers black, with a large white spot on the inner webs of all except the mesial ones; throat chestnut; a dark blue band across the upper part of the chest; rest of under parts white or rufescent white. Bill, legs, and feet black.

Length.—To end of outer tail feathers 7·5 inches, of which the tail is 4·5; middle tail feathers 2 inches; wing 4·8. The female is distinguished by the smaller chestnut patch on the forehead, less intense tints, whiter under parts, and the narrowness of the band across the chest.

Hab.—Europe, Palestine, Africa, Natal, Malacca, Penang, Tenasserim, Burmah, Sumatra, Borneo, China and Celebes; also Persia, Beloochistan, Afghanistan, Eastern Turkestan, Nepal and the whole Continent of India and Ceylon. Other recorded localities are Behar, Darjeeling, Quilon in Travancore, Nicobar Islands, Assam and Pegu. In Sind, as in other parts of India, it is a winter visitant. Said to breed in Persia at heights from about 4,000 to 8,000 feet in the months of April and May. Hume says they also breed along the whole line of the Himalayas from Cabul to Assam. The nests are made of pellets of clay mingled with fur, straw, &c. The eggs are 3—4 in number, thickly spotted with brownish red and inky purple. In size the eggs vary from 0·7 to 0·84 inch in length and from 0·5 to 0·55 in breadth.

138. Hirundo hyperythra, *Blyth, J. A. S. Beng.* xviii. p. 814; *Kelaart, Prodr. Cat.* p. 118; *Layard, Ann. and Mag. Nat. Hist.* xii. p. 170; *Blyth, Ibis*, 1867, p. 306; *Holdsw., P. Z. S.* 1872, p. 419; *Legge, B. Ceylon*, p. 592; *Hume, Str. F.* 1879, p. 84; *Sharpe, Cat. B. Br. Museum*, x. p. 167. Cecropis hyperythra, *Gould, B. Asia* i. pl. 30; *Jerd., Ibis*, 1871, p. 352; *Hume, Str. F.* 1877, p. 266.—The RUFOUS-STREAKED SWALLOW.

Above purplish blue or deep steel blue, streaked with fulvous on the hind neck; wing coverts like the back; bastard wing, primary coverts, and quills blackish, externally glossed with steel-blue; feathers of lower rump and upper tail coverts steel-blue, tipped with rufous; tail blackish, the feathers glossed with steel blue. Crown of the head like the back: lores dusky, surmounted by a narrow line of rufous from the base of the forehead, extending over the eye and forming a scarcely perceptible eyebrow; sides of hinder crown, ear coverts, cheeks, sides of neck and entire under surface of body deep chestnut, very plainly marked with narrow blackish shaft lines, a little broader on the ear coverts and throat; thighs and under tail coverts chestnut, the longer under tail coverts tipped or subterminally spotted with blue, the longest entirely blue; the under wing coverts and axillaries chestnut with distinct blackish shaft lines near the edge of the wing. (*Sharpe.*) "Bill deep brown, in some specimens blackish, the base of the lower mandible reddish; legs and feet vinous brown; iris sepia brown. (*Legge.*)

Length.—6·4 inches; wing 4·55; tail 2·95; tarsus 0·55; culmen 0·4.

Hab.—Ceylon. Breeds in the N. and N.-W. Provinces from April to June.

139. Hirundo Javanica, *Sparrm., Mus. Carls.* ii. pl. 100; *Vieill., N. Dict. d' Hist. Nat.* xiv. p. 523; *Temm., Pl. Col.* iv. pl. 83; *Gray, Gen. B.* i. p. 57; *Temm. and Schleg., Faun. Jap. Aves,* p. 32; *Cab., Mus. Hein. Th.* i. p. 46; *Wall, Ibis,* 1860, p. 147; *Salvad., Ucc. Born.* p. 126; *Bourd., Str. F.* 1876, p. 374; *Fairb., Str. F.* 1877, p. 392; *Sharpe, Journ. Lin. Soc. Zool.* xiii. p. 498; *Hume and Dav., Str. F.* 1878, p. 43; *Ramsay, Proc. Lin. Soc. N. S. Wales* iii. p. 275; *Hume, Str. F.* 1879, pp. 47, 84; *Legge, B. Ceylon,* p. 597; *Hume, Str. F.* 1880, p. 120; *Davison, Str. F.* 1883, p. 345; *Sharpe, Cat. B. Br. Mus.* x. p. 142; *Murray, Avif. Brit. Ind.* ii. p. 263, No. 776. Hirundo frontalis, *Quoy et Gaim., Voy. de'l Astrol. Zool.* i. p. 204, pl. 12, fig. 1. Hirundo domicola, *Jerd., Madr. Journ.* xiii. p. 173; *Blyth, Cat. B. Mus. As. Soc.* p. 198; *Kelaart, Prod. Cat.* p. 118; *Layard, Ann. and Mag. N. Hist.* xii. p. 170; *Jerd., B. Ind.* i. p. 158; *Holdsw., P. Z. S.* 1872, p. 418; *Jerd, Ibis,* 1871, p. 351. Hypurolepis domicola, *Gould, B. Asia* i. pl. 32; *Hume, Nests and Eggs Ind. B.* p 73; *id., Str. F.* 1874, p. 155. Hypurolepis Javanica, *Oates, B. Br. Burm.* i. p. 308.—The Nilghiri or Tropical House Swallow.

Above glossy black or dull steel-blue, the white bases of the feathers of the hind neck showing through; a broad band on the forehead; also the chin, throat, upper breast, cheeks, and ear coverts deep ferruginous; lores dusky; wings and tail dark brown, slightly glossed with steel-blue; the tail with an oval white spot on all the tail feathers, except those of the central pair; under surface of the body pale ashy, albescent on the abdomen; breast with dusky shaft streaks; sides of the upper breast with a bluish patch; sides of the body and flanks dull smoky brown; under tail coverts ashy, the feathers with white tips and subterminal patches of black.

Length.—5 inches; wing 4·2; tail 2·1; depth of fork 0·3; tarsus 0·4; bill from gape 0·65.

Hab.—Ceylon and Southern India, also British Burmah, Malay Peninsula, Java, Sumatra, Borneo, the Phillipine Islands, Celebes and some of the further islands. It is recorded from Mynall in Travancore, from Coonoor, Ootacamund (Nilghiris) and Bangalore. In British Burmah it was procured by Mr. Davison at Mergui in Tenasserim. Theobald found them breeding in Tenasserim during April. They not only build under the roofs of bungalows and in verandahs of houses, but also in caves and under boats which are unused. The nests are made of mud, cup-like in shape, and are lined with feathers. The eggs, normally three in number, are white, speckled with reddish.

140. Hirundo erythropygia, *Sykes, P. Z. S.* 1832, p. 83; *Jerd., Madr. Journ.* xi. p. 237 (1840); *Blyth, Ibis,* 1866, pp. 237, 357; *Gray, Hand-l. B.* i. p. 69, No. 806 (1869); *Brooks, Ibis,* 1869, pp. 46, 47; *Blyth, Ibis,* 1870, p. 161; *Cock. and Marsh., Str. F.* 1873, p. 350; *Adam, t. c.* p. 370; *Aitken, Str. F.* 1875, p. 212; *Hume, t. c.* p. 318; *Butler t. c.* p. 451; *Walden, Ibis,* 1876, p. 338; *Butler, Str. F.* 1877, p. 226; *Davidson and Wenden, Str. F.* 1878, vol. ii. p. 76; *Murray, t. c.* p. 113; *Legge, B. Ceylon,* p. 594 (1879); *Hume, Str. F.* 1879, p. 84; *Butler, Cat. B. Sind, &c.,* p. 13 (1879); *id., Cat. B. S. Bom. Pres.* p. 14 (1880); *id., Str. F.* (1880), p. 377; *Wardlaw-Ramsay, Ibis,* 1880, p. 48; *Vidal, Str. F.* 1882, p. 43; *Butler. t. c.* p. 377; *Reid, Str. F.* 1881, p. 18; *Davison, Str. F.* 1882, p. 292; *Davison, Str. F.* 1883, p. 345; *Seebohm, Ibis,* 1883, p. 169; *Murray, Avif. Brit. Ind.* ii. p. 266, No. 780. Hirundo daurica (*non Pall.*), *Blyth, Cat. B. Mus. As. Soc.* p. 198 (1849, pt.); *Layard, Ann. and Mag. Nat. Hist.* xii. p. 170 (1873); *id. and Kelaart, Prodr. Cat. App.* p. 58 (153); *Cass., Cat. Hirund Mus. Philad. Acad.* p. 4 (1853); *Horsf. and Moore, Cat. B. E. I. Co. Mus.* i. p. 92 (1854, pt.); *Jerd., B. Ind.* i. p. 160 (1862, pt.); *Boulger, P. Z. S.* 1866, p. 568; *Holdsw., P. Z. S.* 1874, p. 419; *Murray, Vert. Faun. Sind,* p. 103 (1884). Cecropis erythropygia, *Gould, B. Asia* i. pl. 29 (1868); *Jerd., Ibis,* 1871, p. 352; *Blyth, B. Burm.* p. 127 (1875); *Fairb., Str. F.* 1876, p. 254. Lillia erythropygia, *Hume, Nests and Eggs Ind. B.* p. 76 (1873); *id., Str. F.* 1877, p. 255.—The RED-RUMPED SWALLOW

Adult.—General colour above deep purplish blue with white striations where the bases of the feathers show through; the wing coverts like the back; quills blackish externally, glossed with dull blue; rump and upper tail coverts deep ferruginous, the longer coverts deep purplish blue; tail feathers blackish, glossed with dull blue; crown of head like the back, from which it is almost separated by a nuchal collar of deep ferruginous, the sides of the hinder crown, and sides of the neck being of the latter colour and converging on to the nape, the nuchal collar being only interrupted by a few dark blue plumes in the form of spots; a narrow frontal line and a streak over the eye deep ferruginous; lores whitish, tipped with dusky; ear coverts pale rufous with dusky shaft streaks; cheeks, throat, and under surface of body whitish, slightly marked with rufous on the breast and flanks; the whole of the under parts narrowly streaked with dusky blackish shaft lines, disappearing on the under tail coverts, the long ones of which are deep blue-black with whitish bases; under wing coverts and axillaries rather deeper fulvous than the breast, with nearly obsolete dusky shaft lines, which are, however, more plainly developed on the small wing coverts near the edge of the wing; quills dusky below, paler along the edge of the inner web. (*Sharpe.*) to Bill, legs and feet black; iris brown. (*Legge.*)

Total length.—6·2 inches; culmen 0·35; wing 4·45; tail 3·11; tarsus 3·5.

Hab.—All over India, to Nepal, Himalaya, Siberia, N.-E. Asia, Persia, Beluchistan and Afghanistan. In Ceylon rarely. Occurs in Sind, the Deccan, Kutch, Kattiawar, Rajputana and N. Gujerat; also the Punjab, N.-W. Provinces and Oudh, Bengal, Central, and Southern India. It is a permanent resident of the plains of India, and breeds from April to August. The nest, according to Hume, is usually fixed to the under surface of some ledge of rock or the roof of some cave or building, and is constructed of fine pellets of mud or clay, making up a tubular passage terminating in a bulb-like chamber some 4 to 7 inches in diameter. The eggs are pure white, and generally four in number. The nest chamber is lined sometimes thickly and sometimes thinly with feathers only as a rule, but occasionally with a mixture of these and fine grass. During the breeding season the old birds, like all the other species, fly round about their nest morning and evening, uttering quite a variety of rather pretty somewhat musical notes. During the day they remain near, and one of them generally in the nest, or the pair may be seen perched on some stone below the nest sitting for an hour at a time, preening their feathers, the male every now and then singing a few notes.

Family.—MOTACILLIDÆ.

Nine-quilled Passeres with bill generally of moderate length, slender, straight, and more or less deflected at the tip; rictus nearly smooth; wings long and pointed; tertiaries lengthened and nearly as long as the primaries; tail long; tarsus long and slender; toes moderate; hind claw long and slightly curved. No bastard primary; plumage either black and white, or grey and *white with* a good deal of yellow.

The family Motacillidæ comprises two groups of birds, the species of each bear a very close resemblance one to another. They live almost on the ground, though some do perch on trees, and their natural habitat is by the river side, on the margins of lakes, damp ground, meadows, marshes and irrigated fields; some of the Anthinæ or Pipits, however, affect bare stony plains and perch on trees. Their habits are peculiar and characteristic. Living as they do on the ground they run at a great speed by short jerky movements, and when still, wag their tails up and down continually. Their food is chiefly insects, but some eat grain and seeds also. They breed mostly on the ground or on the ledges of rock, and lay whitish or clay-coloured eggs. A few species only breed in India proper, and those chiefly in the Himalayas and Cashmere, the rest (a considerable number) are migratory, and visit India only during winter.

Gen. **Motacilla**.—*Linn.*

Bill moderate, slender and compressed at the tip, profile of culmen straight from the base of the bill to the tip; nostrils apert; wings, with nine long primary quills, the first two subequal and longest; tertiaries equal to the primaries in length, or nearly so; tarsus long and slender; hind toe short with slightly curved claw.

Owing to the many stages of plumage in which the species of this large family of birds are met with in India, and also to the insufficient materials for comparison and study, I consider it best to follow Mr. Sharpe as closely as possible in the description and key to the plumage of each species, as the admirable manner in which he has worked them out, with the immense mass of materials at his hand, leaves nothing to be added or desired.

141. Motacilla personata, *Gould, B. Asia.* iv. pl. 63; *Blyth, Ibis,* 1865, p. 49; *Blanf., Ibis,* 1873, p. 219; *Severtz., Turkest. Jevotn.* pp. 66, 139; *Hume and Henders., Lahore to Yark.,* p. 224; *Hume, Str. F.* 1873, pp. 29-30; *Ball. Str. F* 1874, p. 440; *Brooks, t. c.* p. 456; *id.,* 1875, p. 259; *Scully, Str. F.* 1876, p. 150; *Brooks, Str. F.* 1877, p. 472; *Blanf., t. c.* p. 246; *Hume, t. c.* p. 329; *Seebohm, Ibis,* 1878, p. 344; *Brooks, Str. F.* 1878, ii. p. 140; *Legge, B. Ceylon,* p. 219; *Hume, Str. F.* 1879, p. 103; *Wardlaw-Ramsay, Ibis,* 1880, p. 60; *Reid, Str. F.* 1881, p. 48; *Murray, Avif. Brit. Ind.* ii. p. 274, No. 784. Motacilla dukhunensis, *Jerd., B. Ind.* ii. p. 218 (*nec Sykes*). Motacilla Cashmeriensis, *Brooks, Pr. As. Socy. Beng.* 1871, p. 289; *id, J. A. S. Beng.* xli. p. 82; *id., Str. F.* 1874, p. 456.—The Black-faced Wagtail.

Adult male.—A broad frontal band extending to the front of the eye and forming a narrow supercilium, white; sides of the face, ear coverts, chin, throat, lower parts from below the breast and under wing coverts white; crown and nape black; breast black; back, rump and upper tail coverts grey, the upper tail coverts darker; primaries dusky brown, the outer webs darker; secondaries and tertiaries darker brown, margined on their outer webs and tipped with white; the secondaries margined for the basal half on their inner webs with white; tail black, the two outermost feathers on each side white, except a dark brown margin on their inner webs. Bill and legs black; irides brown.

Length.—7·5 to 8 inches; wing 3·6 to 3·7 inches; tail 4·5 to 4·75; bill at front 0·75.

Hab.—Ceylon, also Sind, Punjab, N.-W. Provinces, Oudh, Central Provinces, Beloochistan, Persia, South Afghanistan, East Turkistan; also in Rajputana. A winter visitant throughout India; breeds in Persia and Cashmere.

The Wagtails of India have been fully treated of by Mr. Hume, in Vols. I. and II. of *Stray Feathers*, in respect to the distinctness of the several species occurring in India, and the outcome of his investigations has placed the present species under the name it bears here. "In winter," Mr. Hume says, "both *M. personata* and *dukhenensis*=*alba* entirely lose in both sexes the black of the head, which is replaced in the male by a dark, in the female by a light, grey. The black of the chin, throat, and breast, is reduced in *dukhenensis*=*alba* to a moderately broad more or less crescentic pectoral band with two ill-defined broken blackish stripes running up the side of the neck, as it were from the points of the crescent, which stripes never, he thinks, entirely disappear, though in some specimens they become almost obsolete; the broad white frontal band remains unchanged in width or nearly so in the adult male, though its colour is less pure; but in the female it is greatly diminished in width so as in some specimens to become almost obsolete; while in all specimens it is more or less overlaid with sordid grey. In *personata*, on the other hand, the whole breast *always* remains black, and though the chin and upper part of the throat are white, the lower part of the throat is still more or less speckled with black. In the perfect winter plumage of both species, the amount of the black on the breast, sides of the neck and throat at once serve to distinguish the two species, but specimens of *alba* changing into winter plumage often (so far as the amount of black on the throat is concerned) exactly resemble the perfect winter plumage of *personata*, and the only ready and unfailing diagnosis of the two species is that *in both sexes, and at all seasons, the ear coverts and aural region are in personata* black, blackish or dark grey; in *dukhenensis*=*alba* pure white or greyish or sordid white."

Sharpe (*Cat. B. Br. Mus.* x. p. 481) says that old birds in winter plumage are remarkably like the summer plumage, and have the same black ear coverts, the chin, however, is white, as well as a good deal of the throat and the forepart of the cheeks, so that a narrow black stripe is left between the white lores and white cheeks, running from the base of the bill to the ear coverts. It seems certain, he adds, that old birds have the white chin spot for a short time only, for December specimens have nearly got the full black chin.

The female in breeding plumage (*Gilgit, Scully*,) exactly resembles the male. *Length.*—6·5 inches; culmen 0·5; wing 3·5; tail 3·3; tarsus 0·9.

142. Motacilla madraspatensis, *Gm.*, *Syst. Nat.* i. p. 961; *Gould, B. Asia*, pl 61; *Holdsworth, P. Z. S.* 1872, p. 458; *Severtz., Turkest. Jevotn.* pp. 66, 139; *Murray, Str. F.* 1878, p. 113; *Legge, B. Ceylon*, p. 107; *Hume, Str. F.* 1879, p. 103; *Reid, Str. F.* 1881, p. 47; *Davison, ibid*, 1881, p. 310; *Murray, Avif Brit. Ind.* ii. p. 277, No. 787. Motacilla madraspatana, *Blyth, J. A. S. B. Beng.* xvi. p. 429; *Bp. Consp. Av.* i. p. 251; *Jerd., B. Ind.* ii. p. 217; *Hume, Nests and Eggs Ind. B.* p. 377; *id., Str. F.* 1873, p. 28; *Fairbank, Str. F.* 1876, p. 200; *Dresser, Ibis*, 1876, p.

177; *Brooks, Str. F.* 1877, p. 472; *Murray, Hdbk., Zool. &c., Sind.* p. 165; *id., Vert. Zool. Sind,* p. 164; *Davison and Wenden, Str. F.* 1878, p. 348; *Seebohm, Ibis,* 1883, p. 92. Motacilla picata, *Frankl., P. Z. S.* 1831, p. 119.—The PIED WAGTAIL.

Head, lores, sides of the face, nape, ear coverts, chin, throat, breast, back, rump and upper tail coverts black; a broad white stripe from the nostrils over the eye as a supercilium and extending to the nape; primaries and their coverts, secondaries, tertiaries and inner webs of greater coverts dark brown; the primaries and their coverts narrowly, the secondaries, tertiaries, median and greater coverts tipped, and broadly margined on their outer webs with white, forming a conspicuous wing patch; the basal half of all the primaries and secondaries white on the inner webs, and tipped with white; the inner webs of the innermost narrowly margined with white; tail black, the two outermost feathers on each side white, except a margin of dark brown on their inner webs, which is broader on the next outermost; breast, belly, vent, under tail and wing coverts white; edge of the wing and thigh coverts white, with a few dark spots. Bill and legs black; irides dark brown.

Length.—8·25 to 9 inches; wing 3·75 to 4; tail 4; bill at front 0·5; tarsi 1·0.

Hab.—Ceylon and nearly throughout India, extending into the Eastern Himalayas; westward to Cashmere, and thence to Turkestan. Occurs in Sind, Kutch, Rajputana, Guzerat, Concan and Deccan, Khandeish, Berars, Central and Southern India, and Sikkim. The localities quoted are,—Kumaon, Nepal, Behar, Mhow, Saugor, Kamptee, Deccan, Madras, Travancore and Ootacamund.

According to Hume, the Pied Wagtail breeds throughout India from north to south only, avoiding the low country of Bengal Proper. It ascends to mountains of Southern India, and breeds at Ootacamund. The months are generally March, April and May. They nest in the neighbourhood of water in holes in banks, also crevices in rocks, under stones, in drains, holes in walls, and in fact anywhere. The normal number of eggs is four. They differ much in size and shape, and vary from a long to a broad oval more or less pointed towards the small end. The ground colour of the eggs varies from the pale brownish to greenish white, and the markings are clouds, smudges, streaks, spots and specks of earthy brown, dark olive brown and sometimes purplish brown.

143. Motacilla melanope, *Pall., Reis. Russ. Reichs.* iii. *App.* p. 696; *Gm., Syst Nat.* i. p. 997; *Dresser, B. Eur.* iii. p. 251, pl. 128; *Legge, B. Ceylon,* p. 610; *Murray, Avif. Brit. Ind.* ii. p. 278, No. 788. Motacilla boarula, *Linn., Mant.* p. 517; *Gm., Syst. Nat.* i. p. 997; *Gould, B. Eur.* ii. pl. 147; *Bp., Comp. List. B. Eur. and N. Amer.* p. 19; *Blyth and Wald., B. Burm.* p. 97. Motacilla sulphurea, *Bechst., Naturg. Deutschl.* iii. p. 459; *Blanf., East. Pers.* ii. p. 233; *Seebhom, Hist. Br. B.* ii. p. 263. Calobates sulphurea, *Kaup., Naturl. Syst.* p. 33; *Jerd., B. Ind.* ii. p. 220, No. 592; *Butler and Hume, Str. F.* 1875, p. 489; *Butler, Str. F.* 1877. p. 230. Calobates boarula, *Swinh., Ibis,* 1870, p. 346; *Hume, Str. F.* 1873, p. 201; *id., Nests and Eggs Ind. B.* p. 381; *Murray, Hdbk Zool., &c. Sind,* p. 167; *id., Vert. Zool. Sind,* p. 166. Calobates melanope, *Swinh., P. Z. S.* 1861. p. 364; *Brooks, J. A. S. B.* xli. p. 82; *Fairb., Str. F.* 1876, p. 260; *Bourd., t. c.* p. 401; *Tweed., Ibis,* 1877, p. 310; *Hume, and Dav., Str. F.* 1878, p. 362; *Davison and Wenden, Str. F.* 1878, ii. p. 84; *Hume, Str F.* 1829, pp. 63, 103, 161; *Scully, t. c.* p. 315; *Vidal, Str. F.* 1880, p. 69; *Reid, Str. F.* 1881, p. 48; *Davison, Str. F.* 1882, p. 310; *id., Str. F.* 1883, p. 395; *Oates, B. Br. Burm.* i. p. 159.—The GREY AND YELLOW WAGTAIL.

Head, nape, sides of the face and back pale grey, with an olive tinge; rump and upper tail coverts pale greenish yellow; chin, supercilium and throat white, rest of under surface yellow, purest on the middle of the abdomen, under tail coverts and flanks; primaries dusky brown, lighter on the margin of their inner webs, and darker on the outer; secondaries dusky brown, white on both webs at their bases, forming a conspicuous wing band; tertiaries dark brown, also white at their bases, and edged on both webs with yellowish, narrow on the outer, and broad on the inner webs, being a continuation of the basal white patch; tail dark brown, nearly black, the feathers with greenish yellow edging, the outermost feathers whiter and dark shafted; the next also white, both the shaft and outer web for three-fourths their length dark brown. Bill black; legs pale brown; irides brown.

Length.—7·25 to 7·5 inches; wing 2·25 to 2·5; longest tertiaries the length of the first three primaries; tail 3·8; bill at front nearly 0·5. In summer plumage the chin and throat are black, and the under parts dark yellow; the upper surface is clear blue grey, with a slight wash of olive yellow on the back and crown; rump and upper tail coverts sulphur yellow, tinged with olive; a short streak from the eye over the ear coverts and a moustacial stripe white; three middle pairs of tail feathers black, slightly edged with yellow on the outer webs; the next two pairs black on the outer webs and white on the inner; the outer pair all white; wing coverts dark brown, edged paler; quills dark brown; the tertiaries edged broadly with yellowish white. The birds found in India during winter with a buff-coloured throat and eyebrow are immature.

Hab.—Central and Southern Europe, N.-E. Africa, Australia and Asia Minor. Occurs throughout India to Nepaul and Ceylon as a winter visitant; also in Sind, Punjab, and N.-W. Provinces; Beloochistan, Persia and Afghanistan; Kutch, Kattiawar, Jodhpore, Jeypore, North Guzerat, Concan, Deccan, and Central and Southern India; also the Indo-Burmese countries, China, the Malay Peninsula, Sumatra, Java and Borneo. Breeds in Cashmere, according to Brooks, along the mountain streams at elevations of above 6,000 feet during the month of May. Eggs, 4—5 in number, nearly uniform in shape and size, broad ovals at the larger end and much compressed and pointed at the smaller end. Typically the ground colour is yellowish or brownish white, closely mottled and clouded all over with pale yellowish brown or brownish yellow. In length the eggs vary from 0·68 to 0·73 and in breadth from 0·53 to 0·55.

144. Motacilla borealis, *Sundev., Œfv. K. Vet.-Akad. Forh. Stockh*; *Sharpe, Cat. B. Br. Mus.* x. p. 522; *Murray, Avif. Brit. Ind.* ii. p. 281, No. 792. Budytes flava melanocephala, *DeSelys-Longchamps, Faun. Belg.* p 88. Motacilla viridis, *Gray, Gen. B.* i. p. 203. Budytes viridis, *Jerd., Madr. Journ.* xiii. p. 132; *Blyth, J. A. S. B.* xvi. p. 430; *Bp., Consp. Av.* i. p. 250; *Jerd., B. Ind.* ii. p. 222, No. 593; *Holdsworth, P. Z. S.* 1872, p. 458; *Wald. and Layard, Ibis*, 1872, p. 97; *Blyth and Wald., B. Burm*, p. 96; *Seebohm and Harvie-Brown, Ibis*, 1876, p. 122; *Brooks, Ibis*, 1877, p. 208; *Legge, B. Ceylon* p. 617; *Oates, B. Brit. Burm.* i. p. 161. Budytes cinereocapillus (*nec. Savi.*) *Hume, Ibis*, 1869, p. 357; *Brooks, J. A. S. Beng.* xli. p. 82; *Adam, Str. F.* 1873, p. 384; *Hume, Str. F.* 1874, p. 237; 1875, p. 489; *id., Oates, l c.* p. 142; *Fairb., Str. F.* 1876, p. 260; *Hume and Dav., Str. F.* 1878, pp. 363, 518; *Ball, Str. F.* 1878, ii. p. 219; *Davison and Wenden, l. c.* p. 84; *Brooks, l. c.* p. 139; *Hume, Str. F.* 1879, pp. 65, 103, 161; *Vidal, Str. F.* 1880, p. 69; *Davison, Str. F.* 1882, p. 310; *id., Str. F.* 1883, p. 396.—The GREY-HEADED WAGTAIL.

Male and female in breeding plumage.—Whole head from bill to the nape deep slaty; lores and ear coverts nearly black; a narrow indistinct line over the lores; a short streak of white occasionally behind the eye, frequently absent; upper plumage dull greenish yellow; upper tail coverts brown, margined with yellowish; median and greater coverts brownish black, edged and margined with yellowish white; quills brown, the secondaries and tertiaries margined with yellowish white on the outer webs; four central pair of tail feathers black; the two outer pairs black at base and white on the terminal portion, the junction being oblique; chin white, also a line from the gape along the dark suborbital and loreal patch; the whole lower plumage bright yellow, slightly blotched and pencilled here and there on the throat and breast with dusky; a little dusky on the lower throat.

In winter the head becomes greenish yellow like the back, and the ear coverts also become yellowish; the eyestreak is distinct, and the under surface of the body duller yellow. *The young* are more or less fulvous or white below, and there are spots on the throat and breast. Bill blackish brown; the base of the lower mandible yellowish; iris brown; legs, feet and claws dark horn colour. (*Oates.*)

Length.—7 inches; wing 3·2; tail 3·1; tarsus 0·9; bill from gape 0·7; culmen 0·5.

Hab.—From Northern Scandinavia, across Northern Europe and Siberia, occurring on migration throughout Southern Europe down to South Africa, and being met with in winter throughout the plains of India, the Burmese countries and the Malay Peninsula. (*Sharpe.*) It occurs at Kandahar and throughout S. Afghanistan ; also in the N.-W. Provinces, Punjab, and Sind. It is recorded from Nepal, Behar, Mhow, Calcutta, Poona and Sholapore in the Deccan, Madras, Assam, Pegu, Tenasserim and Ceylon. In Burmah Oates says it is abundantly distributed over the plains of Arrakan and Pegu, and in the Northern and Central portions of Tenasserim as far south of the Malay Peninsula. Its breeding habitat is Europe, where it is said to place its nest on the ground under cover of a tussock on the side of a ditch. The nest is made of fine roots and fibres, and lined with horsehair and wool. Eggs, 4—5 in number, white, spotted with grey. In fact it has a very wide distribution in India during winter, being then found in swampy lands, grass fields, meadows and paddy fields.

Gen. Limonidromus.—*Gould.*

General form and characters of *Motacilla*, but with the plumage uniform ; feet pale ; bill long and exceeding in length the outer toe and claw. Intermediate between the Wagtails and Pipits both in structure and habits.

145. Limonidromus indicus, *Gould, B. Asia.* iv. pl. 67 *Holdsworth, P. Z. S.* 1872 ; *Walden, Ibis,* 1874, p. 239; *Salvad., Ucc. Born.* p. 261 ; *Hume, Str. F.* 1874, p. 239; 1875, p. 142 ; *Blyth and Wald., B. Burm.* p. 16 ; *Bourd., Str. F.* 1876, p. 401 ; *Hume and Dav., Str. F.* 1878, p. 364 ; *Legge, B. Ceylon,* p. 614 ; *Hume, Str. F.* 1879, pp. 65, 103 ; *Vidal, Str. F.* 1880, p. 69; *Bingham, l. c.* p. 189; *Oates, B. Brit. Burm.* i. p. 164; *Davison, Str. F.* 1883, p. 397; *Sharpe, Cat. B. Br. Mus.* x. p. 532; *Murray, Avif. Brit. Ind.* ii. p. 283, No. 794. Motacilla indica, *Gm., Syst. Nat.* i. p. 962 ; *Gray, Gen. B.* i. p. 203. Nemoricola indica, *Blyth, J. A. S. B. Beng.* xvi. p. 429; *Bp., Consp.* i. p. 251 ; *Jerd., B. Ind.* ii. p. 226, No. 595 ; *Hume, Str. F.,* 1873, p. 450; *Armstrong, Str. F.,* 1876, p. 329.—The BLACK-BREASTED WAGTAIL.

Above dull olive brown, the upper tail coverts dark brown, the lateral ones with whitish margins; ear coverts and lesser wing coverts like the back ; cheeks, chin, throat, lores, eyelids, and supercilium extending from the bill to the nape, and whole under surface of the body yellowish white ; two black bands across the breast, the upper one entire and the lower one interrupted in the middle; median and greater series of wing coverts dark brown with broad yellowish white tips forming two bands across the coverts ; quills brown, the 2nd to the 7th primaries with a patch of yellowish white on the outer webs near their bases ; all the primaries and secondaries with an abrupt margin of yellowish white near their tips on the outer webs ; tertiaries brown, broadly tipped with olive green ; tail with two central feathers olive brown like the back, and washed externally with olive ; remainder of the feathers blackish, obsoletely tipped with white ; outermost feathers white except at the base, where it is brown ; penultimate feather dark brown, with the terminal third of the inner web white; under wing coverts dull white, washed with olive; axillaries white, washed with olive yellow; irides black; upper mandible dusky brown; lower mandible fleshy white; legs and feet purplish white.

Length.—6·3 to 6·6 inches; wing 3·1; tail 2·7; tarsus 0·85; culmen 0·55.

Hab.—Eastern Siberia and N. China, ranging in winter into the Indian Peninsula and Ceylon, the Andaman Islands and the Burmese countries. (*Sharpe.*) It also occurs in Cochin-China, the Malay Peninsula, Sumatra and Borneo. In Burmah, Oates says, it is uncommon in Pegu; it was only once met with by Armstrong in the Irrawaddy delta In the Tenasserim division it appears to be tolerably abundant. In Ceylon as well as in South India it is fairly common on the Nilghiris and in Coonoor, also in Malabar on the Coast. Jerdon procured it at Nellore, and it is said to be not very uncommon about Calcutta, also in Assam. It is quite a forest-loving species, being found in well-wooded localities and in shady orchards. It is usually seen solitary, feeding on insects.

Gen. **Anthus**.—*Bechst.*

Plumage sombre, generally mottled and lark-like, the feathers of the back with dark centres and pale edges; feet pale; bill straight, stout and shorter than in *Motacilla*; profile of culmen swollen from the centre to the tip. No scutellations on upper part of back of tarsus; the outstretched feet do not reach beyond the tail; 1st to 3rd quills longest; tertials long.

146. Anthus Richardi, *N. Dict. d'Hist. Nat.* xxvi. p. 491; *Temm., Pl. Col.* iii. pl. 101; *McGill., Br. B.* ii. p. 199; *Hume, Ibis,* 1869, p. 120; *Blanf., East Persia* ii. p. 236; *Seebohm, Ibis,* 1878, p. 343; *Sharpe, Cat. B. Br. Mus.* x. p. 564; *Murray, Avif. Brit. Ind.* ii. p. 289. Corydalla Richardi, *Vigors, Zool. Journ* ii. p. 397; *Bp. Consp., Av.* i. p. 247; *Kelaart, Prod. Faun. Zeyl. Cat.* p. 121; *Jerd., B. Ind.* ii. p. 231, No. 599; *Blanf., Ibis,* 1870, p. 466; *Holdsw., P. Z. S.* 1871, p. 458; *Hume, Str. F.* 1874, p. 239; *Ball, t. c.* pp. 416, 479, 496; *Blyth and Wald., B. Burm.* p. 95; *Armstrong, Str. F.* 1876, p. 330; *Hume and Davison, Str. F.* 1878, p. 365; *Ball, Str. F.* 1878, ii. p. 220; *Cripps, t. c.* p. 288; *Legge, B. Ceylon,* p. 621; *Hume, Str. F.* 1879, p. 103; *Oates, B. Br. Burmah* i. p. 166. Cichlops monticolus, *Hodgs., Icon. ined. in Br. Mus. Passeres,* pls. 121, 124, fig. 1. Corydalla sinensis, *Bp. Consp.* i. p. 247; *David et Oust. Ois Chine,* p. 311.—RICHARDS' or the LARGE MARSH PIPIT.

Upper surface of the body, including the scapulars and wing coverts, brown, the feathers edged with fulvous; lower back and rump more uniform, the feathers centred with dusky; primaries, secondaries and tertiaries brown, the primaries narrowly, and the secondaries and tertiaries broadly edged with fulvous; the first primary ashy white externally; tail dark brown, with ashy fulvous margins, the outermost pair of feathers nearly entirely white, the next with a large triangular patch of white on the inner web; supercilium, chin, cheeks, throat and axillaries fulvous white ; ear coverts sandy rufous or fulvous brown ; under surface of the body pale fulvous, darker on the flanks, thighs and vent, and striated on the breast, lower throat and foreneck with dusky brown. Bill brown, yellowish at the base of the lower mandible ; irides brown ; legs flesh colour.

Length.—7 to 8 inches ; wing 3·6 to 3·9 ; tail 3·4 ; tarsus 1·2 ; culmen 0·6.

Hab.—Central and Eastern Asia where it breeds, migrating to India and Ceylon in winter, also into Southern China, the Moluccas and the Burmese countries ; occurring also in parts of Europe. It is found from Nepaul and the Himalayas to the extreme South ; more rare, however, in Southern India and the Carnatic. Jerdon adds that it is tolerably abundant in Lower Bengal, Ceylon and countries to the eastward. According to Oates it is excessively common in all the vast plains in the south of Pegu. It has been procured in Tonghoo and in Karenne, also throughout Tenasserim and the Thoungyeen Valley. It is common in the Malay Peninsula, and has been got in Siam. It abounds in all the rice-fields and swampy lands covered with grass, and numbers are generally found together ; but this fact would not admit of their being called gregarious. Nothing of its nidification in India is yet known.

147. Anthus striolatus, *Blyth, J. A. S. B.* xvi. p. 435 ; *Bp. Consp* i. p. 248 ; *Layard, Ann. and Mag. Nat. Hist.* xii. p. 268 ; *Blanf., J. A. S. Beng.* xli. p. 61 ; *Sharpe, Cat. B. Br. Mus.* x. p. 568 ; *Murray, Avif. Brit. Ind.* ii. p. 290, No. 801. Corydalla striolata, *Kelaart, Prodr. Fauna Zeyl. Cat.* p. 121 ; *Jerd., B. Ind.* ii. p. 232, No. 601 ; *Holdsw., P. Z. S.* 1872, p. 453 ; *Brooks, Str F.* 1873, p. 369 ; *Walden, Ibis,* 1874, p. 140 ; *Ball, Str. F.* 1874, p. 417 ; *Hume and Davison, Str. F.* 1878, p. 366 ; *Legge, B. Ceylon,* p. 628 ; *Hume, Str. F.* 1879, p. 103 ; *Butler, Cat. B. Bom. Pres.* p. 56 ; *Oates, B. Br. Burmah* i. p. 167. Cichlops thermophilus, *Hodgs., Icon. ined. Passeres,* pl. 122A.—BLYTH'S PIPIT.

Like *Anthus Richardi*, except that the triangular patch of white on the inner web of the penultimate tail feathers in *Anthus Richardi* is about two inches in length, or never less than an inch and-a-half, but in this species it is never quite an inch ; the tarsus is also shorter, and the markings on the breast more numerous.

Length.—7 to 8 inches ; wing 3·5 ; tail 3 ; tarsus 1·05 ; culmen 0·6.

Hab.—Throughout India and Ceylon, occurring as far west as Sind. It has also been met with in Burmah and the Andaman Islands. Jerdon records it from Saugor in Central India, Nellore and Darjeeling. It is also stated to be found in South India generally (Madras, Travancore), also in Dinapoor, Sultanpoor (Punjab), Sikkim and Nepaul. Visits India in September, and leaves again by the 15th April.

148. Anthus rufulus, *Vieill, N. Dict. d'Hist. Nat.* xxvi. p. 494 ; *Blyth, J. A. S. B.* xvi. p. 437 ; *Bp., Consp. Av.* i. p. 248 ; *Layard, Ann.*

and Mag. Nat. Hist. xii. p. 268; *Murray, Avif. Brit. Ind.* ii. p. 291, No. 803. Anthus cinnamomeus, *Rupp., Neue Wirb.* p. 103; *Sharpe, Cat. B. Br. Mus.* x. p. 574. Anthus malayensis, *Eyton, P. Z. S.* 1839, p. 104; *Blyth, J. A. S B.* xi. p. 797; *Hume, Str. F.* 1874, p. 497; *Tweed., Ibis*, 1877, p. 310; *Hume and Davison, Str. F.* 1878, p. 366; *Hume, Str. F.* 1879, pp. 65, 103. Agrodroma agilis, *Jerd., Madr. Journ.* xi. p. 33. Cichlops ubiquitarius, *Hodgs., Icon. ined. in Br. Mus. Passeres*, pl. 122A. Anthus caffer, *Sundev., Œfv. K. Vet. Akad. Forh. Stockh*; *Layard, Ibis*, 1869, p. 368. Anthus raalteni, *Bp. Consp. Av.* i. p. 248. Corydalla rufula, *Kelaart, Prodr. Fauna. Zeyl. Cat.* p. 121; *Jerd., B. Ind.* ii. p. 232; *Blanf., Ibis*, 1880, p. 469; *Holdsw., P. Z. S.* 1872, p. 458; *Hume, Nests and Eggs, Ind. B.* p. 384; *Brooks, Str. F.* 1873, p. 359; *Ball, Str. F.* 1874, p. 416; *Hume, t. c.* p. 497; *Blyth and Walden, B. Burm.* p. 96; *Fairb., Str. F.* 1876, p. 260; *Armstrong, t. c.* p. 330; *Bourd., t. c.* p. 401; *Fairb., Str. F.* 1877, p. 407; *Legge, B. Ceylon*, p. 625; *Hume, Str. F.* 1879, p. 103; *Vidal, Str. F.* 1880, p. 69; *Reid, Str. F.* 1881, p. 49; *Davidson, Str. F.* 1882, p. 310; *Oates, B. Br. Burm.* i. p. 168; *Davison, Str. F.* 1883, p. 397; *Scully, Str. F.* viii. p. 317. Corydalla rufulus, *Murray, H'dbk., Zool., &c., Sind*, p. 160; *id., Vert. Zool. Sind*, p. 172.—The Indian Tit Lark.

Head, nape, back, scapulars and upper tail coverts olive brown, the feathers with dark mesial streaks; rump unstreaked pale olive; supercilium fulvous white; chin white; throat, breast and rest of under surface, including the under wing coverts, fulvous white, deeper on the breast and sides of the throat, the feathers of which are centred darker; primaries, secondaries, tertiaries and wing coverts brown; the primaries slightly paler brown and edged externally with fulvous white; the secondaries edged with light olive brown and tipped whitish; the tertiaries broadly edged externally with pale olive or fawn brown, all, except the innermost tertiaries, fulvous and basally whitish on their inner webs; tail dark brown, the two centre feathers shorter than the others, pale brown and margined narrowly with pale olive; the outermost feathers on each side white, except a narrow margin on the inner web, which is brown; the next feather also white, with a dark shaft, and a wider brown margin on the inner web. Bill dusky, yellowish at base of lower mandible; irides brown; legs pale yellowish brown.

Length.—6·5 to 7 inches; wing 3 to 3·25; tail 2·5; tarsus 1; bill at front 0·4.

Hab.—The whole of Southern Africa, extending up the eastern side of that continent to N.-E. Africa, and occurring even in Egypt; also throughout India and Ceylon, the Burmese countries and Malayan Peninsula, extending to Java, Sumatra, Borneo and the Phillipines. (*Sharpe.*) In India it is found in Sind, Punjab, N.-W. Provinces, Bengal, Assam, British Burmah and Nepaul: also Beloochistan, Afghanistan and Eastern Turkestan. Common in the Concan and Deccan; breeds in Sind during April and May. Eggs 3—4, of a greenish colour, with numerous brown mottlings all over, chiefly at the larger end. It is one of the most common birds, and is abundantly spread over all India, except in the higher elevations. In Burmah as elsewhere it is partial to open grass plains and dry paddy fields.

Family.—FRINGILLIDÆ.

Birds with conical bill, usually entire at the tip, the lower mandible generally of the same proportions as the upper, but in some deeper; margin of bill not toothed or indented; wings moderate; tail moderate or short, even, rounded or emarginate; feet fitted for walking on the ground. They are chiefly ground-feeders, and while some may be said to be omnivorous, others feed almost exclusively on grain. They nidificate on trees, holes in rocks, or banks of nullahs and river-beds. Plumage generally plain, in some only sandy. They are usually possessed of much intelligence, and there are among them some of the most familiar birds, which are the most appreciable songsters. The gizzard of many is thick and muscular, and in such cases the birds swallow stone, or gravel, to assist the trituration of the seeds they feed on.

Sub-Family.—FRINGILLINÆ.

Bill variable in size and form, more or less conical and thick, short and bulged in some or thick and elongate.

Gen. Petronia.—*Kaup.*

General characters of the sub-family; culmen and gonys slightly curved, the depth at base nearly equal to the length; commissure scarcely sinuated; nostrils exposed.

149. Petronia flavicollis, (*Frankl.*), *Blyth, Cat. B. Br. Mus. As. Soc.* p. 120; *Irby, Ibis*, 1861, p. 231; *Sharpe, Cat. B. Br. Mus.* xii. p. 293; *Murray, Avif. Br. Ind.* ii. p. 308, No. 830. Fringilla flavicollis, *Frankl., P. Z. S.* 1831, p. 20. Gymnoris flavicollis, *Blyth, J. A. S. B.* xiii. p. 948; *Adam, Str. F.* 1873, p. 388; *Hume, Nests and Eggs, Ind. B.* p. 461; *Ball, Str. F.* 1874, p. 421; *Blanf., East. Pers.* ii. p. 256; *id., Str. F.* 1877, p. 249; *Vidal, Str. F.* 1880, p. 72; *Reid, Str. F.* 1881, p. 56. Passer flavicollis, *Jerd., B. Ind.* ii. p. 368; *Butler, Str. F.* 1875, p. 497; *Murray, Vert. Zool. Sind*, p. 184; *Sharpe, Ibis*, 1886, p. 486; *Legge, B. Ceylon*, p. 605.—The YELLOW-THROATED SPARROW.

Male.—Head, neck, back, rump, scapulars and under tail coverts pale earthy brown; a pale or fulvous supercilium, more distinct in females; chin white; throat-spot yellow; the rest of the under surface whity brown, albescent on the vent and under tail coverts; primaries and secondaries dull brown, the primaries edged paler and tipped whitish, as are also the secondaries; tertiaries broadly edged and tipped with fulvous; lesser wing coverts chestnut; median and greater coverts dull brown, tipped with fulvous white, forming two conspicuous wing bars; edge of the wing white; tail dull brown, the outermost feathers on each side paler.

The female wants the chestnut on the wing, and is more brown in colour beneath; the throat-spot, too, is less bright; upper mandible black, lower yellowish at the base; irides brown; legs pale brown.

Length.—5·5 inches; wing 3·4; tail 2; tarsus ·7.

Hab.—Ceylon, the Malabar countries, Travancore and Mysore, also Sind, Punjab, N.-W. Provinces, Beloochistan, Persia, Rajputana, Kutch, (Kattiawar, Jodhpore), N. Guzerat, Deccan and Concan. Other localities are Shiraz, Bushire, Fao, all over Sind, Kutch, Saharunpore, Lucknow, Etawah, Allahabad, Mhow, Indore, Saugor, Mahableshwar.

Breeds throughout India nearly during the months of April and May, also in June, in holes in trees in which a little grass is placed, but thickly lined with feathers, hair, tow, or any suitable fibrous material. Eggs, three to four, dull and glossless, moderately elongated ovals, greenish white or glossless white, thickly streaked, smudged and blotched with brownish.

Gen. Passer.—*Briss.*

Bill broad at base, slightly scooped at tip; 2nd and 3rd quills longest; nostrils partly covered by plumes.

150. Passer domesticus (*Linn.*), *Pall. Zoogr. Rosso. Asiat.* ii. p. 29; *McGill., Brit. B.* i. p. 340; *Shelley, B. Egypt,* p. 148; *Blanf., East. Pers.* ii. p. 254; *Hume, Str. F.* 1878, ii. p. 64; *Legge, B. Ceylon,* p. 600; *Murray, Avif. Brit. Ind.* ii. p. 310, No. 832. Fringilla domestica, *Linn., Syst. Nat.* i. p. 323. Pyrgita domestica, *Cuv. Regne. Anim.* i. p. 385. Passer indicus, *Jerd and Selby, Ill. Orn.* iii. p. 118; *Jerd., B. Ind.* ii. p. 362; *Hume, Nests and Eggs, Ind. B.* p. 457; *Blanf., East. Persia,* ii. p. 254; *Oates, B. Br. Burm.* I. p. 346; *Murray, Vert. Zool. Sind,* p. 183.—The COMMON HOUSE-SPARROW.

Male.—Head and nape dark grey; lores, feathers below the eye, sides of the lower mandible, chin, throat and breast black; mantle and scapulars chestnut with dark mesial streaks; rump and upper tail coverts ashy brown; lesser wing coverts chestnut, the last row or series of feathers dark brown at the base and tipped with white; the greater series dark brown, edged with rufescent and tipped with fulvous white; primaries, secondaries, and tertiaries dusky brown, edged with rufous, paler and narrow on the primaries, which are darkish brown on the middle of their outer webs; tertiaries tipped with fulvous white; sides of the face and neck and entire under surface white, the flanks cinereous; tail dusky or pale brown, the feathers edged with fulvous brown.

The female is pale earthy or light brown, with a fulvous supercilium extending to the nape and the lower parts less pure white; bill horny brown; legs dusky; irides light brown.

Length.—5·25 to 6 inches; wing 3; tail 2·25; tarsus 0·65; culmen 0·4.

Hab.—Ceylon, and throughout India to the Himalayas, Assam and Upper Pegu; also Beluchistan, Persia, and Afghanistan. Its nidification is too well known to need description.

Sub-Family.—PLOCEINÆ,—Weaver Birds.

Bill thick at base, with the keel projecting on the forehead and arched to the tip; wings rounded; 1st quill very short; tarsi and toes strong, scutate; hind toe long and strong.

Gen. Ploceus,—*Lin.*

General characters of the sub-family

151. Ploceus phillipinus, *Lin., Syst. Nat.* i. 305; *D' Aub. P. E* 135, 2; *Reich.-Sing.* t. 36, p. 283; *Murray, Avif. Brit. Ind.* ii. p. 338, No. 873. Ploceus phillipensis, *Briss., Orn.* iii. 232, pl. xii. f. i. Ploceus maculata, *P. L. S. Mull. Suppl.* 150; *ex P. E.*; *Hume, Str. F.* vi. 399. · Ploceus baya (*Blyth*), *apud Jerd., B. Ind.* ii. 343, No. 694; *Murray, Hdbk., Zool. &c., Sind*, p. 176.—The Common Weaver Bird.

Adult Male in Breeding Plumage.—Forehead, crown, sides of the neck and breast bright yellow; lores, sides of the face, ear coverts, chin and throat dull brown, paler on the chin; back brown, the feathers with yellow edgings; rump paler brown, edged lighter; upper tail coverts a dirty buff colour or rufous white; wing coverts dull brown, the greater series and the primary coverts narrowly edged with greyish white; primaries, secondaries and tertiaries dull brown, the primaries with a narrow edging of pale yellow on their outer webs, also on the secondaries; tertiaries broadly edged yellowish white; tail dull brown, the feathers faintly and narrowly edged with yellowish green; abdomen, vent and under tail coverts dull white, also the thigh coverts; the middle of the abdomen and thigh coverts tinged yellowish; edge of the wing fulvous white. Bill black; irides brown; legs yellowish brown.

Length.—5·5 inches; extent 8·5; wing 2·75; tail 1·75; bill at front 0·6.

The *female* is like the male, but wants the yellow crown and breast, and the chin and throat are whitish or rufous white.

Hab.—Throughout India to Ceylon, Assam, Burmah and Nepaul. Common everywhere in Sind with the two next species, as well as in the Punjab, N.-W. Provinces and Bengal, also Central and Southern India, the Concan and Deccan, Kutch, Kattiawar, Jodhpore and N. Guzerat. Breeds freely in company with *manyar*. Nest non-pensile, being attached to the upper stalks of reeds, with the leaves interwoven, and smaller than that of *bengalensis* or *manyar*, less large in the body, and generally with a long and narrow tubular entrance. In Ceylon it is said by Parker to be thinly scattered throughout the Northern Province; most numerous in the Manaar district, breeding from December to March in the Northern Province and from May to July in the North-West. They resort to their breeding quarters early in

October. The unfinished-like nests are inhabited by the males. Breeds wherever found from April to June. Eggs white, 3, 4 or 5 in number. All the species of this genus are taken young by natives, and taught to perch on the hands and to perform various feats.

152. Ploceus manyar, *Horsf.*, *Trans. Lin. Socy.* xiii. p. 160; *Hume Str. F.* vi. p. 399; *Jerd.*, *B. Ind.* ii. p. 348; *Hume*, *Nests and Eggs Ind. B.* p. 440; *Blyth*, *B. Burm.* p. 92; *Oates*, *Str. F.* v. p. 160; *Hume*, *Str. F.* viii. p. 106; *Legge*, *B. Ceylon*, p. 646; *Murray*, *Vert. Zool. Sind*, p. 181; *Oates*, *B. Br. Burm.* i. p. 360; *Murray*, *Avif. Br. Ind.* ii. p. 339, No. 875. Euplectes striatus, *Blyth*, *J. A. S. B.* xi. p. 873.—The STRIATED WEAVER BIRD.

Adult Male in Breeding Plumage—Forehead and crown bright golden yellow; lores, cheeks, chin and throat and sides of the neck blackish or sooty brown; back, rump and upper tail coverts brown, the feathers edged with fulvous white; wing coverts, primaries, secondaries and tertiaries concolorous with the back, the primaries edged yellowish, and the secondaries, wing coverts and tertiaries whitish or fulvous white; tail brown, the feathers edged greenish; breast and flanks fulvous white, with mesial dark streaks; abdomen and under tail coverts white, tinged fulvous; bill black; irides brown; legs pale brown.

Length.—5·8 inches; wing 2·75; extent 9; tail 1·75; bill at front 0·56. *Females* and males in non-breeding plumage want the yellow head, and have a pale supercilium, and the chin and throat are whitish.

Hab.—Northern and Central India to Assam and Burmah. Occurs in Sind, Punjab, N.-W. Provinces, Oudh, Bengal, Deccan, Concan, Travancore, Kutch, Kattiawar and N. Guzerat. Breeding season same as the last. The nest is generally suspended from the top of four or five leaves of high bulrush or elephant grass, which are also incorporated into the nest. The entrance tube is not as long as that of *P. baya*.

Sub-Family.—ESTRELDINÆ.

Bill large, conic, more or less bulged or slender; wings short, rounded; the 1st primary minute as in *Ploceus*.

Gen. Amadina.—*Swains.*

Bill thick, as long as deep; culmen arched, prolonged behind on the forehead; tarsi stout, moderate. These birds inhabit grassy or reedy ground and cultivation generally, feeding on rice, grain and other seeds.

153. Amadina malacca *(Lin.)*, *Jerd.*, *B. Ind.* ii. p. 352, No. 697. Loxia malacca, *Lin.*, *Syst. Nat.* i. p. 300; *Edward*, *Birds*, pl. 356, fig. 2; *Murray*, *Avif. British*, *Ind.* ii. p. 341, No. 878.—The BLACK-HEADED MUNIA.

Head, neck and breast rich black; back, wings and tail pure cinnamon red, the upper tail coverts brighter, tinged with a glistening lustre; under surface of the body from below the breast white; middle of abdomen and vent black. Bill bluish, the tip yellowish; irides dark brown; legs plumbeous.

Length—4·5 inches; wing 2·6; tail 1·5.

The young is pale cinnamon brown above, whitish below, and dusky about the head and neck.

Hab.—Southern India and Ceylon, a few stragglers, according to Jerdon, being found in Central India and even in Bengal. On the Malabar Coast it is extremely abundant, frequenting long grass by the sides of rivers and tanks; also grain and cane-fields. The nest is placed among reeds, and is a rather large or nearly round or oval structure made of grass with the entrance on one side. The eggs, according to Jerdon, are 4—6 in number, and in colour pure white. Hume says he had notes of eggs sent to him from the Coimbatore district, also from the Bhundara district, and describes them as somewhat elongated ovals, from 0·6 to 0·75 inch in length, and from 0·44 to 0·5 in breadth.

154. Amadina atricapilla (*Vieill.*), *Oates.*, *B. Br. Burm.* i. p. 366; *Murray, Avif. Brit. Ind.* ii. p. 342, No. 879. Loxia atricapilla, *Vieill.*, *Ois. Chant.* p. 53. Coccothraustes sinensis, *Briss.*, *Orn.* iii. p. 235. Munia rubronigra, *Hodgs.*, *As. Res.* xix. p. 156; *Jerd.*, *B. Ind.* ii. p. 353, No. 698; *Legge, B. Ceylon*, p. 625; *Blyth, B. Burm.* p. 92; *Oates, Str. F.* v. p. 160; *Hume, and Dav.*, *Str. F.* vi. p. 401 (footnote). Munia atricapilla, *Hume, Nests and Eggs Ind. B.* ii. p. 444; *Salv.*, *Ucc. Born.* p. 265; *Wald.*, *Trans. Zool. Soc.* ix. p. 208. Munia sinensis, *Daud. et Oust.*, *Ois Chine* p. 324. Amadina rubronigra, *Hume, Str. F.* viii. p. 107; *Scully, Str. F.* viii. p. 32:—The CHESTNUT-BELLIED MUNIA.

Head, neck and breast black; remainder of the plumage chestnut turning to glistening fulvous on the rump, upper tail coverts and the outer edges of the tail feathers; centre of abdomen, vent and under tail coverts black. Bill and feet plumbeous; iris dark brown.

Length.—4·5 inches; wing 2·1; tarsus 0·55; bill from gape 0·45.

The young are pale fulvous throughout; lighter below than above.

Hab.—Ceylon and Northern India; found throughout Lower Bengal and along the foot of the Himalayas as far as Dehra Dhoon; also in the N.-W. Provinces. It has also been procured in Southern India, also in Ceylon; rare in the latter country, but is much more common in Assam and Burmah, throughout the Malay Peninsula, the Islands of Sumatra and Borneo, South-West China, and the Indo-Burmese countries. In Burmah it occurs in all parts of the province. It everywhere affects grassy land in flocks of from 6 to 12; breeds from June to August in Burmah, placing the nest in a clump of elephant grass. Eggs generally five, pure white. Oates says that the nest of this bird is very often tenanted by a snake, and great care should be taken not to insert the hand without previous examination.

155. Amadina punctulata (*Linn.*), *Oates, B. Br. Burm.* i. p. 368; *Murray, Avif. Br. Ind.* ii. p. 342, No. 880. Loxia punctulata, *Linn., Syst. Nat.* i. p. 302. Loxia undulata, *Lath., Ind. Orn.* i. p. 387. Munia undulata, *Jerd., B. Ind.* ii. p. 354, No. 699. Munia punctulata, *Hume, Nests and Eggs Ind. B.* p. 444; *Legge, B. Ceylon*, p. 656. Munia subundulata, *Godw Aust., P. Z. S.* 1874, p. 48; *Hume, Str. F.* iii. p. 398; *Oates, Str. F.* v. p. 162. Munia superstriata, *Hume, Str. F.* i. p. 481 (footnote); *Hume and Dav., Str. F.* vi. p. 402. Munia punctularia, *Blyth and Wald., B. Burm.* p. 93. Lonchura punctulata, *Hume, Str. F.* iii. p. 156. Munia Inglisi, *Hume, Str. F.* v. p. 39. Amadina punctulata, A. subundulata, A. superstriata, and A. Inglisi, *Hume, Str. F.* viii. p. 107. Amadina superstriata, *Oates and Hume, Str. F.* x. p. 232.—The BARRED MUNIA.

Back as far as the rump chocolate brown, the shafts slightly paler and the feathers of the rump barred with whitish; upper tail coverts glistening yellow fulvous; chin, throat, ear coverts and sides of the neck chestnut; heads and neck behind ruddy brown; tail brown, the edges of the feathers glistening yellow or fulvous; primaries and secondaries brown, the edges and tertiaries the same chocolate brown as the upper surface; under wing coverts buff; under surface of the body white with zigzag markings of brownish fulvous; lower abdomen, vent and under tail coverts unmarked whitish. Bill and legs plumbeous; iris deep reddish brown.

Length.—4·7 inches; wing 2·1; tail 1·7; tarsus 0·6; bill from gape 0 45

Hab.—Throughout India and Ceylon. Common in the North, spreading into Assam and Burmah. It is found throughout the Indo-Burmese countries, and is recorded from Arrakan, Pegu, Tavoy and Tenasserim. Occurs in the Himalayas and the south of India on the edges of the Nilghiris; also in various parts of the Carnatic, Central India and Bengal. In the Punjab, Sind, N.-W. Provinces, and Rajputana it is rarely seen. It frequents gardens, groves and orchards, and is quite a familiar bird. It builds in thorny bushes, chiefly about fields. Acacias are generally selected. The nest is not unlike that of other species of Munia, and the eggs glossless white.

156. Amadina striata, *Linn., Syst. Nat.* i. p. 306; *Hume, Str. F.* viii. p. 107; *Oates, B. Br. Burm.* i. p. 365; *Murray, Avif. Br. Ind.* ii. p. 344, No. 884. Fringilla leuconota, *Temm., Pl. Col.* 500, fig. 2. Munia striata, *Jerd., B. Ind.* ii. p. 356; *Hume, Nests and Eggs Ind. B.* p. 448; *Wald., Ibis*, 1874, p. 144; *Legge, B. Ceylon*, p. 600. Munia leuconota, *Blyth, B. Burm.* p. 93.—The WHITE-BACKED MUNIA.

Upper surface of the body rich dark brown, darkest on the forehead; all the feathers, except those on the forehead, conspicuously white-shafted; ear coverts and sides of the neck the same as the back; cheeks, chin, throat, and upper breast, dark blackish brown; wings and tail dark, nearly blackish brown; middle tail feathers exceed the outermost by 0·5 inch; lower breast, abdomen, and vent white; flanks brown with white shafts. Under tail coverts darker brown with less conspicuous shaft lines; upper mandible blackish, the lower one bluish; iris reddish brown; legs greenish horny.

Length.—4·5 inches; wing 2; tail 1·6; tarsus 0·5; bill 0·4.

Hab.—Peninsular India. Abundant on the Malabar Coast, sparingly in other parts of India, in the Northern Circars, Lower Bengal, Arrakan, and Ceylon. In the Andamans and Nicobars it is replaced by A. fumigata, *Wald.*, and A. semistriata, *Hume*. Its habits do not differ from those of the preceding species. Breeds throughout the peninsula of India, the eastern portions of the Central Provinces, Orissa, Lower and Eastern Bengal, and Arrakan. The breeding season, according to Hume, varies according to locality. In the Nilghiris, he says, they appear to lay in July and August. In Yercaud a nest was taken in the last week of September. The eggs are regular, somewhat elongated ovals, pure white, and perfectly devoid of gloss. They vary in length from 0·55 to 0·65 inch, and in breadth from 0·42 to 0·47.

157. Amadina malabarica (*Linn.*), *Jard. and Selby, Ill. Orn.* 2nd Ser. pl. 34; *Reich., Sing.* t. 150; *Jerd., B.Ind.* ii. p. 357, No. 703; *Murray, Hdbk., Zool., &c., Sind,* p. 177; *Murray, Vert. Zool. Sind,* p. 182; *Legge, B. Ceylon,* p. 662; *Murray, Avif. Br. Ind* ii., p. 345, No. 885.—The PLAIN BROWN MUNIA.

Head, back and scapulars pale earthy brown, the feathers of the head centred darker, giving it a rufescent brown appearance; rump pale earthy brown; upper tail coverts white, barred with dusky; primaries, secondaries and tertiaries dusky brown; the secondaries and tertiaries rufescent brown on their outer webs and tipped very slightly with whitish; wing coverts like the back, the first three or four from the edge of the wing whitish; chin, throat, breast, belly, and under tail coverts greyish white, the flanks and sides of the breast in some specimens with transverse bars of rufescent; under tail coverts white; tail dark brown, edged with dark reddish brown, the central feathers broadly so, and prolonged 0·75 beyond the others. Bill plumbeous; legs pale brown; irides deep brown.

Length.—5 inches; tail 2; wing 2·1; bill at front 0·4.

Hab.—Ceylon, Southern and Central India, Malabar, Sind, Punjab, N.-W. Provinces, Deccan, Concan, Kutch, Kattiawar, Jodhpore, Jeypore, N. Guzerat, and in fact nearly throughout India, but not extending to the countries towards the east. Breeds everywhere it is found, but chiefly in the more arid tracts and nearly throughout the year if the record of its nidification in different parts of the country has been properly ascertained. They build in thorny bushes, generally making a large globular nest of fine grass and loosely put together. The eggs are pure glossless white.

Padda (Amadina) *Oryzivora,* the well-known Java Sparrow, is naturalized now in various parts of India, and is also occasionally found as a straggler about Colombo. It is not, however, in the proper sense, a native of India or Ceylon, but the following characters will suffice for its identification. Cheeks and ear coverts white; chin, throat, a line bordering the ear coverts, the forehead, and whole top of head black; above, also the neck, breast, and upper abdomen bluish grey; abdomen, sides, thighs and vent vinous; under tail coverts white; rump, upper tail coverts and tail black.

158. Amadina Kelaarti, *Blyth, Ibis,* 1867, p. 299: *Holdsw., P. Z. S.* 1872, p. 464; *Legge, B. Ceylon,* p. 650; *Hume, Str. F.* vii. p. 410. Amadina pectoralis, *Blyth, J. A. S. B.* 1851, xx. p. 178; *Kelaart, Prod. Cat.* p. 126.—The CEYLON OR KELAART'S MUNIA.

Above brown, the feathers with pale shafts, forehead blackish; wings, rump, tail, throat, foreneck and cheeks deep brown black; upper tail coverts mixed brown, white and fulvous; breast brown; abdomen and under tail coverts black, the latter with white mesial streaks, rest of under surface barred with white and black; bill livid; feet dark plumbeous.

Length.—4 inches; wing 2·1 to 2·2; tail 1·5; central tail feathers 0·4 inch longer.

Hab.—Ceylon, to which island it is confined. Breeds, according to Mr. F. B. Armstrong, on high trees (as the mango), about 15 feet from the ground. Eggs unspotted white.

Family, ALAUDIDÆ.

Bill typically longer and more slender than in most *Fringillidæ;* short and thick in many; wings broad; tertiaries elongated, pointed; hind toe and claw long, the latter curved; plumage brown, more or less striated. (*Jerd.*).

Gen. **Mirafra.** –*Horsf.*

Bill thick, much compressed, the culmen curved and convex, the tip of the upper mandible wide above and inflexed; wings short, rounded; primaries scarcely longer than the secondaries and tertials; 1st quills short, half the length of the second, which is shorter than the third; tail short, even.

159. Mirafra affinis, *Jerd., Madr. Journ.* xiii. pt. ii. p. 136; *id., B. Ind.* ii. p. 417, No. 755; *Hume, Nests and Eggs Ind. B.* p. 474; *Ball, Str. F.* ii. p. 422; *Blyth and Wald., B. Burm.* p. 95; *Hume, Str. F.* viii. p. 108; *Legge, B. Ceylon* p. 634; *Murray, Avif. Br. Ind.* ii. p. 349, No. 891. Mirafra microptera, *Hume, Str. F.* i. p. 483; *id., Nests and Eggs Ind. B.* p. 475; *id., Str. F.* iii. p. 159; *Oates, Str. F.* v. p. 163; *Hume, Str. F.* viii. p. 108; *Oates, B. Br. Burm.* i. p. 376.—The MADRAS BUSH LARK.

Entire upper surface of the body dusky brown, each feather edged with pale rufous; wing coverts brown, edged with rufous; quills dusky brown, edged with bright rufous on the outer webs of the primaries and secondaries, and pale rufescent on both webs of the tertiaries; inner webs of the primaries pale rufous at the base; tail brown, edged with pale rufous, more conspicuous on the outermost feathers; lores and cheeks mixed rufous and brown; chin and throat white; superciliary streak pale fulvous; under surface of the body white, faintly tinged with fulvous, the breast streaked with dark brown. Bill dusky, fleshy beneath; legs fleshy; irides hazel.

Length.—5·5 to 6 inches; wing 2·9 to 3·25; tail 1·75 to 2; tarsus 1; culmen, 0·5; hind claw 0·45.

Hab.—Ceylon and Southern India generally. It is recorded from the Malabar Coast, Carnatic, Mysore and the Southern portion of the tableland, extending, according to Jerdon, to Goomsoor and Midnapore in Bengal. It is found also in Burmah and Cochin-China. In Burmah, Oates says it is very abundant at Thayetmyo and its immediate neighbourhood. In gardens and compounds as well as on road-sides and patches of jungle it is common. He found a nest in July, which is said to have been made of grass partially domed, like the last species, and placed in a hoof mark under a tuft of grass and overhung by a small bush. The eggs, two in number, were white, thickly spotted with rusty brown. Hume says it lays 3—4 eggs, 0·81 × 0·56 in size.

Gen. **Pyrrhulauda**.—*Smith.*

Bill short, very stout, sides compressed; culmen arched; commissure straight; wings long; tertiaries lengthened; 1st primary small; tail moderate; toes small.

160. Pyrrhulauda grisea, *Scop., Son. Voy.* t. 113, 2; *Jerd., B. Ind.* ii. p. 424, No. 760; *Hume, Str. F.* i. p. 212; *id.*, vol. vii. p. 66; *Gray, Handlist B.* No. 7834; *Murray, Hdbk., Zool., &c., Sind*, p. 186; *Legge, B. Ceylon*, p. 637; *Murray, Avif. Br. Ind.* ii. p. 352, No. 896. Pyrrhulauda crucigera, *Tem., Pl. Col.* 269, 1.—The BLACK-BELLIED FINCH-LARK.

Male.—Forehead and cheeks white, or fulvous white; crown of the head, back, scapulars, rump and upper tail coverts grey brown, with a slight tinge of rufescent on the back, the feathers centred dusky; cheeks whitish; primaries, secondaries, and wing coverts brown, the feathers edged paler; chin, throat, breast, sides of the neck and entire lower surface black; the flanks, sides of breast and abdomen greyish white; bill pale brown; legs fleshy; irides dark brown.

Length.—4·75 to 5 inches; wing 3; tail 2; bill at front 0·37. The *female* is readily distinguishable by the absence of the black under surface and a more rufescent tinge on the upper.

Hab.—Ceylon, Sind, Punjab, N-W. Provinces, Oudh, Bengal, Kutch, Kattiawar, Rajputana (Jeypore and Jodhpore), N. Guzerat, Concan, Deccan, Central and South India. Affects open plains and ploughed lands. Breeds all over the plains of India from January to August—the first brood being batched in February and March and the second in July and August. Eggs have also been taken in April and May. The nest is always on the ground, and placed in some small depression on open fallow plains. The eggs are moderately elongated ovals, having a greenish or greyish white ground, densely mottled, speckled and spotted, or finely streaked with various shades of yellowish and earthy brown. Hume adds that with the exception of the eggs of *Alauda raytal*, these are the smallest of all our Indian Lark's eggs, 0·65 × 0·8 by 0·5 × 0·62.

Gen. **Alauda**—*Linn.*

Bill cylindrical, conical or subulate; nostrils concealed; wings very long, no spurious quill; 1st, 2nd and 3rd primaries longest, tips of the lesser quills marginate; tail forked, short or moderate; head crested.

161. Alauda gulgula, *Frankl., P. Z. S.* 1831, p. 119; *Jerd., B. Ind.* ii. p. 434; *Hume and Dav., Lahore to Yarkand*, p. 269, pl. xxxix.; *Hume, Nests and Eggs* p. 486; *Blyth, B. Burm.* p. 95; *Armstrong, Str. F.* iv. p. 337; *Oates, Str. F.* v. p. 163; *Anderson, Yunnan Exped.* p. 605; *Hume and Dav., Str. F.* vi. p. 409; *Legge, B. Ceylon*, p. 630; *Hume, Str. F.* viii. p. 109; *Scully, Str. F.* viii. p. 338; *Hume, Str. F.* ix. p. 355; *Oates, Str. F.* x. p. 234; *Murray, Avif. Br. Ind.* ii. p. 359, No. 904. Alauda peguensis, *Oates, Str. F.* iii. p. 342. Alauda arvensis (*L.*), *David et Oust. Ois. Chine*; *Oates, B. Br. Burm.* i. p. 373.—The INDIAN SKY LARK.

Head, nape, back, scapulars, and rump dark brown, margined with fulvous, crest moderately long; eye streak pale fulvous; ear coverts dusky with a few brown spots; upper tail coverts like the back, tinged slightly with rufous; wing coverts brown, edged with greyish; primaries and secondaries brown, with rufous or fulvous margins on their outer webs; tail dark brown, outermost feather on each side fulvescent white, except a faint dusky margin on the inner margin of the inner web, the next with the outer web only fulvescent; chin, throat, breast and rest of under surface fulvescent white, deeper on the breast and streaked with dusky; bill horny brown, pale beneath; legs fleshy brown; irides dark brown.

Length.—6 to 6·5 inches; wing 3·25 to 3·75; tail 2·25; bill at front 0·37 to 0·5.

Hab.—Throughout India to Cashmere and Nepaul; Sind, Kutch, Rajputana, N. Guzerat, Concan, Deccan, Beloochistan, Afghanistan, Punjab, N.-W. Provinces and Cashmere. It is said by Blyth to occur in Arracan. Oates found it abundant in Southern Pegu, and according to Dr. Armstrong it is said to be spread over the whole Irrawaddy delta. Davison observed it in the plains between the Sittang and Salween rivers and in the immediate neighbourhood of Moulmein. It ranges throughout India, also the Indo-Burmese countries, and Ceylon. Frequents cultivated lands. Breeds during December. The nest is not unlike that of other larks, and is made in depressions in the ground under the shelter of a stone or tuft of grass. Eggs 3—4, white, or greyish-white mottled with brown. Eggs have been taken in the

Nilghiris, in the Central Provinces, Central India, Punjab, and N.-W. Provinces.

SECTION.—OSCINES CULTIROSTRES.

Family—STURNIDÆ.—Starlings.

Bill straight or very slightly curved, rather long pointed and compressed, often angulated at the base, the tip entire or slightly notched; wings long and pointed; tail moderate; tarsus strong; nostrils on each side covered with feathers. They walk freely on the ground, fly well, are gregarious, and live on fruit, insects, grain, and some on the ordure of cattle. They nidificate under the eaves of roofs or in holes of trees. Some are intelligent and are caged, and taught to utter long and amusing sentences. The Indian species may be said to be divided into Starlings and Mynahs; Glossy Mynahs or Grackles.

Sturnus vulgaris, Linn.

Sub-Family.—STURNINÆ.

Bill with the sides compressed, tip rather blunt and flattened; wings long and pointed; tail rather short; tarsi strong, scutate in front; toes long and strong.

Gen. **Acridotheres.**—*Vieill;* Gracula, *Cuv.*

Bill stouter and shorter than in *Sturnus.* Culmen deflected at tip; nostrils concealed by the frontal plumes; tail rounded; tarsi stout; a naked space usually behind the eye; head crested or sub-crested; its quill rudimentary.

162. Acridotheres, melanosternus, *Legge, B. Ceylon,* p. 670; *Hume, Str. F.* viii. p. 72; *id., Str. F.* ix. p. 295; *Sharpe, Cat. B.* xiii. p. 83.—The Common Ceylon Myna.

Head sub-crested; nape, neck behind, chin, throat and breast glossy black, the latter extending down on to the abdomen; back, scapulars, rump and upper tail coverts brown; sides of the body dark vinous; wing coverts, primaries and secondaries black; outer webs of the earlier primary coverts black; edge of the wing and the base of the primaries white, forming a conspicuous wing patch; tail black, the feathers tipped white; lower abdomen, vent and under tail coverts white. Bill and orbits deep yellow; legs dull yellow; irides reddish.

Length.—9·5 to 10 inches; wing 5·25; tail 3·5; bill at front 0·8 to 0·9.

Hab.—Ceylon, where it is a resident everywhere breeding in holes of trees, roofs of houses and almost anywhere, except on the ground, from February to May. Eggs 4, of a glossy pale green, greenish or deep bluish green colour. Size 1·13 × 0·88.

Gen. **Sturnia**.—*Less.*

General characters same as those of *Acridotheres*. Bill less stout, barely deflected at tip; 1st and 2nd primaries sub-equal; head usually crested.

163. Sturnia pagodarum (*Gmel.*), *Jerd.*, *B. Ind.* ii. p. 329, No. 687; *Hume, Nests and Eggs Ind. B.* p. 432; *Ball, Str. F.* ii. p. 419. Sturnia pagodarum, *Blyth, B. Burm.* p. 90; *Legge, B. Ceylon*, p. 677; *Hume, Str. F.* viii. p. 106. Temenuchus pagodarum, *Murray, Vert. Zool. Sind*, p. 179; *Oates, B. Br. Burm.* i. p. 382. Turdus pagodarum, *Gmel., Syst. Nat.* i. p. 816.—The BLACK-HEADED MYNAH.

Head, with the long crest, nape and lores black; ear coverts, sides of the neck and behind, breast and abdomen, fulvous or pale orange buff, the feathers with mesial whitish streaks; back, scapulars, outer webs of secondaries and tertiaries grey, the innermost tertiaries entirely grey; primaries dark brown, edged with black on their outer webs; edge of wing, under wing, and under tail coverts and the vent white; tail dark brown, the feathers broadly tipped white; the centre feathers grey like the back. Bill bluish at base, rest yellow; irides whitish; legs bright yellow.

Length.—8·5 to 9 inches; wing 4·2; tail 3; bill at front 0·37.

Hab.—Ceylon, India, Cashmere, Assam, Burmah. Common in Southern India and in the Carnatic; also Travancore and the Northern Circars. Extends to Afghanistan; occurs also in Sind, Punjab, N.-W. Provinces, Deccan, and Concan, but not in any numbers; breeds from May to August.

Gen. **Sturnornis**.—*Legge.*

Bill stouter than in *Sturnia*; a triangular patch of bare skin behind the eye

164. Sturnornis senex (*Bonap.*), *Legge, B. Ceylon*, p. 679. Temenuchus senex (*Temm.*), *Gray, Handl. B.* ii. p. 20; *Holdsw., P. Z. S.* 1872, p. 462; *Legge, Ibis*, 1874, p. 23. Heterornis albofrontatus, *Lay., Ann. and Mag. N. H.* xiii. 1854, p. 217. Temenuchus albofrontatus (*Lay.*), *Bly., Ibis*, 1867, p. 299.—The WHITE-HEADED MYNA.

Forehead, forecrown, face, chin, throat and tail coverts white, duller on the latter; centre of crown, nape, hind neck, back, wings and tail black, with a greenish lustre; some of the interscapulars tipped ashy, and those of the hind neck with whitish shafts, more or less conspicuous; foreneck, chest, breast and flanks dusky lavender grey, paling towards the abdomen, each with a mesial stripe; under wing coverts dull blackish; bill and gape plumbeous blue; the legs and feet bluish plumbeous; iris dull white, with a narrow brown inner circle.

Length.—8·3 to 8·5 inches; wing 4·25 to 4·4; tail 3 to 3·1; tarsus 1 to 1·1; bill from gape 1·05 to 1·15.

Hab.—The mountain forests of Ceylon. Habits arboreal; rare.

Gen. **Pastor**.—*Tem.*

Bill short, compressed, curving from the base, slightly deflected at the tip; groove of nostril clothed with short plumes; 2nd quill longest; 1st spurious; tarsus scutate; tail even; head with an occiptal crest.

165. Pastor roseus (*Lin.*), *Gould, Birds of Eur.* pl. 212; *Naum. vogt.* t. 63; *Jerd., B. Ind.* ii. p. 333, No. 690; *Blf., East. Persia* ii. p. 267; *Str. F.* i. p. 208; iii. pp. 208, 495; *Murray, Hdbk., Zool., &c., Sind., B.* 176; *Legge, B. Ceylon*, p. 673; *Murray, Avif. B. Ind.* ii. p. 372, No. 925.—The Rose-coloured Pastor.

Head, crest, crown, neck on the back and nape black, glossed with bluish purple; chin and throat black; entire back, breast, rump and upper tail coverts pale salmon or delicate rose colour; wing coverts black, the lesser series margined with grey, and the greater series glossy black with purple reflections; primaries dark brown, tinged with greenish; some of the secondaries glossy black, also with green reflections, and others only so on the outer web; tail greenish black; under tail coverts black; bill yellowish rose; legs yellowish brown; irides deep brown.

Length.—9 to 9·5 inches; wing 5·25; tail 3; bill at front 0·8.

Hab.—S.-E. Europe, Asia Minor, India, Ceylon and Assam. In the Deccan and the Carnatic they come about November, and this is the time they come in throughout Western India. They are very voracious feeders, and commit great havoc among the jowaree and bajree crops, and in fact corn of any kind, flower buds, and small fruits, as mulberries, capers, &c. A winter visitant in most parts of India; arrives in Sind about the beginning of April in large flocks; in the Punjab and N.-W. Provinces in August. Occurs also as a migrant in Beloochistan, Persia, Afghanistan and Eastern Turkistan.

Sub-Family.—LAMPROTORNINÆ.—Grackles or Hill Mynahs.

Bill stouter than in the *Sturninæ*; culmen more or less curved and hooked, tip notched; nostrils more or less hidden by the frontal plumes; wings long or moderate and pointed; tarsi short and stout; plumage glossy. Like the *Sturninæ*, all the species live on fruit and insects, and nidificate in holes of trees or in rocks, and like them associate with cattle.

Gen. Eulabes.—*Linn.*

General characters of the sub-family; head with naked wattles; habits frugivorous; the species hop instead of walk on the ground.

166. Eulabes religiosa (*Linn.*), *Jerd.*, *B. Ind.* ii. p. 337, No. 692; *Hume*, *Nests and Eggs Ind. B.* p. 435; *Fairbank*, *Str. F.* v. p. 407; *Ball*, *Str. F.* vii. p. 221; *Legge*, *B. Cyelon*, p. 682. Mainatus religiosa (*Linn.*), *Sharpe*, *Cat. B. Br. Mus.* xiii. p. 99 Gracula religiosa, *Linn.*, *Syst. Nat.* i. p. 164; *Blyth*, *Cat.* p. 108; *Murray*, *Avif. Brit. Ind.* ii. p. 373, No. 927.—The Southern Hill Mynah or Grakle.

Whole plumage glossy purplish black, with green reflections on the lower back and upper tail coverts; under surface less bright; wings and tail deep black; 1st seven primaries with a white spot, forming a conspicuous wing band; wattles begin from behind the eye, and over the auricular region, form a large loose lappet and again extend upward to the side of the hind crown. A small nude space under the eye. Bill orange; wattles deep yellow; irides dark brown.

Length.—10 inches; wing 5·6; tail 2·8; culmen 1.

Hab.—Ceylon to 1,500 feet elevation, the forests of Malabar, Wynaad, Coorg, and the Northern Circars. Found in parties of 5—6. Generally confined to the large forests. Breedsf rom March to October. Eggs like those of *Acridotheres*, 2 in number, 1·3 × 0·88.

167. Eulabes ptilogenys, *Blyth*, *J. A. S. B.* 1846, xv. p. 285; *id.*, *Cat. B. Mus. As. Soc. Beng.* p. 108; *Kelaart*, *Prod. Cat.* p. 125; *Layard*, *Ann. and Mag. Nat. Hist.* 1854, xiii.; *Holdsw. P. Z. S.* 1872, p. 463; *Legge*,

Ibis, 1874, p. 25; *id.*, *B. Ceylon*, p. 685. Mainatus ptilogenys (*Blyth*), *Sharpe*, *Cat. B. Br. Mus.* xiii. p. 513.—The CEYLON GRACKLE.

Entire plumage glossy black, with strong metallic reflection of purple on the head, hind neck, breast and thighs; back tinged with greenish bronze, also the wings and abdomen; a white bar across the wing formed by a patch on each of the first 6—7 quills; yellow lappets on each side of the nape only; bill orange red, the base of upper mandible as far as the nostrils black; lower mandible black for one-half its length; irides greyish white.

Length.—10·75 to 11 inches; wing 6 to 6·25, tail 2·5 to 3; tarsus 1·3 to 1·4; bill from gape 1·4.

Hab.—Ceylon, where it is a resident and breeds during June, July, and August. Eggs of the usual type, 2 in number, 1·3 × 0·97.

Family.—PITTIDÆ.

Bill strong, moderately long or nearly as long as the head, culmen convex, slightly curved; nasal aperture basal, oblong, covered by membrane; tarsus long, seldom equal or longer than the tail. Plumage brilliant. They nidificate in open nests and lay spotted eggs.

168. Pitta brachyura (*Linn.*), *Royle*, *Ill. Bot. Him.* pl. 7, fig. 3; *Jerd.*, *Madras Journ.* x. p. 25; *Kelaart*, *Prod. Faun. Zeyl.* p. 122; *Legge*, *Ibis*, 1874, p. 18; *Ball*, *Str. F.* vii. p. 213; *Sclater*, *Cat. B. Br. M.* xiv. p. 423; *Murray*, *Avif. Br. Ind.* ii. p. 380, No. 938. Corvus brachyurus, *Linn.*, *Syst. Nat.* i. p. 158. Pitta bengalensis, *Vieill.*, *Enc. Meth.* p. 685; *Jerd.*, *B. Ind.* i. p. 503. Pitta coronata, *Hume*, *Nests and Eggs Ind. B.* p. 224; *Ball*, *Str. F.* ii. p. 406; *id.*, v. p. 416; *Butler and Hume*, *Str. F.* iii. p. 470; *Fairbank*, *Str. F.* iv. p. 257; *Legge*, *B. Ceylon*, p. 687.—The INDIAN PITTA OR GROUND THRUSH.

Upper surface of the body green; vertical stripe on top of the head black, bordered on each side with pale yellowish or buffy brown; supercilium buffy white; lores and cheeks black, also the wings, which have a broad white basal band and white tips to the feathers; rump, lesser wing coverts and upper tail coverts bright light blue; back, scapulars and greater wing coverts green; under surface of the body fawn colour, the throat white, but the middle of the abdomen and under tail coverts scarlet; under wing coverts black with a broad white patch; bill black; culmen paler; feet yellowish.

Length.—7 inches; tail 1·5; wing 4.

Hab.—Ceylon, the Indian Peninsula, Assam, Arracan, Tenasserim and Ceylon. Recorded localities in India are Simla, Bareilly, Behar, Assam, Kattywar, Sikkim, Mysore, Travancore, Coorg, Raipur, Mallegaum, Ahmednuggur, Khandalla, Belgaum, Calicut, Ootacamund, Madras, Malabar, the Godavery Valley and Mount Abu. This species breeds wherever it is found from May to August. The nest is a globular structure with an aperture on one side composed of dry leaves, twigs, and roots. The eggs are irregular ovals, glossy, china-white, speckled and spotted with maroon, dark purple and brownish purple. In size they vary from 0·96 to 1·07 inches in length and by 0·81 to 0·9 inches in breadth.

ORDER—MACROCHIRES.

Gape wide; bill short, broad at base; keel curved to the tip; tail generally forked.

Family—CYPSELIDÆ.

Bill short, broad at base, depressed, compressed at tip; gape wide; wings long and pointed; tarsi short.

Sub-Family—CYPSELINÆ—Swifts.

Wings very long and curved, scimitar-like; toes short, hinder one generally directed forwards; claws curved and sharp; tail short, of 10 feathers only; rictal bristles absent; keel of sternum large; posteriorly entire.

Gen. Cypselus—*Illiger*.

Bill with the sides gradually compressed to the tip; nostrils partially feathered; second quill longest; tail generally forked; tarsi short, plumed to the toes; toes all directed forward.

169. Cypselus melba (*Linn.*), *Edw.*, *B.* pl. 27; *Naum. vogt.* 147 i.; *Gould*, *B. Eur.* pl. 53, 2; *Jerd.*, *B. Ind.* p. 175, No. 98; *Murray*, *Hdbk. Zool.*, *&c.*, *Sind*, p. 124; *id.*, *Vert. Zool.*, *Sind*, p. 105, *Legge*, *B. Ceylon* p. 317; *Murray*, *Avif. Br. Ind.* ii. p. 388, No. 950.—The Alpine Swift.

Above wood-brown, glossy purple on the back; wings darker brown; under surface white, except a broad dusky bar across the breast; rump, on the sides, under tail coverts and tarsal plumes brown; bill black; irides deep brown; toes brown with an orange tinge.

Length.—8 to 9 inches; wing 8·5 to 8·75, 2·5 inches beyond the tip of the tail, which is forked, and 3 inches in length; outer feathers 3·75.

Hab.—S.-W. Europe, Palestine, W. Asia, Africa, Greece, Beloochistan, Afghanistan and Persia are other countries where it is found. It also occurs as a migrant, passing through the Punjab, N.-W. Provinces, Sind, Kutch, Kattiawar, Guzerat, and the Deccan during winter. Ceylon, and, according to Jerdon, it is not rare in South India all along the Western Ghats from Honore to Cape Comorin, extending its daily flight often to the Western Coast, and occasionally eastwards to Salem, Madura, and even Madras; abundant on the Nilghiris and on the Malabar Coast.

170. Cypselus affinis, *Gray*, *Ill. Ind. Zool.* pl. 35, 2; *Jerd.*, *B. Ind.* i. p. 177, No. 100; *Str. F.* i. p. 166; *Murray*, *Zool.*, *&c.*, *Sind*, p. 125; *id.*, *Vert. Zool*, *Sind* p. 105; *Legge*, *B. Ceylon*, p. 319.—The Common Indian Swift.

Upper surface brown-black, darker, and glossed greenish on the back; head brownish; forehead paler; under surface brownish black; chin, throat and rump white; bill black; feet brownish; irides deep brown.

Length.—5·5 to 6 inches; wing 5, extends 1·5 beyond tip of tail, which is 1·75.

Hab.—Ceylon, Beloochistan, Persia, Afghanistan, Nepaul and Abyssinia. In India very generally distributed. Occurs in Sind, the Punjab, Deccan, Concan, Kutch, Kattiawar, Jodhpore and N. Guzerat. Wherever it is found, it breeds in large colonies under the eaves of roofs and in untenanted buildings. Mr. Parker records the most northern colony in Ceylon as at Oddisuddan, 15 miles east of Mullaitiva, where they breed from May to November. Eggs 2—4 in number, pure white.

171. Cypselus batassiensis (*Gray*). C. palmarum, *Gray and Hardw., Ill. Ind. Zool.* i. p. 35, fig. i.; *Jerd., B. Ind.* i. p. 180, No. 102; *Legge, B. Ceylon*, p. 322; *Murray, Avif. British Ind.* ii. p. 390, No. 957.—The Palm Swift.

Entire plumage glossy ashy brown or fuscous, darker on the wings and tail, and more albescent on the under surface. Bill black irides brown; feet, dusky reddish; tail much forked, the inner feathers of the fork 1·25 inch shorter than the outer; primaries dark brown, the 1st shorter than the second, and much pointed at the tip.

Length.—5 to 5·5 inches; tail 2·5 (outer feathers); wing 4·5.

Hab.—Ceylon and throughout India in the more moist regions as the Malabar Coast, Carnatic, the Northern Concan, Bengal, the central tableland and the North-West Provinces; in fact, wherever palms grow. Extends to Assam. Hume says they nest solely on the "Tar" (or toddy tree?), which he calls *Borassus flabelliformis*, on the under surface of which it builds its nests. The eggs are long ovals, slightly compressed towards one end and pure white.

Sub-Family.—CHÆTURINÆ.

Characters same as those of *Cypselinæ*; tail feathers ending in a spinous tip; the species comprised in it are mostly of large size, and pale colours.

Gen. Hirundinapus.—*Hodgs.*

Toes three in front; hind toe or hallux shorter than the front toes, opposable and reversible to the front; tarsus naked; tail short, even or wedge-shaped; the naked shafts of the feathers ending in a spinous tip.

172. Hirundinapus indicus, *Hume, Str. F.* i. p. 471; *id., Str. F.* ii. p. 155; iv. p. 286; *Inglis, Str. F.* v. p. 17; *Oates, B. Br. Burm.* i. p. 5; *Murray, Avif. Br. Ind.* ii. p. 392, No. 960. Acanthylis giganteat (*Temm.*), *apud Jerd., B. Ind.* i. p. 172; *Blyth and Wald., B. Burm.* p. 84; *Wardlaw-Ramsay, Ibis*, 1877, p. 459. Chætura gigantea, *apud Legge, Birds Ceylon* p. 314.—The Indian Giant Spine-tail.

Not unlike *H. giganteus*, but differs in having the chin and throa whity brown; a white spot between the eye and base of the bill, and the back and rump much paler brown; bill black; irides dark brown; legs and feet pale purplish or plumbeous.

Length.—9 to 9·25 inches; tail 2·8; wing 7·8 to 8; tarsus 0·75; bill from gape 1·1.

Hab.—Ceylon and Southern India, Andamans, Tenasserim and the Malay Peninsula. It has been obtained in Malabar and the Wynaad, also on the coast at Tellicherry. They occur in large flocks, wherever they are located, and in the early morning and the dusk of the evening are seen in scattered flocks, crossing and recrossing one another, while the setting sun now and again show their glossy plumage. It is said they build upon rocks jutting out in the sea or on rocks in the sea.

Gen. **Collocalia**, *Gray.*—Edible-Nest-Building Swallows.

General characters as in *Cypselus*; hind toe pointing backwards; 2nd quill longest; tail moderate, even, or slightly forked; bill very small, much hooked; feet small. (*Jerd.*)

173. Collocalia Linchi, *Horsf. and Moore, Cat. B. E. I. Co.* i. p. 100; *Wallace, P. Z. S.* 1863, p. 384; *Hume, Str. F.* ii. p. 157; *id., Nests and Eggs Ind. B.* p. 89; *Salvad, Ucc. Born.* p. 121; *Hume and Dav., Str. F.* vi. p. 49; *Hume, Str. F.* viii. p. 85; *Oates, B. Br. Burm.* ii. p. 10. Hirundo fuciphaga, *apud Horsf., Trans. Linn. Socy.* xiii. p. 143. Collocalia fuciphaga, *apud Bl. and Wald., B. Burm.* p. 85. Collocalia francica *apud B. Legge, B. Ceylon.* p. 324.—Horsfield's Swiftlet.

Above glossy bronze-black; chin, throat, sides of the head and of the body ashy-brown, each feather margined paler; abdomen and vent white, streaked with brown; under tail coverts dark brown margined with white; wings and tail glossy black; bill black; irides brown; feet brownish black.

Length.—4 inches; tail 1·75; wing 4; tarsus 0·3; bill from gape 0·4.

Hab.—Ceylon, Java, Borneo, the Malay Peninsula, Tenasserim and Arracan; also the Andaman and Nicobar Islands. The correct distribution of this Swiftlet has not yet been ascertained. Mr. Davison's experience of the species is that they are very familiar birds, coming even into the house, and taking up their quarters in it, day after day. It breeds abundantly in both the Andamans and Nicobars. Eggs pure white, devoid of gloss, long ovals, and average 0·7 × 0·45 inch.

Gen. **Dendrochelidon**, *Boie.* (Macropteryx, *Sws.*)

Hallux not reversible; tarsus short, either naked or feathered; wings long, first two primaries sub-equal; tail long and forked; head sub-crested.

174. Dendrochelidon coronatus (*Tick.*), *Sclater, P. Z. S.*, 1865, p. 617; *Jerd., B. Ind.* i. p. 185, No. 104; *Hume, Nests and Eggs*, p. 92; *id., Str. F.* iii. p. 45; *Hume and Dav., Str. F.* vi. p. 51; *Legge, B. Ceylon*, p. 328; *Hume, Str. F.* viii. p. 85; *Parker, Str. F.* ix. p. 476; *Murray,*

Avif. Brit. Ind. ii. p. 395, No. 968. Hirundo coronata, *Tick., J. A. S. B.* ii. p. 580; xv. p. 2. Macropteryx coronatus, *Blyth, B. Burm.* p. 86; *Wardlaw-Ramsay, Ibis,* 1877, p. 458; *Oates, B. British Burmah* ii. p. 12.—The INDIAN CRESTED TREE-SWIFT.

Upper plumage and sides of the neck ashy, tinged with metallic green on the forehead, crown, and the longer upper tail coverts; lores and a narrow space round the eye black; a narrow white supercilium; chin, moustache and ear coverts ferruginous; under surface of the body pale ashy, whitish on the abdomen, vent and under tail coverts; wing coverts metallic blue; quills brown, suffused with bluish green; tail metallic greenish-brown.

The female differs in having the ear coverts black instead of chestnut, and the chin and moustache ashy like the throat. Bill black; legs blue-black; irides brown.

Length.—9 to 9·5 inches; tail 5·2 to 5·5; wing 6·3; tarsus 0·3; bill from gape 0·8.

Hab.—Ceylon, Central and Southern India, the Malabar Coast, Wynaad, Mysore, Southern Ghauts of Nellore and the whole of British Burmah. In the sub-Himalayan tract, below Gurhwal and Kumaon, the Mandla districts of the Central Provinces, and in Darjeeling, it is said to be extremely common and to breed. At Tissa, in the southern provinces of Ceylon, some weeks prior to the beginning of the rains, these Swfts collect in parties of 200 or more before dark, perhaps, as Mr. Parker surmises, to sleep in the rushes like *Hirundo rustica.* He adds that in the Southern Province they breed in March and July, in the N.-W. in April, and in the Northern in April, June, July, September and October. The nest is a shallow half-saucer, composed of flakes of thin bark agglutinated with saliva. Egg one only, pure white, a long almost cylindrical oval, 0·85 by 0·55. The breeding season lasts from April to June.

Family.—CAPRIMULGIDÆ, *Vigors.*—GOATSUCKERS.

Bill short, flat, and broad, weak and curved; gape wide, extending to below the eyes, and with numerous strong bristles; wings long or short; tail moderate, of ten feathers; tarsi short; toes long, hind toe joined to inner at base; eyes large; plumage mottled and pencilled; habits nocturnal.

Sub-Family.—STEATORNINÆ,—*Gray.*

Bill large, wide, depressed, slightly curved and strongly hooked; gape very wide; base of bill covered with feathers and bipectinated bristles. Hallux partially reversible in some. (*Jerd.*)

Gen. **Batrachostomus,**—*Gould.*

Bill very large, strong, broad and hooked at tip; nostrils narrow, lateral, covered by plumes; no rictal bristles; wings short and rounded; tail long; tarsi feathered.

175. Batrachostomus moniliger, *Blyth, J. A. S. B.* xvii. p. 806; *Jerd., B. Ind.* i. p. 119, No. 105; *Str. F.* ii. p. 350; iv. p. 376; vi. p. 55. Podargus Javensis, *Jerd., 2nd Suppl. Cat.* 253. Batrachostomus Javensis, (*Horsf.*), *Str. F.* vii. p. 147.—The WYNAAD FROGMOUTH.

Above with the throat and breast bright bay or chestnut; a torque of white spots edged black on the upper part of the breast and another below it; belly and lower tail coverts pale isabelline with similar but smaller spots; flanks mottled with dusky; coronal feathers long; occipital feathers tipped white and edged black, forming a nuchal ring continuous with the pectoral collar; supercillium pale rufescent; loral plumes tipped black and white; wing coverts tipped white and edged black; tertiaries pale, mottled dusky, with a minute terminal black and white spot; primaries black; scapulars like the tertiaries; tail mottled and obscurely banded, each band ending in a series of white spots, successively more developed on each outer feather, the lateral halves of the tail separated into two distinct lobes. (*Jerd.*) Bill black; irides hazel.

Length.—10 inches; tail 4·25; wing 4·75; tarsus 0·7; bill from gape 1·2; width at gape 1·1.

Hab.—Ceylon, the Malabar Coast, Wynaad, Coorg, Travancore, and the Central Provinces. Very little is known of its habits or of that of any of the other species of the genus, being a nocturnal bird. Mr. Bourdillon, however, says that, if he is not mistaken, the habits of this species is very shy and retiring, for it never appears to venture into the open, and only commences calling in the breeding season some considerable time after dark, and lives entirely in dense jungle. He adds that it is a very difficult bird to secure.

Sub-Family.—CAPRIMULGINÆ.

Bill small and weak, with bristles at the base; wings long; tail rather long; tarsi short, scaled or plumed; middle toe longest; its claw long and serrated. Found in most parts of the world; all live on insects, which they capture on the wing.

Gen. Caprimulgus.—*Lin.*

General characters as in the sub-family. Bill very short, flexible and broad at base, compressed and bent at the tip; rictal bristles strong and numerous.

176. Caprimulgus asiaticus, *Lath., Ind. Orn.* iii. p. 588; *Jerd., B. Ind.* i. p. 197, No. 112; *Hume, Nests and Eggs* p. 97; *id., Str. F.* iii. p. 46; *Blyth, B. Br. Burm.* p. 46; *Hume and Dav., Str. F.* v. p. 59; *Legge, B. Ceylon*, p. 343; *Brooks, Str. F.* vii. p. 169; *Hume, Str. F.* viii. p. 85; *Murray, Hdbk., Zool., &c., Sind*, p. 126; *id., Vert. Zool. Sind*, p. 106; *Bingham, Str. F.* ix. p. 150; *Oates, B. Br. Burm.* ii. p. 17; *Murray, Avif. Br. Ind.* ii. p. 399, No. 973.—The COMMON INDIAN NIGHT-JAR.

Plumage remarkably soft and lax, pale rufescent ashy; the feathers finely pencilled and mottled with dusky; top of head with narrow longitudinal blackish streaks; neck with a white spot; collar rufescent; wing coverts and scapulars edged with buffy or tawny; quills with a white spot on each of the first four feathers, and mottled at the tip, the exterior feathers with a large white patch near the tips of the inner webs; a central patch of white on the throat. Lower parts and tail irregularly barred and mottled lightly; the tail, in the male, with white spots on the outer tail feathers; *tarsi bare.*

Length.—9 inches; extent 18 to 18·5; wing 5·5 to 6; tail 4·5.

Hab.—Very widely spread in Ceylon and India. Occurs in Sind, the Concan and Deccan, Kutch, Kattiawar, and North Guzerat; recorded also from Upper Pegu and Amherst. Breeds wherever it is found, ascending the lower ranges of the Himalayas to the height of 5,000 or 6,000 feet in spring and summer. The eggs are laid in a depression on the ground. May is the month in which they breed, but eggs have also been taken in April. In Ceylon Mr. Parker has taken eggs in June and July in the Northern Province, and in June and September in the S. E. of the Island. Eggs, two in number, long, cylindrical ovals, of a pinkish stone colour, blotched, clouded, spotted and streaked with different shades of pale reddish and purplish brown. Average size 1·04 × 0·77.

C. mahrattensis may be looked for in Ceylon. A skin in my possession from Mr. Hall of Caltura is not unlike it but it is in too bad a state of preservation to correctly identify it with that species.

177. Caprimulgus atripennis, *Jerd., Ill. Ind. Orn.* pl. 24; *id., B. Ind.* i. p. 196, No. 111; *Murray, Avif. Br. Ind.* ii. p. 401, No. 977. Caprimulgus spilocircus (*Gray*), *Hume, Nests and Eggs Ind. B.* p. 97; *Legge, B. Ceylon* p. 340.—The GHAUT NIGHT-JAR.

Crown and tertiaries cineraceous, minutely mottled with black; the crown with a broad black mesial longitudinal streak; ear coverts ferruginous; wing coverts and scapulars black, with a russet tinge, and bordered broadly with rufescent white; nape feathers tinged with russet; neck in front with a broad white patch; first primary with a white spot on the inner web; the next three with a white patch extending across both webs; none of the quills mottled at the tip; outer tail feathers with a broad white tip; rictal bristles white at base and tipped black.

The female is like the male, except that the white on the tail is tinged with rufous and is much contracted, and the marks on the primaries are narrow, ill-defined and rufescent. Bill pinkish brown; irides brown; feet and legs brown. The nestling is covered with reddish brown down.

Length.—10·5 inches against 12 to 13 inches; wing 6·5 against 8·5 to 9 inches. In colour it has a russet tinge about the nape, breast and back, not mottled at the tip; ear coverts ferruginous.

Hab.—Nearly throughout Ceylon and the Eastern ghauts; also Southern India, and the Malabar Coast. According to Hume, it breeds on the Nilghiris; in Ceylon, in the N.-W. Provinces from March to May, laying two eggs under a bush or at the foot of a tree. The eggs have the usual gloss peculiar to those of the species, and a pale somewhat creamy pink ground, faintly streaked and mottled all over with pale reddish and purple. The average of 6 eggs is 1·16 × 0·84; the length varies from 1·11 inch to 1·25, and the breadth from 0·79 to 0·89 inch.

178. Caprimulgus Kelaarti, *Blyth, J. A. S. B.* xx. p. 175; *id., J. A. S. B.* xiv. p. 208; *Jerd., Ill. Ind. Orn.* pl. 24; *Hume, Str. F.* iv. p. 381; *Legge, B. Celyon,* p. 337; *Murray, Avif. Brit. Ind.* ii. p. 403, No. 980.—The NEILGHERRY NIGHT-JAR.

Plumage above and below light cinereous, tinged on the scapulars and under surface with pale fawn; head, neck, back, scapulars, rump and upper tail coverts mottled and pencilled with black and dusky; ear coverts black, edged with light rufous; a line from below the ear coverts to the gape, also the throat white; first four primaries with a white spot on the under web, all except the middle feathers mottled at the tips; tail feathers tipped with white and margined with dusky. Bill dusky brown; irides brown.

Length.—11·5 inches; tail 5·75; wing 7· to 7·2.

Hab.—Ceylon, the Nilghiris, Central Provinces, and on the Eastern Ghauts. Hume says it breeds throughout Southern India and the Central Provinces from February to August; the eggs, not unlike those of other species, are laid in a depression in the ground under a bush or tuft of grass. They are two in number, and resemble exactly those of *C. indicus* and *asiaticus.*

SUB-ORDER—COCCYGES HETERODACTYLÆ.

Family—TROGONIDÆ.

Bill short, stout, somewhat triangular, strong and curved from the base, the tip and sometimes the margin toothed; gape wide; nostrils and base of bill concealed by long tufts of bristles; wings moderate or short; tarsus short, partially feathered; toes short, two before and two behind, inner toe being turned backwards; tail long and broad, of 12 feathers; plumage soft; skin tender and thin.

Gen. Harpactes, *Swainson.*

Bill strong, broad and deep, conic and much curved; nostrils partially covered by hairs; tarsus half-feathered; orbital region nude. Birds of rich plumage, living in dense forests, and feeding on insects, which, like the *Caprimulgidæ,* they capture in the air.

179. Harpactes fasciatus (*Gmel.*), *Jerd., B. Ind.* i. p. 201, No. 115; *Hume, Str. F.* vii. p. 507. Trogon Malabaricus, *Gould, Monog.* pl. 31. *Legge, B. Ceylon,* p. 269; *Murray, Avif. Br. Ind.* ii. p. 405, No. 983. —The MALABAR TROGON.

Entire head and neck black ; rest of the upper plumage castaneous olive-brown ; lesser wing coverts, tertiaries and some of the secondaries finely streaked with black and white ; breast, belly and lower parts fine crimson red ; tail with the centre feathers more chestnut than the back ; rest black and white. The *female* has the head and neck of the same colour as the body, and the wing coverts and tertiaries are finely banded black and brown ; lower plumage ochreous yellow. Bill deep blue ; orbital skin smalt blue ; irides dark brown ; feet light lavender-blue. (*Jerd.*)

Length.—12 inches ; tail 6 ; wing 5 ; tarsus 0·6 ; bill at front 0·5 ; at gape 1·0.

Hab.—Ceylon and Malabar ; also Central India. Found in the forests of Malabar from the extreme south to about N. lat. 17°, reaching up the ghauts and hill ranges to at least 3,000 feet. Jerdon adds that it prefers the more elevated situations, and keeps to the thickest parts of the woods. It is usually solitary, and sometimes in pairs. Layard says it is found in small parties of three or four, and feeds on various insects.

SUB-ORDER.—ZYGODACTYLI.

Bill various, more or less arched, often straight and angular ; toes two before and two behind ; outer hind toe often reversible.

Family—CUCULIDÆ, *Leach.*—Cuckoos.

Bill rather slender and compressed, curved above, tip hooked ; gape wide ; nostrils in a membranous groove ; wings long ; tail rounded.

Sub-Family—CUCULINÆ.

Tarsi short, feathered and scaled ; bill broad, flattened at base.

Gen. Cuculus.—*Lin.*

3rd quill longest ; two outer feathers of tail shortest ; tarsi feathered below the knee ; outer front toe longest, united at base to the inner toe and reversible.

180. Cuculus canorus, *Linn., Syst. Nat.* i. p. 168 ; *Jerd., B. Ind.* i. p. 322, No. 199 ; *Hume, Nests and Eggs, Ind. B.* p. 133 ; *Wald., Trans. Zool. Soc.* viii. p. 115 ; *Hume, Str. F.* iii. p. 78 ; *Blyth, B. Burm.* p. 79 ; *Hume, Str. F.* iv. p. 288 ; *Wardlaw-Ramsay, Ibis,* 1877, p. 458 ; *David et Oust. Ois. Chine,* p. 65 ; *Legge, B. Ceylon,* p. 221 ; *Anders., Yunnan Exped.* p. 589 ; *Dresser, B. Europe,* v. p. 199, pl. ; *Hume and Dav., Str. F.* vi. p. 156 ; *Hume, Str. F.* viii. p. 88 ; *Scully, Str. F.* viii. p. 253 ; *Oates, Str. F.* x. p. 192 ; *id., B. Br. Burm.*, ii. p. 103 ; *Murray, Hdbk, Zool., &c., Sind.* p. 131 ; *id., Vert. Zool. Sind,* p. 116 ; *id., Avif. Brit. Ind.* ii. p. 408, No. 987.—The European Cuckoo.

Head and upper parts dark ashy, ashy, or pale blue ; breast and belly white, elegantly crossed with wavy bars of black ; the quills are dusky, their inner webs marked with large oval white spots; tail long, the two middle feathers black with white tips, the others dusky, with alternate spots of white on each side of the shafts; legs short, yellow; bill black; yellowish at base beneath; orbits and irides deep yellow. The *young bird* has the whole upper plumage, wings and tail barred with ferruginous and the feathers tipped white; lower plumage, white, barred with brown.

Length.—14 inches; wing 8·75 to 9; tail 7; bill at front 0·75.

Hab.—Europe, N. Africa, China, Formosa, Beloochistan, Persia, S. Afghanistan, Eastern Turkistan, and India generally; Nepaul, Burmah, Ceylon, Upper Pegu, and throughout Western, Central, and Southern India, as a migrant. It arrives in Sind during August and September. Breeds in the Himalayas, round Almorah, Kumaon, and Kotegurh during the latter half of May, selecting the nests of Pipits and Stone-Chats, also *Malacocirci*. The eggs are variable in size and colouring, but the general colour is pure white, thinly freckled and streaked with brownish red and pale purple. Length from 0·88 to 0·95 inch, breadth 0·68 to 0·73.

181. Cuculus poliocephalus, *Latham, Ind. Orn.* i. p. 213; *Jerd., B. Ind.* i. p. 324, No. 201; *id., 2nd Suppl. Cat.* No. 223 bis; *id., Ibis*, 1872, *Suppl. List*; *Legge, B. Ceylon*, p. 231; *Murray, Avif. Br. Ind.* ii. p. 409 No. 989. Cuculus Himalayanus, *Gould, Cent. Him. B.* pl. 54; *Hume, Nests and Eggs, Ind. B.* p. 135.—The Small or Hoary-headed Cuckoo.

Upper surface of the body ashy, tinged sometimes with rufous, and by slightly glossed with green on the back and upper tail coverts; quills brown, glossed greenish, with numerous close large white spots; tail deep ashy or blackish brown, with large white spots on the middle of each feather and on the edge of the inner webs, also at the tip; chin and throat pale ashy; breast tinged with rusty; under surface of the body white, with narrow distant bars of dark brown or buff; under tail coverts white; bill dusky horny; irides reddish brown.

Length.—10 to 10·6 inches; tail 5·1 to 5·2 · wing 5·6; bill at front 0·6; tarsus 0·6.

Hab.—Ceylon; also the Himalayas, migrating to the plains during winter. Jerdon says it has been found as far south as Nellore on the East Coast; at Darjeeling it is said to be tolerably common. Nothing certain, Hume says, is known of the eggs of this species. Mr. Thomson, he adds, says it lays in May and June. Mr. Brooks, when in Cashmere, took an egg supposed to belong to this species from the nest of *Reguloides superciliosus* at Goolmerg, on 2nd June; "It was an elongated cylindrically ovate egg, nearly the same size at both ends, which are obtuse, pure white and glossy; size 0·81 by 0·57 inch.

182. Cuculus Sonneratii, *Lath., Ind. Orn.* i. p. 215; *Jerd., B. Ind.* i. p. 325, No. 220; *Wald., Trans. Zool. Soc.* viii. p. 55; *Blyth, B.*

Burm., p. 80; *Anderson, Yunnan Exped.* p. 587; *Hume and Dav., Str. F.* vi. p. 156; *Legge, B. Ceylon,* p. 233; *Hume, Str. F.* viii. p. 88; *Vidal, Str. F.* ix. p. 54; *Oates, B. Br. Burm.* ii. p. 107; *Murray, Avif. Br. Ind.* ii. p. 410, No. 990.—The BANDED CUCKOO.

General colour above dusky, tinged with greenish and closely barred with rufous; the wing coverts barred with paler rufous or white; outer web of quills rufescent; tail rufous, the feathers dusky on the outer webs; the inner webs narrowly barred, the tip white and with a subterminal broad, dusky bar; beneath, from throat, white, tinged with fulvous on the flanks and marked with numerous narrow dusky cross bars; sides of the head and neck white, barred with dusky; ear coverts dusky.

The young are more coarsely barred than adults, with pale rufescent on a blackish ground; breast white, banded with dusky; central feathers of tail nearly black, the edges scolloped with rufous; outer feathers dusky. (*Jerd.*) Bill dusky; irides brown; legs greenish grey.

Length.—9·5 inches; tail 4·5; wing 4·8; tarsus 0·7; bill from gape 1·1.

Hab.—Ceylon, and Peninsular India also Tenasserim and the Indo-Burmese countries. Jerdon records it from the forests of Malabar and Travancore, where he says it is tolerably common; also from the sides of the Nilghiris and in the Wynaad, and more rarely on the Eastern Ghauts about the latitude of Madras. In Burmah it has been procured at Thayetmyo.

183. Cuculus micropterus, *Gould, P. Z. S.* 1837, p. 137; *Jerd., B. Ind.* i. p. 326, No. 203; *Swinhoe, P. Z. S.* 1871, p. 395; *Blyth and Wald., B. Burm.* p. 79; *David et Oust. Ois. Chine,* p. 64; *Hume and Dav., Str. F.* vi. p. 156; *Legge, B. Ceylon,* p. 228; *Hume, Str. F.* viii. p. 88; *Oates, Str. F.* x. p. 193; *Oates, B. Br. Burm.* ii. p. 104; *Murray, Avif. Br. Ind.* ii. p. 410, No. 991. Cuculus affinis (*A. Hay*), *Blyth, J. A. S. B.* xv. p. 18; *Blyth, B. Burm.* p. 76; *Wardlaw-Ramsay, Tweedd. Mem.* p. 671; *Hume, Str. F.* viii. p. 8. Cuculus striatus (*Drap.*) *apud. Jerd.* i. p. 328, No. 204.—The INDIAN CUCKOO.

Upper parts, including the wings, dark ashy, purer on the forehead; crown, nape, sides of the head and neck, also the cheeks, ashy; chin, throat and breast grey; inner webs of quills barred with white; tail ashy brown, tipped with whitish, and with a subterminal broad dark band; all the feathers with white shaft spots, which become bars on the outermost ones; the edges of the centre feathers scolloped with rufous; abdomen, vent and sides of the body white, banded broadly throughout with black; upper tail coverts brown, tinged with ashy; under tail coverts white, with a few nearly obsolete bars. The *young* are dark brown; the upper surface broadly tipped with rufous, and the head barred with rufous white. Bill dark horny black; legs yellow; irides brown.

Length.—12·5 to 13 inches; tail 6·4 to 6·8; wing 7·5 to 8·5; tarsus 0·85; bill from gape 1·3.

Hab.—Ceylon, and the greater part of Peninsular India; also Central Asia, China, Cochin-China, the Malay Peninsula, and the Indo-Burmese countries.

Oates says it is distributed over Pegu both on the hills and in the plains. It extends also to Assam. Jerdon says it is rare in the South of India, but common in the North; rare on the Malabar Coast and in the Carnatic; it is also rare in Ceylon, but tolerably common in the jungles of Central India, as at Nagpore, Chanda, Mhow, and Saugor, and moderately common in Lower Bengal and on the Himalayas. Habits the same as other members of the genus.

Gen. **Hierococcyx**, *Müller*.

Bill as in *Cuculus* but stouter, wider at gape and much deeper; wings with the 4th quill longest, the 5th subequal with the 2nd; tail nearly even, broad and barred; plumage barred.

184. Hierococcyx varius (*Vahl.*), *Jerd.*, *B. Ind.* i. p. 329, No. 329; *Legge*, *B. Ceylon*, ii. p. 240; *Murray*, *Avif. Br. Ind.* ii. p. 412, No. 993.—The COMMON HAWK CUCKOO.

Upper parts uniform ash grey, darker on the wings and their coverts; foreneck and breast pale rufous, the feathers greyish mesially; abdomen and flanks white, barred with grey and rufous; vent and under tail coverts white; tail grey, tipped with white, crossed with 5—6 narrow undulating bands, and a broad dusky subterminal one; quills barred with white on their inner webs; chin white; throat greyish; bill dusky; lower mandible yellowish; irides gamboge yellow.

Length.—13 to 13·5 inches; tail 6·75; wing 7; bill at front 0·8.

Hab.—Ceylon, Bengal and Northern and Southern India; affects gardens, groves, avenues, &c. Lives like its congeners on caterpillars and other insects.

Gen. **Cacomantis**, *Müller*.

Cuckoos of small size and variable plumage, generally grey or dusky; plumage not barred in the normal adult state; tarsi less plumed than in *Cuculus*.

185. Cacomantis nigra (*Vahl.*), *Jerd.*, *Ibis*, ii. 1872, Plate 1. *Polyphasia nigra*, *Jerd.*, *B. Ind.*, i. p. 333; *Murray*, *Avif. Brit. Ind.* ii. p. 414. Cacomantis passerinus (*Vahl.*), *Legge*, *B. Ceylon*, p. 235.—The INDIAN PLAINTIVE CUCKOO.

Adult uniform dark ashy above, glossed with green, beneath pale ashy; vent and under tail coverts white; quills dusky, with a broad white band on the inner web of each feather; tail blackish, except the middle pair, all the feathers banded and tipped with white; bill blackish, red at base beneath and at the gape; feet reddish yellow; irides ruby red or brownish red. (*Jerd.*)

Length.—9 inches; tail 4·5; wing 4·5; bill at front 0·6; tarsus 0·6.

Hab.—Nearly all over India in moist and woody countries. Abundant on the Malabar Coast, in the Wynaad, and the warmer slopes of the Nilghiris; rare in the Carnatic; uncommon on the eastern ghauts, but plentiful in Central India, and Lower Bengal, up to the foot of the N.-W. Himalayas. Common in Ceylon. Breeds on the Nilghiris in the nests of *Drymoipus inornatus*, the Common Wren Warbler, during September. The eggs, according to Hume, are elongated ovals, occasionally more or less cylindrical. The shell is fine and smooth. The ground colour is a delicate pale greenish blue, blotched and spotted towards the large end with reddish or purplish brown and pale reddish purple. Size 0·78 to 0·81 × 0·53 to 0·57.

Gen. **Surniculus**.—*Lesson*.

Plumage black; tail even or forked; outermost feathers short, the penultimate slightly the longest, and each lateral half curling outwards towards the tip; otherwise as in *Cacomantis*. (*Jerd.*)

186. Surniculus lugubris (*Horsf.*), *Salvad, Ucc. Born.* 179, p. 63; *Blyth and Wald., B. Burm.* p. 80; *Hume and Dav., Str. F.* vi. p. 159; *Anders., Yunnan Exped.* p. 587; *Legge, B. Ceylon*, p. 243; *Hume, Str. F.* viii. p. 86; *Oates, B. Br. Burm.* ii. p. 112. *Murray, Avif. Br. Ind.* ii. p. 414, No. 998. Cuculus lugubris, *Horsf. Trans. Linn. Soc.* xiii. p. 179. Pseudornis dicruroides, *Hodgs., J. A. S. B.* viii. p. 136. Surniculus dicruroides, *Jerd., B. Ind.* i. p. 336, No. 210.—The BLACK FORK-TAILED CUCKOO.

Upper parts glossy black, glossed green and blue; head sub-crested and with a few white feathers on the nape; tail glossy blue-black, the outermost pair of feathers barred and tipped with white; the next pair with only a few white spots near the shaft and very narrowly tipped with white; primaries black, all except the second with a white spot on the inner web; tibial plumes spotted with white; upper tail coverts with some white specks occasionally; lower surface of the body dull black; inner wing coverts the same, with minute white specks. The *young* are black, and the plumage above and below is much spotted with white. Bill black; irides brown; legs plumbeous.

Length.—10 inches; tail 5·3 to 5·75; wing 5·5; tarsus 0·65; bill from gape 1·1.

Hab.—Ceylon, the Indo-Curmese countries, and India generally. Ranges into China, Siam and Cochin-China, and extends down the Malay Peninsula, to Sumatra, Java, and Borneo. It is common on the Malabar Coast, in the Wynaad, Central India, and at Darjeeling. In the Himalayas, Ceylon, Burmah, and Tenasserim, it is said to be not uncommon. Oates says it is found over the whole of British Burmah and Karenne.

Gen. **Chrysococcyx**.—*Boie*.

Bill as in *Cuculus*, but a little more depressed at the base and entire at tip; wings pointed; 2nd quill longer than the 4th; 3rd subequal with the 4th; feathers of the rump and upper tail coverts soft, tarsi short, feathered.

187. Chrysococcyx maculatus (*Gm.*), *Blyth, B. Burm.* p. 80 *Wald., Ibis,* 1876, p. 345; *Wardlaw-Ramsay, Ibis,* 1877, p. 438; *Hume, Str. F.* viii. p. 89; *Bingham, Str. F.* ix. p. 167; *Oates, Str. F.* x. p. 193; *id., B. Br. Burm.* ii. p. 113; *Murray, Avif. Br. Ind.* p. 415, No. 999. Trogon maculatus, *Gm., Syst. Nat.* i. p. 404; *Legge, B. Ceylon,* p. 238. Chrysococcyx smaragdinus, *Blyth, J. A. S. B.* xv. p. 53. Chrysococcyx Hodgsoni, *Moore, in Horsf. and Moore, Cat. Birds, Mus. E. I. Co.* ii. p. 705; *Jerd. B. Ind.* i. p. 338, No. 211; *David et Oust. Ois. Chine,* p. 62. Chrysococcyx Schomburgki, *Gould, P. Z. S.* 1864, p. 73. Lamprococcyx maculatus, *Hume and Dav., Str. F.* vi. pp. 161, 502.—The EMERALD CUCKOO.

Head, neck, and entire upper plumage, including the wings and tail, also the breast, emerald green, with a golden gloss; inner webs of quills marked with white, and the outer tail feathers with large white spots; lower breast and rest of the lower plumage white, crossed with bars of shining or metallic green. Bill yellow, tipped dusky or black; legs and feet brownish green; irides red brown. The young are variously marked; generally the forehead, crown, and nape are rufous, or barred with rufous.

Length.—7 inches; tail 3; wing 4·4; tarsus 0·5; bill from gape 0·85.

Hab.—The Himalayas to Ceylon. Found in the greater portion of Burmah and Tenasserim; also Arracan. Jerdon says it has been procured at Darjeeling and also in Central India.

Gen. **Coccystes**.—*Gloger.*

Head crested; nostrils basal, ovate; 4th quill longest; 3rd and 4th subequal; tail long, graduated; tarsi not plumed.

188. Coccystes jacobinus, *Bodd., Pl. Enl.* 872; *Levail O. A.* t. 208; *Hume, Nests and Eggs, Ind. B.* p. 137; *Murray, Vert. Zool., Sind,* p. 117; *Oates, B. Br. Burmah* ii. p. 118; *Legge, B. Ceylon,* p. 216; *Hume, Str. F.* viii. p. 89; *Murray, Avif. Br. Ind.* ii. p. 417, No. 1002. Oxylophus jacobinus, *Hume, Str. F.* iii. p. 81. Coccystes melanoleucos (*Gmel.*), *Horsf. and Moore, Cat. B.* ii. p. 694; *Jerd., B. Ind.* i. p. 339, No. 210; *Murray, Hdbk., Zool., &c., Sind,* p. 131. Leptosomus afer, *Frankl., Proc. Zool. Soc.* 1831, p. 121. Oxylophus serratus, *Gray, Gen. B.* ii. p. 464.—The PIED-CRESTED CUCKOO.

Entire upper surface black with a greenish gloss; chin, throat, belly, vent, and under tail coverts white or fulvescent white; bases of the primaries white, forming a conspicuous wing patch; tail feathers broadly tipped white, the two middle narrowly; shoulders white; under wing coverts fulvescent white. Bill black; legs bluish; irides red brown.

Length.—13 inches; wing 5·5 to 5·75; tail 6·75 to 7; bill at front 0·75.

Hab.—Throughout India to Nepaul. Common in Ceylon, Central and Southern India, Bengal, Upper Pegu and rare on the Malabar Coast. Lays in February in the Kurnegala district. Mr. Parker says they are scarce in the

N.-W. Province and the interior of Northern Ceylon during the S.-W. monsoon, but in S.-E. Ceylon more numerous than at other times. In Sind, Kutch, Kattiawar, Rajputana and North Guzerat, and in fact wherever it is found, it lays according to the breeding season of the various Babblers, in whose nests it deposits its eggs, from January to July. The eggs, like those of the *Malacocirci*, are a spotless sky blue, and highly glossy, round ovals, varying in length from 0·9 to 0·98 inch, and in breadth from 0·72 to 0·82 inch.

189. Coccystes coromandus (*Linn.*), *Jerd. B. Ind.* i. p. 341; *Hume, Nests and Eggs, Ind. B.* p. 138; *Salvad., Ucc. Born.* p. 67; *Hume, Str. F.* viii. p. 82; *Blyth, B. Burm.* p. 81; *David et Oust. Ois. Chine*, p. 61; *Legge, B. Ceylon*, p. 249; *Hume and Dev., Str. F.* vi. p. 162; *Hume, Str. F.* viii. p. 89; *Scully, t. c.* p. 257; *Murray Avif. Br. Ind.* ii. p. 417, No. 1003. Cuculus coromandus, *Linn., Syst. Nat.* i. p. 171.—The RED-WINGED CRESTED CUCKOO.

Whole head and neck black; the chin, throat, and foreneck fulvous; collar round the neck white; upper parts of the body black, glossed with green; tail and lesser wing coverts black, tinged with greenish blue, the tail tipped with fulvous white, increasing in extent towards the outer feathers; primaries, secondaries, and greater wing coverts deep ferruginous or chestnut, the tips dusky; tertiaries brown; under surface of the body fulvous white, changing to smoky brown on the vent, and dusky black on the under tail coverts; under wing coverts pale ferruginous; flanks greyish brown, with a slight rufescent tinge. The *young* have the upper parts glossed brown and the feathers are edged with rufous.

Bill black; legs plumbeous; irides red brown.

Length.—13 to 18 inches; tail 10; wing 6·4; tarsus 1·1; bill from gape 1·4.

Hab.—Generally spread throughout India, Ceylon, Burmah, and Malayana. Recorded from Siam, China, and Cochin-China, Sumatra, Java, Borneo, and the Phillippine Islands. Occurs abundantly in Pegu and Tenasserim. It is found in Malabar, the Carnatic, and Central India. It has also been obtained in Bengal. It is seen generally singly, flying from tree to tree. It utters a loud call note, which rings through the forest or topes of trees.

Gen. Eudynamys.—*Vig. and Horsf.*

Bill strong, thick, vertically deep, and hooked at tip; 4th quill longest; tarsi not plumed below the joint, flattened in front.

190. Eudynamys honorata (*Linn.*), *Bodd. Tabl. Pl. Enl.* 294, 586; *Lev. O. A.* t. 214; *Legge, B. Ceylon*, p. 251; *Murray, Avif. Br. Ind.* ii. p. 418, No. 1004. Eudynamys orientalis (*Linn.*), *Jerd., B. Ind.* i. p. 342, No. 214; *Cat. Hodgs. Coll. B. M.* p. 119; *Murray, Hdbk. Zool., &c., Sind*, p. 132; *id., Vert. Zool. Sind*, p. 117.—The INDIAN KOEL.

Male.—Entirely black with a greenish gloss ; bill pale greenish ; irides fine crimson ; legs slaty blue.

Length.—15·5 ; wing 7·5 ; bill at front 1.

Female.—Dusky brown with a greenish tinge, spotted with white on the head, scapulars, and wing coverts ; quills, tail, and entire under parts, including the under wing and thigh coverts, barred with white.

Length.—17 to 17·5 inches ; wing 7·75 to 8 ; tail 8.

Hab.—Throughout India, extending to Nepaul, Ceylon, Burmah, Malayana and the Phillippines ; common in the Deccan and Concan, Kutch, Guzerat and Kattiawar. In Sind it is rare, and occurs only during the rains, laying its eggs in the nest of the common crow, *Corvus splendens*. In Ceylon, Mr. Parker's experience is that it is more numerous than the crows, in whose nests they lay their eggs in June and July, consequently, he says, their eggs outnumber those of the crows in some cases. The great disparity, he adds, was noticeable in one instance where one nest contained 3 fresh crows' eggs and 8 koels', which evidently were the laying of three birds! In another 2 crows' and 6 koels' eggs. Koels evidently lay concurrently with the crow.

Sub-Family.—PHŒNICOPHÆINÆ.

Bill moderate or longish ; ridge curved ; nostrils linear ; orbital region generally naked ; wings short ; tail long and graduated ; plumage decomposed and hair-like. Food, chiefly insects.

Gen. Rhopodytes.—*Cab. et Hein.*

Bill much compressed throughout and curved ; nostrils basal, pierced in a slight depression in the horny substance ; wing short, rounded, with the 4th, 5th, and 6th quills nearly equal and longest ; tail much lengthened, graduated ; hallux short ; claws sharp.

191. Rhopodytes viridirostris, *Jerd.*, *Ill. Ind. Orn. Pl.* 3 ; *Jerd.*, *B. Ind.* i. p. 346. Phœnicophaus Jerdoni, *Blyth*, *J. A. S. B.* p. 3 ; *Hume*, *Str. F.* vi. p. 163. Zanclostomus viridirostris, *Legge*, *B. Ceylon*, p. 258, 12-13 ; *Murray*, *Avif. Brit. Ind.* iii. p. 421, No. 1010.—The Small Green-billed Malkoha.

Upper parts dusky cinereous, glossed with greenish ; wings and tail black, glossed with greenish, the tail feathers tipped with white ; under surface of the body greyish, tinged with fawn, paler on the abdomen ; chin and throat with a few black feathers. Bill bright apple green ; nude orbital space cobalt blue ; irides blood red ; legs blackish green.

Length.—15 inches ; tail 10 ; wing 5·25 ; bill at front 1 ; tarsus 1·3.

Hab.—South India and Ceylon ; frequents thick bamboo and bushy jungles, also groves and avenues, where the species feeds on various large insects, as grasshoppers, &c. Breeds, according to Mr. Parker, in March, April and May. The nest he says is from 7 to about 20 feet above the ground, in a thick thorny bush or a young leafy tree. It resembles much that of a pigeon's. It is sometimes made entirely of twigs; occasionally a few leaves are intermingled. Eggs generally two in number, sometimes one only, white, 1·13 × 0·96 inches in length. The nestling has a dark skin covered with light hairs.

Gen. **Phœnicophaes**—*Steph.*

Bill stout, wide at base, and suddenly compressed; more arched than in *Rhopodytes*, the tip bent down. Face nude, papillose.

192. Phœnicophaes pyrrhocephalus (*Forst.*), *Steph., Gen. Zool.* ix. i. p. 59; *Blyth, J. A. S. B.* 1842, p. 927; *Bp., Consp. Gen. Av.* i. p. 98. Phœnicophaus pyrrhocephala, *Blyth, J. A. S. B.* 1845, p. 199; *Kelaart Prod. Cat.*; *Layard, Ann. and Mag. Nat. Hist. Ser.* (5); *Legge. B Ceylon,* p. 255.—The CRIMSON-HEADED MALKOHA.

Crown of the head and the forecheek bright crimson, surrounded by a band of white; hind head and neck black, spotted with white; foreneck entirely black; back and wings black; tail long, black on the lower part, and tipped with white; breast and under parts white. Legs pale blue.

Length.—16 inches; tail 10, wing 5·25; bill at front 1·1; tarsus 1·3.

Hab.—Ceylon. Rather plentiful at Rambharawihara in the S. Province. Found sparingly through the forests of the Northern Province up to Elephant Pass. (*Parker.*)

Sub-Family CENTROPODINÆ, *Bp.*—COUCALS or CROW-PHEASANTS.

Bill strong, deep, compressed; wings rounded; tail long, graduated; tarsi long and scaled; hallux lengthened in some.

Gen. **Centrococcyx**.—*Illiger.*

Bill well curved, high at base; claw of the hallux lengthened, nearly straight.

193. Centrococcyx rufipennis (*Illiger*), *Jerd., B. Ind.* i. p. 348, No. 217; *Str. F.* i. p. 453; *Hume, Nests and Eggs Ind. B.* p. 142; *Legge, B. Ceylon,* pp. 260, 1203; *Murray, Avif Br. Ind.* ii. p. 423, No. 1014.—The COMMON COUCAL OR CROW PHEASANT.

Whole head, neck, lower back, upper tail coverts and under surface of the body rich black, with a purplish gloss; tail glossed with green; upper back and wings deep chestnut; bill black; irides crimson; legs black.

Length.—19 to 20 inches; tail 10; wing 7; bill at front 1·3; tarsus 2; hind claw 1. The *young* vary much in plumage, generally the upper parts are barred with black and rufous, and the lower with dusky and fulvous white; the tail is also banded with greyish.

Hab.—Ceylon, and India generally, frequenting wooded and cultivated localities, especially along the banks of rivers and on the edges of cultivation, where it captures mice, snakes, worms, rats, lizards, and other insects, upon which it feeds. This is the diet of all the members.

All the species build a large, globular, open, or domed nest in the middle of thick thorny bushes or trees. The nest is usually made of dry sticks or twigs lined with a few green leaves. The hole for entrance and exit is made on one side. June to August are the months in which they lay in India. In Ceylon February in the Manaar district and May in the N.-W. provinces. The eggs are from 2 to 5 in number, oval, and measure from 1·3 to 1·55 inch in length, and from 1·12 to 1·25 inch in breadth. In texture they are coarse and chalky, and of a dull white colour, sometimes with a pale yellowish glaze.

194. Centrococcyx chlororhynchus, *Blyth, Ibis*, 1867, p. 702; *Str. F.* vii. p. 372; *Legge, B. Ceylon*, p. 263.—The CEYLON OR GREEN-BILLED COUCAL.

Like *C. rufipennis*, but has a larger bill, of an uniform greenish yellow colour; back and wings dark maroon; head, neck, and under surface of the body ruddy, glossed with amethystine; tail purplish black; irides red.

Length.—18 inches; tail 9; wing 6·5; bill to gape 1·75; tarsus 2.

Hab.—Ceylon, in the upland country, where they breed in April and May. Mr. Parker says the nests are quite similar in structure to those of *C. rufipennis* and are built in varying sites. Three is the usual number of eggs, which are of a creamy white colour with a slight gloss.

Gen. Taccocua.—*Lesson.*

Bill short, or of moderate length, much compressed; culmen arched; gonys straight or slightly concave; nostrils bordered on their upper edge with a tuft of bristly feathers; 3rd and 4th quills nearly equal and longest; tail long, graduated; plumage of the head and superciliary region bristly, of the body stiffish.

195. Taccocua Leschenaulti (*Less.*), *Jerd., B. Ind.* i. p. 352; *Hume, Str. F.* v. p. 218; *Legge, B. Ceylon*, p. 266; *Murray, Avif. Br. Ind.* ii. p. 425, No. 1017. Zanclostomus sirkeer, *Jerd., Cat.* 230; *id., 2nd Suppl. Cat.* 230; *Hume, Nests and Eggs Ind. B.* p. 145.—The SOUTHERN SIRKEER.

Upper surface of the body pale earthy-brown, the feathers of the head inclining to ashy, the shafts of the feathers, also those of the neck and breast, glistening black; upper tail coverts long; lateral tail feathers dark-brown nd broadly tipped with white; throat whitish; foreneck and breast ashy, tinged with ferruginous; abdomen dark ferruginous. Bill cherry red, yellowish at tip; feet plumbeous; irides reddish brown.

Length.—15 to 15·5 inches; wing 5·5 to 5·75; tail 8·0.

Hab.—Ceylon and Southern India on the Nilghiris, also on the Eastern Ghauts and in the Deccan, frequenting grassy slopes near jungle at from 5,000 to 6,000 feet elevation. Feeds chiefly on the ground. Nest similar to that of a crow-pheasant. Breeds in March. Eggs 2—3, white.

Family CAPITONIDÆ.—BARBETS.

Bill stout, somewhat conic, inflated at the sides, moderately long or short, wide at the base and more or less compressed at the tip ; base of upper mandible continued backward to the gape and furnished with numerous stiff bristles, which project forward. Some African species have the mandibles denticulated and grooved at the sides ; wings and tail short, the latter even, or nearly so ; tail feathers 10 in number ; toes in pairs. Plumage gay, and in nearly all the species green is the predominant colour. They breed in holes of trees, and lay from two to four white eggs. Food, fruits and berries. (*Jerd.*)

Gen. Megalæma,—*G. R. Gray.*

Bill nearly as long or slightly longer than the head, more or less wide at the base and compressed at the tip ; culmen slightly arched ; upper mandible somewhat overlapping the lower one ; gape wide ; feet zygodactyle. Habits arboreal, frequenting forests, groves, and tree jungle.

196. Megalæma zeylanica (*Gmel.*), *Blyth, J. A. S B.* 1858, xx. p. 181 ; *Kelaart, Prod. Cat.* p. 127 ; *Layard, Ann. and Mag. Nat. Hist.* xiii. p. 46 ; *Jerd., B. Ind.* i. p. 311 ; *Holdsw*, *P. Z. S.* 1872, p. 429 ; *Legge, B. Ceylon*, p. 208. Megalæma caniceps, *G. R. Gray, Gen. B.* ii. p. 429, 1846 ; *Layard, Ann. and Mag. Nat. Hist.* 1854, p. 446 (xiii.) Bucco zeylanicus, *Gmel., Syst. Nat.* i. p. 408.—The CEYLON BARBET.

Head and neck dark earthy brown, the feathers of the latter with longitudinal pale yellowish shaft streaks ; upper back and wing coverts dark green, the former narrowly centred and the latter finely tipped with yellowish white ; quills dark brown, the edge of the outer webs and inner edge of the primaries and secondaries cream colour ; rest of upper plumage rich green ; throat and breast dark brown, the feathers centred paler ; abdomen green, with a bluish tinge ; tail dark green above, black shafted, below greenish blue ; bill pale brown tinged with orange ; rictal bristles strongly developed ; feathers of the forehead and chin stiff-shafted ; facial nude skin yellow ; legs and feet dull yellow ; iris brown.

Length.—9·2 to 9·5 inches ; wing 4·5 ; tail 2·9.

Hab.—Ceylon. Breeds throughout the year. Mr. Parker's notes are to the effect that its nests have been taken in January, March, April, May, June, July, August, and October. He notes an incident when no less than three other birds simultaneously endeavoured to obtain possession of an existing hole which a pair of these Barbets were improving with a view to nesting in it. These were, he says, Common Mynahs (*A. melanosternus*), Pied Robins and Rollers. Daily fights occurred, but one of the wise Barbets always took the precaution to sit inside the hole, and she could not be ousted from that point of vantage, there being no means of giving her an unexpected "dab" in the back,—a favourite mode of assault among birds. Eventually, by a steady persistence in stopping at home and pecking at her enemies' eyes when the other birds approached, she became the victorious owner of the coveted dwelling.

197. Megalæma flavifrons, (*Cuv.*), *Bonap. Consp. Av.* i. p. 143; *Blyth, J. A. S. B.* 1852, p. 179; *Marsh., Mon. Capit.* pl. 30; *Kelaart, Prod. Cat.* p. 127; *Layard, A. M. N. Hist.* p. 447; *Legge, B. Ceylon*, p. 202. Cyanops flavifrons, *Jerd., B. Ind.* i. p. 314 (note); *Blyth, Ibis*, 1867, p. 297. Bucco flavifrons, *Cuv. Regne. Anim.* i. p. 428.—The YELLOW-FRONTED CEYLON BARBET.

Forehead and a spot at gape bright golden yellow; eyebrow, lores, below the eye, ear coverts, chin, and throat bright verditer blue; head and sides of the neck bright green, the feathers with yellowish white shaft streaks; rest of upper surface grass green, tinged with bluish on the coverts; quills brown, yellow at base of inner web; outer webs of secondaries margined with grass green; under surface of body bright green, lighter on the breast, where the tips are margined lunately with darker green; tail deep green above, bluish on the under surface. Bill brownish black, paler at base of lower mandible.

Length.—9 inches; wing 4; tail 2·75; tarsus 1·10.

Hab.—Ceylon.

Gen. **Xantholæma**,—*Bonap.*

Bill shorter than in *Cyanops*, wider and less compressed; 2nd quill of wing longest and sub-equal to the next three.

198. Xantholæma hæmacephala (*P. L. S. Müll*), *Marsh., Monog. Capit.* pl. xliii.; *Wald., Trans. Zool. Soc.* ix. p. 156; *Hume, Nests and Eggs*, p. 131; *id., Str. F.* iii. p. 77; *Armstrong, Str. F.* iv. p. 311; *Oates, Str. F.* v. p. 144; *Hume and Dav., Str. F.* v. p. 155; *Murray, Vert. Zool. Sind*, p. 117; *Legge, B. Ceylon*, p. 218; *Hume, Str F.* viii. p. 88; *Scully, Str. F.* viii. p. 253; *Bingham, Str. F.* ix. p. 167; *Kelham, Ibis*, 1881, p. 390; *Oates, B. Br. Burm.* ii. p. 136. Bucco hæmacephalus, *P. L. S. Müll., Natursyst. Suppl.* p. 88. Bucco indicus, *Lath., Ind. Orn.* i. p. 205. Xantholæma indica, *Jerd., B. Ind.* i. p. 315, No. 197; *Wald., Ibis*, 1871, p. 162. Megalæma hæmacephala, *Blyth, B. Burm.* p. 74.—The CRIMSON-BREASTED BARBET.

Forehead and forecrown bright crimson; throat and round the eyes pale sulphur yellow; pectoral gorget glistening crimson, edged below with an arrow of rich golden yellow; moustachial streak continued round the throat, above the crimson pectoral gorget and on the crown of the head, black; back and wing coverts green, more or less margined yellowish; primaries and secondaries greenish, the inner webs dusky brown and margined with dull white; tail greenish, tinged with blue; beneath, the abdomen, vent, and under tail coverts fulvous or greenish white, streaked with green; bill black; irides hazel; orbitar skin dull crimson; legs coral red.

Hab.—Ceylon, and India generally, also Burmah, Malayana, Nepaul, Tenasserim and Upper Pegu; Punjab, N.-W. Provinces and Oudh. Occurs in Kutch, Kattiawar and Jodhpore, and probably in North Guzerat also. In Sind it is rare, and occurs as a visitor in September and October, affecting the acacia forests.

In Burmah it is found in every portion of the province, also in Karenne, and wherever it occurs it frequents open country, gardens, compounds, and groves of trees. Its presence is readily known by the note it utters, which is like the hammering of a piece of metal. It breeds in March, April and May, but in Central and Southern India a little earlier, laying 2—3 eggs in a hole of a tree, excavated by itself at no great height from the ground. Eggs pure white, from 0·87 to 1·07 in length × 0·62 to 0·72 in breadth.

199. Xantholæma rubricapilla (*Gmel.*), *Horsf and Moore, Cat. B. Mus. E. I. C.* p. 646; *Legge, B Ceylon,* p. 215. Megalæma rubricapilla, *G. R. Gray, Gen. B.* p. 429; *Kelaart, Prod. Cat.* p. 127; *Layard, Ann. and Mag. Nat. Hist.* xiii. p. 448; *Hume, Str. F.* vii. p. 370.—The SCARLET-FRONTED BARBET.

A narrow frontal streak and a band across the top of the head from eye to eye black; intermediate space scarlet; a spot of golden yellow at base of nostrils; superciliary streak golden yellow, also the lores, cheeks, ear coverts, chin and throat; ear coverts and cheeks edged from the gape to behind the eye with black; occiput and nape green, washed with verditer; sides of the neck verditer blue; upper breast with a scarlet spot edged with yellow; upper plumage dark green, edged with paler green; quills brown, pale yellowish at base of inner webs, externally edged with green; breast light yellowish green, shading into blue green; tail greenish blue on the under surface; rictal bristles black and longer than the bill; bill plumbeous; legs olive brown; irides brown.

Length.—6·25 inches; wing 3·2; tail 1·5; bill at front 0·6; tarsus 0·7.

Hab.—Ceylon, where it is the representative of *X. malabarica* of Southern India. Mr. Parker has taken its eggs in January, March, May and November. It probably breeds throughout the year.

ORDER.—PICI.

Zygodactylous birds, characterized by their striking and singular habits, to which their whole structure is adapted. They have large and strong bills, with the point sharp and wedge-shaped for the purpose of penetrating through the bark of trees in search of insect food in the decayed parts. The neck is short and furnished with strong muscles to enable them to strike with such force as to be heard at a distance. The tongue is long and extensile, at the end of which is a horny barbed probe-like substance, with which it extracts the insects from the crevices. Tail of 12 feathers, ten of them stiff-shafted, pointed at the ends and bent inwards to enable them to support themselves (together with their sharp clawed feet) in the act of climbing the perpendicular branches of trees. They breed in holes of trees, and lay shining white eggs. They are divided into several sub-families, according to the form, length, and strength of their bill, feet, and coloration.

Family.—PICIDÆ.—Woodpeckers.

Bill moderate or long, straight, angular, wedge-shaped; wings moderate; 4th and 5th quills usually longest; tail of 2 small outer feathers and ten with thick and stiff shafts; feet zygodactyle; one toe sometimes absent; plumage varied, black and white, or green, crimson, yellow, and rufous mixed. Males with generally a cheek stripe and a crimson tuft or crest; nostrils apert or concealed by bristles.

Gen. Brachypternus.—*Strickl.*

Bill distinctly curved; lateral ridge absent; nostrils apert; tail cuneate. Hind toe and claw minute.

200. Brachypternus aurantias (*Linn*), *Malh., Mon. Pic.* ii. p. 69, figs. 5—6; *Jerd., B. Ind.* i. p. 295, No. 180; *Hume, Nests and Eggs Ind. B.* p 126; *Str. F.* i. p. 171; *Murray, Hdbk. Zool., &c., Sind,* p. 131; *id., Vert. Zool. Sind,* p. 114. Brachypternus dilutus, *Blyth, J. A. S. B.* iv. p. 550; *Jerd., B Ind.* i. p 297, No. 182; *Str. F.* i. p. 171; *Murray, Hdbk. Zool., &c., Sind,* p. 131; *id., Vert. Zool. Sind* p. 114.—The Golden-backed Woodpecker.

Adult Male.—Head and crest bright crimson; hind neck, lower back, upper tail coverts and tail black; middle of the back black, mixed with greenish yellow; upper back and scapulars rich golden yellow; wing coverts black, changing to greenish yellow, the feathers white-spotted; primaries dusky brown, spotted white on their outer and inner webs; the secondaries and tertiaries greenish yellow on their outer webs, dusky on their inner webs, and also spotted white. Cheeks, sides of the neck, and a stripe from the nostrils to the eyes, white; a dusky stripe through the eyes to and including the ear coverts; chin, throat, sides of the face below the white cheek patch, neck and entire under parts striated black and white, the striations less distinct on the lower abdomen, vent and under tail coverts. Flanks and tibial plumes white, the feathers with black bars. The female has the head black with small white spots on the crown, and a small tuft of crimson behind; bill black; irides reddish brown; feet dusky green.

Length.—10·5 to 12 inches; wing 5·5 to 5·75; tail 4; bill at front 1·25.

Hab.—Throughout the greater part of India to the foot of the Himalayas, Cashmere, Nepaul, and Northern Ceylon. Occurs also in the Punjab, N.-W. Provinces, Khelat and Afghanistan. Breeds all over the plains of India during April, May, June and July, in holes in mango, siris, or other soft-wooded trees, which they excavate themselves. There is no nest except the fine chips, which fall in the act of boring, on which the eggs, generally three in number, are laid. The eggs are a lengthened pyriform oval, milk-white, and glossy. In length they vary from 1·0 to 1·2 inch, and in breadth from 0·77 to 0·85 inch. I agree with Mr. Hume, who very properly points out (*Str. F.* vol. i. p. 171) that the Sind species, *B. dilutus*, is not specifically separable.

201. Brachypternus chrysonotus (*Lesson.*), *Jerd.*, *B. Ind.* i. p. 296, No. 181; *Murray, Avif. Brit. Ind.* ii. 440, No. 1044. Brachypternus puncticollis, *Malh.*, *Mon. Pic.* ii. pl.; *Hume, Str. F.* iv. p. 242; *Legge, B. Ceylon*, pp. 205, 1212.—The LESSER GOLDEN-BACKED WOODPECKER.

Similar to the last, but smaller; the frontal feathers are more mixed with black in the male; the black of the nape is continued lower upon the shoulders, contrasting strongly with the golden orange of the back; wings are of a duller golden. Eyestreak narrower, but darker and more strongly defined, and the white spots are smaller; the white markings of the throat and foreneck are also smaller and consist of round oval points, edged on the sides of the neck by unspotted black; lastly, the white markings of the under parts are narrower, giving a generally dark hue to the breast and abdomen. Bill dark slaty; legs plumbeous green; irides crimson. (*Jerd.*)

Length.—11·5 inches; tail 3·25; wing 5·25; bill at front 1·1.

Hab.—Ceylon, in the northern provinces; Southern India, in the Carnatic and Malabar. Said to occur also on the slopes of the Nilghiris. Breeds during June and July in holes in trees excavated by themselves.

202. Brachypternus ceylonus (*Forst.*), *Blyth*, *J. A. S. B.* 1846, p. 282; *id.*, *Cat. B. Mus. As. Soc. Beng.* p. 56; *Kelaart, Prod. Cat.* p. 128; *Layard, Ann. and Mag. Nat. Hist.* 1854. xiii. p. 449; *Cab. et Heine* v. p. 171; *Holdsw.*, *P. Z. S.* 1872, p. 428; *Legge, B. Ceylon*, pp. 202, 1212. Picus ceylonus, *Forst. Naturf.* xiii. pl. 4.—The RED WOODPECKER.

Similar to *B. chrysonotus*, except that it is a brighter crimson on the head; and the scapulars are a rich golden yellow; the under surface is striated by almost oval spots.

Length.—About 10 inches; wing 5; tail 3·25.

Hab.—Ceylon. Breeds throughout the year.

Gen. **Micropternus.**—*Blyth.*

Bill broad at base; culmen arched; no lateral ridge; wings and tail short; feet small; inner hind toe and claw minute; plumage chestnut bay.

203. Micropternus gularis, *Jerd.*, *B. Ind.* i. p. 294, No. 179; *Hume, Str. F.* v. p. 477 *et. seq.*; *id.*, *Str. F.* vii. p. 470; *Legge, B. Ceylon*, pp. 200, 1212; *Murray, Avif. Br. Ind.* ii. p. 441, No. 1047. Phaiopicus Jerdoni, *Malherbe, Rev. Zool.* 1849, p. 538.—The SOUTH INDIAN RUFOUS WOODPECKER.

Whole upper plumage rufous-bay with cross bands of dusky black; head dusky brown; chin, throat and part of cheeks olivaceous brown, the feathers mottled with white; cheek stripe crimson; under plumage unspotted bay; under tail coverts faintly barred with dusky. Bill black; irides brown.

Length.—7·5 to 9 inches; tail 2·5 to 3; wing 4·8; bill at front 0·9.

Hab.—Ceylon and the forests of Malabar both above and below the Ghauts. Affects forest jungle. It has also been found in the Southern Mahratta Country, where Mr. Elliot obtained it at Dhārwar. He remarks that like many other species of Woodpeckers, the head, scapulars, and tail are generally smeared with a gummy substance. Breeds in Ceylon nearly throughout the year, nesting in the pendant nests of black ants in February, April, and November.

Gen. Chrysophlegma.—*Gould.*

General characters of *Callolophus*, the bill slightly more curved; the lateral ridge traceable only close to the base of the bill · culmen blunt; tail long, cuneate.

204. Chrysophlegma chlorigaster, *Jerd., 2nd Suppl. Cat.* p. 211; *Hume, Str. F.* vii. p. 517. Chrysophlegma chlorophanes, *Jerd., B. Ind.* i. p. 290. Picus chlorophanes, *Vieill., Nouv. Dict. d' Hist. Nat.* xxvi. p. 79.—The Southern Yellow-naped Woodpecker.

Whole head and cheek-stripe red; crest red, the feathers terminating with yellow; back, scapulars, rump and upper tail coverts bright green; ear coverts brownish green; wings greenish, tinged with orange, the outer webs of the quills orange red, the inner webs dusky and with white spots; tail black; under surface of the body dull green; lower abdomen barred and spotted with white. Bill slaty green; under mandible yellow; legs dull green; irides reddish brown.

Length.—9 to 9·7 inches; tail 3·9 to 4; wing 4·7 to 4·8; bill at front 0·9.

Hab.—South India, in Malabar, Travancore, and Ceylon in the interior of the N.-W. Provinces. It is not known whether like *chlorolophus* this species also descends to the ground to feed. Nothing is known of its nidification.

Gen Gecinus.—*Boie.*

Bill slightly widened in its whole length, compressed at the tip; upper mandible with one or more lateral ridges near the culmen, which is slightly arched; anterior and versatile toes nearly equal; head crested; tail long, cuneate.

205. Gecinus striolatus (*Blyth*), *Jerd., B. Ind.* i. p. 287, No. 171; *Hume, Nests and Eggs Ind. B.* p. 125; *id., Str. F.* iii. p. 68; *Blyth and Wald., B. Burm.* p. 76; *Anderson, Yunnan Exped.* p. 585; *Legge, B. Ceylon* p. 194; *Hume and Dav., Str. F.* vi. p. 136; *Cripps, Str. F.* vii. p. 262; *Scully, Str. F.* viii. p. 247; *Hume, Str. F.* viii. p. 87; *Oates, B. Br. Burm.* ii. p. 49; *Murray, Avif. Br. Ind.* ii. p. 447, No. 1057. Picus striolatus, *Blyth, J. A. S. B.* xii. p. 1000; *Sundev., Consp. Av. Pic.* p. 60. Chloropicus striolatus, *Mal., Mon. Pic.* ii. p. 134, pl. lxxvii. fig. 1—3.—Blyth's Striated Green Woodpecker.

Forehead with a narrow black line; rest of the head and upper parts scarlet; back, scapulars, sides of the neck, wing coverts and tertiaries green; supercilium, lores and a stripe under the eye and ear coverts whitish; rump and upper tail coverts golden yellow; tail dusky black, the basal half of the middle feathers barred with white, nearly obsolete on the others; primaries and their coverts dark brown, spotted with white on both webs; secondaries the same, but broadly margined with greenish on the outer webs; sides of the head and ear coverts greyish brown streaked darker; under surface of the body dull green. the edges of the feathers paler and with two black streaks meeting at the tip; under wing coverts white, barred with blackish. The *female* has the red on the head replaced by black. Bill with the upper mandible horn colour, lower mandible yellow, except the horn-colour tip; irides red, surrounded by a white circle; legs olive green.

Length.—11·5 inches; tail 4; wing 5·5; tarsus 1; bill from gape 1·4.

Hab.—The Himalayas, especially abundant in the sub-Himalayan region from Kumaon to Cashmere, and in the low jungles of the N.-W. Provinces, Oudh and the Punjab. It is also recorded from Mount Aboo in Guzerat. It extends throughout the Indo-Burmese countries, the hill tracts of Eastern Bengal, South India, and nearly the whole continent of India down to Ceylon. Breeds in the Dhoons, and almost everywhere it is found. Eggs glossy white, 5—6 in number, varying in size from 1·14 to 1·35 inch × 0·9 to 1·0 inch.

Sub-Family.—CAMPEPHILINÆ.

Bill strong and wide at base, nearly straight; lateral ridge sometimes wanting.

Gen. Chrysocolaptes.—*Blyth.*

General characters of the last; lateral ridge medial at first, then parallel to and nearer the margin; head crested; tail short and square; four central feathers, equal; feet strong; hind toe longer than the anterior one.

206. Chrysocolaptes festivus (*Bodd.*), *Jerd.*, *B. Ind.* i. p. xiv. *Supplement*, No. 167; *Hume. Str. F.* i. p. 373; vii. p. 206; *Legge, B. Ceylon* pp. 191, 1212; *Murray, Avif. Br. Ind.* ii. p. 452, No. 1066. Chrysocolaptes melanotus, *Blyth, J. A. S. B.* xii. p. 1005. Picus goensis, *Jerd., B. Ind.* i. p. 282, No. 167.—The BLACK-BACKED WOODPECKER.

Forehead black, speckled with white; crown and occiput crimson; lores, streak behind the eye to the nape, hind neck and interscapulars white; another black streak from the eye down the sides of the neck; back, scapulars, rump and tail black, tinged with aureous on the scapulars; wing coverts and secondaries bright golden yellow; primaries and their coverts dusky black, the primaries with large roundish spots; chin and throat white, with three black stripes; rest of under surface of the body white, more or less streaked with black, which disappear on the abdomen, vent, and under tail coverts. Bill dusky blackish; legs and feet horny plumbeous; irides crimson.

Length—12·5 to 13 inches; tail 3·5; wing 6·25; bill at front 1·9 to 2.

Hab.—Ceylon, Southern and Central India, and the Southern Mahratta Country. Jerdon says he found it in the juugles of the eastern ghouts, in parts of Mysore, between Bangalore and the Nilghiris, in the Vindhyan mountains near Mhow, and in the hilly and jungly districts of Nagpore, between that and the Nerbudda; also in the Midnapore jungles. In Ceylon Mr. Parker says it occurs in the southern part of the Manaar district. It breeds during March, and feeds generally in low jungle on the lower part of the stems of small trees and bushes. The eggs are laid in large holes in the trunks of trees at from 6 to 20 feet high. Eggs only one, pure white.

207. Chrysocolaptes Stricklandi (*Layard*), *Cab. et Heine, Mus. Hein.* v. p. 160; *Blyth, Ibis*, 1867, p. 297; *Holdsw:, P. Z. S.* 1872, p. 427; *Legge, Ibis*, 1874, p. 15; *id., Str. F.* 1875, p. 200; *Legge, B. Ceylon*, pp. 194, 1212. Brachypternus Stricklandi, *Layard, Ann. and Mag. Nat. Hist.* 1854, xiii. p. 449; *Jerd., B. Ind.* i. p. 298 (*note*).—STRICKLAND'S RED WOODPECKER.

Above scarlet maroon, or maroon, edged with scarlet; lower back and tail coverts brown, the filamentous feathers brilliant scarlet; primaries brown, their outer webs margined with scarlet; inner webs of secondaries with four large circular white spots; the inner primaries with only three of these, the middle two and the first one only; breast buffish, the feathers albescent in the centre and edged with dark brown; sides and abdomen mottled; chin white, with five lines of dark brown running down it; bill light corneous; legs bluish.

Length.—10·8 to 11 inches; wing 5·25; tail 4·25; bill 1·75; tarsus 1.

The female has the head brown with white ocelli, and a pale streak of brown forms an eyebrow. (*Layard*.) Breeds during February in the trunks of trees. Eggs, 2 in number, narrow ovals, more pointed at the large end; dull white in colour.

Hab.—Ceylon.

Gen. **Picus**.—*Linn*.

Bill moderate, compressed, culmen straight and sharp, lateral ridge distinct about midway between the culmen ridge and margin, which it joins about the middle of the length of the bill; gonys long; versatile toe longer than the anterior; plumage black, sometimes spotted or banded with white.

208. Picus mahrattensis, *Lath., Ind. Orn. Suppl.*, p. xxxi.; *Malh., Mon. Pic.* 1. p. 105, pl. xxviii. figs. 1—3; *Sundev., Consp. Av. Pic.* p. 31; *Jerd, B. Ind.* i. p. 274, No. 160; *Hume, Nests and Eggs Ind. B.* p. 122; *Ball, Str. F.* ii. p. 390; *Hume, Str. F.* iii. p. 58; *Legge, B. Ceylon*, p. 184; *Hume, Str. F.* viii. p. 87; *Oates, B. Br. Burm.* iii. p. 37; *Murray, Vert. Zool. Sind.* p. 114; *Murray, Avif. Br. Ind.* ii. p. 458, No. 1077. Picus aurocristatus, *Tick., J. A. S. B.* xxxii. p. 75. Liopipo mahrattensis, *Blyth, B. Burm.* p. 78.—The YELLOW-FRONTED PIED WOODPECKER.

Forehead and crown of head pale yellow; occiput crimson in the male, yellow in the female; lores, ear coverts, round the eyes, sides of neck, chin, throat and upper breast white; a dusky line from the nape extending to the sides of the breast; back, wings, and tail black, banded with white; lower breast and abdomen brown, with pale edges to the feathers; centre of abdomen and vent crimson; under tail coverts whitish, marginally streaked dusky brown. Bill bluish plumbeous, dark on the culmen and tip of both mandibles; eyelids dark brown; irides deep red; legs and feet plumbeous.

Length.—7·5 to 7·75; wing 4 to 4·5; tail 2·5; bill at front 1·1.

Hab.—Ceylon and throughout India. Occurs in Sind, Punjab, N.-W. Provinces, Kutch, Kattiawar, Rajputana (Jodhpore and Sambhur Lake). North Guzerat and the Deccan. Has also been recorded from North Pegu. Although nothing is on record of its nidification in Sind, it is not improbable that it breeds in June and July, as young birds not fully fledged have been collected in September. In other parts of India and also Ceylon it breeds from February to July. Eggs glossy white, two in number.

Gen. **Iyngipicus.**—*Bonap.*

Woodpeckers of small size, with spotted or banded white and black plumage; lateral ridge conspicuous near the culmen; bill barely straight; tail with two middle feathers elongated; outer feathers soft and rounded.

209. Iyngipicus gymnopthalmus (*Blyth*), *Kelaart, Prod. Cat.* p. 128; *Jerd., B. Ind.* i. p. 279 (*note*); *Holdsw., P. Z. S.* 1872, p. 427; *Legge, Str. F.* 1873, p. 433, *id., B. Ceylon*, p. 186. Picus gymnopthalmus, *Blyth, J. A S. B.* xviii. p. 804; *Malh., Mon. Pici.* i. p. 153; *Sundev., Consp. Av. Picin.* p. 8. Iyngipicus gymnopthalmus, *Hargitt, Ibis,* 1882, p. 47; *Parker, Ibis,* 1886, p. 183.—The Ceylon Pigmy Woodpecker.

Above black, banded with white or fulvous white; forehead, top of head and a streak down the back of the neck black; supercilium red; a broad post orbital streak running down the sides of the neck white, followed by a black one, under surface uniform fulvous.

Length.—5 to 5·25 inches; wing 3; tail 1·5; bill at front 0·4; tarsus 0 4.

Hab.—Ceylon, where it is diffused all over the low country. Breeds in the country at Tissa (February to July). Eggs 2—3 in number, blunt ovals, with a slight gloss and pure white. Size 0·62 × 0·53.

ORDER.—PSITTACI.

Toes in pairs; bill, wings and tail various.

Family.—PSITTACIDÆ.

Bill large and powerful, thick and strong, much arched or curved, sometimes notched, the hooked tip overhanging the lower mandible, which is short and obtusely rounded in front with a cutting edge; base of bill covered with a naked skin, in which are situated the small round nasal orifices; wings generally rounded and moderately long; 2nd quill usually the longest; tail various, either short and graduated, or with 2—3 elongated middle feathers; tarsi short, scutate; toes zygodactyle (in pairs); claws curved. The birds com prised in this family are noted for the beauty of their plumage. They are sub-divided chiefly according to the form of the bill and tail into several groups—(1) Psittacinæ, or true Parrots, with a notched or crenate bill and short tails; head not crested. (2) Loriinæ or Lories, species with gaudy plumage and of small size. (3) Palæorninæ or Parrakeets, with long tails, generally wedge-shaped. (4) Platycerninæ, Australian Parrots. (4) The Macaw or Arainæ ; and (5) The Cockatuas

Sub-Family.—PSITTACINÆ.

Bill moderately long, arched, and strong, the edge crenated. Head without crest ; tail short.

Sub-Family.—LORIINÆ—LORIES.

Bill small and compressed, slightly curved, margin of upper mandible sometimes sinuated ; lower mandible slender, conic, longer than high.

Gen. **Loriculus**.—*Blyth.*

Bill small, nearly 0·5 in length, curving from the base ; upper mandible much longer than the lower, sinuated at the margin, moderately hooked and tapering to a fine point; lower mandible small; wings nearly as long as the tail; 1st and 2nd quills longest ; tail short, even, or barely rounded. (*Jerd.*)

210. **Loriculus indicus** (*Gmel.*), *Jerd., B. Ind.* i. p. 265 (note): *Hume, Str. F.* ii. p 186; iii. p 57; *Blyth, B. Burm.* p. 58; *Hume, Str. F.* vii. p. 368; *Legge, B Ceylon*, pp. 180, 1212.—The CEYLON LORIQUET.

Whole head deep red ; nape pale saffron ; foreneck, rump and upper tail coverts crimson; back green, tinged with saffron ; tail bluish green, tipped yellowish, pale verditer ; scapulars, wing coverts and tertiaries dark green ; quills brown, their outer webs green, tinged bluish ; on the lower surface the throat has a patch of verdigris blue ; the lower plumage is green, with a yellowish tinge on the breast, and the under side of the wing is blue ; the under wing coverts shining green. The *female* has not the blue throat patch. Bill coral red, yellowish at tip ; cere red ; irides pale yellowish ; legs pale orange.

Length.—5·5 inches ; tail 1·9; wing 3·5 ; tarsus 0 4 ; bill from gape 0·45.
Hab.—Ceylon, to which island it is confined.

Sub-Family.—PALÆORNINÆ.—*Vigors.*

Bill moderate, upper mandible hooked, the tip overhanging the under mandible ; tail long, the feathers narrow and pointed.

Gen. **Palæornis**.—*Vigors.*

Bill large, under mandible small; cere narrow; 2nd quill of wing longest; two middle feathers of tail very long and slender; culmen rounded, toothed.

211. **Palæornis columboides**, *Vigors, P. Z. S.* 1830; *Lear, Mon. Psitt.* pl. 31 ; *Jerd., Ill. Ind. Orn.* pl. 18; *id., B. Ind.* i. p. 261, No. 151 ; *Hume, Str. F.* ii. p. 21 ; *Legge, B. Ceylon*, p. 1211 ; *Murray, Avif. Br. Ind.* ii. p. 465, No. 1090.—The BLUE-WINGED PAROQUET.

Head, back of neck and interscapulars pale dove grey ; forehead, lores, and below the eye verdigris green ; a black collar edged with verdigris green continued round and meeting at the chin ; lower back, rump and upper tail coverts blue green; wing coverts and scapulars the same, but the feathers edged paler; primary coverts and quills dark blue externally and dusky on the inner webs; centre feathers of the tail blue, tipped with yellowish white; the next pair blue on the outer web, greenish near the base and tipped with yellow; rest green externally and yellow internally; lower tail feathers yellow; neck in front and breast pale dove grey; rest of the under surface pale verdigris green.. The female either wants the collar or has only some slight indication of it. In the male it is the same before the adolescent or adult stage is reached. Bill cherry red above, dusky beneath; legs greenish plumbeous.

Length.— 14·5 to 15 inches; tail 8·75; wing 6; bill at gape 0·75: height nearly 0·9.

Hab.—Ceylon; Southern India, in the jungles of the Malabar Coast from Travancore up to N. L. 17° or so from the level of the sea to 5,000 feet and upwards on the slopes of the Nilghiris. A single specimen from Ceylon only available for identification, and this is questionable as to whether the skin is not one of a feral bird.

212. Palæornis indo-burmannicus, *Hume, Str. F.* vii. p. 458; viii. p. 86; *Bingham, Str. F.* ix. p. 159; *Oates, Str. F.* x. p. 189; *id., B. Br. Burm.* ii. p. 139. Palæornis Alexandri (*Linn.*), *Jerd., B. Ind.* i. p. 257, No. 147; *Blyth and Wald., B. Burm.* p. 54. Palæornis eupatrius (*Linn.*), *Finsch, Die Papageien* ii. p. 11 (part). Palæornis magnirostris (*Ball*), *Hume, Str. F.* iii. p. 55; *Armstrong, Str. F.* iv. p. 307; *Oates, Str. F.* v. p. 143; *Wardlaw-Ramsay, Ibis,* 1877, p. 453; *Hume and Dav., Str. F.* vi. p. 117. Palæornis sivalensis (*Hutton*), *Hume, Nests and Eggs Ind. B.* p. 115.—The LARGE BURMESE PAROQUET.

General colour green, duller and tinged with yellow beneath, and most brilliant on the forehead, crown, lores, feathers round the eyes, back and wings; sides of head green, tinged with yellow; chin and throat with some small black feathers, the base of the latter yellowish; a black stripe from the base of the throat produced upwards on each side of the neck; round the neck a peach-rose coloured collar; primaries and secondaries green, the inner edges of the inner webs brown; wing coverts green; median wing coverts forming a conspicuous red wing spot; middle tail feathers yellowish at tip, blue-green subterminally for two-thirds and greenish at the base; other tail feathers green externally and yellowish on their inner webs. The *female* has not the rose collar, and the stripe on each side of the neck is wanting; the red wing spot is much smaller. Irides and cere yellow; bill yellow at tip, the remainder red; legs orange yellow.

Length.—22 to 24 inches; tail 12—13; wings 8 to 8·4; tarsus 0·7; bill from gape 1·2.

Hab.—Lower Himalayas to Sikkim, the forests of Malabar, Central and South India, Ceylon, Northern Circars, Carnatic, Deccan, Punjab, British

Burmah, and Cochin-China. Breeds during January and February in holes of trees which the birds excavate for themselves, and lay 3—4 white eggs, long ovals, pointed towards one end, and from 1·5 to 1·52 × 0·95 inch in size. Generally found in small colonies.

213. Palæornis torquatus (*Bodd.*), *Jerd., B. Ind.* i. p. 257, No. 148; *Finsch, Die Papageien* ii. p. 17; *Hume, Nests and Eggs* p. 116; *id., Str. F.* ii. p. 13; *Wald., Ibis,* 1874, p. 282; *Blyth, B. Burm.* p. 55; *Hume, Str. F.* iii. p. 56; *Wardlaw-Ramsay, Ibis,* 1877, p. 453; *Oates, Str. F.* v. p. 144; *Legge, B. Ceylon* p. 171; *Hume and Dav., Str. F.* vi. p. 118; *Hume, Str. F* viii. p. 86; *Scully, Str. F.* viii. p. 240; *Oates, Str. F.* x. p. 189; *id., B. Br. Burm.* ii. p. 141; *Murray, Vert. Zool. Sind,* p. 112; *Parker, Ibis,* 1886, p. 183; *Murray, Avif. Br. Ind* ii. p. 467, No. 1093. Psittacus torquatus, *Bodd., Tabl. Enl* pl. p. 32.—The Rose-ringed Paroquet.

Adult Male.—Head and face emerald green; a dark line from the nostrils to the front of the eye, indistinct round the base of the narrow cere; hind neck and nape glaucous or light ashy, succeeded on the sides of the neck by a black demicollar meeting under the chin and followed by another of a peach-rose colour; back, scapulars, and tertiaries dull green; upper tail coverts emerald green; entire under surface pale green, yellowish towards the vent; primaries, their coverts, and secondaries, dark green, their inner webs and under surface dusky; tail feathers dark green, their inner webs and under surface yellowish; the two centre feathers dark green at their base, bluish for the remaining two-thirds, and tipped yellowish, all black shafted; under wing coverts greenish-yellow. The female is entirely green, and wants the rose collar. Bill coral red; irides pale yellow; feet cinereous.

Length.—15·5 to 16·5 inches; wing 6·5 to 7; tail 9·5; bill at gape 1.

Hab.—Throughout India, part of Burmah, Ceylon, Punjab and Sind; extends to the Lower Himalayas, Upper Pegu, and Nepaul. Occurs abundantly in the Concan and Deccan, Kutch, Kattiawar, Jodhpore, and N. Guzerat. Breeds throughout India and Ceylon. The breeding season lasts from January to April. February and March, however, appear to be the chief months in which they lay in colonies. Eggs, pure white, 4 in number.

214. Palæornis cyanocephalus (*Linn.*), *Finsch., Die Papagein* ii. p. 40 (part); *Wald., Ibis,* 1874, p. 284; *Blyth and Wald., B. Burm.* p. 55; *Hume and Dav., Str. F.* vi. p. 118; *Hume; Str. F.* viii. p. 86; *Bingham, Str. F.* ix. p. 161; *Legge, B. Ceylon* pp. 174, 1211; *Murray, Avif. Br. Ind.* p. 468, No. 1094; *Parker, Ibis,* 1876, p. 183. Psittacus cyanocephalus, *Linn., Syst. Nat.* i. p. 14. Psittacus rosa, *Bodd., Tabl. Pl. Col.* p. 53. Psittacus bengalensis, *Gmel., Syst. Nat.* i. p. 325. Palæornis rosa, *Jerd., B. Ind.* i. p. 259 (part). Palæornis bengalensis, *Hume, Str F.* ii. p. 16; iii. p. 56; *Oates Str. F.* vii. p. 46; *id., B. Br. Burm.* ii. p. 145.—The Blue-headed Paroquet.

Head, including the ear coverts, rosy pink, changing to bluish on the crown and nape; a black stripe from each side of the lower mandible, covering the throat and continued as a collar round the neck; upper back, scapulars and wings green; lower plumage tinged with yellow; a patch of deep maroon on the median wing coverts; primaries and secondaries dusky on their inner webs and the outer web of the first primary; rest of the quills green on their outer webs; *under wing coverts bright green.* Central tail feathers blue, *tipped with yellow, others green on the outer webs,* yellowish on the inner, and all tipped with bright yellow. The female has the head plum-blue, the black on the throat and collar are absent, and the wing spot is less conspicuous. Upper mandible orange yellow; lower black; irides yellow; legs grey.

Length.—13·5 inches; tail 8; wing 5·5; tarsus 0·5; bill from gape 0·65.

Hab.—In British Burmah, it ranges through the Indo-Burmese countries into India, where it occurs in Bengal and along the lower ranges of the Himalayas as far as Nepaul. Ceylon, where, according to Mr. H. Parker, it extends at least as far north as a line west of Mullaittiva, and is also found in the island of Manaar. Breeding season same as the last. Eggs, pure white, four in number.

215. Palæornis rosa (*Bodd.*), *Jerd., B. Ind* i. p. 259, No. 149. Palæornis purpureus (*P. L S. Mull*), *Hume, Str. F.* ii. p. 11; *id., Nests and Eggs Ind. B.* p. 116. Psittacus rosa, *Bodd., pl. Enl.* 192 et 888; *Murray, Avif. Br. Ind.* ii. p. 468, No. 1095.—The Western Rose-headed Paroquet.

Very similar to *P. cyanocephalus*, except that the rump and lower back are bluish; also the under wing coverts and the outer webs of the next pair of feathers to the central pair; the outer webs of the first and second primaries are narrowly edged with pale yellow and the tips of the central tail feathers are white and not yellow; the crown and nape too are more lilac than bluish, and the under surface of the body a pale yellowish green.

Length.—14 to 15 inches; tail 8·5; wing 5·25.

Hab—Ceylon and throughout India, extending into the Himalayas and Assam. On the Malabar Coast it is extremely common; also on the Eastern Ghauts, the Carnatic, Northern Circars, Central India, Midnapoor, and Lower Bengal. Breeds, according to Hume, throughout the plains of Continental India, high up on Mount Aboo, also throughout the salt range and the lower ranges of the Himalayas, up to heights of from 4,000 to 5,000 feet, from Murree to the Ganges. They commonly lay in April, excavate holes for themselves, and lay from 4 to 6, pure white, but rather soiled, glossless eggs, varying in length from 0·9 to 1·05 inches, and in breadth from 0·75 to 0·86 inch.

216. Palæornis calthropæ (*Layard*), *Ann. and Mag. Nat. Hist.* xiii. p. 462; *Hume, Str. F.* ii. p. 18; vii. p. 367; *Legge, B. Ceylon,* pp. 177, 1211.—The Ceylon Paroquet.

Crown and back plumbeous grey, passing to bluish on the rump and rich dark indigo blue on the middle tail feathers and outer webs of the others; tail yellow beneath and at the tips, sullied along the inner webs of the rectrices above; forehead and cheeks, broad nuchal ring and entire under-parts brilliant green; wings deeper green, paler and yellowish towards the scapulars; throat intense black, with a tendency to form a ring round the neck, but only half surrounds it; upper mandible bright coral red, with a white tip; lower mandible reddish; irides white; in the female the rump is brighter blue, and the tail is mingled green and indigo blue; bill blackish.

Length.—14 to 15 inches; tail 8·6; wing 5·3; tarsus 0·6.

Hab.—Ceylon, to which island it is peculiar. Breeds during February. Mr. Parker however mentions in MS. that he observed the species feeding young in the nest in July in the Kurnegala district.

SUB-ORDER—COCCYGES ANISODACTYLÆ.

Family, UPUPIDÆ, *Bp.*—Hoopoes.

Bill long, sides compressed to tip; nostrils small and at base; wings long and rounded; tail long; outer toe united to middle; hind toe long.

Sub-Family.—UPUPINÆ.—*Bp.*

Bill with prominent keel, tip sharp; claws long, curved, sharp and strong.

Gen. Upupa.—*Linn.*

Bill slender and curved throughout; nostrils covered with membranous scale; tarsi broadly scaled; head crested.

217. Upupa ceylonensis (*Reich.*), *Jerd., Suppl.* vol. ii.; *Hume, Str. F.* iii. p. 90; vii. p. 517; *Murray, Avif. Br. Ind.* ii. p. 470, No. 1098. Upupa nigripennis (*Gould*), *Jerd., B. Ind.* ii. p. 392, No. 255; *Hume, Nests and Eggs Ind. B.* p. 163; *Legge, B. Ceylon,* pp. 278, 1213.—The Indian Hoopoe.

Whole head and neck cinnamon-rufous, the feathers of the crest broadly tipped with black; lesser wing coverts cinnamon-rufous, the median series black, tipped with white, and the greater series black, barred across with white; primaries black, with a bar of white near the tip, the first with or without a white spot on the inner web; primary coverts black; tertiaries brown, tinged and edged with rufous; back dull vinous; scapulars barred with black and rufous; rump the same, followed by a transverse white band; upper tail coverts black; tail black, with a white bar across the feathers; chin, throat, breast and upper abdomen rufous-fawn; lower abdomen whitish, streaked with brown; vent and under tail coverts white, in some a few feathers are tipped with black. Bill dark brown; irides red brown; legs plumbeous.

Length.—10·5; tail 4; wing 3 to 3·5; bill from gape 2·2. No white on crest, nor are there any white spots on the first primary.

Hab.—Ceylon, and Southern India, also a part of Central India, the Punjab, and N.-W. Provinces. Breeds from February to May, in India ; in Ceylon, May and June in the Northern Provinces.

According to Jerdon it frequents groves of trees, thin forest jungle, gardens, the neighbourhood of villages and old deserted buildings. Like other species of the genus, it feeds on the ground on insects, grubs, and larvæ. It usually has its crest depressed when feeding, and on the slightest disturbance, erects it. It has an undulatory but vigorous flight.

Family, MEROPIDÆ—Bee-Eaters.

Bill long ; both mandibles curved and sharp ; nostrils partly hidden by short bristles ; wings long and pointed ; tail long and broad ; central feathers generally elongated ; tarsi short ; toes long, two exterior united to middle ; hind toe with a pad beneath.

Gen. Merops.—*Linn.*

Second quill longest ; tail with the two middle feathers elongated ; tarsi scaled ; outer toe longer than inner ; wings reaching to two-thirds the length of tail.

218. Merops viridis, *Linn., Syst. Nat.* i. p. 182 ; *Jerd., B. Ind.* i. p. 205 ; *Hume, Nests and Eggs Ind. B.* p. 99 ; *Str. F.* i. p. 167 ; iii. p. 49 ; *Blyth, B. Burm.* p. 73 ; *Armstrong, Str. F.* iv. p. 304 ; *Hume and Dav., Str. F.* vi. p. 67 ; *Anders., Yunnan Exped.* p. 582 ; *Legge, B. Ceylon*, p. 309 ; *Hume, Str. F.* viii. p. 85 ; *Bingham, Str. F.* ix. p. 152 ; *Murray, Vert. Zool., Sind.*, p. 107 ; *id., Avif. Br. Ind.* ii. p. 471, No. 1099. Merops ferrugiceps, *Hodgs. in Gray's Zool. Misc.* p. 82.—The Common Indian Green Bee-Eater.

Above bright grass green ; below bright green, mixed with verdigris ; lower abdomen and under tail coverts slightly paler and with a bluish tinge ; head, nape, and hind neck burnished with golden ; forehead and fore crown deep rufous, wanting in many specimens from Northern India, as Sind ; eye streak from base of bill through the eye to ear coverts, and a collar on top of the breast, black ; quills reddish, tipped dusky ; tail very dull green, the edges of their inner webs dusky ; elongated portion of the two central feathers dark brown. Bill black ; irides blood red.

Length.—9·75 inches to tip of central tail feathers ; wing 3·5 to 3·75 ; bill at front 1·1.

Hab.—Ceylon and the whole of India, extending to Indo-China. Occurs also at Quetta in Beloochistan Persia and Egypt ; also in Southern India (Travancore), Nepaul and Cashmere. Abundant, nearly throughout British Burmah. Breeds almost all over India, Burmah and Ceylon, laying from 3 to 5 eggs, during March and April, often also in May, in holes in sandy banks. The eggs are little polished alabaster-like balls, nearly spherical in shape, milky white in hue, and brilliantly glossy. They vary in length from 0·68 to 0·82 inch and in breadth from 0·64 to 0·73 inch.

219. Merops phillipinus, *Linn.*, *Syst. Nat. Ed.* 13, 1, p. 183; *Hume*, *Nests and Eggs Ind. B.* p. 101; *Salvad.*, *Ucc. Born.* p. 89; *Blyth*, *B. Burm.* p. 72; *Oates*, *Str. F.* v. p. 143; *Dav. et Oust. Ois. Chine*, p. 72; *Legge*, *B. Ceylon*, p. 306; *Hume and Dav.*, *Str. F.* vi. p. 67; *Hume*, *Str. F.* viii. p. 85; *Bingham*, *Str. F.* ix. p. 152; *Oates*, *B. Br. Burm.* ii. p. 66; *Murray*, *Vert. Zool.*, *Sind*, p. 108; *id.*, *Avif. Br. Ind.* ii. p. 471, No. 1100. Merops Phillipensis (*Linn.*), *Jerd.*, *B. Ind.* i. p. 207, No. 118; *Anders.*, *Yunnan Exped.* p. 581.—The BLUE-TAILED BEE-EATER.

Forehead, crown, nape, and back dull green, tinged with coppery; rump and upper tail coverts bright blue; central tail feathers blue, the projecting elongation black; other tail feathers blue; their inner webs dusky; tertiaries bluish green; primaries and secondaries green externally, and rufescent on their inner webs, all tipped with black; wing coverts green; lores, ear coverts and a line through the eye black; a narrow blue line above this and a pale bluish white one below; chin yellow; throat chestnut; under surface of the body green, with a rufescent tinge; under tail coverts pale blue; under wing coverts bright buff. Bill black; irides bright red; legs plumbeous.

Length.—12 to 12·5 inches; tail 5·5 to 5·7; wing 5·3 to 5·5; tarsus 0·5; bill from gape 2. The female is very slightly smaller.

Hab.—Ceylon, and the whole peninsula of India, also the Andaman Islands, and the whole of British Burmah, being especially abundant in Arrakan and Pegu; somewhat rare in Tenasserim, where, according to Oates, it is partially migratory, and is found also in China, Cochin-China, Siam, the Malay Peninsula, Sumatra, Java, Borneo, Celebes, and the Phillipine Islands. Wherever this Bee-Eater is found it occurs in large flocks, and like *viridis* are very partial to resting on telegraph wires. They are especially numerous about the banks of large streams and rivers, where they nest like *viridis*, in a long tunnel 3 to 5 feet deep, with a chamber at the end. Eggs slightly larger than those of *viridis*, 4 to 5 in number, and of the same colour and gloss.

220. Merops Leschenaulti, *Vieill.*, *Nouv. Dict. d' Hist. Nat.* xiv. p. 17; *Hume and Dav.*, *Str. F.* vi. p. 68. Merops quinticolor (*V.*), *Jerd.*, *B. Ind.* i. p. 208, No. 119. Merops Daudini (*Cuv.*), *Swinhoe*, *P. Z. S.* 1871, p. 348. Merops Swinhœi, *Hume*, *Nests and Eggs Ind. B.* p. 102; *id.*, *Str. F.* ii. p. 163; iii. p. 50; *Armstrong*, *Str. F.* iv. p. 305; *Legge*, *Birds of Ceylon*, p. 312; *Hume*, *Str. F.* vii. p. 455; viii. p. 85; *Parker*, *Str. F.* ix. p. 478; *Murray*, *Avif. Br. Ind.* ii. p. 472, No. 1101. Merops erythrocephalus (*Gm.*), *Blyth and Wald.*, *B. Burm.* p. 274.—The CHESTNUT-HEADED BEE-EATER.

Top of the head, ear coverts, nape and upper back, rich chestnut; lores black, extending as a band under the eye and ear coverts; lower back, wing coverts, and tertiaries green, the latter tinged with bluish; rump and upper tail coverts pale azure or shining blue; quills green, rufous on the inner webs, and all tipped with dusky black; tail even or slightly emarginate, the centre feathers not elongated, bluish on the outer and green on the inner webs; rest green, margined with brown on the inner webs and all tipped with dusky; sides of the face, chin and throat yellow, followed by a collar of chestnut, edged with black, which extends up the sides of the neck; breast bright green; rest of lower plumage green, tinged with blue, which is most conspicuous on the vent and inner tail coverts. Bill black; irides crimson; legs dusky black.

Length.—8·5 inches; tail 3·3 to 3·5; wing 4·2; tarsus 0·4; bill from gape 1·7.

Hab.—Ceylon; Malabar forests; Nilghiris up to 5,500 feet elevation; Mysore, Wynaad, and Southern India generally. It is said to be found sparingly distributed throughout the whole province of Burmah, also in Siam, Cochin-China and China. Occurs in forests and well-wooded parts of the country in small flocks. Breeds during March and April on the slopes of the Nilghiris. A favourite locality in Ceylon is in sloping sandy river banks in dense forests, especially where there is a little open ground in the immediate vicinity where insects can be caught. They bore holes in the sandy parts of the banks to a depth of from 3 to 6 feet, at the bottom of which is a circular chamber about 6 inches in diameter, where, without any nest or lining, they lay from 4 to 6 eggs, pure and glossy white, almost spherical, varying in length from 0·82 to 0·92 inch, and in breadth from 0·72 to 0·81 inch.

Family, CORACIADÆ.—Rollers.

Bill long and broad at the base, tip hooked; nostrils at the base oblique, linear, apert; gape with strong rictal bristles; wings and tail moderately long; and quill longest; tarsi short.

Gen. **Coracias**—*Linn.*

Characters same as those of the Family.

221. Coracias indica (*Linn.*), *Edw. B.* pl. 326; *P. E.* 285; *Jerd., B Ind.* p. 214, No. 123; *Hume, Str. F.* vii. p. 259; *Murray, Hdbk., Zool., &c., Sind,* p. 128; *id., Vert. Zool., Sind,* p. 109; *Legge, B. Ceylon,* p. 281; *Murray, Avif. Br. Ind.* ii. p. 476, No. 1107.—The Indian Roller.

Forehead rufescent brown; head and nape greenish blue; supercilium light blue; hind neck, scapulars, upper back and tertiaries ashy or earthy brown, tinged on the hind neck with vinous; lower back greenish blue; rump, upper tail coverts, lesser coverts, and shoulders cobalt blue, some of the feathers of the upper tail coverts tipped greenish; winglet and primaries pale blue, the latter with a broad band of violet blue in the middle and tipped dark blue; secondaries violet blue, the margins of their inner webs dusky, and the basal half of their outer ones dark green, shading into light blue on their outer margins; tail with the middle feathers dull green, the rest violet blue with a pale sky blue band; chin light fulvous; throat and breast of a vinous colour, with light fulvous shaft-stripes, passing into isabelline on the upper abdomen, where the fulvous streaks are indistinct; lower abdomen, vent, under tail coverts, and under wing coverts pale blue. Bill dusky brown; legs orange; irides red brown; eyelids yellow.

Length.—13·5 inches; wing 7·25; tail 5; bill at front 1·12; tarsus 1.

Hab.—Ceylon; and the whole of India, the Himalayas, Nepaul, N.-W. Provinces, the Punjab, Sind, S. Persia (Bushire), Beloochistan, Kutch, Kattiawar, Jodhpore, Jeypore, North Guzerat, the Concans and the Deccan.

In parts of India it is a resident and breeds in holes of decayed trees, and sometimes in the deep forks of acacia trees, in April and May. Eggs two in number, round, pure white.

Gen. **Eurystomus**.—*Vieillot.*

Bill shorter and much broader than in *Coracias;* base wide, the tip of culmen curved; nostrils narrow; rictal bristles absent; gape wide; wings long; 2nd quill longest; 1st sub-equal; tarsus short; outer toe slightly syndactyle.

222. Eurystomus orientalis (*Linn.*), *Jerd., B. Ind.* i. p. 219, No. 126; *Hume, Nests and Eggs Ind. B.* p. 105; *id., Str. F.* ii. p. 164; *Salvad., Ucc. Born.* p. 105; *Blyth, B. Burm.* p. 72; *David et. Oust. Ois Chine*, p. 73; *Wardlaw-Ramsay, Ibis*, 1877, p. 457; *Hume and Dav., Str. F.* vi. p. 72; *Legge, B. Ceylon*, p. 285; *Hume, Str. F.* viii. p. 85; *Oates, Str. F.* x. p. 186; *id., B. Br. Burm.* ii. p. 70; *Murray, Avif. Br. Ind.* i. p. 477, No. 1109. Coracias orientalis, *Linn., Syst. Nat.* i. p. 159.—The BROAD-BILLED ROLLER.

Whole head, including lores, cheeks, ear coverts and nape dark brown, tinged with greenish blue, which is more conspicuous and decided on the scapulars; back, rump, upper tail coverts, tertiaries and wing coverts, also the primaries, secondaries and their coverts black, the first 6 or 7, with a light blue patch at their bases; tail uniform dark violet; throat and upper breast with broad violet blue shaft stripes; rest of lower plumage dingy greenish blue, brighter on the vent, under tail coverts and under wing coverts. Bill and legs vermilion; eyelids red; irides dark brown; gape yellowish.

Length.—12 to 12·5 inches; tail 4·4 to 4·5; wing 7·6 to 8; tarsus 0·7; bill from gape 1·7.

Hab.—From Ceylon to the base of the Himalayas; Lower Bengal, Assam, the Burmese countries, extending to China, Siam, Cochin-China, and down the Malay Peninsula to Sumatra, Java, and Borneo. According to Oates, it is rare, though locally distributed over the greater part of Burmah. It has been got in Pegu, in the hills north of that town, also at Tonghoo and at Shwaygheen. Capt. W. Ramsay got it on the Karin hills, and Mr. Blanford at Bassein, and Davison's experience is that it is confined to the southern portion of Tenasserim. Oates adds that it is almost crepuscular in its habits. It breeds in the Terai during May in holes of the higher branches of lofty trees. Nothing appears to be known of its eggs, but they also are probably white.

Family.—ALEDINIDÆ—KINGFISHERS.

Bill long, straight, thick, quadrangular, and pointed; tongue short, flat and fleshy; nostrils lateral, oblique; tail short; wings moderate and rounded; tarsi short; plumage thick, of singular brilliancy, in which blue, green and orange are the prevailing colours. Habits solitary. Found near rivers, brooks, streams or stagnant waters, from which they capture fish for subsistence. All kingfishers agree in their manners. They generally perch on some tree or other elevated object overhanging water, and there remain motionless for hours watching till some fish comes under their view, when they will dive down perpendicularly and bring up their prey. The scales of the fish they eat are thrown up in small pellets.

Sub-Family.—ALCEDININÆ.

Bill long, slender, compressed, acute and grooved near the culmen for the greater part of its length; gonys nearly straight.

Gen Alcedo.—*Linn.*

Bill long, slender, straight, compressed, the tip acute; culmen sharp and carinated; commissure straight; 2nd and third quills sub-equal, 3rd slightly the longest, 1st very little shorter; lateral toes syndactyle; inner toe short.

223. Alcedo bengalensis, *Gm.*, *Syst. Nat.* i. p. 450; *Jerd.*, *B. Ind.* i. p. 234, No. 134; *Sharpe*, *Mon. Alced.* p. ii. pl. 2; *Hume*, *Nests and Eggs Ind. B.* p. 107; *Salvad*, *Ucc. Born.* p. 92; *Hume*, *Str. F.* i. pp. 168, 169; iii. p. 52; *Blyth*, *B. Burm.* p. 71; *Armstrong*, *Str. F.* iv. p. 307; *Legge*, *B. Ceylon*, p. 292; *Anders.*, *Yunnan Exped.* p. 580; *Wardlaw-Ramsay*, *Ibis*, 1877, p. 457; *Hume and Dav.*, *Str. F.* vi. p. 81; *Hume*, *Str. F.* viii. p. 86; *Bingham*, *Str. F.* ix. p. 155; *Oates*, *B. Br. Burm.* ii. p. 72.—The LITTLE INDIAN KINGFISHER.

Head and hind neck dusky, each feather tipped with pale blue; a band from the nostrils to the ear coverts rufous; a dark patch at the gape on both upper and lower mandibles. Sides of the neck, chin and throat white; a streak of dusky feathers edged with blue from each corner of the lower mandible dividing the white of the chin and throat and sides of the neck; quills dusky on their inner webs; the outer webs dull greenish blue; scapulars dull bluish green; back, rump and upper tail coverts pale blue; tail blue, tinged with greenish; breast and entire under surface orange brown or ferruginous. Bill blackish above, horny brown below; irides dark brown; legs orange red.

Length.—6·2 to 7 inches; wing 2·75; tail 1·1; bill at front 1·4.

Hab.—Ceylon and throughout India; also China. Occurs also in Beloochistan and S Afghanistan, but is rare. In Kutch, Kattiawar, N. Guzerat, Concan and the Deccan, it is the common form where *A. ispida* does not occur. In Sind it appears to be a seasonal visitant.

In Burmah it affects all the low-lying parts near the sea. It extends as far as East Africa; in the north to Siberia and Japan, and ranges thence to China, Siam, Cochin-China, and the Malay Peninsula, and breeds from March to May, making a narrow hole about 2 feet in depth in some bank overlooking the water, generally about five or six feet above water level. In Ceylon Mr. Parker says December, January and February in the Manaar districts. Correspondents in the Nilghiris, Deccan, the Dhoon, Darjeeling, Cashmere, Kumaon, Ootacamund, Caltura in Ceylon, Ahmednuggur, and other places all agree in regard to the lining of the nest, being composed of small filamentous bones, probably undigested food thrown up in the chamber, on which the eggs are laid. The eggs are glossy white, some oval, and others spherical, about 0·8 × 0·7 inch.

Gen. **Ceryle**.—*Boie.*

Bill long, straight, compressed, and acute at tip; culmen obtuse, somewhat flattened and margined on each side by an indented groove; tail slightly lengthened, rounded; wings long; 2nd and 3rd quills sub-equal; inner toe longer than the hinder.

224. Ceryle rudis (*Linn.*), *Jerd., B. Ind.* i. p. 232, No. 136; *Sharpe, Mon. Alced.* p. 61, pl. 19; *Hume, Nests and Eggs Ind. B.* p. 109; *id., Str. F.* iii. p. 52; *Dresser, B. Eur.* v. p. 125, pl.; *Blyth, B. Burm.* p. 71; *David et Oust. Ois. Chine,* p. 77; *Legge, B. Ceylon,* p. 288; *Oates, Str. F.* v. p. 143; *Hume and Dav., Str. F.* vi. p. 85; *Hume, Str. F.* viii. p. 86; *Bingham, Str. F.* ix. p. 157; *Murray, Hdbk. Zool., &c., Sind,* p. 129; *id., Vert. Zool., Sind,* p. 112; *Oates, B. Br. Burmah,* ii. p. 77.—The PIED KINGFISHER.

Head, hind neck, and a broad streak behind the eye extending down the sides of neck black, finely streaked with white; supercilium white; chin, throat, sides of the neck, and upper breast white; the latter with a few of the feathers tipped black in some specimens; lower parts white, with a broad band of black, and a narrower one also, in males, across the lower breast, and in some specimens a few dark spots on the abdomen and flanks; primaries black; edge of the outer web of the first primary and the bases of the others white, forming a conspicuous white band; primary coverts black; back, rump, upper tail coverts and scapulars black, tipped broadly with white; tail black, the feathers basally and at the tips white. Bill black; legs dusky brown; irides dark brown.

Length.—10·5 to 11 inches; wing 5·5; tail 3; bill at front 2·3.

Hab.—S.-E. Europe, N.-E. Africa, Western Asia, Ceylon, Burmah and Malayana. Found all over India to Nepaul. In Sind it is a resident, and breeds in holes along the banks of the Indus and canals from March to May. Eggs 2—4 in number, oval, white.

Sub-Family.—HALCYONINÆ.

Kingfishers of larger size than the Alcedinidæ, with strong, thick and straight bills, broad at the base, with the culmen flattened and slightly inclining upwards to the tip, groove of upper mandible strongly marked; wings short and broad; tarsus and toes small and feeble, the latter nearly syndactyle; rictus smooth.

Gen. **Halcyon**.—*Swainson.*

Bill long and straight, somewhat quadrangular; lower mandible angulated; nostrils hidden by plumes; 3rd quill longest, 4th and 5th sub-equal; tail short, rounded or even; outer toe nearly as long as the middle one.

225. Halcyon smyrnensis (*Linn.*), *Sharpe, Mon. Alced.* p. 161, pl. 59; *Hume, Nests and Eggs Ind. B.* p. 105; *Dresser, B. Europe*, v. 133, pl.; *Blyth, B. Burm.* p. 70; *Armstrong, Str. F.* iv. p. 306; *Oates, Str. F.* v. p. 143; *Hume and Dav., Str. F.* vi. p. 74; *Legge, B. Ceylon*, p. 298; *Hume, Str. F.* viii. p. 85; *Bingham, Str. F.* ix. p. 154; *Oates, B. Br. Burm.* ii. p. 82; *Murray, Vert. Zool., Sind*, p. 110. Alcedo smyrnensis, *Linn., Syst. Nat.* i. p. 181. Alcedo fuscus, *Bodd., Tabl. Pl. Enl.* p. 54. Halcyon fuscus, *Jerd., B. Ind.* i. p. 224, No. 129.—The WHITE-BREASTED KINGFISHER.

Whole head, neck, abdomen, under tail and lesser wing coverts rich chestnut; scapulars, tertiaries, back, rump and upper tail coverts, also the greater coverts and winglet blue; the scapulars and tertiaries more dull; median wing coverts black; quills blue, broadly tipped with black, with a broad oblique bar of white on the inner webs of the primaries; chin, throat, neck in front and breast white; tail blue, the margins of their inner webs dusky brown, except the centre feathers, which are wholly greenish blue. Bill coral red; feet vermilion red; eyes brown.

Length.—10·5 inches; wing 4·5 to 4·75; tail 3; bill at front 2·25.

Hab.—Ceylon and the Peninsula of India to the base of the Himalayas, extending to the Indo-Burmese countries, Singapore and China. Recorded from the Concans and Deccan, Kutch, Kattiawar, Jodhpore, Sambur, N. Guzerat, Travancore and Nepaul. Breeds all over India nearly, from March to July (in Ceylon June to August), laying 4—7 eggs in a hole excavated by itself in banks of tanks and canals or streams, also in the interior of wells, or on cliffs overlooking rivers. Eggs spherical; some are slightly oval. Like those of its congeners, they are pure white. In length they vary from 1·05 to 1·27 inch and in breadth from 0·97 to 1·12 inch.

226. Halcyon pileata (*Bodd.*), *Sharpe, Mon. Alced.* p. 169, pl. 62; *Hume, Str. F.* iii. p. 51; *Blyth, B. Burm.* p. 70; *Armstrong, Str. F.* iv. p. 306; *Legge, B. Ceylon*, p. 301; *Hume and Dav., Str. F.* vi. p. 74; *Hume, Str. F.* viii. p. 85; *Bingham, Str. F.* viii. p. 193; ix. p. 154; *Oates, Str. F.* x. p. 187; *id., B. Br. Burm.* ii. p. 83. Alcedo pileata, *Bodd., Tabl. Pl. Enl.* p. 41. Alcedo atricapilla, *Gm., Syst. Nat.* i. p. 453. Halcyon atricapillus, *Jerd., B. Ind.* i. p. 226, No. 130. Entomobia pileata, *Salvad. Ucc. Born.* p. 102.—The BLACK-CAPPED PURPLE KINGFISHER.

Whole head black, also the moustache; whole upper parts glossy rich violet purple, brighter on the rump; tail rich violet purple; all except the central pair of feathers margined with black on the outer webs and tipped very narrowly with whitish; lesser and median wing coverts black; primary coverts blue; primaries white, tinged with blue on the outer webs, black at the ends; shafts of the first six black; secondaries and tertiaries blue on the outer webs, all tipped black; wing bar white and conspicuous; chin, throat and neck white, tinged with fulvous; breast pale fulvous, with crescentic brown markings; abdomen white, rest of lower surface, including the under wing coverts, rich fulvous; bill dark red; irides brown; legs coral red.

Length.—11·5 to 12 inches; tail 3·5 to 3·7; wing 4·7 to 5·3; tarsus 0·7; bill from gape 2·8.

Hab.—Ceylon, the Malabar Coast, Bengal, in the Sunderbuns, the Andaman Islands, China, Siam, Cochin-China, Philippines, Sumatra, Borneo, and British Burmah, in which last province it is said by Oates to be abundant in all the maritime portions and up the larger rivers. It feeds both on fish and small reptiles, also insects of sorts.

Gen. **Ceyx**.—*Lacep.*

Bill comparatively large, wide, barely grooved; gonys inclined upwards; culmen flattish; tail short; feet with only three toes, two in front and one behind.

227. Ceyx tridactyla (*Pallas*), *Jerd., B. Ind.* i. p. 229, No. 133; *Sharpe, Mon. Alced.* p. 119, pl. 40; *Hume, Str. F.* iii. p. 51; *Blyth, B. Burm.* p. 71; *Legge, B. Ceylon*, p. 303; *Hume and Dav., Str. F.* vi. p. 80; *Hume, Str. F.* viii. p. 86; *Bingham, Str. F.* viii. p. 193; ix. p. 155; *Oates, Str. F.* x. p. 187; *Murray, Avif. Br. Ind.* ii. p. 486, No. 1123.—The THREE-TOED KINGFISHER.

Lores and base of upper mandible blue-black; forehead, crown and nape rufous, glossed with black; cheeks, ear coverts and lower plumage buffy yellow, tinged with rufescent on the breast; behind the ear coverts a bluish-black spot and below it a patch of white; upper back black, streaked with lustrous blue; lower back, rump and upper tail coverts rich rufous with a lilac gloss; scapulars and lesser wing coverts black, tipped and margined with blue; greater coverts and quills black; the secondaries and tertiaries edged with blue; tail chestnut, tipped narrowly with brown; under wing coverts pale rufous. Bill coral red; irides dark brown; legs red.

Length.—5·4 inches; tail 1·1; wing 2·2; tarsus 0·3; bill from gape 1·55.

Hab.—Ceylon, and the greater part of India; also British Burmah, the Malay Peninsula, Sumatra and Java. It has been recorded from South India and the Deccan; also from Arrakan, Bengal, and Pegu. Affects rocky streams and dense forests. Breeds in Ceylon.

Gen. **Pelargopsis**.—*Gloger.*

Kingfishers with large, stout bills, broad at the base, and the culmen inclining upwards towards the tip; rictus smooth; margin of culmen slightly sinuated; lower mandible angulated; gonys ascending; groove of the upper mandible strongly marked for about two-third its length.

228. Pelargopsis gurial (*Pearson*), *Sharpe, Mon. Alced.* p. 97, pl. 29; *Legge, B. Ceylon*, p. 295; *Murray, Avif. Br. Ind.* ii. 487, No. 1124. Halcyon leucocephalus, *Jerd., B. Ind.* i. p. 222, No. 127; *Hume, Nests and Eggs Ind. B.* p. 105; *Oates, B. Br. Burm.* ii. p. 79 (note).—The BROWN-HEADED or the INDIAN STORK-BILLED KINGFISHER.

Head, lores, cheeks and nape olive brown or dark olive brown; hind neck above the scapulars and scapulars dingy brownish green; quills, sides of lower back, upper tail coverts and tail dull bluish green, the quills tipped with dusky black; the inner webs of all also dusky; middle of back to rump light bright azure blue; chin and throat yellowish white, becoming buffy like the sides of the neck, with which it joins; rest of lower plumage orange buff; bill dark blood red; legs coral red; irides light brown.

Length.—16 inches; tail 4; wing 6; bill at gape 4 inches.

Hab.—Southern India and Ceylon to Bengal and the Himalayas, affecting well-wooded forests. In Malabar Jerdon says it is common; rare in the Carnatic; found occasionally in Central India and the Northern Circars. Breeds in the lower Himalayas during June, and in Ceylon, according to Colonel Legge and Mr. Parker, nearly throughout the year, except the last two or three months. Eggs, 4 in number, round, pure white; size 1·09 × 1·02 inch.

Family.—BUCEROTIDÆ.—HORNBILLS.

A group of large birds distinguished by the enormous size of their bill; which are arched or curved, and have in most species an appendage or casque placed above the culmen from the base to about the middle of the upper mandible, or is as large as the bill itself. This is hollow and cellular internally, and in one or two species solid. The bill is wide at the base and more or less dilated; the tip is acute and the margins denticulated. The casque is small at first and is developed by age. The throat is usually naked, also the sides of the face and the orbital region; eyelids protected by eyelashes; wings short and ample, the 4th and 5th quills longest; secondaries long and nearly equal to the primaries; tail of ten feathers, long, rounded, the centre pair of feathers generally elongated; tarsi short, stout, transversely scutate in front, reticulated behind; outer toe joined to the middle one nearly to the apex; inner toe less so. They live in pairs, and subsist entirely on fruit, which they swallow whole, first tossing it up in the air after breaking it off the tree, and catching it again. They breed in holes of trees, and lay 2—4 white eggs. The male bird is said to plaster up the female during the whole time of incubation until the young are fledged In fact Mr. Wallace vouches for this. Mr. Hume quotes an account of his nesting experience of *D.*

bicornis in Sumatra to the same effect. It is, as he says, "one of those strange facts in Natural History which are stranger than fiction."

Gen. **Anthracoceros**.—*Reich*.

Bill with a long, sharp, acute casque, extending from the base of the bill over two-thirds its length.

229. Anthracoceros coronatus (*Bodd.*), *Jerd.*, *B. Ind.* i p. 245, No. 141; *Hume, Str. F* ii. p. 388. Buceros coronata, *Bodd.*, *Tabl. Pl. Enl.* 873. Hydrocissa coronata, *Elliot, Mon. Bucer.* pl. xii.; *Legge, B. Ceylon* p. 272; *Murray, Avif. Brit. Ind.* ii. 490, No. 1128.—The MALABAR PIED HORNBILL.

Plumage entirely black, except beneath from the breast, the tips of the primaries and secondaries, the three outer tail feathers on each side and the next pair which are white; bill and part of the casque yellowish white; base of both mandibles black, also the hind margin of the casque of the male; a patch of black on the anterior three-fourths in adults; casque large, compressed laterally, protruding back over the crown and ridge.

Length.—3 feet; wing 13 inches; tail 14; bill from gape 7 inches; height of bill with casque 4 inches; naked skin on the throat pale, livid fleshy; irides crimson.

Hab.—Ceylon and Southern India; also Malabar, Goomsoor and Central India. It is said to have different breeding seasons in different parts of Ceylon. In the Manaar district Mr. Parker shot young birds in September, the eggs being probably laid in June or July. Eggs have also been taken in October. In the N.-E. the breeding season is said to be April and May, and in the south March and April. They roost on large trees in large societies, and like other Hornbills immure the females in the nest holes.

Gen. **Tockus**.—*Gloger*.

Bill short, rounded and solid; no casque; ridge elevated and much curved; central tail feathers produced beyond the rest.

230. Tockus gingalensis (*Shaw*), *Cuv.* vii. pl. p. 435. Tockus gingalensis, *Jerd.*, *B. Ind.* i. p. 250; *Legge, B. Ceylon*, pp. 275, 1213, 1224.—The JUNGLE GREY HORNBILL.

Upper part of head and back blackish brown, with a cast of bluish grey; wings bluish grey, the lesser coverts edged with black; cheeks, foreneck, breast, belly, and thighs greyish white; middle feathers of tail bluish grey, the rest tipped with white; bill pale yellowish white, the tip dusky, also the lower mandible; legs dusky; irides reddish.

Length.—2·2 inches; wing 8·5; tail 8·5; bill to gape 4·25.

Hab.—Ceylon, in the N.-W. Provinces, affecting deep forests. Breeds from March to July in natural holes in trunks of living trees at heights of from 40 to 50 feet. Eggs, generally 2 in number, variable in shape, typical ovals or elongated ovals.

ORDER, GEMITORES—PIGEONS AND DOVES.

Bill short, straight, compressed, front half of mandible vaulted and curved at the tip, the base with a soft fleshy membrane, in which are the nostrils;

wings moderate or long; tail variable, of 12, 14, or 16 feathers, even or rounded; tarsi strong. Habits monogamous. Both sexes assist in making the nest, incubating the eggs, and feeding the young. Nests loosely constructed of twigs, straw, and almost any material which could be readily got, and built on trees, roof of buildings or ledges and holes in rocks; eggs two in number, white. They feed on fruit and grain, and in feeding the young disgorge the food from their craw.

Gen. **Crocopus**.—*Bonap.*

Characters those of the Sub-Family; basal portion of bill with the fleshy protuberance occupying one-half its length or nearly as much; third primary sinuated on its inner web.

231. Crocopus chlorigaster, *Blyth, J. A. S. B.* xvii p. 167; *Jerd.*, iii. p. 448, No. 773; *Str. F.* ii. p. 423; *Murray, Hdbk., Zool. &c., Sind*, p. 193; *Tem. Pig.* t. 2; *Murray, Avif. Br. Ind.* ii. p. 498, No. 1142. C. jerdoni, *Strickl.*—The SOUTHERN GREEN PIGEON.

Forehead, crown and nape ashy grey, as also are the lores, sides of the face and ear coverts; neck behind yellowish green, followed on the upper back by a narrow band of ashy grey; back, scapulars, rump and upper tail coverts green, slightly tinged with yellowish on the scapulars; primaries dusky brown, margined on their outer web with pale yellow; the wing coverts broadly margined with the same colour, forming an oblique wing bar; shoulder of wing lilac; tail above greenish at base and ashy grey for the terminal half; under tail coverts dull maroon, the feathers broadly tipped with white; chin and throat greenish yellow; neck in front, breast and abdomen bright yellow, tinged greenish on the flanks; vent mixed green and white; bill whitish; legs and feet yellow; irides carmine.

Length.—11·75 to 12·5 inches; wing 7; tail 5; bill at front 0·75.

Hab.—Ceylon, and nearly throughout the Peninsula of India (*Jerd.*), Malabar Coast, Madras and Southern India generally; Lower Bengal, Oudh, Central Provinces, Khandeish, the Deccan, Sind, and North Guzerat. Rare in Sind, and has only been found on the frontier, at Jacobabad. Breeds from March to June, nesting on trees. Eggs two in number, pure white and glossy, 1·12 to 1·3 in length by 0·9 to 1·0 in breadth.

Gen. **Osmotreron**.—*Bonap.*

General characters as in *Crocopus*; bill more slender; legs red; sexes differ much in plumage.

232. Osmotreron bicincta, *Jerd., B. Ind.* ii. p. 449; *Hume, Nests and Eggs Ind. B.* p. 493; *Blyth and Wald., B. Burm.* p. 144; *Armstrong, Str. F.* iv. p. 337; *Oates, Str. F.* vi. p. 163; *Hume and Dav., Str. F.* vi. p. 411; *Hume, Str. F.* viii. p. 109; *Legge, B. Ceylon*, p. 725; *Oates, Str.*

F. x. p. 235; *id., B. Br. Burm.* ii. p. 308; *Murray, Avif. Br. Ind.* ii. p. 499, No. 1144.—The ORANGE-BREASTED GREEN PIGEON.

Upper surface of the body, including the lesser wing coverts, tertiaries and greater wing coverts green, the two latter broadly edged on the external web with yellow; winglet, primaries, and the primary coverts black; secondaries also black, narrowly margined with yellow; occipital region, nape, hind neck, under wing coverts, axillaries, sides of the body, and central tail feathers ashy; other tail feathers dark ashy, all tipped with greyish white; forehead, front of crown, sides of the head and neck, chin, throat, abdomen, and vent yellowish green; flanks yellow, streaked with dark green; breast orange, separated from the neck by a lilac band across, forming a collar; under tail coverts cinnamon. The *female* has not the lilac and orange breast, and the under tail coverts are pale ashy white, dashed with dull greenish; bill glaucous green; legs pinkish red; irides blue, with an outer circle of red.

Length.—12 inches; tail 4·2; wing 6·3; tarsus 0·8; bill from gape 1.

Hab.—The more moist and wooded portions of India and Ceylon, and also in the greater part of British Burmah. Extends to Assam, Cachar, and countries to the eastward. Recorded from Lower Bengal and the coasts east and west of India. Occurs abundantly in Nepaul, Sylhet, Tipperah, and Arrakan; also the Sub-Himalayan terais of Behar and Oudh, and the Eastern forest regions of the Central Provinces. Breeds in the Nepaul terai from April to June, making a nest generally on the outer branch of a tree. Eggs two in number, oval, and pure white.

233. Osmotreron pompadoura (*Gmel.*), *Jerd., B. Ind.* iii. p. 452, No. 777; *Hume, Str. F.* iii. p. 162; vi. p. 414; *Murray, Avif. Br. Ind.* ii. p. 502, No. 1149. Osmotreron flavogularis, *Blyth, J. A. S. B.* xxvi. p. 225.—The YELLOW-FRONTED GREEN PIGEON.

Forehead yellowish; throat pure yellow; no buff patch on the breast; mantle and wing coverts maroon; rest of upper parts green, including the lores, face and ear coverts; wing coverts edged with bright yellow, also the quills; tail green with a broad mesial dark band and tipped with ashy; under tail coverts green in both sexes, with broad whitish tips; bill glaucous green; irides red, with an outer blue circle.

Length.—10 inches; tail 4; wing 5·5.

Hab.—Ceylon and South India. General habits as the last.

Sub-Family CARPOPHAGINÆ.—FRUIT PIGEONS.

Bill longer than in *Treroninæ*, more slender and depressed at the base; the terminal third corneous; wings long; tail even or rounded, longer than in the *Treroninæ*; feet with broad soles; tarsus short and well feathered; under mandible feathered to nearly the tip. Breeds at high altitudes, and lays but one egg.

Gen. **Carpophaga**.—*Selby.*

General characters of the sub-family; plumage above glossy metallic green or coppery brown.

234. Carpophaga ænea (*Linn.*), *Hume, Nests and Eggs Ind. B.* p. 496; *id., Str. F.* ii. p. 260; iii. p. 163; *Blyth, B. Burm.* p. 144; *Wald., Trans. Zool. Soc.* ix. p. 215; *Armstrong, Str. F.* iv. p. 337; *Inglis, Str. F.* v. p, 39; *Hume and Dav., Str. F.* vi. p. 416; *Hume, Str. F.* viii. p. 109; *Legge, B. Ceylon*, p. 718; *Bingham, Str. F.* ix. p. 194; *Parker, Str. F.* ix. p. 481; *Oates, B. Br. Burm.* ii. p. 301; *Murray, Avif. Br. Ind.* ii. p. 503, No. 1152. Columba ænea, *Linn., Syst. Nat.* i. p. 283. Columba sylvatica, *Tick., J. A. S. B.* iii. p. 581. Carpophaga sylvatica (*Tick.*), *Jerd., B. Ind.* ii. p. 455, No. 780.—The IMPERIAL GREEN PIGEON.

Whole head and neck and entire under parts pearl grey, tinged with ruddy vinaceous; under tail coverts deep maroon; orbital feathers, base of bill and chin whitish; back, rump, upper tail coverts, tertiaries, upper wing coverts and tail shining coppery green; axillaries buff; primaries and secondaries greenish brown, tinged with ashy on the outer webs. Bill greyish, the base dull red; eyelids, legs, and feet lake red.

Length.—17 inches; tail 6·5; wing 9; tarsus 1·1; bill from gape 1·5.

Hab.—Ceylon and the whole of India, to Assam and Sylhet, except the North-West Provinces and the Himalayas. It is also found in Burmah, and extends through the Malay Peninsula to Sumatra and Java. Affects forests and well-wooded parts of the country. Abundant in the Malabar forests, in Central and Southern India, Midnapore and the countries to the north-east generally. Breeds in the Andamans and in Tenasserim, also in the forests of Central India, laying only a single egg in a nest made of twigs in thickets and bamboo bushes. March and April are the months in which it breeds.

Family—COLUMBIDÆ, *Bp.*—PIGEONS AND DOVES.

Bill horny at apex only; tail generally of 12 feathers only; tarsus lengthened; plumage sombre; feet more fitted for walking on the ground. Breeds in holes of rocks, buildings or well.

Sub-Family—PALUMBINÆ.—WOOD PIGEONS.

General characters of the family.

Gen. **Palumbus**.—*Linn.*

Characters those of the sub-family; the distinguishing feature is the patch on each side of the neck.

235. Palumbus Elphinstonei (*Sykes*), *Jerd., B. Ind.* ii. p. 465, No. 786; *id., Ill. Ind. Orn.* pl. 48; *Gould, B. Asia* pt. vi. pl. 12; *Hume, Str. F.* vii. pp. 95, 424; *Murray, Avif. Br. Ind.* ii. p. 507, No. 1158. Palumbus torringtoni (*Kelaart*), *Blyth, Ibis*, 1867; *Hume, Str. F.* vii. p. 424; *Legge, B. Ceylon* p. 693.—The NILGHIRI WOOD PIGEON.

Head and neck ashy; nuchal patch black, with small *white tips;* back of neck and interscapulars cupreous ruddy, slightly glossed with greenish; rest of upper surface of body ruddy brown, dark ashy on the rump and upper tail coverts; wings, including the quills, dusky black, narrowly edged with ruddy cupreous; outer primaries pale edged; tail dull black; under surface of the body ashy, albescent on the throat; neck and breast glossed with green; vent and lower abdomen albescent; bill deep red, tipped with yellow; legs and feet dull red.

Length.—15 to 16 inches; tail 5·75 to 6; wing 8 to 8·25.

Hab.—The Nilghiris and the dense woods above the Khandalla ghauts in the Deccan. Breeds from March to July, laying only a single egg. Nests placed on high trees in dense woods. Egg spotless glossy white, oval, 1·46 × 1·2.

Gen. **Columba**.—*Linn.*

Characters same as those of *Palumbus.*

236. Columba intermedia, *Strickl., Ann Nat. Hist. Ser.* 1. xiii. p. 39; *Jerd., B. Ind.* ii. p. 469, No. 788; *Hume. Nests and Eggs Ind. B.* p. 499; *David et Oust. Ois. Chine*, p. 384 *Hume and Dav., Str. F.* vii. p. 449; *Hume, Str. F.* viii. p. 109; *Scully, Str. F.* viii. p. 339; *Legge, B. Ceylon* p. 698; *Blf., East Pers.* p. 268; *Murray, Vert. Zool. Sind*, p. 202; *Murray, Avif. Brit. Ind.* ii. p. 508, No. 1160. Columba livia, *apud. Bl. B. Burm.* p. 145.—The INDIAN BLUE ROCK PIGEON.

Head, nape, chin, abdomen, vent and upper and under tail coverts dark slaty grey; back, scapulars, secondaries, tertials, inner webs of primaries and rump pale ashy, paler on the rump; the outer webs of the primaries dusky grey, as are also their tips; secondaries broadly tipped dusky, the innermost tertials and greater wing coverts with a subterminal black patch on the outer webs only, forming two black wing bands; neck all round and breast glossy, changeable green and amethystine, in varying lights; throat also slightly tinged with glossy green; under wing coverts white; tail like the upper tail coverts, or a little paler for two-thirds its length, then broadly black, with a very narrow terminal ashy tip; the basal two-thirds or more of the outer web of the outermost feather white. Bill black; cere whitish; irides dull orange; legs pinkish red.

Length.—12 to 13 inches; wing 8·75 to 9; tail 5; bill at front 0·75.

Hab.—Ceylon, and throughout India to the Himalayas, Assam, Burmah, Persia, Beluchistan and Afghanistan in great abundance, congregating in large flocks. Breeds throughout India and Ceylon. Eggs, 2 in number, white and glossy, 1·2 × 1·25. Nesting in mosques, tombs, old buildings, wells, and in holes in rocks and caverns.

Gen. **Alsocomus**.—*Tick.*

Bill small, much compressed; wings long, 2nd quill equal to 4th, the 3rd longest and sinuate on the outer web.

237. Alsocomus puniceus, *Tickell, J. A. S. B.* xi. p. 462; *Jerd., B. Ind.* ii. p. 462, No. 782; *Blyth, B. Burm.* p. 145; *Wardlaw-Ramsay, Ibis,* 1877, p. 147; *Hume and Davison, Str. F.* vi. p. 418; *Legge, B. Ceylon,* p. 698; *Hume, Str. F.* viii. p. 109; *Oates, Str. F.* viii. p. 167; *Bingham, ibid.* p. 196; *Oates, Str. F.* x. p. 235; *Oates, B. Br. Burm.* ii. p. 289; *Murray, Avif. Br. Ind.* ii. p. 509, No. 1154.—The PURPLE WOOD PIGEON.

Whole plumage vinaceous ruddy, inclining to chestnut on the back and wings, the feathers more or less glossed with metallic green and amethystine, especially on the neck; head greyish white; quills blackish, edged slightly with ashy; rump and upper tail coverts dark ashy; tail black; under tail coverts brown; bill livid at base, yellow at tip; legs and feet lake pink; irides orange; orbital skin purplish pink.

Length.—14·8 to 15 inches; tail 6; wing 8·5; tarsus 1; bill from gape 1·1.

Hab.—Ceylon, also Tenasserim and Pegu, and the Eastern portions of Central India, extending to near the sea coast in Midnapoor, and probably eastwards towards Cuttack. To the east of the Bay of Bengal, in Assam, Arrakan, Singbhoom and Tenasserim it is more common. Oates says it is sparingly distributed over many parts of Pegu, and that it is more abundant near Kyakpadien than elsewhere. It has also been procured at Tounghoo and Tonka, where Hume records it from, and which appears to be the southernmost point of its distribution. Eggs similar to those of pigeons, and one in number only.

Sub-Family.—TURTURINÆ.—*Bp.*

Habits terrestrial and arboreal; tail somewhat long, with pale tips to the outer feathers; neck usually adorned with a ring or spot.

Sub-Family, TURTURINÆ.—*Bonap.*

Bill lengthened, slender, the base soft and tumid; wings long; feet short; feathers of the rump rather rigid.

Gen. Turtur.—*Selby.*

Bill slender; wings long, 2nd and 3rd quills longest; tail moderate, rounded or graduated; tarsi scutellated in front, naked; outer toe shorter than the inner.

238. Turtur meena (*Sykes*), *Jerd., B. Ind.* ii. p. 476, No. 793; *Hume, Nests and Eggs* p. 501; *id., Str. F.* iii. p. 163; *Bl., B. Burm.* p. 146; *Hume and Dav., Str. F.* vi. p. 420; *Hume, Str. F.* viii. p. 110; *Scully, Str. F.* viii. p. 340; *Oates, Str. F.* x. p. 235; *id., B. Br. Burm.* ii. p. 292; *Murray, Avif. Brit. Ind.* ii. p. 513, No. 1169. Columba meena, *Sykes, P. Z. S.* 1832, p. 140. Turtur rupicolus (*Pall.*), *Jerd., B Ind.* ii. p. 476, No. 792. Turtur pulchratus, *Hodgs., apud Legge, B. Ceylon,* pp. 711, 1218.—The RUFOUS TURTLE DOVE.

Forehead, crown, nape, hind neck and back ashy brown, suffused with vinous, and the feathers indistinctly edged with rufous; a patch on the neck black with greyish tips; lower back and rump dark ashy, edged paler; upper tail coverts brown, edged with pale rufous; scapulars, tertiaries, lesser and median coverts brown, broadly edged with rufous; greater coverts and secondaries edged with ashy, the innermost ones edged with rufous; primaries dark brown edged with rufous; lower plumage vinous red, tinged with purplish in some, paler on the chin and throat; sides of the body, under wing coverts, vent and *under tail coverts ashy*; central tail feathers ashy brown, the others ashy brown tipped with grey (*Oates*); bill brown, with a tinge of ashy on the basal half; iris orange-red; legs vinous red.

Length.—13 inches; tail 5; wing 7; tarsus 1·1; bill from gape 1.

Hab.—The Himalayas to Nepaul and Ceylon. It is a permanent resident of the hilly portions of Southern India, and of the broken belt of hills that stretch across the continent of India from the northern portions of the Western Ghauts to Cuttack; thence it extends into Eastern Bengal, Khasia hills, Cachar, Assam, and along the bases of the Himalayas as far west as the Sikkim and Nepaul Terais, and again southwards into Arrakan, Pegu and Northern Tenasserim. (*Hume.*) Breeds from December to April, but the majority lay in March, April and May. The number of eggs is two, and like all doves, pure glossy white.

239. Turtur suratensis, *Gm.*, *Tem. Pig.* t. 43; *Jerd.*, *B. Ind.* iii. p. 479, No. 795; *Str. F.* v. pp. 231, 409; *Gray*, *Handlist* No. 9315; *Murray*, *Hdbk.*, *Zool.*, *&c.*, *Sind*, p. 194; *id.*, *Vert. Zool. Sind*, p. 203; *Legge*, *B Ceylon*, p. 705; *Murray*, *Avif. Brit. Ind.* ii. p. 514, No. 1171.—The SPOTTED DOVE.

Forehead greyish white; crown, nape, breast and upper abdomen pale vinaceous, darker on the breast, paling on the lower abdomen and flanks, and albescent on the under tail coverts; chin and throat white; patch on the neck black with narrow rufous tips; back and scapulars isabelline brown, or rufous brown, the feathers with dark shaft-stripes, broadening into a nearly triangular spot at the tip, on each side of which, especially on the scapulars and wing coverts, is a pale rufous or vinaceous spot; in some specimens scarcely a spot, but with this colour edging the feathers; edge of the wing, and the lower series of wing coverts near it greyish white, with faint dark shaft-stripes; primaries and secondaries dusky brown, the first three quills, and some of the secondaries edged with pale or greyish white; primary coverts dark brown; tail with the central feathers brown, the outermost black at the base, and tipped white for the terminal half, and the others with the white tips decreasing in extent; bill blackish; irides hazel, surrounded by a reddish sclerotic membrane; legs reddish.

Length.—12 inches; wing 5·5 to 5·75; tail 5·5, graduated.

Hab.—Ceylon and throughout India nearly to the Himalayas. Replaces *senegalensis* on the Malabar Coast and in Lower Bengal. Jerdon says it is rare in the bare Carnatic land, the Deccan, and N.-W. Provinces. Uncommon in Upper Sind, but less so in Lower Sind. Breeds in India in April and May, and in Ceylon from January to August, but chiefly in May. The average size is 1·01 × 0·79. It occurs, but less abundantly, in Rajputana and N. Guzerat.

240. Turtur risorius (*Linn.*), *Jerd., B. Ind.* ii. p. 481; *Hume, Nests and Eggs Ind. B.* p. 506; *id., Str. F.* iii. p. 165; *Wald. in Blyth's B. Burm.* p. 146; *Dresser, B. Eur.* vii. p. 51; *Dav. et Oust. Ois. Chine*, p. 387; *Cripps, Str. F.* vii. p. 297; *Legge, B. Ceylon*, p. 702; *Hume, Str. F.* viii. p. 110; *Oates. Str. F.* x. p. 235; *Oates, B. Br. Burmah* ii. p. 293; *Blanf., East. Pers.* p. 270; *Murray, Hdbk. Zool. &c., Sind*, p. 194; *id., Vert. Zool., Sind*, p. 204; *Murray, Avif. Br. Ind.* ii. p. 515, No. 1173. Columba risoria, *Linn., Syst. Nat.* i. p. 285.—The INDIAN RING DOVE.

Head pale greyish brown, with a vinous tinge; the forehead albescent; nape and neck pale vinaceous; collar black, a narrow line of white before and behind it; back, scapulars and innermost tertiaries grey brown, as also are the rump and upper tail coverts; primaries and their coverts dusky brown; the primaries margined narrowly with whitish, and their coverts tinged with greyish; edge of the wing, lower series of the median coverts and greater series also pale grey; under wing coverts greyish white; chin and throat albescent; breast and upper abdomen, also the sides of the neck and breast, pale vinaceous; flanks, lower abdomen, vent, thighs and under tail coverts ashy grey, the latter with whitish tips; tail with the central feathers like the back; outermost feathers on each side narrowly margined with greyish white on their outer web, with a broad black band about the middle, greyish at base, and broadly terminated with white, which on the others increase in extent. Bill black; irides crimson; orbital skin whitish; legs pinkish.

Length.—12 to 13 inches; wing 6·5; tail 5; bill at front 0·81.

Hab.—Ceylon and India generally, except the more moist regions, as the Malabar Coast; abundant in Sind, Punjab, N.-W. Provinces, Oudh, Bengal, Rajputana, Kutch, Guzerat, Concan, Deccan, Central and South India, also Beluchistan and Southern Afghanistan. Rare in Burmah. Breeds throughout the year, and in Ceylon from February to July in the Manaar districts. Commonly the eggs are a broad ellipsis in outline, but a few are somewhat pointed at one or both ends. Colour cream white.

241. Turtur humilis (*Temm.*), *Jerd., B. Ind.* ii. p. 482; *Hume, Nests and Eggs Ind. B.* p. 507; *id., Str. F.* ii. p. 269; iii. p. 165; iv. p. 292; *Armstrong, Str. F.* iv. p. 338; *Wald., Trans. Zool. Soc.* ix. p. 219; *David et Oust. Ois. Chine*, p. 388; *Hume and Dav., Str. F.* vi. p. 423; *Hume, Str. F.* viii. p. 110; *Oates, Str. F.* x. p. 235; *id., B. Br. Burm* ii. p. 294; *Murray,*

Hdbk., Zool., &c., Sind, p. 194; *id., Vert. Zool., Sind.* p. 204; *id., Avif. Br. Ind.* ii. p. 516, No. 1174. Turtur tranquebaricus, *Herm., Obs. Zool.* p. 200; *Bly., B. Burm.* p. 145; *Legge, B. Ceylon*, p. 708. Turtur humilior, *Proc. As. Soc. Beng.* 1874, p. 241; *id., Str. F.* iii. p. 279.—The RED TURTLE DOVE.

Male.—Head and nape ashy grey, also the lores and sides of the face, slightly paler on the forehead; collar black, set off by whitish before and behind it; back, scapulars and wing coverts brick red, slightly paler behind the black collar; chin whitish; throat, breast and entire lower surface pale vinous red, white on the vent and lower tail coverts; rump and upper tail coverts deep slaty; primaries, their coverts and secondaries dusky brown; the margin of the primaries, as also the margins and tips of the secondaries, whitish; primary coverts slightly tinged with vinous red on their outer webs; edge of the wing greyish, some of the dark bases of the median coverts showing through; tail with the middle feathers ashy brown, the others greyish black at the base, and broadly tipped with white; outermost feathers on each side white on the exterior web; bill black; irides dark brown; legs purplish red.

Length.—9 inches; wing 5·5 to 5·75; tail 3 to 3·25. The *female* is duller in colour on the back, being more of an earthy brown and much paler below.

Hab.—Ceylon and the drier regions in India, to the foot of the Himalayas. Common in the Punjab, N.-W. Provinces, Oudh, Bengal, Rajputana, Kutch, Guzerat, Concan and Deccan, but less so in Sind. Occurs also in Assam and Northern Burmah. In Sind it affects the northern districts chiefly; seldom seen below Sukkur.

Family, GOURIDÆ.—GROUND-DOVES.

Wings moderate; tarsus longer than in the *Turturinæ*, as are also all the toes; wing shorter and less pointed. The Colonial representatives of the family belong to the *Phapidinæ*.

Sub-Family, PHAPIDINÆ.

General characters as of the family; tarsus not feathered; tail of 12, 14 or 16 feathers.

Gen. **Chalcophaps**—*Gould.*

Bill slender; wings moderately long; 2nd and 3rd quills nearly equal and longest; tail rather short and rounded; tarsus not feathered; plumage rich glossy metallic green.

242. Chalcophaps indica (*Linn.*), *Jerd., B. Ind.* ii. p. 484, No. 798; *Hume, Nests and Eggs Ind. B.* p. 509; *id., Str. F.* ii. p. 269; iii. p. 165; *Salvad., Ucc. Born.* p. 299; *Bourdillon, Str. F.* iv. p. 404; *Blyth, B. Burm.* p. 147; *Dav. et Oust. Ois. Chine*, p. 384; *Hume and Dav., Str. F.* vi. p. 424; *Hume, Str. F.* viii. p. 110; *Legge, B. Ceylon* p. 714; *Oates,*

Str. F. x. p. 235; *Kelham, Ibis,* 1881, p. 528; *Oates, B. Br. Burm.* ii. p. 297; *Murray, Avif. Br. Ind.* ii. p. 517, No. 1175.—The EMERALD DOVE.

Forehead white, continued as a supercilium over the eye; crown, nape, a narrow band down the hind neck and another across the upper back ashy grey; back and wings shining dark emerald green; quills dark brown, the secondaries metallic green on the external web; tertiaries bright metallic green; smaller coverts near the edge of the wing white; on the lower back a narrow band of ashy, followed by a broad black one, then a second ashy one, and lastly a broad band, which with the upper tail coverts is dark ashy brown, tipped darker; sides of the head and neck and the whole under surface of the body deep vinaceous, rather duller on the abdomen; under tail coverts ashy; three central pairs of tail feathers dark brown, tipped paler, the others banded with black and ashy; under wing coverts chestnut; bill red; irides dark brown; eyelids plumbeous; legs dusky red.

Length.—10·5 inches; tail 4; wing 5·8; tarsus 1; bill from gape 0·9.

Hab.—Ceylon and throughout India in forest countries and well wooded districts; not in the drier regions, as Sind, Rajputana, Kattyawar, &c. It is abundant in Lower Bengal; extends to Assam and all the countries on the east of the Bay of Bengal as far as Tenasserim. It also occurs in the Andamans, Nicobars, the Indo-Burmese Countries, South China, Siam, the Malay Peninsula, and all the islands nearly down to Australia. Frequents thick forests and is met with in small parties or in pairs. Breeds from March to July in suitable localities. The nests, according to Hume, are placed in some dense bush or low thick-foliaged tree. They are more regular saucers than those of other doves, composed of roots, grass, or twigs, but comparatively neat and with a central depression. In Ceylon, according to Mr. Parker, they are rarely more than 15 feet off the ground. They breed there in June and July. Eggs two in number, pure white, from 1 to 1·1 inch in length and from 0·82 to 0·86 in breadth.

ORDER, RASORES,—GALLINACEOUS OR GAME BIRDS.

Bill usually short, vaulted, more or less arched and bent down at the tip; nostrils situated in a membrane at the base of the bill; wings usually short; tail variable in length and form; tarsi long and strong, often spurred; hinder toe short and elevated from the ground.

Family.—PHASIANIDÆ.

Bill moderate, strong, vaulted, the tip of the upper mandible hooked over the lower; nostrils apert. Wings moderate or short; tail of from 12 to 18 feathers, long and broad; tarsus moderate or long, spurred in the males; toes long; hind toe raised. This family includes the Peafowls, also the Jungle and Spur fowls and Pheasants.

Sub-Family.—PAVONINÆ—PEAFOWL.

Plumage brilliant green, shot with gold, and ocellated.

243. Pavo cristatus, *Linn.*, *Syst. Nat.* i. p. 267; *Elliot*, *Mon. Phas.* i. pl. v.; *Jerd.*, *B. Ind.* iii. p. 506; *Hume and Marsh.*, *Game Birds* p. 83; *Murray*, *Vert. Zool.*, *Sind*, p. 212; *Legge*, *B. Ceylon* p. 731; *Murray*, *Avif. Br. Ind.* ii. p. 529, No. 1186.—The COMMON PEACOCK.

Feathers of the crest with bare shafts, except at the tip. Whole head, neck, and breast rich purplish blue with gold and green reflections; scapulars, tertiaries and lesser wing coverts rufescent, barred with black; facial skin greyish white; back green, the feathers scale-like in appearance with coppery edges; median coverts deep blue; primaries and tail chestnut; abdomen and under surface black; train green, ocellated. Bill horny brown; irides dark brown.

Length.—Without train, 42 to 48 inches; with train, more than double the length of head to true tail; wing 18.

The pea hen is chestnut brown on the head and nape; neck greenish, edged with whitish brown; upper surface of the body hair brown with undulations; quills brown; tail deep brown, tipped with white; chin and throat white; breast greenish, like the neck; abdomen white; under tail coverts brown.

Length.—38 to 40 inches; wing 16; tail 14. Crest feathers with bare shafts except at the tip.

Hab.—Throughout India proper, extending into Ceylon and Assam. This lovely bird is so well known that any account of its habits would be superfluous. They generally roost at night on high trees, seldom, if ever, on the ground, except perhaps when disturbed at night and are forced to fly down. They pair in the early part of the hot weather, when the peacock has then his full train of upper tail coverts to display to his wives. They lay in July and August. Eggs, pure white, or a rich *café au lait* or reddish buff, with strong glossy shells pitted all over with minute pores. Size 2·55 to 3 × 1·92 to 2·2 inches.

Sub-Family.—GALLINÆ.

Head generally furnished with fleshy crests and wattles; tail of 14 feathers, more or less divaricate, and held demi-erect; upper tail coverts of males elongated and pendant.

Gen. Gallus.—*Linn.*

Head furnished with a fleshy crest; face and wattles nude; tarsus in males spurred; other characters as in the sub-family.

244. Gallus Stanleyi. *Gray and Hardw., Ill. Ind. Zool.* 3, pl. 43; *Gould, B. Asia, Pt.* vi. pl.; *Layard, Ann. and Mag. Nat. Hist.* 1854, p. 62; *Jerd., B. Ind.* iii. p. 540; *Blyth, Ibis,* 1867, p. 307; *Holdsw., P. Z. S.,* 1872, p. 468; *Hume and Marsh., Game Birds* i. p. 323, pl.; *Legge, Ibis,* 1875, p. 403. Gallus Lafayetti, *Legge, B. Ceylon,* p. 736, 1218.—The CEYLON JUNGLE COCK.

Male.—Back of head reddish; neck with long yellowish red hackles mesially streaked with black; rump feathers deep red basally, with heart-shaped terminations of deep metallic blue with purple reflections; feathers falling over the sides of the rump purplish black mesially and margined with deep red; secondaries blue-black; primaries brownish black; greater wing coverts deep reddish chestnut with reddish brown centres; under surface of the body rich glossy red with mesial deep chestnut longitudinal streaks; abdomen and under tail coverts black, also the thighs; upper tail coverts metallic blue, with green and purple reflections; central tail feathers long and curving outwards, of a black colour with deep blue reflections; rest of tail feathers brownish black. Bill brown; lower mandible pale yellow; irides buff; comb, wattles and nude skin on the facial region and head yellowish or purplish red, the comb with a large yellow spot about the middle. Legs and feet pale yellow.

Length.—19 to 25 inches; wing 8·5 to 9·0; tail 8 to 14 to end of central elongated feathers; tarsus 2·75 to 3·2; bill from gape 1·25 to 1·5.

The *female* is smaller, and has the head and neck brown, the upper parts of the latter with irregular black lines externally and mesially yellow; upper parts of the body yellowish brown vermiculated with black; primaries dark brown; secondaries dark buff, barred irregularly with black, with broad black lines; upper breast like the back; feathers of the under surface of the body black basally and yellowish white at the tip; tail reddish brown, mottled with black.

Hab.—Ceylon (Bigawantalawa District, *Armstrong*). Pundaloya and chiefly the Southern districts. Major Legge gives the distribution of the Jungle-fowl as more or less scattered through the dry jungly districts of the low country, and diffused throughout the hills of the Southern and Central Provinces. He says it is rather rare in the jungles of the maritime portions of the Western Province and south-western district, and is not common even in the forests of the interior. It is occasionally brought into Colombo and Galle by natives, but very seldom indeed into the former town. During his rambles in the jungles of the Hewagam and Rayigano Korales he never heard its note; but further inland, in the three and four Korales, in Saffragam, and in the Pasdum Korale, he has listened to its well-known cry; likewise in the hilly jungles of the south-western district. He has not met with it near the sea; but has seen it about Oodogamma, and further up at the base of the ranges it becomes more plentiful. On the eastern slopes of the Morowak Korale, where a drier climate prevails, it finds a more congenial home, and along the Wellaway river and from that eastward it is numerous. In the maritime portions of the south-east it abounds, delighting in the dense Euphorbia scrubs along the sea-coast. From this section of country round the east coast to the north of the island it is very numerous, and inhabits all the northern forests, extending down the west side as far south as the Kuronegala district. In the hills it is resident and breeds commonly up to about 5,000 feet. On the Nuwara-Elliya plateau and up on the Horton Plains it is very abundant during the north-east monsoon, coming up from lower down the hills, and probably, to some extent, from the low country, to feed on the berries of the nilloo. He adds that it is probable many remain throughout the year in these uplands; but as the Horton Plains were only visited in the cool season, he is unable to say whether it is found in that locality to any extent during the wet season. In February and March, they breed on the Horton Plains in great numbers.

This handsome bird, although so very abundant in many parts, is by no means easy to shoot. It dwells entirely in cover, and, though it is fond of frequenting the vicinity of paths and tracks through forest, its sense of hearing is so acute that it removes to a safe distance at the sound of approaching footsteps; and though it will continue to utter its challenge cry of "George Joyce," it gradually makes its way off behind some protecting hillock or rise in the ground which shuts out the road or path from its view. The north-eastern forests are well suited to its habits, the ground being covered with dry leaves, which do not decay so soon as in the humid jungles of the south; and among these, harbouring a multitude of seeds, insects, and grubs, it scratches exactly after the manner of its domestic race. This scratching may often be heard on a still morning at some distance away; and if the bird be behind a mound or little eminence it can be approached if the sportsman is cautious and makes no noise.

The Jungle-fowl roosts at a considerable height from the ground, choosing a good-sized branch to perch upon, and up to which it flies at an early hour in the evening; for the jungle swarms with hostile vermin, and its instinct teaches it to leave *terra firma* before the shades of evening spread a gloom through the thick forest. At daybreak in the morning they fly down from their roost, and while the cocks challenge each other with loud calls of "George Joyce, George Joyce," every now and then flapping their wings as they walk slowly about, the hens, if they have a brood of chicks to tend, lead them out into open places or into roads, where they scratch surrounded by their family, precisely after the manner of a barn-door fowl; and so intent are they in thus seeking food for their young, that I have walked down a road to within shot before disturbing them. The cocks are particularly combative in the breeding season; and when the challenge note is uttered, if there be another cock within hearing, he replies and flaps his wings, the call is continued, the birds approaching each other, and they will sometimes cross a road in so doing, and thus afford a shot. It could never be ascertained whether any actual combats were the result of their meeting, and it is thought that generally one or other of the birds retreats when it sees its antagonist. Layard, however, writes on this subject:—"The cocks fight most desperately in defence of their seraglios, the combat frequently terminating in the death of one of the engaged parties. As they not unfrequently mingle with the fowls of the lonely villages, they cross with the domestic breed, being more than a match in courage for the plebeian dunghill cocks, and armed with tremendous sharp spurs."

"Mr. Mitford, of the Ceylon Civil Service," he continues, "showed me, while at Ratnapura, a hybrid hen; her general appearance and call much resembled that of the wild bird; her eggs also partook of the spotted character; but Mr. Mitford never succeeded in rearing any chicks from them, as they were always addled. The bird was very tame to those with whom she was acquainted, but fled precipitately at the approach of strangers.

"As a rule, Jungle-fowl do not thrive well in confinement; but several exceptions to this have come under my notice, the birds in question having been reared from the nest. Captain F. Bayley successfully kept a cock for years in his beautiful grotto-like aviary at Galle; and Mr. Thwaites of Hakgala had some beautiful examples which I saw on the occasion of my last visit to his bungalow, and which, he informed me, he had had for some years in confinement without their having in any way suffered from their captivity. Mr. Holdsworth likewise conveyed some to England, which the late Rev. Dr. Boake had reared in an aviary at Colombo.

"The sound of the flapping of the wings, which is of course the invitation to battle, has the effect of always drawing two birds together; and the knowledge of this fact has given rise to the device of imitating the noise, by doing which the sportsman can bring the cock up to him, and if he be properly concealed can easily shoot him. The natives make this sound by clapping against their thighs with the palm of the hand hollowed; but Europeans can best do it by making a pad with the handkerchief, and beating it against the palm of the other hand. By this means the exact sound can be made; and I myself once procured a very fine specimen in the Ostenburgh woods by adopting this plan. It is worthy of note that this species (and I believe the same is the case with all the wild Jungle-fowl) does not utter its call before daybreak, like the domesticated varieties; and this fact renders it difficult to surmise how the habit first arose in the latter.

"The male birds have an alarm note, sounding like clock, clock, which they make, if they hear any strange noise, when perched on a branch and about to roost. I kept a wild bird in confinement for a short time, and being very timid it invariably made this note when I approached, at the same time running round the aviary and trying to escape. The 'George Joyce call is, as Mr. Holdsworth remarks, preceded by a sharp monosyllabic note sounding like *tik*. This gentleman likewise says that he has seen the cock, when 'calling,' 'strutting up and down a low horizontal branch of a tree, raising and lowering its head' as it gave out its note.

"I have remarked in my note on 'distribution' that numbers of Jungle-fowl visit the forests in which the undergrowth of 'nilloo,' a species of Strobilanthes, is so abundant, for the purpose of feeding on its berries; and the popular idea obtains that the fruit of this shrub has the effect of stupefying the birds. Certain it is that at this period the Jungle-fowl in the Horton Plains and about Nuwara-Elliya do become affected, and are apparently so "intoxicated" that they may be knocked down with a stick. Mr. Holdsworth, writing on the subject, says that he failed to discover that any thing was known to botanists of the seeds of this plant possessing narcotic qualities; and he suggests that the birds may perhaps eat some noxious fungus growing in the woods where the 'nilloo' thrives.

"Another idea among the Singhalese is that the Jungle-fowl become blind at this season from eating the nilioo-seeds. Mr. Bligh writes me on this subject as follows:—'About that season of the year if village fowls be brought to the hills they rarely escape a serious eye-disease, which rapidly spreads throughout a given district, and in many cases they become totally blind in two or three weeks. This is the disease which the Jungle-fowl evidently catch. A dog of mine caught a Jungle-cock with one eye lost, and evidentty from this cause.'

"The flight of the Jungle-fowl is strong; but they rarely take wing unless suddenly surprised, their usual mode of escape from danger being by running, which they do with considerable speed.

Nidification.—"In the north of Ceylon the Jungle-fowl breeds in the early part of the year (when I have procured its eggs), and most likely at other seasons as well. In the Hambantota district I have met with young chicks in July, and in the neighbourhood of Kadugannawa in December, whilst at Horton Plains, young have been seen in April; and, finally, in the Kukul Korale I have taken its eggs in August. From this it will appear that it breeds throughout the year. The nest is almost always placed on the ground near a tree, under a bush, and beneath the shelter of a fallen log; a hollow is scratched and a few dry leaves placed in it for the eggs to repose upon. I once found a nest in damp soil between the large projecting flange-like roots of the Doon-tree, containing two eggs partly incubated. I have generally found that the eggs do not exceed two in number, but sometimes three and occasionally four are laid. The general colour is creamy, but some eggs are whiter than others; white specks sometimes prevail all over the shell in the same manner as in the ordinary hen's eggs. Sometimes they are closely stippled with brownish specks or minute points of reddish grey, which occasionally tend slightly to form an indistinct zone at one end, either the smaller or larger. They vary from 1·75 to 2·0 inches in length by from 1·24 to 1·49 inch in breadth."

In 1873 Mr. Parker found a nest on the top of a young tree about 30 feet high. He writes me that it had the appearance of a Crow's or a Hawk's nest, of which the Jungle-hen had taken possession. She flew off, and three eggs were found to be in the nest. After incubation the young would have been doubtless carried down by the mother to the ground, just as young ducklings are conveyed from a tree-nest to water.

The young chicks, when slightly larger than a quail, fly well and very strongly; they show their galline nature in displaying a strong affection for the parent. I once shot a hen which was accompanied by a brood of half-grown chicks, and as I approached they ran to and fro by the dead bird until I was close to them, when they flew off.

Mr. Parker found three nests in trees. "One of these," he says, "was almost certainly built by the Jungle-fowl, as I saw it when it was in an unfinished state, the hen having flown off it on my approach. It was twelve feet off the ground, on the top of a low bush, and it was made of sticks and twigs, with a concavity for the eggs, which was lined with twigs only. It resembled a rather large nest of *Carpophaga aenea*. Another nest was on the top of a pollarded tree, 7 feet off the ground. Natives say that they have found the eggs in deserted squirrels' nests."

He obtained eggs in the North Provinces in February, March, May, June, July, August, and September; and in the N.-W. Provinces in February, March, April, May, June, July and September. The average size of 18 eggs from North-West Provinces is 1·81 × 1·37 inches. Soon after coming to Ceylon he caught a tiny chick that was accompanying a Jungle-hen (he presumes, though he did not see the hen) in dense forest, two miles away from a village. He reared it, and to his surprise it appeared to be a hybrid. Its wings and tail had the markings of the Jungle-hen, but its other colouration was more like that of an ordinary village fowl. It lived with my other fowls, and when adult laid 7 eggs, from which four chickens were obtained. Endeavours were made to pair it with a Jungle-cock, but the latter was too wild in captivity.

The natives trap numbers of Jungle-fowl in the forests, in the following manner:—In a place, frequented by these birds, they construct a miniature fence of small sticks or twigs, about 9 inches high, and 40 or 50 feet long. In the middle a gap is left, about 8 inches wide. They then, for several days, scatter food in the immediate neighbourhood, and along the sides of the fence, and around the gap. When the birds have become fully accustomed to feed at this spot, the hunters fix a hair noose in the gap, held by a spring and catch. Many birds are thus captured at one site.

Gen. **Galloperdix**.—*Blyth.*

Bill somewhat lengthened; orbits nude; tail moderately long, of 14 feathers, held erect and folded as in the domestic fowl; tarsus of male with 2 or more spurs; females also spurred.

245. Galloperdix bicalcaratus, *Forst., Ind. Zool.* p. 25, pl. 74; *Pennant., Ind. Zool.* p. 40, pl. 7; *Legge, B. Ceylon*, p. 741. Perdix zeylonensis, *Bonn. et Vieill, Ency. Meth. Orn.* 1, 210, pl. 93, fig. 3. Galloperdix zeylonensis, *Gmel., Edit. Linn. Syst. Nat tom.* 1, part ii. p. 759; *Gould, B. Asia*, pt. 6, p. 67. *Hume, Nests and Eggs, Ind. B.* p. 555. Francolinus ceylonensis, *Less., Trait d'Orn.*, p. 504. Galloperdix zeylonensis, *Blyth, Cat. M. A. S. B. Calc.* p. 241.—The CEYLON SPUR FOWL.

Head black, a line of white down the centre of each feather, becoming obsolete on the centre of the crown; back of neck black, with a mesial white line; shoulders and scapulars deep chestnut with a mesial black dash and a white line inside of it; lower back deep chestnut, freckled with black at the tips; upper and under tail coverts black, also the lesser wing coverts, which are bordered with chestnut at base, and have a buffy spot at tip; primaries brown; remainder of wing deep chestnut; lower surface of body black with a large white spot at the tip of each feather; legs and feet red; iris brownish red. The female is entirely deep chestnut, paler on the under surface and minutely freckled with brown, especially on the secondaries and upper tail coverts; tail purplish black. Bill, orbits, eyes, legs and feet as in the male.

Hab.—Ceylon, to which island it is peculiar, Major Legge says that the spur-fowl in Ceylon inhabits the damp jungles of the west and south-west, the forests of the Central Province permanently up to an altitude of about, 4,500 feet and those of the southern ranges as well, likewise the Eastern Province jungles, but not the northern portion of the island. How far northward of the Matale Hills it extends, he is unable to say; but he has himself not heard it north of Dambulla, nor on the sea-coast beyond the virgil. On the western side it is found in the southern portions of the Kurunegala district, straying as far north as Uswuoa, and about Ambepussa is not uncommon; further south it increases, and is found in various forest and jungle recesses in the Hewagam and Salpiti Korales. In Saffragam and in the Pasdun Korale it is abundant, and extends in numbers throughout the wooded districts between Galle and the southern hills, in which latter it is likewise common. Eastward of the Kolonna Korale it is rare. Major Legge adds, he heard it once on the banks of the Kirindeganga in the Wellawe Korale; but higher up, on the slopes of the mountains, it is again common. In the Friars-Hood jungles and about Nilgalla it is plentiful in parts, though not widely distributed as in the damp woods of the western district. It is found more or less in all the jungles of the coffee-districts, and breeds above 5,000 feet in some parts; in the cool season it is found in the Nuwara-Eliya district, and very probably extends over all the plateau to the Horton Plains. It is very common in the Knuckles forests.

Major Legge says, the "Haban-kukula," so well known in Ceylon on account of its remarkable cackling note, is one of the shiest birds in the island, affecting the most entire concealment, and only emerging from the jungles in the early morning. It is so wary that, although it may occasionally be surprised or heard close to a path in the forest, it immediately becomes aware of the presence of the enemy, and runs off with great speed, instantly disappearing in the thick jungle. It does not, however, confine itself entirely to forests, as I have sometimes found it in Lantana-scrub and detached copses in the south-west of the island; and I have more than once, by rushing into a small thicket with shouts, endeavoured to get it on the wing, but have always failed, as it invariably escaped by darting through the grass and underwood on foot, and thus gained the main portion of the jungle in safety. On the coffee-estates in the Central Province it comes out of the forest the first thing in the morning, and feeds along the edge of the plantations in silence; almost before the sun is up it retreats into its native fastnesses, and about six or half-past commences to call. There is something highly ventriloquistic in its note; and this, combined with the birds moving about, as I believe they always do when they are calling, makes it impossible to get near them by following the sound of their notes. These are given out and answered by the cocks; and if disturbed during the time they are cackling, they will wait a little, and then recommence louder than ever.

Layard writes as follows on their habits:—"After remaining some time concealed, if nothing occurs to excite their fears, a cock-bird, bolder than the rest, will utter a few low notes, not unlike the plaintive cry of a turkey poult; if this is answered from a distance, or the birds are reassured by the silence, the call is changed to a loud piping whistle, of which the following stave gives the nearest representation I can devise:—

"And the birds once more sally out from their concealment. I am convinced that like the Virginian Quail, these birds possess the power of ventriloquism in a great degree. I have often listened to those in my aviary, and could have declared that the calls proceeded from every part of the garden save that in which the performers were located. . . . .

"They fly with great rapidity, but prefer to take refuge in concealment rather than maintain a lengthened flight. One which escaped from a basket in my house flew up to the roof and through the ventilating-holes ; but instead of continuing on the wing at the elevation it had attained, it dropped instantly into a small copse, out of which it was hunted with much difficulty, when it darted through an open door into my kitchen and concealed itself behind a box.

"The males are very pugilistic, and in their manner of fighting reminded me of the game-cock, depressing and elevating the head, imitating each other's actions, &c."

Though they seem to do well in confinement for a short time, I do not think they would ever live long in a state of captivity, their nature being naturally so wild and shy that they are unable to adapt themselves to the confined life of an aviary. I kept a brood or four, which were brought to me quite young, for eight months, at the end of which time they were stricken with some disease which carried them off one by one. They were at all times very shy, hiding behind the artificial cover with which I provided them, and whenever they were frightened flew up against the bamboo covering of the "run" in which I kept them, sadly lacerating their heads. The injuries thus received, however, did not appear to affect their health, as one individual lived for months with a bare skull, which he acquired by dashing his head repeatedly against the roof of the aviary. They were confined with an old male bird, and did very well for about a month. Breeds from April to July. Eggs two in number.

The eggs were of a uniform cream-colour, and one of them was covered with small, white, polished, calcareous specks, similar to those often seen on hen's eggs. They were rather broad ovals in shape; and measured 1·42 and 1·43 inch in length by 1·12 and 1·12 inch in breadth, respectively.

Gen. **Francolinus**.—*Steph.*

Bill very slightly curved at tip ; tail of 14 feathers, even or rounded ; tarsi of male with blank spurs.

246. Francolinus pictus (*Jard. and Selby*), *Jerd., B. Ind.* iii. p. 561, No. 819; *Hume, Str. F.* v. p. 211 ; *id., Nests and Eggs, Ind. B.* p. 538 ; *id. and Marsh., Game Birds,* p. 19, pl. Perdix pictus, *Jard. and Selby, Ill. Orn.* pl. 50.—The PAINTED PARTRIDGE.

Crown of the head dark brown, the feathers edged paler ; forehead and lores, also the cheeks and ear coverts, chestnut ; back and scapulars deep brown, the feathers margined with white ; wings chestnut, banded with black ; lower back, rump, and upper tail coverts with wavy bars of black and white ; tail deep brown, the feathers narrowly barred across ; chin white ; neck all round pale ferruginous ; breast and abdomen variegated black and white, each feather being white with two dark bands, and the shafts and tip black ; under tail coverts chestnut. Bill blackish ; irides dark brown ; legs yellowish red.

Length.—12 inches; wing 6; tail 2·75; tarsus 1·75.

Hab.—Ceylon, Central and Southern India, where it replaces *F. vulgaris.* Found throughout Bundelkund and the Saugor and Nerbudda territories, thence south to Nagpore and the Deccan; west it extends into Khandesh and perhaps Guzerat, and eastwards to the Northern Circars. Like its northern congener, Jerdon adds that it delights in grassy plains and fields, but affects more the open, dry and raised plains with scattered bushes. It breeds during the monsoon (July to September), laying 7—8 eggs, rather of a peg-top shape, broad and obtuse at the large end, and much pointed towards the small end; the colour may be said to be a pale *café au lait.* Size 1·3 to 1·45 by 1·1 to 1·22.

Gen. **Ortygornis.**—*Reich.*

247. Ortygornis ponticeriana, *Gmel., Syst. Nat.* i. p.; *Gray Ill. Ind. Zool.*, pl. 56, fig. 2; *Jerd., B. Ind.* iii. p. 569, No. 822; *Murray, Hdbk., Zool., &c., Sind,* p. 203; *id., Vert. Zool. Sind,* p. 214; *Hume, Nests and Eggs, Ind. B.* p. 542; *Hume and Marsh., Game Birds,* p. 51, pl.; *Legge, B. Ceylon,* p. 748; *Murray, Avif. Brit. Ind.* ii. p. 554, No. 1212.—The Common Grey Partridge.

Forehead, over the eyes, lores, nape and face rufous, the face with dusky freckles; top of the head olive brown; ear coverts rufescent brown; back, scapulars and wing coverts dark chestnut, each feather with two or three transverse buffy bars, bordered with black on both sides; feathers of the rump and upper tail coverts similar, but olive brown instead of chestnut; tail feathers rich chestnut or deep ferruginous, with a broad subterminal dark brown nearly black band, tipped with pale or yellowish white; central tail feathers like the back; beneath the chin and throat are white or creamy, encircled from the base of the lower mandible with dark spots, forming a gular patch; breast and entire lower parts creamy white, or very pale buff, the feathers with transverse dark bars; lower tail coverts ferruginous. The female is like the male, but paler in colour, and wants the spur.

Length.—11·5 to 13·5 inches; wing 5·5 to 6; tail 3·35 to 4; legs bright red; irides brown; the orbital ring with a row of minute white feathers; bill dusky brown.

Hab.—Ceylon and throughout India, Beloochistan and S. Persia. Affects dry, scrubby or bare stony tracts. Delights among *Euphorbia* bushes. In the morning they are generally found in fields or on the edges of cultivation, where they pick up seeds and corn, also insects of all kinds. They afford fair sport with one or two good men, or a good dog and one's wits against the birds. Breeds from February to May, and from July to November, both in Ceylon and India. The eggs are generally laid in a depression in the ground, on which a few blades of grass are laid. Eggs, 6—9 in number, white or clear cream colour, from 1·2 to 1·42 in length, and from 0·95 to 1·12 in breadth. Average of 50, 1·33 × 1·02. In Bengal, either in the deltaic district or in the Eastern Provinces, it does not occur, nor in Assam or Burmah. In the Deccan it ascends to 2,500 feet or more; in the Himalayas and Southern India not above 1,000 feet. In Ceylon, the most inland locality it has been met with is in the valley of Aruvi-aru in the Manaar districts, where it lives—according to Parker—at a distance of 18 miles from the sea at a village called Kunjukulam.

Gen. **Perdicula**.—*Hodgs.*

Bill short, thick, curved; tarsus with a blunt tubercle; wings rounded; outer webs of most of the primaries sinuated; tail short, of 12 feathers. Size small.

248. Perdicula asiatica (*Latham*), *Gould, B. Asia,* part xv. pl. 12; *Temm., Pl. Col.* p. 447; *Hume, Str. F.* vii. p. 156; *Hume and Marsh., Game Birds,* p. 109, pl.; *Legge, B. Ceylon,* p. 752; *Murray, Avif. Brit. India* ii. p. 562. Coturnix pentah, *Sykes, Trans. Zool. Socy.* ii. pl. 3; *Hardw., Ill. Ind. Zool.* 2, pl. 45, fig. 3. Perdicula cambayensis, *apud Jerd., B. Ind.* iii. p. 581, No. 826.—The JUNGLE BUSH QUAIL.

Above rich dark reddish brown, mottled with dull rufous; supercilium rufous white, narrowly edged with black, an indistinct pale line from the gape; feathers of the back of the neck and the back white shafted; scapulars and wing coverts richly marked on their inner webs with pale creamy white and black; primaries red-brown with tawny spots and bars; tail with a few black bars; chin rich chestnut; rest of the under surface white, tinged with rufescent on the lower abdomen, flanks, vent and lower tail coverts, and with numerous cross bars of black, smallest on the throat and sides of the neck. Bill dusky, tinged with reddish; irides light brown; legs yellowish red.

Length.—6·5 to 7·2 inches; wing 3 to 3·5; tail 1·5 to 1·78; tarsus 0·94 to 1; bill from gape 0·5 to 0·6.

Hab.—Generally distributed throughout India, Ceylon, Malabar Coast, the Wynaad, Mysore, Madras, Eastern Ghauts, Western Ghauts, Khandalla, Mahableshwar, Rutnagherry, and South Konkan generally; Chanda, Seoni, Nursingpur, Manbhoom, Rajmahal hills, Mirzapoor, Etawah, Kuchawan Hills, Mount Abu, Lucknow, Umballa, the Dhoon, Mussoorie, Simla, lower Himalayan ranges below Kumaon and Kashmir, are some of the recorded localities given by Mr. Hume, where this species is common. They always keep in small coveys in grass jungle or stubble long enough to hide them. They feed of course on seeds and grains of sorts. Breeds from September to January according to locality, making a nest on the ground under the shelter of some bush or tuft of grass. It is shallow and circular, and lined or made up of grass roots, grass and a few dead leaves. Eggs, 5—7 in number, regular ovals, more or less pointed towards one end, with a faint gloss, and in colour spotless creamy white. Size, from 0·96 to 1·1 in length and 0·79 to 0·9 in breadth.

Sub-Family.—COTURNICINÆ.—QUAILS.

Wings long, rather pointed ; bill moderate ; tarsus not spurred ; tail short, coriceated by the upper tail coverts.

Gen. **Coturnix**.—*Brisson.*

Bill short, straight, very slightly curved at the tip ; tarsi not spurred ; tail short ; wings long and pointed ; 1st and 2nd quills longest.

249. Coturnix communis (*Linn.*), *Bonn.*, *Tabl. Enc. Meth.* p. 217 ; *Bodd*, *Pl. Enl.* 170 ; *Jerd.*, *B. Ind.* iii. p. 586, No. 829 ; *Hume*, *Nests and Eggs Ind. B.* p. 549 ; *Blyth*, *B. Burm.* p. 151 ; *Dav et Oust. Ois. Chine*, p. 396 ; *Dresser*, *B. Eur.* vii. p. 298 ; *Hume*, *Str. F.* viii. p. 111 ; *Scully*, *Str. F.* viii. p. 350 ; *Hume and Marsh.*, *Game Birds* ii. p. 133, pl. ; *Hume*, *Str. F.* x. p. 236 (*note*) ; *Murray*, *Hdbk.*, *Zool.*, *&c.*, *Sind*, p. 203 ; *id.*, *Vert. Zool.*, *Sind*, p. 215 ; *Oates*, *B. Br. Burm.* ii. p. 331 ; *Murray*, *Avif. Brit. Ind.* ii. p. 565, No. 1236.—The COMMON EUROPEAN OR LARGE GREY QUAIL.

Primaries *with pale rufous bars* on their outer webs.—*C. communis.*

Top of head brown, the feathers edged paler ; a mesial buffy line on the crown ; supercilium pale yellowish white, reaching above the ear coverts, which are partially brown ; lores and a line below the eye white ; sides of the neck white; two narrow blackish lines from the sides of the neck to below the throat, the interspace being white; the upper black band not always perfect; chin and throat patch dark brown; breast pale buff, buffy white or rufous, with pale shafts to the feathers; sides of the breast and flanks similar or deeper in colour, with pale shafts; abdomen white, pale rufous, or buff; back, scapulars and upper tail coverts from brown to a rich dark brown, each feather shafted a rich rufous, or buff, with three transverse bars or bands of the same colour on each side, the tips being pale buff; *primaries dusky brown with pale rufous bars on theirs outer webs;* the secondaries with pale tips and the tertials barred buffy on both webs, the borders of the buffy bars darker than the ground colour of the feathers. The female is like the male, but wants the central throat patch, and the breast is spotted with brown or dark brown. She is also much larger.

Length.—7 to 8 inches; wing 4 to 4·5; tail 1·6 to 2·25; irides brown or hazel; legs pale fleshy; bill blackish with a brownish horny tinge above and at the tip.

Hab.—Ceylon and India generally to Nepaul, Sind, Punjab, Beloochistan, Afghanistan, Persia, Arabia, the Deccan, N. Guzerat, Rajputana, Kutch, Kattiwar and Southern and Central India. A rare visitor to Burmah and in the countries S.-E. of the mouths of the Ganges, Chittagong, Arracan and Pegu, where it may be considered a straggler. It is found throughout Europe and nearly the whole of Asia. The greater bulk of these which come into India, Hume says, are migratory. They arrive from the North from Central Asia across the Himalayas, and from the west from Persia, Beluchistan, &c. Hume adds, that arrived within our boundaries, while a certain number remain scattered about, some remaining in the lower ranges and valleys of the Himalayas up to an elevation of 4,000 to 5,000 feet, the greater bulk move forward, southwards and eastwards, and arrive about the middle of October in Sylhet, Bengal, and the Deccan, and frequent the crops of peas, millet, &c., to the end of March; their stay, however, depends much on the supply of food. They migrate invariably at night, and evidently in large numbers at a time. Numbers are netted throughout India, for the table, for quaileries, and the cock-birds for fighting purposes,—a favourite pastime nearly throughout India amongst Mahomedans. Breeds generally in the N.-W. and Upper Provinces of India, laying six eggs, from February to April. Eggs broad ovals, a good deal pointed towards one end. The ground colour is a clear yellowish or reddish buff, thickly speckled and freckled and thinly blotched with reddish brown.

Gen. **Excalfactoria**.—*Bonap.*

General characters similar to those of *Coturnix*. Wings less pointed and more rounded; 1st quill shorter than the second; 3rd, 4th and 5th graduating very slightly from the 2nd.

250. Excalfactoria chinensis (*Linn.*), *Jerd.*, *B. Ind.* ii. p. 591; *Hume, Nests and Eggs Ind. B.* p. 553; *Salvad., Ucc. Born.* p. 311; *Oates, Str. F.* iii. p. 345; *Wald., Trans. Zool. Soc.* ix. p. 224; *Blyth, B. Burm.* p. 151; *David et Oust. Ois. Chine*, p. 397; *Hume and Dav., Str. F.* vi. p. 447; *Hume, Str. F.* viii. p. 111; *Oates, Str. F.* viii. p. 167; *Hume and Marsh., Game Birds* ii. p. 161, pl.; *Bingham, Str. F.* x. p. 196; *Oates, Str. F.* x. p. 236; *Murray, Avif. Br. Ind.* ii. p. 567. Tetrao chinensis, *Linn., Syst. Nat.* i. p. 277. Coturnix chinensis, *Legge, B. Ceylon*, pp. 755, 1218.—The BLUE-BREASTED QUAIL.

A narrow white line from the nostrils to the eye; forehead, feathers round the eye, ear coverts, breast, sides of the neck and of the body slaty blue; abdomen, vent and tail chestnut; upper plumage, wing coverts and tertiaries olive brown, marked with black and pale rufous, and most of the feathers with pale shaft streaks; primaries and secondaries plain brown; chin, throat, and cheeks black; a broad moustachial stripe from the gape white; a broad collar below the black of the throat white, succeeded by a narrow band of black. The female has the upper plumage almost similar to the male; the supercilium, forehead and throat are rufous, enclosing a dull white chin; sides of the head pale rufous, speckled with black; lower plumage pale buff; all but the centre of the abdomen barred with black. Bill bluish black; irides red; eyelids plumbeous; legs bright yellow.

Length.—5·7 inches; tail 1; wing 2·8; tarsus 0·8; bill from gape 0·5.

Hab.—Ceylon, and generally distributed over Eastern India. Occurs in Bengal, Assam, Burmah, Southern and Cochin-China, the Malay Peninsula, Sumatra, Java, and Borneo. In Ceylon it is fairly common, especially towards the south of the island. In Burmah it is generally distributed, but is nowhere common except in Pegu, where it arrives in May in large numbers. In Raipur, Mandla, and the Chanda districts, also in the Tributary Mahals, Singbhoom, Calcutta, Cachar, Sylhet, Khasia hills, as well as in the Dafla hills and in the valley of Nepaul it is fairly common. It is also recorded from Arracan. Open, swampy grassy lands or meadows are their favourite haunts, and they are seldom found far from such spots. They do not appear shy but freely come into the open to feed. Breeds in Ceylon, Pegu, Cachar, Purneah, and the Sub-Himalayan districts from Sikkim or Kasauli. Lays from June to the 1st or 2nd week in September. Eggs, 5—6, broad ovals, of the shape of those of the Common Black Partridge, *café au lait* tinged with olive in colour. In size they vary from 0·95 to 1·04 in length and from 0·7 to 0·8 in width. The females when with their brood make great endeavours to entice away persons in the vicinity of their nests, attempting lameness and feigning a great number of would-be accidents.

Family, TINAMIDÆ.

Bill short, rather slender, and very slightly curved at the tip; tail short or none; tarsi not spurred; hind toe small or wanting.

Gen. **Turnix**.—*Bonap.*

Characters the same as those of the Family; nostrls linear; 1st quill longest; no hind toe.

251. Turnix plumbipes (*Hodgs.*), *Hume, Nests and Eggs Ind. B.* p. 554; *Blyth, B. Burm.* p. 152; *Oates, Str. F.* v. p. 164; *Anders., Yunnan Exped.*-p. 673; *Hume and Dav., Str. F.* vi. p. 450; *Hume, Str. F.* viii. p. 111; *Scully, Str. F.* viii. p. 350; *Hume and Marsh., Game Birds* ii. p. 177, pl.; *Oates, Str. F.* x. p. 236; *id., B. Br. Burm.* ii. p. 337; *Murray, Avif. Brit. Ind.* ii. p. 568, No 1239. Hemipodius plumbipes, *Hodgs., Beng. Sport. Mag.* ix. p. 345. Turnix ocellatus (*Scop.*), *Jerd., B. Ind.* ii. p. 577; No. 833. Turnix pugnax (*Temm.*), *Hume, Str. F.* iii. p. 178; *id., Nests and Eggs Ind. B.* p. 553. Turnix taigoor, *Sykes, Trans. Zool. Soc.* 2, pl.; *Jerd., B. Ind.* iii. p. 495, No. 832; *Hume and Marsh., Game Birds* ii. p. 169, pl.; *Legge, B. Ceylon* pp. 761, 1218.—The INDO-MALAYAN BUSTARD QUAIL.

Above rufous with transverse black lines and pale yellow streaks; below rufescent or pale ferruginous, becoming chestnut on the flanks and undertail coverts; the foreneck, breast and sides of the body lunated with black.

The *female* is a much larger bird, and the plumage is darker; the crown and sides of the head, the sides and back of the neck are spotted with white: chin, throat and breast black; sides of the breast and body lunated with black. Legs and feet plumbeous or pale leaden; irides pearly grey.

Length.—5·6 to 6·25; wing 3·12 to 3·5; tail 1·0 to 1·4; tarsus 0·95 to 1·12; bill from gape 0·7 to 0·81.

Hab.—Throughout India nearly (except Sind, Katthiawar and Jodhpoor, and other similar dry places), extending to Ceylon, Burmah, the Malay Peninsula, Siam, and Cochin-China. It frequents gardens, land covered with grass, also bushes, roadsides, &c. Breeds in July and August, wherever it occurs, laying 4—6 eggs, of a stone grey colour, irrorated with small specks of brown interspersed with larger spots of a neutral tint.

It will be seen that I have made *T. taigoor* a synonym of *T. plumbipes*. There can be no doubt of both species being identical; the rufous tint of the Malayan race can only be considered as climatic. There are no other characters which could be considered sufficient to warrant a separation.

ORDER, GRALLATORES,—WADERS OR SHORE BIRDS.

Tarsi long, rounded; tibia bare to a greater or less extent; hind toe imperfect in most or absent; wings long; neck long or of moderate length, generally in proportion to the length of the legs; bill variable in size and structure. All, except the Ostriches and Emeus (which do not fly) fly well, and stretch their legs out behind them during flight.

Tribe, PRESSIROSTRES.—*Cuvier.*

Hind toe small, absent or moderate; bill depressed at base, and rather compressed on the sides. It comprises the *Otitidæ* or Bustards and Floricans; the *Cursoridæ*, or Courier Plovers; *Glareolidæ* or Swallow Plovers; *Charadriidæ* or Sand Plovers; *Hæmatopodidæ* or Shore Plovers, and the *Gruidæ* or Cranes The Otitidæ are not represented in Ceylon.

Family, CURSORIDÆ.—Courier Plovers.

Tarsi long, slender; bill slender, arched beyond the nostrils, which are in a short triangular groove; wings long and pointed; tail short, of 12 feathers; toes three; no hind toe.

Gen. Cursorius.—*Lath.*

Bill moderately long; tarsi long and slender, scutellated; 1st and 2nd quills longest; tail short.

252. Cursorius coromandelicus, *Gmel., Syst. Nat.* i. p. 781; *Bodd., Pl. Enl.* 892; *Gould, B. As.* pl. 37; *Jerdon, B. Ind.* iii. p. 626, No. 840; *Hume, Str. F.* iv. p. 19; *id., Nests and Eggs Ind. B.* iii. p. 564; *Murray, Hbdk., Zool., &c., Sind,* p. 207; *id., Vert. Zool. Sind.* p. 221; *Legge, B. Ceylon,* p. 977; *Murray, Avif. Brit. Ind.* ii. p. 579, No. 1250.—The Indian Courier Plover.

Forehead and top of head bright chestnut; a small patch of black on the nape; supercilium white, extending to and meeting behind the nape; a black streak from the base of the nostril and through the eye, also extending and meeting behind; chin and throat white or pale buffy white; neck all round pale ferruginous, darkening into deep ferruginous on the breast and upper abdomen; a dark patch in the middle of the abdomen; primaries and their coverts black; under tail coverts white; back, scapulars and wing coverts earthy brown; upper tail coverts the same; tail with outer feathers on each side white, with a black edge subterminally on the inner web; rest, except the middle tail feathers, ashy brown at base, with a subterminal dark band and a white tip; bill black; irides brown; legs creamy white.

Length.—9 to 10 inches; wings 6; tail 2·37; tarsus 2·25.

Hab.—Ceylon and Southern India; also Sind, Punjab, N.-W. Provinces, Oudh, Bengal, Beloochistan, N. Guzerat, Rajputana, Kutch, Kattiawar, Concan and Deccan, affecting open grassy plains, feeding on grass seeds, insects, &c. They are extremely shy, and run with great speed, now and again stopping dead to look back, and when pressed do not fly far. Breeds from March to July, under some tuft of grass or bush, laying 3—4 eggs of a cream or bright buff colour with patches, spots, blotches and smears of pale inky grey either all over or on only some portion of the egg; the markings above this are narrow scratches and streaks of blackish brown.

Family, GLAREOLIDÆ.—SWALLOW PLOVERS.

Bill short, convex, broad at the base, compressed to tip; wings long, first quill longest; tail even or forked; tarsi short, reticulated; three toes in front, one behind, very small; gape large.

Gen. **Glareola**.—*Brisson*.

Tail short and even, or long and forked; other characters as in the family.

253. **Glareola orientalis** (*Leach*), *Linn. Tr.* xiii. 132; *Gould, B. As.* vi. pl. 23; *Schiel., Handlist Dierk.* t. 7, 79; *Jerdon, B. Ind.* iii. p. 631; *Str. F.* ii. pp. 284, 465; viii. p. 371; *Murray, Hdbk., Zool., &c., Sind*, p. 208; *Hume, Nests and Eggs Ind. B.* p. 568; *Legge, B. Ceylon*, p. 980; *Bingham, Str. F.* ix. p. 196; *Oates, Str. F.* x. p. 237; *Kelham, Ibis*, 1882, p. 6; *Oates, B. Burm.* ii. p. 361; *Murray, Vert. Zool., Sind*, p. 222; *id., Avif. Brit. Ind.* ii. p. 581, No. 1253.—The LARGE SWALLOW PLOVER.

Forehead, crown, back of head, sides of neck, ear coverts, back, scapulars and wing coverts hair brown; upper tail coverts white; tail forked, basally white, the feathers broadly tipped with dark brown; chin and throat rufescent, a few of the feathers in some specimens tipped dark brown; a dark line from each side of the mandible to below the neck, enclosing the rufous chin, throat and breast; upper abdomen and flanks earthy brown, with a tinge of rufescent; lower abdomen, vent and under tail coverts white; axillaries and under wing coverts behind chestnut; primaries dark brown, almost black; the shaft of the first primary white; a few of the upper secondaries tipped white; irides dark brown; bill black; gape reddish; legs and feet dusky brown.

Length.—10 to 10·5 inches; wing 7·5; tail 4·25 to 4·5.

Hab.—Ceylon; also Sind, Bengal and the Deccan, and throughout Burmah in suitable localities from February to June. Occurs in Mongolia and China, also Cochin-China, and the Malay Peninsula. Affects fields and open or cultivated land in small flocks. It has, like its congeners, a very rapid and swallow-like flight. Breeds in Sind. Mr. S. Doig, in an article in *Stray Feathers*, vol. viii., p. 375, gives an account of its nidification in company with *Glareola pratincola*. "The breeding ground," he says, "was about 15 acres in extent, and was a salt plain with patches of coarse sedge here and there on it, the whole being surrounded by dense tamarisk and rush jungle, and was situated about half a mile from the bank of the 'Narra.' The nests were slight hollows scraped in the ground, and the greatest number of eggs in any nest was three, which seemed to be the normal number, but some contained only two eggs, of a light dirty green or drab colour, covered all over with dark purple blotches, dense at the broader end, and forming a zone. In shape they are from broad ovals to nearly spherical, and vary in size from 1·1 to 1·35 in length, and from 0·8 to 1·05 in width."

The distribution of the *Glareolidæ* is not perfectly known.

254. Glareola lactea, *Tem., Pl. Col.* 399; *Jerd., B. Ind.* iii. p. 632; *Hume, Nests and Eggs Ind. B.* p. 568; *Str. F.* iii. p. 179; *Blyth, B. Burm.* p. 154; *Hume, Str. F.* viii. p. 112; *Legge, B. Ceylon*, p. 984; *Oates, Str. F.* x. p. 237; *id., B. Br. Burm.* ii. p. 363; *Murray, Hdbk., Zool., &c., Sind* p. 208; *id., Vert. Zool., Sind*, p. 223., *id. Avif., Brit. Ind.* ii. p. 582, No. 1255.—The SMALL SWALLOW PLOVER.

Forehead, crown, back, scapulars and wing coverts pale earthy or grey brown, orbital feathers white; chin, throat and breast much paler than the back; lower abdomen, vent and under tail coverts white; tail basally white; the central feathers broadly dark brown subterminally and tipped with white; the lateral or outer ones on each side narrowly tipped with dark brown, and edged with white; upper tail coverts white; primaries dark brown, the first 3—4 distinctly white shafted and basally whitish on their inner webs; secondaries white, broadly edged on their outer webs and at the tip with brown; primary coverts dark brown, also the under wing coverts; bill black; gape reddish; irides deep brown.

Length.—6·5 to 6·75 inches; wing 5·5 to 5·75; tail 2 to 2·06; bill at front, 0·37, at gape 0·56.

Hab.—Ceylon; also Sind, Punjab, N.-W. Provinces, the Deccan, and British Burmah, affecting the same situations as the last. Oates says that it is found abundantly on the larger rivers in Burmah, except in the southern part of Tenasserim. It breeds in Burmah on sandbanks, also on the banks of the Indus, Ganges, Chenab, Brahmaputra, Nerbudda, Mahanuddy, and in Ceylon. March to April appears to be the breeding season. Eggs, 4 in number, from pale green to stone colour, and marked with dark lines, blotches and spots.

Sub-Family, CHARADRINÆ—PLOVERS.

Bill slender, straight, flattened at the base, compressed and grooved; wings long and pointed; tarsi moderate, 1st quill usually longest; hind toe small or wanting.

Gen. Squatarola.—*Cuv.*

Nasal groove short; bill bulged at the tip; a very minute clawed hind toe present.

255. Squatarola helvetica (*Linn.*), *Jerd., B. Ind.* iii. p. 365, No. 144; *Dresser, B. Eur.* vii. p. 455; *Salvad., Ucc. Born.* p. 313; *Blyth, B. Burm.* p. 153; *Scully, Str. F.* iv. p. 184; *Armstrong, Str. F.* iv. p. 338; *David et Oust. Ois Chine*, p. 424; *Hume and Dav. Str. F.* vi. p. 455; *Hume, Str F.* viii. p. 112; *Legge, B. Ceylon*, p. 929; *Oates, Str. F.* x. p. 237; *id., Burm.* ii. p. 365; *Murray, Vert. Zool., Sind*, p. 224; *Murray, Avif. Brit. Ind.* ii. p. 583, No. 1256. Tringa helvetica, *Linn., Syst. Nat.* 1, p. 250.—The GREY PLOVER.

Winter Plumage.—Forehead, lores, supercilia, chin, abdomen and entire lower surface, including the under tail coverts, white; foreneck, sides of the breast and flanks white, the feathers with sub-triangular or sub-quadrate brownish markings; feathers below the wing from the axilla long and black; head dusky brown, the feathers with narrow tips; rest of the upper plumage dusky brown, the feathers edged and tipped with white or greyish white; tail basally white, with a slightly rufescent tinge terminally, and with 6—7 transverse brown bands or bars In summer the entire lower surface from the chin, except the vent and under tail coverts, is black, also the lores and sides of the neck; forehead, supercilia and sides of the breast white; back and rump, scapulars and wing coverts black, broadly tipped with brown and white; top of head and nape grey brown, the feathers tipped with white; tail white, banded dark brown; primaries dark brown, their inner webs white.

Length.—11 to 12 inches; wing 8; tail 3·25; bill at front 1·25, black; irides dusky; feet dark brown, or dusky brown; weight 7·5 oz.

Hab.—Ceylon; also Sind, Beloochistan Coast, Kutch, Kattiawar, and nearly all over the Indian Coast and Burmah. Occurs in flocks along the sea-coast during winter, especially on mud flats. In the Kurrachee harbour it is numerous on the large island-like flats, especially about Baba Island, associated with the larger and smaller Kentish Plovers.

Gen. **Charadrius**.—*Gmel.*

Bill short and strong; first quill longest; hind toe wanting; other characters as in the sub-family.

256. Charadrius fulvus. *Gm., Syst. Nat.* I, p. 687; *Dresser, B. Eur.* vii. p. 443, pl.; *Hume, Str. F.* i. p. 228; ii. p, 287; *id., Nests and Eggs*, p. 570; *id., Str. F.* iii. p. 179; *Blyth, B. Burm.* p. 153; *Salvad., Ucc. Born.* p. 313; *David et Oust. Ois Chine*, p. 424; *Hume and Dav., Str. F.* vi. p. 455; *Hume, Str. F.* vii. p. 482; *Scully, Str. F.* viii. p. 350; *Legge, B. Ceylon*, pp. 934, 1222; *Oates, B. Br. Burm.* ii. p. 364; *Murray, Avif. Brit. Ind.* ii. p. 584, No. 1257. Charadrius longipes (*Temm.*), *Bonap., Rev. Crit.*, 1850, p. 180; *Jerd., B. Ind.* ii. p. 636, No. 845; *Murray, Vert. Zool., Sind*, p. 224.—The EASTERN GOLDEN PLOVER.

Winter Plumage.—Head dark brown, the tips of the feathers yellow; forehead white or yellowish white, as are also the lores, supercilia, chin, foreneck and the under tail coverts; back, scapulars, rump, upper tail coverts and wing coverts dusky brown, the edges of the feathers with triangular or sub-triangular yellow spots; tail lighter in colour, the feathers also similarly edged with yellow spots; the neck behind, on the sides, and in front buffy, with a dusky tinge and yellow edgings and spots to the feathers; flanks pale brown, spotted with soiled white. In the summer plumage, the upper plumage is much darker, nearly black, the yellow spots less numerous and smaller, the forehead is white, and the cheeks, throat, neck, and entire under parts are black; primaries black, shafts of the first three white; secondaries tipped with white; also the median wing coverts; tail brownish with transverse bands of black.

Length.—10 to 10·5 inches; wing 6·75; tail 2·75; bill at front 0·87; tarsus 1·75; bill dusky at base, black at the tip; irides deep brown.

Hab.—Sind, Punjab, Kutch, Kattiawar, Deccan and India generally, also Burmah, in open plains or in the vicinity of rivers and ploughed fields.

Gen. **Ægialitis.**—*Boie.*

Bill slender, grooved on upper mandible for two-thirds its length; front of bill raised; upper mandible slightly the longer; 1st quill longest. All the Sand Plovers are more or less gregarious in their habits, and feed either on ploughed lands, meadows, edges of marshes and ponds, sandbanks, mud lagoons and banks of rivers and tanks. They run with some speed, making a dead stop now and again to pick up a worm, mollusc, small crustacea or other insects on which they feed. Nearly all are migratory. Eggs, generally 4 in number, of a stone yellow or greenish colour, richly blotched.

257. Ægialitis Geoffroyi, *Wagl., Syst. Av. Charadrius sp.* 19; *Jerd., B. Ind.* iii. p. 638; *Harting, Ibis,* 1870, p. 378, pl. xi.; *Salvad., Ucc. Born.* p. 318; *David et. Oust. Ois. Chine,* p. 426; *Dresser, B. Eur.* viii. p. 475, pl.; *Hume and Dav., Str. F.* vi. p. 455; *Hume, Str. F.* viii. pp. 112, 200; *Legge, B. Ceylon,* p. 939; *Oates, B. Br. Burm.* ii. p. 366; *Kelham, Ibis,* 1882, p. 9; *Murray, Vert. Zool., Sind,* p. 226; *Murray, Avif. Brit. Ind.* ii. p. 586, No. 1259. Cirrepidesmus Geoffroyi, *Hume, Str. F.* i. p. 289; *id., Nests and Eggs Ind. B.* p. 571.—The LARGE SAND PLOVER.

In winter plumage, head, neck, nape, back, sides of the breast, scapulars and wing coverts greyish brown; a streak from the base of the mandible under the eye to the ear coverts slightly darker; forehead, a streak above the eye, chin, throat, sides of the neck and rest of the lower parts white; upper tail coverts dull white or pale grey brown; primaries and their coverts dark brown; outer web near the tips and the tips of the secondaries white; longest tertial reaches to between the 3rd and 4th primaries. In summer plumage the forehead, lores, ear coverts and beneath the eye are black; on each side of the forehead is a white spot; the neck and breast rufous; the throat and chin white; head tinged with rufescent, and the upper parts margined with the same; the shafts of the feathers of the back, scapulars and wing coverts in both stages are dark; primaries dark brown; the outer webs of the inner ones white, also the tips of the secondaries.

Length.—8 to 9·25 inches; expanse 17 to 19 inches; wing 5·4 to 5·98; tail 2; bill at front 1; tarsus 1·5; legs greenish; bill black; irides brown.

Hab.—Sind, Beloochistan Coast, Persian Gulf, Bengal, Rajputana, Kutch, Kattiawar and India generally during winter; also Burmah. Extremely common along the sea coast and at the mouths of the Indus in large flocks, where they may be seen running along the sandbanks for small crustacea, insects, molluscs, &c.

258. Ægialitis mongolica (*Pall.*), *Harting, Ibis*, 1870, p. 384; *Salvad., Ucc. Born.* p. 316; *Hume, Str. F.* iii. p. 170; *Blyth, B. Burm.* p. 153; *Armstrong, Str. F.* iv. p. 339; *Legge, B. Ceylon*, p. 942; *Kelham, Ibis*, 1882, p. 10; *Murray, Avif. Brit. Ind.* ii. p. 586, No. 1260. Charadrius mongolicus, *Pall., Reis. Russ. Reichs.* iii. p. 700. Charadrius mongolicus, *Pall., Zoogr. Rosso-Asiati.* ii. p. 136. Charadrius pyrrhothorax, *Temm. in Gould, B. Eur.* pl. 299. Ægialitis pyrrhothorax, *Jerd., B. Ind.* iii. p. 639, No. 847; *Murray, Hdbk., Zool., &c., Sind*, p. 209; *id., Vert. Zool., Sind* p. 226. Cirrepidesmus mongolicus, *Hume, Str. F.* i. p. 230; ii. p. 289; *id., Nests and Eggs Ind. B.* p. 571. Ægialitis mongolus, *Hume and Dav., Str. F.* vi. p. 455; *Oates, Str. F.* x. p. 237.—The LESSER SAND PLOVER.

In both winter and summer plumage similar to *Æ. Geoffroyi*, but smaller in all measurements.

Length.—7 to 7·25 inches; expanse 15 inches; wing 5 inches; tail 1·87; bill at front 0·75; tarsus 1·25. The tertials reach to between the first and second primaries; bill black; irides brown; legs dusky plumbeous.

Hab.—Sind, Beloochistan Coast, Persian Gulf, Afghanistan, and India generally also Burmah and Ceylon, along the sea shore and banks of rivers, not far inland.

259. Ægialitis cantiana (*Lath.*), *Jerd., B. Ind.* iii. p. 647, No. 848; *Armstrong, Str. F.* iv. p. 340; *Dresser, B. Eur.* vii. p. 483. pl.; *Hume and Dav., Str. F.* vi. p. 456; *Legge, B. Ceylon* p. 947; *Oates, Str. F.* x. p. 237; *id., B. Br. Burm.* ii. p. 368; *Murray, Vert. Zool., Sind*, p. 226; *Murray, Avif. Brit. Ind.* ii. p. 587, No. 1261. Charadrius cantianus, *Lath., Ind. Orn. Suppl.* pl. lxvi. Ægialophilus cantianus, *Hume, Str. F.* i. p. 230; *id., Nests and Eggs*, p. 571.—The KENTISH PLOVER.

Male in Winter Plumage.—Forehead, streak over the eye extending to the ear coverts, chin, throat, ring round the neck, breast, abdomen and under tail coverts white; outer tail feathers on each side also white, with a subterminal dusky spot on the inner web; crown, nape, neck behind, a streak from the base of the bill under the eye, cheeks, back, scapulars, sides of breast and tertial earthy or greyish brown, the feathers with darker shafts; in some

(February specimens) the feathers are tinged with rufous, and those on the fore part of the crown, very slightly (absent in most) white-tipped; tail earthy or grey brown, darker subterminally, and all, except the central feathers, tipped pale fulvous or white; primaries dusky brown, 4th, 5th and 6th with a patch of white on their outer webs; secondaries edged and tipped terminally with white; edge of the wing and under wing coverts white.

In nuptial plumage, the white of the forehead extends broadly over the eye and beyond it, behind which on the forecrown is a patch of black followed by a reddish or reddish brown patch, tinged with grey. The streak from the base of the bill through the eye to the ear coverts is black, and there is a large patch of black on each side of the breast; back, scapulars and tertials greyish brown; the 1st primary is the longest; primaries dusky brown; wing coverts grey brown, the greater series tipped with white; secondaries white at their base and tips; under wing coverts, chin, throat and under parts white; the tail is like the back, the middle feathers longest and dusky brown near the tip, the outer ones on each side white.

Length.—6·75 inches; wing 4·3; tail 2; bill at front ·75; bill black; irides brown; feet dusky greenish.

Hab.—Ceylon, South India, Sind, Beloochistan, Persia, Afghanistan, Punjab, N.-W. Provinces, Oudh, Bengal, Rajputana, Kutch, and Guzerat. Abundant along the coast about the Delta of the Irrawaddy, and also at various points in Tenasserim. It is also recorded from Arracan. In Ceylon, Major Legge found it breeding in June and July on the banks of salt lagoons, in the south-east portion of the Island.

260. Ægialitis dubia (*Scop.*), *Salvad.*, *Ucc. Born.* p. 316; *Blyth*, *B. Burm.* p. 153; *David et Oust. Ois. Chine*, p. 429; *Anderson, Yunnan Exped.* p. 676; *Hume, Str. F.* vii. p. 227 (note); *Oates, Str. F.* x. p. 237; *id.*, *B. Br. Burm.* ii. p. 370; *Murray, Avif. Brit. Ind.* ii. p. 588, No. 1262. Charadrius dubius, *Scop.*, *Del. Flor. et Faun. Insub.* ii. p. 93. Charadrius curonicus, *Gm.*, *Syst. Nat.* i. p. 692. Charadrius phillipinus, *Lath.*, *Ind. Orn.* ii. p. 745. Charadrius fluviatilis, *Bechst.*, *Gemeinn Naturg. Deutschl.* iv. p. 422. Ægialitis phillipensis (*Scop.*), *apud. Jerd.*, *B. Ind.* ii. p. 640, No. 849. Ægialitis fluviatilis, *Hume, Str. F.* i. p. 230; ii. p. 289; *id.*, *Nests and Eggs, Ind. B.* p. 572. Ægialitis curonica, *Wald. in Blyth's B. Burm.* p. 154; *Dresser, B. Eur.* vii. p. 491; *Legge, B. Ceylon*, p. 952.—The Lesser Ringed Plover.

A narrow streak above the base of the bill continued behind, under, and through the eye to the ear coverts black; crown of head and ring round the neck black; a patch of white on the forehead above the black frontal streak; chin, throat, and under parts from below the black collar, including the under coverts, white; nape and upper plumage cinereous or greyish brown; primaries dusky brown; tail with the middle feathers paler than the lateral ones, except the outermost on each side, which are white, with a dusky spot on the inner web; under wing coverts white.

Length.—7 to 7·25 inches; wing 4·5; tail 2·5; bill at front 0·56; bill black; rides brown; legs yellowish.

Hab.—Ceylon and throughout India, also throughout Burmah, Sind, Beloochistan, Persia, Afghanistan, E. Turkestan, Nepaul, and Cashmere. Extremely common in rice fields and along the banks of the Indus. Breeds in the Deccan and Central Provinces during April and May. Eggs, three in number, broad ovals, elongated and pointed towards one end, of a fawn, drab or buffy stone colour, speckled and spotted with hieroglyphic-like lines and figures of brownish purple, blackish brown or black. Size 1·1 to 1·23 × 0·8 to 0·87.

261. Ægialitis Jerdoni, *Legge, P. Z. S.* 1880, p. 39; *id., Birds of Ceylon,* p. 956; *Murray, Avif. Brit. Ind.* ii. p. 588, No. 1263. Ægialitis minutus (*Pall.*), *apud. Jerd., B. Ind.* ii. p. 641; *Legge, Str. F.* iii. p. 372; *Hume and Davison, Str. F.* vi. p. 456; *Hume, Str F.* viii. pp. 112, 199; *Oates, Str. F.* x. p. 238; *id., B. Br. Burmah,* ii. p. 371. Ægialitis phillipinus (*Lath.*), *apud. Hume, Str. F.* p. 179.—The LITTLE INDIAN RINGED PLOVER.

Similar to *Æ. dubia,* from which it differs in being smaller, in having the edges of the eyelids swollen and protuberant, and in having the basal half of the lower mandible yellow. Another point of difference, according to Mr. Hume, is that in summer the legs of *Æ. Jerdoni* do not become yellow as in *Æ. dubia.*

Length—6 inches; tail 2 2; wing 4·1; tarsus 9; bill from gape 5·5. The female is rather larger, approaching in size the male of *Æ. dubia.*

The Little Indian Ringed Plover is generally distributed over Burmah, but is nowhere very abundant. Oates procured it near Thayetmyo and also in Southern Pegu, along the banks of the canal. Capt. Wardlaw-Ramsay got it at Tounghoo, and Mr. Davison observed it in Tenasserim about the latitude of Moulmein. It occurs in suitable localities over the whole of India and Ceylon, the Indo-Burmese Countries, and Cochin-China, where Dr. Tiraud procured many specimens near Saigon. Oates says it is probably a constant resident in Burmah, notwithstanding the fact that all his specimens were procured in the winter season. In the rains, when sandbanks are submerged, its area of distribution must become very restricted, and it is likely at this time of the year to escape observation. Major Legge found it breeding in Ceylon. Eggs similar to *Æ. dubia,* both in size and colouration.

Sub-Family, VANELLINÆ.—LAPWINGS.

Bill rather compressed, straight, convex at the tip; nostrils in a long lateral groove; wings pointed and long; tail broad; hind toe short. Generally very active and lively birds. Nearly all winter visitants in India. Feed on worms, slugs, molluscs, &c., either along the sea-shore, or river banks, or the edges of tanks and marshes ; also in ploughed fields.

Gen. **Chettusia**.—*Bp.*

Head not crested ; plumage ashy ; otherwise as in *Vanellus.*

262. Chettusia gregaria, *Pallas, Zoogr.* ii. t. 56 ; *Gould, B. Eur.* pl. 292 ; *Jerd., Birds Ind.* iii. p. 644, No. 852 ; *Str. F.* i. 231 ; iv. 13 ; *Murray, Hbdk., Zool., &c., Sind* p. 210 ; *id., Vert. Zool. Sind,* p. 229 ; *Legge, B. Ceylon,* p. 759 ; *Murray, Avif. Brit. Ind.,* ii. p. 590, No. 1265.—The Black-sided Lapwing.

Forehead, supercilium extending to the occiput, lower belly, vent and under tail coverts white ; top of head, a narrow band from the base of the bill through the eye, and the middle of the abdomen black ; back of neck, back, and scapulars olivaceous brown, tinged greyish ; sides of head and neck pale rufous, passing to greyish or brownish on the breast ; primaries black ; secondaries white ; tail and upper tail coverts white, with a broad subterminal black band, tipped with white ; outermost feathers white.

Length.—12·5 to 13 inches ; wing 8·5 ; tail 3·5 ; tarsus 2·3 ; bill at front 1·2. In the young the black abdominal patch is wanting. The females are much duller than the males in colour.

Hab.—Ceylon, also Sind, Beloochistan, Persia, Afghanistan, Punjab, N. W. Provinces, Oudh, the Concan, Deccan, Kutch, Kattiawar, Rajputana and Central India. Frequents grassy plains in parties of from five to twenty. Its flesh is said to be very delicate.

Gen. **Lobivanellus**.—*Strickl.*

A lappet of skin in front of the eye extending to the base of the bill ; hind toe very small.

263. Lobivanellus indicus, *Bodd., P. E.* 807 ; *Gould, B. E.* pl. 78 ; *Hume, Str. F.* iii. p. 648 ; *id.* vii. p. 67 ; *Hume, Nests and Eggs, Ind. B.* p. 574. Lobivanellus goensis, *Jerd.,* iii. p. 648, No. 855 ; *Murray, Hbdk., Zool., &c., Sind,* p. 211 ; *id., Vert. Zool. Sind,* p. 232 ; *Legge, B. Ceylon,* p. 962 ; *Murray, Avif. Brit. Ind.* ii. p. 592, No. 1269.—The Red-wattled Lapwing or "Did he do it."

Head, nape, back of the neck, chin, throat, neck in front and breast black ; a broad streak from behind the eye along the sides of the neck, also the abdomen and upper and lower tail coverts white ; tail white, with a subterminal dark band and broadly tipped white ; back, scapulars and tertials pale brown ; primaries and their coverts black ; greater wing coverts like the back basally, and broadly edged and tipped with white, forming a conspicuous wing band.

Length.—12·5 to 13 inches; wing 9·5; tail 4·75·, bill at front 1·27; wattles red.

Hab.—Throughout India and Ceylon, Beluchistan, Persia, and Afghanistan. In India it is everywhere common, during both winter and summer, and breeds from April to July. It is an extremely noisy bird, and especially so during the breeding season. Its vulgar name, "Did he do it," is very appropriately given, being its continuous cry, with "Pity to do it," the place resounding with its almost endless echoes, till the intruder is out of reach of its nest. The nest is usually a small depression in the earth, with or without lining of any kind, and made in the vicinity of a marsh. The eggs are generally of a deep green colour, irregularly marked with blotches and streaks of a brownish black.

Gen. **Sarciophorus**.—*Strickl.*

Wattles yellow; bill rather slender; hind toe absent.

264. Sarciophorus bilobus (*Gmel.*), *Jerd., B. Ind.* ii. p. 649; *Blanf., Ibis*, 1870, p. 470; *Blyth, B. Burm.* p. 153. Charadrius malabaricus, *Bodd. Tabl. Pl. Enl.* p. 53; *Murray, Avif. Brit. Ind.* ii. p. 594, No. 1271. Charadrius bilobus, *Gmel., Syst. Nat.* i. p. 691. Lobipluvia malabarica, *Hume, Nests and Eggs Ind. B.* p. 477; *Hume, Str. F.* viii. p. 112; *Legge, B. Ceylon*, p. 966; *Parker, Str. F.* ix. p. 482; *Hume, Str. F.* x. p. 238 (*note*); *Oates, B. Br. Burm.* ii. p. 375; *Murray, Vert. Zool., Sind*, p. 230.—The YELLOW-WATTLED LAPWING.

Breeding Plumage.—Head and nape black; ear coverts white, extending behind the nape; chin and throat black; neck in front and behind, also the back, scapulars and tertiaries pale brown; breast slightly darker, edged with dark brown; rest of the under surface including the upper and lower tail coverts white; tail white, with a black band subterminally and white tip, except three of the lateral tail feathers, which are white, with a subterminal dusky spot on the outer web of the third feather; primaries and their coverts black; the inner webs of the primaries white, decreasing in extent to the inner ones; secondaries basally white, and terminated with black; greater wing coverts like the back, but broadly tipped and edged with white, forming a conspicuous white wing band.

Length.—11 to 11·75 inches; wing 8·25; tail 3·25; bill at front 1; irides brown; bill yellow at the base, the rest black; wattles yellow.

Hab.—Nearly throughout India, Burmah and Ceylon. Both in India and Ceylon it is a resident, frequenting dry stony or grassy plains usually in company with *Cursorius coromandelicus.* Breeds from June to August on the edges of cultivated land. The eggs are not unlike those of *L. indicus*, but smaller, and have a stone colour ground, with deep brown and nearly black blotches. In the winter plumage, the chin and throat and the black edges to the feathers of the breast below are wanting, and the upper plumage is duller or paler brown.

Sub-Family, ÆSACINÆ.—Stone Plovers.

Bill strong and thick; no hind toe; nostrils linear, in a groove near the base of the bill; gonys strongly angulated.

Gen. Æsacus.

Bill long, sub-curved, the lower edge of the under mandible wide in the middle, then curving to a point.

265. Æsacus recurvirostris (*Cuv.*), *G R. Gray, M. G. B.* pl. 142; *Jerd., B. Ind.* iii. p. 652, No. 858; *Hume, Nests and Eggs, Ind. B.* p. 579; *id., Str. F.* ii. p. 182; *Blyth, B. Burm.* p. 152; *Str. F.* vol. v. p. 121; *Hume, Str. F.* vi. p. 458; *Oates, Str. F.* vii. p. 50; *Hume, Str. F.* viii. p. 112; *Legge, B. Ceylon,* p. 974; *Oates, B. Br. Burm.* ii. p. 357; *Murray, Hdbk., Zool., &c., Sind,* p. 211; *id., Vert. Zool. Sind,* p. 231; *Murray, Avif. Brit. Ind.* ii. p. 594, No. 1272 (*Karwanak: Chota Taloor,* Sind).—The Large Stone Plover.

Forehead and a broad line down the sides of the face white; a broad dark streak on each side from the base of the lower mandible; feathers round and behind the eye white, broadly bordered with dark brown; chin, throat, abdomen, and under tail coverts white; top of head, neck behind, back, scapulars and tertials pale brown, the feathers distinctly dark-shafted; neck in front white, in some specimens obtained in April greyish brown; the breast ashy, contrasting with the pure white of the rest of the under surface; primaries black, the first three quills with a patch of white on their terminal thirds, and the last three basally and at tip white, with a subterminal black band; lesser wing coverts dark brown; median and greater coverts pale greyish brown, the latter white tipped; secondaries dark brown, their inner webs white; tail pale brown at base, with a subterminal white band and a broad black tip, except the outermost feather, which is white at the base and more broadly tipped with black; bill black, greenish at the base; irides yellow; legs yellow.

Length.—20 inches; wing 10·5; tail 4·37; tarsus 3·5; bill at front 3, at gape 3·75.

Hab.—Nearly throughout India and Ceylon, along the sea coast and banks of large rivers. From the stomach of a specimen got in the Kurrachee harbour ten calling crabs (*Gelasimus annulipes*) were extracted. Breeds in Ceylon during February. Eggs have been taken by Mr. C. Murray, C.C.S., in S.-E. Ceylon, and by Mr. Parker on an island north of Manaar in the Adam's Bridge line of banks, where it is said to be a permanent resident. The nest is a mere depression in the ground.

Gen. **Œdicnemus.**—*Cuv.*

Bill longer than the head, straight and slightly depressed at the base; culmen raised near the point; mandible angulated beneath; nostrils in the middle of the bill in a longitudinal slit; toes three; tail graduated.

Œdicnemus crepitans.

266. Œdicnemus crepitans, *Temm., Man. d' Orn.* p. 348; *Jerd., B. Ind.* iii. p. 654; *Hume, Str. F.* i. p. 232; *id., Str. F.* iii. p. 182; *Blyth, B. Burm.* p. 152; *Oates, Str. F.* xi. p. 238; *Murray, Vert. Zool. Sind*, p. 232; *Murray, Avif. Brit. Ind.* ii. p. 546, No. 1273. Charadrius œdicnemus, *Linn., Syst. Nat.* i. p. 255. Charadrius scolopax, *S. G. Gmel., Reisse Russ.* iii. p. 87, pl. 16. Œdicnemus indicus, *Salvad., Ass. Soc. Ital. Sc. Nat.* viii. p. 380; *Hume, Nests and Eggs, Ind. B.* p. 581. Œdicnemus scolopax, *Dresser, B. Eur.* vii. p. 401, pl.; *Legge, B. Ceylon*, p. 969; *Oates, B. Br. Burm.* ii. p. 356.—The STONE PLOVER OR BASTARD FLORICAN.

Lores white, with a few brown spots; chin and throat white; a distinct narrow moustachial stripe from the base of the lower mandible; head, neck, back, scapulars and upper tail coverts reddish ashy, each feather with a mesial dusky streak; breast the same as the back; belly white; under tail coverts reddish ashy; tail white basally, all the feathers except the middle ones tipped with black; thigh coverts white; primaries black, the first three quills with a patch of white at their terminal third, and the last three white basally and at tip with a subterminal dark band; edges of the greater wing coverts white, forming a wing band.

Length.—16 inches; wing 9; tail 4·5; bill at front 1·5; irides and orbits yellow: also the legs and feet.

Hab.—Throughout India, including Burmah; also Ceylon and Persia. Affects stony places, waste land, grassy plains, dry river beds and the sides of sloping banks ; runs very swiftly, especially when first surprised, stops short now and again after the manner of *Cursorius isabellinus,* and squats close to the ground, depending for safety on the colour of its plumage, which is like that of the ground. Its flight is strong and steady, but it seldom uses its wings, except when hard pressed; usually turns out in the evening in quest of food, which consists chiefly of worms. The young are said to run from the nest within three hours of their birth. It is not uncommon to meet with parties of this bird in looking for Oobara (*H. Macqueenii*) among Grewia bushes, and perhaps from this circumstance and its lineated plumage it is called the "*chota* or small Taloor." It is, as Jerdon says, a favourite quarry for the Sparrow Hawk and the Besra. Its flesh is as much esteemed almost as that of the Houbara, being highly flavoured. Breeds in Sind from February to April and in Ceylon from May to September. It makes no nest, the eggs being laid in a small depression in the ground, usually sheltered by a stone. The eggs are only two in number, occasionally three have been found.

Family, HÆMATOPODIDÆ, *Bp.*—Sea Plovers.

Feet with three toes, and a very small hind toe; bill long, strong, front half compressed, tip blunt ; wing long and pointed.

Sub-Family, STREPSILINÆ.—*Bp.*

Characters those of the Family; bill slightly curved upwards.

267. Strepsilas interpres (*Linn.*), *Jerd., B. Ind.* ii. p. 656; *Salvad., Ucc. Born.* p. 320; *Blyth, B. Burm.*, p. 154; *Dresser, B. Eur.* vii. p. 555, pl.; *Hume, Str. F.* iv. p. 464; *Murray, Vert. Zool., Sind*, p. 233; *Legge, B. Ceylon*, pp. 900, 1222; *Oates, Str. F.* x. p. 238; *id., B. Br. Burm.* ii. p. 376; *Murray, Avif. Brit. Ind.* ii. p. 597, No. 1274. Cinclus interpres, *Hume, Str. F.* i. p. 233; ii. p. 292. Tringa interpres, *Linn., Syst. Nat.* i. p. 248.—The Turnstone.

Strepsilas interpres.

In winter the crown and hinder part of the head are dusky, edged very narrowly with greyish brown, the lores pale brown, or in some specimens greyish brown; the chin and throat are white, also a patch on each side of the neck, bordered in front along the sides of the white throat patch with dusky or dark brown; upper back, scapulars, rump, breast and sides of the breast dusky or dark brown, according to season, edged with rusty or brownish red; some of the scapulars partly edged with white; tertials long, reaching beyond the fifth quill, edged and tipped with rufous or red brown; lesser wing coverts, like the upper back, white at the shoulder; the secondary or greater coverts tipped with white, forming a conspicuous wing bar; primaries and secondaries black, the inner webs of the former and tips of the latter white; back, lower surface of the body from below the breast, also the thigh and upper and lower tail coverts white; a patch of black on the rump; tail feathers white, with a subterminal black band, except the central ones, which are entirely black. In the summer or breeding plumage, the forehead, a band over the eye, lores and a patch behind the eye are white; the crown of the head is also white, broadly streaked with black. There is also a black streak behind the white frontal patch, continued to the front and below the eye on each side joining the black streak from the lower mandible, and getting lost on the neck, whence springs a black demicollar not extending on the upper surface of the neck, which, like the head, is white with dark streaks; back of neck white, extending down the sides between the black demicollar and sides of the breast; chin white, throat and breast deep black; upper back and scapulars black, the feathers broadly edged and tipped with red rust colour, some wholly so, especially the scapulars; lesser and median wing coverts black, broadly edged and tipped with bright rust colour; the tips of the greater or secondary coverts white, forming a wing band; quills black, the inner webs and part of the outer webs of the last two or three basally white; secondaries like the quills, but broadly white on their inner webs, and also narrowly tipped white; tertials dark brown, edged and tipped with rusty; back, entire lower surface below the breast, and upper tail coverts white; rump with a patch of black; tail as in the winter plumage; irides deep brown; legs orange yellow.

Length.—8 to 8·5 inches; wing 6; tail 2·5.

Hab.—India generally, and Ceylon along the sea-shores, and sometimes inland along the banks of large rivers. Its geographical range is very wide, being found in Europe, America, and Africa, and throughout Asia in suitable localities. In Sind it is extremely common in the Kurrachee harbour and at the mouths of the Indus. It occurs also on the Sambhur lake, and on the banks of the river at Poona, in the Deccan; also on the Beluchistan Coast and in the Persian Gulf. In Ceylon it is rather rare.

Gen. **Dromas**.—*Payk.*

Bill long, lower mandible strongly angulated; tarsus long; wings reach beyond the tip of the tail; feet webbed; hind toe long and slender.

268. Dromas ardeola, *Paykl., Handlist Ac. Vet. Stockhlm.* t. 8; *Jard. and Selby, Ill. Orn.* pl. 157; *Jerd., B. Ind.* iii. p. 658; *Str. F.* ii. p. 293; vii. p. 186; viii. p. 383; *Murray, Hbdk., Zool., &c., Sind,* p. 212; *id., Vert. Zool. Sind,* p. 234; *Legge, B. Ceylon,* p. 986; *Murray, Avif. Brit. Ind.* ii. p. 598, No. 1275.—The CRAB PLOVER.

Whole head, neck all round, chin, throat, breast, entire lower parts, back, upper and lower tail coverts and upper tertials white; generally a dark loreal spot; mantle and interscapulars black; primaries and secondaries black, their inner webs white; greater wing coverts black; tail reddish ashy, as also are some of the tertials near their tips; bill black, 2·5 inches in length; irides brown.

Length.—15 to 15·5 inches; wing 8·75 to 9; tail 2·5.

Hab.—Indian coasts, Ceylon, Africa, Red Sea, Seychelles, Madagascar, Beluchistan Coast and the Persian Gulf. Common in Sind in the Kurrachee harbour. Breeds in the Persian Gulf near Bushire; also in Ceylon. Mr. Hume has given an account of its nidification in vols. vii. and viii. of *Stray Feathers.* There is said to be no nest, and the eggs are laid in a burrow, about 4 feet deep in the loose sand; but whether this was dug by the bird or was that of a crab remained a question, the holes being, it was said, too narrow to admit the bird. Mr. Parker adds to his account of the nesting of these birds in Ceylon (*Str. F. Vol. ix.*) one from his Overseer. He says:—

"I have had no opportunity of visiting the place myself since the 16th June, 1881. I now give his account of them, premising that he has always proved most trustworthy in his accounts of birds and nests, and is particularly observant. The details regarding the nests were noted down by him on the spot. In confirmation of his account, I may add that a few days previously, on another bank, I found an uncompleted nest-hole in a similar position, with footprints which appeared to be those of the Crab-Plover leading into and out of it, and that I saw several of these birds on the sand banks.

"The bank of loose sand in which the nests were found rose several feet out of the water, with a long gradual slope to the windward, and a short steep one on the leeward side; this ended before reaching the water, near which the sand rose little above the water level. In this leeward face 17 nests were excavated in a row, the entrances being from 2 to 3 feet above the flatter gound below. All the holes were nearly horizontal, and were carried in square from the line of the edge of the slope. Their distances apart varied from about 6 to 9 feet. All the tunnels were straight, excepting one which curved considerably to the left; and the majority of the egg-chambers were on one side of the tunnel, a few being in line with it. The entrance tunnels were from 3 to 3½ inches in diameter, and from 4 to 5 feet long, excluding the chambers, which were circular in plan, 6 inches in diameter, and 6 inches high. All contained young, 2 or 3 in number; 5 nests had 3 young ones each.

They were laid on the bare sand, except in one instance where a few bits o sea-weed formed a slight bed for them. The parents, none of which were in the nests, flew around the heads of the party while the nests were being examined, uttering a croaking cry, and seeming much excited. The shape and size of the holes were ascertained by packing them carefully with cloth in advance of the excavation."

Gen. **Hæmatopus**—*Linn.*

Bill straight, long, very slightly bent upwards; nostrils linear in a long cleft; toes three, all placed forward; no hind toe.

269. Hæmatopus ostralegus, *Linn.*, *Syst. Nat.* I, p. 257; *Jerd.*, *B. Ind.* ii. p. 659; *Hume, Str. F.* i. p. 234; *Blyth, B. Burm.* p. 154; *Dresser, B. Eur.* vii. p. 567; *Hume, Str. F.* viii. p. 112; *Legge, B. Ceylon*, p. 987; *Murray, Vert. Zool.*, *Sind*, p. 235; *Murray, Avif. Brit. Ind.* ii. p. 599, No. 1276. Hæmatopus osculans, *Swinh.*, *P. Z. S.* 1871, p. 405; *Dav. et Oust. Ois Chine*, p. 432.—The Oyster Catcher.

Entire head, neck, breast, upper back, scapulars and tail black; lower orbital feathers white; lower back and entire lower parts white, also a ring round the throat; primaries black, the inner webs and part of the outer webs of all except the first two quills white, the white on the outer webs of the innermost primaries spreading to the edges; secondaries basally and narrowly at tip white, with a subterminal black band; greater coverts and some of the secondaries and lower tertiaries white, forming a large wing patch; lesser and primary coverts black; bill orange yellow, or bright scarlet, 3·5 to 3·75 inches long; irides lake red; orbits orange.

Length.—16 to 17 inches; wing 10·5; tail 4; tarsus 2·25.

Hab.—Europe, Siberia, India, Ceylon, Afghanistan, Beloochistan, Persian Gulf, Sind, the Eastern and Western Coasts of India; in fact, has a very wide distribution. Inhabitant of the sea-shores, being seldom found inland. It lives chiefly on molluscs, worms, &c., and is said to easily disengage limpets from the rocks, and to pluck out the oysters from their half-opened shells, with its admirably adapted, wedge-shaped bill. Oyster-Catchers feed in the mornings and evenings and also at night, and are at all times watchful and shy in their habits.

Tribe, LONGIROSTRES.—*Cuv.*

A family of wading birds, in which Cuvier includes the snipe, godwits, ibises, curlews, phalaropes, &c., at the end of which come the avocets. These are nearly all migratory birds, and associate in flocks during winter. The characters by which this tribe is chiefly distinguished are the long slender bill, and long and pointed wing; the hind toe is usually present but wanting in some.

Family, SCOLOPACIDÆ.

Bill long, straight, compressed, soft, the point enlarged; the mandibles furrowed for half their length; upper mandible slightly longer than the lower; nostrils lateral, situated basally in a groove and covered by membrane; feet moderate, slender, three toed, not webbed; hind toe present; plumage varied and rich.

Gen. Scolopax —*Linn,*

Characters same as those of the Family; lower mandible channelled only to the middle; wings long, 1st quill longest; tibia feathered to the knee.

270. Scolopax rusticola, *Linn., Syst. Nat.* i. p. 243; *Jerd., B. Ind.* iii. p. 670; *Blyth, B. Burm,* p. 157; *Anders., Str. F.* iii. p. 356; *Dresser, B. Eur.* vii. p. 615, pl.; *Hume and Dav., Str. F.* vi. p. 458; *Hume, Str. F.* viii. p. 112; *Bingham, Str. F.* viii. p. 196; *Hume and Marsh., Game Birds* iii. p. 311, pl.; *Murray, Avif. Brit. Ind.* ii. p. 603, No. 1781. Scolopax rusticula, *Dav. et Oust. Ois. Chine; Legge, B. Ceylon,* p. 806; *Oates, B. Br. Burm.,* p. 380; *Murray, Vert. Zool., Sind,* p. 238.—The Woodcock.

The peculiar shape of the head of this esteemed bird is almost a sufficient character to identify it among others. The head is more obtusely triangular than round; the eyes are placed above its middle, near the top, and the ears are nearly on a level with the corner of the mouth. Crown of the head ashy, or ashy grey; the nape and back part of the head with four transverse alternate bands of black and rusty red or chestnut brown; a dark streak from the gape to the eye; the orbital feather pale buff; back, scapulars, wing coverts, and upper tail coverts, marbled, spotted, barred, streaked and variegated with black, white, grey, red, brown, rufous and yellow, that it is not possible to describe them with accuracy; chin pale yellowish brown, or nearly white; throat and breast pale brown, barred transversely with dark brown; primaries blackish, with triangular spots of pale reddish brown on both webs; secondaries and tertiaries blackish, but with the markings more elongated and reaching to the shaft. The whole under parts are yellowish white, numerously barred with transverse dark undulating lines; tail black, with spots and bars on both webs, the tips ashy grey above and silvery white below; tibia feathered to the knee. The female is larger, and only differs from the male in this respect and its duller tints.

Length.—14 to 16 inches; wing 8 to 8·25; tail 3·25; bill at front 3 to 3·2 (upper mandible); tarsi 1·5 to 1·8; irides dark brown; legs livid fleshy, as also is the bill with a tinge of grey.

Hab.—Europe, Egypt, India, including Burmah, Ceylon and Java. It is a summer resident on the wooded ranges of the Himalayas, and a winter visitant to the Nilghiris and the higher ranges of Southern India and Ceylon, parts of the Punjab, Nepaul, Sylhet and Bengal, frequenting damp situations, and feeding on worms, snails, slugs, &c. In Sind it is extremely rare, and is known only by two specimens obtained at Kurrachee. It is also said to occur in North Canara and the Concan, also in Persia, Beloochistan and Afghanistan. It breeds in the Himalayas during June, laying buff-coloured eggs blotched with reddish brown.

Gen. **Gallinago.**—*Steph.*

Characters the same as in *Scolopax*. Tibia not feathered to the knee; tail of 16—28 feathers.

271. Gallinago nemoricola (*Hodgs.*), *Jerd., Ill. Ind. Orn.* pl. 9; *id., B. Ind.* iii. p. 672; *Hume, Str. F.* vi. p. 459; *id. and Marsh., Game Birds*, p. 325; *Legge, B. Ceylon*, p. 816; *Murray, Avif. Brit. Ind.* ii. p. 604, No. 1282.—The Wood Snipe.

Top of the head black, with rufous yellow longish markings; upper part of the back black, the feathers margined with pale rufous yellow and often smeared bluish; scapulars the same, some of them with zigzag markings; long dorsal plumes black with zigzag marks of rufous grey, as are most of the wing coverts; winglet and primary coverts dusky black, faintly edged whitish; quills dusky; lower back and upper tail coverts barred reddish and dusky; tail with the centre feathers black at the base and chestnut, with dusky bars towards the tip; laterals dusky with whitish bars; beneath the chin white; the sides of the neck ashy, smeared with buff and blackish; breast ashy, smeared with buff and obscurely barred; the rest of the lower plumage, with the thigh coverts, whitish, with numerous dusky bars; lower tail coverts rufescent, with dusky marks, and the under wing coverts barred black and whitish. Bill reddish brown, paler at base beneath; irides dusky brown; legs plumbeous green. (*Jerd.*)

Length.—12·5 to 13 inches; wing 5·75; tail 2·5; bill at front 2·6; tarsus 1·75.

Hab.—The Himalayas, Nilghiris, Coorg, Wynaad and other elevated regions in Southern India, also Ceylon, affecting brushwood and swampy ground.

272. Gallinago stenura (*Kuhl.*), *Jerd.*, *B. Ind.* iii. p. 674; *G. F. L. Marshall, Str. F.* i. p. 423; *Cripps, Str. F.* i. p. 496; *Hume, Str. F.* ii. p. 294; *Hume and Dav., Str. F.* vi. p. 459; *Murray, Vert. Zool., Sind,* p. 239; *Legge, B. Ceylon,* p. 816; *Oates, B. Br. Burm.* ii. p. 383; *Murray, Avif. Brit. Ind.* ii. p. 605, No. 1284. Scolopax stenura, *Kuhl., Bonap. Osserv. Sulla, sec. Ediz. Regn. Anim. Cuv. Monog. Scolopax,* p. 121.—The PIN-TAIL SNIPE.

Crown dark brown or black, with a mesial longitudinal pale line; face white, divided by a dark line from the nostrils to the eye and extending to the ear coverts; there is also in some specimens a faint line from the ear coverts to in front of the neck on each side, but not meeting; chin and throat white; neck in front and behind pale fawn brown, barred, streaked or spotted with brown or dark brown; sides of the abdomen like the breast, and transversely barred; middle of abdomen white, barred in some specimens; upper back scapulars and wing coverts brown, darker on the mantle and scapulars, the feathers of which are broadly edged with yellow and spotted and streaked with rusty; the scapulars, tertials and wing coverts barred with the same; lower back, rump and upper tail coverts rufescent brown, barred with dusky; under wing lining and axillaries white, distinctly and richly barred with blackish brown; tail basally dark brown, followed by a large oval rufous or rufous buff patch, and a narrow subterminal dark band, tipped pale rufous or the colour of the oval patch; primaries and their coverts, also the secondaries, pale brown or dusky, narrowly margined at the tip with white, both webs unicolorous.

Length.—9·75 to 10 inches; wing 4·8 to 5·4; tail 2 to 2·5; tarsus 1·12 to 1·25. Females are larger. Legs and feet plumbeous with a greenish tinge; irides deep brown; bill 2·2 to 2·6; gape and base of bill greenish; rest of bill pale horny, with a dusky tip for about one-third its terminal length. In the females the bills average from 2·45 to 2·7.

Hab.—Ceylon and nearly throughout India; rare in the Punjab, N.-W. Provinces and Sind, also in Rajputana, Kutch, and Kattiawar; fairly common in N. Guzerat, Central India and Khandeish. In Bombay the Concan generally, and the Deccan, as well in the Nizam's Provinces it is plentiful, also in Lower Bengal, east and west of the Brahmapootra. It is recorded from Arracan, Pegu, Tenasserim, the Andamans and Nicobars, where it is most commonly met with. This snipe is a migrant; arrives in Sind about the middle of August, and leaves about the end of March or middle of April. Rice fields, mud swamps, and the vicinity of large rivers, jheels and tanks, where there are sedges and rushes, are the selected spots of the Pin-tail, at least in Sind.

273. Gallinago scolopacina, *Bonap., Comp. list, B. Eur. and N. Amer.* p. 52; *Jerd., B. Ind.* iii. p. 674, No. 871; *Hume, Nests and Eggs Ind. B.* p. 586; *Hume and Dav., Str. F.* vi. p. 459; *Legge, B. Ceylon,* p. 820; *Murray, Vert. Zool., Sind,* p. 240; *Murray, Avif. Brit. Ind.* ii. p. 606, No. 1285. Scolopax gallinago, *Linn., Syst. Nat.* i. p. 244. Scolopax cœlestis, *Frenzl., Beschr. der Vogel und ihrer Eier in der Gegend Von Wittenberg,* p. 58. Gallinago gallinaria (*Gm.*), *Cripps, Str. F.* vii. p. 302; *Hume, Str. F.* viii. p. 112; *Bingham, Str. F.* viii. p. 112. Gallinago cœlestis, *Dresser, B. Eur.* vii. p. 641, pl.; *Hume and Marsh., Game Birds* iii. p. 359; *Oates, B. Br. Burmah,* p. 381.—The COMMON SNIPE.

Crown of the head black, with a mesial longitudinal white, yellowish, or rusty white line; a superciliary on each side from the base of the upper mandible of the same colour, and a dark streak below it to the eye; sides of the head spotted with dusky grey, tinged ferruginous brown; chin and throat white, or nearly white; neck on the sides and in front yellowish white, spotted with brown; breast white, brown, pale yellowish or ferruginous on the upper part, and spotted with dusky; the sides greyish white, barred with dark brown; back and scapulars velvetty black, the feathers broadly edged with yellow, and barred and spotted with chestnut brown; the yellow edges to the feathers forming four conspicuous lines on the back; upper tail coverts barred with alternate bars of dusky black and pale yellowish brown, somewhat rufescent; the under tail coverts pale yellowish fawn, also barred with dusky or dark brown; the middle of the abdomen is white, in some specimens tinged with pale buffy fawn; axillaries and flanks white, barred with dusky or dark brown, but not so broadly, close and numerous as in *Stenura;* under wing lining white, a few bars only on the edge of the wing; a white patch always conspicuous in the centre of the wing; greater and lesser wing coverts dusky or dark brown, barred with rufescent, and edged and tipped with pale white or cream colour; primaries dusky or dark brown, *the first with its outer web white;* secondaries dusky or dark brown, broadly tipped with white; the outer edges of their inner webs white, and striated with dusky; the inner webs of the primaries also whitish basally and mottled minutely with dusky; tertiaries rufescent, barred with dark brown; tail black at the base, with an oval patch of rusty orange or ferruginous, then a subterminal narrow band, and tipped with buffy or pale reddish yellow, in some specimens white; legs pale green; bill terminally for one-third or more of its length deep brown, the rest basally horny brown with a green and yellowish tinge; its length from gape, of males 2·39 to 2·7; at front 2·43 to 2·75; of females 2·62 to 3·0 at front rather flat at the tip.

Length, Male.—9 to 11 inches; wing 4·9 to 5·5; tail 2·5 to 2·8. *Females* larger.

Hab.—Ceylon and throughout India and Burmah as a winter visitant, also Persia, Beluchistan and Afghanistan. Arrives in Sind about the beginning of September and leaves in April, and with the Jack Snipe is tolerably abundant everywhere. It is a very vigilant bird, and in consequence difficult to shoot, especially in bogs and moist localities where rushes are present. In such retreats, three, four or half-a-dozen may be seen at a time, walking leisurely, with head erect, and constantly on the alert; and at the first note of alarm, they rise, and soon get out of gunshot. This species, it need hardly be mentioned, is held in much esteem for the table.

Gallinago gallinula. The Jud-Cock.

274. Gallinago gallinula (*Linn.*), *Jerd.*, *B. Ind.* iii. p. 676; *Hume, Str. F.* iii. p. 182; *Blyth, B. Burm.* p. 157; *Dav. et Oust. Ois. Chine,* p. 479; *Dresser, B. Eur.* vii. p. 653; *Hume and Dav., Str. F.* vi. p. 459; *Cripps, Str. F.* vii. p. 302; *Hume, Str. F.* viii. p. 112; *Legge, B. Ceylon* p. 828; *Hume and Marsh., Game Birds* iii. p. 373, pl.; *Hume, Str. F.* x. p. 239 (note); *Oates, B. Br. Burm.* ii. p. 384; *Murray, Vert. Zool., Sind,* p. 241; *Murray, Avif. Brit. Ind.* ii. p. 608, No. 1286. Scolopax gallinula, *Linn., Syst. Nat.* i. p. 244.—The Jack Snipe or Jud-Cock.

Crown of the head with a mesial longitudinal black streak from the top of the upper mandible; on each side of this a yellowish or cream-coloured streak extending above the eye as a superciliary, and in some specimens separated from the orbital region by a dark streak; a dusky line from the gape to the eye, and another from below it curving downwards to the ear coverts; the space between the two streaks white or cream colour; chin and throat white, greyish, or pale brown; sides of the head greyish, greyish white, or brownish white, spotted with brown and pale red; neck behind and nape ferruginous or greyish brown, streaked or spotted with dusky; breast pale yellowish brown or dusky, spotted or dashed with darker brown; abdomen white; flanks dashed with brown and pale ferruginous; axillaries pure white, with faint, almost obsolete dusky markings; back and scapulars rich black, with bronze green and purple reflections, the feathers of the upper back and scapulars edged on their outer webs broadly with rich cream yellow, forming two conspicuous longitudinal bands along each side; lower back and rump glossy blue black (specimens in August very narrowly margined with albescent); primaries dusky, the basal half of the first paler, *not white*; inner primaries narrowly margined at the tip with albescent; secondaries dusky, broadly tipped with white; tertiaries dusky on their inner webs, spotted and streaked with reddish or yellowish brown on their outer webs; tail dusky or dark brown, edged near the tips with pale ferruginous; under tail coverts white; legs and feet pale greenish; irides deep brown.

Length.—8·5 inches; bill dark brown at the tip, 1·6 to 1·8 inches in length at front; wing 4 to 4·6 inches; tail 1·8 to 2·2.

Hab.—Ceylon and throughout India, and more plentiful than the common snipe, with which it is generally associated. In Sind small parties begin to arrive about the 26th August, or a few days earlier than the common snipe. It is a difficult bird to flush, seldom rising until nearly trampled upon. It prefers deep cover at all times, but I have often seen them on the oozy, semi-fluid mud of back waters, where there was not even a stubble for cover.

Gen. **Rhynchæa**.—*Cuv.*

Bill shorter than in *Gallinago*, curved downwards at the tip; wings rounded; tarsi long; tibia nearly entirely bare.

275. Rhynchæa capensis, *Linn.*, *Syst. Nat.* 1, p. 246. Rhynchæa Bengalensis, *Jerd.*, *B. Ind.* ii. p. 677; *Hume*, *Nests and Eggs Ind. B.* p. 586; *Salvad.*, *Ucc. Born.* p. 335; *Blyth*, *B. Burm.* p. 157; *Butler*, *Str. F.* iv. p. 15; v. p. 223; *Dav. et Oust. Ois. Chine* p. 480; *Wardlaw-Ramsay*, *Ibis*, 1877, p. 469; *Hume and Dav.*, *Str. F.* vi. p. 459; *Cripps*, *Str. F.* vii. p. 302; *Hume*, *Str. F.* viii. p. 112; *Legge*, *B. Ceylon* p. 800; *Bingham*, *Str. F.* ix. p. 197; *Hume and Marsh.*, *Game Birds* iii. p. 381, pl.; *Oates*, *Str. F.* x. p. 239; *Murray*, *Vert. Zool.*, *Sind*, p. 242; *Oates*, *B. Br. Burm.* ii. p. 386.

Rhynchæa capensis, *Murray, Avif. Brit. Ind.* ii. p. 609, No. 1287.—The Painted Snipe.

Crown of the head with a broad mesial longitudinal line, bordered by dark brown, nearly black feathers, which form a line from the sides of the upper mandible to the nape, where it is broader than in front; a yellowish buff circle round the eye, and a line behind it; chin and throat whitish, the feathers with some faint dusky spots; neck in front and breast olive brown, the feathers with white spots and bars; the feathers on the lower part of the sides and middle of the breast nearly dark brown, forming a dark pectoral band, another similar band below this with a white interspace, but not meeting on the breast; hind neck olivaceous, finely marked with dark transverse striæ; mantle and scapulars dark brown, with dark margined buffy yellow and white bars; wing coverts and tertiaries pale olive, with black margined transverse bands or bars of rufous buff, broader and more conspicuous on the tertiaries; outer web of the first primary grey brown, the rest paler, and all with 5—6 buff or rufous buff ocelli; the interspaces between the basal three ocelli deep black, and between the terminal ones greyish brown; inner webs of primaries with white bars and dark wavy lines and marblings; secondaries ashy grey ocellated with buff on their outer webs, the interspaces basally black, and terminally with dark brown wavy lines; their inner webs, like the primaries, with white bars and wavy lines, and the tips margined with white, the patterns showing through paler on the under side of the wing; tail ashy grey, with buff ocelli on both webs, and tipped with buff; abdomen, vent and under tail coverts white. The female has the lores, sides of the face, upper breast and back of neck chestnut, the feathers edged whitish on the upper breast; back, scapulars and wing coverts, also the tertiaries, dark olive with narrow, close, black striæ, the outermost tertials white, otherwise as in the male. Bill reddish brown; irides deep brown; legs and feet greenish.

Length.—9 to 10 inches; wing 4·9 to 5·2; tail 1·5 to 1·8; bill at front 1·8 to 2 inches.

Hab.—Sind, Kutch, Kattiawar, Rajputana, Central India, Punjab, N.-W. Provinces, British Burmah and Ceylon. Breeds in Sind during May and June, and in nearly all localities where it occurs.

Gen. **Limicola**.—*Koch.*

Characters same as *Rhynchæa*; bill broad and depressed.

276. Limicola platyrhyncha (*Temm.*), *Salvad., Ucc. Born.* p. 322; *Dresser, B. Eur.* viii. p. 3, pl.; *Hume and Dav., Str. F.* vi. p. 461; *Hume, Str. F.* viii. p. 113; *Legge, B. Ceylon,* p. 896; *Oates, Str. F.* x p. 240; *id., B. Br. Burm.* ii. p. 387; *Murray, Vert. Zool., Sind,* p. 252; *Murray, Avif. Brit. Ind.* ii. p. 610, No. 1288. Tringa platyrhyncha, *Temm., Man d'Orn.* p. 398; *Jerd., B. Ind.* ii. p. 692, No. 886; *Blyth, B. Burm.* p. 156.—The Broad-billed Sandpiper.

In winter, the crown of the head, back, scapulars and wing coverts are ashy brown, tinged with rufous; neck and cheeks white, spotted with brown; primaries and tail brown, the latter edged with pale reddish ashy; lower parts white; the flanks, breast and under tail coverts tinged with rufous. In summer dress the Broad-billed Sandpiper has the crown of the head brownish black, varied with greyish; the neck on the sides and in front greyish white, with black spots, and tinged with buffy; chin white, with a few dark spots; lower back black, with fulvous white or rufous margins to the feathers.

Length.—6·5 to 6·75 inches; wing 3·9 to 4·32; bill at front 1·27 to 1·37; tarsi 0·94; irides deep brown; legs and feet dusky black.

Hab.—Ceylon and the Indian Coast generally. Occurs commonly at Kurrachee and along the Mekran Coast, also at Kutch and in Bengal. Recorded from Arracan, also from Pegu, and Amherst in Tenasserim. Frequents sea-coasts and tidal rivers.

Sub-Family, TRINGINÆ,—Stints, &c.

Bill rather long, flat and wide, keeled near the tip, somewhat flexible; nostrils in a groove, extending two-thirds the length of the bill; wings long; toes divided or narrowly webbed.

Gen. Tringa.—*Linn.*

Toes edged by membrane; wings with the first quill longest; bill straight or slightly bent and obtuse at the extremity.

277. Tringa minuta, *Leisl. Nacht., zu Bechst. Naturg. Deutsch* i. p. 74; *Jerd., B. Ind.* ii. p. 690, No. 884; *Dresser, B. Eur.* viii. p. 29, pl.; *Hume, Str. F.* i. p. 242; *Legge, Str. F.* i. p. 491; *id., B. Ceylon*, p. 884; *Murray, Vert. Zool., Sind*, p. 257; *Oates, B. Br. Burm.* ii. p. 389; *Murray, Avif. Brif. Ind.* ii. p. 611, No. 1290.—The Little Stint.

In winter the upper parts are ashy or pale earthy brown, the feathers of the back, scapulars, tertials and lesser and median wing coverts mesially dusky or dark brown, and in some very narrowly edged with whitish. There is a dark spot in front of the eye, and a pale white supercilium; the chin, throat, centre of the breast and rest of the under surface, including the vent, axillaries and under tail coverts, are white; sides of the breast ashy brown; primaries mostly white shafted, dusky brown, slightly paler on their inner webs; secondaries white basally, and also narrowly tipped with white; greater wing coverts tipped with white, forming a conspicuous wing band; rump, upper tail coverts and two central tail feathers dusky or dark brown; lateral tail feathers pale ashy.

Length.—6·6 inches; expanse 13·1; tail 2·3; tarsus 0·9; wing 3·8; bill at front 0·6; irides deep brown; legs black.

Hab.—Nearly throughout Europe, India and Ceylon, also Java, Formosa, Australia and China. In Sind, along the coast; also in the Kurrachee harbour; inland on the large pieces of water and on the Munchur Lake, this Little Stint is extremely common, also on the Mekran Coast, the Punjab, N.-W. Provinces, Oudh, Bengal, Burmah, and Ceylon. Occurs in Persia, Beluchistan (Quetta), Afghanistan, and in fact has a very wide distribution. In the Concan, Deccan and Southern India generally it is equally abundant.

278. Tringa subminuta, *Midd., Sib. Reise. Vog.* p. 222. *Taf.*, xix. p. 6; *Legge, B. Ceylon*, p. 889; *Oates, B. Br. Burm.* ii. p. 391; *Murray, Avif. Brit. Ind.* ii p. 612, No. 1291. Tringa damacensis (*Horsf.*), *apud Hume, Str. F.* i. p. 243. Tringa salina (*Pall.*), *apud Legge, Str. F.* i. p. 491; *Dresser, B. Eur.* viii. p. 33; *Blyth and Wald., B. Burm.*, p. 156. Tringa ruficollis (*Pall.*), *apud. Wald. Trans. Zool. Soc.* ix. p. 234; *Hume, Str. F.* viii. p. 113; *Oates, Str. F.* x. p. 240.—The LONG-TOED STINT.

Summer Plumage.—Forehead, top of head and nape dark brown, each feather with an edging of rich rufous on the terminal half; lores, cheek and ear coverts the same; an albescent patch in front of the eye above the lores; upper part of the throat pure white; lower throat streaked with small marks of pale rufous brown; sides of throat, neck, upper breast and sides of body pale rufous brown, each feather with a central dark brown streak; lower breast, abdomen and vent pure white; under tail coverts white, each feather with a long, narrow central brown streak; thighs rufescent; upper neck mixed brown and pale rufous; whole upper plumage, including the scapulars and tertiaries, rich blackish brown, each feather broadly tipped with bright rufous; rump and upper tail coverts glossy black, few of the feathers of the latter obsoletely tipped white; centre tail feathers black, edged with rufous, the others pale brown, tipped and margined internally with white; axillaries white, a little brown at their bases; under wing coverts pale brown, edged with white; shaft of first quill sordid whity brown, those of the others dark hair brown; primaries and secondaries dark brown, all tipped with white except the first six primaries; all the primaries except the first three with a median narrow margin of white on the outer web; upper coverts brown, all more or less tipped and margined with dull white. In winter it resembles *T. minuta* in general appearance, but the upper plumage is darker; the forehead and face where white in *T. minuta* are streaked with brown in *T. subminuta*; the greater wing coverts and secondaries are very narrowly tipped with white, and the sides of the neck and the chest are thickly marked with brown streaks. Iris brown; bill olive-brown; legs and toes pale brown; claws nearly black.

Length.—6·2 inches; tail 1·4; wing 3·7; tarsus 0·8; middle toe and claw nearly an inch; bill from gape 7·5. The female is of the same size. This Stint may be recognized by the great length of its toes, the middle one, including its claw, measuring frequently little short of an inch in length. It resembles *T. minuta* in having the outer tail feathers brown, but differs in having the shafts of all the primaries brown, except that of the first quill, which is dull white. From *T. Temmincki* it may be separated by the colour of its outer tail feathers as well as by its long toes. (*Oates.*)

Hab.—Arracan, Pegu and Tenasserim. Found also seasonally in N.-E. Siberia through China and Mongolia to Burmah, extending on the west to Bengal, the Eastern Coast of India and Ceylon, and ranging southwards to the Malay Peninsula, Java, Borneo, Celebes, and the Phillipines.

279. Tringa Temmincki, *Leisler, Nacht. zu Bechst. Naturg. Deutsch.* i. p. 63; *Jerd., B. Ind.* iii. p. 691; *Dresser, B. Eur.* viii. p. 45, pl.; *Hume, Str. F* i. p. 244; iii. p. 183; *Blyth, B. Burm.* p. 156; *David et Oust. Ois. Chine,* p. 43; *Hume and Dav., Str. F.* vi. p. 461; *Hume, Str. F.* viii. p. 113; *Legge, B. Ceylon,* p. 892; *Murray, Vert. Zool., Sind,* p. 251, *Oates, B. Br. Burm.* ii. p. 392; *Murray, Avif. Brit. Ind.* ii. p. 613, No. 1292.—TEMMINCK'S, or the WHITE-TAILED STINT.

Upper parts as in *minuta*; chin, throat and supercilia white; a dark spot in front of the eye; breast and lower neck ashy brown; belly, vent and under tail coverts white; four central tail feathers dusky brown, the rest white; legs pale horny green, or greenish olive.

Length.—6 to 6·25 inches; wing 3·8; bill at front 0·7; irides deep brown.

Hab.—As the last and associated with it everywhere.

280. Tringa subarquata, *Gould, Nov. Comm. Petrop.* xix. p. 471, t. xviii.; *Jerd., B. Ind.* ii. p. 689; *Blyth, B. Burm.,* p. 156; *Dresser, B. Eur.* viii. p. 59; *Hume and Dav., Str. F.* vi. p. 460; *Legge, B. Ceylon,* p. 879; *Oates, Str. F.* x. p. 240; *Murray, Avif. Brit. Ind.* ii. p. 615, Pelidna subarquata, *Oates, B. Br. Burm.* ii. p. 394; *Salvad., Ucc. Born.* p. 322.—The CURLEW STINT.

Winter Plumage.—Bill curved downwards. Head, on the crown and sides, back of the neck and nape light greyish brown, streaked with darker brown and dusky black, with an olivaceous gloss; face and supercilia white, and a dark streak from the gape to the eye; sides of the neck and in front greyish, streaked with brown; breast the same; abdomen and upper and lower tail coverts white; back, scapulars and wing coverts ashy-brown, the shafts darker; tail ashy grey, edged with white; primaries dusky brown, also the secondaries, which are tipped with white; axillaries white; lesser coverts grey, the shafts darker. Bill black; irides brown; legs dusky grey.

Length.—8 to 10 inches; wing 5; tail 1·75; bill at front 1·6. In summer plumage the forehead is whitish, mixed with pale reddish brown; supercilia pale yellowish white; chin white; head, neck and nape ferruginous with dark margins; throat, breast and upper abdomen chestnut; in a specimen obtained on 20th May the feathers are all narrowly edged with white; back, scapulars and tertiaries black; also the lesser coverts, the feathers edged with chestnut.

Hab.—India generally, and Ceylon, also Beluchistan, Persia and Afghanistan. Recorded from Cashmere and Egypt, also from Australia and Java. Common also in the low tidal portions of the plains between the Pegu and Sittang rivers and in the Irrawady delta. Recorded also from Arracan and the Tenasserim Coast. Found commonly along the Sind and Mekran Coasts and on the large dhunds, not far inland. It occurs in Kutch and Kattiawar and on the Bombay Coast in some numbers, also in the Kurrachee harbour.

Gen. Machetes—*Cuv.*

Bill straight; first and second quills of wing longest; outer toe united as far as the first joint; hind toe short and elevated.

281. Machetes pugnax (*Linn.*), *Dresser, B. Eur.* viii. p. 87, pl.; *Hume and Dav., Str. F.* vi. p. 460; *Hume, Str. F.* viii. p. 112; *Scully, Str. F.* viii. p. 357; *Legge, B. Ceylon* p. 873; *Oates, Str. F.* x. p. 240; *Murray, Avif. Brit. Ind.* ii. p. 616, No. 1296. Tringa pugnax, *Linn., Syst. Nat.* i. p. 247. Philomachus pugnax, *Jerd., B. Ind.* ii. p. 687; *Murray, Vert. Zool., Sind*, p. 248.—The Ruff.

In winter the plumage of these birds is very variable, the upper parts are from pale earthy to rich brown, the feathers with black or dark brown central spots and fulvous edges; the head, nape and neck behind paler; chin and throat white; neck in front and breast pale earthy or grey brown, the feathers margined at the tip with white; abdomen, vent and under tail coverts white; primaries dark brown; secondaries paler, edged and margined at the tip with white; greater coverts tipped white, forming a wing band; the lesser and median ones black, edged with rufous or reddish brown, also the greater coverts in some stages. The plumage is so variable, that out of 50 skins or more, no two birds would be found alike. During summer or in their breeding plumage the males acquire a ruff, which is very variously coloured and stands erect behind the head, the face is covered with reddish tubercles and the upper parts and breast marked with transverse bars. Bill dusky; irides brown; legs fleshy yellow.

Length.—12 to 12·5 inches; wing 7·25; tail 2·5; bill at front 1·3; tarsus 2.

Hab.—Throughout India and Ceylon, and in great numbers during winter. Occurs also in Beloochistan, Persia and Afghanistan. Breeds in Europe. During spring on their return to the breeding grounds, generally the fens, they become very pugnacious, the females being "*causa terrima belli.*" Being polygamous, the Ruffs, on hearing the cry of a female or seeing one, immediately rouses itself, and begins a fight with others; their combats are described as being both desperate and long; at the end of the fight the female, it is said, becomes the mate or prize of the victor. Buffon says—"They not only contend with each other in a single recounter, but they advance to combat in marshalled ranks." "Their actions in fighting," according to Selby, "are very similar to those of a game cock, with the head lowered, and the beak held in a horizontal position, the ruff and every feather distended, the former sweeping the ground as a shield;" and he adds "that in such feuds their contests are often attended by fatal consequences."

Gen. **Calidris**.—*Cuv.*

Hind toe wanting, otherwise as in *Tringa*.

282. Calidris arenaria (*Linn.*), *Jerd., B. Ind.* iii. p. 694; *Hume, Str. F.* i. p. 244; *Salvad., Ucc. Born.* p. 322; *Armstrong, Str. F.* iv. p. 343; *Hume, Str. F.* iv. p. 465; *Dresser, B. Eur.* viii. p. 101, pl.; *Hume, Str. F.* viii. p. 113; *Oates, Str. F.* x. p. 240; *Murray. Vert. Zool., Sind,* p. 252; *Oates, B. Br. Burm.* ii. p. 398; *Murray, Avif. Brit. Ind.* ii. p. 617, No. 1297.—The SANDERLING.

In winter the forehead, lores, cheeks, chin, throat, breast, neck in front, belly, thighs, vent and under tail coverts white; crown of the head, sides of the neck and breast, back and scapulars cinereous or ashy brown, the feathers with dark shafts; shoulders and edge of the wing dark brown; median and greater coverts like the back, dark shafted and tipped white; primaries dark brown, all white shafted; their inner webs ashy, and the four middle ones white on their outer webs, forming in the closed wing a wedge-shaped spot; secondaries brown or dusky, tipped with white; rump and upper tail coverts brown, edged with white; tail brownish ash, edged with white, the two central feathers darker than the rest; bill black, 0·93 to 1 inch in length.

Length.—7·5; wing 4·75; tail 2; tarsus 0·92; irides deep brown; legs black.

Hab.—Kurrachee (Sind), Beluchistan Coast, Persia, Ceylon, Kutch, Guzerat, Concan and South India, also the Laccadives, the West Coast, and the Irrawaddy delta. Extremely abundant everywhere, associated with the Stints on the sea-shore.

Sub.-Family, TOTANINÆ.—SAND-PIPERS.

Bill grooved as far as, or beyond, the middle, moderately long, the tip hard and pointed; nostrils narrow; hind toe long and slender, barely reaching the ground.

Gen **Actitis**.—*Ill.*

Groove of the bill extending quite to the tip; 1st quill of wing longest.

283. Actitis hypoleucos (*Linn.*), *Jerd., B. Ind.* iii. p. 699, No. 893; *Blyth, B. Burm.* p. 155; *Murray, Vert. Zool., Sind,* p. 253; *Murray, Avif. Brit. Ind.* ii. p. 619, No. 1300. Tringa hypoleucos, *Linn., Syst. Nat.* i. p. 250. Tringoides hypoleucos, *Hume, Nests and Eggs Ind. B.* p. 588; *id., Str. F.* ii. p. 299; iii. p. 183; *Salvad., Ucc. Born.* p. 326; *Hume, Str. F.* viii. p. 113; *Legge, B. Ceylon,* p. 867; *Oates, Str. F.* x. p. 241. Totanus hypoleucos, *Dresser, B. Eur.* viii. p. 127; *Bingham, Str. F.* ix. p. 197.—The COMMON SAND-PIPER.

Forehead, crown, nape and back of the head ashy brown, streaked with dark narrow lines; supercilium white, also the orbital ring, chin and throat; sides of the face pale ashy with brown streaks; middle of the breast white, the sides mottled or streaked with brown, or entirely brown; back, scapulars, tertiaries and lesser wing coverts ashy brown, glossed with green, and with fine transverse dark lines; greater wing coverts ashy brown, tipped with white, which with the white bases of the secondaries form a conspicuous wing band; primaries and their coverts dark brown, the latter tipped with white, and all, except the first primary, and sometimes the second also, with a large white spot on their inner webs; lower back, rump and upper tail coverts ashy brown, with dark transverse bars; four central feathers of the tail like the back, the rest tipped with white and with dark spots along their edges; beneath white. Bill dusky; irides brown; legs pale green.

Length—7 to 8 inches; wing 4·5; tail 2·4; tarsus 0·97 to 1; bill 0·97.

Hab.—Affects the sea coast as well as lakes, &c., inland. Occurs throughout India, Burmah, Malacca, Ceylon, &c.; also Beloochistan, Persia, and Afghanistan.

284. Actitis ochropus (*Linn.*), *Jerd.*, *B. Ind.* iii. p. 698, No. 892; *Blyth*, *B. Burm.* p. 155; *Murray*, *Vert. Zool.*, *Sind*, p. 254. Tringa ocrophus, *Linn.*, *Syst. Nat.* i. p. 250; *Murray*, *Avif. Brit. Ind.* ii. p. 619, No. 1301. Totanus ochropus, *Hume*, *Str. F.* iii. p. 183; *Dresser*, *B. Eur.* viii. p. 135, pl.; *David et Oust. Ois. Chine*, p. 465; *Hume and Dav.*, *Str. F.* vi. p. 462; *Legge*, *B. Ceylon*, p. 862. Helodromas ochropus, *List.*, *Br. B. Brit. Orn. Union.*; *Oates*, *B. Br. Burm.* ii. p. 400.—The Green Sandpiper.

In winter plumage the forehead, crown, nape and back of the neck are deep or dusky brown, the feathers streaked with white; a dark streak from the base of the bill to the eye and a white one above it; chin and throat white; back and scapulars olive brown, or brown glossed with greenish, each feather edged with small roundish spots, the spots on the scapulars distinctly margined behind with deep brown; primaries and their coverts and secondaries deep brown, none of them white-shafted; wing coverts dusky brown; *axillaries dusky or dark brown, with narrow oblique white bars;* abdomen, vent and upper and under tail coverts white; tail white, broadly barred with deep brown, the middle feathers having four bars, and those next to them decreasing in number, the outer feathers on each side being pure white with sometimes a dusky subterminal spot on the outer web; legs and feet greenish grey; bill black; irides brown.

Length.—9·5 to 10 inches; wing 5·5 to 6; tail 3; bill 1·37; tarsus nearly 1·5.

Hab.—Throughout India, Ceylon, Beloochistan, Persia and Afghanistan, frequenting the banks of rivers, edges of lakes and large sheets of water; a winter visitant, seldom seen along the sea coast. Occurs throughout Europe, Asia and Africa, extending to Burmah and the Malay Peninsula.

Gen. **Totanus.**—*Bech.*

Bill slightly curved at tip, groove half the length of the bill ; tarsi with narrow scales in front, otherwise as in *Actitis.*

285. Totanus glareola (*Gm.*), *Salvad., Ucc. Born.* p. 327 ; *Hume, Str. F.* iii. p. 183 ; *Dresser, B. Eur.* viii. p. 143, pl. ; *Legge, B. Ceylon,* p. 857 ; *Murray, Avif. Brit. Ind.* ii. p. 620, No. 1302. Tringa glareola, *Gm., Syst. Nat.* i. p. 677. Actitis glareola, *Jerd., B. Ind.* iii. p. 697 ; *Blyth, B. Burm.* p. 155. Rhyacophila glareola, *Hume and Dav., Str. F.* vi. p. 462 ; *Hume, Str. F.* vii. p. 488 ; viii. p. 113 ; *Oates, Str. F.* x. p. 240.—The Wood Sand-Piper.

Winter Plumage.—Crown of the head, forehead, nape and back of the neck dusky brown, the feathers with narrow white or greyish edgings ; a dark streak from the base of the bill to the eye, and a white one above it ; chin and throat rather sullied ; foreneck and breast the same, but suffused with ashy brown, darker on the sides, where the feathers are indistinctly dark shafted ; back, scapulars and tertials dusky, the feathers edged with white or greyish white spots ; axillaries white, with transverse oblique dusky brown spots ; primaries, secondaries and their coverts dusky brown, the shaft of the first quill and the tips of the later inner ones white ; the greater wing coverts margined and tipped with white ; rump, upper and lower tail coverts and abdomen white ; tail with the central feathers longest and barred with black and white alternately, the barrings oblique, the rest less broadly barred and decreasing on the outer ones to dusky markings on the outer webs only ; legs pale olive green ; irides deep brown.

Length.—8·5 to 9 inches ; wing 5 ; tail 2 ; bill at front 1·2 ; tarsus 1·5.

Hab.—Common nearly throughout India, also Ceylon, and in Beloochistan, Persian Gulf, and Afghanistan during winter.

286. Totanus canescens (*Gmel.*), *Dresser, B. Eur.* viii. p. 173, pl. ; *Hume, Str. F.* i. p. 247 ; iii. p. 183 ; *Armstrong, Str. F.* iv. p. 344 ; *Oates, B. Br. Burm.* ii. p. 402 ; *Murray, Avif. Brit. Ind.* ii. p. 621, No. 1303. Scolopax totanus, *Linn., Syst. Nat.* i. p. 245. Scolopax canescens, *Gmel., Syst. Nat.* i. p. 668. Totanus glottis (*Linn.*), *Jerd., B. Ind.* iii. p. 700 ; *Blyth, B. Burm.* p. 155 ; *Legge, B. Ceylon,* p. 840 ; *Murray, Vert. Zool., Sind,* p. 255.—The Green Shanks.

In winter the forehead, except a few brown streaks in the middle, sides of the face, chin, throat, neck in front, and entire lower parts, including the under tail coverts, are white, also the lower back, rump and upper tail coverts ; a dark streak from the base of the bill to the eye ; crown of the head, sides of the neck and nape dusky, the feathers streaked whitish or greyish white ; sides of the breast white, mottled with ashy brown; upper back and scapulars brown, the feathers edged whitish; scapulars distinctly dark shafted, also the tertiaries; primaries dark brown, the shaft of the first quill white, and the edges and tips of the inner ones also white ; secondaries ashy brown, tipped white; tail white with narrow transverse dark bars, the outer ones nearly pure white; bill slightly curved upwards, dusky greenish, 2·2 in length ; irides brown.

Length.—14 to 14·5 inches ; wing 2·2 ; tail 3·75 ; tarsus 2·75.

Hab.—India generally during winter, also Burmah and Ceylon, along the sea coast, lakes, rivers, &c. Widely distributed. Recorded from N.-E. Europe, Red Sea, Africa and Australia. Like all the *Totaninæ* it is excellent eating.

287. Totanus stagnatilis, *Bechst., Orn. Taschenb.* ii. p. 292; *Jerd., B. Ind.* iii. p. 701 ; *Dresser, B. Eur.* viii. p. 151, pl.; *Blyth, B. Burm.* p. 155; *Hume, Str. F.* viii. p. 113; *Murray, Vert. Zool., Sind,* p. 255; *Legge, B. Ceylon,* p. 844; *Oates, B. Br. Burm.* ii. p. 403, *Murray, Avif. Brit. Ind.* ii. p. 621, No. 1304.—The LITTLE GREEN SHANK.

In winter the plumage of the upper parts are the same as *Totanus glottis ;* shoulder of the wing black; entire under parts white ; sides of the breast not so much spotted or streaked with dark brown; bill not curved upwards as in *glottis ;* tail banded white and dusky.

Length.—10·5 inches; wing 5·25; tail 2 ; bill 1·62; tarsus 2·25; legs pale green; irides brown.

Hab.—The same as *glottis* and usually associated with it. Mr. Parker, of Ceylon, who is a very keen observer, says that he must defend this engaging Green Shank from the charge of being a greedy feeder; "intent on gobbling up everything that comes in its way in the shortest possible time." He says :

"When the bird is seen from a considerable distance and without glasses, it exhibits great apparent greediness; but, so far as I observed, it is by no means really greedy. It may be seen preening itself in the midst of its food supply. But more positive evidence than this is forthcoming. In the Mannar district, where I for sometime lived in a small house at the edge of a rice field, I often, with my binoculars, watched these birds feeding in the field at a distance of 10 or 15 yards. The water in which they fed was muddy, and the insects in it were invisible. The bird, therefore, inserted its bill deeply in the water, and moved it very rapidly from side to side to disturb them. On their rising to the surface it rushed after and secured them."

288. Totanus calidris (*Linn.*), *Jerdon, B. Ind.* ii. p. 702; *Hume, Str. F.* i. p. 248; ii. p. 299; *Blyth, B. Burm.* p. 155; *Dresser, B. Eur.* viii.

p. 157, pl.; *Hume, Str. F.* viii. p. 113; *Legge, B. Ceylon*, p. 852; *Murray, Vert. Zool., Sind*, p. 256; *Oates, B. Br. Burm.* ii. p. 404; *Murray, Avif. Brit. Ind.* ii. p. 622, No. 1305. Scolopax calidris, *Linn., Syst. Nat.* i. p. 245. —The RED SHANK.

Winter Plumage.—Forehead, crown, nape, back of the neck, upper back and scapulars cinereous or glossy olive brown, the feathers on the back and scapulars dark shafted; supercilium and orbital ring white; chin and throat white; sides of the face greyish white, with narrow brown streaks; neck in front and breast greyish white, with dusky or greyish brown linear markings; primaries dusky, their inner webs white; the first quill white shafted, and some of the inner ones white tipped; secondaries white; tertials like the back; wing coverts olive brown, the greater ones tipped with white; axillaries, under wing coverts, abdomen, vent and under tail coverts white; lower back white; upper tail coverts and tail white, barred with dusky.

Length.—11·5 inches; tail 2·7; wing 6·45; bill at front 1·7 to 1·9, reddish at the base, its terminal half dark brown; tarsus 2; irides brown; legs red.

Hab.—India generally and Ceylon during winter. Sind, Persia, Beloochistan and Afghanistan, Southern and Western India, N.-W. Provinces, Oudh, and Burmah generally. Breeds in the North of Europe.

289. Totanus fuscus (*Linn.*), *Jerd., B. Ind.* iii. p. 702, No. 896; *Hume, Str. F.* i. p. 248; *Dresser, B. Eur.* viii. p. 165, pl.; *Cockburn, Str. F.* iv. p. 509; *Hume, Str. F.* viii. p. 113; *Legge, B. Ceylon*, p. 848; *Murray, Vert. Zool., Sind*, pp. 255, 256; *Murray, Avif. Brit. Ind.* ii. p. 622, No. 1306. —The SPOTTED RED SHANK.

In winter the forehead, crown, nape, back of the neck and upper back ashy grey, finely streaked with dusky; supercilium white, and a dusky streak from the base of the bill to the eye; chin and throat white, sides of face white with some fine dusky streaks; breast and under parts mottled and barred with dingy ash brown and dull fulvous, or greyish white; upper back, scapulars, shoulder of wing and lesser coverts a glossy olive brown, darker on the upper back and tertiaries, all the feathers spotted on the edges with white; the wing coverts also tipped with white; lower back white; rump barred with undulating lines of ashy brown and white; tail also barred the same; primaries dark brown, the inner ones pale brown, tipped and mottled with white; secondaries barred white and pale brown; legs deep orange red; bill blackish orange at the base beneath.

Length.—13 inches; wing 6·75; tail 2·5; tarsus 2·8; bill 2·4.

Hab.—Throughout India during winter, also Ceylon and the Province of Burmah; usually solitary or in very small parties. It is a sea-shore bird, but is also found on the edges of rivers, lakes, mud-banks, &c. It is said to swim well, and also to dive when in danger.

Gen. **Terekia**.—*Bonap.*

Bill recurved, long, slender; tarsi short; toes narrowly webbed; hind toe less than half the size of the outer one.

290. Terekia cinerea, *Guldenst., N. Comm. Soc. Imp. Petrop.* xix. p. 473, t. xix; *Jerd., B. Ind.* iii. p. 682, No. 876; *Dresser, B. Eur.* viii. p. 195, pl.; *Hume, Str. F.* i. p. 237; ii. p. 296; *Armstrong, Str. F* iv. p. 341; *Hume and Dav., Str. F.* vi. p. 460; *Legge, B. Ceylon*, p. 836; *Murray, Vert. Zool., Sind*, p. 246; *Murray, Avif. Brit. Ind.* ii. p. 624, No. 1309.—The TEREK SAND-PIPER or PIGMY CURLEW.

Forehead, chin, throat, sides of the head and neck in front greyish white with ashy striæ; back, scapulars, tertials, rump and upper tail coverts ashy brown, the feathers with dark shafts; feathers of the median wing coverts narrowly tipped with white; primaries dark brown, the 1st quill with a white shaft; secondaries dusky, broadly terminated with white; shoulder and edge of the wing dark brown; tail concolorous with the back, the tips bordered with white; sides of the breast ashy grey, the feathers mesially darker; lower breast, abdomen, vent and under tail coverts white. In an advanced stage of plumage—March—the entire upper parts are darker, the scapulars are terminated with black, the chin and throat become pale ashy grey, and there is a distinct fulvous orbital ring, the forehead and face become fulvescent, and the inner primaries tipped with white.

Length.—10 inches; wing 5 to 5·2; bill at front 1·9 to 2, orange at the base, the rest dusky or dark brown; tail 2 to 2·5; legs and feet pale orange; irides brown.

Hab.—Sind, the Mekran Coast, Kutch, Kattiawar, N. Guzerat, Northern and Southern India, Burmah and Ceylon generally, affecting the sea coast, creeks and channels during winter. Found also in N.-E. Europe and New South Wales. According to Jerdon it breeds in Northern Asia, and is extensively distributed over Europe, Asia and Australia.

Sub-Family, LIMOSINÆ.—GODWITS.

Bill much lengthened, curved or straight from the base, or turned upwards; tail short and even; toes long, united at the base.

Gen. **Limosa**, *Briss.*

Bill sub-curved at the tip, inclined upwards; 1st quill longest; outer toe united to the middle as far as the first joint; tibia bare for more than two-thirds its length; tarsi long; hind toe half the length of the outermost.

291. Limosa ægocephala (*Linn.*), *Jerd., B. Ind.* ii. p. 681; *Dresser, B. Eur.* viii. p. 211; *Blyth, B. Burm.* p. 155; *Hume, Str. F.* vii. p. 356; *Legge, B. Ceylon*, p. 832; *Hume and Marsh., Game Birds*, iii. p. 409, pl.; *Oates, Str. F.* x. p. 239; *Murray, Vert. Zool., Sind*, p. 243; *Oates, B. Br.*

Burm. ii. p. 409; *Murray, Avif. Brit. Ind.* ii. p. 626, No. 1311.—The BLACK-TAILED GODWIT.

In winter plumage, the entire head, back of the neck, back, scapulars and breast pale earthy grey, darker on the scapulars and back, where each feather is dark shafted; superciliary stripe, chin, throat, also the abdomen and under tail coverts white; rump white, the feathers of the upper tail coverts black for their terminal half; tail white at the base, the terminal two-thirds tipped black, the outer feathers for their terminal third only, and all more or less narrowly tipped white; primaries and their coverts dusky brown, the inner primaries basally white, and all white on their inner webs; secondaries dusky terminally, white basally, and some of the tertials with their outer webs white; greater wing coverts broadly edged with white, also some of the hinder primary coverts; shoulder of wing dusky brown, also the lower back; neck in front and flanks greyish white.

Length.—16 to 18 inches; wing 7·75 to 8·75; tail 3·12 to 3·5; bill at front 3·7 to 4·5, of a dull reddish colour at base and dusky at the tip; legs dusky greenish; irides dark brown.

Hab.—Nearly throughout India and Ceylon during winter. Rare in Southern India, the Concan and the Deccan. Common in Kutch, Kattiawar and Rajputana, also in Beloochistan, Persia and Afghanistan. In Sind this species is numerous, everywhere behind the tall grass, along the edges of the Munchur Lake, in the shallow pools, wading up to their body, and often swimming across deeper spots if beyond its standing depth. It is held in much esteem for the table, being equal to Jack and the Common Snipe, especially those which have been feeding in rice fields.

Sub-Family, NUMENINÆ.

Bill very long, slender, arcuate and compressed, with the tip hard and rather obtuse.

Gen. Numenius.—*Linn.*

Characters same as those of the Sub-Family; bill curved from the base; upper mandible slightly the longer; tarsi narrowly scutate transversely; hind toe slender with a rudimentary nail.

292. Numenius phæopus (*Linn.*), *Jerd., B. Ind.* iii. p. 684; *Dresser, B. Eur.* viii. p. 227, pl.; *Hume, Str. F.* ii. p. 297; iii. p. 182; *Blyth, B. Burm.* p. 155; *Hume, Str. F.* viii. p. 112; *Legge, Birds, Ceylon,* p. 910; *Oates, Str. F.* x. p. 240; *Murray, Vert. Zool., Sind,* p. 247; *Oates, B. Br. Burm.* ii. p. 411; *Murray, Avif. Brit. Ind.* ii. p. 629, No. 1313. Scolopax phæopus, *Linn., Syst. Nat.* p. 243.—The WHIMBREL.

Forehead and crown dusky brown with a mesial longitudinal streak; lores dark brown; superciliary stripe white, extending from the upper side of the

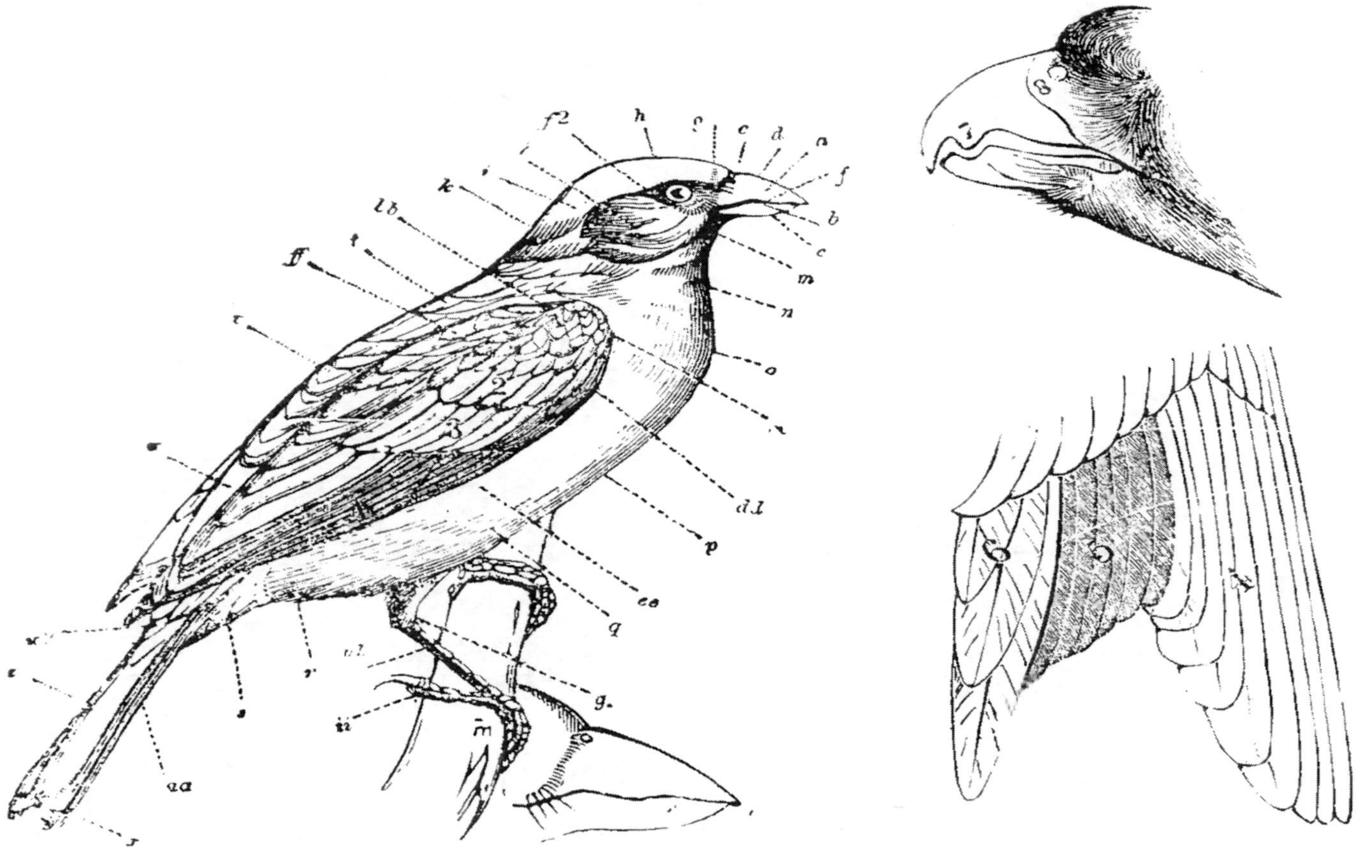

a Upper mandible.
b Lower mandible.
c Nostrils.
d Culmen or keel.
e Gonys.
f Margins of mandibles or commissure.
f2 Ophthalmic region, or orbit.
g Forehead.
h Crown.
i Sinciput or hind head.
k Nape.
l Ear-coverts.
m Chin or mentum.
n Throat.
o Breast.
p The body.
q Belly or abdomen.
r Vent.
s Under-tail coverts.

t Interscapularies or back.
v Lower back.
w Rump.
w2 Upper-tail coverts.
x Tail feathers.
z Central or median tail feathers.
aa Lateral tail feathers.
bb Shoulder of wing.
cc Shoulder joint (lesser wing coverts.)
dd Axilla, or edge of wing.
ee Spurious wing or primary coverts.
ff Scapulars.
gg Thigh or tibia.
hh Tarsus.
ii Toes.

1 Lesser coverts.
2 Median coverts.
3 Greater coverts.
4 Primaries.
5 Secondaries.
6 Tertiaries.
7 Festoon
8 Cere.

upper mandible ; orbital feathers white ; chin and throat white ; neck in front and behind, and breast, ochreous white, the feathers with a dark central longitudinal streak ; flanks, axillaries and under wing coverts white, barred with pale brown, as also are the rump and upper tail coverts; tail brown, brownish white or grey brown, with 6—7 bars of dark brown ; lower back white ; upper back, scapulars and wing coverts dusky or deep brown, the feathers edged pale white or dirty fulvous ; primaries dusky or dark brown, their inner webs as well as both webs of the secondaries with white bars, not reaching the shaft.

Hab.—Throughout most parts of India, Burmah and Ceylon ; also Europe, N. Africa, Egypt and Abyssinia.

Affects the same situations as the Curlew, in small flocks. In the Kurrachee harbour it is oftener seen than the Curlew, and is more shy and difficult to approach, but unlike the Curlew it is often seen on open barren tracts, or sandy flats, far inland, in flocks of 3, 4 or half-a-dozen. It is common all along the sea coast, mud-banks and sandy islands of estuaries of rivers, or of the sea, and like the Curlew is a fine bird for the table ; Jerdon says it is perhaps better than the Curlew, and has been called the "Woodcock" of Bengal.

Numenius arquatus. The Curlew.

293. Numenius arquatus (*Linn.*), *Jerd.*, *B. Ind.* iii. p. 683, No. 877 ; *Dresser*, *B. Eur.* viii. p. 243, pl. ; *Hume*, *Str. F.* iii. p. 182 ; *Murray*, *Vert. Zool.*, *Sind*, p. 247 ; *Oates*, *B. Br. Burm.* ii. p. 412 ; *Murray*, *Avif. Brit. Ind.* ii. p. 630, No. 1314. Scolopax arquata, *Linn.*, *Syst. Nat.* 1. p. 242. Numenius lineatus, *Cuv.*, *Regn. Anim.* 1. p. 521 ; *Blyth. B. Burm.* 1. p. 155 ; *Legge*, *B. Ceylon*, p. 906.—The CURLEW.

Head, neck behind and in front, also the breast, rufescent ashy, or rufescent grey brown, the feathers with dark mesial longitudinal shaft-streaks; upper back and scapulars varying from dusky to dark brown, the feathers broadly edged fulvous or pale rufous; upper abdomen white, the feathers with dusky shaft-streaks; lower abdomen, vent and under tail coverts pure white; lower back white; rump and upper tail coverts also white, with dark shafts; tail fulvous white with transverse brown bars; chin and throat white, also a small space above the eye in some specimens; first five primaries and edge of wing dark brown, their inner webs mottled with white; secondaries dusky brown, with transverse white bars on both webs half across only, the dark markings forming a rude saw, the edges and tips of the feathers white.

Length.—21 to 26 inches; wing 12 to 12·5; tail 4·5; bill at front 5 to 7·25; irides dark brown; legs and feet bluish grey.

Hab.—Throughout most parts of Europe, India, Burmah, Ceylon, N. Africa, Egypt, Abyssinia and Palestine. Common along the sea coast and back waters in great numbers during winter; also along the banks of the Indus and Punjab rivers, and on all large inland sheets of water.

Sub-Family, RECURVIROSTRINÆ.—*Bp.*

Nostrils narrow, membranous; tail short and rounded; tarsi long, covered with reticulated scales; bill long and slender, recurved in one genus.

Gen. **Recurvirostra**.—*Linn.*

Bill long, thin, the keel flattened, the tips turned upwards; toes united by webs; hind toe short.

294. Recurvirostra, avocetta (*Linn.*), *Bodd.*, *P. E.* 353; *Gould, B. Eur.* pl. 289; *Jerd.*, *B. Ind.* iii. p. 248; *Murray, Hdbk., Zool., &c., Sind*, p. 222; *id.*, *Vert. Zool*, *Sind*, p. 258; *Legge, B. Ceylon*, p. 925; *Murray, Avif. Brit. Ind.* ii. p. 631, No. 1316.—The AVOCET, SCOOPER or CROOKED-BILL.

Forehead in some specimens faintly white, otherwise black; crown, lores, nape and back of the neck black; scapulars, lesser wing coverts and upper tertials black; primaries black, some of the inner ones with their inner webs white; secondaries and some of the tertials white; chin, throat, neck in front, lower neck behind, lower back, rump, upper tail coverts and entire under surface white.

Length.—17 to 18 inches; bill 3·5, curved upwards, black; wing 8·5; tail 3; tarsus 3·62; irides red brown; legs pale bluish grey.

Hab.—Throughout India and Ceylon during winter; S.-E. Europe, Lower Egypt, Senegal and Persia. Common in Sind, in large flocks inland, on almost every large sheet of water, especially on the Munchur Lake and along the edges of tanks, &c. Occasionally affects the sea coast and Kurrachee harbour, but by preference the inland waters. Breeds probably in Persia. In Upper India the Avocet is less common; in Kutch, Jodhpore and N. Guzerat rather rare.

Gen. **Himantopus**.—*Briss.*

Bill long and straight; toes webbed only at the base; nostrils linear; hind toe wanting.

295. Himantopus candidus (*Linn.*), *Bonnat. Tabl. Encyl. et. Meth., Orn.* i, p. 24; *Jerd., B. Ind.* ii. p. 704; *Hume, Ibis,* 1870, p. 146; *Dresser, B. Eur.* vii. p. 587, pl.; *Hume and Dav., Str. F.* vi. p. 464; viii. p. 113; *Legge, B. Ceylon* p. 919; *Murray, Avif. Brit. Ind.* ii. p. 632, No. 1317. Himantopus intermedius, *Hume, Nests and Eggs Ind. B.* p. 589 Charadrius himantopus, *Linn., Syst. Nat.* i. p. 255.—The STILT.

In winter plumage, the forehead, lores, chin, throat, entire lower parts, lower back and rump white; crown of the head dusky or dark ash; neck behind ashy grey, the feathers tipped with white; upper back and scapulars brown, the feathers with pale tippings; primaries dark brown, the inner ones tipped white; secondaries also with white tips; central tail feathers very pale grey, the rest white. In the breeding plumage the primaries, secondaries, scapulars tertiaries and upper back are rich glossy black, with greenish reflections; the crown of the head dusky or dark brown, spreading over and below the eyes.

Length.—15 to 16 inches; wing 8·5 to 9; tail 3; bill black, reddish at the base, 2·75 inches in length; tarsi 4·5 to 5·5; irides blood red; legs and feet lake red.

Hab.—India generally, also Burmah and Ceylon, in large flocks during winter, frequenting margins of lakes and ponds, also banks of rivers. Breeds in Sind during June in the Narra Districts. Eggs 2—4 in number, of a pale blue colour, spotted and speckled with dark brown and olive green. Incubation 18 to 20 days. The young are said to leave the nest immediately they are hatched, and hide themselves among very scanty cover. Found also in Beloochistan, Afghanistan, Persia, and probably Mesopotamia.

Family, PARRIDÆ.

Bill long, one and a half or twice the length of the head; nostrils lateral; wing spurred or with a tubercle; tarsi long; toes long with long claws.

Sub-Family, PARRINÆ.

General characters of the Family; feet large; toes and claws very long and thin, to enable the members to walk on marshy or oozy ground and aquatic plants.

Gen. **Hydrophasianus**.—*Wagl.*

1st and 2nd quill of wing equal and longest; primaries with lanceolate appendage to the tips; bill more slender than in *Metopidius*; forehead without a frontal shield; tail long; central feathers much elongated in the breeding season.

296. Hydrophasianus chirurgus (*Scop.*), *Jerd.*, *B. Ind.* iii. p. 709; *Hume, Nests and Eggs Ind. B* p. 592; *id.*, *Str. F.* iii. p. 185; *Salvad.*, *Ucc. Born.* p. 343; *David et Oust. Ois. Chine*, p. 483; *Legge*, *B. Ceylon*, p. 914; *Oates*, *B. Br. Burm.* ii. p. 360; *Murray*, *Vert. Zool.*, *Sind*, p. 259. Tringa chirurgus, *Scop. Del. Flor. et. Faun. Insubr.* ii. p. 92. Parra sinensis (*Gm.*), *Syst. Nat.* 1, p. 709. Hydrophasianus sinensis, *Blyth and Wald.*, *B. Burm.* p. 157.—The PHEASANT-TAILED JACANA.

In winter plumage, the forehead, crown, a streak from the base of the bill through the eye, extending down each side of the neck on to the breast and forming a pectoral gorget; also the back of the neck dusky or pale hair brown, the feathers on the forehead and crown tipped with white; supercilium white, and a pale golden yellow line from behind the eye; back, scapulars, tertials and lesser wing coverts glossy olive, or pale hair brown; the lower back, rump, upper tail coverts and central tail feathers slightly darker, and the lesser wing coverts mottled and barred transversely with white. Shoulder of wing spurred. First primary with an appendage, the shaft of 2nd, 3rd and 4th quills also in some specimens hair like at the tip, all dark brown, and, except the first and second, broadly white on their inner and outer webs; greater coverts and secondaries, chin, throat, neck in front, abdomen, vent and under tail coverts white; tail 3·5 to 4 inches. In breeding plumage the for ehead, crown, entire face, chin, throat and neck in front white. There is a black patch on the nape; and the neck behind is shining golden yellow, edged on the sides with black; back, scapulars and tertiaries dark olive brown, with purplish reflections; rump and upper tail coverts bronzed dark brown; tail black; breast and entire lower parts dark or deep dusky brown; shoulder of wing spurred; wing coverts white; primaries as in the winter plumage.

Length.—18 to 20 inches; irides dark brown; bill plumbeous at the base and tipped greenish, 1·25 in length; tail 10 to 11 inches; wing 8 to 8·5; tarsus 2·12; middle toe and claw 3 inches; hind toe and claw 2 inches.

Hab.—Throughout India, Ceylon and British Burmah. Common in Sind on the Munchur and other Lakes, also in the Punjab and N.-W. Provinces. Breeds in India generally from May to September, making a large floating nest. Eggs, pear-shaped, of a beautiful bronze colour.

Family, RALLIDÆ.

Bill compressed, short, pointed, thick, wedge-shaped; nostrils in a short groove; legs stout; toes long; tarsi moderate; tail short.

Sub-Family, GALLINULINÆ.—WATER-HENS.

Bill with the keel advancing on the forehead, where there is usually a casque; toes long and slender or bordered by a scolloped web; wings short and rounded; hind toe long.

Gen. **Porphyrio**.—*Briss.*

Bill very thick ; casque large ; mid-toe as long as tarsi, slender, not fringed with web.

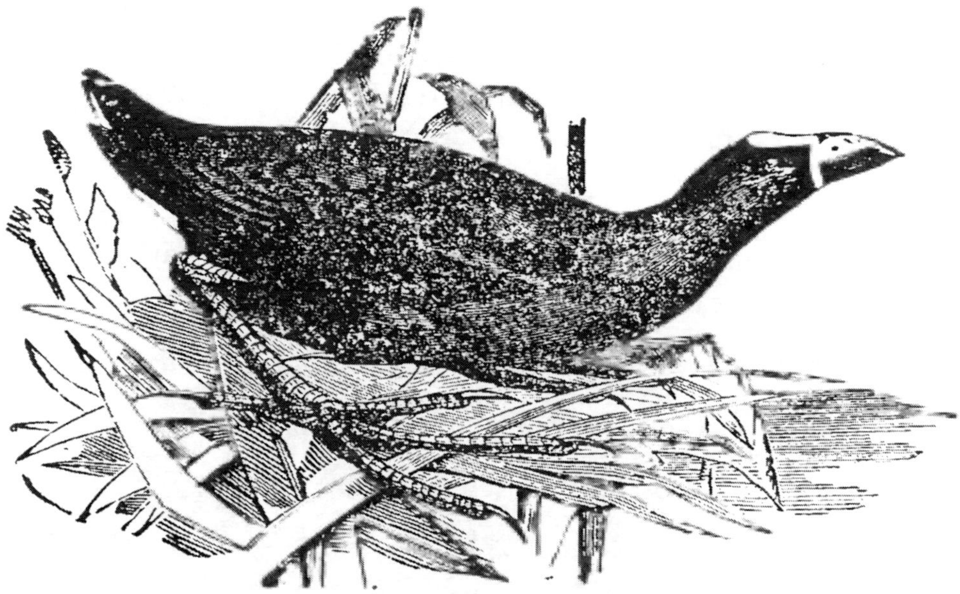

Porphyrio poliocephalus. The Purple Coot.

297. Porphyrio poliocephalus (*Lath.*), *Jerd.*, *B. Ind.* iii. p. 713 ; *Blyth*, *B. Burm.* p. 161 ; *Butler*, *Str. F.* iv. p. 20 ; *Oates*, *Str. F.* vi. p. 165 ; *Elliot*, *Str. F.* vii. p. 22; *Legge*, *B. Ceylon* p. 795 ; *Murray*, *Vert. Zool.*, *Sind*, p. 260; *Oates*, *B. Br. Burm.* ii. p. 351 ; *Murray*, *Avif. Brit. Ind.* ii. p. 635, No. 1320. *Parker*, *Ibis* 1886, p. 187. Gallinula poliocephala *Lath.*, *Ind. Orn. Suppl.* p. lxviii. Porphyrio neglectus, *Scheg. Mus. P. B. Ralli*, p. 53 ; *Hume*, *Str F.* i. p. 249 ; *Hume*, *Nests and Eggs* p. 594 ; *id. Str. F.* iii. p. 185.—The Purple Coot.

Occiput and nape, lores, and round the eyes greyish, clouded with purple ; cheeks, chin and throat the same, but with more of a purple tinge; neck in front and breast pale bluish ; lower breast, abdomen, flanks, vent and thigh coverts dark purplish blue ; under tail coverts white ; back of neck, back, rump, and upper tail coverts purplish blue; scapulars, wing coverts and outer webs of primaries pale greenish blue, the inner webs of primaries, secondaries and tertials dark brown or black; tail black, the feathers on the outer web edged with bluish.

"Nestling black-haired ; bill white ; the base and sides crimson ; casque purple or lilac; legs reddish purple; toes lilac ; spur on winglet prominent." (*Parker MS.*)

Length.—18 inches ; wing 10 to 10·2; tail 4·5 ; bill at gape 1·62 ; tarsi 3·62 ; mid-toe 3·62 ; casque and spot at base of bill cherry red; bill red ; irides red ; legs crimson.

Hab.—Throughout India, Ceylon and British Burmah ; also in Persia, Beloochistan and Afghanistan. Common in Sind in suitable localities, but I do not believe they are anywhere as numerous as on the Munchur Lake, where, among the rushes, they are with the Bald Coot simply innumerable.

Breeds in Ceylon in the Manaar district in January and February. In Sind and India generally from May to September, making a nest of rushes, &c., in the reedy grass. Eggs prettily marked on a greenish ground with spots, blotches and streaks of a reddish colour, lake red or rich red.

Gen. **Fulica**.

Bill moderate ; nostrils lateral ; casque small ; wing with a tubercle at the shoulder ; tail short ; toes with lobate membrane.

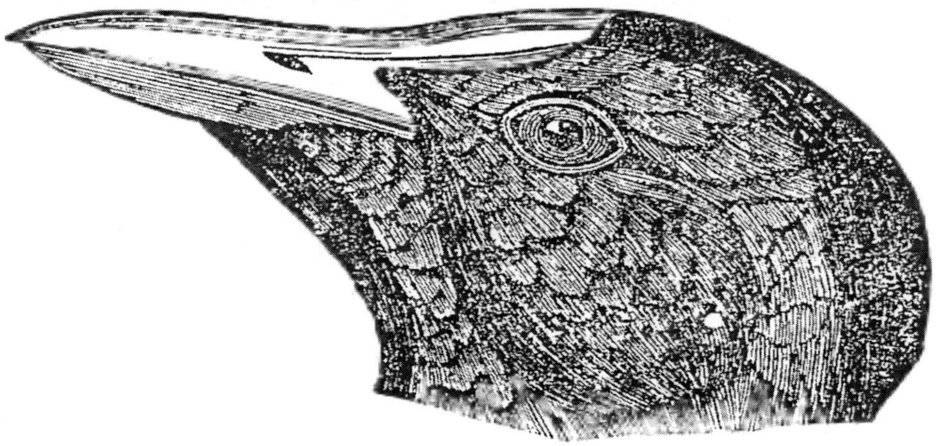

Fulica atra.

298. Fulica atra, *Linn., Syst. Nat.* 1, p. 257 ; *Jerd., B. Ind.* iii. p. 715 ; *Hume, Str. F.* i. p. 249 ; *id., Nests and Eggs* p. 595 ; *Blyth, B. Burm.* p. 162 ; *Wardlaw-Ramsay, Ibis,* 1887, p. 472 ; *Dresser, B. Eur.* vii. p. 327 ; *Murray, Vert. Zool., Sind,* p. 261 ; *Oates, B. Br. Burm.* ii. p. 352 ; *Murray, Avif. Brit. Ind.* ii. p. 636, No. 1321.—The Bald Coot.

Upper plumage black ; hoary, dark ash, lead colour or dusky brown below ; a spot below the eye, and the outer edge of the wings white ; frontal disc or casque white ; also the bill, which in the breeding season is tinged pale red ; irides blood red ; legs dull green, with a yellow, green, and red garter in the breeding season.

Length.—15 to 16 inches ; wing 7·5 to 7·75 ; tail 2 ; bill at gape 1·41.

Hab.—Throughout India, Ceylon and British Burmah ; also Europe (central and south), Egypt, Assam, Nepaul, Persia, Beloochistan and Afghanistan. Not recorded by Colonel Legge, but has been since found as a straggler in the interior of the Central Province, in 1887, but is very rare. In India, it is numerous in suitable localities, but on the Munchur Lake in Sind, as Mr. Hume says (*Str. F.* vol. i. 249), "they would have to be counted not by thousands, but by hundreds of thousands. * * * You can shoot nothing without knocking over some of these wretched coots." He also adds "that in no part of the world has he even seen such incredible multitudes of coot as are met with in Sind ; in the Munchur Lake *par excellence*."

Gen. **Hypotænidia**.—*Reich.*

Bill moderately long, straight or slightly arched, compressed at the base, cylindrical at the tip ; upper mandible grooved for two-thirds of its length ; nostrils lateral, linear, and situated in the groove ; lower part of tibia naked ; tarsi long and robust ; toes long and slender, three before and one behind ; anterior toes entirely divided ; wings short and rounded ; 3rd and 4th quills longest.

299. Hypotænidia striata (*Linn.*), *Wald., Trans. Zool. Soc.* viii. p. 95 ; *Hume, Nests and Eggs Ind. B.* p. 605 ; *Blyth, B. Burm.* p. 161 ; *Hume, Str. F.* iii. p. 189 ; *Hume and Dav., Str. F.* vi. p. 468 ; *Legge, B. Ceylon*, p. 775 ; *Hume and Marsh., Game Birds* ii. p. 245, pl. ; *Oates, Br. Burm.* ii. p. 339 ; *Murray, Avif. Brit. Ind.* ii. p. 638, No. 1323. Rallus striatus, *Linn., Syst. Nat.* i. p. 262.—The BLUE-BREASTED BANDED RAIL.

Top of head, nape and hind neck chestnut ; upper plumage, including the wing coverts and tertiaries, blackish brown, each feather broadly edged with olive brown and barred with white ; primaries, secondaries and tail dark brown, barred with white ; lores, cheeks, ear coverts, sides of the neck, foreneck and breast bluish grey, tinged somewhat with rufescent ; sides of the body, lower abdomen, vent, under tail and thigh coverts, also the under wing coverts, dark brown, barred with white ; centre of abdomen dull white ; bill rosy pink on the basal half ; remainder horn colour or yellowish green ; irides red ; legs and feet dull greenish or olive brown. The young has not the chestnut head and bluish breast.

Length.—9·8 to 11·5 inches ; wing 4·5 to 5 ; tail 1·5 to 2·25 ; tarsus 1·3 to 1·62 ; bill from gape 1·32 to 1·82.

Hab.—Southern India, along the bases of the Neilgherries, the Wynaad, Malabar Coast, Southern Konkan, in the Rutnagherry districts and Southern Ceylon. It also occurs in Lower Bengal in the deltaic districts, in the neighbourhood of Calcutta too, as well as in Sylhet, Cachar, Khasia Hills, and the Assam Valley to Sadiya. In Arracan it is said to be fairly common, while in Burmah, Oates says, it is found throughout the whole province, Tenasserim included. Breeds in all localities where they occur, from May to October, making a small nest of grass on the ground near water, surrounded by thick vegetation. Eggs, seven in number, of a pinkish stone colour blotched with pale purple. In length they vary from 1·28 to 1·41 inches, and from 0·98 to 1·13 in width.

Gen. **Rallus**.—*Linn.*

Bill moderately long, straight or slightly curved at tip; shoulder with a small spur; other characters as in *Hypotænidia.*

300. Rallus indicus, *Blyth, J. A. S. B.* xviii. p. 820; *Jerd., B. Ind.* iii. p. 726; *Hume, Str. F.* iii. p. 416; *Blyth, B. Burm.* p. 162; *David et Oust. Ois. Chine* p. 489; *Legge, B. Ceylon* p. 778; *Hume, Str. F.* viii. p. 113; *Hume and Marsh., Game Birds* ii. p 257, pl.; *Oates, B. Br. Burm.* ii. p. 342; *Murray, Avif. Brit. Ind.* ii. p. 638, No. 1324.—The INDIAN WATER RAIL.

Above, including the sides of the neck, scapulars and tertiaries olive brown, sometimes with a ruddy tinge, each feather with a broad black mesial streak; a dark streak from the lores continued under the eye to the ear coverts; a broad white supercilium from above this to the nape; wing coverts dark olive brown, some of them tipped with whitish, and all broadly edged with ruddy; primaries and secondaries brown, some of the inner ones margined with ruddy; chin and throat plumbeous; cheeks, foreneck, breast and centre of abdomen plumbeous ashy, the feathers more or less fringed with ruddy; sides of the abdomen and of the body, axillaries and vent blackish, barred with white; under tail coverts white, each feather with a large black central patch; under wing coverts black, with white margins. Bill dull red, dusky on the culmen and tip; irides red brown; legs and feet dirty pale green.

Length.—10 to 10·5 inches; tail 2·2; wing 5·2; tarsus 1·6; bill from gape 1·6.

Hab.—Ceylon and from Bengal to Nepaul. Recorded from Arracan by Blyth. Frequents patches of rush and grass at the edges of swamps and ditches. A migrant to India. According to Jerdon it is a rare bird in Central and Southern India, and has chiefly been found in the cold season.

Gen. **Rallina**.—*Reich.*

Base of bill not prolonged over the forehead, feet shorter than in the Rails.

301. Rallina euryzonoides (*Lafresn.*), *Tweed., P. Z. S.* 1877, p. 767; *Legge, B. Ceylon*, p. 772; *Hume, Str. F.* viii. p. 113; *Hume and Marsh., Game Birds* ii. p. 237, pl.; *Oates, Str. F.* x. p. 242; *Oates, B. Br. Burm.* ii. p. 340; *Murray, Avif. Brit. Ind.* ii. p. 639. No. 1325. Gallinula euryzonoides, *Lafresn., Rev. Zool.* 1845, p. 368. Rallus zeylanicus, *Gm., Syst. Nat.* I. p. 716. Porzana ceylonica, *Blyth, Cat. B. Mus. As. Soc. Beng.* p. 285; *Jerd., B. Ind.* ii. p. 725; *Hume, Str. F.* i. p. 440; iii. p. 188; *Bourdillon in Blyth's B. Burm.* p. 162. Rallina ceylonica, *Wald. in Blyth's B. Burm.*, p. 162.—The BANDED CRAKE.

Whole head, neck all round and breast chestnut; upper plumage, wings and tail rich olive brown with a ruddy tinge on the back, rump, scapulars and tertiaries; quills with white bars on the inner webs; chin and throat whitish; abdomen, vent, under tail coverts, sides of the body and under wing coverts broadly barred with dark brown and white. Bill with the base of the upper mandible and the greater portion of the lower green; remainder of bill dark brown; irides blood red; eyelids grey; legs black. (*Oates.*)

Length.—10 inches; tail 2·2; wing 5·5; tarsus 1·75; bill from gape 1·3.

Hab.—In Ceylon it arrives in October in considerable numbers, coming to that island in an exhausted condition. It remains there till June.

Mr. Parker observes "that when slightly alarmed they walk with the head and tail erect, taking dainty little steps, as though on tip-toe. When more frightened they run a short distance with the head down, but the tail still erect, then take a few slow cautious steps followed by another little run. When passing through the sedge they make a clucking noise." This is, of course, the general habits of all Rails.

Thayetmyo in British Burmah, where Oates had a live specimen sent to him by Colonel Horace Browne.

It has been found in Sikkim, Bhootan, Nepaul and in Goomsoor in the Ganjam Districts. Mr. Hume got a specimen from the Assamboo Hills, and Mr. Brooks in Cawnpore. It has also been got near Cuttack and in Mainpuri near Lucknow. About Calcutta, and also near Madras, it has also been obtained, but all these were apparently stragglers during severe winter.

Sub-Family, RALLINÆ.—RAILS.

Forehead with a nude shield; bill compressed, slender; toes shorter than in the *Gallinules*; shoulder of wing with a tubercle or short spur.

Gen. **Porzana**.—*Vieill.*

Wings moderate, rounded; tail short; toes long, about the length of the tarsus.

302. Porzana Bailloni (*Vieill.*), *Dresser, B. Eur.* vii. p. 275, pl.; *Legge, B. Ceylon*, p. 766; *Hume and Dav., Str. F.* vi. p. 467; *Scully, Str. F.* viii. p. 358; *Hume and Marsh., Game Birds* ii. p. 203, pl.; *Oates, B. Br. Burm.* ii. p. 344; *Murray, Avif. Brit. Ind.* ii. p. 641, No. 1328. Rallus Bailloni, *Nouv. Dict. d'Hist. Nat.* xxviii. p. 548. Crex pygmæa, *Naum. Naturg. Vog. Deutschl.* ix. p 567. Porzana pygmæa, *Jerd., B. Ind.* iii. p. 723, No. 910; *Murray, Vert. Zool., Sind*, p. 264. Zaporna pygmæa, *Hume, Nests and Eggs, Ind. B.* p. 603.—The PIGMY RAIL OR BAILLON'S CRAKE.

Head and hind neck wood brown; back, scapulars and wing coverts yellowish brown with an olive tinge, the feathers with numerous irregular, white, black-edged spots; supercilium, cheeks, chin and throat grey; breast and upper abdomen bluish grey; the sides, vent and under tail coverts black, with transverse white bars; primaries dusky brown; outer web of 1st quill yellowish white; secondaries with zigzag white lines bordered with black; tertiaries yellowish brown, with a tinge of olive, spotted or streaked irregularly with white, which have edgings of black; tail dusky brown; bill dark green; irides reddish; legs fleshy brown.

Length.—7 to 7·75 inches; wing 3·67; tail 1·75 to 2; bill at front 0·62; tarsus 1·0; mid-toe and claw 1·5.

Hab.—Sind, Punjab, N.-W. Provinces and Oudh, also Bengal, Nepaul, Rajputana, Kutch, Guzerat, Concan and Deccan, and generally throughout India and Burmah, also Ceylon. It is also an inhabitant of Beloochistan and Afghanistan, and probably Persia also. In Central and Southern India it is said to be not uncommon.

Breeds during July and August in the plains of Upper India and in the lower ranges of the Himalayas about rice swamps and marshy pools. Eggs, six in number, oval, slightly pointed towards one end; a pale olive stone colour or greenish drab, thickly freckled and mottled with faint dusky clouds and streaks. In length they vary from 1·1 to 1·22 and in width from 0·83 to 0·91 inch.

The habits of this species is not unlike the other Rails, but, as a rule, it is more shy and retiring, and when disturbed, runs with great speed on the lotus leaves or other aquatic herbage, and conceals itself among the thickest of the coverts it frequents.

303. Porzana fusca (*Linn.*), *Jerd., B. Ind.* iii. p. 724, No. 911; *Blyth, B. Burm.* p. 161; *Legge, B. Ceylon* p. 769; *Hume and Marsh., Game Birds* ii. p. 217; *Oates, B. Br. Burm.* ii. p. 346; *Murray, Avif. Brit. Ind.* ii. p. 642, No. 1330. Rallus fuscus, *Linn., Syst. Nat.* i. p. 262. Rallina fusca, *Hume, Nests and Eggs, Ind. B.* p. 604; *Hume, Str. F.* viii. p. 113.—The RUDDY CRAKE.

Forehead as far back as the eyes, the sides of the head and neck, the foreneck, breast and upper abdomen rich ferruginous; chin and throat whitish; sides of the body and lower abdomen olivaceous; flanks, vent and under tail coverts dark brown, irregularly and indistinctly barred with white; the whole upper plumage, wings and tail olive brown; under wing coverts brown edged with white. The female has the ferruginous of the lower parts paler and the white of the throat extends lower down; irides crimson; eyelids plumbeous, the edges red; bill greenish brown; legs and toes red; hinder parts of leg fuscous. (*Oates.*)

Length.—8·5 inches; tail 1·75; wing 3·8; tarsus 1·4; bill from gape 1·0.

Hab.—Ceylon, Southern and Central India, Punjab, N.-W. Provinces, and Rajpootana (rare). Common in Lower and Eastern Bengal, also in British Burmah. Breeds during July and August on the Woolar Lake in Cashmere, also in Burmah, where, according to Oates, it is a permanent resident. It is also recorded from Arracan and the Malay Peninsula.

Gen. **Gallinula.**—*Briss.*

Bill moderate, curved slightly at the tip; nostrils in a groove, placed about the middle of the upper mandible; bill extending on to the forehead and forming a small shield; shoulder of wing with a tubercle or spur; toes very narrowly edged by membrane.

Gallii ula chloropus. The Water or Moor Hen.

304. Gallinula chloropus (*Linn.*), *Jerd., B. Ind.* iii. p. 716, No. 905; *Hume, Nests and Eggs Ind. B.* p. 397; *id., Str. F.* i. p. 250; iii. p. 187; *Blyth, B. Burm.* p. 162; *Dresser, B. Eur.* vii. p. 313, pl.; *Hume and Dav., Str. F.* vi. p. 466; *Legge, B. Ceylon,* p. 781; *Murray, Vert. Zool., Sind,* p. 262; *Oates, B. Br. Burm.* ii. p. 347; *Murray, Avif. Brit. Ind.* ii. p. 645, No. 1333; *Parker, Ibis,* 1886, p. 187. Gallinula Burnesi, *Blyth, J. A. S. B.* xiii. p. 736.—The Moor Hen.

Top of head, nape and back of neck dusky olive brown; back, scapulars, tertiaries, wing coverts and upper tail coverts shining olive brown; primaries, secondaries and tail dusky brown, the outer web of the 1st quill white; a pale fulvous brown streak from behind the nostril on each side to the eye, and a patch of the same colour on the side of the head including the ear coverts; under each eye a white spot; chin and throat white; breast dark bluish ashy, the feathers tipped with pale or dirty fulvous; lower abdomen white; vent feathers black; under tail coverts white; feathers on the flanks long and lax, those falling on the thighs pale brown with a mesial white streak; bill reddish at base, greenish yellow at tip; irides red; an orange garter above the knee.

Length.—12 to 13 inches; wing 6·75; tail 3; bill at gape 1·1. In mature plumage the entire head and neck are dark brown, almost black, and the upper plumage darker olive brown.

Hab.—Diffused throughout India, Ceylon and parts of Burmah, also Central and South Europe, Africa and Java. Occurs also in Beluchistan, Persia, Afghanistan, Eastern Turkestan, Nepal and Cashmere, affecting small rivers and marshes. In the dhunds and jheels in Sind, also in the Deccan, Guzerat and Rajputana, it is extremely common, swimming about freely. During the day, on retreating to the edges of the tanks or dhunds, it lives concealed among the reeds and rushes. It is less shy towards evening when it creeps along the margins of the waters among the long reeds in quest of aquatic insects, worms and seeds. Breeds from March to August. The nest is a large structure of withered reeds and rushes, placed near the brink of the water; the female lays from 4 to 6 eggs; in shape they are long, oval or ovate pyriform, of a stone colour, with a pinkish tinge, speckled, spotted and blotched with reddish brown or red. It is said that the female never quits its nest without covering her eggs with the leaves of the surrounding herbage. The young are able to swim immediately they are hatched. In the N.-W. Provinces of Ceylon Parker says it is numerous, and a regular immigrant; in the extreme south-east a permanent resident, while throughout the east of the Island it is only known as one of the rarest species.

305. Gallinula phœnicura (*Penn.*), *Jerd.*, *B. Ind.* ii. p. 720, No. 907; *Hume, Nests and Eggs Ind. B.* p. 599; *Murray, Vert. Zool., Sind,* p. 263; *Murray, Avif. Brit. Ind.* ii. p. 645, No. 1334. Rallus phœnicurus, *Pennant in Forst. Zool. Ind.* p. 19, pl. ix. Erythra phœnicura, *Wald., Trans. Zool. Soc.* viii. p. 94; *Salvad., Ucc. Born.* p. 340; *Legge, B. Ceylon,* p. 786; *Oates, B. Br. Burm.* ii. p. 348.—The WHITE-BREASTED WATER HEN.

Forehead, lores, entire face, chin, cheeks, throat, neck, breast and abdomen white; crown of the head, nape, neck behind, back, scapulars, wings, flanks and tail black, with greenish reflections; outer web of first quill white; lower abdomen, vent and under tail coverts deep chestnut; bill yellow with a tinge of green; irides blood red.

Length.—12 to 13 inches; wing 6·5; tail 2·5; bill at front 1·5.

Hab.—Ceylon, Sind and throughout the Indian Peninsula and Burmah. In Sind not uncommon along the canals and the Indus. Breeds in Ceylon in the Manaar Districts from January to March, in the N.-W. Provinces from May to December, and in India generally from May to August. Eggs greyish, with a light reddish tinge, spotted and blotched with various shades of red and bluish grey; affects generally the heavy undergrowth along the edges of canals.

Gen. **Gallicrex**.—*Blyth.*

Bill as in *Gallinula*, with the base of the bill extending on to the forehead and forming a fleshy protuberance; toes long; hind toe and claws about half the length of the mid-toe; claws curved.

306. Gallicrex cinereus (*Gm.*), *Hume, Nests and Eggs Ind. B.* p. 596; *Wald., Trans. Zool. Soc.* ix. p. 229; *Oates, Str. F.* v. p. 165; *Wardlaw-Ramsay, Ibis,* 1877, p. 477; *Legge, B. Ceylon,* p. 791; *Murray, Vert. Zool. Sind,* p. 261; *Oates, B. Br. Burm.* ii. p. 349; *Murray, Avif. Brit. Ind.* ii. p. 646, No. 1335. Fulica cinerea, *Gmel., Syst. Nat.* i. p. 702. Gallinula cristata, *Lath., Ind. Orn.* ii. p. 779. Gallicrex cristatus, *Jerd., B. Ind.* iii. p. 716; *Blyth and Wald., B. Burm.* p. 161.—The WATER COCK.

Male in Breeding Plumage.—Dull black, the feathers of the back, wing coverts, rump and upper tail coverts more or less edged with light brown; tertials dark brown, edged with pale whity brown; edge of the wing white; quills dusky, the shaft of the 1st quill white; tail blackish brown, the outer feathers edged with pale brown; lower wing coverts dusky with whitish edges; bill greenish yellow, fine red at the base; the crest about one inch long, fleshy red; irides red; legs dull red.

Length.—16 to 17 inches; extent 23; wing 8·5; tail 3·5; tarsus 3. (*Jerd.*)

Female.—Top of head dull black or dusky brown; back of neck, back, scapulars, wing coverts and tertiaries the same, the feathers edged with fulvous, more broadly on the back and wings; tail the same; sides of the face, including a broad supercilium fulvous, in some with a rufescent tinge; chin and throat fulvous white; neck in front, breast and entire under parts brownish fulvous, the feathers with narrow transverse bars; thigh coverts the same; primaries and secondaries dusky brown; outer web of first quill fulvous.

Length.—13 to 14 inches; wing 7; tail 2·5; bill at gape 1·25; tarsus 2·5.

Hab.—Ceylon, Sind, Lower Bengal, Tennaserim, South and Central India, Burmah and Malayana. Affects large swamps and marshes, also the vicinity of rivers, where several may be seen in the early morning, issuing from the thick cover of tamarisk, fringing the banks, and running along the edge of the water.

ORDER, HERODIONES.

Bill large, long, stout and strong, pointed and in some slightly curved; tarsi generally long and scutellate; tail short; tibia bare for a considerable space. The Order comprises the Storks, Herons and Ibises.

Family, CICONIDÆ.—STORKS.

Bill long and stout, compressed to the tip; nostrils narrow, pierced through the bill and situated near the base of the culmen; tail moderate; front toes united at the base.

Breeds in inaccessible places in parts of Bengal and Burmah, constructing a large nest of sticks, and laying 2—3 whitish eggs, not unlike those of the Vultures; huge broad ovals, in size from 2·87 to 3·3 in length, and from 2·1 to 2·55 in breadth.

307. Leptoptilus Javanicus (*Horsf.*), *Jerd., B. Ind.* iii. p. 732; *Salvad., Ucc. Born.* p. 358; *Blyth, B. Burm.* p. 159; *Legge, B. Ceylon* p. 113; *Sharpe, Ibis,* 1819, p. 72; *Oates, Str. F.* x. p. 242; *id., B. Br. Burm.* ii. p. 263; *Murray, Avif. Brit. Ind.* ii. p. 648, No. 1337. Ciconia javanica, *Horsf., Trans. Linn. Soc.* xiii. p. 188.—The LESSER ADJUTANT.

Head and neck covered with a few soft decomposed feathers; crown of head bony and perfectly bare; ruff and lower plumage white; upper plumage, wings and tail dark brown with a slightly greenish gloss. Bill dirty yellowish; top of head dirty green; nude parts and neck tinged with yellow, seasonally red; irides whitish; legs dusky black.

Length.—52 to 55 inches; tail 10; wing 25; tarsus 9; bill from gape 10·5.

Hab.—Ceylon and over nearly the whole of India in small numbers, frequenting marshes, paddy fields and edges of lakes and rivers. Common in Southern India and the Malabar Coast; rare in Central India and the Upper Provinces. Occurs in Bengal, Assam, Sylhet, and Burmah, extending from the latter down the Malay Peninsula. Habits same as the last.

Gen. **Xenorhynchus**.—*Bp.*

Bill very large, stout and solid, the tip turned up; 2nd and 3rd quills longest.

308. Xenorhynchus asiaticus, *Lath., Ind. Orn.* ii p. 670; *Murray, Vert. Zool. Sind*, p. 266; *Oates, B. Br. Burm.* ii. p. 364. Ardea Indica, *Lath., Ind. Orn.* ii. p. 701; *Murray, Avif. Brit. Ind.* ii. p. 648, No. 1338. Mycteria australis, *Shaw, Trans. Linn. Soc.* v. p. 34; *Jerd., B. Ind.* iii. p. 734. Mycteria indica, *Hume, Nests and Eggs Ind. B.* p. 607; *id., Str. F.* iii. p. 189. Xenorhynchus australis, *Blyth and Wald., B. Burm.* p. 158; *Legge, B. Ceylon*, p. 1117; *Oates, Str. F.* x. p. 242.—The BLACK-NECKED STORK.

Head and neck rich dark glossy green, glossed on the hind head with purple; lesser, median and greater coverts and scapulars, also the interscapulars and tail dark brown, mixed with rich bluish green with a golden tinge; rest of plumage white; bill black; legs reddish.

Length.—52 to 56 inches; wing 24; tail 9; bill at front 12·5 inches.

Hab.—Ceylon, Sind, Punjab, N.-W. Provinces, Oudh, Bengal, Rajputana, Kutch, Guzerat, Concan, Deccan and the greater part of India, extending to Malayana; also Burmah. In Central and North India it is, as in Sind, extremely common along the banks of rivers and on the edges of tanks and marshes.

Breeds nearly all over India in well-watered tracts, where lakes, jheels, swamps and marshes abound, and from September to December. The site for building is generally the higher branches of peepul or seesum trees. Nest very large and composed of twigs and sticks. Eggs, 4 in number, pure white and not unlike those of the last. Size 2·65 to 3·13 × 1·98 to 2·3 inch.

Gen. **Ciconia.**—*Linn.*

Keel of bill straight; 3rd and 4th quills longest; hind toe elevated.

309. Ciconia alba (*Belon.*), *Bodd., Tab. Pl. En.* 866; *Gould, B. Eur.* pl. 283; *Jerd., B. Ind.* iii. p. 736, No. 919; *Str. F.* iv. p. 22; *Murray, Hdbk., Zool., &c., Sind,* 225; *id., Vert. Zool., Sind.* p. 267; *Legge, B. Ceylon,* p. 1119; *Murray, Avif. B. Ind.* ii. p. 649, No. 1340.—The WHITE STORK.

Head, crown, nape, chin, throat, breast and back pure white; greater wing coverts glossy black, shaded with grey towards the shafts; primaries, secondaries and tertiaries black; nude orbitar area black; legs red; irides brown.

Length.—44 inches; wing 23 to 25; tail 10; bill at front 7·5 to 7·75.

Hab.—Ceylon, Sind, the Deccan, Concan, Rajputana, Kutch, Guzerat and Central India; also the Punjab, N.-W. Provinces, Oudh, and Bengal. Along the banks of the Indus and the edges of lakes and swamps; in Sind it is not uncommon during winter. Feeds on lizards, molluscs, &c.

310. Ciconia leucocephala (*Gm.*), *Bodd., Tab. Pl. Enl.* 906; *Jerd., B. Ind.* iii. p. 737, No. 920; *Murray, Hdbk., Zool., &c., Sind,* p. 226; *id., Vert. Zool., Sind,* p. 267; *Murray, Avif. Brit. Ind.* ii. p. 649, No. 1341. Ardea leucocephala, *Gmel., Syst. Nat.* i. p. 642. Melanopelargus episcopus, *Hume and Henders., Lah. to Yark.,* p. 295; *Hume, Nests and Eggs Ind. B.* p. 609. Dissura episcopus, *Hume, Str. F.* viii. p. 114; *Legge, B. Ceylon,* p. 1119; *Oates, B. Br. Burm.* ii. p. 265. Dissura episcopus, *Bodd. F.* vi. p. 469.—The WHITE-NECKED STORK.

Head black; back of neck glossed with purple, also the upper back, breast and upper abdomen; neck white; primaries and upper tail coverts glossed with green, also the lower back; tail white; irides crimson; eyelids and nude orbitar area plumbeous; throat purplish; bill black, reddish on the anterior half; feet red. "Nestling had the inner circle of the iris brown, surrounded by a narrow black ring from an outer one of pale golden orange. Bill black; tip and edges vinous." (Parker *MS.*)

Length.—36 to 37 inches; extent 70; wing 20; tail 7; bill at front 6.

Hab.—Ceylon; also Sind, Punjab, N.-W. Provinces, Oudh, Bengal, Kutch (?), Rajputana (?), Guzerat, Concan, Deccan, South and Central India; also British Burmah. In Ceylon it breeds from December to February on large trees overhanging the northern rivers, or at tanks.

Family. ARDEIDÆ.—HERONS.

All the members of the *Ardeidæ* family swarm throughout India and Ceylon in suitable localities. All are permanent residents and breed from May to

September. Their nests are generally loosc structures, some more or less compact, and built of twigs, &c., on trees, standing in the vicinity of water, and particularly on those in the middle of large sheets of water. Eggs, 3 to 4, glossless, and in colour from pale sea green to bluish green, but it is not uncommon to find single nests containing from 8 to 10 eggs, differing in shape, size and colour.

The following, from Hume's *Nests and Eggs*, gives the average size of the eggs of the different species :—

Ardea cinerea.....................	2·27	×	1·66
Ardea purpurea..................	2·17	×	1·56
Herodias alba	2·11	×	1·55
Herodias garzetta	1·73	×	1·22
Demiegretta gularis	1· 7	×	1· 3
Bubulcus coromanda	1·71	×	1·32
Ardeola grayi........	1·48	×	1·17
Butorides javanica	1·64	×	1·23

An account by Layard of the breeding of *Herodias garzetta* and kindred species in Ceylon, conveys exactly what is observable in the breeding season of the *Ardeidæ* in India generally, and along the canals, &c., in the Narra Districts, and other large sheets of water in Sind.

During this season on almost all the large pieces of water in India, unfrequented and distant from human habitation, in which trees are standing out of reach, except by boats, large colonies of ibises, spoonbills, cormorants, snake-birds, night-herons, &c., may be seen. During the day, except by the droppings of the birds, which coat the branches so thickly with lime, little suspicion would be excited of the spot being a heronry, as most of the birds, except a few sitting close, are away feeding, but towards eve, hundreds would be seen coming to roost, amid a continuous cackling. The report of a gun amongst them would present a scene scarcely describable. If disturbed before they have begun to lay, they are said to entirely desert the spot, and carry away almost every stick they had used in building and to begin operations afresh in a distant locality.

Gen. **Ardea**—*Linn.*

Bill slender, the tip scooped ; upper mandible with a groove from the nostril, but not extending to the tip ; nostrils covered partially by membrane ; 2nd and 3rd quills longest ; tarsi long and scutellate in front.

311. Ardea goliath, *Temm., Pl. Col.* 474; *Rupp., Faun. Abyss.* pl. 26; *Jerd., B. Ind.* iii. p. 739; *Hume, Nests and Eggs Ind. B.* p. 610, No. 621 ; *id., Str. F.* i. p. 105; vii. p. 490.—The GIANT HERON.

Upper plumage dark blue grey ; short occipital crest and rest of head dark brown ; sides of the head and entire neck chestnut brown ; chin and throat white ; neck in front white with black streaks ; breast and abdomen dark chestnut brown. The young bird is dull grey above, the head, ear coverts and back of neck are pale rufous cinnamon. Bill dusky above, beneath and tip greenish ; irides pale yellow ; legs blackish. (*Jerd.*)

Length.—55 to 65 inches ; wing 24 ; tail 10 ; bill at front 8 ; tarsus 9 ; standing height nearly 4 feet.

Hab.—Ceylon and Bengal, near Calcutta, also the Khasia hills. Nothing certain appears to be known of its nidification.

312. Ardea cinerea, *Linn., Syst. Nat.* i. p. 235 ; *Naum, Vogt.* t. 220 ; *Gould, B. Eur.* pl. 274 ; *Jerd., B. Ind.* iii. p. 741 ; *Hume, Str. F.* i. p. 253 ; *Murray, Hdbk., Zool., &c., Sind,* p. 226 ; *Hume, Nests and Eggs Ind. B.* p. 610 ; *Dresser, B. Eur.* vi. p. 217, pl. ; *Legge B. Ceylon,* p. 1127 ; *Oates, B. Br. Burm* ii. p. 245 ; *Murray, Avif. Brit Ind.* ii. p. 652, No. 1345. —The Common Heron.

Ardea cinerea. The Common Heron.

Forehead, sides of the head and crown white ; a narrow streak from the base of the upper mandible over each eye, and another above it merging into the long occipital feathers, black ; neck behind bluish ashy ; in front white, with two rows of black elongate spots ; breast and under surface white ; back and wing coverts bluish ashy grey ; primaries black ; scapulars silvery grey ; tail bluish ashy ; bill dark yellow, brown on the upper mandible ; irides yellow ; nude oribitar area greenish.

Length.—39 inches; wing 18; tail 8; bill at front 5.

Hab.—Ceylon and throughout India. In Sind the Mohannas or fishermen use this species as a decoy in the capture of wild fowl. Each boat has usually from 5 to 10 birds. Their eyelids are sewn up, and they stand motionless on the cross bar of the rudder gear or perched along the edges of the boat. They are fed daily, and during summer, when the occupation of wild fowl catching has ceased, serve the fishermen as food in the absence of anything better. Breeds throughout India from April to July, building nests on trees in small parties. In Ceylon from January to March; colour of eggs sea green; size from 2·08 to 2·48 in length and 1·48 to 1·79 in breadth.

313 Ardea purpurea, *Linn.*, *Syst. Nat.* i. p. 236; *Jerd.*, *B. Ind.* iii. p. 743; *Hume*, *Nests and Eggs Ind. B.* p. 611; *Salvad.*, *Ucc. Born.* p. 345; *Blyth*, *B. Br. Burm.* p. 159; *Dresser*, *B. Eur.* vi. p. 217, pl.; *Legge*, *B. Ceylon* p. 1132; *Oates*, *Str. F.* x. p. 243; *id.*, *B. Br. Burm.* ii. p. 245; *Murray*, *Vert. Zool.*, *Sind*, p. 269; *Murray*, *Avif. Brit. Ind.* ii. p. 653, No. 1346.—The Blue Heron.

Head glossy black, with a lengthened black crest, the two middle feathers of which extend 3—4 inches beyond the rest; sides of the head rusty yellow, with three longitudinal narrow black lines, one extends behind the head, and is continued down the neck, and two lateral ones from the eyes to the breast; chin and throat white; neck in front variegated with rufous black and purple, the feathers on the top of the breast long and acuminated, purplish white; back, wings, and tail reddish ash; scapulars purple, long, forming a brilliant plume on each side; breast and flanks deep brownish red, rest of under parts a little paler. Bill deep yellow; orbitar skin greenish yellow; tarsus reddish brown. The nestling, Mr. Parker says, has black hair.

Length.—36 to 42 inches; wing 15·5; tail 5·75; bill at front 5·37; tarsus 5·25.

Hab.—Throughout India and Ceylon, extending into Burmah. Habits and nidification the same as those of the Common Heron. In Ceylon, however, Mr. Parker took eggs in the Manaar District during January and February, and near Vihankulam early in February.

Gen. **Herodias**. *Boie.*

Bill moderately long, slender, straight and compressed to the tip; plumage white. In breeding plumage with a long dorsal train composed of lax decomposed feathers, and pectoral plumes in some. The following key given by Mr. Hume will probably be found useful:—

Species.	Non-breeding plumage.	Breeding plumage.				Dimensions.				
	Bill.	Bill.	Crest.	Dorsal train.	Pectoral plumes.	Bill at front.	Wing.	Tarsus.	Nude portion of tibia.	Mid-toe and claw.
H. alba, *Linn.* *Jerd.*, *B. Ind.* iii. 744.	Yellow.	Black...	None.........	Long; extending 5 inches beyond tail.	None	5·0	17·2	7·91	5·2	4·7
H. intermedia, *V. Haselt.* *Jerd.*, *B. Ind.* iii. 745.	Yellow.	Black...	None.........	Long; about 7—8 inches beyond tail.	Of long decomposed feathers.	2·68 to 3·09	11·15 to 12·65	4·1 to 4·6	2·8 to 3·1	3·62 to 4·05
H. garzetta, *Linn.* *Jerd.* *B. Ind.* iii. 746.	Black...	Black...	Of 2 narrow feathers, 5-6 inches long.	Long; curling up at point, scarcely extending beyond the tail.	Of long, narrow, ordinary feathers.	3·1 to 3·6	9·8 to 11·4	3·7 to 4·5	1·8 to 2·76	2·75 to 3·15

314. Herodias alba (*Linn.*), *Jerd., B. Ind* ii. p. 744; *Blyth, B. Burm.* p. 159; *Legge, B. Ceylon* p. 1138; *Murray, Vert. Zool., Sind*, p. 270; *Murray, Avif. Brit. Ind.* ii. p. 655, No. 1347. Ardea alba, *Linn., Syst. Nat.* i. p. 239; *Dresser, B. Eur.* vi. p. 231, pl. Ardea torra (*Buch.*), *Frankl. P. Z. S.* 1831, p. 123. Herodias torra, *Salvad., Ucc. Born.* p. 347; *Scully, Str. F.* viii. p. 360. Ardea egretta, *apud Hume, Nests and Eggs Ind. B.* p. 613.—The LARGE WHITE HERON.

In Breeding Plumage.—Whole plumage pure white; dorsal train of decomposed feathers extending about 4—5 inches beyond the tail; no crest, nor pectoral plumes. No dorsal train in non-breeding plumage. Bill yellow in winter, black in summer; irides pale yellow.

Length.—34 to 36 inches; tail 6; wing 13·5 to 17; tarsus 5·2 to 6·1; bill at front 4 to 5; from gape 5·5.

Hab.—Throughout India, Ceylon, and Burmah; nidificates on trees in small parties; eggs pale bluish green.

315. Herodias intermedia (*Von Hasselt*), *Salvad., Ucc. Born.* p. 348; *Blyth, B. Burm.* p. 159; *Legge, B. Ceylon*, p. 1141; *Murray, Vert. Zool., Sind*, p. 270; *Oates B. Br. Burm.* ii p. 247. *Murray, Avif. Brit. Ind.* ii. p. 655, No. 1348. Ardea nigrirostris (*Gray*), *Hardw., Ill. Ind. Zool.*, pl. Herodias plumifera, *Gould, B. Austr.* vi. pl. 57. Ardea intermedia, *Von Hass., Wagler, Ibis*, 1829, p. 659; *Hume, Nests and Eggs Ind. B.* p. 615. Herodias egrettoides, *Jerd., B. Ind.* ii. p. 745.—The LESSER WHITE HERON.

Breeding Plumage.—Whole plumage pure white; dorsal train exceeding the tail by 7—8 inches; a long soft tuft of pectoral feathers; no crest, no dorsal nor pectoral plumes in winter. Bill black in summer, yellow with a black tip in winter; facial skin green; irides yellow.

Length.—26 to 28 inches; tail 5·5; wing 11·5 to 12·5; tarsus 4·3; bill at front 2·68 to 3·09.

Hab.—Generally distributed throughout India, Ceylon and Burmah, but rare in the latter and in Southern India. Breeds during July and part of August, in colonies and generally in the company of other species of Herons, Ibises, &c. The nest is not unlike that of its congeners, composed of thin twigs, lined or not with coarse sedge, but generally more closely packed. Eggs, 4 in number, broad ovals, rather pointed towards one end; pale sea or bluish seagreen, 1·68 to 2·08 in length, and 1·3 to 1·52 in breadth.

316. Herodias garzetta (*Linn.*), *Jerd., B. Ind.* ii. p. 746; *Hume, Str. F.* iii. p. 190; *Legge, B. Ceylon* p. 1144; *Murray, Vert. Zool., Sind*, p. 270; *Oates, B. Br. Burm.* ii. p. 248; *Murray, Avif. Brit Ind.* ii. p. 655, No. 1349. Ardea garzetta, *Linn., Syst. Nat.* i. p. 237; *Hume, Nests and Eggs Ind. B.* p. 616; *Dresser, B. Eur.* vii. p. 239.—The LITTLE BLACK-BILLED WHITE HERON.

Breeding Plumage.—Whole plumage white; crest of 2—3 narrow feathers about five inches long; dorsal train scarcely extending beyond the tail and curled upwards at tip; pectoral plumes long and pointed. In *non-breeding plumage* there is neither a crest nor a dorsal train. Bill always black; base of lower mandible yellowish; irides yellow; facial skin greenish yellow; tarsus black.

Length.—25 inches; tail 4; wing 9·6 to 11·4; bill from gape about 4; at front 3·1 to 3·6.

Hab.—India, Ceylon and Burmah. Breeds in June, July, and part of August. Nidification similar to *H. intermedia*; eggs of the same colour, but from 1·6 to 1·8 in length, and 1·25 to 1·38 in breadth.

Gen. **Demi-egretta.**—*Blyth.*

Bill long and more slender than in *Herodias*; adult plumage dark, otherwise as in *Herodias.*

317. Demi-egretta gularis, *Bosc., Act. Soc. H. N.* i. t. 2; *Meyer, Zool. Ann.* i. t. 1; *Hume, Str. F.* i. p. 254; *Murray, Avif. Brit. India* ii. p. 655, No. 1351. Ardea gularis (*Bosc.*), *Legge, B. Ceylon,* p. 1136. Demi-egretta schistacea (*Licht.*), *Hemp. and Ehr. Sym. Phys.* t. 6. Demi-egretta asha, *Sykes, Cat.* 171; *Jerd., B. Ind.* iii. p. 747, No. 928; *Murray, Hdbk., Zool., &c., Sind,* p. 227.—The Ashy Egret.

Adult.—In breeding season, deep slaty blue; chin, throat, sides of the head, nearly to the gape and the base of the ear coverts, white; an occipital crest and dorsal train of decomposed feathers, concolorous with the upper parts, and not reaching quite to the end of the tail; pectoral plumes narrow and pointed; bill reddish yellow, dusky above; nude orbitar skin yellowish green; legs blackish; feet and lower part of tarsus yellowish.

Length.—24 to 27 inches; wing 10 to 11·4; tail 3 to 3·8; irides yellow; bare portion of tibia 2·2 to 2·9; bill 3·5 to 4·1; tarsus 3·9 to 4·4; mid-toe and claw 2·3 to 2·6. Affects the mud flats in the Kurrachee harbour.

The young or intermediate stage of plumage is white throughout, some of the wing coverts being greyish.

Hab.—Sind, Mekran, Arabian and Western Coasts, also the Eastern Coast to Ceylon. Nidification the same as the Herons. Eggs, a rounded oval, pale blue, 4—6 in number, 1·83 × 1·42 inch.

Bubulcus.—*Pucher.*

Bill shorter than in the *Demi-egretta*; legs longer; plumes during the breeding season yellow.

318. Bubulcus coromandus (*Bodd.*), *Salvad., Ucc. Born.* p. 350; *Legge, B. Ceylon,* p. 1147; *Oates, Str. F.* x. p. 243; *id., B. Br. Burm.* ii. p. 251; *Murray, Vert. Zool., Sind,* p. 271; *Murray, Avif. Brit.*

Ind. ii. p. 657, No. 1353. Cancroma coromanda, *Bodd., Tabl. Pl. Enl.* p. 54. Buphus coromanda, *Jerd., B. Ind.* iii. p. 749; *Blyth, B. Burm.* p. 160; *Bingham, Str. F.* ix. p. 197. Ardea coromanda, *Hume, Nests and Eggs Ind. B.* p. 618.—The Cattle Egret.

In breeding plumage the head, sides of the face, neck in front (except a narrow mesial line, which is white) nape and part of the hind neck, and the decomposed elongate feathers brilliant orange, the filamentose feathers of the back reaching to the end of the closed wings, rest of the plumage pure white; legs yellowish green, the joints tinged plumbeous; bill deep orange yellow; orbitar skin yellowish, with a pinkish tinge; irides pale yellow; mid-claw serrated.

Length.—21 inches; wing 10·25; tail 4; bill at front 2·5; tarsus 3·5. In winter the plumage is entirely white.

Hab.—Sind and throughout India, Burmah and Ceylon. It has gained the name of the Cattle Egret from its being always found amongst cattle when grazing, usually perched on their heads or backs. It is seldom, like the other species, seen wading in water. Feeds chiefly on insects, small frogs or tadpoles. Breeds from April to July. Eggs, 4—5, pale sea-green.

Gen. **Ardeola**.—*Boie*.

Tibia feathered nearly to the knee; tarsus shorter than in *Bubulcus*; toes also shorter.

319. Ardeola grayi (*Sykes*). *Hume, Nests and Eggs, Ind. Birds* p. 619; *Blyth, B. Burm.* p. 160; *Legge, B. Ceylon*, p. 1150; *Scully, Str. F.* viii. p. 361; *Murray, Avif. Brit. Ind.* ii. p. 658, No. 1354. Ardea grayi, *Sykes, P. Z. S.*, 1832, p. 158. Ardeola leucoptera, *apud Jerd., B. Ind.* iii. p. 751.—The Pond Heron or Paddy Bird.

In summer dress the head is greyish or buffy yellow with an elongate white crest; neck in front, except a fulvous mesial line, back of the neck, and also breast, with the elongated feathers a little paler than the head; scapulars pale greyish brown; elongated dorsal feathers dark maroon; rest of the plumage white; tarsal plumes fulvous or pale buff; bill yellowish, bluish at the base and tipped black; orbitar skin greenish yellow; irides bright yellow; legs and feet dull greenish.

In winter the crown of the head and nape are dark brown, the feathers with narrow mesial shaft-streaks; neck behind, on the sides and breast fulvous or pale buff, the feathers edged with dusky brown; back and scapulars grey brown or pale ashy brown; lower back, rump, upper and under tail coverts, also the tail and abdomen, pure white; thigh coverts fulvous; primaries white, park shafted, the outer webs of the first three quills and also their tips greyish brown; secondaries pure white; wing coverts white, tinged very slightly in some specimens with greyish.

Length.— 18 to 19 inches; wing 8 to 8·5; tail 3; bill at front 2·5.

Hab.—Ceylon, Sind and throughout India, and the Burmese countries. Breeds from May to August nesting in trees. Eggs, 4—6, pale bluish green, elongated ovals, 1·35 to 1·62 in length by 1·1 to 1·25 in breadth. Abundant in all moist localities, at the edges of ponds, ditches, marshes, and lakes, and especially in rice fields.

Gen. **Butorides.**—*Blyth.*

Bill moderately long and stout; tibia feathered nearly to the knee; inner toe short; head crested.

320. Butorides javanica (*Horsf.*), *Jerd., B. Ind.* iii. p. 752; *Wald., Trans. Zool. Soc.* viii. p. 100; *Hume, Nests and Eggs Ind. B.* p. 620; *Blyth, B. Burm.* p. 160; *Legge, B. Ceylon*, p. 1153; *Murray, Vert. Zool., Sind*, p. 272; *Oates, B. Br. Burm.* ii. p. 254; *Murray, Avif. Brit. Ind.* ii. p. 659, No. 1358. Ardea javanica, *Horsf., Trans. Linn. Soc.* xiii. p. 190.—The Little Green Bittern.

Forehead and crown glossy black, also the long occipital crest; a streak from behind the eye including the ear coverts white, in some with a fulvescent tinge; another streak, which is black, below the eye; back and sides of the neck, also the breast and abdomen, greyish brown, ashy brown in some; chin and a streak down the front of the neck white; back and scapulars green, the feathers lengthened, lanceolate and white-shafted; the tertials white edged; wing coverts glossy green, edged with pale buff or fulvous; secondaries margined round their tips with yelllowish white; tail dark slaty; under tail coverts greyish; quills dark slaty, narrowly tipped with white; bill black above, pale yellow beneath; legs yellowish green.

Length.—16 to 16·75 inches; wing 6·75; tail 2·5; bare part of tibia 0·5; irides bright yellow; nude orbitar skin dull green.

The young bird—or bird of the year—is very differently marked. The head is black, with the feathers narrowly striated mesially with rufescent; sides of the neck and breast and lower parts fulvescent white, the feathers edged with dark brown; chin, throat and a line down the neck white; back and scapulars brown with a greenish tinge; the scapulars with a minute triangular white spot at the tip. Primaries and secondaries dusky brown, each with a triangular white or fulvous white spot at the tip; primary coverts the same; wing coverts brown, broadly edged with rufescent, each feather with a rufescent or white triangular spot at the tip; edge of the wing fulvescent white.

Hab.—Ceylon, Sind and throughout the greater part of India, extending to Burmah; also the Malay Peninsula and islands as far as Australia, affecting water-courses, wooded streams, nullahs and large open lakes. Habits nocturnal, generally issuing from its retreat at about sunset. Breeds in June and July, making nests in small companies on low trees or bushes. Eggs 4—6 in number, greenish white.

Gen. **Ardetta**.—*Gray*.

·Bill rather slender and straight; toes and claws long; tarsus short, otherwise as in *Butorides*. Habits nocturnal.

321. Ardetta flavicollis (*Lath.*), *Jerd.*, *B. Ind.* iii. p. 753; *Blyth*, *B. Burm.* p. 160; *Wald.*, *Trans. Zool. Soc.* ix. p. 236; *Hume*, *Str. F.* viii. p. 114; *Murray*, *Avif. Brit. Ind* ii. p. 660, *No.* 1357. Ardea flavicollis, *Lath.*, *Ind. Orn.* ii. p. 701; *Hume*, *Nests and Eggs Ind. B.* p. 621. Ardeiralla flavicollis, *Salvad.*, *Ucc. Born.* p. 353; *Legge*, *B. Ceylon*, p. 1159; *Oates*, *B. Br. Burm.* ii. p. 255.—The Blue Bittern.

"In the breeding season the plumage is dull cinereous black; chin and throat with the feathers tipped white, or with red brown; the larger feathers of the neck are mixed with white, red brown and dusky black, each feather having some black at the base and tip, and more or less red brown on one web only; a stripe of golden yellow down the side of the neck, widening inferiorly; feathers of the back forming the dorsal plume, lengthened, but not decomposed; the feathers of the breast dark ashy, slightly lengthened, abdomen dusky, mixed with whitish; inner wing coverts dusky reddish. The young bird has the feathers slightly edged with rufous, and the throat and neck less richly coloured than in the adult; bill livid red, dusky on the culmen, cere livid purple; irides yellow in some with an outer circle of red; legs pale brown, with a tinge of green in some, reddish brown in others."

Length.—23 to 24 inches; wing 8·5; tail 3; bill in front 3·5; tarsus 2·5. (*Jerdon.*)

Hab.—Sind, Punjab, N.-W. Provinces, Deccan, Concan and nearly throughout India, extending to Ceylon and Burmah. Affects swamps, rice fields and beds of rushes and reeds. Breeds in Sind. Mr. Doig obtained the eggs of a colony of these birds in the month of May on the Narra Canal. He says—"Once the sun is well up, they are seldom seen, unless actually beaten out of the dense tamarisk and reed jungle in which they lie hid." They are nocturnal feeders; the nests are formed of tamarisk twigs, with sometimes a few aquatic weeds on which the eggs are laid; always four in number, broad ovals, sharp at both ends, and nearly white in colour; size from 1·5 to 1·85×1·15 to 1·30 inches.

322. Ardetta cinnamomea (*Gmel.*), *Jerd.*, *B. Ind.* iii. p. 755; *Hume*, *Nests and Eggs*, *Ind. B.* p. 622; *Salvad.*, *Ucc. Born.* p. 354; *Blyth*, *B. Burm.* p. 160; *Hume and Dav.*, *Str. F.* vi. p. 483; *Cripps*, *Str. F.* vi. p. 308; *Hume*, *Str. F.* viii. p. 114; *Oates*, *Str. F.* x. p. 243; *id.*, *B. Br. Burm.* ii. p. 256; *Murray*, *Vert. Zool.*, *Sind*, p. 274; *Murray*, *Avif. Brit. Ind.* ii. p. 661, No. 1338. Ardea cinnamomea, *Gmel.*, *Syst. Nat.* 1. p. 643. Ardeiralla cinnamomea, *Legge*, *B. Ceylon*, p. 1162.—The Chestnut Bittern.

Top of head, back and scapulars chestnut, the feathers centred slightly darker; chin and throat white, with a median chestnut line; foreneck and breast chestnut, the feathers slightly darker mesially, and the edges of those on the breast fulvous; a median fulvous line on the foreneck; thigh coverts also chestnut; primaries, secondaries and tail dark brown; wing coverts like the back, but more fulvous; flanks buffy, the feathers mesially streaked with dusky; abdomen, vent and under tail coverts white with a fulvous tinge in some; bill yellow, dusky superiorly; orbitar skin yellow; irides yellow; legs yellowish with a greenish tinge.

Length.—15 to 16 inches; wing 6; tail 1·75; bill at front 1·8 to 2; tarsus 1·9 to 2.

In immature plumage the upper parts, wing coverts, scapulars, neck in front and breast, also the thigh coverts reddish brown or slightly darker, the feathers of the back and breast margined from ferruginous buff to fulvous.

Hab.—Ceylon, Sind, and nearly throughout India, and Burmah also Malayana. Breeds in July and August, nesting on the ground at the edges of swamps or on the small embankments between the paddy fields. Eggs, generally six in number, dull white in colour.

323. Ardetta sinensis, *Gmel., Syst. Nat.* i. p. 642; *Jerd., B. Ind.* ii. p. 755; *Hume, Nests and Eggs*, p. 623; *id., Str. F.* i. p. 308; ii. p. 311; iii. p. 193; *Salvad., Ucc. Born.* p. 354; *Blyth, B. Burm.* p. 160; *Legge, B. Ceylon*, p. 1156; *Oates, Str. F.* x. p. 243; *Kelham, Ibis*, 1882, p. 196; *Murray, Vert. Zool., Sind*, p. 274; *Oates, B. Br. Burm.* ii. p. 257; *Murray, Avif. Br. Ind.* ii. p. 661, No. 1359.—The LITTLE YELLOW BITTERN.

Top of head cinnamon rufous, the feathers centred broadly with black, giving it quite a black appearance; neck behind, back, scapulars, tertiaries and wing coverts deep cinnamon-rufous, the feathers margined with fulvous or bright buff; primaries and secondaries, greater wing coverts and tail black; edge of wing and under wing coverts fulvous white; chin and throat white, with a median buff line; sides of the breast deep brown, margined with buff; breast bright buff, margined paler; abdomen, vent and under tail coverts buffy white; legs yellowish green; bill pale yellow, brownish superiorly.

Length.—13 inches; wing 5·25; tail 1·75; bill at front 2; tarsus 1·7 to 1·8; mid-toe 1 inch.

Hab.—Ceylon, Sind, Bengal, Kutch, Deccan, and nearly throughout India; and Burmah generally, extending to the Malay Peninsula and Islands of Java, Borneo and Sumatra. It is less common than the last, and frequents similar situations, *i.e.*, high reeds and thickets. All the species are nocturnal feeders, and remain hid during the day in dense cover. Breeds during July and August in similar situations as the last. Eggs, four in number, pale green.

Gen. **Botaurus**.—*Briss.*

Bill rather short, stout and rounded; tip scooped; the upper mandible curved to the tip and longer than the lower; tarsi short; nostrils narrow, situated near the base of the bill; 1st to 3rd quills of wing longest.

324. Botaurus stellaris, *Linn., Syst. Nat.* i. p. 230; *Jerd., B. Ind.* iii. p. 757; *Hume, Nests and Eggs Ind. B.* p. 624; *Dresser, B. Eur.* vi. p. 281, pl; *Murray, Vert. Zool., &c., Sind,* p. 275; *Oates, B. Br. Burm.* ii. p. 258; *Murray, Avif. Brit. Ind.* ii. p. 662.—The COMMON EUROPEAN BITTERN.

Forehead, crown and nape glossy black, also a moustachial stripe; sides of the face and ear coverts buff, with narrow dusky streaks; feathers of the sides of the neck long and lax, bright buff, and with irregular black transverse bars; hind neck bare, covered by the feathers of the foreneck; chin and throat fulvous, with a median rufescent line; foreneck and breast the same, each feather with irregular dark brown, nearly black bars and spots; lower breast with long, lax, feathers, which are buff, with broad longitudinal black stripes; flanks the same; abdomen rufous buff, with narrow dark mesial streaks; back and scapulars black, the feathers edged, barred and mottled with buff tail buff, thickly mottled and with zigzag markings of dusky; primaries and secondaries dark brown barred with rufous; wing coverts buff, barred and mottled with dusky brown; bill pale yellow, dusky above; orbits yellow; irides gamboge yellow; legs greenish yellow.

Length.—30 inches; wing 13·5; tail 4·5; tarsus 3·75 to 3·9.

Hab.—Ceylon, Sind, the Deccan, Punjab, N.-W. Provinces, Oudh, Bengal, and nearly all India, Burmah, and Central and Southern Europe, Persia, Nubia, Beluchistan and S. Afghanistan. In Ceylon it is extremely rare and is only an occasional straggler. A single skin, in not very good condition, was received at this Institute last year from Mr. Warburton of Caltura, for identification. It is not recorded, I find, by Col. Legge, nor by previous writers.

The Bittern is a shy solitary bird; it is never seen on the wing during the day, but sits hid among the reeds, rushes and other rank vegetation that prevail in the marsh or bog, where it may have taken up its abode. It is said to defend itself fiercely against a dog or falcon, with both its bill and claws, the bill with its extremely sharp point being however chiefly made use of. It is said to have been esteemed in falconry, owing to its habit, when flown at, of ascending in spiral circles, high up in the air, to keep above its enemy. Selby adds—"Should this manœuvre fail, it then prepares for the descent of the hawk, by setting its sharp bill perpendicularly upwards, upon which its antagonist frequently transfixes itself." Its boom or note is said to resemble the bellowing of a bull. It is also often uttered while the bird is soaring in the air, but the sound is feeble, compared with the hollow booming noise which it makes at night during the breeding season. Jerdon says it is excellent eating, not fishy in the smallest degree, and has a high game flavour.

Gen. **Nycticorax**.—*Steph.*

Bill long, sharp, the gape extending below the eyes; nostrils in a lateral groove covered by membranous scale, wings with the 2nd and 3rd quills longest; claw of mid-toe serrated; tarsi irregularly scaled.

325. Nycticorax griseus (*Linn.*), *Bodd., Tab. P. E.* 758, 759; *Naum., Vogt.* t. 225; *Gould, B. Eur.* pl. 279; *Jerd., B. Ind.* iii. 758, No. 937; *Dresser, B. Eur.* vi. p. 299, pl.; *Hume, Str. F.* viii. p. 114; *Murray, Vert. Zool., Sind,* p. 276; *Legge, B. Ceylon,* p. 1165; *Murray, Avif. Brit. Ind.* ii. p. 663, No. 1362. Nyctiardea nycticorax, *Hume, Nests and Eggs, Ind. B.* p. 624. Ardea grisea, *Linn., Syst. Nat.* i. p. 235; *Str. F.* vi. p. 415; *Murray, Hdbk., Zool., &c., Sind,* p. 228 (*Gadri,* Sind).—The Night Heron.

Forehead and supercilium, also the chin, throat and a narrow mesial line on the foreneck white; under tail coverts, breast and abdomen white, with a creamy tinge; top of head and nape, also the back and scapulars black, glossed with green; lengthened crest feathers 6—7 inches long, narrow and white, tipped with brown; hind neck, wing coverts, tail and sides of the body ashy grey; first three quills emarginate near the tip; bill black, yellow at base of lower mandible; orbitar skin yellowish green; irides blood red.

Length.—22 to 23 inches; wing 12·5; tail 3·75; bill at front 2·8; tarsus 3.

Hab.—Ceylon, Sind, Beloochistan, Persia, Afghanistan and throughout India and Burmah. It is a permanent resident in India, and breeds in societies from May to September. The nest is a loose structure of twigs. Eggs, 3—4, glossless pale sea-green; size 1·92 × 1·35.

Gen. **Gorsachius**.—*Pucher.*

Bill moderate, higher than broad at base; tarsus moderate; tibia feathered for the greater portion of its length; feet and toes long; neck thick.

326. Gorsachius melanolophus (*Raffles*), *Salvad., Ucc. Born.* p. 355; *Blyth, B. Burm.* p. 160; *Legge, B. Ceylon,* p. 1169; *Murray, Avif. Brit. Ind.* ii. p. 664, No. 1363. Ardea melanolopha, *Raffles, Trans. Linn. Soc.* xiii. p. 326. Botaurus limnophilax, *Salvad., Ucc. Born.* p. 355. Gorsachius melanolophus, *Hume, Str. F.* ii. p. 312; *Bourdillon, Str. F.* iii. p. 524; *Hume, Str. F.* viii. p. 114.—The Malayan Tiger Bittern.

Forehead, crown and a long occipital crest purplish black; sides of the head and back of the neck chestnut, as are also the back, rump, wing coverts, scapulars and tertiaries, but these parts are closely barred with undulating narrow bars of black; winglet black, broadly tipped with white; the first two or three primary coverts black, tipped with white; the others chestnut and also white tipped; primaries slaty black, tipped with white and with a subterminal patch of chestnut; secondaries also tipped with white; upper tail coverts and tail slaty brown; chin and throat whitish; front and sides of the neck and breast dull rufous grey; the centre of the throat and middle line of the neck and breast streaked with black, light buff and chestnut; under surface of the body dull chestnut, marked irregularly with black lines and white patches; under tail coverts white. Facial skin green; legs and feet greenish olive; irides greenish yellow.

Length.—19 inches; tail 3·5; wing 10·3; tarsus 2·5; bill from gape 2·3.

Hab.—Southern India and Ceylon; also Tennasserim, Arracan, and the Nicobars.

Family, TANTALIDÆ.

Bill long, stout, rounded, curving downwards in many, flat in others; wings long; tail rather short; toes webbed at the base.

Sub-Family, TANTALINÆ.

Bill long, slender and curved; sides compressed to the tip, or thick and rounded; tail even; inner toe shorter than outer; hind toe long.

Gen. Tantalus.—*Linn.*

Bill rounded, long and curved downwards; nostrils at the base of the bill; head and cheeks bare; tibia naked for half its length.

327. Tantalus leucocephalus, *Penn. in Forst. Ind. Zool.* p. 20, pl. 10; *Gmel. Syst. Nat.* i. p. 649; *Jerd., B. Ind.* ii. p. 761, No. 938; *Hume, Nests and Eggs, Ind. B.* p. 626; *Blyth, B. Burm.* p. 158; *Hume and Dav., Str. F.* v. p. 484; *Newton, Str. F.* viii. p. 415; *Legge, B. Ceylon,* p. 1100; *Oates, Str. F.* x. p. 244; *id., B. Br. Burm.* ii. p. 267; *Murray, Vert. Zool., Sind,* p. 276; *id., Avif. Brit. Ind.* ii. p. 665, No. 1364.—The Pelican Ibis.

Plumage white; quills and tail richly glossed greenish black; tertiaries white, tinged with rosy, with a dark band near the end and a white tip, the feathers lax and decomposed; lesser and median coverts glossy green, edged with white; greater coverts white; bill yellow, the tip greenish, as are the naked orbits, head and gular skin; irides pale yellow brown; grey in some; legs fleshy red.

Length.—40 to 42 inches; expanse 71; wing 20; tail 6·25; tarsus 8·1.

Hab.—Extremely common throughout India, Burmah and Ceylon, frequenting rivers, tanks, marshes, &c., generally in small parties of ten or a dozen. Breeds from May to August on high trees. In Ceylon rather earlier. Eggs, 3—4, glossless dull white, with a thick compact shell. Of its habits the following account from Mr. Parker will be found interesting:—"Some years since a young, well-feathered bird was caught, and was brought to me in a starving condition, having wandered from the nests about a mile and a half away. In three days he had appointed himself the general guardian of the establishment, in which position he evidently felt great satisfaction in driving away goats, dogs, fowls, &c. This he effected by walking after them with his wings fully expanded, and he seemed so large and so human that nothing ventured to dispute his authority. He also had a curious custom of dragging long sticks or pieces of creeper up to the house when he was hungry, and, after worrying and shaking them, pretending to eat them, as though to show to what a pass his hunger had brought him ! I never observed it at any other time. He always objected to being turned out of the house, holding his head as high as possible, inclining his bill upward, his head half turned round, while short croaks and snaps of his mandibles expressed his disapproval of this treatment. He slept on the roof, facing the wind ; even in strong gales this was his favourite site. In the early morning he soared aloft, and took one long hearty flight all round the neighbourhood at a good elevation, after which he did not leave the ground until he flew up at dusk to his perch on the roof.

"Colonel Legge mentions Blyth's reference to this bird's habit of feeling in the sand with its foot. Had Blyth observed the bird catching fish in shallow water he would have noticed that this is its mode of feeding. While it holds its bill in the water just above the mud, its mouth being half open, it drives the fish out of the mud or through the water with one foot or the other, in the direction of its bill. As some frightened fish makes a dart through the triangle formed by the bill and the mud there is a sudden snap, and the unlucky fish is generally caught by the tail before he can get clear through. If so, the bill holds the tail like a vice, the fish is slowly raised in the air, a slight jerk brings its body between the mandibles, where a few nips soon prepare it for its downward journey into the long neck-pouch. My tame bird did not follow the fish if he missed them, but, without raising his head, continued to drive others with his foot. This bird also had a queer habit of putting his head into any empty biscuit tin or large canister, and tapping the side of the tin with one foot, while he listened to the sounds with open mouth, and the silliest of expressions on his face. I have seen him experiment in this way with a pair of boots, but the result was evidently not altogether satisfactory. There was not much music to be extracted from a pair of boots, he found."

These birds have a habit, in common with *Anastomus oscitans*, of soaring to immense heights on fine cloudless days, and descending almost vertically, in a zig-zag line. I have known them drop in this manner from a height at which they were invisible in the blue sky. One first hears a rushing sound,—like that made by a Falcon when swooping on some hapless teal,—as the bird descends, and in five seconds after the speck is descried in the air the bird is on the ground. It does not simply come down by the action of gravity ; this can be seen when the descent is made from lower elevations. It requires a great impetus while circling round, and suddenly turning itself sideways, and changing its direction, throws almost the whole of this into its headlong descent.

In Ceylon this bird usually breeds in company with *Pelecanus philippinensis*, and in the same trees, but at a lower level. The eggs are laid chiefly in February and March, in both south-east and northern Ceylon, but some are also laid in January. The usual number is 4. Some are sparingly spotted.

The young have the cheeks and ear coverts grey; head and neck brown; lower plumage smoky white, darker across the abdomen and on the sides of the body.

Sub-Family, PLATALÆINÆ,—SPOONBILLS.

Bill flat, spathulate, long and rounded at the tip.

Gen. Platalea.—*Linn.*

Bill thin, flat, dilated and rounded at the tip (spathulate), otherwise as in *Tantalus;* toes connected by a small membrane extending as far as the second joint of the outer and the first joint of the inner one.

328. Platalea leucorodia (*Linn.*), *Bodd. Tab. Pl. En.* 405; *Gould, B. Eur.* pl. 286; *Jerd., B. Ind.* iii. p. 763; *Murray, Hdbk., Zool., &c., Sind,* p. 229; *Murray, Vert. Zool., Sind,* p. 227; *Legge, B. Ceylon,* pp. 1096, 1223, No. 1365; *Murray, Avif. Brit. Ind.* ii. p. 666.—The SPOONBILL.

Plumage pure white, except a buffy yellow patch on the upper breast, extending sometimes on to the back; orbitar skin orange yellow, also the skin of the gullet; head crested; bill and legs black, spotted or barred with yellowish; the tip yellowish during winter; irides blood red; legs black; nude facial skin and gular pouch orange yellow.

Length.—31 to 36 inches; wing 14 to 16; tail 6·25 to 6·5; bill at front 7 to 8·5.

The young have the shafts and tips of the primaries black.

Hab.—Ceylon, Sind, Beloochistan, Persia, Afghanistan and throughout India, frequenting rivers, lakes, &c.

Breeds throughout India nearly. Especially common in Sind and Ceylon. Nests made in trees; eggs white, chalky, broad ovals, and elongated 2·4 to 2·95 inch in length and 1·65 to 1·95 in breadth.

Sub-Family, ANASTOMINÆ.

Bill thick, stout, gaping in the middle.

Gen. Anastomous.—*Illiger.*

Bill long, curved, thick, solid, gaping in the middle, compressed at the sides; tail nearly even; nostrils basal, at the edge of the upper mandible; tarsi reticulated; tibia naked for half its length; toes webbed at the base.

329. Anastomous oscitans (*Bodd.*), *Jerd., B. Ind.* iii. p. 765 ; *Hume, Nests and Eggs, Ind. B.* p 630 ; *Blyth, B. Burm.* p. 158 ; *Hume, Str F.* iii. p. 192 ; *Hume, Str. F.* viii. p. 114 ; *Legge, B. Ceylon*, p. 1103 ; *Oates, Str. F.* x. p. 244 ; *Murray, Vert. Zool., Sind*, p. 277 ; *id., Avif., Brit. Ind.* ii. p. 666.—The SHELL IBIS.

Young.—Plumage light grey, darker on the head and neck, the feathers on the latter hair-like ; upper back, scapulars, primaries and secondaries, also the winglet and tail black, with purple reflections ; nude skin of the chin and front of the eyes greenish black ; in a later stage of plumage the head, sides of the face, nape and neck behind are dusky brown, the feathers short ; neck in front, breast, lower parts, back, wing coverts and tail pure white, the primaries and secondaries also, their shafts black, also the shafts of the winglet ; the first three primaries broadly margined with black on their outer and inner webs, their tips black ; the inner webs of the primaries margined only to the notch ; tertials white, also black shafted ; the upper series slaty grey, with their webs lax and disunited. In the breeding plumage the bird is entirely white ; bill greenish black ; nude orbitar and gular skin blackish ; irides grey or pale brown ; legs blackish.

Length.—29 to 30 inches ; wings 15 to 16 ; tail 7 ; bill at front 6·5 to 8 ; tarsus 5·25 to 5·5.

Hab.—Ceylon, Sind, Beloochistan, Persia, Punjab, N.-W. Provinces, Oudh, Bengal, Guzerat, and the Deccan ; abundant in Bengal and Central India, also Burmah ; chiefly found in the vicinity of rivers, lakes and marshes ; resident in some parts of India as in Sind, where it breeds from July to September in company with *Threskiornis melanocephalus.* Eggs, creamy white, from 2 to 2·52 inches in length and from 1·48 to 1·82 in breadth. In Ceylon the breeding season appears from Mr. Parker's notes to be later, viz., December. The nests are as usual built of sticks from 18 to 24 inches in diameter, with an egg cavity 8 or 9 inches wide, lined with aquatic stems and fine twigs. Usually four eggs are laid.

Sub-Family, IBIDINÆ.

Bill more slender, long and curved, as in *Anastomous.*

Gen. Threskiornis.—*Gray.*

Bill nearly square at base, curved ; upper mandible with a lateral groove extending to the tip ; nostrils situated at its base ; tail short ; hind toe half as long as the mid-toe ; head and neck nude ; scapulars and tertials lengthened and decomposed ; feathers of the breast elongated ; plumage white.

330. Threskiornis melanocephalus (*Lath.*), *Jerd., B. Ind.* iii. p. 768 ; *Hume, Nests and Eggs, Ind. B.* p. 632 ; *Murray, Vert. Zool., Sind*, p. 278 ; *Murray, Avif. Brit. Ind.* ii. p. 667, No. 1367. Tantalus melanocephalus, *Lath., Ind. Orn.* ii. p. 709. Ibis melanocephalus, *Salvad., Ucc. Born.*

p. 359; *Blyth, B. Burm.* p. 158; *Legge, B. Ceylon,* p. 1106; *Oates, B. Br. Burm.* p. 268.—The WHITE IBIS.

Head and neck nude; lower neck, back wings and their coverts, primaries, secondaries, entire under surface from the breast and also the tail, white; scapulars and tertials lengthened, their outer webs disunited, and of a greyish colour. In another stage of plumage the quills are black with green reflections; bill and legs black; irides blood red.

Length.—29 to 30 inches; wing 14; tail 5·75; bill at front 6; tarsus 4.

Hab.—Ceylon, Sind, Mekran Coast, Persia, Rajputana, Kutch, Guzerat, Concan, Deccan, and nearly throughout India, and Burmah. A resident wherever found; breeds from July to September. Eggs, 4—6, white, or dingy white, with a slight bluish tinge when fresh; size 2·5 × 1·75. In Ceylon it builds among a crowd of other waders, and breeds generally from January to April according to the district. The eggs in some cases, Mr. Parker says, had very faint sienna spots near the obtuse end. Many having a broken zone of them. Usually the eggs are elongated ovals but some are compressed towards the large end. The shells are course and glossless and of a very pale blue colour. The average size of 20 eggs is given by Mr. Parker as 2·54 × 1·69.

Gen. **Falcinellus.**—*Bech.*

Bill long and slender, more so than in *Threskiornis*: tarsus longer; 2nd and 3rd quills longest.

Falcinellus igneus. The Glossy Ibis.

331. Falcinellus igneus (*Linn.*), *Jerd.*, *B. Ind.* iii. p. 770; *Hume, Nests and Eggs, Ind. B.* p. 635; *Blyth, B. Burm.*, p. 158; *Elliot, P. Z. S.* 1877, p. 503; *Hume, Str. F.* viii. p. 114; *Doig, Str. F.* viii. p. 377; *Oates, Str. F.* x. p. 245; *Murray, Vert. Zool., Sind,* p. 279; *id., Avif. Brit. Ind.* ii. p. 669, No. 1370. Tantalus falcinellus, *Linn., Syst. Nat.* i. p. 241. Scolopax rufa, *Scop. Ann.* i. p. 93. Numenius igneus, *S. G. Gmel., Nov. Comm. Petrop.* xv. p. 460, t. 18. Plegadis falcinellus, *Dresser, B. Eur.* vi. p. 335, pl.; *Legge, B. Ceylon,* p. 1109; *Oates, B. Br. Burm.* ii. p. 271.—The Glossy Ibis.

Head, on the crown and sides, deep greenish dark brown, glossed with metallic purple, the feathers lanceolate; neck, nape, chin and throat, also the back and breast, deep rich reddish brown or chestnut red; lower back, rump, wing coverts and tail dark green, with bronze and purple reflections; primaries dark brownish black, tinged with green; tertiaries dark red brown; legs blackish green, with a blue garter above the knee; claw of mid-toe scooped or hollow below, and forming a sharp edge on one side; irides brown; lores nude.

Length.—22 to 23 inches; wing 10·5 to 11; bill at front 6 to 6·5; tarsus 4·5. Birds of the year are dark brown, the feathers of the head, chin and throat margined with white or lineated; back greenish brown, very little glossed; under parts dusky.

Hab.—Ceylon, Sind, Beloochistan, Persia, Afghanistan, Punjab, N.-W. Provinces, Oudh, Bengal, Rajputana, Kutch, Central India, Guzerat and the Deccan: also Burmah. Recorded also from Arracan. It is not known from the Concan, but possibly occurs there, being a bird essentially affecting paddy fields, marshes and jheels. Breeds in Sind, also in Ceylon, whereas in the case of some of the other waders, the breeding time varies with the season and abundance of food. The latter is said by Mr. Parker to cause it to be earlier in some years than in others. Generally it may be said to breed from February to April, size 2·07 × 1·35.

ORDER,—NATATORES.

Feet more or less fully webbed; tarsi compressed, generally short, except in the *Phœnicopteridæ;* bill various; wings also variously developed. The first tribe of the order is *Lamellirostres,* or birds with thick depressed bills usually covered with soft skin, the tip commonly called the "nail," above being horny; the edges of the bill are serrated, forming lamellar teeth, which serve as a sieve.

Family, PHŒNICOPTERIDÆ.

Bill thick, rounded, rather compressed on the sides, suddenly bent downwards in the middle: tarsi and thighs long, the latter naked; tarsi scutellate.

Gen. **Phœnicopterus**.—*Linn.*

Margin of bill lamellate and dentate; nostrils in a groove covered by membrane; neck very long; 1st and 2nd quill of wing longest; other characters as in the Family.

332. Phœnicopterus antiquorum (*Tem.*) *Bodd.*, *Tab. P. E.* 63; *Naum. Vogt.* t. 233; *Gould.*, *B. Eur.* pl. 287; *Murray, Avif. Brit. Ind.* ii. p. 669, No. 1371. Phœnicopterus roseus (*Pall.*), *Jerd.*, *B. Ind.* iii. p. 775, No. 944; *Hume, Str. F.* i. p. 257; *Murray, Hdbk., Zool., &c., Sind,* p. 230; *Legge, B. Ceylon,* pp. 1092-1222.—The Flamingo.

Plumage throughout of a rosy white in the adult bird; primaries and secondaries black; primary and greater wing coverts white, dark shafted and broadly tipped with black, rest of the wing coverts and tertiaries rosy red; axillaries and under wing coverts rosy red; bill rosy, broadly black at the tip; legs and feet rosy red.

Length.—48 to 54 inches; wing 16 to 16·5; tail 6; bill 4 to 4·12. Birds of the year have scarcely any rosy tinge, and the plumage, especially of the upper parts, is mixed with dusky.

Hab.—Ceylon, South India, Beloochistan, Persia, Afghanistan, Punjab, N.-W. Provinces, Oudh, Bengal, Central India, Rajputana, Kutch, Guzerat, Concan and Deccan. Everywhere in flocks of thousands on all the lakes, rivers, &c., especially in Sind. Mr. Hume (*Str. F.* i. p. 257) truly describes them "as occurring in countless myriads, seen either massed upon the water, as huge rosy islands, or floating above it like a sunset cloud in all the large lakes of Sind. On taking flight, the exposure of the rosy upper and under wing coverts turns the mass into a gigantic brilliant rosy scarf, waving to and fro in mighty folds as it floats away." They are also common about the Kurrachee harbour, chiefly on the mud flats and in Clifton Bay; usually they are in large parties drawn up in line. When feeding they have their necks and heads bent down in such a position that the upper mandible rests on the ground; with it they stir up the limpid ooze in search of animalculæ, minute crustacea, fish, &c., on which they live. Like the Cranes the Flamingoes also have sentinels posted to give warning of danger; their flesh is not considered good, but the Mohannas or fishermen caste on the Indus consider it palatable, the fishy taste being lost on their palates, owing to their principal diet being fish. The ancients considered it choice food, and the Egyptians, at the present day, are partial to the flesh. From the tongue they are said to extract an oil which they use for flavouring certain viands.

They have been found breeding at Fao in Mesopotamia; the nest is as curious as the structure of the bird, being a truncated cone, built entirely of stiff clayey mud, on which the parent bird sits either astride or with its long legs folded under it. Eggs, 2 in number, white, and very chalky. In Ceylon the breeding season appears to be March. Mr. Parker says he has received information of two sites, one in the South-East and another in the North-East, both being in very wild unfrequented little known districts. The nests are said to be raised up in the marshy flats and to have a saucer-like concavity on the top. The birds are said to sit on the nest with their legs doubled under them.

Family, ANATIDÆ.—*Vigors.*

Bill flat and broad, laminated at the sides; food insects and tender aquatic plants, which they obtain in shallow muddy places.

Sub-Family, PLECTROPTERINÆ.—*G. R. Gray.*

Bill long and broad, tip horny; knee and above bare; tarsi with squarish scales; hind toe long; wing with one or more spurs on the shoulders; a fleshy carbuncle at base of upper mandible; plumage glossy black.

Gen. **Sarkidiornis**.—*Eyton.*

Characters those of the Sub-Family; 1st and 2nd primaries sub-equal and longest.

333. Sarkidiornis melanonotus. *Penn. in Forst. Ind. Zool.* p. 21, pl. 11; *Newton, Str. F.* viii. p. 415; *Murray, Avif. Brit. Ind.* ii. p. 677, No. 1379. Sarcidiornis melanonota, *Jerd., B. Ind.* iii. p. 785; *Hume, Nests and Eggs, Ind. B.* p. 636; *Blyth, B. Burm.* p. 165; *Hume and Marsh., Game Birds*, iii. p. 91, pl.; *Legge, B. Ceylon*, p. 1063; *Oates, B. Br. Burm.* iii. p. 275; *Murray, Vert. Zool., Sind*, p. 286.—The COMB DUCK.

Top of the head and back of neck black, spotted with white, more so on the back of the neck; cheeks, sides and front of the neck white with a few black spots; breast and entire under parts white; chin and throat white; back, scapulars, tertiaries and wing coverts glossy black, glossed with purple; upper tail coverts glossed greenish; primaries and secondaries black; the lesser wing coverts glossed with purplish green; tail black; bill of male with a fleshy protuberance; irides dark brown; bill black.

Length.—28 to 30 inches; wing 13 to 15; tail 6. Female is smaller, and less brightly coloured.

Hab.—Sind, Punjab, N.-W. Provinces, Oudh, Bengal, Rajputana, Kutch, Kattiawar, Guzerat, Concan and Deccan, South India and Ceylon; also British Burmah.

A straggler in Sind. Breeds in the N.-W. Provinces during July and August. In Ceylon it is said to breed in the Manaar districts from January to March, usually on trees in the proximity of large sheets of water.

334. Nettapus coromandelianus (*Gmel.*), *Jerd., B. Ind.* iii. p. 786; *Blyth, B. Burm.* p. 165; *David et Oust. Ois. Chine*, p. 501; *Legge, B. Ceylon*, p. 1066; *Hume and Marsh., Game Birds*, iii. p. 101, pl.; *Oates, B. Br. Burm.* ii. p. 272; *Murray, Avif. Brit. Ind.* ii. p. 677, No. 1380. Anser coromandeliana, *Gmel., Syst. Nat.* i. p. 522. Nettapus coromandelicus (*L*), *Hume, Nests and Eggs, Ind. B.* p. 638. Nettapus coromandus (*L.*), *Hume, Str. F.* iii. 192.—The COTTON TEAL.

Forehead, crown and nape hair brown, remainder of the head, whole neck and lower plumage white; collar round the neck black in front, glossy green on hind neck; a second demi-collar from the breast upwards below this; under tail coverts dark brown mottled with white; upper plumage glossy green; the secondaries are broadly tipped with white and the primaries also, their basal halves are dark brown; upper tail coverts white, freckled with brown; tail brown; under wing coverts greenish black. The female has a line from the lores through the eye dusky black, surmounted by a dirty white supercilium; rest of the head, whole neck and the upper breast dull white mottled with brown; lower plumage dull white; upper tail coverts white, freckled with brown. In winter the male is like the female, but has always the white patch on the primaries. Bill black; irides red. Mr. Parker describes the nestling as covered with black and greyish white down, the centre of the forehead, crown, occiput and nape are black, bordered by greyish white; a black line passes from the bill through the eye to the hind head; below this greyesh white; rest of the body black; iris dark brown, nearly black.

Length.—13 inches; tail 3; wing 6·5.; tarsus 1; bill from gape 1 1.

Hab.—Nearly throughout India, also Ceylon and Burmah, except the drier regions as Sind, Kutch, Rajputana. Breeds in July and August in the holes of trees, laying from 8 to 10 eggs, of a delicate ivory white colour. They generally affect swamps, marshes, and inundated ponds and ditches.

Sub-Family, TADORNINÆ (Anatinæ, *Sw.*)

Plumage rufous; bill flattened towards the tip, with horny termination; hind toe long and slightly lobed.

Dendrocygna, *Sw.*—WHISTLING DUCKS.

Bill rather large, of uniform width; secondaries long, also the tarsi; 2nd, 3rd and 4th primaries sub-equal and longest.

335. Dendrocygna Javanica (*Horsf.*), *Hume and Dav., Str. F.* vi. p. 486; *Legge, B. Ceylon*, p. 1069; *Hume and Marsh., Game Birds*, iii. p. 109, pl.; *Oates, B. Br. Burm.* ii. p. 273; *Murray, Vert. Zool., Sind*, p. 287; *Murray, Avif. Brit. Ind.* ii. p. 678, No. 1381. Anas javanica, *Horsf. Trans.. Linn. Soc.* xiii. p. 199. Dendrocygna aswuree, *Jerd., B. Ind.* iii. p. 789. Dendrocygna arcuata (*Cuv.*), *apud Hume, Nests and Eggs, Ind. B.* p. 639; *Oates, Str. F.* v. p. 169.—The LESSER WHISTLING TEAL.

Top of head and occiput dull wood brown, and a narrow streak of the same continued down the middle of the back of the neck from behind the nape; sides of the face and neck fulvous brown; chin and throat albescent; lower neck and breast yellowish chestnut, gradually passing into the light chestnut of the under surface of the body; vent and under tail coverts albescent;

back and scapulars dusky brown, the feathers edged with dingy fulvous chestnut, forming lunules; upper tail coverts chestnut; tail brown, tipped slightly paler; primaries and secondaries black; greater coverts and tertiaries dusky brown; lesser and median coverts deep maroon; axillaries black; bill dusky brown, darker at the tip; irides deep brown; eyelids bright yellow to pale golden; legs plumbeous.

Length.—17·5 to 18 inches; wing 8 to 8·5; tail 2 to 2·12; bill at front 1·5 tarsus 1·75.

Hab.—Sind, Punjab, N.-W. Provinces and the Indian Peninsula generally, but not in the more arid tracts, where water is not abundant, as in the interior of Rajputana. According to Hume, there is scarcely any suitable locality within the limits of the Indian empire, including Burmah, Ceylon, the Andamans and Nicobars, in which this species does not occur either as a permanent resident or a seasonal visitant. It is essentially a tree duck, and in the breeding season especially affects the larger pieces of water, in the vicinity of trees. At other times it is found in nearly every suitable piece of water. It nidificates on trees, making a nest of twigs, &c., or occupies old nests of Herons and Ibises. In Sind it has been found breeding in great numbers on the Eastern Narra, and I have taken a nest of 11 eggs at the One Tree Tank, six miles from Kurrachee. Mr. Doig, who took its eggs in the Narra, found 10 as the greatest number from any one nest. "The nests," he says, "were composed of green twigs, and in some instances of leaves of the large bulrush trodden down to make a platform." In Ceylon Mr. Parker has found nests in the Southern Province in June and July, and in the Northern in January, February, March, April and May. The average of 20 eggs he gives as 1·85 × 1·44. Mr. Hume (*Game Birds*) records instances of the curious fact of this species carrying its Young in its feet from the nest to the water. Mr. Kemp in the Futtehpore District adds his testimony to the fact, having obtained an egg from off a narrow ridge where the bird was seen to carry it just before he shot it. Mr. Hume says—"He heard of their being seen flying down to the water with ducklings on their backs, and that twice he saw them carrying these in their claws. On one of these occasions, between 8 and 9 A.M., he saw a duck carry down her whole brood of seven, one at a time, from a hole in a huge mango tree to the water, she passing each time within three yards of his face. In regard to the smaller race of this species mentioned in *Str. F.* ix. p. 486. I have examined a large series of skins of this species, and cannot but conclude that the more elongated feathers of the sides are not sufficient to constitute a species, nor can the very small differences in size be taken into consideration.

336. Dendrocygna fulva (*Gmel.*), *Sclater and Salv.*, *P. Z. S.* 1876, p. 372; *Hume and Marsh.*, *Game Birds*, iii. p. 119, pl.; *Oates*, *B. Br. Burm.* ii. p. 274; *Murray Avif. Brit.*, *Ind.* ii. p. 679, No. 1382. Anas fulva, *Gmel.*, *Syst. Nat.* 1. p. 530. Dendrocygna major, *Jerd.*, *Madras*

Journal, 1840, p. 218; *id.*, *Ill. Ind. Orn.* pl. xxiii ; *Hume, Str. F.* iii. p. 1293.—The LARGER WHISTLING TEAL.

Top of head and sides of the face rufescent brown, slightly paler on the cheeks; chin and throat albescent, a broad ring or patch of white in the middle of the neck; a broad black line down the back of the neck from below the nape; back, scapulars, primaries, secondaries, tertials and greater wing coverts dark brown, the feathers of the back with rufescent or chestnut edging, forming lunules; lesser wing coverts dark maroon; breast yellowish chestnut, gradually passing into the light chestnut of the under parts of the body; vent, under and upper tail coverts white or fulvous white; tail dark brown; bill plumbeous; irides brown; legs and feet plumbeous.

Length.—20·5 to 21 inches; wing 9·25; tail 2·5 to 2·8; bill from gape 2 to 2·4; tarsus 2·25.

Hab.—Ceylon, Sind, Punjab, N.-W. and Central Provinces, Oudh, Bengal, Rajputana, Kutch, Guzerat, Concan and Deccan, also S. India in suitable localities; also Burmah. In Ceylon it is a rare straggler in the Central Province.

Gen. **Casarca**.—*Bp.*

Bill moderate; culmen with a knob at the base; nail at tip large; hind toe lobed; wing spurred; plumage from buffy orange to bright orange.

337. Casarca rutila, *Pall.*, *Hist. d' Egypt*, t. x. p. 1; *Gould, B. Eur.* pl. 358; *Jerd.*, *B. Ind.* iii. p. 791; *Str. F.* i. 260; iv. 198; *Murray*, *Hdbk., Zool., &c., Sind; Hume, Game Birds, Ind.* p. 123. Tadorna casarca, *Dresser, B. Eur.* vi. p. 461, pl.; *Legge, B. Ceylon*, p. 1070; *Oates, B. Br. Burm.* ii. p. 277. (Vern. *Mungh*, Sind).—The RUDDY SHELLDRAKE or BRAHMINY DUCK.

Male.—Head, on the crown and sides buff, darkening on the nape and hind neck, and gradually passing into deep orange or orange fulvous on the upper back and breast; a seasonal glossy black band round the middle of the neck in males (not present in all specimens); chin buff; upper back, scapulars and breast in front deep orange brown, orange fulvous, or rufescent, the colour being variable; in some specimens the feathers are edged paler; lower back ochreous, the feathers finely vermiculated with black; rump black, also the upper tail coverts and tail, which have a greenish gloss; lower abdomen and under tail coverts deep chestnut; in females and in males out of season, and without the black neck collar, the entire under surface from the breast is pale chestnut or fulvous chestnut, sometimes with the feathers round the vent darkening into deeper chestnut; wing spurred at the bend; primaries dark brown; greater coverts and outer webs of secondaries glossy purplish green, forming a broad speculum; lesser and median covers white, sometimes with a buffish tinge; tertials like the back, some of the feathers finely vermiculated with brown at the tips; under wing coverts and axillaries white, also the edge of the wing.

The *female* wants the black collar at all seasons, and is generally duller in colour, the head being very pale buffy white; the crown and neck in some mouse grey; bill black; irides dark brown; legs black.

Length.—Males, 24·5 to 27 inches; wing 14·5 to 15·5; tail 5·5 to 6; tarsus 2 to 2·4; bill at gape 2.

Hab.—Ceylon, Sind, Persia, Beloochistan, Afghanistan, E. Turkistan, Punjab, N.-W. Provinces, Oudh, Nepaul, Bengal, Rajputana, Central India, Kutch Guzerat, the Concan, Deccan and Southern India.

The Ruddy Shelldrake is a winter visitant to India. In Sind it is found on all the large lakes and brooks and along the Indus river in great numbers; and on the Munchur especially; like geese, large parties resort to the fields of sprouting wheat in the the early morning and at night-fall, and do much damage.

They are extremely shy and wary birds, and as Mr. Reid, in *Game Birds*, remarks—"It will not only keep a sharp look-out on its own account, but will fly along the Jheel side before the gunner, uttering its warning note and put every bird on the *qui vive*."

Sub-Family, ANATINÆ.

Hind toe small, not bordered by a membrane; bill even in width throughout, or wider at the tip; lamellæ numerous, fine and bristly.

Gen. Spatula—*Boie.*

Bill longer than the head, narrow at the base, broad at the tip, shovel-like; nail small; lamellæ fine and bristly.

Spatula clypeata. The Shoveller.

338. Spatula clypeata (*Linn.*), *Bodd. Tab. P. E.* pp. 971, 972; *Gould, B. Eur.* pl. 300; *Jerd., B. Ind.* iii. p 796; *Str. F.* iv. p. 199; *Murray, Hdbk., Zool., &c., Sind,* p. 235; *id., Vert. Zool. Sind,* p. 220; *Hume and Marsh., Game Birds, Ind.* p. 141; *Legge, B. Ceylon,* p. 1086; *Murray, Avif. Brit. Ind.* ii. p. 682. (*Vern., Alipat,* Sind).—The SHOVELLER.

Male.—Head and neck all round deep or dark brown with glossy green reflections; back brown; scapulars and breast white; rump and upper tail coverts glossy brown black; sides of the rump white; tail brown, the outer feathers white, the rest edged with white; primaries dusky brown, white shafted; secondaries the same, their outer webs rich bright green and forming the speculum; lesser wing coverts pale blue; greater wing coverts dusky brown, tipped with white, forming a bar across the wing; tertials long and pointed, pale blue on their outer webs, purplish black on the inner ones, the tips of some of the elongated ones white; abdomen rich chestnut brown or brownish red; lower tail coverts black, glossed greenish; flanks chestnut brown, the feathers finely vermiculated with dark brown; bill black; legs orange; irides yellow.

Length.—19 to 20 inches; wing 9 to 10; tail 3·5 to 4; tarsus 1·2 to 1·4; bill from gape 2·9 to 3.

The *female* is slightly smaller, averaging 19 inches in length at the outside; wing 8 to 9. The head is pale reddish brown, with dusky shaft-streaks; breast pale brownish rufous, with dusky brown spots; back dusky brown, the edges and tips of the feathers paler and rufous white; lesser wing coverts tinged with pale blue; speculum green, and a white bar across the wing as in the male.

Hab.—Ceylon, Sind, Beloochistan, Persia, Afghanistan, Nepaul, Cashmere, Eastern Turkestan, Punjab, N-W. Provinces and Oudh, Bengal, Central India, Rajputana, Kutch, Guzerat, Concan, Deccan, and South India.

Winter visitors to India, affecting all the lakes, marshes, ponds, &c., feeding on worms, larvæ, tadpoles, seeds, and young shoots of aquatic plants. They are not naturally shy, as in village ponds they are frequently seen dabbling about, or standing in the shallow edge of ponds, while the inhabitants are drawing water or bathing.

Gen. **Anas**, *Linn.*

Bill slightly longer than the head, of nearly uniform width throughout; tertials long and pointed; tail wedge-shaped; nostrils near the base of the bill; middle tail feather curled.

339. Anas pæcilorhyncha, *Forst., Ind. Zool.* p. 23, pl. 13; *Jerd., B. Ind.* iii. p. 799; *Hume, Nests and Eggs, Ind. B.* p. 643; *Blyth, B. Burm.* p. 165; *Hume and Marsh, Game Birds*, iii. p. 165, pl.; *Legge, B. Ceylon*, p. 1073; *Murray, Vert. Zool. Sind*, p. 292; *Oates, B. Br. Burm.* ii. p. 282; *Murray, Avif. Brit. Ind.* ii. p. 684.—The Spotted Billed Duck.

Top of head to the nape behind dark sepia brown, also a line from the base of the upper mandible through the eye, ending in a point behind; supercilium, sides of the face and neck dingy fulvous, minutely speckled with brown; lower neck, breast and abdomen the same, the brown spots larger than on the upper neck, and increasing in size on the breast, abdomen and flanks; chin and throat unspotted fulvous; upper back, scapulars and lesser and median wing coverts hair brown ; lower back and rump black ; primaries deep brown ; secondaries brown on their inner webs ; speculum on their outer webs, rich emerald glossy green, tipped with black, the black tips of the innermost narrowly edged with white ; greater wing coverts sepia brown at base, with a subterminal white band and tipped with black; tertiaries white on their outer webs and hair brown on their inner ; tail deep brown, the central feathers darker ; vent and under tail coverts nearly black ; under wing coverts white ; bill black, with a spot of red at the base, and yellow at the tip ; legs and feet vermilion red ; irides deep brown.

Length.—23·5 to 25·9 ; wing 10·5 to 11 ; tail 4·75 to 5·75 ; tarsus 1·85 to 1·93 ; bill from gape 2·5 to 2·75. Females are slightly smaller.

Hab.—A permanent resident in India. Breeds in Sind and the Punjab. Found in large numbers in Ceylon, Sind, Beloochistan, Persia, the drier parts of the Punjab and Rajputana, also in the N.-W and Central Provinces, Oudh, Kutch, Guzerat and the Deccan.

Affects large lakes, ponds, brushy or weedy tanks, and often the banks of rivers, feeding on worms, molluscs, insects, larvæ, young shoots of grass, &c. Mr. Hume says (*Game B.* iii, p. 168) "that the breeding season of this duck varies a great deal with locality ;" in the N.-W. Provinces and Oudh, also the eastern portions of Rajputana and the Punjab, July, August and September are the months ; in Guzerat, October. In Sind Mr. Doig obtained eggs at the latter end of April and May on a small island covered with long grass in the middle of the Narra.

Gen. **Dafila** (*Leach.*), *Gray, Gen. Birds,* iii. p. 615.

Tail with the central feathers narrow and much lengthened beyond the rest ; neck long ; bill elevated at the base, of nearly uniform width ; 1st primary of wing longest.

Dafila acuta. The Pintail.

340. Dafila acuta (*Linn.*), *Jerd., B. Ind.* iii. p. 803; *Dresser, B. Eur.* vi. p. 531, pl.; *Hume, Str. F.* iii. p. 193; *Scully, Str. F.* iv. p. 200; *id., Str. F.* viii. p. 363; *Hume and Marsh., Game Birds*, iii. p. 189, pl.; *Oates, Str. F.* x. p. 245; *Murray, Vert. Zool., Sind*, p. 297; *Oates, B. Br. Burm.* ii. p. 279; *Linn., Syst. Nat.* i. p. 202; *Blyth, B. Burm.* p. 166; *Murray, Avif. Brit. Ind.* ii. p. 689, Anas acuta (*L.*) *Legge, B. Ceylon*, p. 1076.—The PINTAIL.

Male.—Entire head, face, chin and throat umber brown, the feathers on the crown slightly darker and with a ferruginous tinge; back of the neck dark brown, nearly black; lower neck, breast and abdomen white; a white line running up on each side of the neck to the occiput; back, sides of the breast and flanks marked with transverse unduiations of black and white; upper tail coverts cinereous or pale fulvous brown; under tail coveıts deep velvet black; tail with the central feathers black, much elongated, and glossed with greenish, the others dusky brown and margined with white; primaries dusky greyish brown, the shafts much paler; secondaries dusky brown on their inner webs, their outer webs forming the speculum, dark greenish bronze, edged with black and tipped broadly white; upper part of the speculum edged with pale ferruginous; tips of the greater coverts, like the lesser and median coverts, are dusky brown; scapulars black, edged with yellowish; tertiaries long and pointed, deep black and edged with whitish; bill black, with a bluish tinge on the sides of the upper mandible; legs and feet slaty or blackish grey; irides dark brown.

Length.—22 to 29 inches; wing 10·3 to 11·75; tail 7·5 to 8; bill 2 to 2·45.

Females.—Smaller. *Length.*—20 to 22·5; wing 9·3 to 10.

Female.—Forehead and crown, also back of the head, nape and neck dark brown, the feathers with fulvous edgings; sides of the face, chin, throat and foreneck fulvous with brown spots and streaks, which become longer and darker on the lower neck; breast and the lower parts fulvous with obscure crescentic brownish markings on the breast, flanks and sides of the rump and large spots on the lower abdomen; back and scapulars dark brown, with lunate or crescentic markings of white and pale buff about the middle of each feather, and edged with whitish; greater and lesser wing coverts dusky brown, with margins and tips of white; primaries a shade lighter; speculum brownish bronze, unglossed, the tips of the feathers white; tertiaries dusky brown, margined with white; tail long, pointed, dark brown, with imperfect bars and streaks of white or yellowish white; under tail coverts fulvous white, with brown spots.

Hab.—Sind, Beloochistan, Persia, Afghanistan, Punjab, N.-W. and Central Provinces, Oudh, Bengal, Kutch, Concan, Deccan, Guzerat, Central and Southern India and Ceylon. Hume says—"There is no district in the Empire, from Ceylon to Kashmir, and from Kashmir to Sadya, Munipoor and

Moulmein, where the Pintail does not occur in greater or less abundance except in South Tenasserim."

The Pintail affects the large broads or dhunds and lakes, and is seldom seen except in large parties. It is held in much esteem for the table, and for this purpose is netted in great numbers with the Gadwall and other water birds. On the Munchur Lake the fowlers net from 100 to 200 daily, and a sportsman in suitable localities could obtain two or three dozens at least as a good day's sport, besides other game. Hume, like myself, thinks that, on the whole, next to the Mallard, the Pintail is the best duck for the table in India, the Gadwall ranking third.

Gen. **Querquedula,** *Steph., Gray, Gen. B.* iii. p. 616.

Bill of uniform width, as long as the head, and slightly raised at the base; nail horny, hooked and narrow; lamellæ not apparent; wings long, second quill longest; secondaries long and pointed; tail wedge-shaped.

341. Querquedula crecca (*Linn.*), *Bod. Tab. P. E.* p. 946; *Gould, B. Eur.* pl. 364; *Jerd., B. Ind.* iii. p. 806; *Dresser, B. Eur.* vi. p. 507, pl.; *Murray, Hdbk., Zool., &c., Sind,* p. 235; *Oates, B. Br. Burm.* ii. p. 285. *Murray, Avif. Br. Ind.* ii. p. 692. Anas crecca, *Linn., Syst. Nat.* i. p. 204; *Legge, B. Ceylon,* p. 1083; *Hume, Game Birds, Ind.* iii. p. 206. (*Kardo,* Sind; *Moorghabi,* Hind.).—The Common Teal.

Forehead, crown, face, cheeks, throat and upper neck in front rich chestnut brown; chin black, a narrow dark line round the base of the bill, followed by a white or buffy one on the side, which meets a similar coloured superciliary stripe, and another under the eye; behind the eye, between the hind superciliary and lower eye-streak is a broad glossy green, or dark green patch, which meets on the back of the neck; breast rufescent or white, tinged with reddish and spotted with black; upper abdomen white; lower abdomen in some minutely barred with brownish; flanks barred with brown or blackish brown; upper back and scapulars marked with undulating white and black transverse bars; lower back dark brown, with faint traces only of paler transverse bars; tail hair brown or dusky brown, the feathers edged with white; under tail coverts black, the feathers on the sides creamy yellow; primaries dusky brown, edged on their outer webs and tipped darker; first six secondaries velvet black on their outer webs; next four or five forming the speculum glossy green, and followed by the black outer web of the first tertial; lesser and median coverts dusky or greenish brown; greater coverts the same and tipped with white or yellowish white, forming a border to the speculum above; bill black, or brownish black; irides brown; legs and feet greyish or plumbeous.

Length.—14·5 to 15·75 inches; wing 7 to 8; tail 2·9 to 3·5.

The female has the head, neck and upper part dusky brown; the feathers edged with white or fulvous white on the head and neck and lunated on the back; speculum as in the male, but slightly duller; chin and throat white, with black spots; breast and flanks white and spotted with dark brown abdomen white; under tail coverts with brown streaks.

Length.—13·5 to 14·7 inches, with a wing of 6·5 to 7·5.

Hab.—Ceylon, Sind, Beloochistan, Persia, Afghanistan, Punjab, N.-W. and Central Provinces, Rajputana, Kutch and throughout India and Burmah.

Abundant wherever it occurs, frequenting tanks, rivers, ponds and jheels, &c.

342. Querquedula circia (*Linn.*), *Jerd., B. Ind.* iii. p. 807; *Dresser, B. Eur.* vi. p. 513, pl.; *Hume, Nests and Eggs*, p. 644; *Scully, Str. F.* iv. p. 201; *Hume and Marsh*, *Game Birds*, iii. p. 215, pl.; *Bingham, Str. F.* ix. p. 198; *Murray, Vert. Zool., Sind*, p. 301; *Oates, B. Br. Burm.* ii. p. 286; *Murray, Avif. Brit. Ind.* ii. p. 693. Anas circia, *Linn., Syst. Nat.* i. p. 204; *Blyth, B. Burm.*, p. 166; *Legge, B. Ceylon*, p. 1080.—The Garganey Teal.

Querquedula circia. The Garganey or Blue-winged Teal.

Male.—Forehead purplish brown, finely streaked with white; crown of the head, occiput, nape and a line half way down the back of the neck dark umber or blackish brown, bounded on each side by a white superciliary streak, which extends to the sides of the neck; face, sides of the neck, cheeks, throat and neck chestnut brown, the feathers with white mesial streaks; chin black, breast and upper abdomen yellowish brown, tinged in some specimens with ferruginous, and with broad crescentic dark brown markings; lower abdomen white or yellowish white, with, in some specimens, transverse, dusky striæ behind; flanks with transverse undulations of black and white; axillaries white with black bases; back brownish black, the feathers edged with yellowish brown; primaries dark brown on their outer webs and tips, pale wood brown on their inner webs, in some specimens narrowly edged with whitish; wing spot on outer web of secondaries dull green, slightly glossed and tipped with white, the white tips forming the second bar across the wing; greater coverts ashy grey or bluish ashy, broadly tipped with white; lesser and median coverts ashy grey, or bluish ashy; scapulars long and lanceolate, black, with a mesial white shaft, and narrowly edged greyish white or white; tertiaries dusky brown, edged with white on their outer webs; rump and upper tail coverts dark brown, with bars of yellowish white; tail dark brown, the feathers edged with yellowish or fulvous white; under tail coverts yellowish white with black spots; bill black above, brownish on the lower mandible; irides brown; legs and feet greenish grey or plumbeous.

Length.—15·5 to 16·5 inches; wing 7·2 to 8; tail 3·2 to 3·5; bill 1·75 to 1·85.

The *female* has the chin and throat white; head on the crown brown with spots and streaks of a darker shade; back of neck brown, the feathers edged with white; eye-streak faint; speculum dull and indistinct, bordered above and below with white; breast and abdomen greyish white, spotted with brown.

Length.—14·5 to 15 inches, with a wing of from 7 to 7·5.

Hab.—The same as *Q. crecca.*

Not found in as great numbers as *Q. crecca*, affects the same situations, and is considered excellent for the table. It is chiefly a nocturnal feeder, concealing itself in the jheels and dhunds, among the high grass, during the day; when disturbed it usually returns to the same spot. Hume says "that at nights in some parts of the country they come in such crowds into the paddy fields as to destory acres of crop at one visit; their food, like *Q. crecca*, is chiefly vegetable, as tender shoots and leaves of water plants, seeds, bulbs, &c., but on the sea coasts, especially the Sind and Mekran Coast, where they are frequently found in some numbers, crustacea, slugs, fry of fish and algæ form their diet."

Sub-Family, FULIGULINÆ, *Sw.*—Diving Ducks.

Bill elevated at base, flat and broad towards the tip; nail strong, broad and horny; tarsi short, rather compressed; toes long, webbed to the end; hind toe short; tail short and rounded.

Gen. **Fuligula**, *Steph.*; Branta, *Boie.*; *Gray, Gen. B.* iii. p. 620.

Bill nearly as long as the head, moderately wide, tip depressed; nail large; lamellæ distinct; wings moderate, 1st quill longest.

343. Fuligula rufina, *Pall., Zoogr. t.* 79; *Bodd. Tab. P. E.* 928; *Gould, B. Eur.* pl. 369; *Jerd., B. Ind.* iii. p. 811; *Str. F.* iv. p. 201; *Murray, Hdbk., Zool., &c., Sind*, p. 238; *Hume, Game Birds, Ind.* iii. p. 253; *Legge, B. Ceylon*, p. 1087; *Murray, Avif. Brit. Ind.* ii. p. 697. (*Rattoba*, Sind; *Lallseeree*, Punjab.)—The Red-crested Pochard.

Male.—Crown of the head, with an elongated crest of a silky texture and dull yellow colour; head on the sides, cheeks, chin and throat rich chestnut, with a tinge of rose red or reddish bay; nape and a line continued down the back of the neck black; lower neck, breast, sides of the breast and abdomen black, in some specimens the abdomen is a chocolate brown; flanks white; back pale brown, or yellowish brown; the scapulars with a fulvous tinge; end of the wing and a large spot on the sides of the back white; primaries brown on their outer webs and at their tips, white on their inner webs; secondaries white, with sub-terminal dark tips; tertiaries pale brown; rump and upper tail coverts nearly black; tail dark brown; bill bright vermilion; legs and feet vermilion or reddish orange; irides reddish brown.

Length.—20·5 to 22 inches; wing 10 to 10·75; tail 3·0 to 4·0; bill 2·3 to 2·5.

Females are not much smaller, and average from 20 to 21 inches. Forehead and crown dark brown; the neck on the back and nape slightly paler; crest much less developed; sides of the face and neck brownish white; speculum greyish white; breast and flanks yellowish brown, some of the feathers edged paler; shoulder of wing greyish white; tail yellowish brown, legs and feet reddish brown; back rufous or yellowish brown, some of the feathers edged paler.

Hab.—Ceylon, Sind, Beloochistan, Persia, Afghanistan, Punjab, N.-W. Provinces, Bengal, Guzerat, Kutch, Rajputana, the Deccan and throughout India generally, except perhaps in Southern India.

It is said to breed in parts of Persia. Occurs everywhere in large numbers during winter from the latter end of October to about the middle of April; a few, however, remain beyond the 10th of April. They are not very shy in their wild state, except in well-shot districts, and usually large bags may be made of this duck in a single day; they swim well and dive equally well, remaining a long while under water. Large lakes and rivers, and situations where there is much deep water, are the natural resorts of this duck.

Mergus merganser. The Goosander.

Family, PODICIPIDÆ.

Tarsus compressed; primaries short; feet lobed; tail very short, almost wanting; bill slightly curved above at the tip.

Podiceps.—*Latham.*

Bill straight, moderately stout; nostrils oblong, lateral, in a short groove; wings short; tarsus scutellate; hallux bordered by a web.

344. Podiceps minor (*Linn.*), *Bodd., Tab. P. E.* p. 905; *Gould, B. Eur.* pl. 392; *Hume, Str. F.* i. p. 268; *id., Nests and Eggs, Ind. B.* p. 646; *id., Str. F.* iii. p. 193; *Oates, Str. F.* viii. p. 168; *id., Str. F.* x. p. 245; *Murray, Avif. Brit. Ind.* ii. p. 769. Podiceps fluviatilis (*Tunst.*), *Legge, B. Ceylon*, pp. 1059 and 1222. Podiceps phillipensis (*Gm.*), *Jerd., B. Ind.* iii. p. 822; *Str. F.* i. p. 268; iv. p. 203; *Murray, Hdbk., Zool., &c., Sind*, p. 242; *id., Vert. Zool., Sind*, p. 312. Tachybaptes fluviatilis, *List. Brit. B. Orn. Union*, p. 204.—The LITTLE GREBE OR DAB-CHICK.

Crown of the head and nape dark blackish brown, or sepia brown, glossed with greenish; sides of the face, neck on the sides and in front chestnut red; chin dull black; breast sepia brown, mixed with white; flanks pale ferruginous; rest of under parts silky white; under wing coverts buff; primaries pale brown, buffy white basally; secondaries white, margined with brown; back, scapulars and tertials glossy brownish black, with a greenish tinge; bill blackish, paler at the base; irides red brown; legs greenish black or dusky green.

Length.—8 to 9 inches; wing 4; bill at front 0·75; tarsus 1·25.

Hab.—Throughout Europe, Africa and Asia. Recorded from throughout Ceylon, India, Beloochistan, Persia, Afghanistan, Eastern Turkestan, Nepaul and British Burmah.

Family, PROCELLARIDÆ—PETRELS, &c.

Bill long, straight, compressed, very deeply grooved, tip strong, arched and hooked; nostrils tubular, situated at the base of the bill, and exposed.

Sub-Family, PROCELLARINÆ—STORMY PETRELS.

Nostrils at base of bill divided by a septum; hind toe generally present; bill slender, compressed; tarsus moderate.

Gen. Daption.—*Stephens.*

Wings long; tail moderate; bill hooked at the tip, and very weak.

345. Daption capensis (*Linn.*), *Gould, B. Austr.* vii. pl. 53; *Sharpe, Rep. Trans. Venus Exped.*, p. 118; *Hume, Str. F.* vii. pp. 442, 463; viii. p 115; *Legge, B. Ceylon*, p. 1056; *Oates, B. Br. Burm.* ii. p. 438; *Murray, Avif. Brit. Ind.* ii. p. 710, No. 1413. Procellaria capensis, *Linn., Syst. Nat.* i. p. 213.—The CAPE PETREL.

Whole head, chin, sides and back of the neck, upper back and lesser wing coverts sooty brown; lower back, upper tail coverts, scapulars and tertiaries white, each feather tipped with sooty brown; secondaries more broadly tipped; median and greater wing coverts with the outer webs and the tips of the inner sooty brown; remainder of the inner web white; primaries blackish, with a broad white marginal band on the inner web; basal two-thirds of tail white, remainder sooty brown; lower plumage from the chin white; under tail coverts tipped with sooty brown.

Length.—About 14 inches; tail 4; wing 9; tarsus 1·7; bill from gape 1·5. (*Oates.*)

Bill blackish brown; irides and feet dark brown. (*Gould.*)

Hab.—Obtained by Mr. Hume in the Straits between Ceylon and the mainland. Oates says it is certain to be found in the vicinity of the Burmese Coast at times.

Gen. **Puffinus**.

Bill longer than the head, slender, compressed at the point; lower mandible deflected at the tip; nostrils in a double tube, extending along the under surface of the bill; tarsus moderate, compressed; toes three in front, rather long; hind toe rudimentary; 1st quill longest.

346. Puffinus chlororhynchus, *Lesson, Traite*, p. 613; *Newton*, *Ibis*, 1861, p. 181; 1867, p. 359; *Legge, B. Ceylon*, p. 1054; *Oates, B. Br. Burm.* ii. p. 439; *Murray, Avif. Brit. Ind.* ii. p. 712, No. 1415.—The GREEN-BILLED SHEARWATER.

Whole plumage sooty brown, darkest on the wings and tail; paler beneath and tinged with glaucous on the chin and throat.

Irides dusky; bill dusky greenish; legs fleshy white. (*Legge.*)

Length.—About 15 inches; tail 5·3; wing 1·09; tarsus 1·8; bill from gape 2.

Hab.—Indian Ocean, breeding in the Mauritius and neighbouring islands, where it deposits its single egg under stones and in burrows. Has been met with on the Coast of Ceylon, and will probably be found to occur in the Bay of Bengal and the Burmese Coast.

ORDER—GAVIÆ.

Family, LARIDÆ, *Vig.* Lestridæ, *Kaup.*

Bill straight, compressed; wings long and pointed; tail long; tarsi with transverse scutes in front; hind toe usually short.

Sub-Family, STERCORARINÆ.—*G. R. Gray.*

Base of bill covered with a cere, tip hooked; 1st quill longest; nostrils median.

Gen. **Stercorarius**.—*Briss.*

Keel of bill covered with a bony or membranous cere; 1st quill longest.

347. Stercorarius antarcticus (*Less.*), *Gray, Gen. B.* iii. p. 653 (1845); *Buller, B. of New Zeal.* p. 267 (1873); *Saunders, P. Z. S.* 1876, p. 321. Lestris antarcticus (*Less.*), *Trait d'Orn.* p. 616 (1831). Lestris catarrhactes (*Linn.*), *Hutton, Ibis*, 1865, p. 277.—THE ANTARCTIC SKUA OR THE CAPE HEN OF SAILORS, ALSO SEA-HEN.

General colour glossy wood brown, dark on the head and paler on the neck and under surface, and passing into dark sepia brown on the back, scapulars, and wing coverts; neck feathers with fine light brown shaft streaks; the scapulars with brownish grey central spots at the tips; the edges of the wing coverts slightly paler than the centre of the feathers; primaries black towards the tips, and white thence to the base; the outer web of the 1st quill wholly black; secondaries white at the base; tail black brown, primary and tail feather shafts white; tail beneath pale at the base.

Adult.—Wing 17·0 inches; tail 6·5; tarsus 3·2; middle toe (with claw) 3·0; bill to gape 2·5; height at base 1·0. "*Length.*—24·0" (*Macgillivray fide Layard*). Iris dark brown; bill brownish black; legs and feet black.

Young.—Nestling. "Dark brown, mottled with white." (*Hutton.*)

Immature bird from Campbell Island. *Measures.*—Wing 16·5 inches; tail 6·5; tarsus 3·0; middle toe (without claw) 2·5; bill to gape (straight) 2·5; height at base 0·88.

The Ceylon specimens are pale brown throughout, the neck feathers with light shafts and greyish tips; the under surface feathers tipped with greyish; wing coverts with the central portions near the tip fulvous, becoming paler at the extremities of the feathers.

Mr. H. Saunders finds that the largest birds are from the Southern Ocean, between the Cape of Good Hope and New Zealand, and that those from the South Atlantic have a tendency to a pale frill of acuminate feathers.

A fine immature example of this skua was brought to Major Legge at Colombo, in October 1875, by a native, who stated that it had been caught by another man near Maravilla, on the Negombo and Chilaw canal. The bird's wing was cut; it was very tame, and it had the appearance of having been accustomed to the society of man, although the native asserted that it had been caught only a few weeks.

The habitat of this large skua is the southern seas, from the edge of the pack-ice northward to the Cape of Good Hope and the shores of Australia. Between these parallels it is found in the vicinity of the existing islands, but does not occur from New Zealand eastward to Cape Horn, where, again, it is found at the Straits of Magellan and the Falkland Islands. Its most northerly ordinary limit in the Pacific appears to be Norfolk Island, but it has occurred as far north as Rockingham Bay. It was procured by the naturalists of

H. M. S. "Challenger" at Tristan d'Acunha, Kerguelen Island, and the Falkland Islands. Captain Hutton states it is very numerous on Kerguelen Island and Prince Edward's Island, breeding there, and that it is very rare north of lat. 45° S. At the Cape, Layard observed it in April; but it does not seem to be common there. Gould likewise records it from the Cape of Good Hope and near Cape Horn, and remarks that he saw it nowhere so abundant as off the coasts of Tasmania, near Storm Bay. Major Legge has seen it frequently off the west coast of Australia, and in the Bight between King George's Sound and Bass's Straits. The occurrence of one specimen only on the coasts of New Zealand is noticed by Mr. Buller.

Habits.—The skuas (or parasitic gulls, as they are sometimes called) subsist largely on the food taken by gulls, terns, and petrels, which they chase until they drop their booty. This species, which is one of the largest of its family, is a bird of bold, fierce disposition and powerful flight, often wandering far from land in company with the petrels which affect the Southern Ocean, and associating with them, in order to rob them of the food which they pick up in the wake of vessels. Major Legge adds that he has seen it steadily cruising round a flock of "Cape Pigeons," watching for an opportunity to launch itself after these assiduous toilers of the sea: catching sight of one which has picked something up, a few vigorous strokes of its pinions give it the required impetus, and it descends with a rush upon the bird, turning and twisting after it with almost motionless pinions. Dr. M'Cormack, of H. M. S. "Erebus," speaks of a fierce skua (evidently this species) which haunted the breeding-place of the Albatross at the Auckland Isles, ever on the watch to pounce down and devour this bird's egg on her quitting it in search of food. It is said to prey on the flesh of other birds at Kerguelen Land, avoiding the water. Major Legge confined one in an aviary containing a Ceylon wood-owl and a Malay bittern (Gorsachius, melanolophus); it proved to be, as might have been expected, a most ravenous bird, gobbling up the owl's meat whenever it dropped from the perch above, or chasing the bittern round the aviary and snatching its food from its bill, and this after it had amply fed itself. It had a hoarse cackling cry, which it chiefly gave vent to when hungry.

This skua has been found breeding on the Crozets, Kerguelen Land, and Prince Edward's Island, and, according to Captain Hutton, lays its eggs on low flats, among moss and grass two or three feet high, making no nest. The eggs, two or three in number, are described by Layard from specimens brought from the Crozets, as "pale brown-green, spotted chiefly at the obtuse end, with large and distinct pale purple and brown blotches;" they measure 3·0 by 2·08 (2″ 1‴) inches. An egg from the Chatham Islands is described by Captain Hutton as olive-brown, with large brown and purplish-grey spots, length 3·1 by 2·1 inches.

Sub-Family, LARINÆ.—*Bp.*

Bill long, straight above, and slightly curved at the tip.

Gen. Larus.—*Linn.*

Bill moderate, strong, compressed, cultrated, bent down at the tip; lower mandible angled beneath; nostrils linear, lateral, longitudinal, pervious; tibia naked; tarsi moderate; toes palmated; hind toe free, short and high on the tarsus; wing long.

348. Larus brunneicephalus, *Jerdon, Madras Journ.* xii. p. 225; *id., Birds, Ind* iii. p. 832; *Holdsworth, P. Z. S.* 1872, p. 480; *Str. F.* i. p. 278; iv. p. 203.; vi. p. 291; *Murray, Hdbk., Zool., &c., Sind*, p. 247; *id., Vert. Zool., Sind*, p. 318; *Legge, B. Ceylon*, p. 1049; *Murray, Avif Brit. Ind.* ii. p. 717, No. 1421.—The BROWN-HEADED GULL.

Summer Plumage.—Entire head and neck sooty brown, darker where it terminates; orbital feathers white posteriorly; back and wings light grey; nape, hind neck, upper tail coverts and tail, also the under parts, white; first primary black; inner web white at the base and with a white subterminal band, the second has both webs white at the base and a smaller terminal spot, the third is grey, with still less black and no white, and so on, lessening to the seventh; the other quills are grey; bill and feet red, the bill darkish at the tip; irides white. (*Jerd.*)

Length.—15·8 to 16·5 inches; wing 11·5 to 13·0; tail 4·5 to 5·5.

In winter, the head, neck all round, entire lower parts and upper tail coverts, also the edge of the wing, are white; tail white with a black band, narrowly edged with white terminally; a dark spot before and behind the eye; quills black, white at their bases, and, except the first two, all tipped with white; secondaries dark brown, tipped with white; tertials and upper plumage as in summer.

Hab.—Ceylon, Sind, along the coast and inland, Mekran Coast, Persian Gulf, Bengal, Kutch, Guzerat and the Deccan. Occurs also in Burmah.

349. Larus ichthyætus, *Pall., It.* ii. *App.*, No. 27; (*Caspian*) *id., Zoogr. Rosso. As.* ii. p. 322; *Tristram, Ibis*, 1868, p. 30; (*Palestine*) *Shelley, B. of Egypt*, p. 307; *Dresser, B. Eur.* pt. xviii.; *Str. F.* i. p. 276; *Murray, Hdbk., Zool., &c., Sind*, p. 247; *id., Vert. Zool., Sind*, p. 319; *Legge, B. Ceylon*, p. 1046; *Murray, Avif. Brit. Ind.* ii. p. 717, No, 1422. Kroikocephalus ichthyætus (*Pall.*), *Jerd., B. Ind.* iii. p. 831.—The GREAT BLACK-HEADED GULL.

Summer Plumage.—Entire head and upper half of neck black; orbital feathers white; mantle, back, scapulars and wings bluish grey; entire lower parts, tail, and upper tail coverts white; in immature plumage the tail has a black band; primaries with a black band, increasing in width to the outermost one, which has the whole of the outer web and half of the inner web black; rest of the first primaries grey, tipped with white; bill wax yellow, vermilion red at the tip, with a black bar across both mandibles; the extreme tip orange yellow.

Length.—28·5 to 29 inches; wing 19·0 to 20·0; bill at front 2·6 to 2·7; tail 7·5 to 7·7.

Hab.—Ceylon, South India (Madras), Sind and Mekran Coasts, also the larger inland lakes of Sind, Persian Gulf, the Punjab, N.-W. Provinces, Bengal, the Concan (Bombay).

Sub-Family, STERNINÆ.—*Bp.*

Bill long or moderate, entire, straight, compressed and pointed; the lower mandible angled; nostrils longitudinal; wings long and pointed; tail short and even, or long and forked; tarsus short and slender; toes short, webbed.

The common residence of this Family is the sea-shore, mouths or banks of large rivers and lakes. They are always in large flocks, and especially so in the breeding season.

They continue long on the wing, and are quick in all their evolutions, darting upon their finny prey, rising in the air, or gliding along near the surface of the water. They are commonly divided as Marsh, River, Sea, and Oceanic Terns, according to their habits and structure.

Gen. Hydrochelidon—*Boie.*

Bill rather long, slender, gently arched on the culmen; gonys with the ascending portion short; tail short, slightly forked; feet not fully webbed.

350. Hydrochelidon hybrida, *Pall., Zoogr. Ross. Asiat.* ii. p. 388; *Oates, Str. F.* iii. p. 348; *Murray, Avif. Brit. Ind.* p. 719, No. 1424. Sterna Javanica, *Horsf., Trans. Linn. Soc.* xiii. p. 198. Hydrochelidon Indica, *Jerd., B. Ind.* iii. p. 837; *Hume, Nests and Eggs, Ind. B.* p. 648. Sterna innotata, *Beavan, Ibis,* 1868, p. 404. Hydrochelidon hybrida, *Salvad., Ucc. Born.* p. 372; *Saunders, P. Z. S.* 1876, p. 640; *Dresser, B. Eur.* viii. p. 315, pl.; *Legge, Birds of Ceylon,* p. 996; *Oates, B. Br. Burm.* ii. p. 419.—The WHISKERED TERN.

Forehead, crown, nape and back of neck glossy black; lores and chin white; throat and breast pale bluish ash; abdomen dusky; under tail coverts white, also the edge of the wing; mantle, wings, upper tail coverts and tail bluish ash; external tail feathers white; under wing coverts white; bill lake red; irides brown; legs and feet dull red.

Length.—11 to 13 inches; wing 8·5 to 9·75; tail 3·75 to 4·5; bill at front 1·5.

Hab.—Throughout India, Burmah and Ceylon, affecting lakes and the sea coast.

351. Hydrochelidon leucoptera (*Meisn and Schinz.*), *Dresser, B. Eur.* viii. p. 321, pl.; *Saunders, P. Z. S.* 1876, p. 641; *Hume, Str. F.*

viii. p. 115; *Legge, B. Ceylon,* p. 1000; *Murray, Avif. Brit. Ind.* ii. p. 719, No. 1425. Hydrochelidon nigra (*Linn.*), *apud. Salvad., Ucc. Born.* p. 372. Sterna leucoptera, *Meisn and Schinz., Vog. Schweiz.* p. 264.—The WHITE-WINGED BLACK TERN.

Head, neck, back, scapulars, innermost secondaries and entire under parts (except the under tail coverts which are white) deep glossy black; primary quills blackish grey, fading to greyish white on the outer portions of the inner webs, except on the terminal portion shafts of the feathers white; secondaries light french grey; lesser wing coverts, edge of the wing, tail, and upper tail coverts white; large coverts french grey; under wing coverts black and blackish grey; edge of the wing mottled with white. Bill reddish black; irides dark brown; legs and feet vermilion red, with a coral tinge.

In winter the forehead and crown are white, nape and occiput dark grey, also the back and scapulars; rump and upper tail coverts pale greyish white; throat, foreneck, under tail coverts, and under wing coverts white; a black spot in front of the eye; breast greyish.

Length.—9·5 inches; tail 3; wing 8·2; tarsus 0·75; bill from gape 1·25.

Hab.—Throughout India, Burmah and Ceylon, affecting lakes, rivers and sea coasts.

Gen. **Gelochelidon**.—*Linn.*

Nostrils with plumes reaching the opening; first quill of wing longest; tail forked; tarsus rather long; bill moderate; culmen slightly curved and with projecting gony.

352. Gelochelidon anglica (*Mont.*), *Jerd., B. Ind.* ii. p. 836; *Salvad., Ucc. Born.* p. 371; *Blyth, B. Burm.* p. 163; *Hume, Str. F.* vi. p. 491; *Murray, Avif. Brit. Ind.* ii. p. 720, No. 1427. Sterna anglica, *Mont., Orn. Dict. Suppl. Saunders, P. Z. S.* 1876, p. 644; *Dresser, B. Eur.* viii. p. 295, pl.; *Hume, Str. F.* viii. p. 115; *Legge, B. Ceylon,* p. 1011; *Oates, Str. F.* x. p. 246; *id., Birds, Br. Burm.* ii. p. 422. Gelochelidon anglicus, *Jerd., B. Ind.* ii. p. 836. Gelochelidon nilotica, *Murray, Vert. Zool., Sind,* p. 320. Sterna nilotica (*V. Hass.*), *Hume, Str. F.* i. p. 281.—The GULL-BILLED TERN.

In summer forehead, lores, head on the crown, nape and back of the neck silky or deep black; sides of the face, chin, throat, breast and under parts white; mantle, wings and tail light grey, wings reach about two inches beyond the tail, the first primary is rather a hoary grey, the rest light grey, their tips and inner webs next the shaft dusky brown, the margins for their basal two-thirds greyish white; shafts white; secondaries and tertiaries light grey; under wing coverts white; tail light grey, the feathers white-shafted; bill, legs and feet black, the latter with sometimes a reddish tinge; irides dark brown.

Length.—14·5 to 16·2 inches; wing 13 to 14·5 inches, reaching the tail by from 2·0 to 2·7 inches; bill at front 1·5 to 1·7; tarsus 1·5.

In winter the black head is replaced by a white grey streaked head, and a few dusky spots behind and round the eye.

Hab.—Ceylon, Sind, Beloochistan, Persia, Bengal, Rajputana, Kutch, the Concans, and Deccan. Has been recorded from Arracan and met with on the coast of the Irrawady delta near Elephant Point and the mouth of the Bassein Creek. Affects the large inland pieces of water, especially numerous on the Munchur Lake in Sind, and the salt water creeks in the deltaic districts. Arrives about the middle of September and leaves about the third week in May.

Gen. **Sterna**.—*Linn.*

Characters the same as *Gelochelidon*. Front toes united by indented web; hind toe short.

353. Sterna caspia, *Pall, Nov. Comm. Petrop.* xiv. p. 582; *Hume, Str. F.* i. p. 280; *Oates, Str. F.* iii. p. 347; *Saunders, P. Z. S.* 1876, p. 656; *Dresser, B. Eür.* viii. p. 289, pl.; *Hume, Str. F.* viii. p. 115; *Parker, Str. F.* ix. p. 487; *Legge, B. Ceylon*, p. 1008; *Oates, Str. F.* x. p. 246; *Murray, Vert. Zool., Sind*, p. 427; *Oates, B. Br. Burm.* ii. p. 427. *Murray, Avif. Brit. Ind.* ii. p. 721, No. 1428. Sylochelidon caspius, *Jerd., B. Ind.* ii. p. 835.—The Caspian Tern.

Summer Plumage.—Crown of the head, nape, and back of the neck and ear coverts velvet black; chin, throat, face, breast, the neck in front and behind and entire under parts white; mantle, wings and tail pale blue grey or pearl grey; the first five or six primaries slaty grey, their shafts white; under wing coverts white. In winter the head is white with a few dark feathers on the nape; bill vermilion red, paler towards the tip; irides brown; legs and feet black.

Length.—18·0 to 20·0 inches; wing 16·0 to 17; tail 4·5 to 5·75; bill at front 2·6 to 2·75; tarsus 1·5 to 1·75.

Hab.—Sind, Beloochistan Coast, Persian Gulf, the Punjab, N.-W. Provinces and Oudh. Affects the sea coasts, larger rivers, jheels, lakes and other inland pieces of water. Breeds in N.-W. Ceylon, where Mr. Parker (*Str. F.* x. p. 487) found a colony breeding.

354. Sterna Bergii, *Licht., Verzeich*, p. 80; *Hume, Nests and Eggs, Ind. B.* p. 655; *id., Str. F.* i. p. 283; iv. p. 470; *Saunders, P. Z. S.* 1876, p. 657; *Hume, Str. F.* viii. p. 116; *Parker, Str. F.* ix. p. 490; *Legge, B. Ceylon*, p. 102; *Murray, Vert. Zool., Sind*, p. 322; *Murray, Avif. Brit Ind.* ii. p. 721, No. 1429. Sterna cristata, *Steph. in Shaw's Gen. Zool.* xiii. i. p. 146. Sterna velox, *Rupp., Atlas*, p. 21, t. 13. Thalasseus cristatus, *Jerd., B. Ind.* ii. p. 842; *Blyth, B. Burm.* p. 163. Thalasseus Bergii, *David. et Oust. Ois Chine*, p. 523.—The Large Crested Sea Tern.

Forehead, lores, sides of the face, neck in front and behind, chin, throat, breast, and all the lower parts white; crown of the head, including the eye, crest and nape glossy black; back, wings and tail dusky grey; inner webs of primaries next the shaft dark brown, the margins white; inner primaries unicolorous silvery or hoary grey, margined with white; secondaries white on their inner webs and tips. Bill pale yellow; irides dark brown; legs and feet black.

Length.—17·0 to 18·5 inches; wing 14·0 to 14·6; bill at front 2·6 to 2·8.

Hab.—Ceylon and the coasts of India generally to the Persian Gulf. Occurs commonly in the Kurrachee harbour, along the Mekran Coast and the Persian Gulf and Burmah. Breeds in the Gulf of Oman, on the Island of Astola, nearly opposite Jask, whence thousands of eggs have been collected during May and June. The eggs are typically broad ovals, strongly pointed towards the small end, but considerably elongated. Varieties are not uncommon. The ground colour varies from white, greenish and pinkish white to pale buff, pale yellowish, and again pale pinkish stone colour to the richest and warmest salmon pink; the markings are of two colours, an intensely deep burnt sienna brown, often quite black in its intensity, and a pale inky purple, which has an appearance of lying beneath the surface of the shell. In some eggs the inky purple markings are almost entirely wanting, in others more numerous and extensive than the dark ones. In others these dark markings are comparatively thinly sprinkled or dense; again there are some with huge blotches and spots about the larger end. The eggs vary from 2·3 inches to 2·71 in length and 1·63 to 1·78 in breadth; the average of 2 dozens was 2·45 × 1·71.

355. Sterna media, *Horsf., Trans. Linn. Soc.* xiii. p. 198; *Saunders, P. Z. S.* 1876, p. 655; *Hume, Str. F.* v. p. 301; *Dresser, B. Eur.* viii. p. 285, pl.; *Hume and Dav., Str. F.* vi. p. 493; *Hume, Str. F.* viii. p. 116; *Legge, B. Ceylon*, p. 1030; *Murray, Vert. Zool., Sind*, p. 321; *Oates, B. Burm.* ii. p. 421; *Murray, Avif. Brit. Ind.* ii. p. 723, No. 1431. Sterna bengalensis, *Less. Traite d'Orn.* p. 621; *Hume, Nests and Eggs, Ind. B.* p. 655; *id., Str. F.* i. p. 284; ii. p. 318; iv. p. 474. Thalasseus bengalensis, *Jerd., B. Ind.* iii. p. 483; *Blyth, B. Burm.* p. 193.—The ALLIED TERN.

Summer Plumage.—Forehead, crown, nape, back of the neck and occipital crest glossy black; lores, face, sides of the neck, breast and entire lower parts white; mantle and wings light silvery or satin grey, paler on the tail; the outer web of the external feathers greyish white; primaries dusky grey, the inner webs margined with white, and the portion next the shaft dusky; wings extend two inches beyond the end of the tail; inner webs of secondaries white. Bill yellow; irides deep brown; legs and feet black.

Length.—15·5 to 16·5 inches; wing 12·2 to 12·25; tail 6 to 6·7; bill at front 2·5; tarsus 1·0 to 1·2.

In winter plumage the entire forehead and lores are pure white, the crown white, the feathers centred dusky; occiput dusky, the feathers slightly margined with white; a spot in front of the eye and a line behind it black.

Hab.—The sea coasts of Sind, Beloochistan, Bengal, Bombay, Madras, Malabar Coast, Burmah and Ceylon. A maritime species abundant in Ceylon, the Kurrachee harbour, mouths of the Indus, and the tidal creeks.

356. Sterna seena, *Sykes, P. Z. S.* 1832, p. 171; *Hume, Nests and Eggs, Ind. B.* p. 650; *id., Str. F.* iii. p. 193; *Saunders, P. Z. S.* 1876, p. 645; *Anders., Yunnan, Exped.* p. 693; *Hume, Str.* F. viii. p. 116; *Legge, B. Ceylon,* p. 1003; *Oates, B. Br. Burm.* ii. p. 423; *Murray, Vert. Zool., Sind,* p. 323; *Murray, Avif. Brit. Ind.* ii. p. 724, No. 1433. Sterna aurantia, *Gray and Hardw., Ill. Ind. Zool.* i. pl. 69, fig. 2. Seena aurantia, *Jerd., B. Ind.* ii. p. 838; *Blyth, B. Burm.* p. 163; *Wardlaw-Ramsay, Ibis,* 1877, p. 472; *Oates, Str. F.* v. p. 169.—The INDIAN RIVER TERN.

Forehead, crown, nape and back of the neck, also a circle enclosing the eye, glossy black; sides of the face, chin and throat white; breast and abdomen pearly greyish white; under tail coverts white; tail pale grey, the external feathers white; back, secondaries, tertiaries and wing coverts pale or ashy grey; primaries hoary or silvery grey, the inner webs of the first three light brown, edged with dusky; under wing coverts white; upper tail coverts like the back. In winter plumage the head is white, except a circle of black or dusky round the eye and on the ear coverts. Bill bright yellow, tipped dusky; irides brown legs and feet red.

Length.—15·0 to 16·3 inches; wing 11·0 to 11·5; bill at front 1·5; tarsus 0·56 to 1·0; tail 7·0 to 7·5.

Hab.—Throughout India, Burmah and Ceylon, also in Beloochistan and Persia. A permanent resident in Sind; affects the river and lakes, also jheels. In Sind it breeds in June and July; March and April in Tenasserim, depositing three eggs in a slight depression in the sand. Considerable numbers breed together. The eggs are various shades of buff, streaked, blotched and spotted with brown. Size 1·5 to 1·75 inch × 1·17 to 1·32.

357. Sterna melanogastra, *Temm., Pl. Col.* p. 434; *Salvad, Ucc. Born.* p. 377; *Saunders, P. Z. S.* 1876, p. 645; *Hume and Dav., Str. F.* vi. p. 492; *Legge, Birds, Ceylon,* p. 1006; *Oates, B. Br. Burm.* ii. p. 424; *Murray, Avif. Brit. Ind.* ii. p. 724; No. 1434. Sterna Javanica, *Horsf., Zool. Res. in Java, Gen. Cat.*; *Jerd., B. Ind.* iii. p. 840; *Hume, Nests and Eggs,* p. 652; *Murray, Vert. Zool., Sind,* p. 323.—The BLACK-BELLIED TERN.

Head and nape black; neck behind black; scapulars, tertials and wing coverts light grey; lores, sides of the face, ear coverts, chin and throat white; neck in front and breast pearly grey; abdomen, vent and under tail coverts brownish black.

Bill orange yellow; irides brown; legs vermilion red.

Length.—12 inches; wing 9·3; tail 6; bill at front 1·43; tarsus 1. In winter the head is white with dusky streaks, the abdomen is like the back and not black, and the bill tipped with dusky.

Hab.—Throughout India, Burmah and Ceylon. Spread throughout the Burmese and Indo-Burmese Countries. Affects inland waters, ponds, marshes and rivers. Breeds all over the Empire, in company with the preceding and in similar situations. Eggs also very similar, but smaller from 1·18 to 1·5 × 0·95 to 1·02 inches.

358. Sterna Dougalli, *Mont., Dict. Orn. Suppl. Saunders, P. Z. S.* 1876, p. 652; *Dresser, B. Eur.* viii. p. 273, pl.; *Legge, Str. F.* iii. p. 376; *id., Birds, Ceylon,* p. 1033; *Murray, Avif. Brit. Ind.* ii. p. 725, No. 1435. Sterna paradisea, *Keys and Blas. Wirb. Eur.* p. 247. Sterna gracilis, *Gould, P. Z. S.* 1847, p. 222; *id., B. Austr.* vii. pl. 27. Sterna korustes, *Hume, Str. F.* ii. p. 318.—The ROSEATE TERN.

In summer the crown and nape are deep glossy black; back and upper surface of the wings delicate, light french grey; rump and upper tail coverts white, washed with grey; rest of the plumage pure white, except that the under surface of the body is tinged with a delicate light rose colour; first primary with the outer web black, the rest with the outer webs hoary grey; inner webs of the primaries dark grey, broadly margined to the tip of the feather with white; bill red at the base, otherwise black; iris dark brown; legs reddish orange.

In *winter* the forehead and cheeks are wnite; crown and nape brownish black, slightly marked with white; lesser wing coverts along the edge brownish; no trace of rose colour on the under parts, otherwise as in the summer plumage. (*Dresser.*) Legs and feet bright vermilion red; claws black; irides deep brown; bill black; gape and base of lower mandible varied from reddish fleshy to vermilion red. (*Davison.*)

Length.—14·5 to 15 inches; tail 7 to 7·5; wing 8·5 to 8·7; tarsus 0·7; bill from gape 2·0; fork of tail about 4.

Hab.—Ceylon, Tenasserim, off the mouth of the Loynah Creek, also the Bassein estuary. It has a wide range, being found in Europe, Africa and America. It is also met with in various parts of India, Ceylon and the Andaman Islands, extending down to Australia. Frequents only the sea coasts. Breeds on isolated sandbanks. In Ceylon, Mr. Parker found a colony nesting in June on a low sand bank on Adam's Bridge. The nests were depressions in the sand, and contained one or two eggs, of the same type as those of the last, pale, buff, blotched, streaked and spotted with brown.

359. Sterna hirundo, *Linn., Syst. Nat.* i. p. 957; *Gould, B. Europe,* pl. 417; *Jerd., B. Ind.* iii. p. 839; *Murray, Avif. Brit. Ind.* ii.

p. 726, No. 1436. Sterna fluviatilis, *Naum. Vogl.* t. p. 712; *Hume, Str. F.* p. 282; iv. 472; *Legge, B. Ceylon*, p. 1015.—The EUROPEAN TERN.

Whole head and nape black; plumage above grey; upper tail coverts white; tail pale grey, the feathers white on their inner web; chin, throat, ear coverts and sides of the neck pure white; rest of the lower parts pearly greyish white; lower tail coverts white. Bill deep red; irides brown; legs red.

Length.—12·5 inches; wing 9·8 to 10·3; tail 4·5; bill at front 1·4; tarsus 1.

In winter the forehead and top of the head are white, mixed round the eyes, occiput and nape with blackish.

Hab.—Ceylon, Central and Southern India and Sind, along the River Indus to the Punjab and the Cashmere lakes.

360. Sterna Saundersii, *Hume, Str. F.* iv. p. 496; v. p. 326; *Murray, Hdbk., Zool., &c., Sind*, p. 249; *id., Vert. Zool., Sind*, p. 325; *Legge, B. Ceylon*, p. 1023; *Murray, Avif. Brit. Ind.* ii. p. 727, No. 1438.—SAUNDERS' LITTLE TERN.

"A triangular frontal patch, the angles reaching to within 0·12 of the eyes, white; a very broad stripe through the lores to the eye black; a narrow white line intervenes between this stripe and the upper mandible. The whole crown, occiput, short occipital crest and sides of occiput as low as the lower margin of the eye velvet black, the central two-thirds of the lower eyelid white, and no black below this; all the rest of the sides of head and neck, chin, throat, entire under parts, wing lining and exterior tail feather pure white; the first three primaries black with black shafts and broad white margins on their inner webs; their greater coverts dusky black; the whole of the rest of the upper surface, including wings and tail, and excepting parts and feathers already described, a most delicate satin grey, contrasting in the strongest manner with the early black primaries.

"*Length.*—9·12 inches; expanse 19·25; tail 3·0; wing 6·43; bill at front 1·12, from gape 1·5; tarsus 0·6; legs and feet dusky yellowish olive; bill yellow, broadly tipped dusky; irides blackish brown."—(*Str. F.* v. p. 326.)

Hab.—Ceylon and Kurrachee in Sind; also the coast. This species is extremely common at Kurrachee, and along the coast during the latter part of April, also in May and June, in which months it breeds at Kurrachee on the bare plains between Kurrachee and Clifton at Ghizree and on the Moach. The eggs are usually laid in a small depression in the saline soil, the birds selecting, wherever possible, spots where there is a little loose shelly sand. In Ceylon Mr. Parker has taken eggs in June. Eggs glossless and often chalky, two or three in number, oval and pointed at one end; of a drab, buff, or stone colour, streaked, blotched and spotted, of a dark or deep brown or reddish brown colour generally at the larger end ; size 1·26 × 0·90 ; is the average of twenty-four.

361. Sterna sinensis, *Gm., Syst. Nat.* i. p. 608 ; *Saunders, P. Z. S.* 1876, p. 662 ; *Hume, Str. F.* v. p. 325 ; viii. p. 116 ; *Legge, B. Ceylon*, p. 1019 ; *Murray, Avif. Brit. Ind.* ii. p. 728, No. 1439. Sternula minuta (*Linn.*), *Hume, Nests and Eggs, Ind. B.* p. 654 (part) ; *Oates, Str. F.* iii. p. 349. Sterna minuta, *apud Wald. in Blyth's B. Burm.* p. 163. Sternula sinensis, *David et Oust. Ois. Chine*, p. 627. Sterna Gouldi, *Hume Str. F.* v. p. 326 ; *Oates, Str. F.* x. p. 247.—The EASTERN LITTLE TERN.

Summer Plumage.—Forehead, continued back to a point on either side just over the eye, white ; crown, nape, the upper part of the hind neck and a streak from the nostrils through the eye to the nape, deep black ; upper plumage pale grey, becoming paler and whitish on the upper tail coverts and tail ; first two primaries nearly black, margined on their inner webs with white ; remaining primaries and secondaries grey, the latter tipped with white on the outer webs ; shaft of the first primary white, that of the second more or less white ; remainder of the plumage white. *In winter* the crown is white, gradually turning to dusky and running into the nape, which remains black, the black of the nape extending to behind the eye ; the band from the nostril to the eye is lost, there being merely a dusky spot in front of the eye ; rest of plumage as in summer. Irides brown : bill yellow, broadly tipped with black ; legs and feet orange yellow.

Length.—10 inches ; tail 4 ; wing 7·0 ; tarsus 0·75 ; bill from gape 1·7 ; fork of tail 2·2.

Hab.—The greater part of India and Ceylon. In Burmah it is recorded by Oates from Southern Pegu. Affects all the larger rivers within tidal influence. Breeds in Burmah during March and April, depositing 2—4 eggs in a small depression in a sandbank. The nests are shallow saucers, similar to those of *Sterna Saundersi*, and as Mr. Parker in MSS. observes scratched out in little ridges of gravelly or shelly sand. Eggs similar to those of *S. Saundersi* and like them extremely variable in size and coloring.

362. Sterna anæsthetus, *Scop., Del. Flor. et Faun. Insubr.* ii. p. 92 ; *Saunders, P. Z. S.* 1876, p. 664 ; *Butler, Str. F.* v. p. 301 ; *Hume, Str. F.* viii. p. 116 ; *Legge, B. Ceylon*, p. 1040 ; *Oates, B. Br. Burm.* ii. p. 431 ; *Murray, Vert. Zool., Sind*, p. 325 ; *Murray, Avif. Brit. Ind.* ii. p. 728, No. 1440. Sterna panayensis, *Gm., Syst. Nat.* 1. p. 607. Onychoprion anæsthetus, *Jerd, B. Ind.* iii. p. 844 ; *Salvad, Ucc. Born.* p. 374. Haliplana anæstheta, *David. et Oust. Oist. Chine*, p. 528.—The PANAYAN TERN.

" A frontal band, extending backwards over the eyes for about 0·15 inch behind the posterior angle of the eye, pure white ; a broad black stripe through the lores, to and behind the eyes joining the black of the occiput ; forehead and crown inside the white band and entire occiput and nape velvet black; chin, throat, sides of the neck, axillaries, under wing coverts, lower tail coverts, edge of the wing along carpal joint and ulna white; the breast, abdomen and flanks white, shaded with pale french grey; back of the neck the same; back, wings and tail sooty brown; upper back strongly shaded with bluish grey, as are also some of the tail feathers; lesser wing coverts behind the white edge of the wing blackish brown; the primaries a darker brown, their shafts brown on the upper surface; outer web of first primary almost black, the rest greyish white on their inner webs, towards their bases; external tail feathers white for the basal half on both webs, greyish brown on the inner web for the terminal half. In winter the entire under surface is pure white, and there is a dark spot in front of the eye; head greyish white or white, the feathers mesially spotted or striped dusky; a black collar at the base of the occiput, extending on each side nearly to the eye.

"Bill dusky reddish, red towards the base of the lower mandible; legs coral red; bill, legs and feet black.

"*Length.*—14·75 inches; wing 9·62; tail 7; bill at front 1·6."—(*Str. F.* vi. p. 474.)"

Hab.—Sind, Beloochistan (Mekran Coast), Persian Gulf, the Concan and the Laccadives, Burmah and Ceylon. Mr. Hume found them breeding on the Vingorla rocks on the Western Coast.

363. Sterna fuliginosa, *Gm., Syst. Nat.* i. p. 605; *Hume, Str. F.* iv. p. 477; *Saunders, P. Z. S.* 1876, p. 666; *Dresser, B. Eur.* viii. p. 307 pl; *Legge, Birds, Ceylon,* p. 1037; *Murray, Vert. Zool., Sind,* p. 326; *Oates, B. Br. Burm.* ii. p. 432; *Murray, Avif. Brit. Ind.* ii. p. 729, No. 1441. Onychoprion fuliginosus, *Salvad, Ucc. Born.* p. 373. Haliplana fuliginosa, *Dav. et. Oust. Ois. Chine,* p. 528.—The Sooty Tern.

Forehead and a streak from the base of the bill to the eye white; sides of the face, chin, throat, neck in front, breast and entire under parts white; top of head, nape, neck behind, back, scapulars and wings sooty black; under wing coverts white; tail forked, external feathers on each side white on their outer web, rest are white at the base; legs and feet black; irides brown; web of outer side of mid-toe reaches to the root of the claw.

Length.—16·5 to 17·5 inches; wing 10·5 to 11·8; tail 6·9 to 7·5; tarsus 0·95 to 1; bill at gape 2·0 to 2·4; bill at front 1·6 to 1·7.

Hab.—Ceylon, Sind and Mekran Coasts, also Persian Gulf, (Bushire), the Concan (Bombay), and Malabar Coast. Breeds on the Laccadive Islands during January and February.

Gen. **Anous**.—*Leach.*

Bill long, slender, slightly curved at the tip, angle well marked; nostrils in a groove; wings long; tarsus short; claw of mid-toe serrated.

364. Anous stolida (*Linn.*), *Gould, B. Austr.* vii. pl. 34; *Jerd., B. Ind.* iii. p. 845; *Salvad., Ucc. Born.* p. 379; *Hume, Str. F.* ii. p. 320; *Saunders, P. Z. S.* 1876. p. 669; *Hume, Str. F.* viii. p. 116; *Legge, B. Ceylon,* p. 1043; *Murray, Vert. Zool., Sind,* p. 326; *Oates. B. Br. Burm.* ii. p. 434; *Murray, Avif. Brit. Ind.* ii. p. 730, No. 1442.—The COMMON NODDY.

A black line from the base of the bill to the eye; forehead white; crown fulvous or yellowish grey; neck, nape, chin, throat, breast, greater and lesser wing coverts, under wing coverts, upper and under tail coverts and tail dark chocolate brown; back and primaries darker, or blackish brown; legs and feet black; irides brown.

Length.—*Male,* 15 inches; wing 11·5; tail 6·5; bill at front 1·6.

Hab.—Ceylon, Sind and Mekran Coasts, also the Bay of Bengal, Laccadives and the West Coast.

ORDER.—STEGANOPODES.

Feet entirely webbed; hind toe articulated on the inner side of the tarsus and joined to the inner front toe by web; legs short; wings long.

Family PHÆTONTIDÆ.

Bill Tern-like, moderate, stout, straight, the culmen curved, and the margins finely serrated; nostrils pervious; tail with the two central feathers much elongated; lower part of tibia naked.

Gen. Phæton.—*Lin.*

Characters same as those of the family.

365. Phæton flavirostris, *Brandt. Bull. Acad. Sc. St. Petersb.* ii. p. 349; *Hume, Str. F.* ii. p 323; v. p. 498; viii. p. 116; *Legge, Birds, Ceylon,* p. 1172; *Oates, B. Br. Burm.* ii. p. 225; *Murray, Avif. Brit. Ind.* p. 732, No. 1447. Phæton candidus (*Briss.*), *apud. Jerd., B. Ind.* ii. p. 850. —The WHITE TROPIC BIRD.

Entire plumage white, except a mark in front of the eye continued as a broad band down the sides of the head; the first four primaries with the outer web; the shaft and a narrow portion of the inner web to within an inch of the tip; the basal portion of the shaft of the next few primaries; a broad band along the median wing coverts, greater portion of the tertiaries and the tips of the scapulars; also the shafts of the lengthened tail feathers and the basal two-thirds of the others which are black; longer flank feathers streaked with slate colour. Bill in the dry specimen pale-yellow, with a pale plumbeous line along the central portion of both mandibles; tarsus and basal portion of feet yellow; rest of feet black. (*Oates.*)

Length.—30 inches; tail 18; wing 10·6; tarsus 0·9; bill from gape 2·5.

Hab.—Ceylon, also Ross Island (Andaman Group). Breeds on Ascension Island. Oates says that a specimen of this Phæton was captured at a considerable distance from the sea in Cachar.

366. Phæton indicus, *Hume, Str. F.* iv. p. 481; *Butler, Str. F.* v. p. 302; *Hume and Dav., Str. F.* vi p. 493; *Hume, Str. F.* viii. p. 116; *Legge, Birds Ceylon*, p. 1173; *Murray, Vert. Zool., Sind*, p. 327; *Oates, B. Br. Burm.* ii. p. 226; *Murray, Avif. Brit. Ind.* ii. p. 733, No. 1448. Phæton ætherius (*Linn.*), *apud. Hume, Str. F.* i. p. 286; ii. p. 323.—The SHORT-TAILED TROPIC BIRD.

"A conspicuous broad, black crescent in front of the eye, and a narrow black line from the gape to nostrils and nostrils to culmen, dividing the feathers from the bill; the whole forehead, front part of the crown, ear coverts and entire lower parts, including wing lining and axillaries, pure white; a black line from the posterior angle of the eye, running round the back of the nape, where it forms a more or less conspicuous half collar; hind crown and nape inside the half collar white, each feather with a triangular black bar near the tips; carpal joint of wing, four or five posterior primaries, all the secondaries, the primary coverts, except those of the first five quills, the greater and median coverts pure white; winglet, greater coverts, shafts and outer webs of the first five primaries, together with a narrow stripe along the shaft of the inner web, black; the extreme tips and inner webs of these feathers white; tertiaries and their greater coverts black, narrowly margined on the exterior webs and tipped with white; the lesser secondary coverts similar; the entire back, rump, scapulars, and upper tail coverts white, closely barred with black, the bars being slightly cuspidate on the upper back, and the longest scapulars almost devoid of barring; tail feathers white, their bases black shafted, and the lateral feather mostly with an arrow-head bar or spot near the tip; irides deep brown; legs and hallux and its web white, tinged bluish and creamy yellow; rest of feet and claws black.

"*Male—Length*, excluding elongated tail feathers, 16·85 to 17·8 inches; central feathers project beyond the rest of the tail 3 to 5·9; expanse 37 to 39·5; tail from vent, including elongated feathers, 7·5 to 10·3; wing 10·75 to 11·8; bill at front 2·2 to 2·45; tarsus 1·0 to 1·13; mid-toe and claw 1·55 to 1·8. *Female—Length*, 18·05 exclusive of elongated feathers, which project 4 inches beyond the others; expanse 39; tail from vent, including elongated feathers, 9·0; wing 11·7, bill at front 2·4; tarsus 1."

Ceylon and Beloochistan coasts. This is Mr. Hume's description of specimens secured by him, in the Gulf of Oman on the Mekran Coast; whether it is the immature of *P. æthereus*, or a new species, is yet a moot question. Captain Butler, in 1877 (*Str. F.* v. p. 302) also secured two specimens on the Mekran Coast between Oormara and Gwadur, and these, Mr. Hume says, are precisely similar to the four specimens secured in the Bay of Bengal. Mr. Davison also observed it at the extreme southern point of Tenasserim and off Cape Negrais.

Family.—FREGATIDÆ.

Wings highly developed. The single species *known to occur in India* lives almost entirely in the air, taking its prey on the wing. Form and habits Raptorial.

Gen. **Fregata** *Briss.*

Bill much hooked at the tip ; wings long ; tail forked, long ; tarsi partially feathered ; claws short and curved.

367. Fregata aquila (*Linn.*), *Salvad., Ucc. Born.* p. 364 ; *Hume, Str. F.* viii. p. 116 ; *Legge, Birds of Ceylon*, p. 1204 ; *Murray, Avif. Brit. Ind.* ii. p. 734, No. 1449. Pelecanus aquilus, *Linn., Syst. Nat.* i. p. 216. Attagen aquilus, *Jerd., B. Ind.* iii. p. 853. Tachypetes aquilus, *Sharpe, Rep. Trans. Venus Exped.* p. 151.—The FRIGATE BIRD.

Glossy black throughout. The young with the head, neck and lower abdomen white.

Length.—37 inches ; wing 26 ; tail 9·5 ; tarsus 0·8 ; bill from gape 5·0 ; Gular pouch scarlet ; bill pale blue.

Hab.—Ceylon, the Màlabar Coast and the Bay of Bengal.

368. Fregata minor (*Gm.*), *Buller B. of New. Zeal.*, p. 342 (1873) ; *Salvadori, Nicelli di Borneo*, p. 364 (1874) ; *Sclater & Salvin, P. Z. S.* 1878, p. 650 ; *Hume, Str. Feath.* 1879, p. 116 (*List B. of Ind.*). Pelecamus minor, *Gm. Lyst. Nat.* 1, p. 572. Attagen ariel, *G. R. Gray, Gen. B.* iii. p. 669 (1845, *ex Gould, MS.*) *Layard Ann. & Mag. Nat. Hist.* 1854, xiv. p. 271. Attagen minor (*Gm.*), *Holdsw. P. Z. S.* 1872, p. 482. Petite Frigate, *Buffon Hist. Nat.* ; Lesser Frigate, *Lath.*—MAN-OF-WAR BIRD, OF SAILORS ; FRIGATE PELICAN OF SOME.

Male—(N.-W. of Australia). Plumage black, the feathers of the back long and lanceolate, glossed near the tips with lively green, above which the webs are illumined with an amethystine hue, but not bronzed as in the next species wing coverts the same ; tertials passing into brown at the tips ; beneath brownish-black, glossed with green and purplish ; on the lower flanks a patch of white.

Male.—Iris red ("black ? " in Admiralty Island specimen, *P. Z. S.* 1877, p. 555) ; bill grey ; skin of throat red ; eyelid black ; legs and feet black.

Adult—(Australia ; Brit., Mus.). Wing 20·7 to 21·5 inches ; tail 13·0 to 14·5 ; depth of fork 6·0 to 7·5 ; tarsus 0·7 ; middle toe 1·85 ; claw (straight) 3·9, length of culmen, exclusive of hooked tip, 2·8. *Male*—(Raine Island ; "Challenger" coll.). Wing 20·5 to 21·0 ; tail 13·5 ; bill to gape (straight) 4·1, width at gape 0·93.—*Female*—(Ceylon ; Poole coll.) Wing 20·2.

Female.—(Raine Island). Head and neck black, the feathers glossed with green; back blackish brown, the feathers pointed as in the male; chest, upper breast, and flanks white, passing round upon the hind neck; lower wing coverts broadly margined with greyish white, pouch not so large as in the male.

The example in the Poole collection corresponds with these in all respects.

Obs.—All examples (so sexed) of females which have been examined have these white markings on the under surface; but I am of opinion that when old they attain the dark plumage, owing to the light coloration being the immature characteristic.

Female.—"Iris red; eyelid, legs, and feet red; skin of throat not so red as in the male." (*J. Murray.*)

Young in down (Raine Island). White the down thick and long; the interscapulary region and scapulars, which are in feather, blackish-brown, with pale margins; bill to gape 2·85 inches.

Immature.—"Iris black; bill and feet whitish, with a shade of blue." (*J. Murray.*)

Head, neck, and chest whitish, washed with cinnamon-reddish, passing into brownish on the breast; abdomen white; back brownish; wing-coverts brown, margined with greyish.

"This species, Major Legge says, being smaller in the wing than *F. aquila*, may be distinguished from it, in the adult male plumage, by the white patch on the flanks. It is said by him to be a frequent visitor to the shores of Ceylon, and, as in the case of many other tolerably rare sea-birds, is generally met with on the west coast. Layard, who first recorded it, thus writes; 'Mr. Brodie, of the Ceylon Civil Service, first shot this species on Calpentyn Lake; and I subsequently saw two, which were killed from the lighthouse in Colombo in February 1853; one passed into my possession, the other into the museum of the Ceylon Branch of the Royal Asiatic Society. I frequently saw them during the month flying at immense altitudes over the coast.' Next in order are the observations of Mr. Holdsworth, who writes that he saw them on many occasions at Aripu during the strength of the South-West monsoon, and they were generally in parties of five or six, at a considerable height above the shore. In June 1877 an immature example was shot at Jaffna by Mr Smart, of the C.C.S. As regards his own experience, Major Legge says he has seen Frigate-birds, both at Colombo and Galle, during the months of May, June, and July. The three examples he observed were all passing southwards along the coast. The range of this Frigate-bird is not so extensive as that of its larger congener. From the Indian Ocean, to which it can only be considered a frequent straggler, it extends eastwards through the Malay Archipelago to Polynesia and the Australian seas, and ranges as far north as the China coasts, where Swinhoe procured it at Amoy. Salvadori records it from Borneo doubtfully, but notes it from Batchian, the Aru Islands, and the Moluccan seas; and at the Admiralty Islands it was obtained by the "Challenger" naturalists. It has been procured on the south coast of new Guinea, and in Torres Straits it is a common bird. At Raine Island it was found breeding many years ago by Commander Ince, R.N., and more recently by the naturalists of the "Challenger." It is further recorded from Port Darwin, Cape York, and Rockingham Bay. On the North-West coast it is equally well distributed. As regards the Pacific Ocean, it is found at New Caledonia, but is said not to extend into Central Polynesia like the larger species. Southwards it extends to the coasts of New Zealand, where it has once occurred ; but it has not been observed in Tasmanian waters.

"Though far less has been written concerning the habits of this species than of its larger congener, the well-known "Man-of-war" bird of the Atlantic, whose powers of flight were, years ago, so well described by that graphic writer Audubon, yet it possesses the same power of wing and marvellous speed when chasing its prey. No oceanic species has such an expanse of wing, in proportion to the small size and light weight of its body, as the Frigate-bird, not even the Albatross, justly renowned for its length of wing and majestic flight, can boast of so much power in relation to the work to be done, for although its bones are peculiarly light, yet its frame is massive and heavy compared with the aerial form of the "Man-of-war" bird. A glance at the living bird or at the freshly killed specimen immediately displays these peculiarities ; the immense quills and great length of the ulna and humerus bones conduce to form an ample wing which completely hides the almost diminutive frame which has to be propelled. It is no wonder, therefore, that the Frigate bird sails along against the wind perfectly motionless, as if propelled by some invisible power, or that, in robbing the gannet or tern of their prey, a few powerful strokes of its great pinions impart such a momentum that it is enabled to rush like a rocket upon the frightened sea-birds, and catching the fish as it falls from their bills, to rise again on its course as easily as it descended.

The Frigate bird takes its food entirely on the wing, either pursuing flying-fish, on which it subsists largely, swooping on other sorts which happen to show themselves near the surface, sweeping down on crabs and cuttle-fish, or pursuing gannets, terns, and gulls and catching the food which they drop from their bills before it reaches the water. Commander Ince, in writing to Mr. Gould, remarks that he found in the females of those shot at Raine Island "young turtles, fish, cuttle-fish, and small crabs." Major Legge adds that he has seen these birds soar round in short circles over a shoal of fish, now and then remaining suspended for a second or two over some particular spot. At this time the wings were kept extended after the manner of a kestrel's, when it ceases for a moment to ply its pinions. At Galle and Colombo, where he observed the birds spoken of, they were sailing along with their wings quite motionless, and were progressing slowly along against a moderate breeze without any apparent exertion, the secret of which is to be found in the great impetus given to the bird's frame by a few powerful strokes of its immense wings. Mr. Holdsworth aptly remarks of the examples he saw at Aripu: "Their action, as they hung as it were against the gale, slowly swaying first on one side, then on the other, strongly reminded me of the behaviour of a large paper kite when it has mounted high in the air." I learn from my correspondent, Mr. Parker, that the bird shot by Mr. Smart, when wounded, flew at his dog and seized him by the nose, beating the dog off.

Nidification.—Large numbers of this species nest on Raine Islet, Torres Straits, and there must be other localities in the Australian seas where it breeds. In Raine Islet Commander Ince, R.N., found it breeding on the south-west corner of it, the nests being constructed of small sticks collected from shrubs and herbaceous plants which alone clothe the Island. The eggs were two in number, larger than those of the gannets (Sula serrator and Sula cyanops (?)), and pure white. He remarks that on one occasion he killed the old birds from a nest which contained one young one, and that on revisiting the spot he found the young bird had been removed to another nest, the owners of which were feeding it as if it had been their own.

Family, PELECANIDÆ.—*Leach.*

Bill stout, straight, broad at the base, compressed at the tip, edges irregularly serrated; feet webbed; face nude.

Sub-Family, SULIDÆ.

Bill short, straight, curved and hooked at tip.

Gen.- **Sula.**

Characters those of the Sub-Family. Plumage black and white.

369. Sula cyanops, *Sundev., Phys. Salsk. Tidskr.* 1837, p. 218, t. 5; *Legge, Birds of Ceylon,* p. 1180; *Hume, Str. F.* viii. p. 116; *Murray Avif. Brit. Ind.* ii. 734, No. 1450. Sula personata, *Gould, P. Z S.* 1846, p. 21; *id., B. Austr.* vii. pl. 77. Dysporus cyanops, *Oates, B. Br. Burm.* ii. p. 231.—The Masked Booby.

Face to behind the eyes and throat nude; entire head, neck, back, rump, upper tail coverts and entire lower parts white, with a slight fulvous tinge; primaries, secondaries and tertials, also the tail, black; irides lemon yellow; bill horny, blackish at the base; both mandibles denticulated for one-half their length from tip.

Length.—32·5 inches; bill at front 4; gape 4·87; tail from vent 8·0; tarsus 2·25; wing 16·5; legs and feet pale bluish grey.

Hab.—Sind and Beloochistan (Mekran Coast), Bengal, Ceylon, and the Western Coast of India near Alibag, whence Mr. W. F. Sinclair, C.S., sent me living specimens.

370. Sula australis, *Steph., Gen. Zool.* xiii. p. 104; *Hume, Str. F.* v. p. 318. Pelecanus sula, *Linn., Syst. Nat.* i. p. 218. Sula fusca (*Linn.*). *apud Jerd., B. Ind.* iii. p. 851. Dysporus sula, *David et Oust Ois Chine*, p. 530; *Oates, B. Br. Burm.* ii. p. 229. Sula leucogastra, *Bodd., Tabl. pl. Enl.* p. 57 (1783); *Sclater and Salv. P. Z. S.*, 1878 p. 657. Sula fiber (*Linn.*), *apud Gould, B. of Austr.* vii. pl. 78 (1848); *Blyth, Cat. B. Mus. A. S. B.* p. 296 (1849); *Jerdon, B. of Ind.* iii. p. 851 (1864); *Holdsw. P. Z. S.* 1872, p. 482; *Salvadori, Ucc. di Born.* p. 389 (1874).—The "BOOBY" OF SAILORS; DUSKY GANNET OF SOME.

Breast, abdomen, sides of the body, vent and under tail coverts white; sides of the under tail coverts, also under wing coverts, marked with brown on the edges of the feathers; remaining plumage umber brown; the feathers of the back, scapulars, and rump edged with whity brown; quills and tail dark umber brown; irides white; bill creamy white, with a bluish tinge in veins; pouch, gape, lores and orbital space pale hoary greenish yellow; legs and feet pale yellow. (*Hume.*)

Adult—(British Museum). Head, entire neck, and upper surface glossy chocolate-brown, paling round the bill in some specimens, whilst in others the head and neck are darker throughout than the back; wings and tail blackish-brown; from the chest to the under tail coverts, including the flanks, pure white, the longer under tail coverts tipped with brown; axillaries white; under wing brown, with a white band formed by the median coverts.

"Iris white; bill creamy white, with a bluish tinge. in veins; pouch, gape, lores, and orbital spaces, pale hoary greenish yellow; legs and feet pale-yellow, with a greenish tinge on tarsi; claws white; with a bluish tinge." (*Hume.*) "Iris very pale yellow; bill and orbits primrose-yellow, blotched before and beneath the eye with pale bluish; eyelash light ash-grey; legs and feet pale yellow." (*Gould.*)

Adult female.—(Laccadives). *Length.*—31·7 inches; wing 16·1; tail 8·0; tarsus 2·0; bill from gape 5·1, at front 4·1 (*Hume*).—*Adult*—(Pacific) *Length*—32·9 inches; wing 16·96; tail 8·21; tarsus 1·83; middle toe 2·73 (*Finseli*). (Tenasserim, Brit. Mus.) wing 16·5; tail 7·0; tarsus 1·86; middle toe 2·95; bill to gape 4·3, at front 3·6 (West Indies, Brit. Mus.); wing 15·1 inches; tail 8·0; tarsus 1·7; bill at front 3·76. (Locality (?). : (Brit. Mus.); wing 15·7 inches; tarsus 1·8; middle toe 3·05; claw (straight) 0·49.

Note.—This species has fourteen tail feathers.

Young.—The nestling is covered with brownish down, darker on the back than on the chest; but when first hatched the young are naked.

Immature.—(Ceylon). Iris bluish white; bill pale bluish, orbital skin and round the gape tinged with green; legs and toes greenish yellow; webs yellow; claws dusky. Face not bare beyond the posterior angle of the eye.

Entire upper surface, head and neck, down to the centre of the chest, uniform pale sepiak-brown; under surface from the chest pale brownish, defined against the dark colour of the foreneck by a distinct line across the chest;

axillaries and a bar across the under wing white; the bases of the feathers of the under surface whitish.

An example received alive in February was in the above plumage, corresponding to other specimens. In April the head and neck begins to darken, blackish-brown feathers appearing among the sepia-brown plumage; at the same time the white feathers of the under surface begin to appear, the scapulars and tail feathers moult completely in a month, and in May the under surface is mingled white and brownish.

An example in the British Museum, labelled "Tenasserim," has the head and neck uniform brown, but the feathers of the back tipped with whitish, conspicuously on the rump, where it forms a whitish patch, and also across the lower part of the hind neck, forming there a pale band, the underparts white, extending somewhat up the middle of the throat; some of the feathers of the fore neck are tipped with white. This specimen in not quite mature.

Obs.—This gannet belongs to a section of the genus Sula, for which the title Dysporus is adopted by some writers; but the type of this genus of Illiger's appears to have been another species with different characteristics, namely, the common European gannet (Sula bassana, Linn.); and I agree with Mr. Hume that it cannot well be adopted. The characteristics of the section to which the present species belongs consist in the bare gular skin not extending down the throat as a stripe more or less extended, but terminating in a curve across the chin. In the Atlantic and on the coasts of South America the white-breasted gannet assumes a smaller form, which some writers separate from, and others unite with, the present. According to the former, it is the *Sula parva* of Gmelin (Syst. Nat i. p. 579). A male procured by Von Pelzeln near Rio Janeiro measured—total length only 21 inches.

Distribution.—This well-known bird (the "Booby" of sailors) is a casual visitor to the coasts of Ceylon, being, however, generally seen on the western side of the Island. Mr. Holdsworth, the first naturalist to record it from our region, writes thus of it:—"In February and March 1868 I had many opportunities of watching a pair of Boobies which frequented the neighbourhood of the Arípu pearl-banks, about ten miles from the land. They used often to perch on a large iron buoy close to my usual anchorage at night. I only saw them during that one season." In 1871 I saw an example of this species myself sitting on a buoy at the entrance to Galle harbour; and in the same locality Captain Wade-Dalton, of the 73rd Regiment, has seen several, being likewise the possessor of a specimen which flew against the lighthouse at Galle and was killed. At the latter end of 1875 or beginning of the following year the immature bird above described was captured near Kalutara (Caltura), and kindly given to me by my friend Sir Charles Layard, into whose hands it had passed. A second immature example was seen by me on the 19th December, 1876, flying about the Colombo Roads, and finally setting on the "Drunken-Sailor" buoy near the fort. Since my departure from the Island a further example, now in the Colombo Museum, was procured at Kalutara.

"This species is widely spread, inhabiting the entire tropical zone, and wandering north and south from it. In the Bay of Bengal Mr. Hume has noticed it, and it is numerous between Penang and Singapore, near the Cocos Islands and Preparis Island, or in that part of the Bay between the Andamans and Burmah. He likewise records it from the Laccadive group, where he saw it at the Cherbaniani reef and near Pere-mull-par. It occurs at the Seychelles, and is occasionally seen as far south as the Mauritius, frequenting also the tropical portion of the east coast of Africa and portions of the Red Sea. In the Atlantic it is found at St. Helena and Ascension, breeding in considerable numbers at Boatswain-bird Island. In the West Indies it has been noticed at the windward Islands and on the coast of Venezuela; and from Honduras Mr. Saloin records it.

"Turning eastward of the Bay of Bengal we find it recorded from Formosa and Shanghai by Swinhoe, and northward of the latter place Pére David says he has not seen it, notwithstanding a species of gannet is included in the "Fauna japonica" by Temminck and Schlegel under the name of S. fusca, which may have been this species.

"To the Philippines it appears to be a rare straggler. Cuming procured it in the Island of Mindanas; but Mr. Everett and recent Collectors have not met with it in this group. It is found among various Islands in the Pacific, among which the Figi group may be mentioned, whence Hartlaub records it. On the North coast of Australia and about Torres Straits it is not uncommon; andI observe that Mr. Ramsay, in his list of Australian birds, notes it from Cape York, the Gulf of Carpentaria, and Port Darwin, as also from the south coast of New Guinea. Salvadori records it from Sumatra, Borneo, Celebes, Ternate, Amboina, and new Guinea; and recently Herr Meyer speaks of a specimen having been brought from Minahassa, in Celebes.

Habits.—This species does not appear to lead the active life which makes the various species of white gannet so conspicuous; it has not the same vigorous, rapid flight, every now and then plunging from great heights like a thunderbolt into the sea, which, when sailing in the Cape or Australian seas, one cannot fail to notice at once in the case of Sula serrator or S. capensis; but it appears to fly leisurely along, nearer the water than these its congeners, now and then sweeping down after some unlucky fish. While affecting the vicinity of the shore it frequently sits on small rocks or on some isolated buoy, which kind of perch it invariably chooses when it is to be had. Its favourite food in the tropics seems to be flying-fish, which it may often be seen chasing, flying after them and dashing on them in a slanting direction. It not unfrequently comes on board ship at night, perching usually on the extremity of the yard-arm, and while taking its rest now and then twisting its head stupidly from side to side, which habit, no doubt, has given rise to its name of Booby among sailors.

The example which I kept in confinement was a greedy bird, snapping up fish and pieces of meat, and devouring them like a cormorant as rapidly as I threw them into it. It perched much on an upright stone which I had placed in the ground for the purpose, but now and then it betook itself to a lower perch and sat upright; but sometimes it placed itself in a position of ease by resting the centre of its breast on the stake, and thus balanced its body in a horizontal position, with the neck held out straight. It walked well, taking short strides, but without the waddling gait which one would have expected from the backward position of its legs. Its voice was a hoarse harsh crake, reminding one of the creaking of a heavy gate on rusty hinges; while moulting, particularly when its neck lost many of the feathers, bare places being visible here and there, it seemed unable to swallow, and shook its food out of its bill with a jerkling motion of the head; this continuing for some time, it became very dull, and one day, while poking its head through the bamboos into the adjoining aviary, a sea-eagle, which occupied the next compartment seized it by the neck. After this, though it had really sustained no injury, it pined and its eyes gradually closed up, until I was obliged to put an end to its unhappy existence.

Dr. Cunningham, in his exhaustive notice of the common gannet or Solan goose (S. bassana) says (Ibis, 1866, p. 13):—"The name gannet is intimately conected with our modern English gander, both words being modifications of the ancient British 'gan' or 'gans,' which is the same word with the modern German 'gans,' which in its turn corresponds with the old High German 'kans,' the Greek *χήν*, the Latin anser, and the Sanskrit 'hansa,' all of which possess the same signification, *viz.*, a goose."

Nidification.—This widely distributed gannet breeds at certain fixed localities throughout the tropical portions of the globe. Its nearest breeding station to Ceylon may, perhaps, be in the Malay Archipelago; but it is known to nest at Rodriguez, and also in the Red Sea, as Von Heuglin was informed by Arab fishermen that there were colonies on the islands of the Dahlak Archipelago; but he did not visit them himself. On Boatswain-bird Island this gannet breeds in considerable numbers. According to Mr. Gill it nests on the top of this rocky islet, and also on some isolated rocks off the north-west corner of Ascension. The single egg is laid on the bare ground, and is chalky white in colour.

"An egg of this gannet, kindly lent me by Mr. F. G. Penrose, and taken at Boatswain-bird Island, is an oval, somewhat pointed at one end; the exterior of the shell is chalky white and the texture rather smooth; beneath, the shell shows pale green where the chalky material has been scratched off. It measures 2·66 by 1·73 inch. Other specimens, belonging to Canon Tristram, the loan of which I have been favoured with, are of similar shape and texture, but vary in width; two measured 2·4 by 1·5 and 2·38 by 1·57 inch."

Sub-Family, PELECANINÆ.

Bill long, flattened, compressed and hooked at tip; tail short; lower mandible and throat with a membranous pouch; orbits nude.

Gen. Pelecanus.—*Lin.*

Characters those of the Sub-Family; second quill of wing longest; secondaries nearly as long as the quills; a membranous mandibular and gular pouch.

Pelicans live in large congregated flocks and feed entirely on fish. They fly high into the air, and go vast heights by circling; they do not however obtain their prey by diving either under water from the surface, nor by diving into it after the manner of sea gulls and terns, but arrange themselves in some suitable or likely spot on the water in two, three or even four rows, or if there is not a sufficient number, form a large semi-circle, and beat the water on the surface with their wings, clapping also their huge bills, and so drive the fish towards a shallow spot, where with their bills they gorge all they get. They breed either on high trees or according to situation low thorny ones, making a huge nest of sticks. Not more than from five to twenty breed on one tree. Eggs, three in number, white and extremely chalky.

371. Pelecanus manillensis, *Gm., Syst. Nat.* i. p. 571. Pelecanus phillipensis, *Gm. Syst. Nat.* i. p. 571; *Jerd., B. Ind.* iii. p. 858, No. 1004; *Hume, Nests and Eggs, Ind. B.* p. 658; *id., Str. F.* viii. p. 116; *Murray, Vert. Zool., Sind,* p. 330; *Oates, B. Br. Burm.* ii. p. 326; *Murray, Avif. Brit. Ind.* ii. p. 737, No. 1454. Pelecanus rufescens, *apud. Elliot. P. Z. S.* 1869, p. 583 (part). Pelecanus phillipinensis, *Blyth, B. Burm.* p. 164; *Legge, Birds Ceylon,* p. 1198.—The SPOTTED-BILLED OR GREY PELICAN.

Breeding Plumage.—Head, neck and upper plumage greyish white or in some pure white, with dark bases visible only on lifting the feathers; feathers of the head long, soft, silky and greyish brown, forming a mane-like ridge to the upper back; occipital crest short, the feathers slightly recurved, of a brownish colour and tipped with white; scapulars white at the base, of a grey colour and black shafted; upper back and scapulars with the feathers sharply pointed; lower back, rump and flanks rich vinaceous, the shafts like those of the upper tail coverts hair brown; lesser and median coverts like the back; greater coverts grey, black shafted; primaries dusky grey, white at the base; secondaries and tertiaries dusky grey; feathers of the tail grey, black shafted; the basal half or more of the inner webs and shafts white; under tail coverts, greyish white, mottled with brown and like the under wing coverts tinged with vinaceous; bill pale bluish, tinged with fleshy, the tip yellowish; mandibular and gular pouch dusky; the gular pouch with reddish venations and tinged ochreous or yellow; irides pale or dusky brown; legs fleshy. *In non-breeding plumage* there is no vinaceous tinge.

Length.—60 to 62 inches; wing 24 to 25·5; tail 8 to 8·7; tarsus 2·9 to 3·1; bill at front 12·5 to 14·3.

Hab.—Sind, Kutch, Rajputana, Guzerat, Deccan and Bengal, also Southern India, Burmah, and Ceylon. Breeds in vast numbers about the end of October, also in February and March, in the Persian Gulf, Ceylon, and parts of Burma. The average size of 20 eggs is 3·15 × 2·09.

Sub-Family, GRACULINÆ OR PHALACROCORACIDÆ.

Bill moderately long, straight and hooked at the tip; face partially nude also the gullet, which is capable of distension; wings moderate; upper and lower tail coverts short: tail with stiff feathers.

Gen. Phalacrocorax.—*Briss.*

Characters the same as those of the Sub-Family.

372. Phalacrocorax carbo (*Linn.*), *Dav. et. Oust. Ois. Chine*, p. 532; *Dresser, B. Eur.* vi. p. 151, pl.; *Legge, Birds of Ceylon*, p. 1182; *Doig. Str. F.* vii. p. 468: *Hume, Str. F.* viii. p. 116; *Oates, B. Br. Burm.* ii. p. 231; *Murray, Avif. Brit. Ind.* ii. p. 738, No. 1456. Pelecanus carbo, *Linn., Syst. Nat.* i. p. 216. Pelecanus sinensis, *Shaw and Bodd., Bat. Misc.* pl. 529. Graculus carbo, *Jerd., B. Ind.* iii. p. 861; *Hume, Nests and Eggs*, p. 659; *Murray, Vert. Zool., Sind*, p. 330.—The LARGE CORMORANT.

In summer or breeding plumage, the head and neck are black with white feathers intermixed; nape with a short black erectile crest; lower neck, breast and entire under surface, except a white thigh patch, glossy black; rump, upper tail coverts and tail black; chin and a fillet of white running up to the eye white, bounded behind by a black band; primaries and their coverts dull black; scapulars, tertials, greater, median and lesser wing coverts bronze brown, the feathers margined with black; legs and feet black; bill brownish; irides deep or sea-green; facial skin pale greenish; gular pouch yellow, spotted bluish in some.

Length.—32 to 35 inches; wing 13·2 to 14·7; tail 7 to 7·5; bill at front 2·3 to 2·5.

In winter the neck is black; the white feathers and white thigh patch disappear.

Hab.—Ceylon, Sind, North-West Provinces, Western and Central India, also Beloochistan and Persia, extending to Eastern Turkestan, Nepaul and Cashmere. Distribution almost universal.

Breeds wherever found. In Sind in the middle of the Samara Dhund in the Eastern Narra Districts. Nest a platform of sticks, lined with grass and rushes. Eggs 4 to 6 in number, white or greenish white, glossless, and of a chalky texture.

Whether on sea or on the inland lakes, Cormorants make terrible havoc among the fishes inhabiting the waters they affect. Sometimes, though seldom so seen, they swoop down from mid-air on the object of their prey, and pursue it under the surface of the water with great dexterity and unerring certainty. They, however, must necessarily rise to the surface to swallow their prey, and this trait no doubt has led to their being trained by fishermen for the purpose of catching fish when not employed. In Sind as well as in China and other countries fishermen always have a dozen or more of these birds sitting, lazily on the cross beam of the prow of their boats, quite sullen and stern ; the whole deportment of the bird gives it the aspect of an unrelenting tyrant.

In fishing a leathern collar is put round their necks, to prevent the fish being swallowed, and it is said the fishermen in Sind make a livelihood by the amount of fish caught by Cormorants when their nets fail. They are not, however, hooded, as falcons are, when unemployed.

373. Phalacrocorax fuscicollis, *Steph., Gen. Zool.* xiii. pt. 1. p. 91 ; *Legge, B. Ceylon*, p. 1182 ; *Hume and Dav., Str. F.* vi. p. 496 ; *Hume, Str. F.* viii. p. 116; *Oates, B. Br. Burm.* ii. p. 233 ; *Murray, Avif. Brit. Ind.* ii. p. 739, No 1457. Phalacrocorax sinensis, *Steph., Gen. Zool.* xiii. pt. 1. p. 96. Graculus sinensis (*Shaw*), *Jerd., B. Ind.* iii. p. 862 ; *Hume, Nests and Eggs, Ind. B.* p. 660; *Murray, Vert. Zool., Sind*, p. 331. Graculus fuscicollis, *Blyth, B. Burm.* p. 164 ; *Oates, Str. F.* v. p. 170.—The WHITE-TUFTED CORMORANT.

Breeding Plumage.—Whole plumage deep black ; glossed with blue and green, the feathers of the back and wing coverts with black margins ; a tuft of decomposed soft white feathers about an inch in length on either side of the head just behind the ear coverts ; the female has not the white tufts.

Non-Breeding Plumage.—Adult Male.—Entire head and neck glossy black ; back, scapulars, rump and upper tail coverts-bronze, some of the feathers of the back and wing coverts margined with black ; throat white ; cheeks, pale brown ; entire lower surface black. *No white thigh or cheek patch.* Bills gular skin and orbits as in the last ; irides bluish green ; feet black.

Length.—24 to 27 inches ; wing 11 ; tail 6 ; bill at front 2·25. In the breeding plumage the forehead and sides of the head are speckled with white, there is a white tuft of feathers behind the ears, and the chin is white.

Hab.—Sind, Kutch, Guzerat, Rajputana, the Deccan, Burmah and Southern Ceylon. Very abundant and resident wherever it occurs. Breeds during November ; in some parts as early as July and August. The average size of 19 eggs is 2·02×1·36 inch.

374. Phalacrocorax pygmæus (*Pall.*), *Dresser, B. Eur.* vi. p. 173, pl. ; *Legge, B. Ceylon*, p. 1191 ; *Murray, Avif. Brit. Ind.* ii. p. 740 No. 1458. Pelecanus pygmæus, *Pall., Reis. Russ. Reichs.* ii. p. 715. Graculus javanicus, *Jerd., B. Ind.* iii. p. 863 ; *Murray, Vert. Zool., Sind*, p. 332. Graculus melanognathos, *Hume, Nests and Eggs, Ind. B.* p. 660. Graculus pygmæus, *Blyth, B. Burm.* p. 164.—The LITTLE CORMORANT.

In Summer Plumage.—A white triangular patch on the head; lores and a line through the eyes white; a few white hair-like feathers on the nape and sides of the neck; chin black; whole body glossy black; head with a short occipital crest; wing coverts, scapulars, secondaries and terttiaries glossed silvery, the feathers margined with black; bill brownish or purplish brown; gular and orbital skin livid fleshy; legs dusky.

Length.—19 to 20 inches; wing 8·5; tail 5·5; bill at front 1·25; tarsus 1·3.

Hab.—Sind, Punjab, N.-W. Provinces, Kutch, Guzerat, Rajputana, Concan, the Deccan, Burmah and Ceylon. Breeds wherever found from August to December according to locality. Eggs 4—5 in number; chalky white. The average size of 19 eggs in Mr. Parker's possession is 1·74 × 1·14 inches; the length is from 1·54 to 1·88 inch and the breadth from 1·03 to 1·22 inch.

Sub-Family, PLOTINÆ.

Pill with edges finely notched; neck longer than the body.

Gen. **Plotus.**—*Lin.*

Bill long, straight, slender; second and third quills longest; nostrils basal, covered by a shield; tail long and rounded.

Plotus melanogaster.

375. Plotus melanogaster (*Penn.*), *Jerd., B. Ind.* iii. p. 865, No. 1008; *Hume, Nests and Eggs Ind. B.* p. 661; *Str. F.* vol. i. p. 469; *id., Str. F.* i. p. 194; *Blyth, B. Burm.* p. 165; *Legge, B. Ceylon*, p. 1194; *Hume and Dav., Str. F.* vi. p 496; *Oates, Str. F.* x. p. 248; *Murray, Hdbk, Zool., &c. Sind.*, p. 249; *id., Vert. Zool. Sind*, p. 332; *id. Avif. Brit. Ind.* ii. p. 741, No. 1459. Anhinga melanogaster, *Penn., Ind. Zool.* p. 27, pl. 12 (*Sili*, Sind).—The INDIAN SNAKE BIRD.

Head, nape and neck brown, the feathers edged with pale ferruginous; back of the neck slightly darker; chin and throat white, also a line from below the eye to half way down the neck, and a narrow streak from the base of the bill; back and entire under surface glossy black; primaries, secondaries, tertiaries, scapulars and wing coverts black, very slightly glossed; some of the inner secondaries, all the wing coverts, scapulars and tertials mesially wnite; upper tail coverts and tail black, the central feathers with barred ridges; under wing coverts black; legs and feet black; bill dusky on the upper mandible, yellowish on the lower; irides yellow.

Length.—32 to 33 inches; wing 13·2 to 14; tail 8·3 to 9·2; bill at front 3·5.

Hab.—Sind, Bengal, Rajputana, Kutch, Guzerat, Concan, Deccan and India generally; also Burmah and Ceylon, extending to the Malay Peninsula.

Breeds in Ceylon and wherever found from June to December in large societies. Eggs, white or bluish white, with a chalky coat. The average size of 20 eggs 52·14 inch 1·38; the length is from 1·95 inch to 2·27 inch, and the breadth from 1·26 to 1·44.

GENERAL INDEX.

ENGLISH INDEX.

Distribution Table of the Birds of the Island of Ceylon.

Number.	No. in Murray's Avifauna of British India.	Jerdon's Nos.	Species.	S. India.	Deccan.	Concan.	Guzerat.	Kutch.	Central Prov.	Central India.	Rajputana.	Bengal.	Oudh.	N.-W. Provinces.	Punjab.	Afghanistan.	Beloochistan.	Sind.	British Burmah.	Nepaul.
1	8	6	Neophron ginginianus, *Lath.*	×	×	×	×	×	×	×	×	×	×	×	×	...	...	×	...	×
2	9	50	Circus cyaneus, *Lin.*	...	×	...	...	...	×	...	...	...	×	×	×	...	...	...	...	×
3	10	53	Circus melanoleucus, *Forst.*	×	×	×	...	...	×	×	×	×	...	...	...	...	...	...	×	×
4	11	52	Circus pygargus, *Lin.*	×	×	×	×	×	×	×	×	×	×	×	×	...	×	×	×	×
5	12	51	Circus macrurus, *S. G. Gm.*	×	×	×	×	×	×	×	×	×	×	×	×	×	×	×	×	×
6	13	54	Circus æruginosus, *Lin.*	×	×	×	×	×	×	×	×	×	×	×	×	×	×	×	×	×
7	15	22	Astur trivirgatus, *Tem.*	×	×	×	...	...	×	...	...	×	...	...	...	...	...	...	×	×
8	16	23	Astur badius, *Gm.*	×	×	×	×	×	×	×	×	×	×	×	×	×	×	×	×	×
9	19	24	Accipiter nisus, *Lin.*	×	×	×	×	×	×	×	×	×	×	×	×	×	×	×	×	×
10	20	25	Accipiter virgatus, *Temm.*	×	...	×	×	...	×	×	×	...	×	×	×	...	...	...	×	×
11	23	47	Buteo plumipes, *Hodgs.*	×	...	...	...	...	...	...	...	...	×	×	...	...	...	...	×	×
12	32	33	Nisaëtus fasciatus, *Vieill.*	×	×	×	×	×	×	×	×	...	×	×	×	×	×	×	...	×
13	33	31	Nisaëtus pennatus, *Gm.*	×	×	×	×	×	×	×	×	...	×	×	×	×	×	×	×	×
14	34	37	Lophotriorchis kieneri, *Geoff.*	×	...	...	...	...	...	×	...	...	...	...	...	...	...	...	×	...
15	35	32	Neopus malayensis, *Tem.*	×	×	×	...	...	×	×	...	...	...	×	...	...	...	...	×	×
16	36	36	Spizaëtus nipalensis, *Hodg.*	×	×	×	...	...	...	...	...	×	×	×	×	...	...	...	×	×
17	37	35	Spizaëtus cirrhatus, *Gm.*	×	×	×	...	...	×	×	...	×	...	...	...	...	...	...	...	×
18	42	39*bis.*	Spilornis melanotis, *Jerd.*	×	×	×	...	...	×	...	...	×	...	...	...	...	...	...	×	...
19	48	43	Haliaëtus leucogaster, *Gm.*	×	...	×	×	×	×	...	×	×	×	×	×	...	...	×	×	...
20	50	55	Haliaëtur indus, *Bodd.*	×	×	×	×	×	×	×	×	×	×	×	×	...	×	×	×	×
21	51	56	Milvus govinda, *Sykes.*	×	×	×	×	×	×	×	×	×	×	×	×	×	×	×	×	×
22	55	59	Elanus cæruleus, *Desf.*	×	×	×	×	×	×	×	×	×	×	×	×	...	...	×	×	×
23	57	57*ter.*	Pernis ptilorhynchus, *Tem.*	×	×	×	...	...	×	×	×	×	×	×	×	...	...	...	×	×
24	58	58	Baza lophotes, *Cuv.*	×	...	...	...	...	×	...	...	×	...	...	...	...	...	...	×	×
25	60	...	Baza ceylonensis, *Legge*	...	...	...	...	...	...	...	...	...	...	...	...	...	...	...	...	...
26	64	8	Falco communis, *Gm.*	×	×	×	×	×	×	×	×	×	×	×	×	×	×	×	×	×
27	65	9	Falco peregrinator, *Sund.*	×	×	...	...	...	×	×	...	...	×	×	×	×	...	...	×	×
23	70	14	Falco severus, *Horsf.*	×	...	...	...	...	...	...	...	×	×	×	×	...	...	...	×	×
29	71	16	Falco chiquera, *Daud.*	×	×	×	×	×	×	×	×	×	×	×	×	×	×	×	...	×
30	74	17	Cerchneis tinnuncula, *Lin.*	×	×	×	×	×	×	×	×	×	×	×	×	×	×	×	×	×
31	77	19*bis.*	Cerchneis amurensis, *Radde*	...	×	×	...	...	...	×	...	...	...	×	×	...	...	...	×	×
32	78	40	Pandion haliaëtus, *Lin.*	×	×	×	×	×	×	×	×	×	×	×	×	...	×	×	×	×
33	79	41	Polioaëtus ichthyaëtus, *Horsf.*	...	...	×	...	×	×	×	×	×	×	×	×	...	...	...	×	×
34	81	72	Ketupa ceylonensis, *Gm.*	×	×	×	...	...	×	×	×	×	×	×	×	×	×	×	×	×
35	85	71	Bubo nipalensis, *Hodgs.*	*	...	...	...	...	...	...	...	...	...	...	...	...	...	...	×	×
36	91	74*bis.*	Scops sunia, *Hodgs.*	×	...	...	...	...	...	...	...	...	...	×	...	...	...	...	...	×
37	95	75*qt.*	Scops malabaricus, *Jerd.*	×	×	×	×	...	...	×	...	×	×	×	×	×	...	×	...	...
38	...	...	Scops minutus, *Legge*	...	...	...	...	...	...	...	...	...	...	...	...	...	...	...	...	...
39	104	81*bis.*	Ninox scultulata, *Raffl.*	×	×	×	...	...	...	×	×	×	...	×	×	...	...	...	×	×
40	107	77	Glaucidium radiatum, *Tick.*	×	...	×	...	...	×	...	...	×	...	×	...	...	...	...	×	×
41	...	...	Glaucidium castanonotum, *Blyth*	...	...	...	...	...	...	...	...	...	...	...	...	...	...	...	...	...
42	117	63	Syrnium indranee, *Sykes*	×	×	×	...	...	...	...	...	...	...	...	...	...	...	...	×	...
43	118	60	Strix flammea, *Lin.*	×	×	×	×	×	×	×	×	×	×	×	×	×	×	×	×	×
44	120	62	Phodilus badius, *Horsf.*	...	...	...	...	...	...	...	×	×	...	...	...	...	...	...	×	×

* Also the Malabar Coast.

Number.	No. in Murray's Avifauna of British India.	Jerdon's Nos.	SPECIES.	S. India.	Deccan.	Concan.	Guzerat.	Kutch.	Central Prov.	Central India.	Rajputana.	Bengal.	Oudh.	N.-W. Provinces.	Punjab.	Afghanistan.	Beloochistan.	Sind.	British Burmah.	Nepaul.
45	127	663	Corone splendens, *Vieill.*	×	×	×	×	×	×	×	×	×	×	×	×	...	...	×	×	×
46	129	660*bis.*	Corone macrorhynchus, *Wagl*	×	×	×	...	...	×	×	×	×	×	×	×	...	...	×	×	×
47	...	...	Cissa ornata, *Wagl*	...	...	...	...	...	...	...	...	...	...	...	...	...	...	...	...	...
48	151	473*bis.*	Oriolus diffusus, *Sharpe*	×	...	×	...	...	...	...	...	×	...	...	...	...	...	...	×	...
49	155	472	Oriolus melanocephalus, *Lin*	×	×	×	...	...	...	×	...	×	×	×	×	...	...	...	×	×
50	161	278	Buchanga atra, *Herm*	×	×	×	×	×	×	×	×	×	×	×	×	×	×	×	×	×
51	162	280	Buchanga longicaudata, *Hay*	×	...	...	...	...	×	×	...	...	...	...	...	...	...	...	...	×
52	165	281	Buchanga cærulescens, *Lin.*	×	...	...	...	...	...	×	...	...	×	×	...	...	...	...	...	×
53	...	...	Dissemuroides edoliformis	...	...	...	...	...	...	...	...	...	...	...	...	...	...	...	...	...
54	168	285	Dissemurus paradiseus, *Lin.*	×	...	...	...	...	...	...	...	...	×	×	...	...	...	...	...	×
55	169	469	Irena puella, *Lath*	×	...	...	...	...	...	...	...	...	...	...	...	...	...	...	×	...
56	170	265	Tephrodornis pondicerianus, *Gm.*	×	×	×	×	×	×	×	×	×	×	×	×	...	...	×	×	×
57	...	...	Tephrodornis affinis, *Blyth*	...	...	...	...	...	...	...	...	...	...	...	...	...	...	...	...	...
58	174	267	Hemipus picatus, *Sykes.*	×	...	...	...	...	×	...	...	×	×	×	×	...	...	...	×	...
59	165a	287	Artamus fuscus, *Vieill.*	×*	×	...	...	...	...	×	...	×	...	...	...	...	...	...	×	...
60	182	270	Graucalus macii, *Less*	×	...	...	...	...	×	×	×	...	×	×	×	...	...	...	×	×
61	191	272	Pericrocotus flammeus, *Forst*	×‡	...	×	...	...	...	...	...	...	...	...	...	...	...	...	...	...
62	194	276	Pericrocotus peregrinus, *Lin.*	×	×	×	×	×	×	×	×	×†	×	×	×	...	...	×	×	×
63	202	268	Lalage sykesi, *Strickl.*	×	×	×	...	...	...	×	...	×	...	...	...	...	...	...	×	...
64	206	299	Hemichelidon ferruginea, *Hodgs.*	...	...	...	...	...	...	...	...	...	...	×	...	...	...	...	×	×‡
65	...	...	Alseonax muttui, *Layard*	...	...	...	...	...	...	...	...	...	...	...	...	...	...	...	...	...
66	207	297	Alseonax latirostris, *Raffl*	×	×	×*	...	...	...	×	...	...	×	×	×	...	...	...	×	×
67	211	323	Muscicapa albicilla, *Pall*	...	...	×	...	...	...	×	...	×	×	×	...	...	...	...	×	×
68	212	323*ter.*	Muscicapa hyperythra, *Cab.*	...	...	...	...	...	...	×	...	...	...	×	...	...	...	...	...	...
69	217	481	Pratincola caprata, *Lin.*	×	×	×	×	×	×	×	×	×	×	×	×	×	×	×	×	...
70	...	...	Hypothymis ceylonensis *Sh.*	...	...	...	...	...	...	...	...	...	...	...	...	...	...	...	...	...
71	237	292	Rhipidura albifrontata, *Sharpe*	×	×	×	×	×	×	×	×	×	×	×	...	...	...	×	×	...
72	238	288	Terpsiphone paradisi, *Lin.*	×	×	×	×	×	×	×	×	×	×	×	×	...	×	×	...	×
73	242	295	Culicicapa ceylonensis, *Sws.*	×	...	...	...	...	×	×	...	×†	×	×	...	...	...	...	×	×
74	...	...	Stoporala sordida, *Wal*	...	...	...	...	...	...	...	...	...	...	...	...	...	...	...	...	...
75	258	304	Siphia rubeculoides, *Vig*	×	...	...	...	...	...	...	...	×	×	×	×	...	...	...	×	×‡
76	259	306 / 305	Siphia tickelliæ, *Bly*	×	×	×*	×	...	×	×	×	×	×	×	...	...	...	...	×	...
77	261	300	Siphia nigrorufa, *Jerd.*	×	...	...	...	...	...	...	...	...	...	...	...	...	...	...	...	...
78	277	582	Sylvia affinis, *Bly*	×	×	×	×	×	×	×	×	×	×	×	×	×	×	×	...	...
79	283	559	Phylloscopus nitidus, *Bly*	×	...	...	...	...	...	×	...	×	×	×	...	...	×	×	...	×
80	284	560	Phylloscopus viridanus, *Bly*	×	...	...	...	...	...	×	...	×	×	×	...	...	...	...	×	×
81	287	556	Phylloscopus magnirostris, *Bly.*	×	×	×	...	...	×	×	...	×	×	×	×	...	...	...	×	×
82	309	515	Acrocephalus stentoreus, *Hemp*	×	×	×	×	×	×	×	×	×	×	×	×	×	×	×	×	×
83	310	516	Acrocephalus dumetorum, *Bly.*	×	×	×	×	×	×	×	×	×	×	×	×	...	...	×	×	×

* Malabar Coast. † Andamans. ‡ Sikkim.

Number.	No. in Murray's Avifauna of British India.	Jerdon's Nos.	SPECIES.	S. India.	Deccan.	Concan.	Guzerat.	Kutch.	Central Prov.	Central India.	Rajputana.	Bengal.	Oudh.	N.-W. Provinces.	Punjab.	Afghanistan.	Beloochistan.	Sind.	British Burmah.	Nepaul.
84	312	{ 520 / 521 }	Locustella certhiola, *Pall.*	...	...	...	...	...	...	×	...	×	×	×	...	...	...	...	×	...
85	330	442	Schœnicola platyura, *Jerd.*	×	...	...	...	...	...	...	...	...	...	...	...	...	...	...	...	...
86	340	543,544	Prinia inornata, *Sykes*	×	×	×*	×	×	×	×	×	×§	×	×	×	...	×	×	×	×
87	341	545	Prinia sylvatica, *Jerd.*	×	×	×	×	×	×	×	×	×§	×	×	×	...	...	×	...	×
88	343	534,535	Burnesia socialis, *Sykes* ...	×	×	×	...	...	×	×	×	×§	×	×	×	...	...	...	...	×
89	346	530	Sutoria sutoria, *Forst*	×	×	×	×	×	×	×	×	×	×	×	×	×	×	×	×	×
90	352	536	Cisticola gracilis, *Franklin.*	...	×	×	...	...	×	×	...	×	...	...	...	...	...	...	×	×
91	356	539	Cisticola cisticola, *Tem.* ...	...	×	×	×	×	×	×	...	...	...	×	×	...	...	×	×	×
92	365	355	Geocichla citrina, *Bly*......	×	...	...	...	...	×	...	...	×	...	...	...	...	...	...	×	×‡
93	366	357	Geocichla wardi, *Jerd*......	×	...	...	...	...	...	...	...	...	...	×	×	...	...	...	...	×
94	...	...	Geocichla spiloptera, *Blyth.*	...	...	...	...	...	...	...	...	...	...	...	...	...	...	...	...	...
95	...	...	Geocichla imbricata, *Layard*	...	...	...	...	...	...	...	...	...	...	...	...	...	...	...	...	...
96	...	...	Merula kinnisi, *Blyth.* ...	...	...	...	...	...	...	...	...	...	...	...	...	...	...	...	...	...
97	385	351	Monticola cyanus, *Lin.* ...	×	×	×	×	×	×	×	×	×	×	×	×	×	×	×	×	×
98	388	507	Erithacus brunneus, *Jerd.*.	×	...	...	...	...	...	...	...	×	...	×	...	...	...	...	...	×‡
99	393	514	Erithacus cæruleculus, *Jerd*	×	×	×	×	×	×	×	×	×	×	×	×	×	×	×	×	×
100	416	468	Ægithina tiphia, *Lin.*	×	×	×	×	×	×	×	×	×	×	×	...	...	...	...	×	×‡
101	421	464	Chloropsis malabaricus, *Gm*	×	×	...	...	...	...	×	...	...	...	...	...	...	...	...	...	...
102	423	463	Chloropsis Jerdoni, *Bly*...	×	...	...	...	...	...	...	...	×	...	...	...	...	...	...	...	...
103	428	446	Hypsipetes ganeesa, *Sykes.*	×	×	×	...	...	...	...	...	...	...	...	...	...	...	...	...	...
104	448	450	Xenocichla icterica, *Strickl*	×	...	*	...	...	...	...	...	...	...	...	...	...	...	...	...	...
105	449	462	Pycnonotus hæmorrhous, *Gm.*	×	×	×	×	×	×	×	×	×	×	×	×	...	...	×	...	...
106	457	452	Pycnonotus luteolus, *Less.*	×	...	*	...	...	...	×	...	×	...	...	...	...	...	...	...	...
107	...	...	Kelartia penicillata, *Blyth.*	...	...	...	...	...	...	...	...	...	...	...	...	...	...	...	...	...
108	...	...	Rubigula melanictera, *Gmel.*	...	...	...	...	...	...	...	...	...	...	...	...	...	...	...	...	...
109	...	...	Myiophoneus Blighi, *Holdsw.*	...	...	...	...	...	...	...	...	...	...	...	...	...	...	...	...	...
110	493	479	Thamnobia fulicata, *L.* ...	×	×	×	...	...	...	×	...	...	...	...	...	...	...	...	...	...
111	495	475	Copsychus saularis, *L.* ...	×	×	×	...	...	×	×	...	×§	...	×	×	...	...	...	×	×‡
112	498	476	Cittocincla tricolor, *Vieill.*	×	...	*	...	...	...	×	...	×§	...	...	...	...	...	...	×	×‡
113	...	...	Argya rufescens, *Blyth.* ...	...	...	...	...	...	...	...	...	...	...	...	...	...	...	...	...	...
114	...	...	Pomatorhinus melanurus, *Blyth.*	...	...	...	...	...	...	...	...	...	...	...	...	...	...	...	...	...
115	...	...	Garrulax cinereifrons, *Blyth.*	...	...	...	...	...	...	...	...	...	...	...	...	...	...	...	...	...
116	...	...	Crateropus striatus, *Sws.*	...	...	...	...	...	...	...	...	...	...	...	...	...	...	...	...	...
117	...	...	Pyctorhis nasalis, *Legge* ...	...	...	...	...	...	...	...	...	...	...	...	...	...	...	...	...	...
118	601	398	Dumetia albigularis, *Blyth*	×	×	...	×	...	...	...	...	...	...	...	...	...	...	...	...	...
119	...	...	Elaphrornis palliseri, *Blyth*	...	...	...	...	...	...	...	...	...	...	...	...	...	...	...	...	...
120	...	...	Scotocichla fuscicapillum, *Blyth*	...	...	...	...	...	...	...	...	...	...	...	...	...	...	...	...	...
121	...	...	Alcippe nigrifrons, *Blyth.*	...	...	...	...	...	...	...	...	...	...	...	...	...	...	...	...	...
122	668	...	Parus cinereus, *Bonn. et Vieil.*	×	...	...	...	...	×	×	...	§ B	×	×	×	×	...	...	×	×
123	702	257	Lanius erythronotus, *Vigors*	×	×	×	×	×	×	×	×	×	×	×	×	×	×	×	...	×

* Malabar. ‡ Sikkim. § Assam

Number.	No. in Murray's Avifauna of British India	Jerdon's Nos	SPECIES.	S. India.	Deccan.	Concan.	Guzerat.	Kutch.	Central Prov.	Central India.	Rajputana.	Bengal.	Oudh.	N.-W Provinces.	Punjab.	Afghanistan.	Beloochistan.	Sind.	British Burmah.	Nepaul.
124	704	261	Lanius cristatus, *Lin.*	×	...	...	...	...	...	§	B	×	×	×	×	...	×	×	×	×
125	705	...	Lanius lucionensis, *Lin.*	...	...	...	...	...	...	†	...	...	...	...	...	...	...	...	×	...
126	723	253	Sitta frontalis, *Swains*	×*	×	×	...	...	×	×	...	×	...	...	...	...	...	...	×	...
127	733	234	Cinnyris asiatica, *Lath*	×	×	×	×	×	×	×	×	×	×	×	×	×	×	×	×	×
128	735	235	Cinnyris lotenia, *Linn*	×	×	...	...	...	...	...	...	...	...	...	...	...	...	...	...	...
129	736	233	Cinnyris minima, *Sykes*	×	...	...	...	...	...	...	...	...	...	...	...	...	...	...	...	...
130	737	232	Cinnyris zeylonica, *Lin*	×	×	...	...	...	...	...	...	§×	...	...	...	...	...	...	...	...
131	748	631	Zosterops palpebrosa, *Temm*	×	×	×	...	...	×	×	×	×	×	×	×	...	...	×	×	×
132	...	...	Zosterops ceylonensis	...	...	...	...	...	...	...	...	...	...	...	...	...	...	...	...	...
133	757	238	Dicæum erythrorhynchum, *Lath.*	×	×	×	...	...	×	×	...	×§	...	...	...	...	...	...	×	×
134	761	240	Prionochilus squalidus, *Burton*	...	...	...	...	...	...	...	...	...	...	×	...	...	...	...	×	×
135	...	...	Prionochilus vincens, *Sclater*	...	...	...	...	...	...	...	...	...	...	...	...	...	...	...	...	...
136	771	...	Cotile obsoleta, *Cab*	...	...	...	×	×	...	...	...	...	...	...	...	...	×	×	...	...
137	772	82	Hirundo rustica, *Lin.*	×	×	×	×	×	×	×	×	§	×	×	×	×	×	×	×	×
138	...	...	Hirundo hyperythra, *Blyth*	...	...	...	...	...	...	...	...	...	...	...	...	...	...	...	...	...
139	776	83	Hirundo javanica, *Sparrm.*	×	...	...	...	...	...	...	...	...	...	...	...	...	...	...	×	...
140	780	85	Hirundo erythropygia, *Sykes*	×	×	×	×	×	×	×	×	×	×	×	×	×	×	×	...	×
141	784	591	Motacilla personata, *Gould.*	...	...	...	...	...	...	...	×	...	...	×	×	×	×	×	...	...
142	787	589	Motacilla madraspatensis, *Gm.*	×	×	×	×	×	×	×	×	×‡	...	×	×	...	×	×	...	×
143	788	592	Motacilla melanope, *Pall*	×	...	...	...	...	×	×	×	×	×	×	×	×	×	×	×	×
144	792	593	Motacilla borealis, *Sundev.*	×	×	...	...	...	×	×	...	×§	...	×	×	×	×	×	×	×
145	794	595	Limonidromus indicus, *Gould.*	*×	...	...	...	...	...	...	...	×§	...	...	...	...	...	...	×	...
146	800	599	Anthus Richardi, *Vieill.*	×	...	...	...	...	...	...	...	×	...	...	...	...	...	...	×	×
147	801	601	Anthus striolatus, *Blyth*	×	...	...	...	...	×	×	...	‡	...	×	×	...	...	...	×	×
148	803	600	Anthus rufulus, *Vieill*	...	×	×	...	...	...	...	...	×§	×	×	×	×	×	×	×	×
149	830	711	Petronia flavicollis, *Frankl.*	*×	×	×	×	×	×	×	×	...	×	×	×	×	×	×	...	...
150	832	706	Passer domesticus, *Linn.*	×	×	×	×	×	×	×	×	×	×	×	×	×	×	×	...	...
151	873	694	Ploceus phillipinus, *Lin.*	×	×	×	×	×	×	×	×	×	×	×	×	×	×	×	×	×
152	875	695	Ploceus manyar, *Horsf.*	...	...	×	×	×	×	×	...	×§	×	×	×	...	...	×	...	...
153	878	697	Amadina malacca, *Lin*	×	...	*	...	...	...	×	...	×	...	...	...	...	...	...	...	...
154	879	698	Amadina atricapilla, *Vieill.*	×	...	...	...	...	...	...	...	§	×	×	×	...	...	...	×	...
155	880	699	Amadina punctulata, *Lin.*	×	...	×	...	...	×	×	×	§	×	×	×	...	...	×	×	...
156	884	701	Amadina striata, *Linn*	×	...	*	...	...	×	...	...	×	...	...	...	...	...	...	×	...
157	885	703	Amadina malabarica, *Linn.*	×	×	×	×	×	×	×	×	×	×	×	×	...	×	×	...	...
158	...	...	Amadina kelaarti, *Blyth.*	...	...	...	...	...	...	...	...	...	...	...	...	...	...	...	...	...
159	891	755	Mirafra affinis, *Jerd*	×	...	*	...	...	...	...	...	×	...	...	...	...	...	...	×	...
160	896	760	Pyrrhulauda grisea, *Scop*	×	×	×	×	×	×	×	×	×	×	×	×	...	...	×	...	...
161	904	767	Alauda gulgula, *Frankl.*	×	×	×	×	×	×	×	×	×	×	×	×	...	...	×	×	×
162	...	...	Acridotheres melanosternus, *Legge.*	...	...	...	...	...	...	...	...	...	...	...	...	...	...	...	...	...
163	916	687	Sturnia pagodarum, *Gmel.*	×	×	×	...	...	...	...	...	§×	×	×	×	...	...	×	×	...
164	...	...	Sturnornis senex, *Bonap*	...	...	...	...	...	...	...	...	...	...	...	...	...	...	...	...	...
165	925	690	Pastor roseus, *Lin.*	×	×	×	×	×	×	×	§×	×	×	×	×	×	×	×	×	...

* Malabar. † Andamans. ‡ Sikkim § Assam.

Number.	No in Murray's Avifauna of British India.	Jerdon's Nos.	Species.	S. India.	Deccan.	Concan.	Guzerat.	Kutch.	Central Prov.	Central India.	Rajputana.	Bengal.	Oudh.	N.-W. Provinces.	Punjab.	Afghanistan.	Beloochistan.	Sind.	British Burmah.	Nepaul.
166	927	692	Eulabes religiosa, *Lin*	×	...	*	...	...	...	...	...	...	...	...	...	...	...	...	...	...
167	...	...	Eulabes ptilogenys, *Blyth.*	...	...	...	...	...	...	...	...	...	...	...	...	...	...	...	...	...
168	938	345	Pitta brachyura, *Lin.*	*×	×	×	×	...	×	×	×	×	×	×	×	...	...	...	×	‡
169	950	98	Cypselus melba, *Lin*	×	×	×	×	×	...	...	...	...	×	×	×	×	×	×	...	...
170	952	100	Cypselus affinis, *Gray*	...	×	×	×	×	...	...	×	...	...	...	×	×	×	×	...	×
171	957	102	Cypselus batassiensis, *Gray*	...	×	*	...	...	×	...	...	×§	...	×	...	...	...	...	...	...
172	960	96	Hirundinapus indicus, *Hume*	×	...	*	...	...	...	...	...	...	...	...	...	...	...	...	×	...
173	967	...	Collocalia Linchi, *Horsf. & Moore*	...	...	...	...	...	...	...	...	...	...	...	...	...	...	...	×	...
174	968	...	Dendrochelidon coronatus, *Tick.*	×	*	...	...	...	×	×	...	...	...	×	...	...	...	...	×	‡
175	971	105	Batrachostomus moniliger, *Blyth*	×	...	*	...	...	×	...	...	...	...	...	...	...	...	...	...	...
176	973	112	Caprimulgus asiaticus, *Lath.*	...	×	×	×	×	...	...	×	...	...	...	?	...	...	×	×	...
177	977	111	Caprimulgus atripennis, *Jerd.*	×	...	*	...	...	...	...	...	...	...	...	...	...	...	...	...	...
178	980	...	Caprimulgus Kelaarti, *Blyth*	×	...	...	...	...	×	...	...	...	...	...	...	...	...	...	...	...
179	983	115	Harpactes fasciatus, *Gmel.*	...	*	...	...	...	...	×	...	...	...	...	...	...	...	...	...	...
180	987	199	Cuculus canorus, *Lin.*	×	×	×	×	×	×	×	×	×	×	×	×	×	×	×	×	×
181	989	201	Cuculus poliocephalus, *Lath.*	×	×	...	...	...	...	...	...	...	...	...	...	...	...	...	...	×
182	990	202	Cuculus sonnerati, *Lath.*	×	*	...	...	...	...	...	...	...	...	...	...	...	...	...	×	...
183	991	203	Cuculus micropterus, *Gould.*	×	*	...	...	...	...	×	...	×§	...	...	...	...	...	...	×	...
184	993	209	Hierococcyx varius, *Vahl.*	×	...	...	...	...	...	...	...	×	...	×	...	...	...	...	...	...
185	997	208	Cacomantis nigra, *Jerd.*	×	...	...	...	...	...	×	...	×	...	...	...	...	...	...	...	...
186	998	210	Surniculus lugubris, *Horsf.*	*	...	...	...	...	...	×	...	...	...	...	...	...	...	...	×	‡
187	999	211	Chrysococcyx maculatus, *Gm.*	...	...	...	...	...	...	×	...	...	...	...	...	...	...	...	×	‡
188	1002	212	Coccystes Jacobinus, *Bodd.*	*	×	×	×	×	×	×	×	×	×	×	×	...	...	×	...	×
189	1003	213	Coccystes coromandus, *Linn.*	...	*	...	...	...	×	×	×	×	...	...	...	...	...	...	×	...
190	1004	214	Eudynamys honorata, *Linn.*	...	×	×	×	×	...	...	...	...	...	...	...	...	...	...	×	×
191	1010	216	Rhopodytes viridirostris, *Jerd.*	×	×	...	...	...	...	...	...	...	...	...	...	...	...	...	...	...
192	...	...	Phœnicophaes pyrrhocephalus, *Forst.*	...	...	...	...	...	...	...	...	...	...	...	...	...	...	...	...	...
193	1014	217	Centrococcyx rufipennis, *Illigr.*	×	×	×	×	×	×	×	×	...	...	...	...	...	...	...	...	...
194	...	...	Centrococcyx chlororhynchus, *Blyth*	...	...	...	...	...	...	...	...	...	...	...	...	...	...	...	...	...
195	1017	219	Taccocua Leschenaulti, *Less.*	×	×	×	...	...	...	...	...	...	...	...	...	...	...	...	...	...
196	...	...	Megalæma zeylanica, *Gmel.*	...	...	...	...	...	...	...	...	...	...	...	...	...	...	...	...	...

* Malabar. ‡ Sikkim. § Assam.

Number.	No. in Murray's Avifauna of British India.	Jerdon's Nos.	SPECIES.	S. India.	Deccan.	Concan.	Guzerat.	Kutch.	Central Prov.	Central India.	Rajputana.	Bengal.	Oudh.	N.-W. Provinces.	Punjab.	Afghanistan.	Beloochistan.	Sind.	British Burmah.	Nepaul.
197	...	..	Megalæma flavifrons, *Cuv.*	...	...	...	...	...	...	...	...	...	...	...	...	...	...	...	...	...
198	1031	197	Xantholæma hæmacephala, *P. L. S. Mull.*	×	×	×	×	×	×	×	×	×	×	×	×	...	?	×	×	×
199	...	...	Xantholæma rubricapilla, *Gmel*	...	...	...	...	...	...	...	...	...	...	...	...	...	...	...	...	...
200	1043	180, 182	Brachypternus aurantias, *Linn.*	×	×	×	×	×	×	×	×	×	×	×	×	×	×	×	...	×
201	1044	181	Brachpyternus chrysonotus, *Less.*	×	*	×	...	...	...	...	...	...	...	...	...	...	...	...	...	...
202	...	...	Brachypternus ceylonus, *Forst*	...	...	...	...	...	...	...	...	...	...	...	...	...	...	...	...	...
203	1047	179	Micropternus gularis, *Jerd.*	*	×	...	...	...	...	...	...	...	...	...	...	...	...	...	...	...
204	1055	175	Chrysophlegma chlorigaster, *Jerd.*	×	*	...	...	...	...	...	...	...	...	...	...	...	...	...	...	...
205	1057	171	Gecinus striolatus, *Blyth*	×	...	...	×	...	...	×§	§	×	×	×	×	×	...	...	×	×
206	1066	167	Chrysocolaptes festivus, *Bodd*	×	×	...	...	...	...	×	×	...	...	...	...	...	...	...	...	...
207	...	...	Chrysocolaptes Stricklandi, *Layard*	...	...	...	...	...	...	...	...	...	...	...	...	...	...	...	...	...
208	1077	160	Picus mahrattensis, *Lath.*	...	×	×	×	×	...	×	×	...	×	×	×	...	×	×	×	...
209	...	...	Iyngipicus gymnopthalmus, *Blyth*	...	...	...	...	...	...	...	...	...	...	...	...	...	...	...	...	...
210	...	...	Loriculus indicus	...	...	...	...	...	...	...	...	...	...	...	...	...	...	...	...	...
211	1090	151	Palæornis columboides, *Vigors*	×	*	...	...	...	...	...	...	...	...	...	...	...	...	...	...	...
212	1091	147	Palæornis indo-burmannicus, *Hume*	×	×	*	...	...	×	...	...	×	×	×	×	...	...	...	×	‡
213	1093	148	Palæornis torquatus, *Bodd.*	×	×	×	×	×	×	×	×	×	×	×	×	...	...	×	×	×
214	1094	...	Palæornis cyanocephalus, *Lin.*	...	...	...	...	...	...	...	...	×	×	×	×	...	...	...	×	×
215	1095	149	Palæornis rosa, *Bodd.*	×	×	×	×	×	×	§×	×	×	×	×	×	...	...	...	×	×
216	...	...	Palæornis calthropæ, *Layard*	...	...	...	...	...	...	...	...	...	...	...	...	...	...	...	...	...
217	1098	255	Upupa ceylonensis, *Reich*	×	...	...	...	...	...	...	...	...	...	×	×	...	...	...	...	...
218	1099	117	Merops viridis, *Linn*	×	×	×	×	×	×	×	×	×	×	×	×	×	×	×	×	×
219	1100	118	Merops phillipinus, *Linn*	×	×	×	×	×	×	×	×	×	×	×	×	×	×	×	×	×
220	1101	119	Merops Leschenaulti, *Vieill*	×	...	...	...	...	...	...	...	×	...	...	...	...	...	...	×	...
221	1107	123	Coracias indica, *Linn.*	×	×	×	×	×	×	×	×	×	×	×	×	×	×	×	×	×
222	1109	126	Eurystomus orientalis, *Linn*	...	...	...	...	...	...	...	§	×	×	×	...	...	...	...	×	...
223	1110	134	Alcedo bengalensis, *Gm*	×	×	×	×	×	×	×	×	...	...	×	×	×	×	×	...	...
224	1116	136	Ceryle rudis, *Linn.*	×	×	×	×	×	×	×	×	×	×	×	×	...	×	×	×	×
225	1118	129	Halcyon smyrnensis, *Linn*	×	×	×	×	×	×	×	×	×	×	×	×	...	...	×	×	×‡
226	1119	130	Halcyon pileata, *Bodd*	...	*	...	...	...	...	...	...	×	...	...	...	...	...	...	×	...
227	1123	133	Ceyx tridactyla, *Pall.*	×	×	×	...	...	...	...	...	×	...	...	...	...	...	...	...	...
228	112[illegible]	127	Pelargopsis gurial, *Pearson*	c×	...	*	...	...	×	×	...	×	...	×	...	...	...	...	...	...

Number.	No. in Murray's Avifauna of British India.	Jerdon's Nos.	SPECIES.	S. India.	Deccan.	Concan.	Guzerat.	Kutch.	Central Prov	Central India	Rajputana.	Bengal.	Oudh.	N.W. Provinces.	Punjab.	Afghanistan.	Beloochistan	Sind.	British Burmah.	Nepaul.
229	1128	141	Anthracoceros coronatus, *Bodd.*	*×	...	...	...	...	...	×	...	...	...	...	...	...	...	...	...	...
230	...	...	Tockus gingalensis, *Shaw.*	...	...	...	...	...	...	...	...	...	...	...	...	...	...	...	...	...
231	1142	773	Crocopus chlorigaster, *Blyth*	×	×	...	×	...	...	×	...	×	×	...	...	...	...	×	...	...
232	1144	774	Osmotreron bicincta, *Jerd.*	...	...	...	...	...	×	×		×	×	...	...	...	...	...	×	×
233	1149	777	Osmotreron pompadoura, *Gmel.*	×	...	...	...	...	...	...	...	...	...	...	...	...	...	...	...	...
234	1152	780	Carpophaga ænea, *Linn.*	×	...	*	...	...	×	×	...	×	...	...	...	...	...	...	×	×
235	1158	786	Palumbus Elphinstonei, *Sykes*	×	×	×	...	...	..	...	...	...	...	...	...	...	...	...	...	...
236	1160	788	Columba intermedia, *Strickl.*	×	×	×	×	×	×	×	×	×§	×	×	×	×	×	×	×	×‡
237	1164	782	Alsocomus puniceus, *Tickell.*	...	...	...	..	...	×	×	§	×	...	...	...	...	...	...	×	...
238	1169	793	Turtur meena, *Sykes*	×	×	×	×	...	...	...	§	×‖	...	...	...	...	...	...	×	×
239	1171	795	Turtur suratensis, *Gmel.*	×	×	×*	×	×	×	×	×	×	×	×	×	×	...	×	...	...
240	1173	796	Turtur risorius, *Linn.*	×	×	×	×	×	×	×	×	×	×	×	×	×	×	×	×	...
241	1174	797 *bis*	Turtur humilis, *Tem.*	...	×	×	×	×	×	×	×	×	×	×	×	...	×	×	×	...
242	1175	798	Chalcophaps indica, *Linn.*	×	?	...	...	...	...	N.	A.	§×	...	?	...	...	..	...	×	...
243	1186	803	Pavo cristatus, *Linn.*	×	×	×	×	×	×	×	×	§×	×	×	...	...	...	×	...	...
244	...	...	Gallus Stanleyi, *Gray*	...	...	...	...	...	...	...	...	...	...	...	...	...	...	...	...	...
245	...	...	Galloperdix bicalcaratus, *Forst*	...	...	...	...	...	...	...	...	...	...	...	...	...	...	...	...	...
246	1215	819	Francolinus pictus, *Jard. and Selby*	×	×	...	×	...	×	×	...	...	...	...	...	...	...	...	...	...
247	1219	822	Ortygornis ponticeriana, *Gmel*	×	×	...	×	×	×	×	×	...	×	×	×	×	×	×	...	...
248	1231	826	Perdicula asiatica, *Lath*	×	×	×	×	...	×	×	...	×	×	×	×	...	...	...	...	...
249	1336	829	Coturnix communis, *Linn.*	×	×	×	×	×	×	A.	×	Sy.	×	×	×	×	×	×	×	×
250	1238	...	Excalfactoria chinensis, *Linn*	...	...	...	...	Sy.	×	×	‖	§×	...	...	...	...	...	...	×	×‡
251	1239	832 } 833 }	Turnix plumbipes, *Hodgs.*	...	...	...	...	...	...	...	...	...	×	×	×	...	...	...	×	...
252	1250	840	Cursorius coromandelicus, *Gmel.*	×	×	×	×	×	?	...	×	×	×	×	×		...	×	×	...
253	1253	842	Glareola orientalis, *Leach.*	...	×	...	...	...	...	...	...	×	...	...	...	...	...	×	×	...
254	1255	843	Glareola lactea, *Tem*	...	×	...	...	...	...	...	...	...	...	×	×	...	...	×	×	..
255	1256	844	Squatarola helvetica, *Linn.*	×	...	...	...	×	...	...	...	×	...	...	...	...	×	×	×	...
256	1257	845	Charadrius fulvus, *Gm.*	×	×	...	...	×	...	...	...	?	...	×	×	...	...	×	×	...
257	1259	846	Ægialitis Geoffroyi, *Wagl.*	×	...	×	...	×	...	...	×	×	...	...	...	...	×	×	×	...
258	1260	847	Ægialitis mongolica, *Pall.*	×	...	×	...	×	...	...	...	×	...	...	...	×	×	×	×	...
259	1261	848	Ægialitis cantiana, *Lath.*	×	×	×	×	×	...	...	×	×	×	×	×	×	×	×	×	...
260	1262	849	Ægialitis dubia, *Scop*	×	...	×	×	×	×	×	×	×	×	×	×	×	×	×	×	×
261	1262	850	Ægialitis Jerdoni, *Legge*	...	...	...	×	×	...	...	...	×	...	...	...	...	...	×	×	...
262	1265	852	Chettusia gregaria, *Pall.*	...	...	×	...	×	...	×	×	...	×	×	×	×	×	×	...	...
263	1269	855	Lobivanellus indicus, *Bod.*	×	...	×	×	×	×	×	×	×	×	×	×	×	×	×	×	×

* Malabar. ‡ Sikkim. § Assam. ‖ Khasia Hills. Sy. Sylhet.

Number.	No. in Murray's Avifauna of British India.	Jerdon's Nos.	SPECIES.	S. India.	Deccan.	Concan.	Guzerat.	Kutch.	Central Prov.	Central India.	Rajputana.	Bengal.	Oudh.	N.-W. Provinces.	Punjab.	Afghanistan.	Beloochistan.	Sind.	British Burmah.	Nepaul.
264	1271	856	Sarciophorus bilobus, *Gmel.*	×	×	×	×	×	×	×	×	×	×	×	×	…	…	×	×	×
265	1272	858	Æsacus recurvirostris, *Cuv.*	×	×	×	×	×	×	×	×	×	×	×	×	…	…	×	×	…
266	1273	859	Œdicnemus crepitans, *Tem.*	×	×	×	×	×	×	×	×	×	×	×	×	…	×	×	×	…
267	1274	860	Strepislas interpres, *Linn.*	×	×	…	…	…	…	…	×	…	…	…	…	…	×	×	…	…
268	1275	861	Dromas ardeola, *Paykull*	…	…	×	×	×	…	…	…	…	…	…	…	…	×	×	…	…
269	1276	862	Hæmatopus ostralegus, *Linn*	×	…	×	…	×	…	…	…	×	…	…	…	×	×	×	…	…
270	1281	867	Scolopax rusticola, *Linn*	×	…	×	…	…	…	…	…	×	×	×	×	×	×	×	…	×
271	1282	868	Gallinago nemoricola, *Hodgs*	×	…	…	…	…	…	…	…	…	…	×	…	…	…	…	…	…
272	1284	870	Gallinago stenura, *Kuhl.*	…	×	×	×	×	…	N×	A×	×	…	×	×	×	×	×	×	…
273	1285	871	Gallinago scolopacina, *Bonap*	×	×	×	×	×	×	×	×	×	×	×	×	×	×	×	×	…
274	1286	872	Gallinago gallinula, *Linn*	×	×	×	×	×	×	×	×	×	×	×	×	×	×	×	×	…
275	1287	873	Rhynchœa capensis, *Linn.*	×	…	…	×	×	×	×	×	…	×	×	×	…	×	×	×	…
276	1288	886	Limicola platyrhyncha, *Tem*	×	…	×	×	×	…	…	…	×	…	…	…	…	×	×	×	…
277	1290	884	Tringa minuta, *Leisl.*	×	×	×	×	×	×	×	×	×	×	×	×	×	×	×	×	…
278	1291	..	Tringa subminuta, *Midd*	×	…	…	…	…	…	…	…	×	…	…	…	…	…	×	×	…
279	1292	885	Tringa temmincki, *Leisl.*	×	…	…	…	…	…	…	…	×	…	…	…	…	…	×	×	…
280	1294	882	Tringa subarquata, *Gould.*	×	×	×	×	×	×	×	×	×	×	×	×	×	×	×	×	×
281	1296	880	Machetes pugnax, *Linn.*	×	×	×	×	×	×	×	×	×	×	×	×	×	×	×	×	×
282	1297	888	Calidris arenaria, *Linn.*	×	×	×	×	×	×	×	×	×	×	×	×	×	×	×	×	×
283	1300	893	Actitis hypoleucos, *Linn.*	×	×	×	×	×	×	×	×	×	×	×	×	×	×	×	×	…
284	1301	892	Actitis ochropus, *Linn.*	×	×	×	×	×	×	×	×	×	×	×	×	×	×	×	×	…
285	1302	891	Totanus glareola, *Gmel*	×	×	×	×	×	×	×	×	×	×	×	×	×	×	×	×	…
286	1303	894	Totanus canescens, *Gmel.*	×	×	×	×	×	×	×	×	×	×	×	×	…	…	×	×	…
287	1304	895	Totanus stagnatilis, *Bechst.*	×	×	×	×	×	×	×	×	×	×	×	×	…	…	×	…	…
288	1305	897	Totanus calidris, *Linn*	×	×	×	×	×	×	×	×	×	×	×	×	×	×	×	×	×
289	1306	896	Totanus fuscus, *Linn*	×	…	×	×	×	…	…	…	×	…	…	…	…	×	×	×	…
290	1309	876	Terekia cinerea, *Gould*	×	…	×	×	×	…	…	…	×	…	×	…	…	×	×	×	…
291	1311	875	Limosa ægocephala, *Linn.*	×	…	×	×	×	…	…	×	…	…	…	…	×	×	×	×	…
292	1313	878	Numenius phæopus, *Linn.*	×	…	×	×	×	…	…	…	×	…	…	…	…	×	×	×	…
293	1 14	877	Numenius arquatus, *Linn.*	×	×	×	×	×	…	…	×	×	×	×	×	×	×	×	×	…
294	1316	899	Recurvirostra avocetta, *Linn.*	×	×	×	×	×	…	…	×	×	×	×	×	×	×	×	×	…
295	1317	898	Himantopus candidus, *Linn*	×	×	×	×	×	×	×	×	×	×	×	×	×	×	×	×	…
296	1319	901	Hydrophasianus chirurgus, *Scop.*	×	…	…	…	×	×	×	×	×	×	×	×	…	…	×	B.	…
297	1320	902	Porphyrio poliocephalus, *Lath*	×	×	×	×	×	×	×	×	×	×	×	×	×	×	×	×	…
298	1321	903	Fulica atra, *Linn*	×	×	×	×	×	×	×	×	×	×	×	×	×	×	×	×	×
299	1323	913	Hypotænidia striata, *Linn.*	×	*	×	…	…	‖	…	B.	×	§	…	…	…	…	…	…	…
300	1324	914	Rallus indicus, *Blyth*	×	…	…	…	…	…	×	syl.	×	§	…	…	…	…	…	×	×
301	1325	912	Rallina euryzonoides, *Lafresn.*	×	…	…	…	…	…	…	syl.	×	‡	×	×	…	…	…	×	×

Note.—Marks in the column Beloochistan refer chiefly to the coast of that country.

Number.	No. in Murray's Avifauna of British India.	Jerdon's Nos.	SPECIES.	S. India.	Deccan.	Concan.	Guzerat.	Kutch.	Central Prov.	Central India.	Rajputana.	Bengal.	Oudh.	N.-W. Provinces.	Punjab.	Afghanistan.	Beloochistan.	Sind.	British Burmah.	Nepaul.
302	1328	910	Porzana Bailloni, *Vieill.*	×	×	×	×	×	×	×	×	×	×	×	×	×	×	×	×	...
303	1330	911	Porzana fusca, *Linn*	×	...	...	...	C	...	×	×	×	...	×	×	...	...	...	...	...
304	1333	905	Gallinula chloropus, *Linn.*	×	×	×	×	×	×	?	×	×	×	×	×	×	×	×	×	×
305	1334	907	Gallinula phœnicura, *Penn.*	×	×	×	×	×	...	...	×	×	×	×	×	...	×	×	×	...
306	1335	904	Gallicrex cinereus, *Gm.*	×	...	...	...	...	...	×	...	×	...	...	...	...	...	×	×	...
307	1337	916	Leptoptilos javanicus, *Horsf.*	×	...	...	...	...	×	×	×	×	?	?	×	...	...	...	×	...
308	1338	917	Xenorhynchus asiaticus, *Lat*	×	×	×	×	×	×	×	×	×	×	×	×°	...	...	×	×	...
309	1340	919	Ciconia alba, *Belon*	...	×	×	×	×	×	×	×	×	×	×	×	...	...	×	...	...
310	1341	920	Ciconia leucocephala, *Gm.*	×	×	×	×	?	...	×	?	×	×	×	×	...	...	×	×	...
311	1342	921	Ardea goliath, *Temm*	...	...	...	...	...	...	...	‖	...	...	...	...	...	...	...	...	...
312	1445	923	Ardea cinerea, *Linn.*	×	×	×	×	×	×	×	×	×	×	×	×	×	×	×	×	...
313	1346	924	Ardea purpurea, *Linn*	×	×	×	×	×	×	×	×	×	×	×	×	×	×	×	×	...
314	1347	925	Herodias alba, *Linn.*	×	×	×	×	×	×	×	×	×	×	×	×°	×	×	×	×	...
315	1348	926	Herodias intermedia, *Von Hasselt.*	×	×	×	×	×	×	×	×	×	×	×	×	×	×	×	×	...
316	1349	927	Herodias garzetta, *Linn.*	×	×	×	×	×	×	×	×	×	×	×	×	×	×	×	×	...
317	1351	928	Demi-egretta gularis, *Bosc.*	×	...	...	...	×	...	...	...	×	...	...	...	...	×	×	...	...
318	1353	929	Bubulcus coromandus, *Bodd.*	×	×	×	×	×	×	×	×	×	×	×	×	×	×	×	×	...
319	1354	930	Ardeola grayi, *Sykes*	×	×	×	×	×	×	×	×	×	×	×	×	×	×	×	×	...
320	1356	931	Butorides javanica, *Horsf.*	×	×	×	×	×	×	×	×	×	×	×	×	×	×	×	×	...
321	1357	932	Ardetta flavicollis, *Lath*	×	×	×	×	×	...	...	...	×	×	×	×	...	...	×	×	...
322	1358	933	Ardetta cinnamomea, *Gmel.*	×	×	×	×	×	..	...	...	×	×	×	×	...	...	×	×	...
323	1359	934	Ardetta sinensis, *Gmel.*	×	×	×	×	×	...	...	...	×	×	×	×	...	...	×	×	...
324	1361	936	Botaurus stellaris *Linn.*	×	×	×	...	×	...	...	...	×	×	×	×	×	×	×	×	...
325	1362	937	Nycticorax griseus, *Linn.*	×	×	×	×	×	×	×	×	×	×	×	×	×	×	×	×	...
326	1363	...	Gorsachius melanolophus, *Raf*	×	...	...	...	...	...	...	...	N	...	...	...	...	...	...	...	...
327	1364	938	Tantalus leucocephalus, *Penn.*	×	×	×	×	×	×	×	×	×	×	×	×	×	×	×	×	...
328	1365	939	Platalea leucorodia, *Linn.*	×	×	×	×	×	...	...	×	×	×	×	×	×	×	×	×	...
329	1366	940	Anastomous oscitans, *Bodd.*	×	×	×	×	×	×	×	×	×	×	×	×	...	×	×	×	...
330	1367	938	Threskiornis melanocephalus, *Lath.*	×	×	×	×	×	...	...	×	×	...	...	×	...	×	×	×	...
331	1370	943	Falcinellus igneus, *Linn.*	×	×	...	×	×	×	×	×	×	×	×	×	×	×	×	×	...
332	1371	944	Phœnicopterus antiquorum, *Tem.*	×	×	×	×	×	×	×	×	×	×	×	×	×	×	×	×	...
333	1379	950	Sarkidiornis melanonotus, *Pen.*	×	×	×	×	×	...	...	×	×	×	×	×	...	...	×	×	...
334	1380	951	Nettapus coromandelianus, *Gmel.*	×	×	×	×	×	×	×	×	×	×	×	×	...	×	×	×	...
335	1381	952	Dendrocygna javanica, *Horsf.*	×	×	×	×	×	×	×	..	×	×	×	×	...	...	×	×	...
336	1382	953	Dendrocygna fulva, *Gmel.*	×	×	×	×	×	×	×	...	×	×	×	×	...	...	×	×	...
337	1383	954	Casarca rutila, *Pall*	×	×	×	×	×	×	×	×	×	×	×	×	×	×	×	×	×
338	1386	957	Spatula clypeata, *Linn.*	×	×	×	×	×	×	×	×	×	×	×	×	×	×	×	...	×
339	1388	959	Anas pœcilorhyncha, *Forst.*	×	×	×	×	×	×	...	...	...	×	×	×	×	×	×	×	...

Note.—Marks in the column Beloochistan refer chiefly to the coast of that country.

Number.	No. in Murray's Avifauna of British India.	Jerdon's Nos.	SPECIES.	S. India.	Deccan.	Concan.	Guzerat.	Kutch.	Central Prov.	Central India.	Rajputana.	Bengal.	Oudh.	N.-W. Provinces.	Punjab.	Afghanistan.	Beloochistan.	Sind.	British Burmah	Nepaul.
340	1393	962	Dafila acuta, *Linn.*	×	×	×	×	×	×	×	...	×	×	×	×	×	×	×	×	...
341	1395	964	Querquedula crecca, *Linn*	×	×	×	×	×	×	×	×	×	×	×	×	×	×	×	×	...
342	1396	965	Querquedula circia, *Linn.*	×	×	×	×	×	×	×	×	×	×	×	×	×	×	×	×	...
343	1399	967	Fuligula rufina, *Pall.*	...	×	×	×	×	×	×	×	×	×	×	×	×	×	×	...	...
344	1411	975	Podiceps minor, *Linn.*	×	×	×	×	×	×	×	×	×	×	×	×	×	×	×	×	×
345	1413	...	Daption capensis, *Linn.*	...	...	...	...	...	...	...	...	...	...	...	...	...	...	...	...	...
346	1415	...	Puffinus chlororhynchus, *Lesson*	...	...	...	...	...	...	...	...	×	...	...	...	...	...	...	×	...
347	1416	...	Stercorarius antarticus, *Less*	...	...	...	...	...	...	...	...	...	...	...	...	...	...	...	...	...
348	1421	980	Larus brunneicephalus, *Jerdon*	...	×	...	×	×	...	...	...	×	...	...	...	...	×	×	×	...
349	1422	979	Larus ichthyætus, *Pall.*	×	...	×	...	...	...	...	...	×	...	×	...	...	×	×	...	...
350	1424	984	Hydrochelidon hybrida, *Pall*	×	×	×	×	×	×	×	×	×	×	×	×	×	×	×	×	...
351	1425	...	Hydrochelidon leucoptera, *Meisn and Schinz*	×	×	×	×	×	×	×	×	×	×	×	×	×	×	×	×	...
352	1427	983	Gelochelidon anglica, *Mont.*	...	×	×	...	×	...	...	×	×	...	...	...	...	×	×	×	...
353	1428	982	Sterna caspia, *Pall*	...	...	...	...	...	...	...	...	...	×	×	×	...	×	×	...	...
354	1429	989	Sterna Bergii, *Licht*	×	...	×	...	×	...	...	...	×	...	...	...	...	×	×	×	...
355	1431	990	Sterna media, *Horsf.*	×	...	×	...	...	...	...	...	×	...	...	...	...	×	×	×	...
356	1433	985	Sterna seena, *Sykes*	×	×	×	×	×	×	×	×	×	×	×	×	×	×	×	×	...
357	1434	987	Sterna melanogastra, *Temm*	×	×	×	×	×	×	×	×		×	×	×	×	×	×	×	...
358	1435	...	Sterna Dougalli, *Mont.*	...	...	...	...	...	...	...	...	×	...	...	...	...	...	...	×	...
359	1436	986	Sterna hirundo, *Linn*	×	...	...	...	...	...	...	...	...	...	...	×	...	...	×	...	...
360	1438	...	Sterna Saundersii, *Hume*	...	...	...	...	...	...	...	...	...	...	...	...	...	...	×	...	...
361	1439	988	Sterna sinensis, *Gm.*	...	...	...	...	...	...	...	...	×	...	...	...	...	...	×	×	...
362	1440	992	Sterna anæsthetus, *Scop*	...	...	×	...	...	...	...	...	...	...	...	...	...	×	×	×	...
363	1441	...	Sterna fuliginosa, *Gm.*	...	...	*	...	...	...	...	...	...	...	...	...	...	×	×	...	...
364	1442	993	Anous stolida, *Linn*	...	...	...	...	...	...	...	...	×	...	...	...	...	×	×	...	...
365	1447	997	Phæton flavirostris, *Brand.*	...	...	...	...	...	...	...	...	×	...	...	...	...	...	...	...	...
366	1448	...	Phæton indicus, *Hume*	...	...	...	...	...	...	...	...	×	...	...	...	...	×	×	×	...
367	1449	1000	Fregata aquila, *Linn*	...	...	*	...	...	...	...	...	×	...	...	...	...	...	...	...	...
368	...	...	Fregata minor	...	...	...	...	...	...	...	...	...	...	...	...	...	...	...	...	...
369	1450	...	Sula cyanops, *Sundev*	...	...	×	...	...	...	...	...	×	...	...	...	...	×	×	...	...
370	1451	998	Sula australis, *Steph*	...	...	...	...	...	...	...	...	×	...	...	...	...	...	...	×	...
371	1454	1004	Pelecanus manillensis, *Gm.*	×	×	...	×	×	...	...	×	×	...	...	...	...	...	×	×	...
372	1456	1005	Phalacrocorax carbo, *Linn.*	×	×	×	×	×	×	×	×	×	×	×	×	×	×	×	×	×
373	1457	1006	Phalacrocorax fuscicollis, *Steph*	...	×	...	×	×	...	...	×	...	...	...	...	...	...	×	×	...
374	1458	1007	Phalacrocorax pygmæus, *Pall.*	...	×	...	×	×	...	...	×	...	...	...	...	...	...	×	×	...
375	1459	1008	Plotus melanogaster, *Penn.*	...	×	×	×	×	...	...	×	×	...	...	...	...	...	×	×	...

Note.—Marks in the column Beloochistan refer chiefly to the coast of that country.